New Progress of Regulations and Judicial Practice of Intellectual Property

Deli Cheng · Xinmiao Yu · Klaus Bacher
Editors

New Progress of Regulations and Judicial Practice of Intellectual Property

Editors
Deli Cheng
Shanghai International College
of Intellectual Property
Tongji University
Shanghai, China

Xinmiao Yu
Shanghai International College
of Intellectual Property
Tongji University
Shanghai, China

Klaus Bacher
Judge of Federal Court of Justice
Berlin, Germany

ISBN 978-981-97-6094-7   ISBN 978-981-97-6095-4 (eBook)
https://doi.org/10.1007/978-981-97-6095-4

Jointly published with Tongji University Press Co., Ltd.
The print edition is not for sale in China (Mainland). Customers from China (Mainland) please order the print book from: Tongji University Press Co., Ltd.

© Tongji University Press Co. Ltd. 2025. This book is an open access publication.

Open Access This book is licensed under the terms of the Creative Commons Attribution 4.0 International License (http://creativecommons.org/licenses/by/4.0/), which permits use, sharing, adaptation, distribution and reproduction in any medium or format, as long as you give appropriate credit to the original author(s) and the source, provide a link to the Creative Commons license and indicate if changes were made.
The images or other third party material in this book are included in the book's Creative Commons license, unless indicated otherwise in a credit line to the material. If material is not included in the book's Creative Commons license and your intended use is not permitted by statutory regulation or exceeds the permitted use, you will need to obtain permission directly from the copyright holder.
The use of general descriptive names, registered names, trademarks, service marks, etc. in this publication does not imply, even in the absence of a specific statement, that such names are exempt from the relevant protective laws and regulations and therefore free for general use.
The publishers, the authors, and the editors are safe to assume that the advice and information in this book are believed to be true and accurate at the date of publication. Neither the publishers nor the authors or the editors give a warranty, express or implied, with respect to the material contained herein or for any errors or omissions that may have been made. The publishers remain neutral with regard to jurisdictional claims in published maps and institutional affiliations.

This Springer imprint is published by the registered company Springer Nature Singapore Pte Ltd.
The registered company address is: 152 Beach Road, #21-01/04 Gateway East, Singapore 189721, Singapore

If disposing of this product, please recycle the paper.

Preface

In the new century, competition among major powers is gradually showcased in the competition of science and technology. Intellectual property rights are powerful tools for competition among nations. The role of intellectual property as a national development strategic resource and a core element of international competitiveness has become more prominent. The "Outline for Building a Powerful Intellectual Property Country (2021–2035)" is a major top-level design for the development of intellectual property in the next 15 years by the Chinese government in the new era. It is a grand blueprint and significant milestone for building a strong country by intellectual property. The development of the new situations provides a broad space for the research and study of intellectual property rights.

Intellectual property rights are the cornerstone of the system for protecting and stimulating innovation. "Innovation is the first driving force for development, and protecting intellectual property rights is protecting innovation." Since the reform and opening up, China's intellectual property industry has continued to develop and has embarked on a path of intellectual property development with Chinese characteristics, achieved historic achievements, and strongly supported innovation. The progress of intellectual property has strongly supported the realization of the goal of building an innovative country and building a moderately prosperous society in an all-round way. However, it is not so easy to master and use intellectual property proficiently. Intellectual property, as a new subject matter of law, is in constant change; intellectual property is highly technical, complex, professional, and international, which makes the study and research of intellectual property more complicated. The analysis and understanding of classic cases of intellectual property is an important way to master intellectual property theory and practice.

"The life of law lies not in logic, but in experience." This is especially true for intellectual property rights. This experience arises from various typical cases in judicial practice. Cases are living laws and laws in action. Although China is a country with statutory law, legal norms are mainly manifested in legal texts formulated by the legislature, and the system of case law has not been established yet, case studies are of great significance in our country's legislation, justice, and legal education. Enhancing case studies has an important role and significance in improving the socialist legal system, improving the technology of law application and the quality of judicial judgments, and promoting legal education. In the judicial field of intellectual property in China due to the continuous revision of several major laws of intellectual property in recent years, judicial interpretations in this field have also been promulgated frequently. The interpretation of the application of intellectual property law and the principles are still being explored. Therefore, it is a very fantabulous way to study intellectual property law through intellectual property precedents.

Because of this, scholars continue to edit the case review and analysis works. Although it is not full of sweat and cattle, it has also sprung up. However, the current case analysis is mostly based on the practice of China's courts and is aimed at the application needs of domestic students. There are not many case evaluations for teaching international students. Based on the analysis of previous cases, this book has made good explorations in the following aspects:

First of all, in the arrangement of the style, the book is structured into main parts: the first part is new amendments about intellectual property right around the world, especially in China and Germany because they have made great changes in recent years. Then we chose some typical cases according to several major jurisdictions of intellectual property rights. The classic cases of the United States, Germany, and China were selected in the order of patent, trademark, copyright, and unfair competition. Most of them are appeals or retrial cases of the Supreme Court. Each case is divided into two parts. The first part is the reasoning and analysis of the courts on the application of the law and the liability. The second part is a case analysis, this part was completed by German scholars, American scholars and Chinese scholars. The presiding judge of the Intellectual Property Division of the Federal Court of Justice of Germany, Dr. Klaus Bacher, is in charge of writing the German intellectual property case review, and Professor Ann Bartow of the University of New Hampshire in the United States for US cases. Deli Cheng and Xinmiao Yu are in charge of the analysis of selected cases in China.

Secondly, it has a unique style in the selection of cases. This book brings together two types of cases home and abroad. One is the latest influential case in the field of intellectual property rights in the past several years, and the other is the classic intellectual property case in the world. The types of cases involve typical cases in the fields of patents, trademarks, copyrights, unfair competition, etc., involving a wide range of intellectual property laws and a complete range of categories. Some cases have been a sensation, and some legal issues have been raised or clarified for the first time in relevant judgments. Many cases not only have a wide range of social influence, but also have typical legal application significance. Many cases involve facts and legal issues that go beyond the case and the adjudication itself and have greater reference significance. At the same time, we also attached the different opinions of some case judgments, such as the Concurring Opinion and the Dissenting Opinion in the US judgment, reflecting the different understandings of different judges on the application of the law. This part is also very meaningful.

Finally, it has a unique perspective and great practical value. The selection of cases in this book reflects the different legal perspectives of judges and scholars. Bacher is a well-known judge with extensive trial experience in the field of intellectual property rights in Germany and the European Union. Through many years of practice, he chose cases with educational value to study. The American scholar Professor Bartow has been teaching in universities for many years, and the cases she helped select are also of very high learning and research value.

This book is suitable for reading and use by teachers and students of law school and judges.

Shanghai, China	Deli Cheng
Shanghai, China	Xinmiao Yu
Berlin, Germany	Klaus Bacher

Editorial Board

Editor-in-chief

Deli Cheng
Xinmiao Yu
Klaus Bacher (Germany)

Deputy Editor-in-chief

Ann Bartow (America)
Yuhan Tang
Lanqing Ge
Pengfei Huang
Lili Zhao

Contents

1	**Main Amendments of Chinese Intellectual Property Law**		1
	Deli Cheng and Lili Zhao		
	1.1	General Provisios	1
		1.1.1 Opinions of the Supreme People's Court on Comprehensively Strengthening Judicial Protection of Intellectual Property	1
		1.1.2 Opinions of the Supreme People's Court on Legally Imposing Heavier Punishments for Infringements of Intellectual Property Rights	8
		1.1.3 Guiding Opinions of the Supreme People's Court on the Trial of Intellectual Property Civil Cases Involving e-Commerce Platforms	10
		1.1.4 Official Reply of the Supreme People's Court on Several Issues Concerning the Application of Law to Disputes over Internet-related Intellectual Property Right (IPR) Infringement	13
		1.1.5 Several Provisions of the Supreme People's Court on Technical Investigators' Participation in Litigation Activities Relating to Intellectual Property Cases	15
		1.1.6 Supreme People's Court Guiding Opinions on Unifying the Application of Laws and on Strengthening Searches for Similar Cases (for Trial Implementation)	17
	1.2	Main Amendments of Chinese Copyright Laws and Regulations	19
		1.2.1 Copyright Law of the People's Republic of China	19
		1.2.2 Opinions of the Supreme People's Court on Strengthening the Protection of Copyright and Rights Related to Copyright	34

		1.2.3	Interpretation of the Supreme People's Court Concerning the Application of Laws in the Trial of Civil Disputes Over Copyright	37
		1.2.4	Provisions by the Supreme People's Court on Several Issues Concerning the Application of Law in Hearing Civil Dispute Cases Involving Infringement of the Right of Communication to the Public on Information Networks	42
	1.3	\multicolumn{2}{l}{Main Amendments of Chinese Trademark Laws and Regulations ....}	45
		1.3.1	Trademark Law of the People's Republic of China	45
		1.3.2	Interpretation of Supreme People's Court on Several Issues Concerning the Application of Law in the Hearing of Civil Cases Involving Trademark Disputes	49
		1.3.3	Provisions of the Supreme People's Court on Issues Concerned in the Trial of Cases of Civil Disputes over the Conflict between Registered Trademark or Enterprise Name with Prior Right	55
		1.3.4	Interpretation of the Supreme People's Court on Several Issues Relating to Laws Applicable to Trial of Civil Dispute Cases Involving Protection of Well-known Trademarks	56
		1.3.5	Provisions of the Supreme People's Court on Several Issues Concerning the Trial of Administrative Cases Involving Trademark Authorization and Confirmation	59
		1.3.6	Interpretation by the Supreme People's Court on the Attachment of the Right to Exclusive Use of a Registered Trademark Implemented by People's Courts	65
	1.4	\multicolumn{2}{l}{Main Amendments of Chinese Patent Laws and Regulations ......}	66
		1.4.1	Patent Law of the People's Republic of China	66
		1.4.2	Interpretations (II) of the Supreme People's Court on Several Issues Concerning the Application of Law in the Trial of Cases Involving Patent Infringement Disputes	75
		1.4.3	Provisions (I) of the Supreme People's Court on Several Issues concerning the Application of Law in the Trial of Administrative Cases Involving the Grant and Confirmation of Patents	82

		1.4.4	Interpretation of the Supreme People's Court on Several Issues Concerning the Trial of Cases Involving Disputes Over New Varieties of Plants (2020 Amendment)	89
	1.5	Main Amendments of Chinese Anti-Unfair Competition Laws and Regulations		91
		1.5.1	Anti-Unfair Competition Law of the People's Republic of China	91
		1.5.2	Interpretation of the Supreme People's Court on Some Issues Concerning the Application of Law in the Trial of Civil Cases Involving Unfair Competition	97
		1.5.3	Provisions of the Supreme People's Court on Several Issues Concerning the Application of Law in the Trial of Civil Cases Involving Infringements upon Trade Secrets	101
		1.5.4	Interpretation of the Supreme People's Court on Application of Laws in the Trial of Civil Disputes Over Domain Names of Computer Network	107
	1.6	Main Amendments of Chinese Criminal Laws and Regulations on Crimes of Infringing upon Intellectual Property Rights		110
		1.6.1	The Section of Criminal Law of the People's Republic of China on Crimes of Infringing upon Intellectual Property Rights	110
		1.6.2	Interpretation (III) of the Supreme People's Court and the Supreme People's Procuratorate of Several Issues Concerning the Specific Application of Law in the Handling of Criminal Cases Involving Infringements upon Intellectual Property Rights	114
		1.6.3	Notice by the Supreme People's Procuratorate and the Ministry of Public Security of Issuing the Decision on Amending the Criteria for Launching Formal Investigation into Criminal Cases of Infringement upon Trade Secrets	119
2	**Main Amendments of Germany Patent Act (2021)**			123
	Xinmiao Yu and Yuhan Tang			
	2.1	General Provisions for All IP Procedures		124
	2.2	Patent Procedures and Procedures for Supplementary Protection Certificates		125
	2.3	Utility Model Procedures		126
	2.4	Trade Mark Procedures		126
	2.5	Design Procedures		127
	2.6	Fee Provisions		127
	2.7	Injunctions		129

3 Cases 131

Klaus Bacher, Ann Bartow, Lanqing Ge, Pengfei Huang, and Lu Jin

- 3.1 Civil Cases on Patent Infringement 131
  - 3.1.1 Patent Cases from Germany 131
  - 3.1.2 Patent Cases from the United States 187
  - 3.1.3 Patent Cases from the China 234
- 3.2 Civil Cases on Copyright Infringement 293
  - 3.2.1 Copyright Cases from United States 293
  - 3.2.2 Copyright Cases from China 406
- 3.3 Civil Cases on Trademark Infringement 462
  - 3.3.1 Trademark Cases from United States 462
  - 3.3.2 Trademark Cases from China 500
- 3.4 Civil Cases on Unfair Competition 541
  - 3.4.1 Cases from China 541

Chapter 1
Main Amendments of Chinese Intellectual Property Law

Deli Cheng and Lili Zhao

1.1 General Provisios

1.1.1 Opinions of the Supreme People's Court on Comprehensively Strengthening Judicial Protection of Intellectual Property

Strengthening the protection of intellectual property plays the most important role in improving the system of property rights protection, and also serves as the biggest momentum to enhance our country's economic competitiveness. As a critical part of the intellectual property protection regime, judicial protection of intellectual protection has made contributions that are essential and irreplaceable. Therefore, stronger judicial protection of intellectual property can meet the needs of China in observing international rules and fulfilling international commitments; and more importantly, it reflects an intrinsic requirement of our country to promote high-quality economic development and build a new economic system with more transparency. For the purposes of fully recognizing the significance of strengthening the judicial protection of intellectual property, accurately discerning its initial purpose and positioning, and providing effective judicial services and safeguards to modernize the national governance system and capabilities, the opinions on the court's protection of intellectual property are hereby offered as follows.

D. Cheng (✉)
Shanghai International College of Intellectual Property, Tongji University, Shanghai, China
e-mail: cdl@tongji.edu.cn

L. Zhao
Xiangshan People's Court, Xiangshan Ningbo, China

I. General Requirements

1. With Xi Jinping Thought on Socialism with Chinese Characteristics for a New Era as the guiding principle, efforts shall be made to extensively implement the Opinions on Several Issues concerning Heightening Reform and Innovation in Intellectual Property Adjudication and the Opinions on Strengthening the Protection of Intellectual Property Rights issued by the General Office of the CPC Central Committee and the General Office of the State Council, and to closely revolve around "striving to make the people feel fairness and justice in every judicial case", a goal that serves the overall judicial landscape, the general public and fair justice. There shall also be efforts to improve the procedures of intellectual property adjudication through use of judicial relief and punitive measures, as well as to enhance the systems and mechanisms for intellectual property adjudication, effectively restrain illegal and criminal activities involving intellectual property, and comprehensively elevate the judicial protection of intellectual property. Faster actions shall be taken to modernize the intellectual property adjudication regime and capacity, so as to provide robust judicial services and safeguards to implement the innovation-driven development strategy and cultivate a pro-business environment that is stable, fair, transparent and predicable.

II. Effectively Protecting the Lawful Rights and Interests of Right-Holders Based on the Characteristics of Individual Cases

2. Stronger protection of technological innovations: Judicial interpretations for adjudicating administrative disputes relating to the granting and validation of patents shall be developed to standardize the examination of patents and increase the quality of patents granted. The adjudication of intellectual property cases in terms of patents, new plant varieties, layout designs of integrated circuits, and computer software shall be strengthened, and the scope and intensity of the protection of intellectual property rights shall be aligned with their technological contributions. Technological progress and innovations shall be encouraged in order to maximize the role of technology in supporting and driving both economic and social development. Research on the judicial protection of drug patents shall be intensified, and research and development of new drugs shall be stimulated so as to promote the sound development of the pharmaceutical industry.

3. More rigorous protection of rights and interests in trademarks: The proximity of trademarks, similarity of goods, distinctiveness and popularity of trademarks of which an application for protection is filed shall be taken into account when a trademark infringement dispute or an administrative dispute relating to the granting and validation of trademarks is adjudicated according to the law. Trademarks shall be made more identifiable and distinguishable. Interpretations shall be made within the range of discretion conferred by law to effectively regulate malicious applications for trademark registration by fully leveraging legal rules, so as to ensure that applications for trademark registration will be filed in an orderly and standardized manner. The protection of well-known trademarks shall be strengthened, and the burden of proof on the holders of rights to the trademarks regarding the popularity of trademarks shall be reduced based on the fact that they are well known to all. The protection of geographical indications shall be strengthened to properly settle disputes over rights to geographical indications and ordinary trademarks.

4. More effective protection of copyrights and the relevant rights: Based on the unique quality of different works, the standards for judgment of originality of works shall be meticulously discerned. The relation between the development of information network technologies and the protection of copyrights and the relevant rights shall be properly handled, and the interests between creators, disseminators, business operators and the general public shall be balanced. Efforts to encourage creation, promote industrial development, and safeguard basic cultural rights and interests shall be coordinated to boost cultural innovation and the development of business forms. Some novel cases such as disputes over sports events and electronic sports shall be adequately adjudicated, and the development of emerging forms of business shall be advanced. More research on copyright infringement litigation and copyright protection shall be carried out. The interests of all relevant parties shall be balanced according to the law, and improper profit-making activities shall be prevented.

5. Stronger protection of trade secrets: The boundaries between civil disputes over trade secrets and criminal activities infringing trade secrets shall be accurately established. The rules of burden of proof in civil procedure shall be adequately applied to reduce the burden of right-holders in protecting their rights according to the law. The criteria of determining the crime of infringing trade secrets shall be improved, the scope and methods of calculating heavy losses arising therefrom shall be regulated, and the costs of reasonable remedial measures taken to reduce business losses or restore safety may be deemed as the basis for determining "heavy losses" or "particularly serious consequences" in criminal cases. The protection of trade secrets such as confidential business information shall be strengthened in an effort to ensure fair competition among enterprises and reasonable flow of personnel, as well as to promote technological innovations.

6. Better rules for determining infringement of e-commerce platforms: Acts of infringing intellectual property rights online shall be rigorously restrained and punished, and complaints filed by right-holders on e-commerce platforms shall be responded to effectively. Better channels shall be provided to right-holders to protect their rights by improving the 'notice-delete' rule and other management rules of e-commerce platforms. In order to properly hear disputes over online intellectual property infringement and disputes over malicious complaint and unfair competition, it is required, on one hand, to exempt bona fide providers of infringement notices from any legal liability, urge and guide e-commerce platforms to fulfill statutory obligations, and promote sound development of electronic commerce; and on the other hand, to subject those abusing rights or filing malicious complaints to legal liabilities and properly balance the interests of all parties concerned.

7. Better transfer and application of intellectual achievements: Disputes over the transfer, commercialization and application of intellectual property achievements shall be properly heard by following the principles of respecting the autonomy of will of the parties concerned and lowering the costs of transactions, as well as adequately defining legal relationship, distribution of benefits and assumption of liabilities in the complete process from creation to application of intellectual achievements. Service inventions and non-service inventions shall be clearly defined with an aim to effectively protect property rights of service inventors and safeguard the lawful rights and interests of R&D personnel in receiving bonuses and remunerations for exploitation of their patents.

8. Punishment on intellectual property crimes: Efforts shall be made to severely combat intellectual property crimes, further advance the reform of the trial-centered criminal procedure system, implement the requirements for substantiation of court trials, improve forensic identification procedures, and standardize the system for forensic experts to testify before the court as well as the system for imposing lenient punishments on those admitting guilt and accepting punishment. The boundaries between criminal legal relations and civil legal relations involving intellectual property rights shall be accurately established, and the application of pecuniary penalty shall be strengthened. The crime of obtaining trade secrets through theft, intimidation, inducement or other illegal means and other criminal activities causing great social harm shall be given stricter and heavier punishments, so as to leverage the role of criminal penalty in punishing and deterring intellectual property crimes.

9. Equal protection of lawful rights of both domestic and foreign business entities: Foreign-related intellectual property disputes triggered by international trade and foreign investment shall be properly heard, with equal protection of domestic and foreign market entities, and simplified notarization and certification procedures. A more impartial, efficient and professional dispute resolution mechanism shall be established so as to elevate the impact and creditability of China's intellectual property adjudication at an international level.

III. Working to Resolve Pronounced Problems by Improving the Actual Effects of Judicial Protection

10. Lower costs for protecting intellectual property rights: Judicial interpretations for evidence in civil procedures for intellectual property rights shall be developed, the rules on the allocation of the burden of proof, the system of removing obstruction of evidence and the system of witnesses appearing in court shall be improved. The approaches to collecting electronic evidence shall be expanded, and the application of rules on electronic data shall be accurately discerned. Applications of the parties for evidence preservation, investigation and evidence collection shall be supported so as to ease the burden of proof on the parties concerned.

11. A shorter period for intellectual property litigation: The pilot program of classification of cases shall be conducted so as to promote the separation of complicated cases from simple ones, separation of trivial cases from major ones, and separation of fast-track trial cases from ordinary ones. The reform of intellectual property adjudication shall be further deepened by seamlessly coordinating civil procedures and administrative procedures for patents and trademarks so as to prevent recurrent litigation. Stricter measures shall be taken to meet the requirements for authorized identification, suspension of action, and retrial of a remanded case, so that less time will be wasted. Applications for conduct preservation shall be supported to create good conditions for the timely enforcement of judgments.

12. A higher amount of damages for infringement: Profits generated from infringement shall be determined according to the law by using relevant data from industrial and commercial departments and taxation departments, third-party commercial platforms, infringers' websites or listing documents, as well as industrial average profit margins. The amount of statutory damages shall be reasonably determined by taking comprehensive consideration of market value of intellectual property, subjective faults of infringers, as well as the duration, scope of impact, severity of consequences of infringement. A higher standard for the amount of damages shall be determined for intellectual property infringement with serious consequences, and counterfeit or pirated goods, as well as materials and instruments mainly used for infringement shall be confiscated and destroyed, so as to effectively prevent the recurrence of intellectual property infringement.

13. Prevention of dishonest actions: Disputes over liability for harm caused by malicious institution of intellectual property actions shall be properly heard, and claims for compensation, including attorney's fees and other reasonable costs, shall be supported according to the law. More rules and guidelines for disputes over jurisdiction of intellectual property cases shall be provided so as to regulate malicious delays of litigation, such as deliberate creation of connections to jurisdiction, and abuse of objections to jurisdiction. Research shall be conducted into including dishonest litigants who violate judicial writs, forge evidence, and initiate malicious litigation in the national credit reporting system.

14. Effective enforcement of judicial judgments on intellectual property: The rules for jurisdiction over the enforcement of intellectual property cases shall be comprehensively optimized. Research shall be conducted on improving the working mechanism for conduct preservation and conduct enforcement. An implementation plan and a guideline for enforcement of intellectual property judgments shall be developed, and enforcement of such judgments shall be strengthened by means of information-based online inquiry and control and joint punishment on activities in bad faith, with a view to ensuring that intellectual property judgments can be effectively enforced.

IV. Improving Overall Efficiency in Judicial Protection with Stronger Systems and Mechanisms

15. A more specialized adjudication system for intellectual property: The establishment of specialized intellectual property courts shall be improved according to the current conditions, rules and trends of intellectual property adjudication, the distribution of courts with jurisdiction over intellectual property cases shall be optimized, the appeal mechanism for intellectual property cases shall be enhanced, and the standards for intellectual property adjudication shall be integrated, in an effort to provide specialized adjudication, centralized jurisdiction, streamlined procedures and professional personnel for intellectual property disputes.

16. Further advancement of the 'three-in-one' adjudication system: A better intellectual property case jurisdiction system and coordination system in alignment with the mechanism for 'three-in-one' trials of civil, administrative and criminal cases involving intellectual property rights shall be established to improve the overall efficiency of the judicial protection of intellectual property. Distinctions in the standard of proof between different legal proceedings shall be ascertained, the res judicata of prior adjudication of related cases shall be dealt with according to the law, and the overlapping criminal, administrative and civil cases involving intellectual property rights shall be properly handled.

17. A better technical fact-finding mechanism: The sources of technical investigators shall be moderately increased, a larger pool of technical investigators for courts shall be prepared, and a national mechanism for sharing of technical investigators shall be established. A technical fact-finding mechanism through which technical investigators, technical advisory experts, technical appraisers and expert assessors may participate in litigation activities shall be created so as to improve the neutrality, objectivity and scientific nature of the technical fact-finding process.

18. More effective guidance for intellectual property cases: A guidance system for intellectual property cases that integrates guiding cases, gazette cases and typical cases of the Supreme People's Court shall be established. The role of typical cases in guiding judicial judgments shall be maximized so as to promote unified adjudicative rules.

19. An open court system based on four platforms: The parties' and the public's access to, participation in, and supervision over court hearings shall be maximally ensured based on the transparency of court procedures, trial activities, judgments and decisions, and enforcement information. More publicity activities on World Intellectual Property Day on April 26 shall be launched with the magnified effect of external publicity, so as to promote the society's understanding and recognition of, respect for and trust of the judicial protection of intellectual property.

20. Stronger international exchange and cooperation on intellectual property rights: China shall play an active role in establishing a multilateral system for intellectual property protection, and work with other countries to promote the creation of new international rules. The communication and cooperation with judicial authorities, research institutes and practicing entities in other countries, and international organizations concerning intellectual property shall be strengthened. In order to create greater impact at the international level, researches, discussions and exchanges on intellectual property protection with significant international impact shall be conducted, and more of China's judgments and decisions on intellectual property cases shall be translated into other languages and recommended to the rest of the world.

V. Working Together to Improve Intellectual Property Protection with More Communication and Coordination

21. A more effective alternative dispute resolution mechanism: More channels shall be provided to resolve disputes over intellectual property rights, and the pilot program of judicial confirmation for mediation agreements on intellectual property rights shall be implemented, so that judicial means will play a better role in guiding and driving the establishment of a better alternative dispute resolution mechanism, and the overall efficiency in dispute settlement will be improved.

22. A better collaboration mechanism for intellectual property protection: In order to join forces to protect intellectual property rights, people's courts shall strengthen communication and coordination with public security organs and procuratorial organs in judicial procedures, and step up cooperation with administrative authorities in intellectual property, market regulation, copyright, customs and agriculture in administrative and enforcement procedures.

23. A mechanism for communication, coordination and sharing of information: A mechanism for data exchange with administrative authorities of intellectual property rights shall be established and improved, and big data analysis tools for intellectual property rights shall be applied on a regular basis, with a view to improving the performance of analysis and decision-making abilities.

VI. Supporting Judicial Protection of Intellectual Property with Better Basic Conditions for Adjudication

24. A more competent team of intellectual property judges: The mechanism for secondment and exchange of judges based on a quota system shall be improved. Outstanding judge assistants shall be appointed to work temporarily in the lower courts, and outstanding judges shall be selected to serve in the higher courts. The exchange and sharing of talented personnel in intellectual property rights shall be encouraged. More training opportunities regarding intellectual property rights shall be provided to judicial officers. More supporting members of the judiciary shall be cultivated, and a team of professional adjudication experts shall be built with a selection of competent judges, assistant judges and clerks working together and under the support of technical investigators.

25. Better basic conditions for specialized tribunals and courts: More efforts shall be made to support the development of the Intellectual Property Tribunal of the Supreme People's Court, as well as local intellectual property tribunals and courts, and ensure that specialized intellectual property judicial organs will have a solid organizational structure, competent personnel, a quality office space, and a sufficient operating budget, so as to lay a bedrock of human resources and materials for judicial protection of intellectual property.

26. Informatization for intellectual property adjudication: More modernized and smart judicial equipment shall be provided, and a trans-regional remote intellectual property litigation platform shall be established. Strong efforts shall be made to promote the popularity and application of information technologies in judicial procedures, such as online case filing, online evidence exchange, electronic service, online court hearing, smart voice recognition, electronic filing, and mobile micro courts. The complete adjudication process shall be supported online as part of an effort to make the judicial resolution of intellectual property disputes easier, more efficient and transparent. Extensive use of electronic case files, judgments and decisions, and information about judicial trials shall be supported, and big data in the justice system shall be fully leveraged to ensure smart services and help make accurate decisions.

1.1.2 Opinions of the Supreme People's Court on Legally Imposing Heavier Punishments for Infringements of Intellectual Property Rights

For the purposes of trying cases impartially, imposing heavier punishments for infringements of intellectual property rights ('IPRs') according to the law, effectively deterring infringements, and creating a good law-based business environment, the following opinions are developed in consideration of the actual IPR trial practices.

I. Strengthening the Application of Preservation Measures

1. Where a right holder applies for conduct preservation with respect to conduct that will cause irreparable damage, such as infringement or imminent infringement upon any core technology, well-known brand, hit show or any other IPR, or infringement or imminent infringement upon any IPR at an exhibition, the people's court shall conduct examination and make a ruling in a timely manner according to the law.

2. Where a right holder applies for both an advance judgment to cease infringement and for conduct preservation in an IPR infringement action, the people's court shall conduct examination of both applications in a timely manner according to the law.

3. If a right holder has preliminary evidence proving that there is an IPR infringement and that the evidence may be destroyed or lost, or may be difficult to obtain at a later time, and applies for preservation of evidence, the people's court shall conduct examination and make a ruling in a timely manner according to the law. The preservation of evidence involving highly professional and technical issues may be participated in by technical investigators.

4. Where an alleged infringer destroys or transfers without approval the allegedly infringing products against which preservation measures have been taken, or does such actions to other evidence, a result of which is that the facts of infringement cannot be ascertained, the people's court may presume that the claims of the right holder regarding the certification items relating to the evidence are tenable. Under the circumstances of obstructing actions as provided for by laws, compulsory measures shall be taken according to the law.

II. Making a Judgment to Cease Infringements According to the Law

5. If the facts of infringement have been clear, and it can be determined that an infringement is tenable, the people's court may make an advance judgment to cease the infringement according to the law.

6. Where a right holder adduces evidence to prove the existence of counterfeit or pirated goods or materials and tools mainly used for the production or manufacture of counterfeit or pirated goods and requests the prompt destruction thereof in a civil action, the people's court shall support it, except under special circumstances. Under special circumstances, the people's court may order the disposal of materials and tools that are mainly used for the production or manufacture of counterfeit or pirated goods outside of commercial channels to minimize the risk of further infringement; and where the infringer requests compensation, the people's court shall not support such a request.

III. Increasing Compensation According to the Law

7. A people's court shall make full use of rules and methods such as obstruction of evidence, investigation and evidence collection, evidence preservation, professional assessment, and economic analysis, among others, to direct the parties to proactively, comprehensively, correctly and honestly adduce evidence, improve the scientific nature and rationality of the calculation of the amounts of damages, and fully make up for the losses sustained by right holders.

8. A people's court shall determine the profit generated from an infringement according to the law by proactively using relevant data from the industrial and commercial department and the taxation department, third-party commercial platforms, the infringer's website, publicity materials, or legally disclosed documents, as well as the industry's average profit rate, among others.

9. Where a right holder legally requests the determination of the amount of damages based on the profits generated from an infringement and has adduced evidence, the people's court may order the infringer to provide evidence on the profit generated from the infringement that it or they have; and where a infringer refuses to provide evidence without a good reason or fails to provide evidence as required, the people's court may determine the amount of damages based on the right holder's claim and on-record evidence.

10. For an intentional IPR infringement with serious circumstances, the right holder's request for punitive damages shall be supported according to the law, and the deterrent effect of punitive damages on the intentional infringement shall be maximized.

11. A people's court shall determine the level of statutory damages in a reasonable manner according to the law. Where the infringement has caused heavy loss to the right holder or the infringer has made huge profits therefrom, the people's court may, with a view to fully compensating for the losses of the right holder and effectively deterring the infringement, determine statutory damages on the level that is close to or reaches the ceiling at the request of the right holder.

The factors that the people's court shall consider when determining the level of statutory damages, whichever is higher: whether the infringer's infringement is intentional, whether the infringer engages in infringement which is their main business, whether there are repeated infringements, whether the infringement lasts for a long time, whether the infringement involves a wide range of areas, and whether the infringement may endanger personal safety, destroy environmental resources or damage public interests, among others.

12. Where a right holder requests the inclusion of new reasonable expenses paid to stop the infringement in the level of damages during the second-instance procedure, the people's court may examine it all along with others.

13. A people's court shall, after comprehensively considering factors such as the complexity of the case, the professionalism and intensity of the work, industry practices, and local government guidance prices and based on the evidence provided by the right holder, reasonably determine the attorney fees to be claimed by the right holder for compensation.

IV. Reinforcing Criminal Crackdown

14. The amount of illegal business operations and the level of illegal income arising from committing the crime of infringing upon IPRs through online sales shall be determined by taking into full consideration the electronic data on online sales, transaction records of bank accounts, delivery notes, computer system records of logistics companies, witness testimony, the defendants' confessions, and other evidence.

15. Where an infringer engages in IPR infringement which is their main business, counterfeits the registered trademark of the goods for emergency rescue and disaster relief or epidemic prevention, among others, during a certain period, or successively infringes upon any IPR, constituting a crime, after being given an administrative punishment due to the infringement upon the IPR, a heavier punishment shall be imposed according to the law, and probation shall generally not apply.

16. Illegal income shall be strictly recovered according to the law, the application of pecuniary penalty shall be strengthened, and criminals shall be deprived of the capacity of and conditions for infringing upon IPRs again.

1.1.3 Guiding Opinions of the Supreme People's Court on the Trial of Intellectual Property Civil Cases Involving e-Commerce Platforms

These Guiding Opinions are developed in light of the intellectual property trial practices for the purposes of fairly hearing intellectual property civil cases involving e-commerce platforms, protecting the legitimate rights and interests of all parties in e-commerce in accordance with the law, and promoting the standardized, orderly and healthy development of e-commerce platform business activities.

I. In hearing cases of intellectual property disputes involving e-commerce platforms, the People's Court shall, under the principle of strictly protecting intellectual property rights, punish acts of providing counterfeit, pirated and other infringing goods or services through e-commerce platforms in accordance with the law, actively encourage the parties to follow the principle of good faith and exercise their rights properly in accordance with the law, and properly handle the relationship between the intellectual property owner, the e-commerce platform operator and the business owner operating on the e-commerce platform.

II. In hearing cases of intellectual property disputes involving e-commerce platforms, the people's court shall determine whether the relevant party is the e-commerce platform operator or a business owner operating on the e-commerce platform in accordance with Article 9 of the E-commerce Law of the People's Republic of China (hereinafter referred to as the 'E-commerce Law').

When determining whether an e-commerce platform operator conducts self-operated business, the people's court may consider the following factors: the "self-operating" information marked on the product sales page, the information on the seller marked on the physical product, and the information on the seller marked on the invoice and other transaction documents, among others.

III. Where an e-commerce platform operator knows or should know that a business owner operating on the platform infringes on intellectual property rights, it shall take necessary measures in a timely manner based on the nature of the rights, the specific circumstances and technical conditions of infringement, as well as the prima facie evidence of infringement and the types of service. The necessary measures taken shall follow the principle of reasonable prudence, including but not limited to deletion, blocking, disconnection and other removal measures. If a business owner operating on the platform has repeatedly and deliberately infringed on intellectual property rights, the e-commerce platform operator has the power to take measures to terminate transactions and services.

IV. In accordance with the provisions of Articles 41, 42, and 43 of the e-Commerce Law, the operator of an e-commerce platform may develop specific implementation measures for the platform-wide notification and declaration mechanism according to the type of intellectual property rights and the characteristics of goods or services. However, the relevant measures may not set unreasonable conditions or obstacles to the parties in taking actions to protect their rights in accordance with the law.

V. A notification given by the intellectual property owner to the e-commerce platform operator in accordance with Article 42 of the e-Commerce Law shall typically include: information on the true identity of the intellectual property certificate and the owner; information on the alleged infringing goods or services that can be accurately located; the prima facie evidence of the tort; and a written guarantee of the authenticity of the notification. This notification shall be made in written form.

Where a notification involves patent rights, the e-commerce platform operator may require the intellectual property owner to submit a description of the comparison of technical features or design features, a utility model or design patent right evaluation report, and other materials.

VI. When determining whether the notifier has "maliciousness" as mentioned in paragraph 3 of Article 42 of the e-Commerce Law, the people's court may consider the following factors: submission of falsified or altered property right certificates; submission of expert opinions on comparison of misrepresentation torts; making the notification, knowing that the state of rights is unstable; failure to cancel or correct a notification in a timely manner, knowing that the notification is wrong; and repeated submission of error notifications.

Where an e-commerce platform operator or a business owner operating on the platform files a lawsuit with the people's court on the grounds that it has been harmed by erroneous notification or maliciously making a notification, it may be heard together with cases of intellectual property disputes involving e-commerce platforms.

VII. A statement of non-existence of tort submitted by a business owner operating on the platform to the e-commerce platform operator according to Article 43 of the E-commerce Law typically includes: (1) the true identity of the business owner; (2) information on goods or services that accurately locate and require termination of necessary measures; (3) prima facie evidence for ownership certificates or authorization certificates in which there is no existence of tort; (4) a written warranty of authenticity of the statement. This statement shall be made in written form.

Where the declaration involves patent rights, the e-commerce platform operator may require the business owner operating on the platform to submit materials such as descriptions of the comparison of technical features or design features.

VIII. When determining whether a statement made by the business owner operating on the platform is malicious, the people's court may consider the following factors: whether the forged or invalid certificates of rights and authorization have been provided; whether the statement contains false information or is obviously misleading; whether a statement is still issued, though an effective judgment or administrative decision on the determination of infringement has been attached to the notification; and whether the statement is not be canceled or corrected in a timely manner, knowing that it is wrong.

IX. Where an e-commerce platform operator does not immediately take measures such as taking the product off the shelf in case of an emergency, causing irreparable damage to the legitimate interests of the intellectual property owner, the intellectual property owner may apply to the people's court for preservation measures in accordance with the provisions of Articles 100 and 101 of the Civil Procedure Law of the People's Republic of China.

Where, in case of an emergency, the e-commerce platform operator does not immediately restore the product link or the notifier does not immediately withdraw the notification or stop sending the notification, irreparably damaging the legitimate interests of business owners operating on the platform, they may apply to the people's court for preservation measures in accordance with the provisions prescribed in the preceding paragraph.

Where an application from the intellectual property owner or a business owner operating on the platform complies with the law, the people's court shall support such application according to law.

X. When judging whether the e-commerce platform operator has taken reasonable measures, the people's court may consider the following factors: the prima facie evidence of the tort; the possibility of the tort; the scope of the tort; the specific circumstances of the tort, including whether there exist malicious infringements and repeated infringements; the effectiveness of preventing damage expansion; the possible impact on the interests of the business owners operating on the platform; and the service types and technical conditions of the e-commerce platform.

Where a business owner operating on the platform has evidence to prove that the patent rights involved in the notification have been declared invalid by the National Intellectual Property Administration, and the e-commerce platform operator suspends necessary measures accordingly, and the intellectual property owner requests to determine that the e-commerce platform operator has not taken necessary measures in a timely manner, the people's court shall not provide support.

XI. Where an e-commerce platform operator falls under one of the following circumstances, the people's court may determine that it should be aware of the existence of the tort:

1. Failure to fulfill statutory obligations to develop rules for the protection of intellectual property rights and to examine the operating qualifications of business owners operating on the platform;
2. Failure to Examine the Certificates of Rights of Business Owners that Are Marked as "Flagship Store" or "Brand Store" in Terms of Store Type;
3. Failure to take effective technical means to filter and block the links of infringing products that contain words such as "highly imitated" and "fake goods" and that are relaunched after the complaint is established;
4. Any Other Circumstance Where the Obligations of Reasonable Review and Care Are not Fulfilled.

1.1.4 *Official Reply of the Supreme People's Court on Several Issues Concerning the Application of Law to Disputes over Internet-related Intellectual Property Right (IPR) Infringement*

The higher people's courts of all provinces, autonomous regions, and municipalities directly under the Central Government; the Military Court of the People's Liberation Army; and the Production and Construction Corps Branch of the Higher People's Court of Xinjiang Uygur Autonomous Region:

Recently, relevant sides have offered recommendations on certain issues concerning the application of the law to disputes over Internet-related IPR infringement, and some higher people's courts have also requested the Supreme People's Court for instructions. Upon deliberation, the following official reply ishereby offered.

I. If an IPR holder claims that its or his right has been infringed upon and filed an application for preservation, requiring Internet service providers (ISPs) or e-commerce platform operators to promptly take such removal measures as deletion, block, or disconnection, the people's court shall conduct an examination and make a ruling in accordance with the law.

II. After receiving the notice issued by an IPR holder in accordance with the law, the Internet service providers or e-commerce platform operators shall, in a timely manner, forward the notice from the right holder to the relevant Internet users or businesses on the platform, and take necessary measures based on the prima facie evidence of the tort and type of service; and if any Internet service provider or e-commerce platform operator fails to take necessary measures in a timely manner, the right holder claims that it shall be jointly and severally liable for any additional harm with the relevant Internet users or businesses on the platform, the people's court may support such claim in accordance with the law.

III. If any Internet service provider or e-commerce platform operator fails to receive, within a reasonable period of time after a forwarded statement of non-existence of tort reaches the IPR holder, a notice that the right holder has complained or instituted an action, it shall, in a timely manner, terminate the removal measures taken, such as deletion, block, or disconnection. Delays caused due to exceptional circumstances, such as notarization and certification procedures, beyond the control of the right holder will not be included in the aforesaid period, but the period shall not exceed 20 working days at a maximum.

IV. If the e-commerce platform operators terminate the necessary measures and damage is caused to the IPR holder due to malicious submission of the statement, and the right holder requests corresponding punitive damages in accordance with the provisions of relevant laws, the people's court may support such request in accordance with law.

V. If the contents of the notice issued by an IPR holder are inconsistent with the objective facts, but in the litigation, it or he claims that the notice was submitted in good faith and requests exemption from liability, and can provide the evidence to prove its or his claim, the people's court shall support such claim after examination and verification in accordance with the law.

VI. This Official Reply shall apply to cases for which no final judgment has been rendered after this Official Reply is made; this Official Reply shall not apply to cases for which final judgment has been rendered before the Official Reply is made, those of which the parties apply for retrial, or those that are determined to be retried under the trial supervision procedures.

1.1.5 Several Provisions of the Supreme People's Court on Technical Investigators' Participation in Litigation Activities Relating to Intellectual Property Cases

In order to regulate technical investigators' participation in the litigation activities relating to intellectual property cases, the present Provisions are developed in accordance with the Organization Law of the People's Court of the People's Republic of China, the Criminal Procedure Law of the People's Republic of China, the Civil Procedure Law of the People's Republic of China and the Administrative Procedure Law of the People's Republic of China and in light of judicial practices.

Article 1 When hearing intellectual property cases involving such specialties or technologies as patents, new variety of plants, layout design of integrated circuit, know-how, computer software and monopoly, people's courts may assign technical investigators to participate in litigation activities.

Article 2 Technical investigators are trial support staff.

People's courts may set up a technical investigation office to be responsible for the daily management of technical investigators, assigning technical investigators to participate in litigation activities relating to intellectual property cases and providing technical advice.

Article 3 After the technical investigator participating in the litigation activities relating to an intellectual property case is determined or changed, the parties to the case shall be informed within three days of the determination or change as well as their right to challenge the technical investigator in accordance with the law.

Article 4 The challenge of a technical investigator shall be subject mutatis mutandis to the applicable provisions of the criminal procedure law, civil procedure law and administrative procedure law governing the challenge of relevant other personnel.

Article 5 Any technical investigator that has participated in the litigation activities in a trial procedure shall not participate in the litigation activities of other procedures in the same case.

If a case remanded for retrial enters the procedure of the second instance after the court of first instance renders a judgment, the technical investigator participating in the litigations in the procedure of the original second instance will not be subject to the provisions prescribed in the preceding paragraph.

Article 6 The technical investigator participating in the litigation activities relating to an intellectual property case shall perform the following duties on the technical issues involved in the said case:

(1) Offer a proposal on the controversial focus of technical facts, as well as the scope, order and method of investigation;
(2) Participate in investigation, evidence collection, inquest and preservation;
(3) Participate in inquiries, hearings, pre-trial conferences and trials;
(4) Raise technical investigation opinions;
(5) Assist judges in organizing experts and professionals in relevant technical fields to give their opinions;

(6) Sit in on relevant meetings such as deliberations at the collegial panel;
(7) Complete other related work.

Article 7 For the participation in investigation, evidence collection, inquest and preservation, the technical investigator shall consult relevant technical materials in advance and put forward proposals on the methods, procedures and precautions for investigation, evidence collection, inquest and preservation.

Article 8 When participating in inquiries, hearings, pre-trial conferences and trials for a case, the technical investigator may, with the consent of the judge, raise questions on technical issues involved in the case to the parties and other litigation participants.

The seat in court for the technical investigator is on the left of the judge assistant, and the clerk's seat is on the right of the judge assistant.

Article 9 The technical investigator for a case shall give his/her technical investigation opinions on the technical issues involved in the case prior to the deliberation of the case.

Technical investigation opinions shall be independently issued by the technical investigator with his/her signature, and shall not be disclosed to the public.

Article 10 When a technical investigator sits in on the deliberation of a case, his/her opinions shall be recorded in the transcript of the deliberations, with his/her signature provided.

A technical investigator shall have no right to vote on the judgement of a case.

Article 11 Technical investigation opinions put forward by a technical investigator may serve as a reference for the collegial panel to determine the technical facts.

The collegiate panel shall be responsible for the determination of technical facts.

Article 12 The technical investigator that participates in the litigation activities relating to an intellectual property case shall sign the judgment documents, and his/her signature shall be located below that of the judge assistant and above that of the clerk.

Article 13 Any technical investigator who commits corruption or bribery, practices favoritism for personal gains or deliberately provides false or misleading technical investigation opinions or opinions with material loopholes, in violation of the laws and provisions relating to the trial work, will be investigated for legal liability; if a crime is constituted, the technical investigator will be held criminally liable in accordance with the law.

Article 14 A people's court at higher level may, as required for trial of cases, dispatch the technical investigators of the people's courts at various levels within its jurisdiction.

For the hearing of a case referred to in Article 1 hereof, the people's court concerned may apply to the superior people's court to dispatch technical investigators to participate in relevant litigation activities.

Article 15 The present Provisions shall come into force on May 1, 2019. In case of any discrepancy between the regulations previously promulgated by the Supreme People's Court and the present Provisions, the latter shall prevail.

1.1.6 Supreme People's Court Guiding Opinions on Unifying the Application of Laws and on Strengthening Searches for Similar Cases (for Trial Implementation)

For the purposes of unifying the application of laws and enhancing the judicial credibility, the following opinions on the retrieval of similar cases by people's courts are hereby put forward based on trial practices.

I. For the purpose of these Opinions, "similar cases" means those cases that are similar to the pending cases in terms of basic facts, focus of disputes, and issues concerning the application of laws, in which the judgments made by people's courts have taken effect.

II. A people's court handling a case under any of the following circumstances shall retrieve similar cases:

1. where the case is to be submitted to the professional (presiding) judge meeting or the judicial committee for discussion;
2. where there is no clear judgment rules or uniform judgment rules have not been formed;
3. where the president and division chief judges of the people's court require to retrieve similar cases according to the authority of trial supervision and administration; or
4. other circumstances requiring the retrieval of similar cases.

III. A judge handling the case shall retrieve similar cases based on the China Judgments Online (www.wenshu.court.gov.cn), the trial case database, etc., and be responsible for the veracity and accuracy of retrieval.

IV. The retrieval scope of similar cases generally includes:

1. guiding cases issued by the SPC;
2. model cases issued by the SPC and cases in which the judgments made by the SPC have taken effect;
3. reference cases issued by the higher people's courts of the provinces (autonomous regions or municipalities directly under the Central Government) and cases in which the judgments made by such courts have taken effect; and
4. cases in which the judgments made by the people's court at the next higher level or this people's court have taken effect.

In addition to guiding cases, priority shall be given to cases in the past three years; and where similar cases have been retrieved already in the previous order of precedence, the people's courts are not required to retrieve more cases.

V. The retrieval of keywords, the retrieval of cases correlated to laws, the correlated retrieval of cases, and other methods may be adopted in the retrieval of similar cases.

VI. A judge handing a case shall identify and compare the similarity between the pending case and the retrieval result to determine whether it belongs to a similar case.

VII. For a case for which similar cases should be retrieved as prescribed in these Opinions, the judge handing the case shall give an explanation about the retrieval of similar cases in the deliberations of the collegial panel, the discussions of the professional (presiding) judge meeting, and the trial report, or prepare a special case retrieval report, and file it with the case for reference.

VIII. The retrieval explanation or report of a similar case shall be objective, comprehensive and accurate, including the information such as the subject, time, platform, method, result of the retrieval, the key points of judgments in the similar case, and the focus of disputes in the pending case, and analyzing and explaining whether such similar case is referred to or the application of the results, such as reference to the similar case.

IX. Where a retrieved similar case is a guiding case, the people's court shall make a judgment by reference to the case, except for those which conflict with new laws, administrative regulations, or judicial interpretations or those which have been replaced by new guiding cases.

Where other similar cases are retrieved, the people's court can take them as a reference for making judgments.

X. In a case, where the public prosecution authority, any party to the case or the defender or litigation representative thereof, et. al. submits a guiding case as a ground for prosecution (or defense), the people's court shall respond whether it should rely on the guiding case and explain the reasons in the reasoning of the judgment; where other similar cases are submitted as a ground for prosecution (or defense), it shall respond by means of interpretation or other means.

XI. Where there are inconsistencies in the application of laws in a retrieved similar case, the people's court may, by taking into account factors such as the level of the court, the time of the adjudication and whether such inconsistencies have been discussed by the judicial committee, resolve the differences through the mechanism for resolving differences in the application of laws, in accordance with the Implementation Measures of the Supreme People's Court for Establishing the Mechanism for Resolving Differences in the Application of Laws and other provisions.

XII. The people's courts at all levels shall actively advance the retrieval of similar cases, strengthen the re retrieval and development of technologies and the training of the application thereof, and improve the level of intelligence and precision in the push of similar cases.

All higher people's courts shall make full use of modern information technology to establish their trial case databases so as to lay a solid foundation for the building of a unified and authoritative national trial case database.

XIII. The people's courts at all levels shall summarize and sort out the retrievals of similar cases on a regular basis, and disclose such information to the public in them or courts within their respective jurisdiction in a certain form for reference by judges in the handling of cases, and file such information with the trial management departments of the people's court at the next higher level.

XIV. These Opinions shall be implemented on a trial basis from July 31, 2020.

1.2 Main Amendments of Chinese Copyright Laws and Regulations

1.2.1 Copyright Law of the People's Republic of China

(Adopted at the Fifteenth Session of the Standing Committee of the Seventh National People's Congress on September 7, 1990 and amended for the first time in accordance with the Decision of the 24th Session of the Standing Committee of the Ninth National People's Congress Concerning Amendment to the Copyright Law of the People's Republic of China on October 27, 2001; amended for the second time in accordance with the Decision of the 13th Session of the Standing Committee of the Eleventh National People's Congress Concerning Amendment to the Copyright Law of the People's Republic of China on February 26, 2010; amended for the third time in accordance with Decision of the 23rd session of Standing Committee of the National People's Congress on Amending the Copyright Law of the People's Republic of China on November 11, 2020).

Before revision (effective April 1, 2010)	Revised (effective June 1, 2021)
Chapter I General Provisions	
Article 3 "Works" mentioned in this Law shall include works of literature, art, natural science, social science, engineering technology and the like made in the following forms: (1) written works; (2) oral works; (3) musical, dramatic, quyi, choreographic and acrobatic art works; (4) works of fine art and architecture (5) photographic works; (6) cinematographic works and works created in a way similar to cinematography (7) drawings of engineering designs and product designs, maps, sketches and other graphic works as well as model works; (8) computer software; (9) other works as provided in laws and administrative regulations	Article 3 "Works" mentioned in this Law shall **refer to ingenious intellectual achievements in the fields of literature, art and science that can be presented in a certain form:** (1) written works; (2) oral works; (3) musical, dramatic, quyi, choreographic and acrobatic art works; (4) works of fine art and architecture (5) photographic works; (6) **audiovisual works** (7) drawings of engineering designs and product designs, maps, sketches and other graphic works as well as model works; (8) computer software; (9) **other intellectual achievements that meet the characteristics of works**

(continued)

(continued)

Before revision (effective April 1, 2010)	Revised (effective June 1, 2021)
Article 4 Copyright owners, in exercising their copyright, shall not violate the Constitution or laws or infringe upon the public interests. The state shall supervise and administer the publication and circulation of works according to law	**Article 4** When exercising rights, copyright owners and **copyright-related rights holders** shall not violate the Constitution and laws, or damage public interests. The state shall supervise and administrate the publication and dissemination of works according to the law
Article 5 This Law shall not be applicable to: (1) laws, regulations, resolutions, decisions and orders of state organs; other documents of legislative, administrative or judicial nature; and their official translations; (2) news on current affairs; (3) calendars, numerical tables, forms of general use and formulas	**Article 5** This Law shall not be applicable to: (1) laws, regulations, resolutions, decisions and orders of state organs; other documents of legislative, administrative or judicial nature; and their official translations; (2) **simple factual information;** (3) calendars, numerical tables, forms of general use and formulas
Article 7 The copyright administration department under the State Council shall be responsible for the nationwide administration of copyright. The copyright administration department of the people's government of each province, autonomous region or municipality directly under the Central Government shall be responsible for the administration of copyright within its own jurisdiction	**Article 7 The copyright administration department under the State Council** shall be responsible for the nationwide administration of copyright. **The local copyright authorities at or above the county level** shall be responsible for the administration of copyright within its own jurisdiction
Article 8 Copyright owners and the obligees related to copyright may authorize a collective management organization of copyright to exercise the copyright or the rights related to copyright. The collective management organization of copyright may, after being authorized, claim rights in its own name for the copyright owners and the obligees related to copyright, and may, as a party concerned, participate in the litigation and arbitration activities involved with copyright or the rights related to copyright	**Article 8** Copyright owners and the obligees related to copyright may authorize a collective management organization of copyright to exercise the copyright or the rights related to copyright. **As a non-for-profit legal person, a collective management organization of copyrights lawfully formed may,** with authorization, claim rights in its own name for a copyright owner and a copyright-related right holder, and may, as a party concerned, participate in the litigation, arbitration, and **mediation activities** involved with copyright or the rights related to copyright
A collective management organization of copyright shall be a non-profit organization, and the method of its establishment, its rights and obligations, the collection and distribution of the royalty for copyright licensing, as well as the supervision and management over it shall be separately provided by the State Council	**A collective management organization of copyrights shall collect royalties from users based on the authorization. The standards for the collection of royalties shall be determined by the collective management organization of copyrights and the user representative through negotiation. If the negotiation fails, the parties may apply to the copyright authority of the state for a ruling. If they refuse to accept a ruling, they may institute a lawsuit with the people's court; and the parties may directly institute a lawsuit with the people's court as well**
	A collective management organization of copyrights shall disclose the collection and transfer of royalties, the withdrawal and use of management fees, the unallocated royalties, and other overall situation to the public on a regular basis, and establish a rights information inquiry system for inquiry by right owners, right holders and users. The copyright authority of the state shall supervise and manage collective management organizations of copyrights in accordance with the law For collective management organizations of copyrights, their methods of formation, rights and obligations, and collection and distribution of royalties, as well as supervision over and management of them shall be separately prescribed by the State Council

(continued)

(continued)

Before revision (effective April 1, 2010)	Revised (effective June 1, 2021)
Chapter II Copyright	
Section 1.1 Copyright Owners and Their Rights	
Article 9 "Copyright owners" shall include: (1) authors; (2) other <u>citizens</u>, legal entities and <u>organizations</u> enjoying copyright in accordance with this Law	Article 9 "Copyright owners" shall include: (1) authors; (2) other **natural persons**, legal entities and **unincorporated organizations** enjoying copyright in accordance with this Law
Article 10 "Copyright" shall include the following personal rights and property rights: (1) the right of publication, that is, the right to decide whether to make a work available to the public; (2) the right of authorship, that is, the right to claim authorship and to have the author's name mentioned in connection with the work; (3) the right of alteration, that is, the right to alter or authorize others to alter one's work; (4) the right of integrity, that is, the right to protect one's work against distortion and mutilation; (5) the right of reproduction, that is, the right to produce one or more copies of the work by means of printing, Xeroxing, rubbing, sound recording, video recording, duplicating, or re-shooting, etc.; (6) the right of distribution, that is, the right to provide the public with original copies or reproduced copies of works by means of selling or donating; (7) the right of lease, that is, the right to nongratuitously permit others to <u>temporarily exploit a cinematographic work, a work created in a way similar to cinematography or computer software</u>, unless the computer software is not the main object under the lease; (8) the right of exhibition, that is, the right to publicly display the original copies or reproduced copies of works of fine art and cinematographic works; (9) the right of performance, that is, the right to publicly perform works, and to publicly transmit the performance of works by various means; (10) the right of projection, that is, the right to make, by such technical equipment as projector, episcope, etc., the works of fine art, photographic works, <u>cinematographic works and works created in a way similar to cinematography</u>, etc. reappear publicly; (11) the right of broadcasting, that is, <u>the right to publicly broadcast or disseminate works by wireless means,</u> to disseminate broadcast works to the public by wired dissemination or rebroadcast, and to disseminate broadcast works to the public by audio amplifier or other similar instruments for transmission of signs, sounds or images; (12) the right of information network dissemination, that is, the right to provide the public with <u>works</u> by wired or wireless means, so as to make the public able to respectively obtain <u>the works at the individually</u> selected time and place;	Article 10 "Copyright" shall include the following personal rights and property rights: (1) the right of publication, that is, the right to decide whether to make a work available to the public; (2) the right of authorship, that is, the right to claim authorship and to have the author's name mentioned in connection with the work; (3) the right of alteration, that is, the right to alter or authorize others to alter one's work; (4) the right of integrity, that is, the right to protect one's work against distortion and mutilation; (5) the right of reproduction, that is, the right to produce one or more copies of the work by means of printing, Xeroxing, rubbing, sound recording, video recording, duplicating, re-shooting, or **digital way** etc.; (6) the right of distribution, that is, the right to provide the public with original copies or reproduced copies of works by means of selling or donating; (7) the right of lease, that is, the right to non-gratuitously permit others to temporarily use **the original or copy of audiovisual works** and computer software, unless the computer software is not the main object of lease; (8) the right of exhibition, that is, the right to publicly display the original copies or reproduced copies of works of fine art and cinematographic works; (9) the right of performance, that is, the right to publicly perform works, and to publicly transmit the performance of works by various means; (10) the right of projection, that is, the right to make, by such technical equipment as projector, episcope, etc., the works of fine art, photographic works, **audiovisual works**, etc. reappear publicly; (11) the right of broadcasting, that is, **the right to publicly broadcast or disseminate works by wired or wireless means**, and to disseminate broadcast works to the public by audio amplifier or other similar instruments for transmission of signs, sounds or images, **excluding the right as prescribed in item (12) of this paragraph;** (12) the right of information network dissemination, that is, the right to provide the public with works by wired or wireless means, so as to make the public able to respectively obtain the works at the individually selected time and place;

(continued)

(continued)

Before revision (effective April 1, 2010)	Revised (effective June 1, 2021)
(13) the right of production, that is, the right to fix works on the carrier by cinematography or in a way similar to cinematography; (14) the right of adaptation, that is, the right to modify a work for the purpose of creating a new work of original creation; (15) the right of translation, that is, the right to transform the language of a work into another language; (16) the right of compilation, that is, the right to choose or edit some works or fragments of works so as to form a new work; (17) other rights which shall be enjoyed by the copyright owners A copyright owner may permit others to exercise the rights provided in Items (5) through (17) of the preceding paragraph, and may receive remuneration as agreed upon in the contract or in accordance with the relevant provisions in this Law A copyright owner may wholly or partially transfer the rights provided in Items (5) through (17) of Paragraph 1 of this Article, and may receive remuneration as agreed upon in the contract or in accordance with the relevant provisions in this Law	(13) the right of production, that is, the right to fix works on the carrier **audiovisual works**; (14) the right of adaptation, that is, the right to modify a work for the purpose of creating a new work of original creation; (15) the right of translation, that is, the right to transform the language of a work into another language; (16) the right of compilation, that is, the right to choose or edit some works or fragments of works so as to form a new work; (17) other rights which shall be enjoyed by the copyright owners A copyright owner may permit others to exercise the rights provided in Items (5) through (17) of the preceding paragraph, and may receive remuneration as agreed upon in the contract or in accordance with the relevant provisions in this Law A copyright owner may wholly or partially transfer the rights provided in Items (5) through (17) of Paragraph 1 of this Article, and may receive remuneration as agreed upon in the contract or in accordance with the relevant provisions in this Law
Section 1.2 Ownership of Copyright	
Article 11 Except otherwise provided in this Law, the copyright in a work shall belong to its author The author of a work is the citizen who has created the work Where a work is created according to the intention and under the supervision and responsibility of a legal entity or another organization, such legal entity or organization shall be the author of the work The citizen, legal entity or organization whose name is affixed to a work shall, without the contrary proof, be the author of the work	**Article 11** Except otherwise provided in this Law, the copyright in a work shall belong to its author The author of a work is the **natural person** who has created the work Where a work is created according to the intention and under the supervision and responsibility of a legal entity or **another unincorporated organization**, such legal entity or **unincorporated organization** shall be the author of the work
(Additional)	**Article 12 The natural person, legal person or unincorporated organization whose name is affixed to a work shall, without contrary proof, be the author of the work and have corresponding rights in the work** **Authors and other copyright owners may register their works with a registry recognized by the copyright authority of the state** **The copyright-related rights shall be governed, mutatis mutandis, by the provisions of the preceding two paragraphs**
Article 13 Where a work is created jointly by two or more co-authors, the copyright in the work shall be enjoyed jointly by those co-authors. Co-authorship may not be claimed by anyone who has not participated in the creation of the work If a work of joint authorship can be separated into independent parts and exploited separately, each co-author shall be entitled to independent copyright in the parts that he has created, provided that the exercise of such copyright does not infringe upon the copyright in the joint work as a whole	**Article 14** Where a work is created jointly by two or more co-authors, the copyright in the work shall be enjoyed jointly by those co-authors. Co-authorship may not be claimed by anyone who has not participated in the creation of the work **The copyright of a cooperative work shall be exercised by co-authors upon consensus; and where no consensus has been reached and there is no justified reason, no party shall prevent another party from exercising rights other than transferring and permitting others' exclusive use, and pledging, but the proceeds obtained shall be reasonably distributed to all co-authors**

(continued)

Before revision (effective April 1, 2010)	Revised (effective June 1, 2021)
	If a work of joint authorship can be separated into independent parts and exploited separately, each co-author shall be entitled to independent copyright in the parts that he has created, provided that the exercise of such copyright does not infringe upon the copyright in the joint work as a whole
(Additional)	**Article 16 To use a work produced by adaptation, translation, annotation, sorting, or compilation of an existing work for publication, performance, and production of an audiovisual work, the permission of the copyright owner of the work and the copyright owner of the original work shall be obtained and remunerations shall be paid to the copyright owners**
Article 15 The copyright of a cinematographic work or a work created in a way similar to cinematography shall be enjoyed by the producer, while any of the playwright, director, cameraman, words-writer, composer and other authors of the work shall enjoy the right of authorship, and shall be entitled to obtain remuneration as agreed upon in the contract between him and the producer
The authors of the screenplay, musical works and other works that are included in a cinematographic work or a work created in a way similar to cinematography and can be exploited separately shall be entitled to exercise their copyright independently	**Article 17 The copyright of cinematographic works and TV play works in audiovisual works shall be enjoyed by producers**, but screenwriters, directors, photographers, lyricists, composers, and other authors shall enjoy the right of signature and have the right to obtain remunerations as agreed upon in the contracts signed with producers
The ownership of the copyright of an audiovisual work other than those specified in the preceding paragraph shall be agreed upon by the parties; and where there is no agreement or the agreement is unclear, the copyright shall be enjoyed by the producer, but the author shall have the right of signature and receive remunerations
The authors of script, music, and **other works** that may be used separately shall have the right to separately exercise their right of copyright
Article 16 A work created by a citizen when fulfilling the tasks assigned to him by a legal entity or another organization shall be deemed to be a service work. Unless otherwise provided in Paragraph 2 of this Article, the copyright of such a work shall be enjoyed by the author, but the legal entity or organization shall have a priority right to exploit the work within the scope of its professional activities. During the two years after the completion of the work, the author shall not, without the consent of the legal entity or organization, authorize a third party to exploit the work in the same way as the legal entity or organization does
In the following cases the author of a service work shall enjoy the right of authorship, while the legal entity or organization shall enjoy other rights included in the copyright and may reward the author:	**Article 18** A work created by a **natural person** when fulfilling the tasks assigned to him by a legal entity or another **unincorporated organization** shall be deemed to be a service work. Unless otherwise provided in Paragraph 2 of this Article, the copyright of such a work shall be enjoyed by the author, but the legal entity or **unincorporated organization** shall have a priority right to exploit the work within the scope of its professional activities. During the two years after the completion of the work, the author shall not, without the consent of the legal entity or organization, authorize a third party to exploit the work in the same way as the legal entity or organization does
In the following cases the author of a service work shall enjoy the right of authorship, while the legal entity or **unincorporated organization** shall enjoy other rights included in the copyright and may reward the author:

(continued)

Before revision (effective April 1, 2010)	Revised (effective June 1, 2021)
(1) drawings of engineering designs and product designs, maps, computer software and other service works, which are created mainly with the materials and technical resources of the legal entity or <u>organization</u> and under its responsibility; (2) service works of which the copyright is, in accordance with the laws or administrative regulations or as agreed upon in the contract, enjoyed by the legal entity or <u>organization</u>	(1) **drawings of engineering** designs and product designs, sketch maps, computer software and other service works, which are created mainly with the materials and technical resources of the legal entity or **unincorporated organization** and under its responsibility; (2) **works for hire created by employees of newspapers, periodical presses, news agencies, radio stations, and television stations;** (3) service works of which the copyright is, in accordance with the laws or administrative regulations or as agreed upon in the contract, enjoyed by the legal entity or **unincorporated organization**
Article 18 <u>The transfer of ownership of the original copy of a work of fine art or another work shall not be deemed to include the transfer of the copyright in such a work,</u> however, the right to exhibit the original copy of a work of fine art shall be enjoyed by the owner of such original copy	Article 20 The transfer of the ownership of an original work shall not change the ownership of the copyright **of the work**, but the exhibition rights of an original art work and **photography work** shall be enjoyed by the owner of the original work **Where an author transfers the ownership of an original unpublished art work or photographic work to another, the transferee's exhibition of the original does not constitute an infringement upon the author's right of publication**
Section 3 Term of Protection	
Article 21 In respect of a work of a <u>citizen</u>, the term of protection of the right of publication and of <u>the rights provided in Items (5) through (17) of Paragraph 1 of Article 10 of this Law shall be the lifetime of the author and fifty years after his death, expiring on December 31 of the fiftieth year after his death.</u> In the case of a work of joint authorship, such term shall expire on December 31 of the fiftieth year after the death of the last surviving author The term of protection of the right of publication and of the rights provided in Items (5) through (17) of Paragraph 1 of Article 10 of this Law where the copyright belongs to a legal entity or another organization, or in respect of a service work where the legal entity or <u>organization</u> enjoys the copyright (except the right of authorship), shall be fifty years, expiring on December 31 of the fiftieth year after the first publication of such a work, however, any such work that has not been published within fifty years after the completion of its creation shall no longer be protected by this Law <u>The term of protection of the right of publication and of the rights provided in Items (5) through (17) of Paragraph 1 of Article 10 of this Law in respect of a cinematographic work or a work created in a way similar to cinematography shall be fifty years, expiring on December 31 of the fiftieth year after the first publication of such a work,</u> however, any such work that has not been published within fifty years after the completion of its creation shall no longer be protected by this Law	Article 23 In respect of a work of a **natural person**, the term of protection of the right of publication and of the rights provided in Items (5) through (17) of Paragraph 1 of Article 10 of this Law shall be the lifetime of the author and fifty years after his death, expiring on December 31 of the fiftieth year after his death. In the case of a work of joint authorship, such term shall expire on December 31 of the fiftieth year after the death of the last surviving author For a work of a legal person or **an unincorporated organization**, and a work for hire whose copyright (excluding right of signature) is owned by a legal person or an **unincorporated organization, the protection period for its right of publication shall be 50 years, ending on December 31 of the 50th year after the creation of the work; and the protection period for its rights as prescribed from items (5) to (17) of paragraph 1 of Article 10 herein shall be 50 years, ending on December 31 of the 50th year after the first publication of the work,** but if a work has not been published within 50 years after the completion of the creation, it shall no longer be protected by this Law **For an audiovisual work, the protection period for its right of publication shall be 50 years, ending on December 31 of the 50th year after the creation of the work; and the protection period for its rights as prescribed from items (5) to (17) of paragraph 1 of Article 10 herein shall be 50 years, ending on December 31 of the 50th year after the first publication of the work,** but if a work has not been published within 50 years after the completion of the creation, it shall no longer be protected by this Law
Section 1.4 Limitations on Rights	

(continued)

(continued)

Before revision (effective April 1, 2010)	Revised (effective June 1, 2021)
Article 22 In the following cases, a work may be exploited without the permission from, and without payment of remuneration to, the copyright owner, provided that the name of the author and the title of the work are mentioned and the other rights enjoyed by the copyright owner by virtue of this Law are not infringed upon: (1) use of a published work for the purposes of the user's own private study, research or self-entertainment; (2) appropriate quotation from a published work in one's own work for the purposes of introduction of, or comment on, a work, or demonstration of a point; (3) inevitable reappearance or citation of a published work in newspapers, periodicals, radio stations, television stations or other media for the purpose of reporting current events; (4) reprinting by newspapers or periodicals or other media, or rebroadcasting by radio stations or television stations or other media, of the current event articles on the issues of politics, economy and religion, which have been published by other newspapers, periodicals, radio stations or television stations or other media, except where the author has declared that publication or broadcasting is not permitted; (5) publication in newspapers or periodicals or other media, or broadcasting by radio stations or television stations or other media, of a speech delivered at a public assembly, except where the author has declared that publication or broadcasting is not permitted; (6) translation or reproduction, in a small quality of copies, of a published work for use by teachers or scientific researchers in classroom teaching or scientific research, provided that the translation or reproduction is not published or distributed; (7) use of a published work by a State organ within the reasonable scope for the purpose of fulfilling its official duties; (8) reproduction of a work in its collections by a library, archive, memorial hall, museum, art gallery or similar institution, for the purpose of the display or preservation of a copy of the work; (9) free of charge performance of a published work, that is, with respect to the performance, neither fees are charged from the public nor the remuneration is paid to the performers; (10) copying, drawing, photographing, or video recording of an artistic work located or on display in an outdoor public place; (11) translation of a work published by a Chinese citizen, legal entity or organization, which is created in the Han language (Chinese), into a minority nationality language for publication and distribution within the country;	**Article 24** In the following cases, a work may be exploited without the permission from, and without payment of remuneration to, the copyright owner, provided that the name **or designation of the author** and the title of the work are mentioned and the normal use of the work, or **unreasonably damage the lawful rights and interests of the copyright owner shall not be affected:** (1) use of a published work for the purposes of the user's own private study, research or self-entertainment; (2) appropriate quotation from a published work in one's own work for the purposes of introduction of, or comment on, a work, or demonstration of a point; (3) inevitable reappearance or citation of a published work in newspapers, periodicals, radio stations, television stations or other media for the purpose of reporting news; (4) reprinting by newspapers or periodicals or other media, or rebroadcasting by radio stations or television stations or other media, of the current event articles on the issues of politics, economy and religion, which have been published by other newspapers, periodicals, radio stations or television stations or other media, except where the **copyright owner** has declared that publication or broadcasting is not permitted; (5) publication in newspapers or periodicals or other media, or broadcasting by radio stations or television stations or other media, of a speech delivered at a public assembly, except where the author has declared that publication or broadcasting is not permitted; (6) **translation, adaptation, compilation**, and broadcasting or reproduction, in a small quality of copies, of a published work for use by teachers or scientific researchers in classroom teaching or scientific research, provided that the translation or reproduction is not published or distributed; (7) use of a published work by a State organ within the reasonable scope for the purpose of fulfilling its official duties; (8) reproduction of a work in its collections by a library, archive, memorial hall, museum, art **gallery**, art museum or similar institution, for the purpose of the display or preservation of a copy of the work; (9) free of charge performance of a published work, that is, with respect to the performance, neither fees are charged from the public nor the remuneration is paid to the performers, **nor the performance is for profit;** (10) copying, drawing, photographing, or video recording of an artistic work located or on display in a public place; (11) translation of a work published by a Chinese citizen, legal entity or **unincorporated organization,** which is created in the **national common language and characters**, into a minority nationality language for publication and distribution within the country;

(continued)

(continued)

Before revision (effective April 1, 2010)	Revised (effective June 1, 2021)
(12) translation of a published work into Braille and publication of the work so translated; The provisions in the preceding paragraph shall be applicable to the limitations on the rights of publishers, performers, producers of sound recordings and video recordings, radio stations and television stations	(12) **providing published works for dyslexics in a barrier-free way through which they can perceive;** (13) **other circumstances prescribed by laws and administrative regulations** The provisions of the preceding paragraph **shall apply to restrictions on copyright-related rights**
Article 23 Anyone who compiles or publishes textbooks for the purpose of implementing the nine-year compulsory education or State education planning may, without the permission from the copyright owner, except that the author has declared in advance that the exploitation is not permitted, compile published fragments of works, short written works or musical works, a single work of fine art, or photographic works into the textbooks, however, he shall pay the remuneration as provided, mention the name of the author and the title of the work, and shall not infringe upon other rights which the copyright owner shall enjoy in accordance with this Law The provisions in the preceding paragraph shall be applicable to the limitations on the rights of publishers, performers, producers of sound recordings and video recordings, radio stations and television stations	**Article 25** Those who compile and publish textbooks for the purpose of implementing compulsory education or educational planning of the state may, without permission of copyright owners, compile published fragments of works, short written works, musical works, or single art works, photographic works, or **graphic works** in the textbooks, however, they shall **pay remunerations to copyright owners** according to the provisions, and designate the names or designations of authors, and titles of works, and **shall not infringe upon other rights enjoyed by copyright owners** in accordance with this Law The provisions of the preceding paragraph shall apply to restrictions on copyright-related rights
Chapter III Contracts of Copyright Licensing and Contracts of Copyright Transfer	
Article 26 Where the copyright is pledged, the pledger and the pledge shall handle the registration of pledge at the copyright administrative department of the State Council	**Article 28** Where the **property rights** in copyright are pledged, the pledgor and pledgee shall handle pledge registration **according to the law**
Article 28 The standards of remuneration for the exploitation of a work may be either agreed upon by the parties concerned or be made by the copyright administration department under the State Council in collaboration with other departments concerned. Where the parties concerned fail to reach a clear agreement, the remuneration shall be paid in accordance with the standards of remuneration made by the copyright administration department under the State Council in collaboration with other departments concerned	**Article 30** The standards of remuneration for the exploitation of a work may be either agreed upon by the parties concerned or be made by **the copyright administration department under the State Council** in collaboration with other departments concerned. Where the parties concerned fail to reach a clear agreement, the remuneration shall be paid in accordance with the standards of remuneration made by **the copyright administration department under the State Council** in collaboration with other departments concerned
Chapter IV Publication, Performance, Sound Recording, Video Recording and Broadcasting	**Chapter IV Copyright-Related Rights**
Section 1.1 Publication of Books, Newspapers and Periodicals	
Article 35 When publishing works created by adaptation, translation, annotation, arrangement or compilation of pre-existing works, the publisher shall obtain permission from and pay remuneration to both the owners of the copyright in the works created by means of adaptation, translation, annotation, arrangement or compilation, and the owners of the copyright in the original work	**(Deletion)**
Article 36 A publisher shall be entitled to permit others to exploit the format design of a published book or periodical of his or prohibit others from doing so The term of protection of the right provided in the preceding paragraph shall be ten years, expiring on December 31 of the tenth year after the first publication of the book or periodical that uses such a format	**Article 37**(Same as left)

(continued)

(continued)

Before revision (effective April 1, 2010)	Revised (effective June 1, 2021)
Section 1.2 Performance	
Article 37 A performer (an individual performer or a performing group) who for a performance exploits a work created by another shall obtain permission from and pay remuneration to the copyright owner. A performance organizer who organizes a performance shall obtain permission from and pay remuneration to the copyright owner A performer who for a performance exploits a work created by adaptation, translation, annotation or arrangement of a pre-existing work shall obtain permission from and pay remuneration to both the owner of the copyright in the work created by adaptation, translation, annotation or arrangement and the owner of the copyright in the original work	**Article 38** A performer who for a performance exploits a work created by another shall obtain permission from and pay remuneration to the copyright owner. A performance organizer who organizes a performance shall obtain permission from and pay remuneration to the copyright owner
Article 38 A performer shall, in relation to his performance, enjoy the rights: …… (5) to permit others to reproduce and distribute the sound recordings or video recordings which record his performance, and to receive remuneration for it; ……	**Article 39** A performer shall, in relation to his performance, enjoy the rights: …… (5) to permit others to reproduce, distribute and **lease** the sound recordings or video recordings which record his performance, and to receive remuneration for it; ……
(Additional)	**Article 40 The performance by an actor for completing the performance tasks of the performing entity shall be performance for hire. The actor shall enjoy the right to indicate his or her identity and protect his or her performance image from being distorted. The ownership of other rights shall be agreed upon by the parties. Where the parties have not reached agreement or the agreement is unclear, the right to performance for hire shall be enjoyed by the performing entity** **Where the right of performance for hire is enjoyed by actors, the performing entity may, within its scope of business, use the performance for free**
Section 3 Sound Recording and Video Recording	
Article 40 A producer of sound recordings or video recordings who, for the production of a sound recording or video recording, exploits a work created by another, shall obtain permission from and pay remuneration to the copyright owner A producer of sound recordings or video recordings who exploits a work created by adaptation, translation, annotation or arrangement of a pre-existing work shall obtain permission from and pay remuneration to both the owner of the copyright in the work created by adaptation, translation, annotation or arrangement and the owner of copyright in the original work	**Article 42** A producer of sound recordings or video recordings who, for the production of a sound recording or video recording, exploits a work created by another, shall obtain permission from and pay remuneration to the copyright owner A producer of a sound recording who, for the production of a sound recording, exploits a musical work which has been lawfully recorded as a sound recording by another, does not need to obtain permission from, but shall, as provided in regulations, pay remuneration to the copyright owner; such work shall not be exploited where the copyright owner has declared that such exploitation is not permitted
A producer of a sound recording who, for the production of a sound recording, exploits a musical work which has been lawfully recorded as a sound recording by another, does not need to obtain permission from, but shall, as provided in regulations, pay remuneration to the copyright owner; such work shall not be exploited where the copyright owner has declared that such exploitation is not permitted	

(continued)

(continued)

Before revision (effective April 1, 2010)	Revised (effective June 1, 2021)
Article 42 …… A producer of sound recordings or video recordings who is permitted to reproduce, distribute, lease or disseminate to the public through information network a sound recording or video recording shall obtain permission from and also pay remuneration to both the copyright owner and the performer	**Article 44** …… A licensee that reproduces, issues, and disseminates audio and video recordings to the public through information networks shall concurrently obtain the permission of the copyright owner and performer and pay remuneration to them; and a licensee that leases audio and video recordings shall obtain the performer's permission and pay remunerations to the performer
(Additional)	**Article 45 Where sound recordings are used for wired or wireless public dissemination, or for public broadcasting to the public through technical equipment transmitting sound, remunerations shall be paid to the sound recording producer**
Section 1.4 Broadcasting by A Radio Station or Television Station	
Article 44 A radio station or television station that broadcasts a published sound recording does not need to obtain permission from, but shall pay remuneration to the copyright owner, unless the parties concerned have agreed otherwise. The specific measures shall be provided by the State Council	(Deletion)
Article 45 A radio station or television station is entitled to prohibit the following acts which it has not permitted: (1) rebroadcasting the radio or television which it has broadcasted; (2) recording the radio or television which it has broadcasted in the audio or video carrier and to reproduce the audio or video carrier The term of protection of the rights provided in the preceding paragraph shall be fifty years, expiring on December 31 of the fiftieth year after the first broadcasting of the radio or television	**Article 47** A broadcasting station or television station shall have the right to prohibit the following acts conducted without its permission: (1) Rebroadcasting a radio or television program broadcast **by it by wired or wireless means** (2) Recording and reproducing a radio or television program broadcast by it (3) **Disseminating a radio and television broadcast by it to the public via information networks** The exercising of rights prescribed in the preceding paragraph by a broadcasting station or television station shall not affect, restrict or infringe upon any other's exercising of copyright or copyright-related rights **The protection period for the rights prescribed in the preceding paragraph of this Article** shall be 50 years, ending on December 31 of the 50th year after broadcasting of the radio or television program for the first time
Article 46 A television station that broadcasts another's cinematographic work, work created in a way similar to cinematography or videographic work shall obtain permission from and pay remuneration to the producer. A television station that broadcasts another's videographic work shall also obtain permission from and pay remuneration to the copyright owner	**Article 48** To broadcast another's **audiovisual work** or video recording, a television station shall obtain permission of **the copyright owner of an audiovisual work** or a video producer, and pay remunerations to the copyright owner or video producer; to broadcast another's video recordings, a television station shall obtain permission of the copyright owner and pay remunerations to the copyright owner
Chapter V Legal Liabilities and Law Enforcement Measures	**Chapter V Protection of Copyright and Copyright-Related Rights**

(continued)

(continued)

Before revision (effective April 1, 2010)	Revised (effective June 1, 2021)
(Additional)	**Article 49** In order to protect copyright and copyright-related rights, the right holder may take technical measures Without permission of the right holder, no organization or individual shall deliberately avoid or destroy the technical measures, manufacture, import or provide relevant devices or components for the public for the purposes of avoiding or destroying the technical measures, or deliberately provide technical services for others' avoidance or destruction of the technical measures, except under the circumstances under which avoidance is allowed as prescribed in the laws and administrative regulations For the purpose of this Law, 'technical measures' means effective technologies, devices or components used to prevent or restrict browsing or appreciation of works, performance, and audio and video recordings, or provision of works, performance, and audio and video recordings for the public via information networks without permission of the right holder
(Additional)	**Article 50** Under the following circumstances, technical measures may be avoided, but technologies, devices or components for avoiding technical measures shall not be provided to others, nor other rights enjoyed by right holders according to the law shall be infringed upon: (1) Providing a small amount of published works that cannot be obtained through normal channels for classroom teaching or scientific research at schools and for use by teachers or scientific researchers (2) Providing published works that cannot be obtained through normal channels for dyslexics in a barrier-free way through which they can perceive for non-for-profit purposes (3) The state authorities perform official duties under the administrative, oversight and judicial procedures (4) Testing the security performance of computers and their systems or networks (5) Conducting encrypted search or conducting reverse engineering research on computer software The provisions of the preceding paragraph shall apply to restrictions on copyright-related rights
(Additional)	**Article 51** The following conducts are not allowed without permission of the right holder: (1) Deliberate deletion of or change in the rights management information on works, layout designs, performances, audio and video recordings, or radio and television programs, except for those which cannot be avoided due to technical reasons (2) Provision of information to the public when the provider knows or should have known that the rights management information on works, layout designs, performances, audio and video recordings, or radio and television programs has been deleted or changed without permission

(continued)

(continued)

Before revision (effective April 1, 2010)	Revised (effective June 1, 2021)
Article 47 …… (6) exploiting a work by means of exhibition, <u>making cinematographic productions or a means similar to making cinematographic productions</u>, or by means of adaptation, translation, annotation, etc. without the permission from the copyright owner, unless otherwise provided in this Law; (7) exploiting a work of another without paying the remuneration; (8) <u>without the permission from the copyright owner or obligee related to the copyright of a cinematographic work or a work created in a way similar to cinematography,</u> computer software, sound recordings or video recordings, leasing his work or sound recordings or video recordings, except where otherwise provided in this Law; (9) without the permission from a publisher, exploiting the format design of his published book or periodical; (10) without the permission from the performer, broadcasting or publicly transmitting his live performance or recording his performance; (11) committing other acts of infringement upon copyright and upon other <u>rights</u> related to copyright	**Article 52** …… (6) exploiting a work by means of exhibition, making **audiovisual works**, or by means of adaptation, translation, annotation, etc. without the permission from the copyright owner, unless otherwise provided in this Law; (7) exploiting a work of another without paying the remuneration; (8) without permission of the **copyright holder, performer or audio and video producer** of an **audiovisual work**, computer software, or audio and video recording, the original or copy of his or her work or audio and video recording is leased, except as otherwise prescribed in this Law.; (9) without the permission from a publisher, exploiting the format design of his published book or periodical; (10) without the permission from the performer, broadcasting or publicly transmitting his live performance or recording his performance; (11) committing other acts of infringement upon copyright and upon other **rights** related to copyright
Article 48 He who commits any of the following acts of infringement shall bear the civil liability for such remedies as ceasing the infringements, eliminating the effects of the act, making a public apology or paying compensation for damages, depending on the circumstances; where he damages public interests at the same time, the copyright administration department may order him to cease the act of tort, may confiscate his illegal gains, confiscate and destroy the reproductions of infringement, and impose a fine on him; if the case is serious, the copyright administration department may also confiscate the materials, instruments and equipment, etc. mainly used to make the reproductions of infringement; where his act has constituted a crime, he shall be investigated for criminal liabilities in accordance with the law: (1) without the permission from the copyright owner, reproducing, distributing, performing, projecting, broadcasting, compiling, disseminating to the public through information network his works, except where otherwise provided in this Law; (2) publishing a book where the exclusive right of publication belongs to another;	**Article 53 Whoever conducts any of the following torts shall, as the case may be, assume the civil liabilities as prescribed in Article 52 of this Law; where a tort concurrently damages public interests, the copyright authority shall order the violator to cease the tort, give a warning, confiscate the illegal gains, confiscate and harmlessly destroy and dispose of the infringing copies, as well as the materials, tools, and equipment, among others, that are mainly used to make the infringing copies, and where the illegal business amount exceeds 50,000 yuan, a fine of one to five times the illegal business amount may be imposed; where there is no illegal business amount, or the illegal business amount is difficult to be calculated or is less than 50,000 yuan, a fine of not more than 250,000 yuan may be imposed; and where a crime is constituted, the violator shall be held criminally liable in accordance with the law:** (1) Without permission of the copyright owner, reproducing, issuing, performing, projecting, broadcasting, compiling, disseminating his or her works to the public via information networks, except as otherwise prescribed in this Law (2) Publishing a book whose exclusive right of publication is enjoyed by another

(continued)

1 Main Amendments of Chinese Intellectual Property Law

(continued)

Before revision (effective April 1, 2010)	Revised (effective June 1, 2021)
(3) without the permission from a performer, reproducing, distributing the sound recordings or video recordings of his performance, or disseminating his performance to the public through information network, except where otherwise provided in this Law; (4) without the permission from a producer of sound recordings and video recordings, reproducing, distributing, disseminating to the public through information network the sound recordings or video recordings produced by him, except where otherwise provided in this Law; (5) without the permission, <u>broadcasting or reproducing the radio or television</u>, except where otherwise provided in this Law; (6) without the permission from the copyright owner or obligee related to the copyright, intentionally avoiding or destroying the technical measures taken by the obligee on his works, sound recordings or video recordings, etc. to protect the copyright or the rights related to the copyright, except where otherwise provided in laws or administrative regulations;	(3) Without permission of a performer, **reproducing or issuing** audio and video recordings of his or her performance, or disseminating his or her performance to the public via information networks, except as otherwise prescribed in this Law (4) Without permission of the producer of audio and video recordings, **reproducing, issuing**, or disseminating audio and video recordings produced by him or her to the public through information networks, except as otherwise prescribed in this Law (5) Without permission, **broadcasting, reproducing, or disseminating radio and television programs to the public via information networks,** except as otherwise prescribed in this Law (6) Without permission of the copyright owner or copyright-related right owner, **deliberately avoiding or destroying technical measures, deliberately manufacturing, importing or providing to others devices or components mainly used to avoid or destroy technical measures, or intentionally providing technical services to others to avoid or destroy technical measures,** unless as otherwise prescribed by laws and administrative regulations
(7) without the permission from the copyright owner or obligee related to the copyright, <u>intentionally deleting or altering the electronic information on the management of the rights on the works, sound recordings or video recordings,</u> except where otherwise provided in laws or administrative regulations; (8) producing or selling a work where the signature of another is counterfeited	(7) Without permission of the copyright owner or copyright-related right owner, **deliberately deleting or changing the rights management information on the works, layout designs, performances, audio and video recordings, or radio and television programs, and providing the information to the public when the provider knows or should have known that the rights management information on works, layout designs, performances, audio and video recordings, or radio and television programs has been deleted or changed without permission,** unless as otherwise prescribed by laws and administrative regulations.; (8) Producing or selling a work where signature of another is counterfeited

(continued)

(continued)

Before revision (effective April 1, 2010)	Revised (effective June 1, 2021)
Article 49 The infringer shall, when having infringed upon the copyright or the rights related to copyright, <u>make a compensation on the basis of the obligee's actual losses; where the actual losses are difficult to be calculated, the compensation may be made on the basis of the infringer's illegal gains.</u> The amount of compensation shall also include the reasonable expenses paid by the obligee for stopping the act of tort Where the obligee's <u>actual losses or the infringer's illegal gains cannot be determined</u>, the people's court shall, on the basis of the seriousness of the act of tort, adjudicate a compensation of <u>500,000 Yuan or less</u>	**Article 54** An infringer infringing upon copyright or copyright-related rights **shall make compensation on the basis of the right holder's actual losses arising therefrom or the illegal gains of the infringer; and where the right holder's actual losses or the infringer's illegal gains are difficult to be calculated, compensation may be made on the basis of the royalties. For deliberate infringement upon copyright or copyright-related rights, circumstances are serious, compensation may be made on the basis of the amount not less than one time nor more than five times the amount determined by the aforesaid methods** Where the right **holder's actual losses or the infringer's illegal gains and royalties are difficult to be calculated**, the people's court shall, on the basis of the seriousness of the tort, **adjudicate on a compensation not less than 500 yuan nor more than 5 million yuan** The amount of compensation shall include the reasonable expenses paid by the right holder for stopping the tort **Where a right holder has assumed necessary responsibility for burden of proof, and the account books and materials, among others, concerning the tort are mainly held by the infringer, the people's court may order the infringer to provide the account books and materials concerning the tort; and where the infringer does not provide them, or provides false account books and materials, the people's court may determine the amount of compensation with reference to the claims of the right holder and the evidence produced** **When trying a case of disputes over copyright, the people's court shall, at the request of a right holder, order destruction of infringing copies, except for special circumstances; order destruction of materials, tools, and equipment, which are mainly used for manufacturing infringing copies, without compensation; or under special circumstances, order prohibiting the aforesaid materials, tools, and equipment, from entering commercial channels, without compensation**
(Additional)	**Article 55** When investigating and handling suspected infringement upon copyright and copyright-related rights, the copyright authority may inquire about the relevant parties and investigate the situation concerning the suspected illegal act; carry out on-site inspections of the parties' premises and articles suspected of illegal acts; consult and copy contracts, invoices, account books and other relevant materials concerning the suspected illegal acts; and may seal up or seize the premises and articles suspected of illegal acts When the copyright authority exercises the functions and powers prescribed in the preceding paragraph in accordance with the law, the parties shall provide assistance and cooperation, and shall not reject or obstruct the exercising of such functions and powers

1 Main Amendments of Chinese Intellectual Property Law 33

(continued)

Before revision (effective April 1, 2010)	Revised (effective June 1, 2021)
Article 50 Where a copyright owner or obligee related to copyright has evidence to prove that another is committing or is going to commit an act infringing upon his right, and that his lawful rights and interests will suffer the damage which is difficult to be remedied if he does not stop it in time, he may, before bringing a lawsuit, apply to the people's court for an order to cease the relevant acts or for property preservation The people's court shall handle the application in the preceding paragraph in accordance with Article 93 through Article 96 and Article 99 of the Civil Procedure Law of the People's Republic of China	**Article 56** Where a copyright owner or a copyright-related right holder has evidence to prove that others are committing or are about to commit acts **infringing upon his or her rights and hindering his or her exercising of rights,** and failure to stop the acts in a timely manner will cause irreparable damages to his or her lawful rights and interests, he or she may apply to the people's court for taking measures such as property preservation, ordering certain actions, **or prohibiting certain actions according to the law before instigating a lawsuit**
Article 51 For the purpose of stopping the acts of tort, a copyright owner or an obligee related to copyright may, under circumstances that the evidence may be destroyed or lost or difficult to obtain later on, apply to the people's court for the evidence to be preserved The people's court must, after receiving the application, make an order within 48 h; if the preservation is granted by an order, its implementation shall start immediately The people's court may order the applicant to provide a surety; if the applicant fails to do so, his application shall be rejected If the applicant fails to bring a lawsuit within 15 days after the people's court has adopted the preservation measures, the people's court shall cancel the property preservation	**Article 57** For the purpose of stopping the tort, a copyright owner or a copyright-related right holder may, under circumstances that the evidence may be destroyed or lost or difficult to be obtained later on, apply to the people's court for evidence preservation before initiating a lawsuit according to the law
Article 53 Where a publisher or producer of reproductions is unable to prove the lawful authorization of his publication or production, or the distributor of the reproductions or the lessor of the reproductions of a cinematographic work or a work created in a way similar to cinematography, computer software, sound recordings or video recordings is unable to prove the lawful sources of his distribution or lease of the reproductions, he shall bear the legal liabilities	**Article 59** Where a publisher or producer of reproductions is unable to prove the lawful authorization of his publication or production, or the distributor of the reproductions or the lessor of the reproductions of **audiovisual works**, computer software, sound recordings or video recordings is unable to prove the lawful sources of his distribution or lease of the reproductions, he shall bear the legal liabilities **Where, during the litigation process, an accused infringer claiming that he or she is not liable for tort shall produce evidence to prove that he or she has obtained the right holder's permission, or he or she falls under the circumstances under which use is allowed without permission of the right holder as prescribed in this Law**
Article 54 Where a party concerned does not implement his contractual obligations or his implementation of the contractual obligations does not conform to the stipulated requirements, he shall bear the civil liabilities in accordance with the General Principles of the Civil Law of the People's Republic of China, the Contract Law of the People's Republic of China and other laws	(Deletion)
Article 56 Any party who objects to an administrative penalty may bring a lawsuit to the people's court within three months as of the date when it received the written decision on the penalty. If a party neither bring a lawsuit nor implements the decision within the above time limit, the copyright administration department concerned may apply to the people's court for enforcement	(Deletion)

(continued)

(continued)	
Before revision (effective April 1, 2010)	Revised (effective June 1, 2021)
(Additional)	Article 61 The parties' assumption of civil liabilities due to failure to perform contractual obligations or performance of contractual obligations not according to the agreement, and the parties' exercising of litigation rights, and application for preservation, among others, shall be governed by the provisions of the relevant laws
Chapter VI Supplementary Provisions	
(Additional)	Article 65 Where the protection period for photographic works, right of publication, and rights prescribed from items (5) to (17) of paragraph 1 of Article 10 has expired before June 1, 2021, but it is still within the protection period according to paragraph 1 of Article 23 of this Law, they shall no longer be protected
Article 60 ...... Any infringements upon copyright and the rights related to copyright or breaches of contract committed prior to the entry into force of this Law shall be dealt with under the relevant regulations or <u>policies in force</u> at the time when the infringement was committed	**Article 66** ...... Any infringements upon copyright and the rights related to copyright or breaches of contract committed prior to the entry into force of this Law shall be dealt with under the relevant regulations in force at the time when the infringement was committed

1.2.2 Opinions of the Supreme People's Court on Strengthening the Protection of Copyright and Rights Related to Copyright

(No. 42(2020) of the Supreme People's Court).

For the purpose of strengthening copyright protection in literary, artistic and scientific fields, giving full play to the role of copyright adjudications in regulating, guiding, promoting and protecting cultural development, stimulating the cultural innovative and creative vitality of the whole nation, promoting the socialist cultural and ethical progress, prospering and developing the cultural undertakings and culture industries, strengthening China's cultural soft power and international competitiveness, and serving the high-quality economic and social development, we hereby put forward the following opinions on further strengthening the protection of copyright and rights related to copyright based on the Copyright Law of the People's Republic of China and other related legal provisions, and in light of the judicial practice.

1. The protection of authors' rights and interests shall be reinforced according to law, the interests between disseminators and the general public shall be balanced, the core status of innovation shall be upheld in China's overall modernization drive. The relation between encouraging the development of emerging industries and the protection of right-holders' lawful rights and interests shall be appropriately handled according to law, the relation between stimulating creation and protecting people's cultural rights and interests shall be effectively coordinated, the role of right assignees and licensees in promoting the dissemination of works shall be utilized, copyright and rights related to copyright shall be protected based on laws, the creation and dissemination of intellectual achievements shall be promoted, the development and flourishing of socialist culture and sciences shall be realized.

2. The quality and efficiency of case trials shall be greatly enhanced, the pilot programs of separating cases into simple and complicated ones shall be promoted, the trial period of type cases involving copyright and copyright-related rights shall be shortened with a focused effort. The rules of evidence in IP rights lawsuits shall be improved, the parties to such cases shall be allowed to preserve, fix and submit evidence through blockchain and other means, so as to effectively resolve the difficulties of IP rights-holders in collecting evidence. The requests of parties to such cases for conduct preservation, evidence preservation and property preservation shall be supported according to law, and multiple civil liability methods shall be comprehensively applied to provide right-holders in civil cases with sufficient remedies.

3. The natural person, legal entities and unincorporated organizations who affix the signature thereof in a common way to any work, performance and sound recording shall be presumed as the holder of the copyright or rights related to copyright of such work, performance, and sound recording, unless such presumption can be invalidated by sufficient evidence to the contrary. Comprehensive judgment shall be made for disputes over signature in light of the nature, type, form of expression of the concerned work, performance, and sound recording, and the related industry prevailing practice, public cognition habit, and other factors. Where a right-holder fulfills the preliminary burden of proof, the people's court shall presume that the copyright or rights related to copyright claimed by such right-holder are established, unless such presumption can be invalidated by sufficient evidence to the contrary.

4. Where the signature presumption rule is applicable for the ascertainment of the ownership of copyright or rights related to copyright and the defendant fails to submit evidence to the contrary, the plaintiff is not required to submit the relevant right transfer agreement or other evidence in written form. In judicial procedures, where a defendant claims not to assume the liability of infringement, such defendant shall provide evidence to prove that he or she has procured the license from the right-holder, or is in a circumstance that allows him or her to use the right concerned in the case without the license of the right-holder as prescribed by the Copyright Law.

5. The newly rising development demands of technological development from the Internet, artificial intelligence, big data and other fields shall be attached great importance to, the types of works shall be correctly defined, the standard for identification of works shall be well grasped, cases of new types such as live broadcasting of sports events and online games, data infringement, among others, shall be appropriated handled, so as to promote the regulated development of emerging industries.

6. Where the party to a case requests for the destruction of the infringing copies and the materials and tools used for producing such infringing copies, the people's court shall, except for special circumstances, support such claims in a civil procedure, or order such destruction according to the court's authority in a criminal procedure. Where such infringing copies and the materials and tools used for producing such infringing copies are not fit for destruction, the people's court may order the infringer to dispose of them with appropriate means other than commercial channels, so as to eliminate the risks of further infringement. The destruction or disposal costs shall be borne by the infringer. The infringer's claims for reimbursement, if any, shall not be supported by the people's court.

In criminal procedures, where the right-holder requests that the aforesaid infringing copies, materials and tools used to produce the infringing copies shall be temporarily held from destruction for the reason that they need to be preserved as evidence for the civil or administrative litigation which the right-holder might lodge later, the people's court shall support such claims. Where the right-holder requests the infringer to make compensation for the storage charges that the right-holder had advances for, the people's court shall support such claims.

7. Where the actual losses of the right-holder, the illegal gains of the infringer, and the royalties of rights concerned are difficult to be accounted, factors such as the type of the right under the request of protection, the market value of the concerned works, the infringer's subject fault, the nature, scale, and the seriousness of the damage consequences of the infringement act shall be comprehensively considered, so as to reasonably determine the amount of compensation in accordance with the Copyright Law, its related judicial interpretations and other regulations. Where the infringer deliberately commits the infringement act with serious circumstances and the right-holder requests for the application of punitive compensation, the people's court shall examine such claims and make the related determination according to law. Where the right-holder is able to submit evidence for his or her reasonable costs of right protection, which includes litigation costs, attorney fees, among others, the people's court shall support such claims and separately account each item of the costs when ascertaining the amount of compensation.

8. Where the infringer used to be determined by a valid court ruling or administrative decision as having committed an infringement act, or used to reach a settlement agreement with the right-holder for an infringement act, but continues to commit the same infringement act or repeatedly commits such act in a disguised form, it shall be regarded as having the intent of infringement, the people's court shall fully consider such circumstances when determining the civil liability for infringement.

9. With an instrument of commitment for litigation with good faith and other forms, the parties to a case shall be clearly notified of the possible legal responsibility that they may bear for dishonest litigation, so as to make such parties legitimately exercise their litigation rights, vigorously perform their litigation obligations, actively and honestly submit evidence within a reasonable period, and make truthful and complete statements in the judicial procedure.

10. The mechanisms to incentivize good faith and penalize lack of credibility and the accountability systems shall be further improved, the people's court may legally adopt compulsory measures such as admonishment, penalties, or detention for acts of dishonest litigation such as submitting forged or altered evidence, concealing or destroying evidence, making false statements or providing false testimonies, conducting fake appraisals or falsifying attribution of authorship. Any violation which constitutes a crime shall be investigated for criminal liability.

1.2.3 Interpretation of the Supreme People's Court Concerning the Application of Laws in the Trial of Civil Disputes Over Copyright

(Adopted at the 1246th meeting of the Judicial Committee of the Supreme People's Court on October 12, 2002 and amended in accordance with the Decision of the Supreme People's Court on Amending the Judicial Interpretation of the Supreme People's Court on Several Issues Concerning the Application of Law in the Trial of Disputes Involving Infringement of Patent Rights (II) and Other Eighteen Judicial Interpretations on Intellectual Property Rights adopted at the 1823rd meeting of the Judicial Committee of the Supreme People's Court on December 23, 2020).

Before modification (effective October 15, 2002)	Revised (effective January 1, 2021)
With a view to correctly trial the cases of civil dispute over copyright, some issues concerning the application of laws are hereby interpreted on the basis of the statutory provisions including the General Principles of the Civil Law of the People's Republic of China, the Contract Law of the People's Republic of China, the Copyright Law of the People's Republic of China and the Civil Procedure Law of the People's Republic of China	With a view to correctly trial the cases of civil dispute over copyright, some issues concerning the application of laws are hereby interpreted on the basis of the statutory provisions including the **Civil Code of the People's Republic of China**, the **Copyright Law of the People's Republic of China** and the **Civil Procedure Law of the People's Republic of China**
Article 1 The people's courts accept the civil cases of dispute over copyright as mentioned below: a. The cases of dispute over the possession, infringement and contract of copyright or copyright-related rights and interests; b. The cases of plead for stopping the infringement upon copyright or copyright-related rights and interests before the institution of an action or for attachment of property or evidences before the institution of an action; c. Other cases of dispute over copyright or copyright-related rights and interests	Article 1 The people's courts accept the civil cases of dispute over copyright as mentioned below: a. The cases of dispute over the possession, infringement and contract of copyright or copyright-related rights and interests; b. The cases of plead for stopping the **infringement** upon copyright or copyright-related rights and interests before the institution of an action or for attachment of property or evidences before the institution of an action; c. Other cases of dispute over copyright or copyright-related rights and interests
Article 2 A civil case of dispute over copyright shall be subject to the jurisdiction of the intermediate people's court or above All the higher people's court may, by taking the practical situations of their respective jurisdictions into consideration, determine some of the basic-level people's courts as the first-instance court for trying civil cases of dispute over copyright	Article 2 A civil case of dispute over copyright shall be subject to the jurisdiction of the intermediate people's court or above All the higher people's court may, by taking the practical situations of their respective jurisdictions into consideration, **can be reported to the Supreme People's Court for approval** some of the basic-level people's courts as the first-instance court for trying civil cases of dispute over copyright

(continued)

(continued)

Before modification (effective October 15, 2002)	Revised (effective January 1, 2021)
Article 3 As for the acts infringing upon copyright as found out by the administrative departments of copyright, if any of the parties concerned lodges an action to look into the civil liabilities of the actor, such case shall be accepted by the people's court When trying a civil case of dispute over the infringement of copyright that has already been handled by the administrative department of copyright, the people's court shall examine the case facts in a comprehensive way	**Article 3** As for the acts infringing upon copyright as found out by the administrative departments of copyright, if any of the parties concerned lodges an action to look into the civil liabilities of the actor, such case shall be accepted by the people's court When trying a civil case of dispute over the **infringement** of copyright that has already been handled by the administrative department of copyright, the people's court shall examine the case facts in a comprehensive way
Article 4 A civil action instituted on the ground of infringing upon copyright shall be subject to the jurisdiction of the people's court where the infringing act occurred or where the infringing reproductions were stored or detained and sealed up or where the defendant dwells as provided for in Article 46 and 47 of the Copyright Law The place where the infringing reproductions were stored as mentioned in the preceding paragraph refers to the place where large quantities of infringing reproductions were stored or infringing reproductions were stored or concealed for business purposes. The place of detention and sealing up refers to the place where the infringing reproductions were lawfully sealed up or detained by the administrative departments of customs, copyright, administrations for industry and commerce, etc	**Article 4** A civil action instituted on the ground of infringing upon copyright shall be subject to the jurisdiction of the people's court where the infringing act occurred or where the infringing reproductions were stored or detained and sealed up or where the defendant dwells as provided for in **Article 47** and **48** of the **Copyright Law** The place where the infringing reproductions were stored as mentioned in the preceding paragraph refers to the place where large quantities of infringing reproductions were stored or infringing reproductions were stored or concealed for business purposes. The place of detention and sealing up refers to the place where the infringing reproductions were lawfully sealed up or detained by the administrative departments of customs, copyright and commerce, etc
Article 5 For the joint actions instituted by several defendants of the place where different infringing acts are involved, the plaintiff may select the people's court of the place where the infringing act of either of the defendants occurred as the jurisdictional people's court. Where an action is instituted against only one of the defendants, the people's court of the place where the infringing act of the defendant shall have jurisdiction	**Article 5** For the joint actions instituted by several defendants of the place where different infringing acts are involved, **The plaintiff can choose to file a lawsuit in the people's court where one of the defendants committed the infringement.** Where an action is instituted against only one of the defendants, the people's court of the place where the infringing act of the defendant shall have jurisdiction
Article 6 Where an action is instituted by an organization lawfully established for the collective management of copyright in its own name upon the written authorization of the copyright holder, the people's court shall accept	
Article 7 The manuscripts, original scripts, lawful publications, copyright registration certificates, attestations issued by authentication institutions, contracts for acquiring rights, etc. as submitted by the parties concerned may be adopted as evidences The natural persons, legal persons or other organizations which appear on a work or production as authors shall be deemed as the holder of copyright or copyright-related rights and interests unless there are evidences that prove the opposite	**Article 7** The manuscripts, original scripts, lawful publications, copyright registration certificates, attestations issued by authentication institutions, contracts for acquiring rights, etc. as submitted by the parties concerned may be adopted as evidences The natural persons, legal persons or **unincorporated organization** which appear on a work or production as authors shall be deemed as the holder of copyright or copyright-related rights and interests unless there are evidences that prove the opposite
Article 8 Where any party concerned purchases infringing reproductions by ordering or on-the-spot dealing by himself or authorizing any other person, the physical objects and invoices, etc. obtained thereby may be adopted as evidences The notaries issued by any notary public, without disclosing his own identity to the party that is suspicious of infringement, concerning the evidences obtained by the party concerned in the ways as mentioned in the preceding paragraph or concerning the process of obtaining the evidences shall be adopted as evidences unless there are evidences that can prove the opposite	
Article 9 The phrase "making known to the public" as mentioned in Article 10, Item 1 of the Copyright Law refers to that a work is made to known to unspecified people by the holder of copyright or with the permission of the copyright holder. However, it shall not be based on the condition that the general public has already known it	

(continued)

(continued)

Before modification (effective October 15, 2002)	Revised (effective January 1, 2021)
Article 10 In the case of a "work" as mentioned in Article 15, Paragraph 2 of the Copyright Law, if the copyright holder is a natural person, the provisions of Article 21, Paragraph 1 of the Copyright Law shall be applicable to the term of protection thereof; while in that the copyright holder is a legal person or any <u>other organization</u>, the provisions of Article 21, Paragraph 2 of the Copyright Law shall be applicable to the term of protection thereof	**Article 10** In the case of a "work" as mentioned in Article 15, Paragraph 2 of the Copyright Law, if the copyright holder is a natural person, the provisions of Article 21, Paragraph 1 of the Copyright Law shall be applicable to the term of protection thereof; while in that the copyright holder is a legal person or any **unincorporated organization**, the provisions of Article 21, Paragraph 2 of the Copyright Law shall be applicable to the term of protection thereof
Article 11 Where a dispute arises from the sequence of authorship to a work, the people's court shall handle the case according to the following principles: if there is any agreement concerning the sequence of authorship, such agreement shall apply; if there is no agreement, the sequence of authorship may be determined according to how much labor one had paid to the creation of the work or the sequence of the content of the work or the number and sequence of the strokes of the Chinese characters for the surnames of the authors, etc	
Article 12 According to Article 17 of the Copyright Law which provides that the copyright to an entrusted work, the trustor has the right to use the work within the stipulated scope of use. If both parties fail to agree upon the scope of use of the work, the trustor may gratuitously use the work within the scope of the specific purpose for creating the work	
Article 13 Apart from the situation as provided in Article 11, Item 3 of the Copyright Law, works such as reports and speeches which are written by other people but are revised, finalized and delivered in one's own name, the copyright shall be held by the person who makes the report or speech. The copyright holder may pay appropriate remunerations to the writers	
Article 14 Where the parties concerned agree to create an autobiographical work on the basis of the experiences of a particular person and if they have come to any agreement concerning the possession of copyright, such agreement shall apply. If they have not come to any agreement, the copyright thereof shall be held by the particular person. If the writer of the work has made efforts to the work, the copyright holder may pay appropriate remunerations to him	
Article 15 With regards to a work created by different authors on the basis of a same topic, the authors shall enjoy independent copyright if the expression of the work is completed independently and is creative	
Article 16 The purely factual news which is disseminated through mass media are the news of current affairs as provided in Article 5, Item 2 of the Copyright Law. When disseminating the news of current affairs as written by other persons, the source of the news shall be marked	
Article 17 The word "reprint" as mentioned in <u>Article 32</u>, Paragraph 2 of the Copyright Law refers to the publishing of works by a newspaper or magazine that have already been published by other newspapers or magazines. Any one who reprints a work without marking the authors or the newspaper or magazine that has first published the work shall assume the civil liabilities of clearing up ill effects and making apologies, etc	**Article 17** The word "reprint" as mentioned in **Article 33**, Paragraph 2 of the Copyright Law refers to the publishing of works by a newspaper or magazine that have already been published by other newspapers or magazines. Any one who reprints a work without marking the authors or the newspaper or magazine that has first published the work shall assume the civil liabilities of clearing up ill effects and making apologies, etc
Article 18 The term "artistic work in out-door public places" as mentioned in Article 22, Item 10 of the Copyright Law refers to such artistic works as sculptures, painting, calligraphy works, etc. that are located or displayed in out-door places for social public activities	
Article 19 Publishers and producers shall bear the burden of proof concerning the lawful authorization of its publication or production. Issuers and leasers shall bear the burden of proof concerning the lawful source of the reproductions issued or leased. Anyone who fails to produce evidences shall assume the legal liabilities as provided in <u>Articles 46</u> and <u>47</u> of the Copyright Law	**Article 19** Publishers and producers shall bear the burden of proof concerning the lawful authorization of its publication or production. Issuers and leasers shall bear the burden of proof concerning the lawful source of the reproductions issued or leased. Any one who fails to produce evidences shall assume the legal liabilities as provided in **Articles 47** and **48** of the Copyright Law

(continued)

(continued)

Before modification (effective October 15, 2002)	Revised (effective January 1, 2021)
Article 20 In case any publication has infringed upon the copyright of any other person, the publisher shall assume civil liabilities of compensation according to seriousness of fault or infringement or damages caused, etc Any publisher who fails to give reasonable care to the authorization of the publication or the source or authorship of the contributions or the content of the publication it has edited shall be <u>responsible for making compensations</u> according to the provisions of <u>Article 48</u> of the Copyright Law	**Article 20** In case any publication has infringed upon the copyright of any other person, the publisher shall assume civil liabilities of compensation according to seriousness of fault or infringement or damages caused, etc Any publisher who fails to give reasonable care to the authorization of the publication or the source or authorship of the contributions or the content of the publication it has edited shall **be responsible for making damages** according to the provisions of **Article 49** of the Copyright Law **The publisher bears the burden of proof that it exercised reasonable care**
If the publisher has given reasonable care and the copyright holder cannot produce evidences to prove that the publisher should have known that the publication thereof has constituted an infringement, it shall, according to the provisions of Article 117, Paragraph 1 of the General Principles of the Civil Law of the People's Republic China, assume the civil liabilities of stopping the infringement and refunding the profits gained from the infringement The publisher shall bear the burden of proof to prove that it has given reasonable care	
Article 21 A user of computer software who uses the software without permission or beyond the permitted scope of business use shall assume the civil liabilities as provided in <u>Article 47</u>, Item 1 of the Copyright Law, Article 24, Item 1 of the Regulation on the Protection of Computer Software	**Article 21** A user of computer software who uses the software without permission or beyond the permitted scope of business use shall assume the civil liabilities as provided in **Article 48**, Item 1 of the Copyright Law, Article 24, Item 1 of the Regulation on the Protection of Computer Software
Article 22 Where a contract for the transfer of copyright fails to be made in written form, the people's court shall examine and determine whether the contract establishes <u>according to the provisions of Articles 36 and 37 of the Contract Law</u>	**Article 22** Where a contract for the transfer of copyright fails to be made in written form, the people's court shall examine and determine whether the contract establishes according to the provisions of **Article 490 of the Civil Code**
Article 23 Where any publisher who loses the work of delivered by the holder of copyright for publication so that the publication contract cannot be performed, <u>it shall assume the civil liabilities as provided in Article 53 of the Copyright Law, Article 117 of the General Principles of the Civil Law and Article 122 of the Contract Law</u>	**Article 23** Where any publisher who loses the work of delivered by the holder of copyright for publication so that the publication contract cannot be performed, it shall assume Copyright owners have the right to demand civil liability from publishers in accordance with Articles 186, 238 and 184 of the Civil Code
Article 24 The actual losses of the copyright holder may be computed according to the arithmetic product of the reduced sales volume of the reproductions incurred by the infringement or the sales volume of the infringing reproductions and the unit profits of the reproductions of the copyright holder. If it is difficult to determine the reduction of the sales volume, it shall be the market sales volume of the infringing reproductions	

(continued)

1 Main Amendments of Chinese Intellectual Property Law 41

(continued)

Before modification (effective October 15, 2002)	Revised (effective January 1, 2021)
Article 25 Where it is impossible to determine the actual losses of the copyright holder or the illegal gains of the infringer, the people's court may determine the amount of compensation upon the request of the parties concerned or by applying the provisions of <u>Article 48, Paragraph 2</u> of the Copyright Law upon its own power When determining the amount of compensation, the people's court shall take into comprehensive consideration of the type of the work, reasonable royalties, nature and consequences of the infringing act, etc Where the parties concerned have come into any agreement concerning the amount of compensation according to the provisions of Paragraph 1 of the present Article, such agreement shall apply	**Article 25** Where it is impossible to determine the actual losses of the copyright holder or the illegal gains of the infringer, the people's court may determine the amount of compensation upon the request of the parties concerned or by applying the provisions of **Article 49, Paragraph 2** of the Copyright Law upon its own power When determining the amount of compensation, the people's court shall take into comprehensive consideration of the type of the work, reasonable royalties, nature and consequences of the infringing act, etc Where the parties concerned have come into any agreement concerning the amount of compensation according to the provisions of Paragraph 1 of the present Article, such agreement shall apply
Article 26 The term "reasonable expenses for stopping infringing acts" as mentioned in <u>Article 48, Paragraph 1</u> of the Copyright Law shall include the reasonable expenses of the right holder or the agent entrusted thereby in looking into the infringing acts and obtaining evidences The people's courts may, according to the allegations of the parties concerned and the specific situations of the cases concerned, include the lawyer's fees that conform to the provisions of relevant departments of the state into the range of compensations	**Article 26** The term "reasonable expenses for stopping infringing acts" as mentioned in **Article 49, Paragraph 1** of the Copyright Law shall include the reasonable expenses of the right holder or the agent entrusted thereby in looking into the infringing acts and obtaining evidences The people's courts may, according to the allegations of the parties concerned and the specific situations of the cases concerned, include the lawyer's fees that conform to the provisions of relevant departments of the state into the range of compensations
Article 27 As for the cases instituted on the ground of infringing upon one's copyright that has happened before the Decision (of the Standing Committee of the People's Congress) on Amending the Copyright Law takes effect and the people's court makes the judgment after the Decision has taken effect, the provisions of Article 48 of the Copyright Law may be applied by reference	**(Deletion)**
Article 28 The statute of limitations for the infringement of copyright is <u>two years, starting from the day when the copyright holder knows or should have known of the infringing act.</u> Where the right holder institutes an action after <u>two years,</u> and if the infringing act still exists when the action is instituted and is within the period of copyright protection, the people's court shall rule that the defendant shall stop the infringing act, and the amount of compensations for damages shall be computed till <u>two years</u> further as of the day when the right holder institutes the action with the people's court	**Article 28** The statute of limitations for the infringement of copyright is three years, starting from the day when the damage to rights and copyright holder knows or should have known of the infringing act. Where the right holder institutes an action after three years, and if the infringing act still exists when the action is instituted and is within the period of copyright protection, the people's court shall rule that the defendant shall stop the infringing act, and the amount of compensations for damages shall be computed till three years further as of the day when the right holder institutes the action with the people's court
Article 29 <u>As for the infringing acts as provided in Article 47 of the Copyright Law, the people's court may, apart from imposing civil liabilities upon the actors upon the pleading of the parties concerned, impose civil sanctions to the actors according to the provisions of Article 134, Paragraph of the General Principles of the Civil Law. The amount of fines to be imposed upon may be determined by referring to the relevant provisions of the Regulation of the People's Republic of China on Implementing the Copyright Law</u> In case the administrative department of copyright has already imposed administrative punishments to a same infringing act, the people's court shall not impose any more civil sanctions	**(Deletion)**

(continued)

(continued)

Before modification (effective October 15, 2002)	Revised (effective January 1, 2021)
Article 30 As for the acts of infringing upon copyright prior to October 27, 2001, if the parties concerned pleads to the people's court for ordering the actors to stop infringing acts or for taking measures of attachment of evidences, the provisions of Articles 49 and 50 of the Copyright Law shall apply Where the people's court takes the measures before the institution of an action, it shall handle the case by referring to the provisions of the Interpretation of the Supreme People's Court Concerning the Application of Laws for Stopping Acts of Infringing upon Registered Trademark Rights and for Attachment of Evidences Before An Action Is Instituted	**Article 28** Where the people's court **takes preservation measures before the institution of an action, it shall handle the case by referring to the provisions of the Civil Procedure Law and the Provisions of the Supreme People's Court on Several Issues on the Application of Law to the Examination of Cases of Preservation of Intellectual Property Disputes for Stopping Acts of Infringing upon Registered Trademark Rights and for Attachment of Evidences Before An Action Is Instituted**
Article 31 Unless there are other provisions in the present Interpretation, the cases of civil dispute over copyright as accepted by the people's courts after October 27, 2001, for the acts that happened prior to October 27, 2001, the provisions of Copyright Law prior to its amendment shall apply, while for the acts that happened subsequent to the said date, the provisions of the amended Copyright Law shall apply. As for the civil acts that happened prior to the said but continues after the date, the provisions of the amended Copyright Law shall apply	**Article 31** Except as otherwise provided in this Interpretation, the provisions of the **pre-amended Copyright Law** shall apply to civil disputes involving civil acts that occurred before the amendment of the Copyright Law; the provisions of the **post-amended Copyright Law** shall apply to civil acts that occurred after the amendment of the Copyright Law; and the provisions of the post-amended Copyright Law shall apply to civil disputes involving civil acts that occurred before the amendment of the Copyright Law and continued after the amendment of the Copyright Law The provisions of the amended Copyright Law shall apply to civil acts occurring before the amendment of the Copyright Law and continuing after the amendment of the Copyright Law The provisions of the amended Copyright Law shall apply to **civil acts occurring before the amendment of the Copyright Law and continuing after the amendment of the Copyright Law**
Article 32 Where any of the relevant provisions promulgated in the past is inconsistent with the present Interpretation, the present Interpretation shall prevail	(Same as left)

1.2.4 Provisions by the Supreme People's Court on Several Issues Concerning the Application of Law in Hearing Civil Dispute Cases Involving Infringement of the Right of Communication to the Public on Information Networks

(Adopted by the Judicial Committee of the Supreme People's Court at its 1561st meeting on November 26, 2012, as amended by the Decision of the Supreme People's Court on Amending the Judicial Interpretation of the Supreme People's Court on Several Issues Concerning the Application of Law in the Trial of Disputes over Infringement of Patent Rights (II) and Other Eighteen Judicial Interpretations on

Intellectual Property Rights adopted by the Judicial Committee of the Supreme People's Court at its 1823rd meeting on December 23, 2020).

Before amendment (effective from 1 January 2013)	Revised (effective 1 January 2021)
For the purposes of correctly hearing civil dispute cases involving infringement of the right of communication to the public on information networks, protecting the right of communication to the public on information networks, promoting the sound development of the information network industry, and maintaining the public interest, these Provisions are developed in accordance with the General Principles of the Civil Law of the People's Republic of China, the Tort Law of the People's Republic of China, the Copyright Law of the People's Republic of China, the Civil Procedure Law of the People's Republic of China, and other relevant laws and regulations and in consideration of trial practice	For the purposes of correctly hearing civil dispute cases involving infringement of the right of communication to the public on information networks, protecting the right of communication to the public on information networks, promoting the sound development of the information network industry, and maintaining the public interest, these Provisions are developed in accordance with the Civil Code of the People's Republic of China, the Copyright Law of the People's Republic of China, the Civil Procedure Law of the People's Republic of China, and other relevant laws and regulations and in consideration of trial practice
Article 1 The people's courts shall take into account the interests of right holders, network service providers and the public when exercising their discretionary power in accordance with law during the hearing of civil dispute cases involving infringement of the right of communication to the public on information networks	
Article 2 For the purposes of these Provisions, "information networks" means the Internet, radio and television broadcasting networks, fixed communication networks and mobile communication networks, with computers, TV sets, fixed telephones, mobile phones and other electronic devices as receiving terminals, as well as local area networks open to the public	
Article 3 Where a network user or network service provider provides, on an information network, any work, performance, or sound or audio-visual recording which a right holder has the right of communication to the public on information networks without the consent of the right holder, the people's court shall determine that the network user or network service provider has infringed upon the right of communication to the public on information networks, except as otherwise provided for by laws and administrative regulations If the work, performance, or sound or audio-visual recording is placed on an information network by means such as uploading to a network server, file sharing settings or using file sharing software, allowing members of the public to download, browse or otherwise obtain the work, performance, or sound or audio-visual recording from a place and at a time individually chosen by them, the people's court shall determine that the network user or network service provider has committed the act of provision as mentioned in the preceding paragraph	
Article 4 Where there is evidence to prove that a network service provider has provided any work, performance, or sound or audio-visual recording jointly with others by means such as cooperation, constituting a joint infringement, the people's court shall hold the network service provider jointly and severally liable. If the network service provider is able to provide evidence that it only provides automatic connection, automatic transmission, information storage space, search, link, file sharing technology and other network services so that it does not contribute to the infringement, the people's court shall support such a claim of the network service provider	
Article 5 Where a network service provider provides the alleged work for the public by means such as Web cache or thumbnail, substantively in place of another network service provider, the people's court shall determine that the network service provider has committed the act of provision If the act of provision as mentioned in the preceding paragraph neither affects the normal use of the alleged work nor unreasonably damages the right holder's lawful rights and interests in the work, the people's court shall support a claim of the network service provider that it has not infringed upon the right of communication to the public on information networks	
Article 6 Where the plaintiff has provided preliminary evidence that a network service provider has provided the alleged work, performance, or sound or audio-visual recording but the network service provider is able to prove that it only provides network services and is not at fault, the people's court shall not determine that the network service provider has committed an infringement	

(continued)

(continued)

Before amendment (effective from 1 January 2013)	Revised (effective 1 January 2021)
	Article 7 Where a network service provider abets or aids any network user in infringing upon the right of communication to the public on information networks when providing network services, the people's court shall hold the network service provider liable for the infringement Where a network service provider induces or encourages any network user to infringe upon the right of communication to the public on information networks by means such as language, promotion of technical support, or bonus points, the people's court shall determine that the network service provider has abetted the infringement Where a network service provider which knows or should have known that a network user is using its network services to infringe upon the right of communication to the public on information networks fails to take necessary measures such as removal, blocking, and removal of links or provides aid such as technical support for the user, the people's court shall hold that the network service provider has aided in the infringement
	Article 8 The people's court shall determine whether a network service provider is liable for infringement as an abettor or aider according to the fault of the network service provider. The fault of a network service provider means whether the network service provide knows or should have known a network user's infringement of the right of communication to the public on information networks Where a network service provider fails to conduct proactive examination regarding a network user's infringement of the right of communication to the public on information networks, the people's court shall not determine on this basis that the network service provider is at fault Where a network service provider is able to prove that it has taken reasonable and effective technical measures but it is still difficult for it to discover a network user's infringement of the right of communication to the public on information networks, the court shall determine that the network service provider is not at fault
	Article 9 The people's court shall determine whether a network service provider should have known an infringement based on a clear fact that a network user has infringed upon the right of communication to the public on information networks and by taking into account the following factors: (1) The network service provider's capability of information management, as required according to the nature of services provided, manners of provision of services, and possibility of infringement attributable thereto (2) The type and popularity of the communicated work, performance, or sound or audio-visual recording and the visibility of the infringing information (3) Whether the network service provider has, on its own initiative, chosen, edited, modified, recommended or otherwise dealt with the work, performance, or sound or audio-visual recording (4) Whether the network service provider has proactively taken reasonable measures to prevent infringement (5) Whether the network service provider has set up any convenient programs to receive a notice of infringement and make reasonable response to the notice of infringement in a timely manner (6) Whether the network service provider has taken reasonable measures against a user's repeated infringements (7) Other relevant factors
	Article 10 Where a network service provider recommends popular movies and TV plays by means such as ranking, catalogue, index, descriptive paragraphs or brief introductions when providing network services, allowing the public to access such works directly by means such as downloading from or browsing the network service provider's Web pages, the people's court may determine that the provider should have known a network user's infringement of the right of communication to the public on information networks
	Article 11 Where a network service provider directly obtains any economic benefits from a work, performance, or sound or audio-visual recording provided by a network user, the people's court shall determine that the network service provider has a higher duty of care for the network user's infringement of the right of communication to the public on information networks If a network service provider obtains any benefits from inserting advertisements into a specific work, performance, or sound or audio-visual recording or obtains any economic benefits otherwise related to the communicated work, performance, or sound or audio-visual recording, it shall be determined that the network service provider directly obtains economic benefits as mentioned in the preceding paragraph, however, excluding the general advertising and service charges, among others, collected by a network service provider for providing network services
	Article 12 Under any of the following circumstances, the people's court may determine that a network service provider providing the information storage space service should have known a network user's infringement of the right of communication to the public on information networks, according to the specific facts of the case: (1) Placing a popular movie or TV play in a position where it is easily appreciable to a network service provider, such as a homepage or any other primary page (2) Choosing, editing, organizing, or recommending the themes or contents of popular movies and TV plays or establishing a dedicated ranking for them on its own initiative (3) Otherwise failing to take reasonable measures, although the provision of the alleged work, performance, or sound or audio-visual recording without consent is easily appreciable

(continued)

Before amendment (effective from 1 January 2013)	Revised (effective 1 January 2021)
Article 13 Where a network service provider fails to take necessary measures such as removal, blocking, and removal of links in a timely manner after receipt of a notice submitted by the right holder by letter, fax, email or any other means, the people's court shall determine that the network service provider knows the alleged infringement of the right of communication to the public on information networks	**Article 13** Where a network service provider fails to take necessary measures based on the prima facie evidence and type of service in a timely manner, after receipt of a notice submitted by the right holder by letter, fax, email **or prima facie evidence of infringement,** the people's court shall determine that the network service provider knows the alleged infringement of the right of communication to the public on information networks
Article 14 Regarding the timeliness of a network service provider's taking necessary measures such as removal, blocking, and removal of links, the people's court shall make a determination after comprehensively considering the form of the notice submitted by the right holder, the accuracy of the notice, the difficulty in taking the measures, the nature of network services, the type, popularity and quantity of the involved works, performances, and sound or audio-visual recordings, and other factors	**Article 14** Regarding the timeliness of a network service provider's **Notification of forwarding,** the people's court shall make a determination after comprehensively considering the form of the notice submitted by the right holder, the accuracy of the notice, the difficulty in taking the measures, the nature of network services, the type, popularity and quantity of the involved works, performances, and sound or audio-visual recordings, and other factors
Article 15 A civil dispute case involving infringement of the right of communication to the public on information networks shall be under the jurisdiction of the people's court at the place of infringement or the place of domicile of the defendant. The place of infringement includes the place where the network server, computer terminal or any other equipment used for committing the alleged infringement is located. Where it is difficult to determine both the place of infringement and the place of domicile of the defendant or both of them are located outside China, the place where the computer terminal or any other equipment on which the plaintiff discovers the infringing content is located may be deemed the place of infringement	
Article 16 Upon entry into force of these Provisions, the Interpretation by the Supreme People's Court on Several Issues Concerning the Application of Law in the Trial of Cases Involving Copyright Disputes on Computer Networks (SPC Interpretation No. 11 [2006]) shall be repealed	

1.3 Main Amendments of Chinese Trademark Laws and Regulations

1.3.1 Trademark Law of the People's Republic of China

(Adopted at the 24th Session of the Standing Committee of the Fifth National People's Congress on August 23, 1982; amended for the first time according to the Decision on Amending the Trademark Law of the People's Republic of China as adopted at the 30th Session of the Standing Committee of the Seventh National People's Congress on February 22, 1993; amended for the second time according to the Decision on Amending the Trademark Law of the People's Republic of China as adopted at the 24th Session of the Standing Committee of the Ninth National People's Congress on October 27, 2001; amended for the third time according to the Decision on Amending the Trademark Law of the People's Republic of China as adopted at the 4th Session of the Standing Committee of the Twelfth National People's Congress on August 30, 2013; and amended for the fourth time in accordance with the Decision to Amend Eight Laws Including the Construction Law of the People's Republic of

China adopted at the 10th Session of the Standing Committee of the Thirteenth National People's Congress of the People's Republic of China on April 23, 2019).

Before amendment (Come into force on 1, May, 2014)	After amendment (Come into force on 1, November, 2019)
Chapter I General Provisions	
Article 4 Any natural person, legal person, or other organization needing to acquire the right to exclusively use a trademark on the goods or services thereof in the course of business operations shall apply to the Trademark Office for trademark registration The provisions of this Law regarding goods trademarks are applicable to service trademarks	**Article 4** Any natural person, legal person, or other organization needing to acquire the right to exclusively use a trademark on the goods or services thereof in the course of business operations shall apply to the Trademark Office for trademark registration. A bad faith application for trademark registration for a purpose other than use shall be rejected The provisions of this Law regarding goods trademarks are applicable to service trademarks
Article 19 Trademark agencies shall follow the principle of good faith, abide by laws and administrative regulations, handle trademark registration applications and other trademark-related matters as authorized by clients, and maintain confidential clients' trade secrets known in acting for clients Where the trademark registration applied for by a client may be denied for any circumstances as described in this Law, a trademark agency shall clearly notify the client thereof	**Article 19** Trademark agencies shall follow the principle of good faith, abide by laws and administrative regulations, handle trademark registration applications and other trademark-related matters as authorized by clients, and maintain confidential clients' trade secrets known in acting for clients Where the trademark registration applied for by a client may be denied for any circumstances as described in this Law, a trademark agency shall clearly notify the client thereof
Where a trademark agency knows or should have known that a client's trademark registration application falls under any circumstances as described in Article 15 and 32 of this Law, it may not accept the client's authorization Trademark agencies may not apply for registration of trademarks other than those applied for in acting for clients	Where a trademark agency knows or should have known that a client's trademark registration application falls under any circumstances as described in **Articles 4**, 15 and 32 of this Law, it may not accept the client's authorization Trademark agencies may not apply for registration of trademarks other than those applied for in acting for clients
Chapter III Trademark Registration Examination and Approval	
Article 33 For a preliminarily approved and published trademark, within three months from the date of publication, a prior rights holder or an interested party which believes that paragraph 2 or 3 of Article 13, Article 15, paragraph 1 of Article 16, Article 30, Article 31, or Article 32 of this Law is violated or any person which believes that Article 10, 11, or 12 of this Law is violated may file an opposition with the Trademark Office. If no opposition has been filed upon expiry of the publication period, the registration shall be approved, a certificate of trademark registration shall be issued, and the registered trademark shall be published	**Article 33** For a preliminarily approved and published trademark, within three months from the date of publication, a prior rights holder or an interested party which believes that paragraph 2 or 3 of Article 13, Article 15, paragraph 1 of Article 16, Article 30, Article 31, or Article 32 of this Law is violated or any person that believes that **Article 4**, Article 10, Article 11, Article 12, **or paragraph 4 of Article 19** of this Law is violated may file an opposition with the Trademark Office. If no opposition has been filed upon expiry of the publication period, the registration shall be approved, a certificate of trademark registration shall be issued, and the registered trademark shall be published
Chapter V Declaration of Invalidation of Registered Trademarks	

(continued)

(continued)

Before amendment (Come into force on 1, May, 2014)	After amendment (Come into force on 1, November, 2019)
Article 44 Where a registered trademark violates Article 10, 11, or 12 of this Law, or its registration was acquired by fraud or any other illicit means, the Trademark Office shall declare invalidation of the registered trademark; and any other organization or individual may petition the Trademark Appeal Board to declare invalidation of the registered trademark The Trademark Office shall notify the party concerned in written form of its decision to declare invalidation of the registered trademark. Against the decision of the Trademark Office, the party concerned may apply to the Trademark Appeal Board for a review within 15 days after receiving the notice. The Trademark Appeal Board shall make a decision within nine months after receiving the review application, and notify the party concerned of its decision in written form. Under special circumstances, the time limit may be extended by three months with the approval of the administrative department for industry and commerce under the State Council. Against the decision of the Trademark Appeal Board, the party concerned may institute an action in a people's court within 30 days after receiving the notice	**Article 44** Where a registered trademark violates **Article 4**, Article 10, Article 11, Article 12, **or paragraph 4 of Article 19 of this Law**, or its registration was acquired by fraud or any other illicit means, the Trademark Office shall declare invalidation of the registered trademark; and any other organization or individual may petition the Trademark Appeal Board to declare invalidation of the registered trademark The Trademark Office shall notify the party concerned in written form of its decision to declare invalidation of the registered trademark. Against the decision of the Trademark Office, the party concerned may apply to the Trademark Appeal Board for a review within 15 days after receiving the notice. The Trademark Appeal Board shall make a decision within nine months after receiving the review application, and notify the party concerned of its decision in written form. Under special circumstances, the time limit may be extended by three months with the approval of the administrative department for industry and commerce under the State Council. Against the decision of the Trademark Appeal Board, the party concerned may institute an action in a people's court within 30 days after receiving the notice
Where any other organization or individual petitions the Trademark Appeal Board to declare invalidation of a registered trademark, the Trademark Appeal Board shall, after receiving the application, notify the party concerned in written form, and specify a time limit for submission of defense. The Trademark Appeal Board shall make a ruling to sustain the registered trademark or declare invalidation of the registered trademark within nine months after receiving the application, and notify the party concerned of its decision in written form. Under special circumstances, the time limit may be extended by three months with the approval of the administrative department for industry and commerce under the State Council. Against the ruling of the Trademark Appeal Board, the party concerned may institute an action in a people's court within 30 days after receiving the notice. The people's court shall notify the opposite party in the trademark ruling proceedings to participate in the action as a third party	Where any other organization or individual petitions the Trademark Appeal Board to declare invalidation of a registered trademark, the Trademark Appeal Board shall, after receiving the application, notify the party concerned in written form, and specify a time limit for submission of defense. The Trademark Appeal Board shall make a ruling to sustain the registered trademark or declare invalidation of the registered trademark within nine months after receiving the application, and notify the party concerned of its decision in written form. Under special circumstances, the time limit may be extended by three months with the approval of the administrative department for industry and commerce under the State Council. Against the ruling of the Trademark Appeal Board, the party concerned may institute an action in a people's court within 30 days after receiving the notice. The people's court shall notify the opposite party in the trademark ruling proceedings to participate in the action as a third party
Chapter VII Protection of the Right to Exclusively Use a Registered Trademark	

(continued)

(continued)

Before amendment (Come into force on 1, May, 2014)	After amendment (Come into force on 1, November, 2019)
Article 63 The amount of damages for infringement upon the right to exclusively use a registered trademark shall be determined according to the actual losses suffered by the right holder from the infringement; where it is difficult to determine the amount of actual losses, the amount of damages may be determined according to the benefits acquired by the infringer from the infringement; where it is difficult to determine the right holder's losses or the benefits acquired by the infringer, the amount of damages may be a reasonable multiple of the royalties. If the infringement is committed in bad faith with serious circumstances, the amount of damages shall be the amount, but not more than three times the amount, determined in the aforesaid method. The amount of damages shall include reasonable expenses of the right holder for stopping the infringement Where the right holder has made its best efforts to adduce evidence but the account books and materials related to infringement are mainly in the possession of the infringer, in order to determine the amount of damages, a people's court may order the infringer to provide such account books and materials; and if the infringer refuses to provide the same or provide any false ones, the people's court may determine the amount of damages by reference to the claims of and the evidence provided by the right holder	**Article 63** The amount of damages for infringement upon the right to exclusively use a registered trademark shall be determined according to the actual losses suffered by the right holder from the infringement; where it is difficult to determine the amount of actual losses, the amount of damages may be determined according to the benefits acquired by the infringer from the infringement; where it is difficult to determine the right holder's losses or the benefits acquired by the infringer, the amount of damages may be a reasonable multiple of the royalties. If the infringement is committed in bad faith with serious circumstances, the amount of damages shall be the amount, but not more than **five times** the amount, determined in the aforesaid method. The amount of damages shall include reasonable expenses of the right holder for stopping the infringement Where the right holder has made its best efforts to adduce evidence but the account books and materials related to infringement are mainly in the possession of the infringer, in order to determine the amount of damages, a people's court may order the infringer to provide such account books and materials; and if the infringer refuses to provide the same or provide any false ones, the people's court may determine the amount of damages by reference to the claims of and the evidence provided by the right holder Where it is difficult to determine the actual losses suffered by the right holder from the infringement, the profits acquired by the infringer from the infringement, or the royalties of the registered trademark, a people's court may award damages of **not more than five million yuan** according to the circumstances of the infringement
Where it is difficult to determine the actual losses suffered by the right holder from the infringement, the profits acquired by the infringer from the infringement, or the royalties of the registered trademark, a people's court may award damages of not more than three million yuan according to the circumstances of the infringement	**The people's court that tries a trademark dispute case shall, at the request of the right holder, order destruction of goods on which a registered trademark is falsely used, except under special circumstances; order destruction of materials and tools primarily used for the manufacture of such goods without compensation; or under special circumstances, order prohibition of the said materials and tools from entering commercial channels without compensation Goods on which a registered trademark is falsely used may not enter commercial channels even if the registered trademark so used is removed only**

(continued)

1 Main Amendments of Chinese Intellectual Property Law   49

(continued)

Before amendment (Come into force on 1, May, 2014)	After amendment (Come into force on 1, November, 2019)
Article 68 Where a trademark agency commits any of the following conduct, the administrative department for industry and commerce shall order it to make correction within a prescribed time limit and impose a warning and a fine of but not less than 10,000 yuan but not more than 100,000 yuan on it; its directly liable person in charge and other directly liable personnel shall be fined not less than 5,000 yuan but not more than 50,000 yuan; and if any crime is constituted, criminal liability shall be investigated: (1) Forging or altering any legal document, seal, or signature or using any forged or altered legal document, seal, or signature in handling trademark-related matters (2) Acquiring trademark agency business by defaming other trademark agencies or disturbing the trademark agency market order by other illicit means (3) Violating paragraph 3 or 4, Article 19 of this Law Where a trademark agency commits any conduct mentioned in the preceding paragraph, the administrative department for industry and commerce shall record it into its credit file; and if the circumstances are serious, the Trademark Office and the Trademark Appeal Board may also decide to stop accepting its trademark agency business, and publish it A trademark agency which, in violation of the principle of good faith, infringes upon the lawful rights and interests of clients shall assume civil responsibility in accordance with the law, and the trademark agency association shall, according to its bylaws, take disciplinary actions against it	**Article 68** Where a trademark agency commits any of the following conduct, the administrative department for industry and commerce shall order it to make correction within a prescribed time limit and impose a warning and a fine of but not less than 10,000 yuan but not more than 100,000 yuan on it; its directly liable person in charge and other directly liable personnel shall be fined not less than 5,000 yuan but not more than 50,000 yuan; and if any crime is constituted, criminal liability shall be investigated: (1) Forging or altering any legal document, seal, or signature or using any forged or altered legal document, seal, or signature in handling trademark-related matters (2) Acquiring trademark agency business by defaming other trademark agencies or disturbing the trademark agency market order by other illicit means (3) Violating **Article 4** or paragraph 3 or 4 of Article 19 of this Law Where a trademark agency commits any conduct mentioned in the preceding paragraph, the administrative department for industry and commerce shall record it into its credit file; and if the circumstances are serious, the Trademark Office and the Trademark Appeal Board may also decide to stop accepting its trademark agency business, and publish it A trademark agency which, in violation of the principle of good faith, infringes upon the lawful rights and interests of clients shall assume civil responsibility in accordance with the law, and the trademark agency association shall, according to its bylaws, take disciplinary actions against it **For a bad faith application for trademark registration, administrative punishment such as warning and fine shall be imposed according to the circumstances; and for a bad faith suit over a trademark, the people's court shall impose punishment according to the law**

1.3.2 Interpretation of Supreme People's Court on Several Issues Concerning the Application of Law in the Hearing of Civil Cases Involving Trademark Disputes

(Adopted at the 1246th Session of the Judicial Committee of the Supreme People's Court on 12 October 2002, and amended pursuant to the Decision of Supreme People's Court on Revisions to "Interpretation of Supreme People's Court on Several Issues Concerning the Application of Law in the Hearing of Cases Involving Patent

Infringement (II)" and other 17 Judicial Interpretations Concerning Intellectual Property adopted at the 1823rd Session of the Judicial Committee of the Supreme People's Court on 23 December 2020).

Before amendment (Come into force on 16, October, 2002)	After amendment (Come into force on 1st, January, 2021)
In order to correctly try trademark dispute cases, and in accordance with the provisions of laws such as the General Principles of Civil Law, the Contract Law, the Trademark Law, the Civil Procedure Law, etc., the following interpretations are made regarding several issues relating to the application of the law:	In order to correctly try trademark dispute cases, and in accordance with the provisions of laws such as **the Civil Code of the People's Republic of China**, the Trademark Law, the Civil Procedure Law, etc., the following interpretations are made regarding several issues relating to the application of the law:
Article 1 The following acts shall fall under acts causing other harm to others' exclusive right to use registered trademarks as stipulated in item 5 of Article 52 of the Trademark Law: (1) using words identical or similar to others' registered trademark as an enterprise name and prominently using them on identical or similar goods so as to likely cause misidentification among the relevant public; (2) reproducing, imitating or translating others' registered well-known trademark or the main part thereof and using them as a trademark on non-identical or dissimilar goods so as to mislead the public and possibly cause harm to the interests of the registrant of the well-known trademark; and (3) registering words identical or similar to others' registered trademark as a domain name and conducting e-commerce business in related goods through the domain name so as to likely cause misidentification among the relevant public	**Article 1** The following acts shall fall under acts causing other harm to others' exclusive right to use registered trademarks as stipulated in **item 7 of Article 57** of the Trademark Law: (1) using words identical or similar to others' registered trademark as an enterprise name and prominently using them on identical or similar goods so as to likely cause misidentification among the relevant public; (2) reproducing, imitating or translating others' registered well-known trademark or the main part thereof and using them as a trademark on non-identical or dissimilar goods so as to mislead the public and possibly cause harm to the interests of the registrant of the well-known trademark; and (3) registering words identical or similar to others' registered trademark as a domain name and conducting e-commerce business in related goods through the domain name so as to likely cause misidentification among the relevant public
Article 2 In accordance with the provisions of paragraph 1 of Article 13 of the Trademark Law, whoever reproduces, imitates or translates others' well-known trademark or the main part thereof that are not registered in China and uses them as a trademark on identical or similar goods so as to likely cause confusion among the relevant parties shall bear civil liability to stop the infringement	**Article 2** In accordance with the provisions of **paragraph 2 of Article 13** of the Trademark Law, whoever reproduces, imitates or translates others' well-known trademark or the main part thereof that are not registered in China and uses them as a trademark on identical or similar goods so as to likely cause confusion among the relevant parties shall bear civil liability to stop the infringement

(continued)

1 Main Amendments of Chinese Intellectual Property Law

(continued)

Before amendment (Come into force on 16, October, 2002)	After amendment (Come into force on 1st, January, 2021)
Article 3 Trademark licenses as provided for in Article 40 of the Trademark Law include the following three categories: (1) exclusive license, which means that the trademark registrant licenses a single licensee to use its registered trademark for an agreed period, within a specified territory and in an agreed manner and the trademark registrant may not use the registered trademark as agreed; (2) sole license, which means that the trademark registrant licenses a single licensee to use its registered trademark for an agreed period, within a specified territory and in an agreed manner and the trademark registrant may use the registered trademark but may not license others to use the registered trademark as agreed; and (3) non-exclusive license, which means that the trademark registrant licenses a licensee to use its registered trademark for an agreed period, within a specified territory and in an agreed manner and the trademark registrant may itself use the registered trademark and license others to use the registered trademark	**Article 3** Trademark licenses as provided for in **Article 43** of the Trademark Law include the following three categories: (1) exclusive license, which means that the trademark registrant licenses a single licensee to use its registered trademark for an agreed period, within a specified territory and in an agreed manner and the trademark registrant may not use the registered trademark as agreed; (2) sole license, which means that the trademark registrant licenses a single licensee to use its registered trademark for an agreed period, within a specified territory and in an agreed manner and the trademark registrant may use the registered trademark but may not license others to use the registered trademark as agreed; and (3) non-exclusive license, which means that the trademark registrant licenses a licensee to use its registered trademark for an agreed period, within a specified territory and in an agreed manner and the trademark registrant may itself use the registered trademark and license others to use the registered trademark
Article 4 Interested parties as provided for in Article 53 of the Trademark Law include licensees under licensing contracts for registered trademarks, lawful successors of property rights of registered trademark, etc When exclusive rights to use a registered trademark are infringed, licensees under exclusive licensing contracts may bring an action to the people's courts. licensees under sole licensing contracts may bring an action jointly with the trademark registrant or bring an action by themselves if the trademark registrant does not bring an action. licensees under non-exclusive licensing contracts may bring an action provided that they have been explicitly authorized to do so by the trademark registrant	**Article 4** Interested parties as provided for in **paragraph 1 of Article 60** of the Trademark Law include licensees under licensing contracts for registered trademarks, lawful successors of property rights of registered trademark, etc When exclusive rights to use a registered trademark are infringed, licensees under exclusive licensing contracts may bring an action to the people's courts. licensees under sole licensing contracts may bring an action jointly with the trademark registrant or bring an action by themselves if the trademark registrant does not bring an action. licensees under non-exclusive licensing contracts may bring an action provided that they have been explicitly authorized to do so by the trademark registrant
Article 5 Where a trademark registrant or interested party brings an action because another party infringes upon its/his exclusive rights to use a registered trademark before its/his application for renewal during the grace period for renewal of the registered trademark has been approved, the people's courts shall accept the action	
Article 6 A civil action instituted on the ground that the exclusive right to use a registered trademark has been infringed upon shall be subject to the jurisdiction of the people's court where the infringing act is carried out, where the infringing commodities are stored or sealed up and detained, or where the defendant has his domicile as is provided for in Articles 13 and 52 of the Trademark Law The place where infringing commodities are stored as provided in the preceding paragraph refers to the place where large quantities of infringing commodities are stored or hidden or infringing commodities are regularly stored or hidden. The place of sealing up and detaining shall mean the place where the customs, industry and commerce and other administrative organs seal up and detaining infringing commodities according to law	**Article 6** A civil action instituted on the ground that the exclusive right to use a registered trademark has been infringed upon shall be subject to the jurisdiction of the people's court where the infringing act is carried out, where the infringing commodities are stored or sealed up and detained, or where the defendant has his domicile as is provided for in Articles 13 and **57** of the Trademark Law The place where infringing commodities are stored as provided in the preceding paragraph refers to the place where large quantities of infringing commodities are stored or hidden or infringing commodities are regularly stored or hidden. The place of sealing up and detaining shall mean the place where the customs and other administrative organs seal up and detaining infringing commodities according to law

(continued)

(continued)

Before amendment (Come into force on 16, October, 2002)	After amendment (Come into force on 1st, January, 2021)
Article 7 Where a joint action is brought against multiple defendants in different places where the infringing acts are committed, the plaintiff may choose a people's court of the place where one of the defendants commits the infringing acts as the people's court of the place where the infringing acts are committed. Where an action is brought against only one of the defendants, the people's court of the place where that defendant commits the infringing acts shall have jurisdiction	
Article 8 The "relevant general public" as mentioned in the Trademark Law refers to the consumers relating to a certain type of commodities or services to which the trademark represents and other business operators that are closely connected with the marketing of the aforesaid commodities or services	
Article 9 The term "identical trademarks" as provided in Article 52, Item 1 of the Trademark Law refers to that there are basically no difference in visual perception between the trademark that is charged of infringement and the registered trademark of the plaintiff The term "similar trademarks" as provided in Article 52, Item 1 of the Trademark Law refers to that the trademark charged of infringement and the registered trademark of the plaintiff are similar in the font style, pronunciation, meaning of the words, or in the composition and color of the pictures, or in the overall structure of all the elements combined, or in the cubic form or combination of colors so that the relevant general public may be confused about the origin of the commodity or believe that there exist certain connections between the origin and the commodity which is represented by the registered trademark of the plaintiff	**Article 9** The term "identical trademarks" as provided in **Article 57, Item 1 and 2** of the Trademark Law refers to that there are basically no difference in visual perception between the trademark that is charged of infringement and the registered trademark of the plaintiff The term "similar trademarks" as provided in **Article 57, Item 2** of the Trademark Law refers to that the trademark charged of infringement and the registered trademark of the plaintiff are similar in the font style, pronunciation, meaning of the words, or in the composition and color of the pictures, or in the overall structure of all the elements combined, or in the cubic form or combination of colors so that the relevant general public may be confused about the origin of the commodity or believe that there exist certain connections between the origin and the commodity which is represented by the registered trademark of the plaintiff
Article 10 In accordance with the provisions of Items 1 of Article 52 of the Trademark Law, people's courts shall determine that trademarks are identical or similar under the following principles: (1) taking the general perception of the relevant public as the standard; (2) trademarks should be compared in their entirety as well as their key elements; the comparison should be carried out with the objects of comparison being kept apart; and (3) when determining whether trademarks are similar, the distinctiveness and popularity of the registered trademark for which protection is sought should be considered	**Article 10** In accordance with the provisions of **Items 1 and 2 of Article 57** of the Trademark Law, people's courts shall determine that trademarks are identical or similar under the following principles: (1) taking the general perception of the relevant public as the standard; (2) trademarks should be compared in their entirety as well as their key elements; the comparison should be carried out with the objects of comparison being kept apart; and (3) when determining whether trademarks are similar, the distinctiveness and popularity of the registered trademark for which protection is sought should be considered
Article 11 "Similar goods" as mentioned in Item 1 of Article 52 of the Trademark Law shall mean the goods that have identical functions, uses, production entities, sales channels, target consumers, etc., or goods that the relevant public generally considers to have a certain connection and that are likely to cause confusion "Similar services" shall mean the services that have identical purposes, contents, methods, target consumers, etc., or the services that the relevant public generally considers to have a certain connection and that are likely to cause confusion "Similar goods and services" shall mean that there are certain connections between goods and services, which are likely to cause confusion among the relevant public	**Article 11** "Similar goods" as mentioned in **Item 2 of Article 57** of the Trademark Law shall mean the goods that have identical functions, uses, production entities, sales channels, target consumers, etc., or goods that the relevant public generally considers to have a certain connection and that are likely to cause confusion "Similar services" shall mean the services that have identical purposes, contents, methods, target consumers, etc., or the services that the relevant public generally considers to have a certain connection and that are likely to cause confusion "Similar goods and services" shall mean that there are certain connections between goods and services, which are likely to cause confusion among the relevant public

(continued)

1 Main Amendments of Chinese Intellectual Property Law 53

(continued)

Article 12 When determining whether a commodity or service is similar on the basis of the provisions of Article 52, Item 1 of the Trademark Law, the people's court shall take into comprehensive consideration of the general understanding of the relevant general public about the commodity or service. The Classification Table of Commodities and Services for the International Registration of Trademarks and the Classification Table of Similar Commodities and Services may be referred to in judging whether a commodity or service is similar	**Article 12** When determining whether a commodity or service is similar on the basis of the provisions of **Article 57, Item 2** of the Trademark Law, the people's court shall take into comprehensive consideration of the general understanding of the relevant general public about the commodity or service. The Classification Table of Commodities and Services for the International Registration of Trademarks and the Classification Table of Similar Commodities and Services may be referred to in judging whether a commodity or service is similar
Article 13 When determining the compensation liabilities of the infringer on the basis of Article 56, paragraph 1 of the Trademark Law, the people's court may compute the amount of compensation according to the method of computation as selected by the right holder	**Article 13** When determining the compensation liabilities of the infringer on the basis of **Article 63, paragraph 1** of the Trademark Law, the people's court may compute the amount of compensation according to the method of computation as selected by the right holder
Article 14 The interests obtained from infringement as provided in Article 56, paragraph 1 of the Trademark Law may be calculated as the product of the sales volume of the infringing commodities and the unit profit of the commodities concerned. In case it is impossible to know the unit profit of the commodity, the unit profit shall be the commodity which is represented by the registered trademark	**Article 14** The interests obtained from infringement as provided in **Article 63, paragraph 1** of the Trademark Law may be calculated as the product of the sales volume of the infringing commodities and the unit profit of the commodities concerned. In case it is impossible to know the unit profit of the commodity, the unit profit shall be the commodity which is represented by the registered trademark
Article 15 The losses incurred from infringement as provided in Article 56, paragraph 1 of the Trademark Law may be computed as the product of the reduced sales volume of the commodities concerned resulting from the infringement and the unit profit of the commodities which are represented by the registered trademark	**Article 15** The losses incurred from infringement as provided in **Article 63, paragraph 1** of the Trademark Law may be computed as the product of the reduced sales volume of the commodities concerned resulting from the infringement and the unit profit of the commodities which are represented by the registered trademark
Article 16 In case it is difficult to determine the interests of the infringer gained from the infringement or the losses of the infringed incurred from the infringement, people's courts may determine the amount of compensation according to the request of the parties or by applying the provisions of paragraph 2 of Article 56 of the Trademark Law ex officio When determining the amount of compensation, the people's court shall take into comprehensive consideration of the elements, including the nature, duration and aftermaths of the infringing act, the reputation of the trademark, the amount of royalties for licensing the trademark, the type, time and scope of the license of the trademark, as well as the reasonable expenses incurred in stopping the infringement, and other factors If the parties concerned reach an agreement on the amount of compensation in accordance with Paragraph 1 of this Article, permission shall be granted	**Article 16 If it is difficult to determine the actual loss suffered by the right holder due to infringement, the benefit gained by the infringer from the infringement, or the license fee for the use of the registered trademark**, people's courts may determine the amount of compensation according to the request of the parties or by applying the provisions of **paragraph 3 of Article 63** of the Trademark Law ex officio When **applying paragraph 3 of Article 63 of the Trademark Law** to determine the amount of compensation, people's courts shall take into account the nature, period and consequences of the infringement, **the degree of subjective fault of the infringer**, the reputation of the trademark, the reasonable expenses incurred in stopping the infringement, and other factors If the parties concerned reach an agreement on the amount of compensation in accordance with paragraph 1 of this Article, permission shall be granted
Article 17 "Reasonable expenses incurred in stopping the infringement" as referred to in paragraph 1 of Article 56 of the Trademark Law include reasonable expenses incurred by the right holder or its agent in investigating and collecting evidence on the infringement People's courts may, according to a party's claim and the specific circumstances of a case, include the attorney's fees in line with the provisions of the relevant departments of the state into the scope of compensation	**Article 17** "Reasonable expenses incurred in stopping the infringement" as referred to in **paragraph 1 of Article 63** of the Trademark Law include reasonable expenses incurred by the right holder or its agent in investigating and collecting evidence on the infringement People's courts may, according to a party's claim and the specific circumstances of a case, include the attorney's fees in line with the provisions of the relevant departments of the state into the scope of compensation

(continued)

(continued)

Article 18 The limitation for instituting legal proceedings concerning the infringement of the right to exclusive use of a registered trademark is two years, commencing from the date when the trademark registrant or interested party knows or should have known the infringement and the obligor. Where the trademark registrant or interested party brings a lawsuit after two years, and if the infringement is still continuing when the lawsuit is brought and the right to exclusive use of the registered trademark is still in the period of validity, the people's court shall order the defendant to stop the infringement, and the amount of compensation for the infringement shall be calculated by reckoning back two years from the date when the right holder brought the lawsuit to the people's court	**Article 18** The limitation for instituting legal proceedings concerning the infringement of the right to exclusive use of a registered trademark is **three years**, commencing from the date when the trademark registrant or interested party knows or should have known **the infringement of the right and the obligor.** Where the trademark registrant or interested party brings a lawsuit after **three years**, and if the infringement is still continuing when the lawsuit is brought and the right to exclusive use of the registered trademark is still in the period of validity, the people's court shall order the defendant to stop the infringement, and the amount of compensation for the infringement shall be calculated by reckoning back **three years** from the date when the right holder brought the lawsuit to the people's court
Article 19 Where a trademark licensing contract has not been filed for record, it shall not affect the effectiveness of the licensing contract, unless otherwise agreed upon by the parties A trademark license contract that fails to be placed on the archivist files of the trademark office shall not confront any bona fide third party	**Article 19** Where a trademark licensing contract has not been filed for record, it shall not affect the effectiveness of the licensing contract, unless otherwise agreed upon by the parties
Article 20 The assignment of a registered trademark shall not affect the effectiveness of trademark licensing contracts that have already come into effect before the assignment, unless otherwise stipulated by the trademark licensing contract	
Article 21 When hearing a case of dispute over the infringement upon the exclusive right to use a registered trademark, the people's court may, in accordance with Article 134 of the General Principles of the Civil Law of the People's Republic of China and Article 53 of the Trademark Law and in light of the specific conditions of the case, order the infringer to bear such civil liabilities as stopping the infringement, removing obstructions, eliminating dangers, compensating for losses and eliminating ill effects, etc. It may also make a decision on such civil sanctions as imposing a fine and/or confiscating the infringing goods, the forged trademark logos, and the property especially used for the manufacture of the infringing goods, such as the materials, tools and equipment, etc. The amount of the fine may be determined by reference to the relevant provisions of Regulation for Trademark Law of the People's Republic of China Where the administrative department for industry and commerce has already imposed an administrative punishment against the same infringement upon the exclusive right to use the registered trademark, the people's court shall no longer impose any civil punishment upon it	**Article 21** When hearing a case of dispute over the infringement upon the exclusive right to use a registered trademark, the people's court may, in accordance with **Article 179 of the Civil Code, Article 60 of the Trademark Law** and in light of the specific conditions of the case, order the infringer to bear such civil liabilities as stopping the infringement, removing obstructions, eliminating dangers, compensating for losses and eliminating ill effects, etc. It may also make a decision on such civil sanctions as imposing a fine and/or confiscating the infringing goods, the forged trademark logos, and the property **mainly** used for the manufacture of the infringing goods, such as the materials, tools and equipment, etc. The amount of the fine may be determined by reference to the relevant provisions of **paragraph 2 of Article 60 of the Trademark Law** Where **an administrative department** has already imposed an administrative punishment against the same infringement upon the exclusive right to use the registered trademark, the people's court shall no longer impose any civil punishment upon it

(continued)

(continued)

Article 22 In the hearing of disputes over trademarks, the people's court may, according to the allegations of the parties concerned and the concrete situations of the cases concerned, decide by law whether the registered trademark involved is a well-known one or not The determination of well-known trademarks shall be carried out in accordance with Article 14 of the Trademark Law Where any of the parties concerned pleads for protecting the well-known trademarks as affirmed by the administrative department in charge or the people's court, and the opposite party has no objection to the well-known nature of the trademark involved, the people's court may refuse to make further examinations. If the opposite party has objection, the people's court shall examine the well-known nature of the trademark involved according to Article 14 of the Trademark Law	
Article 23 The provisions of the present Interpretation concerning commodity trademarks shall be applicable to service trademarks	
Article 24 Where any of the previously promulgated provisions is inconsistent with the present Interpretation, the present Interpretation shall prevail	

1.3.3 Provisions of the Supreme People's Court on Issues Concerned in the Trial of Cases of Civil Disputes over the Conflict between Registered Trademark or Enterprise Name with Prior Right

(Adopted at the 1444th Meeting of the Judicial Committee of the Supreme People's Court on 18 February 2008, Amended in accordance with the Decision of the Supreme People's Court on Amending 18 Judicial Interpretations of Intellectual Property including the Interpretations of the Supreme People's Court on Several Issues Concerning the Application of Law in the Trial of Patent Infringement Dispute Cases (II) adopted at the 1823rd Meeting of the Judicial Committee of the Supreme People's Court on December 23, 2020).

Before amendment (Come into force on 1, March, 2008)	After amendment (Come into force on 1, January, 2021)
To correctly try cases of civil disputes over the conflict between registered trademark or enterprise name with prior right, by taking judicial practices into account, these Provisions are formulated in accordance with the Civil Procedure Law of the People's Republic of China, the General Principles of the Civil Law of the People's Republic of China, the Trademark Law of the People's Republic of China, the Anti-unfair Competition Law of the People's Republic of China and other relevant laws	To correctly try cases of civil disputes over the conflict between registered trademark or enterprise name with prior right, by taking judicial practices into account, these Provisions are formulated in accordance with the Civil Procedure Law of the People's Republic of China, <u>the</u> Civil Code of the People's Republic of China, the Trademark Law of the People's Republic of China, the Anti-unfair Competition Law of the People's Republic of China and other relevant laws
Article 1 For a lawsuit filed on the ground that the character or graphic used in the registered trademark of other party infringes upon the plaintiff's copyright, patent right for a design, right to enterprise name or other prior right, if the lawsuit conforms to the provision of Article 108 of the Civil Procedure Law, the people's court shall accept it	**Article 1** For a lawsuit filed on the ground that the character or graphic used in the registered trademark of other party infringes upon the plaintiff's copyright, patent right for a design, right to enterprise name or other prior right, if the lawsuit conforms to the provision of Article 119 of the Civil Procedure Law, the people's court shall accept it

(continued)

(continued)

Before amendment (Come into force on 1, March, 2008)	After amendment (Come into force on 1, January, 2021)
If the lawsuit is filed on the ground that a registered trademark used by other party on approved commodities is identical or similar to the prior registered trademark of the plaintiff, the people's court shall, in accordance with the provision of <u>Item 3 of Article 111</u> of the Civil Procedure Law, notify the plaintiff to apply to the competent administrative authority for settling the issue. But if the lawsuit is filed on the ground that a registered trademark used by other party beyond the approved scope of commodities or by changing the predominant feature of the trademark, splitting it or combining it with others is identical or similar to the registered trademark of the plaintiff, the people's court shall accept it	If the lawsuit is filed on the ground that a registered trademark used by other party on approved commodities is identical or similar to the prior registered trademark of the plaintiff, the people's court shall, in accordance with the provision of **Item 3 of Article 124** of the Civil Procedure Law, notify the plaintiff to apply to the competent administrative authority for settling the issue. But if the lawsuit is filed on the ground that a registered trademark used by other party beyond the approved scope of commodities or by changing the predominant feature of the trademark, splitting it or combining it with others is identical or similar to the registered trademark of the plaintiff, the people's court shall accept it
Article 2 For a lawsuit filed, on the basis of <u>Item 3 of Article 5</u> of the Anti-unfair Competition Law, on the ground that the enterprise name of other party is identical or similar to the prior registered enterprise name of the plaintiff to the extent that it is easy for the public to become confused about the source of the plaintiff's commodity, and if the lawsuit conforms to the provision of Article 108 of the Civil Procedure Law, the people's court shall accept it	**Article 2** For a lawsuit filed, on the basis of **Item 2 of Article 6** of the Anti-unfair Competition Law, on the ground that the enterprise name of other party is identical or similar to the prior registered enterprise name of the plaintiff to the extent that it is easy for the public to become confused about the source of the plaintiff's commodity, and if the lawsuit conforms to the provision of Article 119 of the Civil Procedure Law, the people's court shall accept it

Article 3 The people's court shall, in light of the plaintiff's claim and the nature of the disputable civil legal relationship, in accordance with the Provision on Cause of Action of Civil Cases (for Trial Implementation), determine the cause of action of a case of civil dispute over the conflict between registered trademark or enterprise name and prior right, and apply corresponding laws

Article 4 If the enterprise name of the defendant infringes upon the right to the exclusive use of a trademark or constitutes unfair competition, the people's court may, by taking the plaintiff's claim and the specific situation of the case into account, order the defendant to stop or regularize the use of enterprise name and assume corresponding civil liability

1.3.4 Interpretation of the Supreme People's Court on Several Issues Relating to Laws Applicable to Trial of Civil Dispute Cases Involving Protection of Well-known Trademarks

(Adopted at the 1467th session of the Judicial Committee of the Supreme People's Court on 22 April 2009, and amended in accordance with the Decision of the Supreme People's Court on Amending 18 Judicial Interpretations of the Supreme People's Court Including the Interpretation of the Supreme People's Court on Several Issues Relating to Laws Applicable to Trial of Patent Infringement Dispute Cases (II) adopted at the 1823rd session of the Judicial Committee of the Supreme People's Court on 23 December 2020).

1 Main Amendments of Chinese Intellectual Property Law

Before amendment (Come into force on 1, May, 2009)	After amendment (Come into force on 1, January, 2021)
This Interpretation is enacted in accordance with the Trademark Law of the People's Republic of China, the Anti-Unfair Competition Law of the People's Republic of China, the Civil Procedure Law of the People's Republic of China and other relevant laws and regulations and in light of trial practice for the purpose of protecting well-known trademarks according to the law in the trial of civil dispute cases such as trademark infringement	
Article 1 For the purpose of this Interpretation, well-known trademarks refer to the trademarks that are <u>widely known</u> by the relevant public within the territory of China	**Article 1** For the purpose of this Interpretation, well-known trademarks refer to the trademarks that are **well known** by the relevant public within the territory of China
Article 2 In any of the following civil dispute cases, where the party concerned takes a well-known trademark as the factual basis, the People's Court shall ascertain whether the trademark involved is well known in light of the specific circumstances of the case if it deems necessary: (1) trademark infringement lawsuits on the ground of violation of the provisions of Article 13 of the Trademark Law; (2) trademark infringement or unfair competition lawsuits on the ground that an enterprise name is identical or similar to the well-known trademark of the party concerned; and (3) the defense or counterclaim in compliance with Article 6 hereof	
Article 3 In an of the following civil dispute cases, the People's Court will not ascertain whether the trademark involved is well known: (1) the establishment of the infringement of trademark rights or unfair competition is not based on the fact that the trademark is well-known; or (2) the accused infringement of trademark rights or unfair competition is not established because it does not have the other elements stipulated by law Where a plaintiff files a tort lawsuit on the ground that the defendant has registered or used a domain name identical or similar to the plaintiff's registered trademark, and the defendant has conducted electronic commerce through the domain name for relevant commodity trading, which is sufficient to cause misidentification of the relevant public, the case shall be handled in accordance with the provisions of Item I of the preceding paragraph	
Article 4 When ascertaining whether a trademark is well known, the People's Court shall base its determination on the fact that the trademark is well known, and shall comprehensively consider all the factors as prescribed in Article 14 of the Trademark Law, except that the recognition of trademark as well-known can be made without considering all the factors as prescribed in the said Article according to the specific circumstances of the case	**Article 4** When ascertaining whether a trademark is well known, the People's Court shall base its determination on the fact that the trademark is well known, and shall comprehensively consider all the factors as prescribed in **paragraph 1 of Article 14** of the Trademark Law, except that the recognition of trademark as well-known can be made without considering all the factors as prescribed in the said Article according to the specific circumstances of the case
Article 5 Where a party concerned claims that its trademark is well known, it shall provide the following evidences according to the specific circumstances of the case to prove that its trademark was already well known at the time of occurrence of the accused trademark infringement or unfair competition act: (1) market share, sales territory, profits and taxes, etc. of the commodities for which the trademark is used; (2) time of continuous use of the trademark; (3) means, duration, degree, capital contribution and territorial scope of the publicity or sales promotion activities of the trademark; (4) records that the trademark has been protected as a well-known trademark; (5) market reputation of the trademark; and (6) other facts that prove that the trademark is already well known The time, scope and method of the use of the trademark as mentioned in the preceding paragraph shall include the continuous use of the trademark prior to the approval of registration With regard to such evidences as the length of time of use of the trademark, its ranking in the industry, market survey report, market value assessment report, and whether it has been recognized as a well-known trademark, the People's Court shall objectively and comprehensively examine such evidences in the light of other evidences confirming that the trademark is well known	
Article 6 Where the plaintiff brings a civil lawsuit on the ground that the use of the trademark in dispute infringes its exclusive right to use the registered trademark, and the defendant defends or counterclaims on the ground that the registered trademark of the plaintiff duplicates, imitates or translates the its prior trademark which has not been registered, the defendant shall bear the burden of proof for the fact that its prior trademark which has not been registered is well known	

(continued)

(continued)

Before amendment (Come into force on 1, May, 2009)	After amendment (Come into force on 1, January, 2021)
Article 7 Where a trademark has been recognized as a well-known trademark by a People's Court or <u>the industry and commerce administrative department of the State Council</u> before the trademark infringement or unfair competition takes place, and the defendant does not raise objections to the fact that the trademark is well known, the People's Court shall recognize the trademark. If the defendant raises objections, the plaintiff shall bear the burden of proof for the fact that the trademark is well known Unless otherwise provided in this Interpretation, the People's Court shall not apply the admission rules of evidence in civil litigation to the fact that the trademark is well known	**Article 7** Where a trademark has been recognized as a well-known trademark by a People's Court or **the administrative department** before the trademark infringement or unfair competition takes place, and the defendant does not raise objections to the fact that the trademark is well known, the People's Court shall recognize the trademark. If the defendant raises objections, the plaintiff shall bear the burden of proof for the fact that the trademark is well known Unless otherwise provided in this Interpretation, the People's Court shall not apply the admission rules of evidence in civil litigation to the fact that the trademark is well known
Article 8 For a trademark that is <u>widely known</u> by the public within the territory of China, if the plaintiff has provided the basic evidence proving that the trademark is well known, or the defendant does not raise objections, the People's Court shall recognize the fact that the trademark is well known	**Article 8** For a trademark that is **well known** by the public within the territory of China, if the plaintiff has provided the basic evidence proving that the trademark is well known, or the defendant does not raise objections, the People's Court shall recognize the fact that the trademark is well known
Article 9 Where it is sufficient to mislead the relevant public on the source of commodities with the well-known trademark and the trademark in dispute, or sufficient to cause the relevant public to believe that there is a specific connection between the operators using the well-known trademark and the alleged trademark, such as licensed use or affiliated enterprise relationship, such circumstance shall fall within the scope of "easy to cause confusion" as specified in <u>paragraph 1, Article 13</u> of the Trademark Law Where it is sufficient to cause the relevant public to believe that there is a certain connection between the alleged trademark and the well-known trademark, thereby weakening the distinctiveness of the well-known trademark or derogating the market reputation of the well-known trademark, or improper use of the market reputation of the well-known trademark, such circumstance shall fall within the scope of "misleading the public and causing possible damage to the interests of the registrant of the well-known trademark" as specified in <u>paragraph 2, Article 13</u> of the Trademark Law	**Article 9** Where it is sufficient to mislead the relevant public on the source of commodities with the well-known trademark and the trademark in dispute, or sufficient to cause the relevant public to believe that there is a specific connection between the operators using the well-known trademark and the alleged trademark, such as licensed use or affiliated enterprise relationship, such circumstance shall fall within the scope of "easy to cause confusion" as specified in **paragraph 2, Article 13** of the Trademark Law Where it is sufficient to cause the relevant public to believe that there is a certain connection between the alleged trademark and the well-known trademark, thereby weakening the distinctiveness of the well-known trademark or derogating the market reputation of the well-known trademark, or improper use of the market reputation of the well-known trademark, such circumstance shall fall within the scope of "misleading the public and causing possible damage to the interests of the registrant of the well-known trademark" as specified in **paragraph 3, Article 13** of the Trademark Law
Article 10 Where a plaintiff requests to prohibit the defendant from using, on dissimilar commodities, any trademark or enterprise name that is identical with or similar to the registered well-known trademark of the plaintiff, the People's Court shall make a judgment in light of the specific circumstances of the case and by taking into account the following factors: (1) the distinctiveness of the well-known trademark; (2) the popularity of the well-known trademark among the relevant public of the commodities using the alleged trademark or enterprise name; (3) the degree of association between the commodities using the well-known trademark and the commodities using the alleged trademark or enterprise name; and (4) other relevant factors	

(continued)

1 Main Amendments of Chinese Intellectual Property Law

(continued)

Before amendment (Come into force on 1, May, 2009)	After amendment (Come into force on 1, January, 2021)
Article 11 Where the registered trademark used by the defendant violates Article 13 of the Trademark Law by duplicating, imitating or translating the well-known trademark of the plaintiff, constituting trademark infringement, the People's Court shall, according to the request of the plaintiff, make a judgment to prohibit the defendant from using the said trademark. However, the People's Court shall not uphold the claim of the plaintiff if the registered trademark of the defendant falls under either of the following circumstances: (1) the time limit for applying for cancellation declaration as provided for in paragraph 2, Article 41 of the Trademark Law has expired; or (2) the trademark of the plaintiff was not well-known when the defendant applied for registration	**Article 11** Where the registered trademark used by the defendant violates Article 13 of the Trademark Law by duplicating, imitating or translating the well-known trademark of the plaintiff, constituting trademark infringement, the People's Court shall, according to the request of the plaintiff, make a judgment to prohibit the defendant from using the said trademark. However, the People's Court shall not uphold the claim of the plaintiff if the registered trademark of the defendant falls under either of the following circumstances: (1) the time limit for **applying for invalidation declaration** as provided for in **paragraph 1, Article 45** of the Trademark Law has expired; or (2) the trademark of the plaintiff was not well-known when the defendant applied for registration
Article 12 Where the party concerned claims protection of an unregistered well-known trademark, which shall not be used or registered as provided for in Articles 10, 11 and 12 of the Trademark Law, the People's Court shall not uphold such claim	
Article 13 In a civil dispute case involving the protection of a well-known trademark, the recognition of a well-known trademark by the People's Court shall only serve as a fact of the case and grounds for judgment, and shall not be included in the main body of the judgment; if the case is concluded by mediation, the fact that the trademark is well-known shall not be recognized in the mediation document	
Article 14 In case of any discrepancy between this Interpretation and the relevant judicial interpretations previously promulgated by the Supreme People's Court, this Interpretation shall prevail	

1.3.5 Provisions of the Supreme People's Court on Several Issues Concerning the Trial of Administrative Cases Involving Trademark Authorization and Confirmation

(Adopted at the 1703rd Meeting of the Judicial Committee of the Supreme People's Court on December 12, 2016, Amended in accordance with the Decision of the Supreme People's Court on Amending 18 Judicial Interpretations of Intellectual Property including the Interpretations of the Supreme People's Court on Several Issues Concerning the Application of Law in the Trial of Patent Infringement Dispute Cases (II) adopted at the 1823rd Meeting of the Judicial Committee of the Supreme People's Court on December 23, 2020).

Before amendment (Come into force on 1, March, 2017)	After amendment (Come into force on 1, January, 2021)
For the correct trial of administrative cases involving trademark authorization and confirmation, these Provisions are developed in accordance with the provisions of the Trademark Law of the People's Republic of China, the Administrative Litigation Law of the People's Republic of China and other laws and in consideration of the trial practice	

(continued)

(continued)

Before amendment (Come into force on 1, March, 2017)	After amendment (Come into force on 1, January, 2021)
Article 1 For the purpose of these Provisions, "administrative cases involving trademark authorization and confirmation" means the cases filed with the people's courts by counter parties or interested parties against review of rejection of trademark registration applications, review of disapproval of trademark registration, review of cancellation of trademarks, declaration of invalidation of trademarks and review of declaration of invalidation and other administrative acts made by <u>the Trademark Review and Adjudication Board of the administrative department for industry and commerce under the State Council (hereinafter referred to as the "Trademark Review and Adjudication Board")</u>	**Article 1** For the purpose of these Provisions, "administrative cases involving trademark authorization and confirmation" means the cases filed with the people's courts by counter parties or interested parties against review of rejection of trademark registration applications, review of disapproval of trademark registration, review of cancellation of trademarks, declaration of invalidation of trademarks and review of declaration of invalidation and other administrative acts made by **China National Intellectual Property Administration**
Article 2 The scope of examining the administrative behaviors of trademark authorization and confirmation by the people's courts shall generally be determined according to the claims and grounds of plaintiffs. Where a plaintiff does not make any claim in the litigation, but the relevant identification of the <u>Trademark Review and Adjudication Board</u> has obvious inappropriateness, the people's court may review the relevant matters and render a judgment after all parties state their opinions	**Article 2** The scope of examining the administrative behaviors of trademark authorization and confirmation by the people's courts shall generally be determined according to the claims and grounds of plaintiffs. Where a plaintiff does not make any claim in the litigation, but the relevant identification of **China National Intellectual Property Administration** has obvious inappropriateness, the people's court may review the relevant matters and render a judgment after all parties state their opinions
Article 3 "Identical with or similar to" the name and other items of the People's Republic of China as prescribed in item 1, paragraph 1, Article 10 of the Trademark Law means that a trademark sign is identical with or similar to the name of the state as a whole Where a sign that contains the name of the People's Republic of China and is not identical therewith or similar thereto as a whole may damage state dignity if it is registered as a trademark, the people's court may determine that it falls under the circumstance as prescribed in item 8, paragraph 1, Article 10 of the Trademark Law	
Article 4 Where a trademark sign or its constituent elements are deceptive and easily make the public misunderstand the quality and other characteristics or the origin of the goods and the <u>Trademark Review and Adjudication Board</u> identifies that it falls under the circumstance as prescribed in item 7, paragraph 1, Article 10 of the Trademark Law, the people's court shall grant support thereto	**Article 4** Where a trademark sign or its constituent elements are deceptive and easily make the public misunderstand the quality and other characteristics or the origin of the goods and the **China National Intellectual Property Administration** identifies that it falls under the circumstance as prescribed in item 7, paragraph 1, Article 10 of the Trademark Law, the people's court shall grant support thereto
Article 5 Where a trademark sign or its constituent elements may cause passive and negative effect on the social and public interests and public order of China, the people's court may determine that it falls under the circumstance of "having other adverse effect" as prescribed in item 8, paragraph 1, Article 10 of the Trademark Law Applying for registration of a name of a public figure in the political, economic, cultural, religious, ethnic and other areas as a trademark falls under the circumstance of "having other adverse effect" as prescribed in the preceding paragraph	
Article 6 Where a trademark mark is composed of a place name a administrative division at or above the county level or another foreign place name known to the public and has a meaning different from the place name as a whole, the people's court shall determine that it does not fall under the circumstance as specified in paragraph 2, Article 10 of the Trademark Law	
Article 7 When examining whether a trademark has a distinctive feature, the people's court shall, according to the general knowledge of the relevant public using the commodity designated to use trademark, judge whether the trademark has any distinctive feature as a whole. A trademark sign that contains descriptive elements but does not affect its distinctive feature as a whole or a descriptive sign that is expressed in a unique way and whose source of goods may be identified by the relevant public shall be determined to have distinctive feature	

(continued)

(continued)

Before amendment (Come into force on 1, March, 2017)	After amendment (Come into force on 1, January, 2021)
	Article 8 When a disputed trademark is a sign in foreign language, the people's court shall, according to the general knowledge of the relevant public within the territory of China, examine and judge whether the trademark in foreign language has distinctive feature. Where the inherent meaning of a sign in both Chinese and foreign language may affect its distinctive feature on the commodity designated to use the trademark and the relevant public has relatively low degree of awareness of the inherent meaning and is able to identify the source of goods with the sign, it may be identified that it has distinctive feature
	Article 9 Where an application is filed for the registration of a trademark with the shape or a part of the shape of a commodity as a three-dimensional sign and it is difficult for the relevant public to recognize it as a sign indicating the source of the commodity under general circumstance, the three-dimensional sign has no distinctive feature as a trademark The shape is independently created or firstly used by the applicant, and does not surely make it have the distinctive feature as a trademark Where a sign referred to in the first paragraph is used for a long period of time or is widely used, the relevant public is able to identify the source of the commodity through the sign, it may be recognized that the sign has distinctive feature
	Article 10 Where a disputed trademark is a legal commodity name or a commodity name established by usage, the people's court shall determine it as a common name specified in item 1, paragraph 1, Article 11 of the Trademark Law. A trademark that is a common name of a commodity under the provisions of the law and the national standards and industry standards shall be recognized as a common name. Where relevant public generally believes that a certain name is able to refer to a category of goods, it shall be recognized as a common name "established by usage." A trademark that is listed as a commodity name by professional reference books, dictionaries and other items may be used as reference for recognizing the common name established by usage Common names established by usage shall generally be judged according to the common understanding of the relevant public across the country. A title of a fixed commodity on relevant market formed due to historical traditions, customs, geographical environment and other reasons that is commonly used on the relevant market may be recognized as a common name by the people's court Where a disputed trademark applicant knows perfectly well or should know that the trademark applied to be registered is the name of a commodity established by usage in some regions, the people's court may regard the trademark applied to be registered as a common name The people's court shall examine and judge whether a disputed trademark is a common name generally according to the de facto status on the date when an application is filed for the trademark. Where the de facto status changes when the registration is approved, whether it is a common name shall be judged according to the de facto status when the registration is approved
	Article 11 Where a trademark sign only or mainly describes and explains the quality, main raw materials, function, purpose, weight, quantity, origin and other items of the commodity, the people's court shall determine that it falls under the circumstance as prescribed in item 2, paragraph 1, Article 11 of the Trademark Law. Where a trademark sign or its constituent elements imply the characteristics of the commodity, but do not affect its function of identifying the source of the commodity, it does not fall under the circumstance as prescribed in this item
	Article 12 Where a party claims that a disputed trademark constitutes reproduction, imitation or translation of a famous trademark not registered and should not be registered or should be invalidated according to paragraph 2, Article 13 of the Trademark Law, the people's court shall give comprehensive consideration to the following factors and the mutual impact of the factors, and determine whether it easily causes confusion: (1) the degree of approximation of the trademark sign; (2) the similarity of the commodity; (3) the distinctiveness and popularity of the trademark requested to be protected; (4) the degree of attention of relevant public; and (5) other relevant factors The subjective intent of the trademark applicant and the evidence of actual confusion may be used as a reference factor for determining the possibility of confusion
	Article 13 Where a party claims that a disputed trademark constitutes reproduction, imitation or translation of a famous trademark registered and should not be registered or should be invalidated according to paragraph 3, Article 13 of the Trademark Law, the people's court shall give comprehensive consideration to the following factors, to determine whether the use of a disputed trademark is sufficient to make the relevant public to believe that there is a considerable degree of connection with the famous trademark, thereby misleading the public and resulting in possible harm to the interests of the registrant of the famous trademark:

(continued)

(continued)

Before amendment (Come into force on 1, March, 2017)	After amendment (Come into force on 1, January, 2021)
(1) the distinctiveness and popularity of the reference trademark; (2) whether a trademark sign is sufficiently similar; (3) the information on the commodity designated to use the trademark; (4) the degree of coincidence and attention of relevant public; and (5) the information on the lawful use of a sign similar to the reference trademark by other market participants or other relevant factors	
Article 14 Where a party claims that a disputed trademark constitutes reproduction, imitation or translation of a famous trademark registered and should not be registered or should be invalidated, and the Trademark Review and Adjudication Board upholds its support under the provisions of Article 30 of the Trademark Law, if the disputed trademark has been registered for less than 5 years, the people's court may, after the party state the opinions, try the case under the provisions of Article 30 of the Trademark Law; and if the disputed trademark has been registered for more than 5 years, the people's court shall try the case under paragraph 3, Article 13 of the Trademark Law	**Article 14** Where a party claims that a disputed trademark constitutes reproduction, imitation or translation of a famous trademark registered and should not be registered or should be invalidated, and the **China National Intellectual Property Administration** upholds its support under the provisions of Article 30 of the Trademark Law, if the disputed trademark has been registered for less than 5 years, the people's court may, after the party state the opinions, try the case under the provisions of Article 30 of the Trademark Law; and if the disputed trademark has been registered for more than 5 years, the people's court shall try the case under paragraph 3, Article 13 of the Trademark Law
Article 15 Where a trademark agent, representative or distributor, agent and other agents and representatives in the sense of sales agency relation applies for registration of a trademark identical with or similar to the trademark of the principal or represented party on a identical or similar commodity in its own name without authorization, the people's court shall try the case under the provisions of paragraph 1, Article 15 of the Trademark Law Where, at the stage of consultation for the establishment of an agent or representative relationship, the agent or representative specified in the preceding paragraph applies for registration of a trademark of a principal or represented party, the people's court shall try the case under the provisions of paragraph 1, Article 15 of the Trademark Law Where there is kinship and other specific identity relationships between a trademark applicant and an agent or a representative, it may be presumed that its behavior of trademark registration is maliciously colluded with the agent or representative, and the people's court shall try the case under the provisions of paragraph 1, Article 15 of the Trademark Law	
Article 16 The following circumstances may be recognized as "other relations" as prescribed in paragraph 2, Article 15 of the Trademark Law: (1) The trademark applicant has kinship with the prior user (2) The trademark applicant has labor relation with the prior user (3) The trademark applicant has a business address adjacent to that of the prior user (4) The trademark applicant has negotiated with the prior user on reaching agent and representative relations, but agent or representative relation has not been formed (5) The trademark applicant has negotiated with the prior user on reaching contract and business relations, but contract or business relation has not been formed	
Article 17 Where an interested party of a geographical indication claims that another's trademark shall not be registered or shall be invalidated in accordance with Article 16 of the Trademark Law, if the commodity designated to use the disputed trademark is not identical with the geographical indication product, the interested party of the geographical indication may prove that the disputed trademark is used on the product and is still likely to make the relevant public to mistakenly believe that the product is derived from the region and therefore has specific quality, reputation or other characteristics, the people's court shall grant support thereto If the geographical indication has been registered as a collective trademark or a certified trademark, the right owner or the interested party of the collective trademark or certified trademark may choose to claim rights in accordance with the article or otherwise under Article 13 and Article 30 of the Trademark Law	
Article 18 The prior rights as prescribed in Article 32 of the Trademark Law include the civil rights or other lawful rights and interests to be protected as enjoyed by the parties before the date when an application for the disputed trademark is filed. Where the prior rights no longer exist when a disputed trademark is approved to be registered, the registration of the disputed trademark shall not be affected	

(continued)

(continued)

Before amendment (Come into force on 1, March, 2017)	After amendment (Come into force on 1, January, 2021)
Article 19 Where a party claims that a disputed trademark damages its prior copyright, the people's court shall, under the Copyright Law and other relevant provisions, examine whether the subject claimed constitutes a production, whether the party is a copyright owner, or whether another interested party having the right to claim for copyright and the disputed trademark infringe upon the copyright Where a trademark sigh constitutes a work protected by the Copyright Law, the design manuscript, original copy, contract on rights obtaining, copyright registration certificate before the date of filing an application for claiming for a trademark, and other documents may be used as the preliminary evidence for proving the ownership of copyright Trademark announcement, trademark registration certificate and other items may be used as preliminary evidence for determining that the trademark applicant is an interested party with the right to claim for the copyright of the trademark sign	
Article 20 Where a party claims that a disputed trademark damages its right of name, if the relevant public believes that the trademark sign refers to the natural person, and it is easy to believe that a commodity with the trademark has obtained the permission of the natural person or has specific relation with the natural person, the people's court shall determine that the trademark has damaged the right of name of the natural person Where a party claims for the right of name with its pseudonym, stage name, translated name and other specific names, the specific name has certain reputation, the party has established stable correspondence with the natural person, and relevant public refers to the natural person with the name, the people's court shall grant support thereto	
Article 21 Where the title claimed by a party has certain market reputation, another person applies for registration of a trademark identical with or similar to the title without permission, it easily makes relevant public to have confusion on the source of the commodity, and the party therefor constitutes prior rights and interests, the people's court shall grant support thereto Where a party files a claim on the basis of the short name of an enterprise that has a certain market reputation and has established stable correspondence with the enterprise, the preceding paragraph shall apply	
Article 22 Where a party claims that a disputed trademark damages the copyright of the role image, the people's court shall conduct examination in accordance with Article 19 of these Provisions For a work with copyright protection period, if the name of the work and the name of the role in the work have relatively high reputation, use of the name as a trademark in a relevant commodity easily makes the relevant public mistakenly believes that permission of the right owner has been obtained or there is specific contact with the right owner, and the party claims that it has prior rights and interests, the people's court shall grant support thereto	
Article 23 Where a prior user claims that a trademark applicant preemptively registers a trademark that is primarily used by it and has certain influence by illicit means, if the trademark primarily used has had certain influence, and the trademark applicant knows or should have known the trademark, it may be presumed that it constitutes "preemptive registration by illicit means," except the trademark applicant proves that it did not maliciously use the goodwill of the trademark A prior user proves that its prior trademark has certain period of continuous use, region, sales volume or advertising, the people's court may determine that it has certain influence Where a prior user claims that a trademark applicant applies for registration of a trademark that is primarily used by it and has certain influence on a commodity not similar thereto and violates the provisions of Article 32 of the Trademark Law, the people's court shall not grant support thereto	
Article 24 Where a party disrupts the order of trademark registration, damages public interests, illegally occupies public resources or seeks illicit interests by means other than deceit, the people's court may determine that it belongs to "other illicit means" as prescribed in paragraph 1, Article 44 of the Trademark Law	
Article 25 When judging whether a disputed trademark applicant has "maliciously registered" a famous trademark of another party, the people's court shall give comprehensive considerations to the popularity of the reference trademark, the grounds of the disputed trademark applicant for applying for the disputed trademark, and the specific circumstance of using the disputed trademark, to determine its subjective intent. Where a reference trademark has high popularity and a disputed trademark applicant has no justified reason, the people's court may presume that its registration constitutes "malicious registration" as specified in paragraph 1, Article 45 of the Trademark Law	

(continued)

(continued)

Before amendment (Come into force on 1, March, 2017)	After amendment (Come into force on 1, January, 2021)
Article 26 Independent use by a trademark owner, user by another party with permission and other use without violating the will of the trademark owner may be recognized as the use as specified in paragraph 2, Article 49 of the Trademark Law Where a trademark sign actually used is slightly different from the trademark sign approved to be registered, but does not change its distinctive feature, it may be deemed use of a registered trademark Only transfer or licensing without actual use of a registered trademark or only announcement of the information on trademark registration and statement of enjoying the exclusive right to use the registered trademark shall not be registered as use of a trademark Where a trademark owner has the real intention to use a trademark and has made necessary preparations for the actual use, but a registered trademark has not been actually used for other objective reasons, the people's court may determine that it has justified reason	
Article 27 Where a party clams that the following circumstances of the Trademark Review and Adjudication Board fall under the circumstances of "violating the legal procedures" as prescribed in item 3, Article 70 of the Administrative Litigation Law, the people's court shall grant support thereto: (1) The review reasons put forward by the party are omitted, which causes real impact on the rights of the party (2) A member of the collegial panel is not informed of the review procedures and there is matters that should have been evaded but have not been evaded upon examination (3) Competent party is not notified of participating in the examination and the party expressly raises an objection (4) Other circumstances in violation of the legal procedures	**Article 27** Where a party clams that the following circumstances of the **China National Intellectual Property Administration** fall under the circumstances of "violating the legal procedures" as prescribed in item 3, Article 70 of the Administrative Litigation Law, the people's court shall grant support thereto: (1) The review reasons put forward by the party are omitted, which causes real impact on the rights of the party (2) A member of the collegial panel is not informed of the review procedures and there is matters that should have been evaded but have not been evaded upon examination (3) Competent party is not notified of participating in the examination and the party expressly raises an objection (4) Other circumstances in violation of the legal procedures
Article 28 Where during the process that a people's court tries an administrative case involving trademark authorization and confirmation, the causes for the Trademark Review and Adjudication Board to reject a disputed trademark, disapprove its registration or announce its invalidation no longer exist, the people's court may, on the basis of the new facts, revoke the relevant judgment of the Trademark Appeal Board and order the said Board to render a new judgment according to the changed facts	**Article 28** Where during the process that a people's court tries an administrative case involving trademark authorization and confirmation, the causes for the **China National Intellectual Property Administration** to reject a disputed trademark, disapprove its registration or announce its invalidation no longer exist, the people's court may, on the basis of the new facts, revoke the relevant judgment of the Trademark Appeal Board and order the said Board to render a new judgment according to the changed facts
Article 29 A review application filed by a party on the basis of the newly found evidence after the original administrative behavior, evidence unable to be obtained during the original administrative procedures due to objective reasons or unable to be provided within the prescribed time limit, or new legal basis is not a review application re-filed on the basis of the "same facts and grounds."	**Article 29** A review application filed by a party on the basis of the newly found evidence after the original administrative behavior, evidence unable to be obtained during the original administrative procedures due to objective reasons or unable to be provided within the prescribed time limit, or new legal basis is not a review application re-filed on the basis of the "same facts and grounds."

(continued)

1 Main Amendments of Chinese Intellectual Property Law 65

(continued)

Before amendment (Come into force on 1, March, 2017)	After amendment (Come into force on 1, January, 2021)
During the procedure of review of rejection of a trademark registration application, after the <u>Trademark Review and Adjudication Board</u> preliminarily approves and publishes the trademark applied on the ground that the trademark applied and the reference trademark do not constitute identical or similar trademark used on a same or similar commodity, the following circumstances shall not be deemed re-filing of review application on the "same facts and grounds:" (1) A reference trademark owner or interested party raises an objection according to the reference trademark, the <u>Trademark Office of the administrative department for industry and commerce under the State Council</u> grants support thereto, and the trademark applicant against which an objection is raised applies for review (2) A reference trademark owner or interested party announces it to be invalidated according to the application for the reference trademark after a trademark applied is approved to be registered	During the procedure of review of rejection of a trademark registration application, after the **China National Intellectual Property Administration** preliminarily approves and publishes the trademark applied on the ground that the trademark applied and the reference trademark do not constitute identical or similar trademark used on a same or similar commodity, the following circumstances shall not be deemed re-filing of review application on the "same facts and grounds:" (1) A reference trademark owner or interested party raises an objection according to the reference trademark, the **China National Intellectual Property Administration** grants support thereto, and the trademark applicant against which an objection is raised applies for review (2) A reference trademark owner or interested party announces it to be invalidated according to the application for the reference trademark after a trademark applied is approved to be registered
Article 30 Where a people's court has specifically determined the relevant facts and the application of laws in an effective ruling, a counter party or an interested party institutes a lawsuit against a ruling re-rendered by the <u>Trademark Review and Adjudication Board</u> according to the effective ruling, the people's court shall issue a ruling not to accept the case; and where a case has been accepted, the people's court shall rule to dismiss the lawsuit	**Article 30** Where a people's court has specifically determined the relevant facts and the application of laws in an effective ruling, a counter party or an interested party institutes a lawsuit against a ruling re-rendered by the **China National Intellectual Property Administration** according to the effective ruling, the people's court shall issue a ruling not to accept the case; and where a case has been accepted, the people's court shall rule to dismiss the lawsuit

Article 31 These Provisions shall come into force on March 1, 2017. These Provisions may apply, mutatis mutandis, to the administrative cases involving trademark authorization and confirmation tried by the people's courts according to the Trademark Law amended in 2001

1.3.6 Interpretation by the Supreme People's Court on the Attachment of the Right to Exclusive Use of a Registered Trademark Implemented by People's Courts

(Adopted at the 1,144th Session of the Judicial Committee of the Supreme People's Court on November 22, 2000, and amended by the Decision of the Supreme People's Court to Amend Eighteen Intellectual Property Judicial Interpretations Including the Interpretation (II) by the Supreme People's Court on Several Issues Concerning the Application of Law in the Trial of Cases Involving Patent Right Infringement Disputes adopted at the 1823rd Session of the Judicial Committee of the Supreme People's Court on December 23, 2020).

Before amendment (Come into force on 21, January, 2001)	After amendment (Come into force on 1, January, 2021)
For the purposes of correctly implementing the attachment of the right to exclusive use of a registered trademark and avoiding repeated attachment, issues concerning the attachment of the right to exclusive use of a registered trademark implemented by people's courts are hereby interpreted as follows:	
Article 1 Where a people's court needs to implement an attachment of the right to exclusive use of a registered trademark when taking conservatory measures in accordance with the relevant provisions of the Civil Procedure Law, it shall issue a written Notice of Assistance in Enforcement to the Trademark Office of the State Administration for Industry and Commerce of the People's Republic of China (the "Trademark Office"), specifying the name used in and the registrant and registration certificate number of the registered trademark that the Trademark Office is required to assist in attaching, as well as the duration of attachment and the contents of assistance in enforcement of attachment, including but not limited to prohibiting the assignment and deregistration of the registered trademark, modification of registration items, and registration of pledge of the right to exclusive use of the registered trademark	Article 1 Where a people's court needs to implement an attachment of the right to exclusive use of a registered trademark when taking conservatory measures in accordance with the relevant provisions of the Civil Procedure Law, it shall issue a written Notice of Assistance in Enforcement to the Trademark Office of the **China National Intellectual Property Administration** (the "Trademark Office"), specifying the name used in and the registrant and registration certificate number of the registered trademark that the Trademark Office is required to assist in attaching, as well as the duration of attachment and the contents of assistance in enforcement of attachment, including but not limited to prohibiting the assignment and deregistration of the registered trademark, modification of registration items, and registration of pledge of the right to exclusive use of the registered trademark
Article 2 The duration of each attachment of the right to exclusive use of a registered trademark shall not exceed six months, commencing from the day when the Trademark Office receives the Notice of Assistance in Enforcement. If it is still necessary to continue the attachment of the right to exclusive use of the registered trademark, the people's court shall, prior to the expiry of the duration of attachment, reissue a written Notice of Assistance in Enforcement to the Trademark Office to require continued attachment. Otherwise, the attachment of the right to exclusive use of the registered trademark shall be deemed to have been removed automatically	Article 2 The duration of each attachment of the right to exclusive use of a registered trademark shall not exceed **one year,** commencing from the day when the Trademark Office receives the Notice of Assistance in Enforcement. If it is still necessary to continue the attachment of the right to exclusive use of the registered trademark, the people's court shall, prior to the expiry of the duration of attachment, reissue a written Notice of Assistance in Enforcement to the Trademark Office to require continued attachment. Otherwise, the attachment of the right to exclusive use of the registered trademark shall be deemed to have been removed automatically
Article 3 A people's court shall not repeatedly attach the right to exclusive use of a registered trademark that has already been attached	

1.4 Main Amendments of Chinese Patent Laws and Regulations

1.4.1 *Patent Law of the People's Republic of China*

(Adopted at the 4th Session of the Standing Committee of the Sixth National People's Congress on March 12, 1984; amended for the first time by the Decision on Amending the Patent Law of the People's Republic of China adopted at the 27th Session of the Standing Committee of the Seventh National People's Congress on September 4, 1992; amended for the second time by the Decision on Amending the Patent Law of the People's Republic of China, adopted at the 17th Session of the Standing Committee of the Ninth National People's Congress on August 25, 2000; amended for the third time by the Decision of the Standing Committee of the National People's

1 Main Amendments of Chinese Intellectual Property Law

Congress on Amending the Patent Law of the People's Republic of China adopted at the 6th Session of Standing Committee of the 11th National People's Congress of the People's Republic of China on December 27, 2008; and amended for the fourth time in accordance with the Decision of the Standing Committee of the National People's Congress to Amend the Patent Law of the People's Republic of China adopted at the 22nd Session of the Standing Committee of the Thirteenth National People's Congress of the People's Republic of China on October 17, 2020).

Before Amendment (Come into force on October 1, 2009)	After Amendment (Come into force on June 1, 2021)
Chapter I General Provisions	
Article 2 The "inventions" as used in this Law means inventions, utility models and designs. The term "invention" refers to any new technical solution relating to a product, a process or an improvement thereof. The term "utility model" refers to any new technical solution relating to a product's shape, structure, or a combination thereof, which is fit for practical use	Article 2 The "inventions" as used in this Law means inventions, utility models and designs. The term "invention" refers to any new technical solution relating to a product, a process or an improvement thereof. The term "utility model" refers to any new technical solution relating to a product's shape, structure, or a combination thereof, which is fit for practical use. **"Design" means a new design of the shape, pattern, or a combination thereof, as well as a combination of the color, shape and pattern, of the entirety or a portion of a product, which creates an aesthetic feeling and is fit for industrial application**
The term "design" refers to any new design of a product's shape, pattern or a combination thereof, as well as the combination of the color and the shape or pattern of a product, which creates an aesthetic feeling and is fit for industrial application
Article 6 An invention made by a person in the execution of the tasks of the entity for which he works or made by him by taking advantage of the material and technical means of this entity shall be a service invention. The right to apply for patenting a service invention shall remain with the entity. After the application is approved, the entity shall be the patentee
For any non-service invention, the right to apply for a patent shall remain with the inventor or designer. After the application is approved, the inventor or designer shall be the patentee
For an invention made by a person by taking advantage of the material and technical means of the entity where he works, if there is a contract between the entity and the inventor or designer regarding the right to apply for patent and the ownership of the patent, the contractual stipulations shall prevail	Article 6 **An invention-creation made by a person in the execution of tasks of the entity employing the person or mainly by taking advantage of the entity's material and technical conditions is a service invention-creation. The right to apply for a patent for a service invention-creation belongs to the entity; and after the application is granted, the entity is the patentee. The entity may, in accordance with the law, dispose of its right to apply for the patent for the service invention-creation and the patent right, and promote the exploitation and application of the invention-creation**
For any non-service invention, the right to apply for a patent shall remain with the inventor or designer. After the application is approved, the inventor or designer shall be the patentee
For an invention made by a person by taking advantage of the material and technical means of the entity where he works, if there is a contract between the entity and the inventor or designer regarding the right to apply for patent and the ownership of the patent, the contractual stipulations shall prevail
Article 14 Where any patent for invention owned by a state-owned enterprise or public institution is of great significance to the interests of the state or to the public interests, the relevant competent department of the State Council and the people's government of the province, autonomous region, or municipality directly under the Central Government may, upon approval of the State Council, decide to popularize and apply the patent within the approved scope, and allow designated entities to exploit the patent; and the exploiting entity shall, in accordance with the legal provisions of the state, pay royalties to the patentee	**(Written in Article 49)**

(continued)

(continued)

Before Amendment (Come into force on October 1, 2009)	After Amendment (Come into force on June 1, 2021)
Article 16 The entity to whom a patent is granted shall give to the inventor or designer of the service invention a reward and shall, after exploitation of the patented invention, pay the inventor or designer a reasonable remuneration on the basis of the scope of popularization and application as well as the economic benefits yielded	**Article 15** The entity to whom a patent is granted shall give to the inventor or designer of the service invention a reward and shall, after exploitation of the patented invention, pay the inventor or designer a reasonable remuneration on the basis of the scope of popularization and application as well as the economic benefits yielded **The state encourages entities to which patent rights are granted to implement property right incentives, and enable inventors or designers to rationally share the benefits of innovation in forms such as equities, options, and dividends**
(Addition)	**Article 20 Patent applications and the exercise of patent rights shall adhere to the principle of good faith. Patent rights shall not be abused to damage the public interest or the lawful rights and interests of any other person**
	Any abuse of patent rights to preclude or restrict competition, which constitutes a monopolistic act, shall be handled in accordance with the Anti-monopoly Law of the People's Republic of China
Article 21 The patent administrative department of the State Council and the Board of Patent Appeals and Interferences shall, pursuant to the requirements of objectivity, impartiality, accuracy and timeliness, handle the relevant patent applications and appeals	**Article 21** The patent administrative department of the State Council shall, pursuant to the requirements of objectivity, impartiality, accuracy and timeliness, handle the relevant patent applications and appeals
The patent administrative department of the State Council shall completely, accurately and timely announce the patent information and regularly publish patent gazettes	**The patent administrative department of the State Council shall strengthen the construction of the patent information public service system, release patent information in a complete, accurate, and timely manner, provide basic patent data, publish patent gazettes on a periodical basis, and promote the dissemination and utilization of patent information**
Before an application for patent is published or announced, the functionaries and other relevant persons of the patent administrative department of the State Council shall keep confidential the contents therein	Before an application for patent is published or announced, the functionaries and other relevant persons of the patent administrative department of the State Council shall keep confidential the contents therein
Chapter II Conditions for Granting Patents	
Article 24 An invention for which a patent is applied for does not lose its novelty where, within six months before the date of application, one of the following events occurred:	**Article 24** An invention for which a patent is applied for does not lose its novelty where, within six months before the date of application, one of the following events occurred:
(1) where it was first exhibited at an international exhibition sponsored or recognized by the Chinese Government;	**(1) it is disclosed to the public for the first time in the public interest, when a state of emergency or any extraordinary circumstance occurs in the country;**
(2) where it was first made public at a prescribed academic or technological meeting;	(2) where it was first exhibited at an international exhibition sponsored or recognized by the Chinese Government;
(3) where it was disclosed by any person without the consent of the applicant	(3) where it was first made public at a prescribed academic or technological meeting;
	(4) where it was disclosed by any person without the consent of the applicant

(continued)

(continued)

Before Amendment (Come into force on October 1, 2009)	After Amendment (Come into force on June 1, 2021)
Article 25 For any of the following, no patent right shall be granted:	**Article 25** For any of the following, no patent right shall be granted:
(1) scientific discoveries;	(1) scientific discoveries;
(2) rules and methods for mental activities;	(2) rules and methods for mental activities;
(3) methods for the diagnosis or for the treatment of diseases;	(3) methods for the diagnosis or for the treatment of diseases;
(4) animal and plant varieties;	(4) animal and plant varieties;
(5) substances obtained by means of nuclear transformation;	(5) **nuclear transformation methods and substances obtained in the method of nuclear transformation;**
(6) the design, which is used primarily for the identification of pattern, color or the combination of the two on printed flat works	(6) the design, which is used primarily for the identification of pattern, color or the combination of the two on printed flat works
For processes used in producing products referred to in items (4) of the preceding paragraph, a patent may be granted in accordance with the provisions of this Law	For processes used in producing products referred to in items (4) of the preceding paragraph, a patent may be granted in accordance with the provisions of this Law
Chapter III Application for Patents	
Article 29 Where, within twelve months from the date on which any applicant first filed in a foreign country an application for patenting an invention or utility model, or within six months from the date on which any applicant first filed in a foreign country an application for patenting a design, he or it files in China an application for patenting the same, he or it may, in accordance with any agreement concluded between the said foreign country and China, or in accordance with any international treaty to which both countries are a party, or on the basis of the principle of mutual recognition of the right to priority, enjoy the right to priority	Article 29 Where, within 12 months from the date of filing of the first application for a patent for an invention or utility model in China, **or within six months from the date of filing of the first application for a patent for a design in China,** the applicant files again an application for a patent for the same subject matter with the patent administrative department of the State Council, the applicant may enjoy a right of priority
Where, within twelve months from the date on which any applicant first filed in China an application for patenting an invention or utility model, he or it files with the patent administrative department of the State Council an application for patenting the same, he or it may enjoy the right to priority	
Article 30 Any applicant who claims the right to priority shall make a written declaration when the application is filed, and submit, within three months, a copy of the patent application document which was first filed; if the applicant fails to make the written declaration or to meet the time limit for submitting the patent application document, the claim to the right to priority shall be deemed as having not been made	**Article 30** An applicant which claims a right of priority for an invention or utility model patent shall file a written declaration at the time of application, and within 16 months from the date of filing of the first application, submit a duplicate of the first patent application documents
	An applicant which claims a right of priority for a design patent shall file a written declaration at the time of application, and submit a duplicate of the first patent application documents within three months
	An applicant which fails to file the written declaration or submit the duplicate of the patent application documents within the prescribed time limit shall be deemed to have not claimed a right of priority
Chapter IV Examination and Approval of Patent Applications	

(continued)

(continued)

Before Amendment (Come into force on October 1, 2009)	After Amendment (Come into force on June 1, 2021)
Article 41 The patent administrative department of the State Council shall form a Patent Re-examination Board. If any patent applicant is dissatisfied with the decision of the patent administrative department of the State Council on rejecting the application, it/he may, within three months as of receipt of the notification, appeal to the Patent Re-examination Board for review. The Patent Re-examination Board shall, after the review, make a decision and notify the patent applicant	**Article 41** A patent applicant may file a request with the patent administrative department of the State Council for a review of the decision of the patent administrative department of the State Council to reject its application, within three months of receipt of a notice of the decision. After review, the patent administrative department of the State Council shall make a decision, and notify the patent applicant
Where a patent applicant is dissatisfied with the review decision of the Patent Re-examination Board, it/he may, within three months as of receipt of the notification, bring a lawsuit with the people's court	The patent applicant may file a lawsuit against the review decision made by the patent administrative department of the State Council within three months of receipt of a notice of the decision
Chapter V Duration, Termination and Invalidation of Patents	
Article 42 The duration of an invention patent shall be twenty years, the duration of the patent for a utility model or design shall be ten years, counted from the date of application	**Article 42** The term of a patent for an invention shall be 20 years, the term of a patent for a utility model shall be ten years, and the term of a patent for a design shall be 15 years, all commencing from the date of filing of application
	Where a patent for an invention is granted four years from the date of filing of application and three years from the date of filing of request for substantial examination, the patent administrative department of the State Council shall, at the request of the patentee, provide patent term extension for unreasonable delay in the patenting process for the invention, except for unreasonable delay caused by the applicant
	For the purpose of making up the time required for the assessment and approval of the marketing of a new drug, the patent administrative department of the State Council may, at the request of the patentee, provide patent term extension for an invention patent relating to the new drug approved for marketing in China. The extension may not exceed five years, and the total effective term of the patent after the new drug is approved for marketing shall not exceed 14 years
Article 45 Where, as of the announcement of the granting of the patent by the patent administrative department of the State Council, any entity or individual considers that the granting of the said patent does not conform to the relevant provisions of this Law, it or he may request **the Board of Patent Appeals** and Interferences to invalidate the patent right	**Article 45** Where, as of the announcement of the granting of the patent by the patent administrative department of the State Council, any entity or individual considers that the granting of the said patent does not conform to the relevant provisions of this Law, it or he may request **the patent administrative department of the State Council** to invalidate the patent right
Article 46 The Patent Re-examination Board shall timely examine the request for invalidating a patent, make a decision and notify the petitioner and the patentee. The decision on invalidating the patent shall be registered and announced by the patent administrative department of the State Council	**Article 46 The patent administrative department of the State Council** shall timely examine the request for invalidating a patent, make a decision and notify the petitioner and the patentee. The decision on invalidating the patent shall be registered and announced by the patent administrative department of the State Council

(continued)

(continued)

Before Amendment (Come into force on October 1, 2009)	After Amendment (Come into force on June 1, 2021)
Where any party is dissatisfied with the decision of **the Patent Re-examination Board** on declaring a patent invalid or maintaining a patent, such party may, within three months as of receipt of the notification, bring a lawsuit to the people's court. The people's court shall notify the opposite party in the procedures for requesting invalidation that it or he should participate in the litigation as a third party	Where any party is dissatisfied with the decision of **the patent administrative department of the State Council** on declaring a patent invalid or maintaining a patent, such party may, within three months as of receipt of the notification, bring a lawsuit to the people's court. The people's court shall notify the opposite party in the procedures for requesting invalidation that it or he should participate in the litigation as a third party
Chapter VI Compulsory License for Exploitation of Patents	**Chapter VI Special Licensing for the Exploitation of Patents**
(Addition)	**Article 48** The patent administrative department of the State Council and the departments charged with the administration of patents of the local people's governments shall, in conjunction with the relevant departments at the same level, take measures to enhance public services for patents and promote the exploitation and application of patents
(Addition)	**Article 50** Where a patentee voluntarily files a written declaration with the patent administrative department of the State Council, indicating its willingness to permit any entity or individual to exploit its patent and specifying the royalty payment methods and rates, the patent administrative department of the State Council shall make an announcement and implement an open license. If an open license declaration is filed for a utility model or design patent, a patent evaluation report shall be provided
	A patentee withdrawing an open license declaration shall make the withdrawal in writing, and the patent administrative department of the State Council shall make an announcement. The announced withdrawal of an open license declaration shall not affect the validity of the open license granted earlier
(Addition)	**Article 51** Any entity or individual intending to exploit a patent under an open license shall obtain the patent exploitation license immediately after notifying the patentee in writing and paying the royalty according to the announced royalty payment methods and rates
	During the period of implementation of the open license, the patent annuity paid by the patentee shall be reduced or waived accordingly
	The patentee implementing an open license may grant an ordinary license after negotiating with the licensee over royalties, but shall not grant a sole license or exclusive license for the patent
(Addition)	**Article 52** Where any dispute arises over the implementation of an open license, the parties shall resolve the dispute through consultations; and if the parties are unwilling to consult or consultation fails, they may request the patent administrative department of the State Council to conduct mediation, or file a lawsuit with the people's court
Chapter VII Protection of Patent Rights	

(continued)

(continued)

Before Amendment (Come into force on October 1, 2009)	After Amendment (Come into force on June 1, 2021)
Article 61 Where any dispute over patent infringement involves a patent for invention for the manufacturing process of a new product, the entity or individual manufacturing the identical product shall provide proof on the difference of its own process used in the manufacture of its product from the patented process	**Article 66** Where any dispute over patent infringement involves a patent for invention for the manufacturing process of a new product, the entity or individual manufacturing the identical product shall provide proof on the difference of its own process used in the manufacture of its product from the patented process
Where any dispute over patent infringement involves a patent for utility model or design, the people's court or the patent administrative department may require the patentee or the interested parties to present a patent assessment report issued by the patent administrative department of the State Council, after the retrieval, analysis and assessment of the pertinent utility model or design, as a proof for trying and settling the dispute over patent infringement	Where a dispute over patent infringement involves a utility model patent or a design patent, the people's court or the department charged with the administration of patents may require the patentee or interested party to present a patent evaluation report prepared by the patent administrative department of the State Council after retrieval, analysis, and evaluation of the relevant utility model or design, as evidence for adjudicating or handling the dispute over patent infringement. The patentee, the interested party, **or the alleged infringer may also voluntarily present the patent evaluation report**
Article 63 Whoever counterfeits the patent of anyone else shall, in addition to bearing civil liabilities in accordance with the law, be ordered by the patent administrative department to make a correction and be announced by the patent administrative department; its or his illegal gains, if any, shall be confiscated, and it or he may be fined up to three times the illegal gains. If there is no illegal gain, it or he may be fined up to 200, 000 Yuan. If any crime is constituted, it or he shall be subject to criminal liabilities according to law	**Article 68** Whoever counterfeits a patent shall, in addition to being held civilly liable in accordance with the law, be ordered by the department charged with patent law enforcement to take corrective action, which shall be announced, with the illegal income confiscated, and may be fined not more than five times the illegal income or if there is no illegal income or the illegal income is not more than 50,000 yuan, fined not more than 250,000 yuan; and if it is criminally punishable, the offender shall be held criminally liable in accordance with the law
Article 64 When the patent administrative department investigates into and deals with a suspected counterfeit patent case on the basis of the evidence it has already gathered, it may query the relevant parties so as to find the information relevant to the suspected violation, may conduct an on-site inspection over the site of party suspected of having committed the violation, may consult and copy the contracts, invoices, account books and other materials relating to the suspected violation, may check the products relating to the suspected violation, and may seal up or detain the counterfeit patented product as proved by evidence When the patent administrative department exercises the functions as prescribed in the preceding paragraph according to law, the parties shall assist and cooperate with it and shall not reject or hamper it	**Article 69** In investigating and handling suspected patent counterfeiting acts based on evidence already obtained, the departments charged with patent law enforcement shall have the authority to take the following measures:
	(1) Interviewing the relevant parties and investigating information related to the suspected violations of law
	(2) Conducting on-site inspection of places where the parties are suspected of violations of law
	(3) Consulting and duplicating the contracts, invoices, account books, and other relevant materials related to the suspected violations of law
	(4) Inspecting the products related to the suspected violations of law
	(5) Placing under seal or impounding the products with a counterfeited patent as proved by evidence
	The department charged with the administration of patents may take the measures set forth in subparagraphs (1), (2) and (4) of the preceding paragraph to handle patent infringement disputes at the request of the patentee or the interested party

(continued)

(continued)

Before Amendment (Come into force on October 1, 2009)	After Amendment (Come into force on June 1, 2021)
	When the department charged with patent law enforcement or the department charged with the administration of patents performs the functions prescribed in the preceding two paragraphs in accordance with the law, the parties shall provide assistance and cooperation, and shall not reject or obstruct it
(Addition)	Article 70 The patent administrative department of the State Council may handle patent infringement disputes that have significant influence nationwide at the request of the patentee or interested party
	In handling patent infringement disputes at the request of the patentee or interested party, the department charged with the administration of patents of a local people's government may concurrently handle cases in which the same patent is infringed upon within its administrative region; and may request the department charged with the administration of patents of the local people's government at a higher level to handle cases in which the same patent is infringed upon across different administrative regions
Article 65 The amount of compensation for a patent infringement shall be determined on the basis of the actual losses incurred to the patentee as a result of the infringement. If it is difficult to determine the actual losses, the actual losses may be determined on the basis of the gains which the infringer has obtained from the infringement. If it is difficult to determine the losses incurred to the patentee or the gains obtained by the infringer, the amount shall be reasonably determined by reference to the multiple of the royalties for this patent. In addition, the compensation shall include the reasonable expenses that the patentee has paid for stopping the infringement	Article 71 The damages for a patent infringement shall be determined according to the actual loss suffered by the right holder due to the infringement or the benefits obtained by the infringer from the infringement; or if it is difficult to determine the loss suffered by the right holder or the benefits obtained by the infringer, the damages shall be reasonably determined by reference to the multiple of the royalty for this patent. In the case of an intentional patent infringement with serious circumstances, the damages may be determined as not less than one nor more than five times the amount determined in the aforesaid method
If it is difficult to determine the losses incurred to the patentee, the gains obtained by the infringer as well as the royalty obtained for the patent, the people's court may, by taking into account such factors as the type of patent, nature and particulars of the infringement, etc., decide a compensation in the sum of not less than 10,000 yuan but not more than 1 million yuan	Where it is difficult to determine the loss suffered by the right holder, the benefits obtained by the infringer, and the patent royalty, the people's court may, by taking into account factors such as the type of the patent and the nature and circumstances of the infringement, determine the damages as not less than 30,000 yuan nor more than five million yuan
	The damages shall also include the reasonable disbursements of the right holder for preventing the infringement
	Where the right holder has made best efforts to adduce evidence but the account books and materials relating to the infringement are mainly in the possession of the infringer, in order to determine the damages, the people's court may order the infringer to provide such account books and materials; and if the infringer fails to provide them or provides any false ones, the people's court may award damages by reference to the claims of and the evidence provided by the right holder

(continued)

(continued)

Before Amendment (Come into force on October 1, 2009)	After Amendment (Come into force on June 1, 2021)
Article 66 Where a patentee or interested party has evidence to prove that someone else is committing or is going to commit an infringement upon the patent right, and its (his) lawful rights and interests will be damaged and are difficult to be remedied if the said infringement is not stopped in time, it or he may, prior to initiating a lawsuit, apply to the people's court for taking such measures as ordering the stop of the relevant act When an applicant files an application, it shall provide a guarantee. If it or he fails to do so, the application shall be rejected The people's court shall make a ruling within 48 h as of its acceptance of an application. If it is necessary to extend the time limit in a special circumstance, the time limit may be extended for up to 48 h. If a ruling is made to stop the relevant act, it shall be executed immediately. If any party refuses to accept the ruling, it (he) may apply for one review. The execution of the ruling is not suspended during the process of review If the applicant fails to lodge a lawsuit within 15 days after it takes such measures as ordering the stop of the relevant act, the people's court shall lift the said measure Where there are errors in an application, the applicant shall compensate the party against whom an application is filed for the losses caused by the stop of the relevant act	**Article 72** Where a patentee or interested party has evidence to prove that another person is committing or will commit an infringement upon the patent or an act **of interfering with the patentee's or interested party's realization of rights**, and irreparable harm will be caused to the lawful rights and interests of the patentee or interested party if the infringement is not stopped in a timely manner, the patentee or interested party may, before instituting an action, **apply to the people's court for attachment of property, ordering certain conduct, or prohibiting certain conduct, in accordance with the law**
Article 67 To stop a patent infringement, the patentee or any interested party may apply to the people's court for preserving the evidence when such evidence is likely to be destroyed and hard to be obtained again The people's court may order the applicant to provide a guarantee for the preservation. If the applicant fails to do so, its or his application shall be rejected The people's court shall make a ruling within 48 h after it accepts an application. If it makes a ruling on preserving the evidence, the ruling shall be executed immediately If the applicant fails to initiate a lawsuit within 15 days after the people's court has taken the measure of preserving the evidence, the people's court shall terminate the said measure	**Article 73 In order to stop a patent infringement, a patentee or interested party may, before instituting an action, apply to the people's court according to the law for the preservation of evidence if any evidence may be destroyed or lost or difficult to obtain at a later time**
Article 68 The statute of limitation on an action against an infringement upon a patent right shall be two years counted from the date on which the patentee or any interested party knows about or should have known about the infringing act Where anyone uses an invention after the application for a patent for this invention is published but before the patent right is granted without paying adequate royalties, the statute of limitations for the patentee to claim payment of such royalties shall be two years, commencing from the date when the patentee knows or ought to know that his invention is used by some else. However, if the patentee has known or ought to have known about this fact prior to the date when the patent right is granted, the statute of limitations shall commence from the date when the patent right is granted	**Article 74 The prescriptive period for instituting an action against a patent infringement shall be three years, commencing from the date when the patentee or interested party knows or should have known the infringement and the infringer** Where any other person uses an invention after an application for the invention patent is published and before the patent is granted without paying appropriate royalties, the prescriptive period for the patentee to claim the payment of such royalties shall be three years, commencing from the date when the patentee knows or should have known the use by the other person; however, if the patentee knows or should have known the use prior to the grant date of the patent, the prescriptive period shall commence from the grant date of the patent

(continued)

(continued)

Before Amendment (Come into force on October 1, 2009)	After Amendment (Come into force on June 1, 2021)
(Addition)	**Article 76 Where, in the process of assessment and approval for the marketing of a drug, any dispute arises between the applicant for the marketing of a drug and the relevant patentee or interested party over the patent right related to the drug of which an application for registration is filed, the relevant party may file a lawsuit with the people's court, requesting a judgment as to whether the relevant technical solution of the drug of which an application for registration is filed falls within the scope of protection of any other person's patent on a drug. The medical products administration of the State Council may, within the prescribed time limit, make a decision on whether to suspend the approval of marketing of the relevant drug according to the effective judgment of the people's court** **The applicant for the marketing of a drug and the relevant patentee or interested party may also apply to the patent administrative department of the State Council for an administrative adjudication on any patent dispute related to the drug of which an application for registration is filed** **The medical products administration of the State Council shall, in conjunction with the patent administrative department of the State Council, develop specific connecting measures for the resolution of patent disputes in the stages of approval of drug marketing and application for the marketing of a drug, report such measures to the State Council, and implement them upon consent of the State Council**
Article 72 Where any person usurps the right of an inventor or designer to apply for a patent for a non-service invention, or usurps any other right or interest of an inventor or designer as prescribed in this Law, he shall be subject to an administrative sanction by the entity for which he works or by the competent authority at the higher level	Delet

1.4.2 Interpretations (II) of the Supreme People's Court on Several Issues Concerning the Application of Law in the Trial of Cases Involving Patent Infringement Disputes

(Adopted at the 1676th Session of the Trial Committee of the Supreme People's Court on January 25, 2016 and effective as of April 1, 2016, and amended according to the Decision of the Supreme People's Court on Revising the "Interpretation of the Supreme People's Court on Certain Issues Concerning the Application of Law in the Trial of Cases involving Patent Infringement Disputes (II)" and Other Seventeen

Intellectual Property Related Judicial Interpretations adopted at the 1823rd meeting of the Judicial Committee of the Supreme People's Court on December 23, 2020).

With a view to ensuring correct trial of the cases involving patent infringement disputes, this Interpretation is formulated pursuant to the Civil Code of the People's Republic of China, the Patent Law of the People's Republic of China, the Civil Procedure Law of the People's Republic of China and other relevant laws, and in light of judicial practices.

Article 1 Where a written claim of rights contains two or more rights, the right holder concerned shall specify in the complaint the rights based on which the alleged infringer is being sued for patent infringement. Where such rights are not specified or not clearly stated in the complaint, the competent people's court shall require the right holder to specify the rights concerned; and, where the right holder still fails to do so after relevant situations have been explained thereto, the competent people's court may rule to dismiss the lawsuit.

Article 2 Where the right claimed by a right holder in a patent infringement lawsuit is declared invalid by the patent administrative department of the State Council, the people's court trying the case involving the patent infringement disputes may render a ruling to dismiss the lawsuit filed by the right holder on the basis of the invalid claim of right.

The right holder may file a lawsuit separately if there is evidence proving that the decision to declare the above claim of right invalid is revoked by a binding administrative judgment.

If the patentee files a lawsuit separately, the period for limitation of action shall be calculated from the date of service of the administrative judgment stated in Paragraph 2 of this Article.

Article 3 Where, as a result of obvious violation of Paragraph 3 or Paragraph 4 of Article 26 the Patent Law, written descriptions cannot be used to explain the claims of rights, which does not fall within the circumstances specified in Article 4 hereof and based on which request is made for declaring the patent invalid, the competent people's court trying the case involving the patent right dispute shall in general rule to suspend the lawsuit; if no request is filed for declaring the patent invalid within a reasonable period of time, the people's court may determine the scope of patent protection according to the written claim of rights.

Article 4 Where ordinary technical personnel in the relevant field can clearly arrive at only one unique understanding by reading written claims of rights, written descriptions and attached drawings despite ambiguity in terms of grammar, wording, punctuations, graphics, symbols, etc. in the written claims of rights, written descriptions and the attached drawings, the competent people's court shall make determination according to such unique understanding.

Article 5 When a people's court determines the scope of patent protection, the technical features as described in the preamble and the characterizing portion of the independent claims, and in the reference section and the limitations of the dependent claims shall all be defining.

Article 6 The competent people's court may employ another patent which is related to the patent involved in the case in respect of divisional application, and its patent examination files and binding judgments/rulings on patent licensing affirmation to interpret the rights claimed for the patent involved in the case.

Patent examination files shall include the written materials submitted by patent applicants or patentees during the process of patent examination, re-examination and declaration of invalidity, as well as the notices on examination opinions, meeting minutes, oral hearing records, binding written examination decisions on patent re-examination requests, written examination decisions on the requests for declaring patents invalid, etc. issued by the patent administrative department of the State Council.

Article 7 As regards an exhausted claim of rights for a combination, if an alleged infringing technical solution contains additional technical features on the basis of all the technical features in the claim of rights, the competent people's court shall determine that the alleged infringing technical solution does not fall under the scope of patent protection, unless the additional technical features are unavoidable impurities in normal quantities.

An exhausted claim of rights for a combination referred to the preceding paragraph shall generally not include the claim of rights for traditional Chinese medicine composition.

Article 8 Functional features are technical features that only serve to define structures, compositions, steps, conditions or the relations thereof according to their functions or effects in the relevant invention, unless ordinary technical personnel in this field are able to directly and clearly determine the specific exploitation methods for achieving such functions or effects by reading the claim of rights alone.

Where, as compared to the technical features that are recorded in the written descriptions and the attached drawings and are indispensable for achieving the aforesaid functions or effects, the corresponding technical features of an alleged infringing technical solution adopt substantially the same means to achieve substantially the same functions and effects, and can be contemplated without creative work by ordinary technical personnel in the relevant field at the time of the occurrence of the alleged infringement, the competent people's court shall determine that such corresponding technical features are identical or equivalent to the functional features.

Article 9 Where an alleged infringing technical solution cannot be applied to the use environment defined by the use environment features contained in the claim of rights, the competent people's court shall determine that the alleged infringing technical solution does not fall under the scope of patent protection.

Article 10 Where the preparation methods for an alleged infringing product are neither identical nor equivalent to the technical features in the claim of rights that use preparation methods to define the relevant product, the competent people's court shall determine that the relevant alleged infringing technical solution does not fall under the scope of patent protection.

Article 11 Where the sequence of technical steps is not specified in the claim of rights for a patented method but ordinary technical personnel in the relevant field are directly and clearly of the opinion that such technical steps shall be exploited according to specific sequence after reading the written claims of rights, the written descriptions and the attached drawings, the competent people's court shall decide that such sequence of steps has the role of defining the protection scope of the patent right.

Article 12 Where phrases such as "at least" or "not more than" are adopted in a claim of rights to define numerical features, and ordinary technical personnel in the relevant field are of the opinion that the patented technical solution concerned places special emphasis on the role of such phrase to define technical features after reading the claim of rights, written descriptions and attached drawings, the competent people's court shall not uphold the claim by the right holder that technical features different from such numerical features are equivalent features.

Article 13 Where the right holder proves that the narrowed revision or statement made by the patent applicant or the patentee in respect of the claims of rights, written descriptions and attached drawings in the patent licensing affirmation procedure is negated, the competent people's court shall determine that such revision or statement has not led to the waiver of the technical solution.

Article 14 When determining ordinary consumers' level of knowledge and cognitive ability as regards a design, a people's court shall consider the design space of the type of the products to which the relevant patented design is identical or similar at the time of the occurrence of the alleged infringement. Where the design space is relatively large, the people's court may determine that ordinary consumers are usually unlikely to notice the minor differences between different designs; where the design space is relatively small, the people's court may determine that ordinary consumers are usually more likely to notice the minor differences between different designs.

Article 15 Where an alleged infringing design is identical or similar to one of the patented designs of a complete set of products, the competent people's court shall determine that the alleged infringing design falls under the scope of patent protection.

Article 16 As regards the design patent of a component product with a unique assembly pattern, if an alleged infringing design is identical or similar to the overall design of the component product after assembly, the competent people's court shall determine that the alleged infringing design falls under the scope of patent protection.

As regards the design patent of a component product whose various components have no assembly pattern at all or do not have a unique assembly pattern, if an alleged infringing design is identical or similar to the designs of all the individual components of the component product, the competent people's court shall determine that the alleged infringing design falls under the scope of patent protection; and, if the alleged infringing design lacks the design of a certain individual component or is neither identical nor similar to the design of a certain individual component, the competent people's court shall determine that the alleged infringing design does not fall under the scope of patent protection.

Article 17 As regards the design patent of a product in active variations, if an alleged infringing design is identical or similar to the designs of all the various use states illustrated in the diagram of variations, the competent people's court shall determine that the alleged infringing design falls under the scope of patent protection; if the alleged infringing design lacks the design of a certain use state or is neither identical nor similar to the design of a certain use state, the competent people's court shall determine that the alleged infringing design does not fall under the scope of patent protection.

Article 18 Where a right holder files a lawsuit to request an entity or individual to pay appropriate fees for exploiting the relevant invention during the period from the date of announcement of the invention patent application to the date of announcement of the grant of the invention patent in accordance with Article 13 of the Patent Law, the competent people's court may make determination on reasonable basis by referring to relevant patent royalties.

Where the scope of protection requested by the applicant upon the announcement of the invention patent application is inconsistent with the scope of patent protection upon the announcement of the grant of the invention patent, and an alleged infringing technical solution falls under both of the foregoing two protection scopes, the competent people's court shall determine that the defendant has exploited the relevant invention during the period stated in the preceding paragraph; and, where the alleged infringing technical solution falls under only one of the two protection scopes, the competent people's court shall determine that the defendant has not exploited the invention during the period stated in the preceding paragraph.

Where a party, without the licensing from the patentee and for the purposes of production and business operation, uses, offers for sale of, or sells the products that have been manufactured, sold or imported by another party during the period stated in Paragraph 1 of this Article after the date of announcement of the grant of the invention patent and such another party has paid or promised in writing to pay appropriate fees prescribed in Article 13 of the Patent Law, the competent people's court shall not uphold the claim by the right holder that the aforesaid use, offer for sale and sale has infringed the patent right.

Article 19 Where a product sales contract is established in accordance with the law, the competent people's court shall determine that the sales as prescribed by Article 11 of the Patent Law have been constituted.

Article 20 As regards the re-processing or re-treatment of a follow-up product obtained from the further processing or treatment of a product directly obtained according to patented methods, a people's court shall determine that such re-processing or re-treatment does not belong to the circumstances of the "use of a product directly obtained according to patented methods" as prescribed under Article 11 of the Patent Law.

Article 21 Where a party has clear knowledge that certain products are the materials, equipment, parts and components, intermediate items, etc. specifically for the exploitation of a patent, and yet still provides, without the licensing from the relevant patentee and for the purpose of production and business operation, such products to another party committing the patent infringement, the competent people's court shall uphold the claim by the right holder that the party's provision of such products is an act of assistance for infringement as prescribed by Article 1169 of the Civil Code.

Where a party has clear knowledge that certain products or methods have been granted patent, and yet still actively induces, without the licensing from the relevant patentee and for the purpose of production and business operation, another party committing the patent infringement, the competent people's court shall uphold the claim by the right holder that the inducing act of the party is an act of abetting another party to commit infringement as prescribed by Article 1169 of the Civil Code.

Article 22 Where an alleged infringer raises the defense based on one existing technology or existing design, the competent people's court shall define the existing technology or existing design pursuant to the Patent Law prevailing on the date of patent application.

Article 23 Where the alleged infringing technical solution or design falls within the protection scope of the prior patent right involved in the case, the competent people's court shall not uphold the defense made by the alleged infringer that its technical solution or design has been granted patent and thus does not infringe the patent right involved in the case.

Article 24 Where the recommended national, industrial or local standards clearly indicate the necessary patent-related information, the competent people's court shall in general not uphold the defense made by the alleged infringer that the exploitation of such standards do not need the licensing from the patentee and thus does not infringe such patent right.

Where the recommended national, industrial or local standards clearly indicate the necessary patent-related information and the patentee intentionally acts against the obligation for licensing on fair, reasonable and non-discriminatory terms as committed in formulating the standards in consultation with the alleged infringer on the conditions for the exploitation and licensing of such patent, resulting in the failure to conclude the patent licensing contract, the competent people's court shall, in general, not uphold the claim by the right holder for cessation of the exploitation of the standards, provided that the alleged infringer has no obvious fault in the consultation.

The conditions for the exploitation and licensing of a patent as mentioned in Paragraph 2 of this Article shall be determined upon consultation by the relevant patentee and the alleged infringer. Where no consensus is reached upon sufficient consultation, the parties concerned may request the competent people's court to determine such conditions, in which case the people's court shall, on fair, reasonable and non-discriminatory terms, take into comprehensive consideration the degree of innovation of the patent, the role of the patent in relevant standards, the technical field to which the standards belong, the nature and scope of application of the standards, relevant licensing conditions and other factors to determine such exploitation and licensing conditions.

The provisions on the exploitation of patents involved in standards as otherwise prescribed by laws and administrative regulations shall prevail.

Article 25 Where a party uses, offers for sale of, or sells, patent-infringing products for the purpose of production and business operation without the knowledge that such products are manufactured and sold without the licensing from the relevant patentee, and is able to prove the legitimate sources of such products, the competent people's court shall uphold the request of the right holder that the aforesaid use, offer for sale, or sale be stopped, unless the user of the alleged infringing products furnishes evidence to prove that it has paid reasonable consideration for such products.

For the purpose of Paragraph 1 of this Article, "without the knowledge" shall mean the circumstance where a party has no actual knowledge and ought not to have knowledge.

For the purpose of Paragraph 1 of this Article, "legitimate sources" shall mean the use of legitimate business methods such as lawful sales channels and usual sale and purchase contracts to obtain products. The party who engages in use, offer for sale or sale shall provide relevant evidence consistent with business norms to prove legitimate sources.

Article 26 Where the defendant is found to commit the patent infringement, the competent people's court shall uphold the request of the right holder that the defendant be ordered to stop the infringement; however, the people's court may, instead of ordering the defendant to stop the act against which the lawsuit is filed, order the defendant to pay reasonable fees as appropriate based on the consideration of the interests of the State and the public interest.

Article 27 Where it is difficult to determine the actual loss suffered by a right holder, the competent people's court shall require the right holder to furnish evidence to prove the gains obtained by the infringer from the infringement in accordance with Paragraph 1 of Article 65 of the Patent Law. Where a right holder has provided the prima facie evidence proving the gains obtained by the infringer but the account books and materials related to the acts of patent infringement are mainly controlled by the infringer, the competent people's court may order the infringer to submit such account books and materials; where the infringer refuses to provide such account books and materials without justification or provides false account books and materials, the competent people's court may determine the gains obtained by the infringer from the infringement based on the claims of the right holder and the evidence furnished thereby.

Article 28 Where a right holder and the relevant infringer have legally agreed on the amount of compensation for patent infringement or the methods for calculating the amount of compensation and claim during the patent infringement lawsuit that the amount of compensation shall be determined in accordance with such agreement, the people's court shall uphold such claim.

Article 29 Where the party concerned legally applies for retrial based on the decision on declaring the patent invalid to request for the revocation of the judgment or mediation statement on patent infringement that is rendered by the people's court before the patent is declared invalid but is not enforced, the people's court may render a ruling to suspend the examination in retrial and suspend the enforcement of the original judgment or mediation statement.

If the patentee provides the sufficient and effective guarantee to the people's court to request that the enforcement of the judgment or mediation statement mentioned in the preceding paragraph be continued, the people's court shall approve such request; if the infringer provides sufficient and effective counter-guarantee to the people's court to request that the enforcement be suspended, the people's court shall approve such request. Where the decision declaring the patent invalid is not revoked by the binding ruling/judgment of the people's court, the patentee shall make compensation for the loss suffered by the other party concerned due to the continuation of the enforcement of such decision; where the decision declaring the patent invalid is revoked by the binding ruling/judgment of the people's court, the people's court may directly enforce the property under the above counter-guarantee based on the judgment or mediation statement mentioned in the preceding paragraph provided that the patent is still valid.

Article 30 If a lawsuit is not filed against a decision declaring the patent invalid with the competent people's court within the statutory time limit or the decision is not revoked by the binding ruling/judgment made after the filing of the lawsuit, the competent people's court shall conduct retrial if the party concerned legally applies for retrial based on such decision requesting that the judgment or mediation statement on patent infringement that has been rendered before the declaration of the invalidity of patent and is not yet enforced be revoked. If the party concerned, based on such decision, legally applies for termination of the enforcement of the judgment or mediation statement on patent infringement that has been rendered before the declaration of the invalidity of patent and is not yet enforced, the people's court shall rule to terminate the enforcement.

Article 31 These Interpretations shall come into effect on April 1, 2016. Where there is any discrepancy between relevant judicial interpretations promulgated previously by the Supreme People's Court and these Interpretations, these Interpretations shall prevail.

1.4.3 Provisions (I) of the Supreme People's Court on Several Issues concerning the Application of Law in the Trial of Administrative Cases Involving the Grant and Confirmation of Patents

(Interpretation No. 8 [2020], SPC, adopted at the 1810th Session of the Judicial Committee of the Supreme People's Court on August 24, 2020, and coming into force on September 12, 2020).

For the purposes of correctly trying the administrative cases involving the grant and confirmation of patents, these Provisions are developed in accordance with the Patent Law of the People's Republic of China, the Administrative Procedure Law of the People's Republic of China and other relevant laws and in light of judicial practice.

Article 1 For the purposes of these Provisions, "administrative case involving the grant of a patent" means a case in which a patent applicant files a lawsuit with a people's court against a decision on examining a request for reexamining a patent made by the patent administrative department of the State Council.

For the purposes of these Provisions, "administrative case involving the confirmation of a patent" means a case in which a patentee or a person requesting the declaration of invalidation of a patent files a lawsuit with a people's court against a decision on the examination of a request for declaring the invalidation of a patent made by the patent administrative department of the State Council.

For the purposes of these Provisions, "alleged decision" means a decision made by the patent administrative department of the State Council on the examination of a request for reexamining or declaring the invalidation of a patent.

Article 2 A people's court shall define the terms used in the claims based on the ordinary meaning understood by technicians in the relevant technical field after reading the claims, specification and appended drawings. If the terms used in the claims are clearly defined or explained in the specification and appended drawings, such definitions shall be adopted.

The terms that cannot be defined according to the provisions of the preceding paragraph may be defined based on the technical dictionaries, technical manuals, reference books, textbooks, and national or industry technical standards, among others, generally used by technicians in the relevant technical field.

Article 3 A people's court may, when defining terms in the claims in an administrative case involving the confirmation of a patent, refer to the patentee's relevant statements that have been adopted by an effective judgment of a civil case involving patent infringement.

Article 4 Where there is any evident error or ambiguity in the grammar, characters, numbers, punctuation, graphs or symbols, among others, in the claims, specification or appended drawings, but technicians in the relevant technical field may have a unique understanding through reading the claims, specification and appended drawings, the people's court shall determine based on such unique understanding.

Article 5 Where a party has evidence proving that a patent applicant or a patentee forges or fabricates any relevant technical content such as specific implementation methods, technical effects and data and graphs in the specification and appended drawings against the principle of good faith, and claims accordingly that the relevant claims fail to comply with relevant provisions of the Patent Law, the people's court shall support such a claim.

Article 6 Where the failure to fully disclose specific technical content in the specification results in any of the following circumstances on the patent application date, the people's court shall determine that the specification and claims relating to the specific technical content fail to comply with paragraph 3, Article 26 of the Patent Law:

(1) The technical proposal specified in the claims cannot be implemented.
(2) The implementation of the technical proposal specified in the claims cannot solve the technical problems to be resolved by the invention or utility model.
(3) The technical proposal specified for confirming the claims can solve the technical problems to be resolved by the invention or utility model, but excessive work is required.

Where a party claims merely based on the specific technical content not fully disclosed as provided for in the preceding paragraph that the claims relating to such specific technical content comply with the provision of paragraph 4, Article 26 of the Patent Law that "the claims shall be based on the specification," the people's court shall not support the claim.

Article 7 Where, based on the specification and appended drawings, a technician in the relevant technical field is of the opinion that the claims fall under any of the following circumstances, the people's court shall determine that the claims fail to comply with the provisions of paragraph 4, Article 26 of the Patent Law on clearly defining the scope of patent protection:

(1) The type of subject matter of the invention is unspecific.
(2) The meaning of technical features in the claims cannot be reasonably determined.
(3) There are evident contradictions between technical features and such contradictions cannot be reasonably explained.

Article 8 Where, after reading the specification and appended drawings, technicians in the relevant technical field fail to prepare or prepare through reasonable summary a technical proposal specified in the claims on the date of application, the people's court shall determine that the claims fail to comply with the provision of paragraph 4, Article 26 of the Patent Law that "the claims shall be based on the specification."

Article 9 "The technical features defined by functions or effects" means technical features defined only by functions or effects in the invention-creation, such as structure, components, steps, and conditions, or interrelation between technical features, except that technicians in the relevant technical field can directly and clearly determine the specific implementation methods for realizing the functions or effects through reading claims.

Where the claims, specification and appended drawings disclose no specific implementation methods for realizing the functions or effects of technical features defined by functions or effects as set forth in the preceding paragraph, the people's court shall determine that the specification and claims with such technical features fail to comply with paragraph 3, Article 26 of the Patent Law.

Article 10 Where a drug patent applicant submits supplementary experimental data after the date of application and claims the use of such data to prove that the patent application complies with paragraph 3 of Article 22, paragraph 3 of Article 26 of the Patent Law, and other relevant provisions, the people's court shall conduct examination.

Article 11 Where the parties have any dispute over the veracity of any experimental data, the party submitting the experimental data shall produce evidence to prove the source and formation process of such experimental data. The people's court may notify the person in charge of the experiment to appear in court to make statements on the raw materials, steps, conditions, environment or parameters of the experiment, as well as personnel and institution that completed the experiment, among others.

Article 12 A people's court shall, when determining the technical field of a technical proposal specified in the claims, take into comprehensive consideration the subject matter and all other contents of the claims, records in the specification on the technical field and background technology, as well as the functions and uses realized by the technical proposal, among others.

Article 13 Where the specification and appended drawings fail to clearly state technical effects realized by differentiated technical features in a technical proposal specified in the claims, the people's court may, based on general knowledge in the relevant technical field, determine technical problems actually resolved by the claims as confirmed by technicians in the relevant technical field in light of the relationship between differentiated technical features and other technical features in the claims, as well as the role of differentiated technical features in the technical proposal specified in the claims, among others.

The failure to ascertain or erroneous ascertainment of the technical problems actually resolved in the claims in the alleged decision shall not affect the people's court's legal determination of creativity in the claims.

Article 14 In determining the knowledge level and cognitive ability of general consumers regarding a product with a design patent, the people's court shall take into consideration the design space of the product with a design patent on the date of application. If the design space is relatively large, the people's court may determine that it is generally not easy for general consumers to notice the minor differences among different designs; if the design space is relatively small, the people's court may determine that it is generally easy for general consumers to notice the minor differences among different designs.

In determining the design space provided for in the preceding paragraph, the people's court may take the following factors into comprehensive consideration:

(1) Function and use of the product.
(2) Overall conditions of the existing design.
(3) Usual design.
(4) Compulsory provisions of laws and administrative regulations.
(5) National and industrial technical standards.
(6) Other factors that need to be considered.

Article 15 Where the pictures or photos of a design are contradictory, missing or vague, among others, making it impossible for general consumers to determine the design to be protected based on such pictures or photos and brief descriptions, the people's court shall determine that they fail to comply with the provision of paragraph 2 of Article 27 of the Patent Law on "clearly displaying the design of a product requiring patent protection."

Article 16 A people's court shall, when determining whether a design complies with Article 23 of the Patent Law, comprehensively judge the overall visual effect of the design.

Design features required for realizing particular technical functions or only with limited choices shall have no significant impact on the overall observation and comprehensive judgment of the visual effect of a patent for a design.

Article 17 Where, in comparison with an existing design of any product of a same or similar type, the overall visual effect of a design is identical or substantially identical only with partial subtle differences, among others, the people's court shall determine that such a design "belongs to an existing design" as provided for in paragraph 1 of Article 23 of the Patent Law.

Except for the circumstances provided for in the preceding paragraph, if the difference between a design and an existing design of a product of a same or similar type has no significant impact on the overall visual effect, the people's court shall determine that the design has no "evident difference" as provided for in paragraph 2, Article 23 of the Patent Law.

The people's court shall determine whether products are same or similar in categories according to the use of the design product. The use of the product may be determined by referring to the brief description of the design, classification of the design product, functions of the product, sale or actual use of the product, and other relevant factors.

Article 18 Where, in comparison with another patent for a design of a product of a same type, on which a patent application is filed on a same day, the overall visual effect of a patent for a design is identical or substantially identical only with partial subtle differences, among others, the people's court shall determine that such a design fails to comply with the provision of Article 9 of the Patent Law that "only one patent right can be granted for the identical invention-creation."

Article 19 Where, in comparison with another design of a product of a same or similar type for which a patent application is filed before the date of application and announced after the date of application, if the overall visual effect of a design is identical or substantially identical only with partial subtle differences, among others, the people's court shall determine that such a design constitutes the "same design" as provided for in paragraph 1, Article 23 of the Patent Law.

Article 20 Where, based on any design inspiration from an existing design on the whole, a design with an overall visual effect identical or substantially identical only with partial subtle differences, among others, with a patent for a design, and without unique visual effect is obtained through the conversion, combination or replacement of design features which general consumers can easily think of, the people's court shall determine that the patent for a design has no "evident difference" as provided for in paragraph 2, Article 23 of the Patent Law in comparison with the combination of existing design features.

Under any of the following circumstances, the people's court may determine that there is a design inspiration set forth in the preceding paragraph:

(1) The design features of different parts of products of a same type are combined or replaced.
(2) The existing design discloses the conversion of design features of a product of a specific type for use on a product with a patent for a design.
(3) The existing design discloses the combination of design features of different products of specific types.
(4) The pattern in an existing design is used on a product with a design patent directly or only after minor change.
(5) The features of a single natural object are converted for use on a product with a patent for a design.
(6) A design is obtained simply by adopting basic geometry or only after minor change.

(7) All or part of a design of a building, work, or logo, among others, publicly known by general consumers is used.

Article 21 In determining the unique visual effect provided for in Article 20 of these Provisions, a people's court may take into comprehensive consideration the following factors:

(1) The design space of the product with a patent for a design.
(2) The correlation of product categories.
(3) The number of design features converted, combined and replaced as well as the difficulty thereof.
(4) Other factors that need to be considered.

Article 22 For the purposes of paragraph 3 of Article 23 of the Patent Law, "lawful rights" include the lawful rights or rights and interests in connection with works, trademarks, geographical indications, names, enterprise names, portraits as well as the names, packages and decorations of goods with certain influence, among others.

Article 23 Where a party claims that any of the following circumstances in the procedures for the examination of a request for reexamining or declaring the invalidation of a patent falls under the "violation of legal proceedings" as provided for in subparagraph (3), Article 70 of the Administrative Procedure Law, the people's court shall support the claim:

(1) Omitting the grounds and evidence put forward by the party, which has a substantial impact on the rights of the party.
(2) Failing to legally notify the patent applicant, patentee and the person filing the request for declaring the invalidation of the patent, among others, required to participate in examination procedures, which has a substantial impact on the rights thereof.
(3) Failing to inform the party of members of the collegial group, and any member thereof fails to withdraw although there is any statutory cause for withdrawal.
(4) Failing to give the party against whom an alleged decision was made an opportunity to state opinions on the grounds, evidence and facts determined as the basis for the alleged decision.
(5) Proactively introducing general knowledge or usual design not claimed by the party and failing to solicit the opinions of the party, which has a substantial impact on the rights of the party.
(6) Any other violation of statutory procedures, which may have a substantial impact on the rights of the party.

Article 24 Where an alleged decision falls under any of the following circumstances, the people's court may render a judgment to revoke it partially in accordance with Article 70 of the Administrative Procedure Law:

(1) The alleged decision's determination of partial claims in the claims is erroneous, while the determination of other parts is accurate.

(2) The alleged decision's determination of partial design in the "application for a design patent" as provided for in paragraph 2, Article 31 of the Patent Law is erroneous, while the determination of other parts is accurate.
(3) Any other circumstance where a judgment can be rendered to partially revoke the decision.

Article 25 Where an alleged decision has stated all the grounds and evidence for invalidity claimed by a party and declared the claims null and void, if a people's court is of the opinion that none of the grounds for the invalidity of the claims as determined by the alleged decision are untenable, it shall render a judgment to revoke or partially revoke the decision, and may, as the case may be, render a judgment that the defendant shall make a decision to reexamine the claims anew.

Article 26 Where an examination decision is remade directly based on an effective judgment without introducing new facts and grounds, and a party files a lawsuit against the decision, the people's court shall rule to refuse to accept the lawsuit in accordance with the law, and if the lawsuit has been accepted, rule to dismiss the lawsuit in accordance with the law.

Article 27 Where any ascertainment of facts or application of law in an alleged decision is definitely improper, but the identification conclusion on the grant and confirmation of a patent is accurate, the people's court may, on the basis of correcting the relevant ascertained facts and application of law, render a judgment to dismiss the plaintiff's claims.

Article 28 Where a party claims that relevant technical content belongs to common knowledge or that relevant design features belong to usual design, the people's court may require the party to provide evidence or make an explanation thereon.

Article 29 Where a patent applicant or a patentee provides any new evidence in an administrative case involving the grant and confirmation of a patent to prove that the patent application should not be rejected or the patent right should remain valid, the people's court shall generally conduct examination.

Article 30 Where a person filing a request for declaring the invalidation of a patent provides new evidence in an administrative case involving the confirmation of a patent, the people's court shall generally not conduct examination, except for the following evidence:

(1) The evidence is used to prove common knowledge or usual design that has been claimed in the procedures for examining the request for declaring the invalidation of the patent.
(2) The evidence is used to prove the knowledge level and cognitive ability of technicians in the relevant technical field or general consumers.
(3) The evidence is used to prove the overall condition of the design space or existing design of the product with a patent for a design.
(4) The evidence is used to reinforce the probative force of evidence that has been adopted in the procedures for examining the request for declaring the invalidation of the patent.
(5) The evidence is used to refute the evidence provided by any other party in legal proceedings.

Article 31 A people's court may require the party to provide new evidence as provided for in Articles 29 and 30 of these Provisions.

Where any evidence provided by a party to the people's court required to be provided in accordance with the law in the procedures for examining a request for reexamining or declaring the invalidation of a patent fails to be submitted without any justified reason, the people's court shall generally not adopt the evidence.

Article 32 These Provisions shall come into force on September 12, 2020.

A case pending trial by a people's court of first or second instance after these Provisions come into force shall be governed by these Provisions after these Provisions come into force; but a case, for which an effective judgment has been rendered before these Provisions come into force shall not be retried according to these Provisions.

1.4.4 Interpretation of the Supreme People's Court on Several Issues Concerning the Trial of Cases Involving Disputes Over New Varieties of Plants (2020 Amendment)

(Adopted at the 1,154th Session of the Judicial Committee of the Supreme People's Court on December 25, 2000, and amended in accordance with the Decision of the Supreme People's Court to Amend Eighteen Intellectual Property Judicial Interpretations including the Interpretation (II) of the Supreme People's Court on Several Issues concerning the Application of Law in the Trial of Cases involving Patent Right Infringement Disputes adopted at the 1,823rd Session of the Judicial Committee of the Supreme People's Court on December 23, 2020).

For the purposes of accepting and trying the cases involving disputes over new varieties of plants, in accordance with the relevant provisions of the Civil Code of the People's Republic of China, the Seed Law of the People's Republic of China, the Civil Procedure Law of the People's Republic of China, the Administrative Litigation Law of the People's Republic of China, the Decision of the Standing Committee of the National People's Congress on Establishing Intellectual Property Right Courts in Beijing, Shanghai, and Guangzhou, and the Decision of the Standing Committee of the National People's Congress on Several Issues concerning the Litigation Proceedings of Patent and Other Cases Involving Intellectual Property Rights, relevant issues are hereby interpreted as follows:

Article 1 The cases involving disputes over new varieties of plants accepted by people's courts mainly include the following types:

(1) A case filed for an administrative dispute over the review of the rejection of an application for a new variety of plant.
(2) A case filed for an administrative dispute over the invalidation of the right to a new variety of plant.
(3) A case filed for an administrative dispute over the modification of the name of the right to a new variety of plant.

(4) A case filed for a dispute over compulsory licensing of the right to a new variety of plant.
(5) A case filed for a dispute over the royalty for compulsory licensing of the right to a new variety of plant.
(6) A case filed for a dispute over the ownership of the right to apply for a new variety of plant.
(7) A case filed for a dispute over the ownership of the right to a new variety of plant.
(8) A case filed for a dispute over the contract on the transfer of the right to apply for a new variety of plant.
(9) A case filed for a dispute over the contract on the transfer of the right to a new variety of plant.
(10) A case filed for a dispute over the infringement of the right to a new variety of plant.
(11) A case filed for a dispute over counterfeiting another's right to a new variety of plant.
(12) A case filed for a dispute over the authorship of the developer of a new variety of plant.
(13) A case filed for a dispute over the royalty for a new variety of plant in the temporary protection period.
(14) A case filed for a dispute over an administrative punishment on a new variety of plant.
(15) A case filed for a dispute over the administrative reconsideration of a new variety of plant.
(16) A case filed for a dispute over administrative compensation for a new variety of plant.
(17) A case filed for a dispute over administrative rewards for a new variety of plant.
(18) A case filed for any other dispute over a new variety of plant.

Article 2 When examining a lawsuit involving the right to a new variety of plant filed by a party in accordance with the law, the people's court shall accept the lawsuit in accordance with the law, provided that the conditions for filing a civil case or administrative case set forth in Article 119 of the Civil Procedure Law of the People's Republic of China and Article 49 of the Administrative Litigation Law of the People's Republic of China are met.

Article 3 Cases of types I to V set out in Article 1 of this Interpretation shall be tried by the Beijing Intellectual Property Court as a people's court of first instance. Cases of types 6 to 18 shall be tried by an intellectual property right court, an intermediate people's court at the place where the people's government of the province, autonomous region or municipality directly under the Central Government is located or an intermediate people's court designated by the Supreme People's Court as the people's court of first instance.

An appeal filed by a party against the first instance judgment or ruling of a civil or administrative case involving a dispute over a new variety of plant shall be tried by the Supreme People's Court.

Article 4 Where the jurisdiction of a people's court over a civil case involving the infringement of the right to a new variety of plant is determined by the place where the infringement is committed, the "place where the infringement is committed" means the place where the propagation materials of such authorized new variety of plant are produced, propagated or sold or are repeatedly used to produce propagation materials of another variety for commercial purposes without the license of the owner of the right to the new variety of plant.

Article 5 For a case involving an administrative dispute over the review of the rejection of an application for a new variety of plant, a case involving an administrative dispute over the invalidation of the right to a new variety of plant, or a case involving an administrative dispute over the modification of the name of the right to a new variety of plant, the approval authority for a new variety of plant shall be the defendant; for a case involving a dispute over the compulsory licensing of a new variety of plant, the approval authority for a new variety of plant shall be the defendant; for a case involving a dispute over the royalty for compulsory licensing, the defendant shall be determined according to the claims of the plaintiff and the parties against which the lawsuit is filed.

Article 6 With regard to a case tried by a people's court which involves a dispute over the infringement of the right to a new variety of plant, if the defendant requests the approval authority for a new variety of plant to declare invalidation of the right to a new variety of plant within the period of submitting a statement of defense, the people's court shall generally not suspend the legal proceedings.

1.5 Main Amendments of Chinese Anti-Unfair Competition Laws and Regulations

1.5.1 *Anti-Unfair Competition Law of the People's Republic of China*

(Adopted at the 3rd Session of the Standing Committee of the Eighth National People's Congress of the People's Republic of China on September 2, 1993, revised at the 30th Session of the Standing Committee of the Twelfth National People's Congress on November 4, 2017, and amended in accordance with the Decision to Amend Eight Laws Including the Construction Law of the People's Republic of China adopted at the 10th Session of the Standing Committee of the Thirteenth National People's Congress of the People's Republic of China on April 23, 2019).

Before amendment (Come into force on January 1, 2018)	After amendment (Come into force on April 23, 2019)
Chapter I General Provisions	
Article 1 This Law is enacted for the purposes of promoting the sound development of the socialist market economy, encouraging and protecting fair competition, preventing acts of unfair competition, and safeguarding the lawful rights and interests of businesses and consumers	

(continued)

(continued)

Before amendment (Come into force on January 1, 2018)	After amendment (Come into force on April 23, 2019)
Article 2 Businesses shall, in their production and distribution activities, adhere to the free will, equality, fairness, and good faith principles, and abide by laws and business ethics For the purposes of this Law, "act of unfair competition" means that in its production or distribution activities, a business disrupts the order of market competition and causes damage to the lawful rights and interests of the other businesses or consumers, in violation of this Law For the purposes of this Law, "business" means a natural person, a legal person, or a non-legal person organization that engages in the production or distribution of commodities or the provision of services (commodities and services are hereinafter collectively referred to as "commodities")	
Article 3 The people's governments at all levels shall take measures to prevent acts of unfair competition and create an environment and conditions favorable for fair competition The State Council shall establish a coordination mechanism of anti-unfair competition work to research and decide major anti-unfair competition policies and coordinate the handling of major issues on maintaining the order of market competition	
Article 4 The departments performing the functions of industry and commerce administration of the people's governments at and above the county level shall investigate and dispose of acts of unfair competition, unless a law or administrative regulation requires any other department to do so	
Article 5 The state encourages, supports, and protects public scrutiny, from all organizations and individuals, of acts of unfair competition State organs and their employees shall not support or harbor acts of unfair competition Industry organizations shall strengthen industry self-regulation, provide guidance and rules for their members to compete according to the law, and maintain the order of market competition	
Chapter II Acts of Unfair Competition	
Article 6 A business shall not commit the following acts of confusion to mislead a person into believing that a commodity is one of another person or has a particular connection with another person: (1) Using without permission a label identical or similar to the name, packaging or decoration, among others, of another person's commodity with certain influence (2) Using without permission another person's name with certain influence, such as the name (including abbreviations and trade names) of an enterprise, the name (including abbreviations) of a social organization, or the name (including pseudonyms, stage names and name translations) of an individual (3) Using without permission the principal part of a domain name, the name of a website, or a web page with certain influence, among others, of another person (4) Other acts of confusion sufficient to mislead a person into believing that a commodity is one of another person or has a particular connection with another person	
Article 7 A business shall not seek transaction opportunities or competitive edges by bribing the following entities or individuals with property or by any other means: (1) An employee of the other party to a transaction (2) The entity or individual authorized by the other party to a transaction to handle relevant affairs (3) An entity or an individual that uses power or influence to affect a transaction A business may, in a transaction, explicitly pay a discount to the other party to the transaction, or pay a commission to an intermediary. In either case, the business shall faithfully make an entry in its account book. The business receiving the discount or commission shall also faithfully enter it into its account book A bribery committed by an employee of a business is deemed to have been committed by the business, unless the business has evidence that the act of the employee is irrelevant to seeking a transaction opportunity or competitive edge for the business	
Article 8 A business shall not conduct any false or misleading commercial publicity in respect of the performance, functions, quality, sales, user reviews, and honors received of its commodities, in order to defraud or mislead consumers A business shall not help another business conduct any false or misleading commercial publicity by organizing false transactions or any other means	

(continued)

(continued)

Before amendment (Come into force on January 1, 2018)	After amendment (Come into force on April 23, 2019)
Article 9 A business shall not commit the following acts of infringing trade secrets: (1) Acquiring a trade secret from the right holder by theft, bribery, fraud, coercion, or any other illicit means (2) Disclosing, using, or allowing another person to use a trade secret acquired from the right holder by any means as specified in the preceding subparagraph (3) Disclosing, using, or allowing another person to use a trade secret under its control in <u>violation of an agreement</u> or the requirements of the right holder for confidentiality of trade secrets	**Article 9** A business shall not commit the following acts of infringing upon trade secrets: (1) Acquiring a trade secret from the right holder by theft, bribery, fraud, coercion, **electronic intrusion**, or any other illicit means (2) Disclosing, using, or allowing another person to use a trade secret acquired from the right holder by any means as specified in the preceding subparagraph (3) Disclosing, using, or allowing another person to use a trade secret in its possession, **in violation of its confidentiality obligation** or the requirements of the right holder for keeping the trade secret confidential **(4) Abetting a person, or tempting, or aiding a person into or in acquiring, disclosing, using, or allowing another person to use the trade secret of the right holder in violation of his or her non-disclosure obligation or the requirements of the right holder for keeping the trade secret confidential** **An illegal act as set forth in the preceding paragraph committed by a natural person, legal person or unincorporated organization other than a business shall be treated as infringement of the trade secret**
Where a third party knows or should have known that an employee or a former employee of the right holder of a trade secret or any other entity or individual has committed an illegal act as specified in the preceding paragraph but still acquires, discloses, uses, or allows another person to use the trade secret, the third party shall be deemed to have infringed the trade secret For the purposes of this Law, "trade secret" means technology or business information unknown to the public and of a commercial value for which the right holder has taken corresponding confidentiality measures	Where a third party knows or should have known that an employee or a former employee of the right holder of a trade secret or any other entity or individual has committed an illegal act as **specified in paragraph 1** of this Article but still acquires, discloses, uses, or allows another person to use the trade secret, the third party shall be deemed to have infringed upon the trade secret For the purpose of this Law, "trade secret" means technical, operational or other **commercial information** unknown to the public and is of commercial value for which the right holder has taken corresponding confidentiality measures
Article 10 A business's premium campaign shall not fall under the following circumstances: (1) The information on the types of premiums, conditions for claiming premiums, amount of a prize, or premiums, among others, in the premium campaign is ambiguous, affecting a claim for a premium (2) A premium campaign is conducted by offering non-existent premiums or intentionally pre-determining premium winners (3) In the case of a lottery-based premium campaign, the amount of the top prize exceeds 50,000 yuan	
Article 11 A business shall not fabricate or disseminate false or misleading information to damage the goodwill or product reputation of a competitor	
Article 12 A business engaging in production or distribution activities online shall abide by the provisions of this Law No business may, by technical means to affect users' options, among others, commit the following acts of interfering with or sabotaging the normal operation of online products or services legally provided by another business: (1) Inserting a link or forcing a URL redirection in an online product or service legally provided by another business without its consent (2) Misleading, defrauding, or forcing users into altering, shutting down, or uninstalling an online product or service legally provided by another business (3) Causing in bad faith incompatibility with an online product or service legally provided by another business (4) Other acts of interfering with or sabotaging the normal operation of online products or services legally provided by another business	
Chapter III Investigation of Suspected Acts of Unfair Competition	

(continued)

(continued)

Before amendment (Come into force on January 1, 2018)	After amendment (Come into force on April 23, 2019)
Article 13 The supervisory inspection departments may take the following measures in investigating suspected acts of unfair competition: (1) Entering business premises suspected of acts of unfair competition for inspection (2) Questioning businesses, interested persons, and other relevant entities and individuals under investigation, and requiring them to provide relevant explanations or other materials relating to the acts under investigation (3) Consulting or duplicating agreements, account books, documents, files, records, business letters, and other materials relating to the suspected acts of unfair competition (4) Seizing or impounding property relating to the suspected acts of unfair competition (5) Inquiring about the bank accounts of businesses suspected of acts of unfair competition Before the measures in the preceding paragraph are taken, a written report shall be filed with the primary person in charge of the supervisory inspection department for an approval. Before the measures in subparagraphs (4) and (5) in the preceding paragraph are taken, a written report shall be filed with the primary person in charge of the supervisory inspection department of the people's government at or above the level of a districted city for an approval The supervisory inspection departments shall abide by the Administrative Compulsion Law of the People's Republic of China and other relevant laws and regulations in their investigations of suspected acts of unfair competition, and disclose the investigation and disposition results to the public in a timely manner	
Article 14 When the supervisory inspection departments investigate suspected acts of unfair competition, the businesses, interested persons, and other relevant entities and individuals under investigation shall faithfully provide relevant materials or information	
Article 15 The supervisory inspection departments and their employees shall have an obligation to keep the trade secrets known in their investigations confidential	
Article 16 Any entity or individual shall have the right to report a suspected act of unfair competition to the supervisory inspection department, which shall process the report in a timely manner as legally required after receiving it The supervisory inspection departments shall publish their telephone numbers, mailing boxes, or e-mail addresses for receiving reports, and keep informants confidential. In the case of a report with the informant choosing not to withhold its identity and with relevant facts and evidence provided, the supervisory inspection department shall notify the informant of the disposition result	
Chapter IV Legal Liability	
Article 17 A business causing any damage to another person in violation of this Law shall assume civil liability according to the law A business whose lawful rights and interests are damaged by any act of unfair competition may institute an action in a people's court	**Article 17** A business causing any damage to another person in violation of this Law shall assume civil liability according to the law A business whose lawful rights and interests are damaged by any act of unfair competition may institute an action in a people's court The amount of compensation for the damage caused to a business by any act of unfair competition shall be determined as per the actual loss of the business incurred for the infringement or if it is difficult to calculate the actual loss, as per the benefits acquired by the tortfeasor from the infringement. **If a business infringes upon a trade secret in bad faith with serious circumstances, the amount of compensation may be determined to be more than one time but not more than five times the amount determined by the aforesaid method.** The amount of compensation shall also include reasonable disbursements made by the business to prevent the infringement Where a business violates Article 6 or Article 9 of this Law, and it is difficult to determine the actual loss suffered by the right holder due to the infringement or the benefits acquired by the tortfeasor from the infringement, a people's court may, based on the circumstances of the infringement, render a judgment to award compensation in the amount of not more than **five million yuan** to the right holder

(continued)

(continued)

Before amendment (Come into force on January 1, 2018)	After amendment (Come into force on April 23, 2019)
The amount of compensation for the damage caused to a business by any act of unfair competition shall be determined as per the actual loss of the business incurred for the infringement or if it is difficult to calculate the actual loss, as per the benefits acquired by the tortfeasor from the infringement. The amount of compensation shall also include reasonable disbursements made by the business to prevent the infringement Where a business violates Article 6 or Article 9 of this Law, and it is difficult to determine the actual loss incurred by the right holder for the infringement or the benefits acquired by the tortfeasor from the infringement, a people's court may, based on the circumstances of the infringement, render a judgment to award compensation in the amount of not more than three million yuan to the right holder	

Article 18 Where a business commits any act of confusion in violation of Article 6 of this Law, the supervisory inspection department shall order it to cease the illegal act, and confiscate illegal commodities. If the amount of illegal operations is 50,000 yuan or more, it may also be fined not more than five times the amount of illegal operations; or if there is no amount of illegal operations or the amount of illegal operations is less than 50,000 yuan, it may also be fined not more than 250,000 yuan. If the circumstances are serious, its business license shall be revoked
A business whose registered enterprise name is in violation of Article 6 of this Law shall, in a timely manner, undergo name modification registration; and before its name is modified, the original enterprise registration authority shall substitute its unified social credit code for its name

Article 19 Where a business bribes another person in violation of Article 7 of this Law, the supervisory inspection department shall confiscate its illegal income, and impose a fine of not less than 100,000 yuan nor more than three million yuan on it. If the circumstances are serious, its business license shall be revoked

Article 20 Where, in violation of Article 8 of this Law, a business conducts any false or misleading commercial publicity of its commodities or help another business conduct any false or misleading commercial publicity by organizing false transactions or any other means, the supervisory inspection department shall order it to cease the illegal act, and impose a fine of not less than 200,000 yuan nor more than one million yuan or if the circumstances are serious, a fine of not less than one million yuan nor more than two million yuan on it, and in the latter case, its business license may be revoked
A business publishing any false advertisements in violation of Article 8 of this Law shall be punished in accordance with the Advertising Law of the People's Republic of China

(continued)

(continued)

Before amendment (Come into force on January 1, 2018)	After amendment (Come into force on April 23, 2019)
Article 21 Where a business infringes a trade secret in violation of Article 9 of this Law, the supervisory inspection department shall order it to cease the illegal act, and impose a fine of not less than 100,000 yuan nor more than 500,000 yuan or if the circumstances are serious, a fine of not less than 500,000 yuan nor more than three million yuan on it	**Article 21** Where a business or **any other natural person, legal person or unincorporated organization** infringes upon a trade secret in violation of Article 9 of this Law, the supervisory inspection department shall order the violator to cease the illegal act, shall **confiscate any illegal income**, and impose a fine of not less than 100,000 yuan nor more than **1 million yuan,** or, if the circumstances are serious, a fine of not less than 500,000 yuan nor more than **5 million yuan**
Article 22 Where a business conducts a premium campaign in violation of Article 10 of this Law, the supervisory inspection department shall order it to cease the illegal act, and impose a fine of not less than 50,000 yuan nor more than 500,000 yuan on it	
Article 23 Where a business causes any damage to the goodwill or product reputation of a competitor in violation of Article 11 of this Law, the supervisory inspection department shall order it to cease the illegal act and eliminate adverse effects, and impose a fine of not less than 100,000 yuan nor more than 500,000 yuan or if the circumstances are serious, a fine of not less than 500,000 yuan nor more than three million yuan on it	
Article 24 Where a business interferes with or sabotages the normal operation of online products or services legally provided by another business in violation of Article 12 of this Law, the supervisory inspection department shall order it to cease the illegal act, and impose a fine of not less than 100,000 yuan nor more than 500,000 yuan or if the circumstances are serious, a fine of not less than 500,000 yuan nor more than three million yuan on it	
Article 25 Where a business engages in any unfair competition in violation of this Law, if it voluntarily eliminates or mitigates the harmful consequences of its illegal act, among other statutory circumstances, a lighter or mitigated administrative punishment may be imposed on it according to the law; or if the illegal act is minor and corrected in a timely manner without any harmful consequences, no administrative punishment shall be imposed on it	
Article 26 Where a business receives any administrative punishment for engaging in unfair competition in violation of this Law, the supervisory inspection department shall enter it into the credit record of the business, and publish it according to the provisions of the relevant laws and administrative regulations	
Article 27 Where the property of a business held civilly, administratively, and criminally liable for a violation of this Law is insufficient to cover all the liabilities, its property shall be first used for its assumption of civil liability	
Article 28 Where a supervisory inspection department's performance of duties under this Law is interfered with or its investigation is refused or impeded, the supervisory inspection department shall order the violator to take corrective action, and may impose a fine of not more than 5,000 yuan on the violator which is an individual or a fine of not more than 50,000 yuan on the violator which is an entity, and the public security authority may impose a public security administration punishment on the violator	
Article 29 A party may, according to the law, apply for administrative reconsideration or file an administrative lawsuit against a decision of the supervisory inspection department	
Article 30 Disciplinary action shall be taken according to the law against an employee of a supervisory inspection department who abuses power, commits dereliction of duties, makes falsehood for personal gains, or divulges any trade secret known in investigation	
Article 31 Where a violation of this Law is criminally punishable, the offender shall be held criminally liable according to the law	

(continued)

(continued)

Before amendment (Come into force on January 1, 2018)	After amendment (Come into force on April 23, 2019)
(Addition)	Article 32 In the civil trial procedure for infringement of a trade secret, if the right holder of the trade secret provides prima facie evidence that it has taken confidentiality measures for the claimed trade secret and reasonably indicates that the trade secret has been infringed upon, the alleged tortfeasor shall prove that the trade secret claimed by the right holder is not a trade secret as described in this Law If the right holder of a trade secret provides prima facie evidence to reasonably indicate that the trade secret has been infringed upon, and provide any of the following evidence, the alleged tortfeasor shall prove the absence of such infringement: (1) Evidence that the alleged tortfeasor has a channel or an opportunity to access the trade secret and that the information it uses is substantially the same as the trade secret (2) Evidence that the trade secret has been disclosed or used, or is at risk of disclosure or use, by the alleged tortfeasor (3) Evidence that the trade secret is otherwise infringed upon by the alleged tortfeasor
Chapter V Supplemental Provision	
Article 32 This Law shall come into force on January 1, 2018	Article 33 (Same as left)

1.5.2 Interpretation of the Supreme People's Court on Some Issues Concerning the Application of Law in the Trial of Civil Cases Involving Unfair Competition

(Adopted at the 1412th meeting of the Judicial Committee of the Supreme People's Court on December 30, 2006. Amended in accordance with the Decision of the Supreme People's Court to Amend Eighteen Intellectual Property Judicial Interpretations including the Interpretation (II) of the Supreme People's Court on Several Issues concerning the Application of Law in the Trial of Cases involving Patent Right Infringement Disputes adopted at the 1,823rd Session of the Judicial Committee of the Supreme People's Court on December 23, 2020.)

Before amendment (Come into force as of February 1, 2007)	After amendment (Come into force as of January 1, 2021)
In order to correctly hear the civil cases involving unfair competition, lawfully protect the legitimate rights and interests of business operators, and maintain the market competition order, this Interpretation is formulated according to the General Principles of the Civil Law of the People's Republic of China, the Anti-unfair Competition Law of the People's Republic of China, and the Civil Procedure Law of the People's Republic of China and by considering the experiences and actual situation of the trial practice	In order to correctly hear the civil cases involving unfair competition, lawfully protect the legitimate rights and interests of business operators, and maintain the market competition order, this Interpretation is formulated according to the **Civil Code of the People's Republic of China**, the Anti-unfair Competition Law of the People's Republic of China, and the Civil Procedure Law of the People's Republic of China and by considering the experiences and actual situation of the trial practice

(continued)

(continued)

Before amendment (Come into force as of February 1, 2007)	After amendment (Come into force as of January 1, 2021)
	Article 1 Those commodities that have certain market popularity within the territory of China and are known by the relevant public shall be regarded as "well-known commodities" prescribed in Item (2) of Article 5 of the Anti-unfair Competition Law. The people's court shall, when affirming well-known commodities, take into consideration the time, region, volume and targets for selling such commodities, the duration, degree and scope for any publicity of such commodities, as well as the protection situation as well-known commodities, and make comprehensive judgments. The plaintiff shall assume the burden of proof for the market popularity of its commodities Where an identical or similar name, package or decoration with that specific to a well-known commodity is used within a different region, if the later user can prove its good faith in using it, it will not constitute the unfair competition prescribed in Item (2) of Article 5 of the Anti-unfair Competition Law. Where the later business activities are conducted within the same region and it is sufficient to cause confusion, and if the first user pleads the court to order the later to add other marks to distinguish the sources of its commodities, the people's court shall support it
	Article 2 The name, package and decoration of commodities that have notable characteristics for distinguishing the source of commodities shall be regarded as the "specific name, package and decoration" prescribed in Item (2) of Article 5 of the Anti-unfair Competition Law. If it is under any of the following circumstances, the people's court shall not affirm them as the specific name, package and decoration of well-known commodities: (1) the name, graphics or model commonly used by the commodities; (2) the name of the commodities that only directly indicates the quality, main raw materials, functions, uses, weight, quantity or any other characteristic of the commodities; (3) the shape formed only due to the nature of the commodities, the shape of the commodities that should be formed in order to obtain technical effects, and the shape that produces substantive value to the commodities; or (4) the name, package or decoration of the commodities that has no notable characteristic In case the notable characteristic occurs upon use under any circumstance prescribed in Item (1), (2) or (4) of the preceding paragraph, it can be confirmed as a specific name, package and decoration Where the specific name, package or decoration of a well-known commodity contains the name, graphics, or model common to the said commodity in question, or directly indicates the quality, main raw materials, functions, uses, weight, quantity or any other characteristic of the said commodity, or contains the place name, if any other party uses it for objectively describing commodities, it will not constitute an unfair competition
	Article 3 In case the decoration of the business place, the pattern of business tools, or the clothes of business staff of a business operator, etc. constitutes an overall business image with a unique style, it may be affirmed as the "decoration" prescribed in Item (2) of Article 5 of the Anti-unfair Competition Law
	Article 4 Where it is sufficient to cause the relevant public to misunderstand the source of a commodity, including the misunderstanding of such a specific relationship as licensed use or affiliation with the business operator of a well-known commodity, it shall be affirmed as "causing the confusion with the well-known commodity of someone else, and making the purchasers mistake it to be a well-known commodity" prescribed in Item (2) of Article 5 of the Anti-unfair Competition Law The use of a fundamentally similar name, package or decoration of a commodity or the one that is hardly different from the counterfeited one in terms of visual effect on the same commodity shall be regarded as "sufficiently to cause the confusion with the well-known commodity of someone else" The identity or similarity with the specific name, package or decoration of a well-known commodity may be affirmed by referring to the principles and methods for judging identical or similar trademarks
	Article 5 In case the name, package or decoration of a commodity is a mark that can not be used as a trademark as prescribed in Paragraph 1 of Article 10 of the Trademark Law, and the relevant party requests the court to protect it according to Item (2) of Article 5 of the Anti-unfair Competition Law, the people's court shall support it
	Article 6 An enterprise name registered by the enterprise registration authority, and a foreign enterprise name used within the territory of China for commercial use shall be affirmed as an "enterprise name" prescribed in Item (3) of Article 5 of the Anti-unfair Competition Law. A business name in the enterprise name that has certain market popularity and is known by the relevant public may be affirmed as a "enterprise name" prescribed in Item (3) of Article 5 of the Anti-unfair Competition Law The name of any natural person used in the business operation of commodities shall be affirmed as a "name" prescribed in Item (3) of Article 5 of the Anti-unfair Competition Law. The pen name or stage name of any natural person that has certain market popularity and is known by the relevant public may be affirmed as a "name" prescribed in Item (3) of Article 5 of the Anti-unfair Competition Law
	Article 7 The commercial use within the territory of China, including the use of the specific name, package or decoration of a well-known commodity, or the enterprise title or name of a commodity, commodity packages or commodity exchange documents, or for advertisements, exhibitions or other commercial activities, shall be affirmed as the "use" prescribed in Items (2) and (3) of Article 5 of the Anti-unfair Competition Law

(continued)

(continued)

Before amendment (Come into force as of February 1, 2007)	After amendment (Come into force as of January 1, 2021)
	Article 8 In case a business operator commits any of the following acts, which is sufficient to cause the misunderstanding of the relevant public, it may be affirmed as a "false or misleading publicity" prescribed in Paragraph 1 of Article 9 of the Anti-unfair Competition Law: (1) conducting one-sided or contrastive publicity of goods; (2) conducting the publicity of goods by taking undecided scientific viewpoints or phenomena as the facts for final conclusions; or (3) conducting the publicity of goods by using ambiguous language or other misleading means The publicity of goods by obviously exaggerating means, if it is insufficient to cause the misunderstanding of the relevant public, shall not be affirmed as the "false or misleading publicity" The people's court shall affirm the false or misleading publicity according to daily life experiences, the general attention of the relevant public, the misunderstanding caused, as well as the actuality of the publicity objects, etc
	Article 9 In case the relevant information is unknown to and is difficult to be obtained by the relevant personnel in the relevant field, it shall be affirmed as "unknown to the public" prescribed in Paragraph 3 of Article 10 of the Anti-unfair Competition Law If it is under any of the following circumstances, it may be affirmed that the relevant information is not unknown to the public: (1) The information is the common sense or industrial practice for the personnel in the relevant technical or economic field; (2) The information only involves the simple combination of dimensions, structures, materials and parts of products, and can be directly obtained through the observation of products by the relevant public after the products enter into the market; (3) The information has been publicly disclosed on any publication or any other mass medium; (4) The information has been publicized through reports or exhibits; (5) The information can be obtained through other public channels; or (6) The information can be easily obtained without any price
	Article 10 In case the relevant information has actual or potential commercial value, and can bring competitive advantage for the obligee, it shall be affirmed as "capable of bringing about benefits to the obligee, and having practical applicability" prescribed in Paragraph 3 of Article 10 of the Anti-unfair Competition Law
	Article 11 In case the obligee adopts proper protection measures suitable for the commercial value or other specific situation in order to prevent information leakage, it shall be confirmed as "confidentiality measures" prescribed in Paragraph 3 of Article 10 of the Anti-unfair Competition Law The people's court shall confirm whether the obligee has adopted confidentiality measures according to the features of the relevant information carrier, the confidentially willingness of the obligee, the identifiability degree of the confidentiality measures, the difficulty for others to obtain it by justifiable means and other factors In case any of the following circumstances is sufficient to prevent the divulge of any classified information, it shall be affirmed that the obligee has adopted the confidentiality measures: (1) Limiting the access scope of the classified information, and only notifying the contents to relevant persons that should have the access to the information; (2) Locking the carrier of the classified information up or adopting any other preventive measure; (3) Indicating a confidentiality mark on the carrier of classified information; (4) Adopting passwords or codes on the classified information; (5) Concluding a confidentiality agreement; (6) Limiting visitors to the classified machinery, factory, workshop or any other place or putting forward any confidentiality request; or (7) Adopting any other proper measure for guaranteeing the confidentiality of information
	Article 12 The business secrets obtained through independent development and research or reverse engineering shall not be affirmed as an infringement upon business secrets prescribed in Items (1) and (2) of Article 10 of the Anti-unfair Competition Law The "reverse engineering" mentioned in the preceding paragraph refers to the relevant technical information on the products as obtained through dismantling, mapping or analyzing the products gotten from technical means or other public channels. In case any party knows the business secrets of someone else by unjustifiable means and then claims its acquisition as lawful for the reason of reverse engineering, it shall not be supported

(continued)

(continued)

Before amendment (Come into force as of February 1, 2007)	After amendment (Come into force as of January 1, 2021)
Article 13 The name list of customers among business secrets shall generally refer to the name, address, contact information, trading habits, trading intent, and trading contents of customers that consist of the specific client information different from relevant public information, and include the name roll of customers that collects a great deal of customers as well as the specific customers that have kept a long-term and stable trading relationship Where a customer is relied on an employee and thus conducts market transactions with the employer of the said employee, after this employee leaves his post, if it could be proved that this customer voluntarily chooses to conduct market transactions with the said employee or his new employer, it shall be affirmed that no unfair means is adopted, unless it is otherwise stipulated between this employee and his former employer	
Article 14 In case any party claims that someone else has infringed upon its business secret, it shall assume the burden of proof to prove that its business secret meets the statutory requirements, the information of the other party is similar or substantially similar to its business secret, and the other party has adopted unfair means. In particular, the evidence for proving that its business secret meets the statutory requirements shall include the carrier, specific contents, commercial value of this business secret as well as the specific confidentiality measures adopted for this business secret	
Article 15 In the case of infringement upon any business secret, if the licensee of the license contract for sole use of the business secret lodges a lawsuit, the people's court shall accept it according to law In case the licensee of the license contract for exclusive use lodges a lawsuit jointly with the obligee, or the licensee lodges a lawsuit alone under the circumstance that the obligee does not want to do so, the people's court shall accept it according to law In case the licensee of the license contract for common use lodges a lawsuit jointly with the obligee, or the licensee lodges a lawsuit alone upon written authorization of the obligee, the people's court shall accept it according to law	
Article 16 When the people's court adjudicates the civil liability of stopping the infringement on any business secret, the time for stopping the infringement shall generally be extended to the time when this business secret has become known to the general public In case the time for stopping the infringement adjudicated according to the preceding paragraph is clearly improper, the tortfeasor may be ordered to stop the use of this business secret within a certain term or scope under the circumstance that the competitive advantage of the obligee to this business secret is protected	
Article 17 The determination of damages for the acts infringing on business secrets as prescribed in Article 10 of the Anti-unfair Competition Law may be governed by the methods of determining damages for patent infringements by analogy, and the determination of damages for the unfair competition acts prescribed in Article 5,9 or 14 of the Anti-unfair Competition Law may be governed by the methods of determining damages for infringing upon registered trademark rights by analogy In case a tort causes any business secret to be known by the general public, the damages shall be determined according to the commercial value of this business secret. The commercial value of this business secret shall be determined according to the research and development costs, the proceeds from implementing this business secret, possible benefits, and the time for maintaining the competitive advantage to this business secret, etc	
Article 18 The civil cases of the first instance involving the unfair competition prescribed in Article 5,9, 10 or 14 of the Anti-unfair Competition Law shall generally be subject to the jurisdiction of the intermediate people's court Each higher people's court may, according to the actual situation of its jurisdiction and upon approval of the Supreme People's Court, determine some grass-roots people's courts to accept the civil cases of the first instance involving unfair competition, and those grass-roots people's courts that have been approved to hear civil cases involving intellectual property may continue the acceptance of cases involving unfair competition	
Article 19 This Interpretation shall come into force as of February 1, 2007	

1.5.3 Provisions of the Supreme People's Court on Several Issues Concerning the Application of Law in the Trial of Civil Cases Involving Infringements upon Trade Secrets

(Adopted at the 1810th Session of the Judicial Committee of the Supreme People's Court on August 24, 2020, and coming into force on September 12, 2020. Interpretation No. 7 [2020], SPC).

For the purpose of correctly trying civil cases concerning the infringements upon trade secrets, these Provisions are developed in accordance with the provisions of the Anti-Unfair Competition Law of the People's Republic of China, the Civil Procedure Law of the People's Republic of China, and other relevant laws, and in light of the judicial practice.

Article 1 A people's court may determine the information on structure, raw materials, components, formulas, materials, samples, styles, propagation materials of new plant varieties, processes, methods or their steps, algorithms, data, computer programs and their relevant documents, among others, relating to technology as technical information set forth in paragraph 4, Article 9 of the Anti-Unfair Competition Law.

A people's court may determine the information on creativity, management, sale, finance, plans, samples, bidding materials, clients' information and data, among others, relating to business activities as business information set forth in paragraph 4, Article 9 of the Anti-Unfair Competition Law.

For the purpose of the preceding paragraph, "clients' information" includes a client's name, address, contact information, and trading practices, intention, content, and other information.

Article 2 Where a party claims that a specific client falls under a trade secret only on the ground that the party maintains long-term stable trading relationships with the client, the people's court shall not support the claim.

Where a client, based on the trust in an individual employee, conducts transactions with the entity to which the employee belongs, if the employee, after leaving his or her office, is able to prove that the client voluntarily chooses to conduct transactions with him or her or his or her new employer, the people's court shall determine that the employee has not obtained the trade secret of the right holder by improper means.

Article 3 Where any information requested for protection by a right holder is not generally known and easily accessible by relevant personnel in the relevant field when an alleged infringement occurs, the people's court shall determine that the information is not known by the public as provided for in paragraph 4, Article 9 of the Anti-Unfair Competition Law.

Article 4 Under any of the following circumstances, a people's court may determine that the relevant information is known by the public:

(1) The information falls under common sense or industry practices in the field to which it belongs.

(2) The information only involves such contents as the product size, structure, materials, and simple combination of components, which may be directly obtained by relevant personnel in the field to which the party belongs through the observation of products on the market.
(3) The information has been disclosed to the public in any open publication or any other media.
(4) The information has been disclosed to the public through public seminars, exhibitions, and other methods.
(5) The information may be obtained by relevant personnel in the field to which the party belongs through other public channels.

New information formed after reviewing, improving or processing the information known by the public shall be deemed as not known by the public, if such new information complies with Article 3 of these Provisions.

Article 5 The people's court shall determine the reasonable confidentiality measures taken by a right holder to prevent the leakage of a trade secret prior to the occurrence of any alleged infringement as the corresponding confidentiality measures set forth in paragraph 4, Article 9 of the Anti-Unfair Competition Law.

A people's court shall determine whether a right holder has taken corresponding confidentiality measures based on such factors as the nature of the trade secret and its carrier, the commercial value of the trade secret, identification degree of confidentiality measures, degree of correspondence between confidentiality measures and the trade secret, and the right holder's willingness to keep the trade secret confidential.

Article 6 Under any of the following circumstances, if it is sufficient to prevent the leakage of a trade secret under normal circumstances, a people's court shall determine that the right holder has taken corresponding confidentiality measures:

(1) A confidentiality agreement has been signed or confidentiality obligations have been agreed upon in the contract.
(2) Confidentiality requirements are raised to employees, former employees, suppliers, clients, and visitors, who are able to access and obtain trade secrets in such forms as bylaws, training, rules and regulations, and written notification.
(3) Visitors' access to factory premises, workshops and other production or distribution premises involving the trade secret is restricted or such premises are differentiated for separate management.
(4) Trade secrets and their carriers are differentiated for separate management by such methods as marking, classification, isolation, encryption, sealing-up, limiting the scope of persons who are able to access or obtain the trade secrets and their carriers.
(5) Measures are taken to prohibit or restrict the use of, access to, storage in or reproduction from computer equipment, electronic equipment, network equipment, storage equipment, and software that can access or obtain trade secrets.
(6) Employees leaving their office are required to register, return, clear and destroy the trade secrets accessed or obtained by them and their carriers, and continue to assume the confidentiality obligation.
(7) Taking other reasonable confidentiality measures.

Article 7 Where any information for which protection is requested by a right holder has realistic or potential commercial value as it is not known by the public, the people's court may, upon examination, determine that the information has commercial value as provided for in paragraph 4, Article 9 of the Anti-Unfair Competition Law.

Where any periodic achievement formed in production and distribution activities complies with the provisions of the preceding paragraph, the people's court may determine upon examination that the achievement has commercial value.

Article 8 Where an alleged infringer obtains a right holder's trade secret in a manner that violates legal provisions or recognized business ethics, the people's court shall determine that the alleged infringer has obtained the trade secret of the right holder by other improper means as set forth in paragraph 1, Article 9 of the Anti-Unfair Competition Law.

Article 9 Where an alleged infringer directly uses any trade secret in its production and distribution activities, or uses any trade secret after the modification or improvement thereof, or adjusts, optimizes or improves relevant production and distribution activities based on any trade secret, the people's court shall determine that the alleged infringer has used the trade secret as set forth in Article 9 of the Anti-Unfair Competition Law.

Article 10 The people's court shall determine the confidentiality obligation assumed by a party in accordance with legal provisions or the confidentiality obligation agreed upon in a contract as a confidentiality obligation set forth in paragraph 1, Article 9 of the Anti-Unfair Competition Law.

Where the parties have not agreed on the confidentiality obligation in their contract, but the alleged infringer knows or should have known that the information obtained by it or him belongs to the trade secret of the right holder according to the principle of good faith and the contract nature, purpose, conclusion process, and trading practices, the people's court shall determine that the alleged infringer shall assume the obligation to keep confidential the trade secret obtained by it or him.

Article 11 A people's court may determine operators and managers of and other personnel having labor relations with a legal person or an unincorporated organization as employees or former employees set forth in paragraph 3, Article 9 of the Anti-Unfair Competition Law.

Article 12 A people's court may, when determining whether an employee or a former employee has channels or opportunities to obtain a right holder's trade secret, consider the following factors in relation thereto:

(1) His or her duties, responsibilities and authority.
(2) The job undertaken by him or her or task assigned to him or her by the entity.
(3) Specific circumstances of his or her participation in production and distribution activities relating to the trade secret.
(4) Whether he or she keeps, uses, stores, reproduces, controls or otherwise accesses or obtains any trade secret and the carrier thereof.
(5) Other factors that need to be taken into consideration.

Article 13 Where there is no substantial difference between any alleged infringing information and relevant trade secret, the people's court may determine that the alleged infringing information is substantially identical to the trade secret set forth in paragraph 2, Article 32 of the Anti-Unfair Competition Law.

A people's court may consider the following factors when determining whether it is "substantially identical" to that set forth in the preceding paragraph:

(1) The degree of similarity and difference between the alleged infringing information and the trade secret.
(2) Whether it is easy for the relevant personnel in the relevant field to think of the difference between the alleged infringing information and the trade secret when an alleged infringement occurs.
(3) Whether the alleged infringing information is substantially different from the trade secret in terms of purposes, use methods, objectives, and effects, among others.
(4) Situation relating to the trade secret in public fields.
(5) Other factors that need to be taken into consideration.

Article 14 The people's court shall determine the alleged infringing information obtained through independent development or reverse engineering as not constituting the infringement upon trade secrets as set forth in Article 9 of the Anti-Unfair Competition Law.

For the purpose of the preceding paragraph, "reverse engineering" means obtaining relevant technical information of a product obtained from any public channel by technical means through disassembling, survey and mapping, and analysis of the product.

Where an alleged infringer that has obtained the trade secret of the right holder by improper means claims no infringement upon the trade secret on the ground of reverse engineering, the people's court shall not support the claim.

Article 15 Where the respondent is attempting to obtain, disclose, use or allow any other person to use, or has obtained, disclosed, used or allowed any other person to use the trade secret claimed by a right holder by improper means, the people's court may render a ruling to take preservation measures in accordance with the law, if the failure to take preservation measures will make it difficult to enforce the relevant judgment or cause other damage to any party or cause irreparable damage to the right holder's lawful rights and interests.

Where any of the circumstances set forth in the preceding paragraph falls under emergency set forth in Article 100 or Article 101 of the Civil Procedure Law, the people's court shall render a ruling within 48 h.

Article 16 Where a natural person, legal person or unincorporated organization other than dealers infringes upon any trade secret, if the right holder claims that the infringer shall assume civil liability in accordance with Article 17 of the Anti-Unfair Competition Law, the people's court shall support the claim.

Article 17 Where a people's court renders a judgment on the civil liability for ceasing the infringement upon a trade secret, the time for cessation of infringement shall generally last until the trade secret has been known by the public.

Where the time for cessation of infringement as determined in a judgment according to the provisions of the preceding paragraph is evidently irrational, the people's court may, under the premise of legally protecting the competitive advantages of the right holder in terms of the trade secret, render a judgment that the infringer shall cease using the trade secret within a certain period or scope.

Article 18 Where a right holder requests a judgment ordering an infringer to return or destroy the carrier of any trade secret, or clear any information on trade secret under the control of the infringer, the people's court shall generally support the request.

Article 19 Where a trade secret is known by the public due to infringement, a people's court may take into consideration the commercial value of the trade secret when determining the amount of compensation in accordance with the law.

A people's court shall, when determining the commercial value set forth in the preceding paragraph, take into consideration such factors as research and development cost, income obtained from the exploitation of the trade secret, available benefits and period of time during which competitive advantages may be maintained.

Article 20 Where a right holder requests the determination of actual loss caused due to infringement by reference to the royalty of the trade secret, the people's court may determine the actual loss based on such factors as the licensing nature, content, actual performance, as well as the nature, circumstances and consequences of the infringement.

A people's court may, when determining the amount of compensation in accordance with paragraph 4, Article 17 of the Anti-Unfair Competition Law, take into consideration such factors as the nature, commercial value, research and development cost, and degree of innovation of the trade secret, competitive advantages it may bring, the infringer's subjective fault as well as the nature, circumstances and consequences of the infringement.

Article 21 Where a party or a person that is not a party to the case applies in writing to the people's court for taking measures to keep confidential evidence and materials involving the trade secret of the party or the person that is not a party to the case, the people's court shall take necessary confidentiality measures during preservation, exchange of evidence, cross-examination, entrusted authentication, questioning, court trial and other legal proceedings.

Whoever, in violation of the requirements for confidentiality measures set forth in the preceding paragraph, discloses any trade secret without authorization or uses any trade secret other than in legal proceedings or allows any other person to use any trade secret accessed or obtained in legal proceedings shall assume civil liability in accordance with the law. If any of the circumstances set forth in Article 111 of the Civil Procedure Law is constituted, the people's court may take compulsory measures in accordance with the law. If it is criminally punishable, the offender shall be held criminally liable in accordance with the law.

Article 22 A people's court shall, when trying a civil case concerning the infringement upon any trade secret, examine the evidence formed in criminal proceedings for the crime involving the infringement upon trade secret in a comprehensive and objective manner according to legal procedures.

Where a party to a civil case concerning the infringement upon a trade secret and its agent ad litem are unable to collect on their own the evidence relating to an alleged infringement, which is kept by the public security authority, procuratorial authority or people's court due to any objective reason and apply for investigation and evidence collection, the people's court shall approve the application, except that it may affect ongoing criminal proceedings.

Article 23 Where a party claims the determination of the amount of compensation in a civil case involving the same infringement upon trade secret based on the actual loss or illegal income determined by an effective criminal judgment, the people's court shall support the claim.

Article 24 Where a right holder has provided prima facie evidence on the benefits obtained by the infringer from the infringement, but the account books and materials relating to the infringement upon trade secret are possessed by the infringer, the people's court may, upon the application of the right holder, order the infringer to provide such account books and materials. If the infringer refuses to provide such account books or materials without any justified reason or fails to provide them in a truthful manner, the people's court may determine the benefits obtained by the infringer from the infringement based on the claim of and evidence provided by the right holder.

Article 25 Where a party requests the suspension of trial of a civil case concerning the infringement upon any trade secret on the ground that a criminal case involving the same alleged infringement upon trade secret has not been concluded, the people's court shall support the request if it deems after soliciting the opinions of the parties that the trial result of the criminal case must be taken as the basis.

Article 26 Where the licensee of a sole licensing contract on the exclusive use of a trade secret files a lawsuit against an infringement upon a trade secret, the people's court shall accept the lawsuit in accordance with the law.

Where the licensee of an exclusive license contract files a lawsuit jointly with the right holder, or separately under the circumstance that the right holder does not file any lawsuit, the people's court shall accept the lawsuit in accordance with the law.

Where the licensee of a simple license contract files a lawsuit jointly with the right holder, or separately upon the right holder's written authorization, the people's court shall accept the lawsuit in accordance with the law.

Article 27 A right holder shall clarify the specific content of a trade secret claimed before the conclusion of first-instance court debate. If only certain aspects can be specified, the people's court shall try the specified part.

Where a right holder separately claims in second-instance proceedings the specific content of a trade secret that are not clarified in first-instance proceedings, the people's court of second instance may conduct mediation regarding the claim related to the specific content of the trade secret on a voluntary basis, and shall inform the party to file a separate lawsuit if mediation fails. If both parties agree on the joint trial of the case by the people's court of second instance, the people's court of second instance may try the case on a consolidated basis.

Article 28 Where a people's court tries a civil case concerning the infringement upon a trade secret, the law when the alleged infringement occurs shall apply. If the alleged infringement has occurred before the law is amended and continues after the law is amended, the amended law shall apply.

Article 29 These Provisions shall come into force on September 12, 2020. For any discrepancies between these Provisions and any judicial interpretation previously issued by the Supreme People's Court, these Provisions shall prevail.

A pending case in a people's court of first or second instance after these Provisions come into force shall be governed by these Provisions after these Provisions come into force; but a case, for which an effective judgment has been rendered before these Provisions come into force shall not be retried according to these Provisions.

1.5.4 Interpretation of the Supreme People's Court on Application of Laws in the Trial of Civil Disputes Over Domain Names of Computer Network

(Adopted at the 1182nd meeting of the Judicial Committee of the Supreme People's Court on June 26, 2001. Amended in accordance with the Decision of the Supreme People's Court to Amend Eighteen Intellectual Property Judicial Interpretations including the Interpretation (II) of the Supreme People's Court on Several Issues concerning the Application of Law in the Trial of Cases involving Patent Right Infringement Disputes adopted at the 1,823rd Session of the Judicial Committee of the Supreme People's Court on December 23, 2020.)

Before amendment (Come into force as of July 24, 2001)	After amendment (Come into force as of January 1, 2021)
In order to correctly try the civil disputes concerning the acts of the registration, and use of computer network domain name, etc.(hereinafter referred to as disputes over domain name), the following interpretations are issued according to provisions of the General Principles of Civil Law of the People's Republic of China (hereinafter referred to as the General Principles of Civil Law), the Law of the People's Republic of China on Anti-Unfair Competition (hereinafter referred to as the Law on Anti-Unfair Competition), the Civil Procedure Law of the People's Republic of China (hereinafter referred to as the Civil Procedure Law):	In order to correctly try the civil disputes concerning the acts of the registration, and use of computer network domain name, etc.(hereinafter referred to as disputes over domain name), the following interpretations are issued according to provisions of the **Civil Code of the People's Republic of China**, the Law of the People's Republic of China on Anti-Unfair Competition, the Civil Procedure Law of the People's Republic of China (hereinafter referred to as the Civil Procedure Law):

(continued)

(continued)

Before amendment (Come into force as of July 24, 2001)	After amendment (Come into force as of January 1, 2021)
Article 1 When the party concerned brings an action to the people's court of the disputes over the acts of the registration, and use of computer network domain name, etc., if the action is proved to comply with the provisions of Article 108 of the Civil Procedure Law after examination, the people's court shall accept the action	**Article 1** When the party concerned brings an action to the people's court of the disputes over the acts of the registration, and use of computer network domain name, etc., if the action is proved to comply with the provisions of **Article 119** of the Civil Procedure Law after examination, the people's court shall accept the action
Article 2 The case of dispute over domain name infringement shall be ruled by the intermediate people's court of the place where the infringement act is committed or the place of domicile of the defendant. If the place where the infringement act is committed or the place of domicile of the defendant is hard to determine, the place where the computer terminal or other equipments by which the plaintiff found that domain name, are located may be regarded as the place where the infringement act is committed Cases of disputes over domain name involving foreign elements include the cases of disputes over domain name in which one or both of the parties are foreigners, stateless persons, foreign enterprises or organizations, international organizations, or the domain name is registered in foreign countries. The jurisdiction of the cases of disputes over domain name involving foreign elements taking place within the territory of the People's Republic of China shall be determined according to the provisions of Chapter 4 of the Civil Procedure Law	
Article 3 The cause of the case of dispute over domain name shall be determined by the nature of the legal relation of the dispute between the two parties concerned, and the domain name of computer network shall be added at the beginning; if the nature of the legal relation of the dispute is hard to determine, it can be generally called the case of dispute over domain name of computer network	
Article 4 When trying cases of dispute over domain name of computer network, the people's court shall come to the conclusion that the acts of the defendant of registering or using the domain name, etc.constitute infringement or unfair competition if the following conditions are met: (1) the civil rights and interests that the plaintiff asked for protection are legal and valid; (2) the domain name or the main part of the domain name of the defendant has constituted duplication, imitation, translation or transliteration of the well-known trademark of the plaintiff; or is the same as or similar to the registered trademark of the plaintiff so that the public may take it for the registered trademark of the plaintiff by mistake; (3) the defendant doesn't enjoy rights or interests of the said domain name or its main part, neither does he have proper reasons to register or use that domain name; and (4) the defendant is registering or using that domain name through malice	

(continued)

(continued)

Before amendment (Come into force as of July 24, 2001)	After amendment (Come into force as of January 1, 2021)
Article 5 The people's court shall come to the conclusion that the defendant is malicious if the acts of the defendant are proved to be under any of the following circumstances: (1) registering the well-known trademark of others as domain name for commercial purposes; (2) registering or using the domain name which is the same as or similar to the registered trademark or domain name of the plaintiff for commercial purposes, intentionally causing confusion with the products, services provided by the plaintiff or with the website of the plaintiff, and misleading the network users to visit his website or other online sites; (3) having offered to sell or rent that domain name for high price or to transfer it by other means to get improper profits; (4) having not used or having not prepared to use the domain name after registration, and intentionally preventing the right owner from registering that domain name; and (5) other circumstances of malice If the defendant has adduced evidence to prove that the domain name he held has already been well-known before the dispute arises, and that the domain name can be distinguished from the registered trademark, domain name, etc.of the plaintiff, or he is under other circumstances which can prove his innocence, the people's court may come to the conclusion that he is not malicious	
Article 6 When trying cases of disputes over domain name, the people's court may determine whether the involved registered trademark is well-known according to the request of the parties concerned and the specific circumstances of the case	
<u>**Article 7** When trying cases of dispute over domain name, the people's court shall apply the corresponding provisions of law to the circumstances complying with the provisions of Article 4 of this Interpretation that constitute infringement according to the relevant provisions of law; those that constitute unfair competition may apply the provisions of Article 4 of theGeneral Principles of Civil Law and the first paragraph of Article 2 of the Law on Anti-Unfair Competition</u> <u>The cases of disputes over domain name involving foreign elements shall be handled according to the relevant provisions of Chapter 8 of the General Principles of Civil Law</u>	**(Deletion)**

(continued)

(continued)

Before amendment (Come into force as of July 24, 2001)	After amendment (Come into force as of January 1, 2021)
Article 8 Where the people's court has determined that the acts of registering or using domain name, etc.have constituted infringement or unfair competition, it can rule that the defendant should stop the infringement, write off the domain name, or rule that the plaintiff should register and use that domain name according to the request of the plaintiff; where actual damages are caused to the right owner, the people's court may rule that the defendant compensate the plaintiff for the losses	**Article 7** Where the people's court has determined that the acts of registering or using domain name, etc.have constituted infringement or unfair competition, it can rule that the defendant should stop the infringement, write off the domain name, or rule that the plaintiff should register and use that domain name according to the request of the plaintiff; where actual damages are caused to the right owner, the people's court may rule that the defendant compensate the plaintiff for the losses **If the infringer intentionally infringes with serious circumstances, the plaintiff has the right to request punitive compensation from the people's court**

1.6 Main Amendments of Chinese Criminal Laws and Regulations on Crimes of Infringing upon Intellectual Property Rights

1.6.1 The Section of Criminal Law of the People's Republic of China on Crimes of Infringing upon Intellectual Property Rights

(Adopted by the Second Session of the Fifth National People's Congress on July 1, 1979, revised by the Fifth Session of the Eighth National People's Congress on March 14, 1997, and amended according to the NPC Standing Committee's Decision Concerning Punishment of Criminal Offenses Involving Fraudulent Purchase adopted at the Sixth Session of the Standing Committee of the Ninth Ntional People's Congress on December 29, 1998, Amendment to the Criminal Law of the People's Republic of China adopted at the 13rd Session of the Standing Committee of the Ninth National People's Congress on December 25,1999, Amendment (II) to the Criminal Law of the People's Republic of China adopted at the 23rd Session of the Standing Committee of the Ninth National People's Congress on August 31, 2001, Amendment (III) to the Criminal Law of the People's Republic of China adopted at the 25th Session of the Standing Committee of the Ninth National People's Congress on December 29, 2001; Amendment (IV) to the Criminal Law of the People's Republic of China adopted at the 31st Session of the Standing Committee of the Ninth National People's Congress on December 28, 2002, Amendment (V) to the Criminal Law of the

People's Republic of China adopted at the 14th Session of the Standing Committee of the Tenth National People's Congress on February 28, 2005, Amendment (VI) to the Criminal Law of the People's Republic of China adopted at the 22nd Session of the Standing Committee of the Tenth National People's Congress on June 29, 2006, Amendment (VII) to the Criminal Law of the People's Republic of China adopted at the 7th Session of the Standing Committee of the 11st National People's Congress on February 28, 2009, Decision of the Standing Committee of the National People's Congress on Amending Some Laws adopted at the Tenth Session of the Standing Committee of the 11st National People's Congress on August 27, 2009, Amendment (VIII) to the Criminal Law of the People's Republic of China adopted at the 19th Session of the Standing Committee of the 11st National People's Congress on February 25, 2011, Amendment (IX) to the Criminal Law of the People's Republic of China adopted at the 16th Session of the Standing Committee of the 12nd National People's Congress on August 29, 2015, Amendment (X) to the Criminal Law of the People's Republic of China adopted at the 30th Session of the Standing Committee of the 12nd National People's Congress on November 4, 2017, and Amendment (XI) to the Criminal Law of the People's Republic of China adopted at the 24th Session of the Standing Committee of the 13rd National People's Congress on December 26, 2020).

Before the amendment (effective November 4, 2017)	After the amendment (effective March 1, 2021)
Chapter III Crimes of Undermining the Order of Socialist Market Economy	
Section 7. Crimes of Infringing Upon Intellectual Property Rights	
Article 213. Using an identical trademark on the same merchandise without permission of its registered owner shall, if the case is of a serious nature, be punished with imprisonment or criminal detention of less than three years, with a fine, or a separately imposed fine; for cases of a more serious nature, with imprisonment of over three years and less than seven years, and with fine	Article 213. Whoever, without the permission of the owner of a registered trademark, uses a trademark identical with the registered trademark on the same kind of goods or **services** shall, if the circumstances are serious, be sentenced to imprisonment of not more than three years and a fine or be sentenced to a fine only; or if the circumstances are especially serious, be sentenced to imprisonment of not less than three years nor more than **ten years** and a fine
Article 214. Knowingly selling merchandise under a faked trademark with a relatively large sales volume shall be punished with imprisonment or criminal detention of less than three years, with a fine or a separately imposed fine; in cases involving a large sales volume, with imprisonment of more than three years but less than seven years, and with fine	Article 214. Whoever knowingly sells goods on which a false registered trademark is used shall, if **the amount of illegal income is relatively large or there is any other serious circumstance**, be sentenced to imprisonment of not more than three years and a fine or be sentenced to a fine only; or if **the amount of illegal income is huge or there is any other especially serious circumstance**, be sentenced to imprisonment of not less than three years nor more than **ten years** and a fine

(continued)

(continued)

Before the amendment (effective November 4, 2017)	After the amendment (effective March 1, 2021)
Article 215. Forging or manufacturing without authority or selling or manufacturing without authority other's registered trademarks or identifications shall, for cases of a serious nature, be punished with imprisonment or <u>criminal detention, or restriction</u> for less than three years, with a fine or a separately imposed fine; for cases of a especially serious nature, with imprisonment of over three years and less than <u>seven years</u>, and with fine	**Article 215.** Whoever forges or produces without permission the labels of another person's registered trademark or a registered trademark that are forged or produced without permission shall, if the circumstances are serious, be sentenced to imprisonment of not more than three years and a fine or be sentenced to a fine only; or if the circumstances are especially serious, be sentenced to imprisonment of not less than three years nor more than **ten years** and a fine
Article 216. Whoever counterfeits other people's patents, and when the circumstances are serious, is to be sentenced to not more than three years of fixed-term imprisonment, criminal detention, and may in addition or exclusively be sentenced to a fine	
Article 217. Whoever, for the purpose of reaping profits, has committed one of the following acts of copyright infringement and gains a fairly large amount of illicit income, or when there are other serious circumstances, is to be sentenced to not more than three years of fixed-term imprisonment, <u>criminal detention</u>, and may in addition or exclusively be sentenced to a fine; when the amount of the illicit income is huge or when there are other particularly serious circumstances, he is to be sentenced to not less than three years and not more than <u>seven years</u> of fixed-term imprisonment and a fine: (1) copy and distribute written, musical, <u>movie, televised, and video works</u>; computer software; and other works without the permission of their copyrighters; (2) publish books whose copyrights are exclusively owned by others; (3) duplicate and distribute audiovisual works without the permission of their producers; (4) produce and sell artistic works bearing fake signatures of others	**Article 217.** Whoever falls under any of the following circumstances to, for profits, infringe upon any copyright **or any right related to copyright** shall, if the amount of illegal income is relatively large or there is any other serious circumstance, be sentenced to imprisonment of not more than three years and a fine or be sentenced to a fine only; or if the amount of illegal income is huge or there is any other especially serious circumstance, be sentenced to imprisonment of not less than three years nor more than **ten years** and a fine: (1) Reproducing and distributing or **communicating to the public through an information network** any written work, musical work, **work of fine arts, audiovisual work**, computer software, or other work **set out by a law or administrative regulation without the permission of its copyright owner** (2) Publishing any book of which another person has the exclusive right of publication (3) Reproducing and distributing or **communicating to the public through an information network** any audio or video recording without the permission of its producer (4) **Reproducing and distributing any audio or video recording of, or communicating to the public through an information network, any performance without the permission of its performer** (5) Producing or selling any work of fine arts on which the signature of author is fake (6) **Intentionally evading or disrupting the technical measures taken by a copyright owner or the holder of a right related to the copyright to protect the copyright or right related to the copyright in a work or audio or video recording, among others, without the permission of the copyright owner or right holder**
Article 218. Whoever, for the purpose of reaping profits, knowingly sells the duplicate works described in Article 217 of this Law, and gains a huge amount of illicit income, is to be sentenced to not more than <u>three years</u> of fixed-term imprisonment, <u>criminal detention</u>, and may in addition or exclusively be sentenced to a fine	**Article 218.** Whoever, for profits, knowingly sells any infringing reproductions set forth in Article 217 of this Law shall, if the amount of illegal income is huge **or there is any other especially serious circumstance**, be sentenced to imprisonment of not more than **five years** and a fine or be sentenced to a fine only

(continued)

1 Main Amendments of Chinese Intellectual Property Law

(continued)

Before the amendment (effective November 4, 2017)	After the amendment (effective March 1, 2021)
Article 219. Whoever engages in one of the following activities which encroaches upon commercial secrets and <u>brings significant losses to persons having the rights to the commercial secrets</u> is to be sentenced to not more than three years of fixed-term imprisonment, <u>criminal detention,</u> and may in addition or exclusively be sentenced to a fine; or is to be sentenced to not less than three years and not more than <u>seven years</u> of fixed-term imprisonment and a fine, <u>if he causes particularly serious consequences</u>: (1) acquire a rightful owner's commercial secrets via theft, <u>lure by promise of gain</u>, threat, or other improper means; (2) disclose, use, or allow others to use a rightful owner's commercial secrets which are acquired through the aforementioned means; (3) disclose, use, or allow others to use, in violation of <u>the agreement with the rightful owner</u> or the rightful owner's request of keeping the commercial secrets, the commercial secrets he is holding Whoever <u>acquires, uses, or discloses</u> other people's commercial secrets, <u>when he knows or should know</u> that these commercial secrets are acquired through the aforementioned means, is regarded as an encroachment upon commercial secrets <u>The commercial secrets referred to in this article are technical information and operation information that are unknown to the public, can bring economic profits to their rightful owners, are functional, and are kept as secrets by their rightful owners</u> The rightful owners referred to in this Article are owners of the commercial secrets and users who have the permission of the owners	**Article 219.** Whoever commits any of the following conduct to infringe upon a trade secret shall, if **the circumstances are serious**, be sentenced to imprisonment of not more than three years and a fine or be sentenced to a fine only; or if **the circumstances are especially serious**, be sentenced to imprisonment of not less than three years nor more **ten years** and a fine: (1) Obtaining a right holder's trade secret by theft, **bribery**, **fraud**, coercion, **electronic intrusion**, or any other illicit means (2) Disclosing, using, or allowing any other person to use a trade secret obtained from a right holder by any means as mentioned in the preceding paragraph (3) Disclosing, using, or allowing any other person to use a trade secret known by him or her in violation of **confidentiality obligations** or the right holder's requirements for keeping the trade secret confidential **Whoever knows** any conduct set forth in the preceding paragraph but still **acquires, discloses, uses, or allows any other person to use** the trade secret shall be punished for infringing upon the trade secret For the purposes of this article, 'right holder' means the owner of a trade secret and any person permitted by the owner to use the trade secret
(Addition)	**Article 219 (I):** Whoever steals, pries into, buys, or illegally provides any trade secret for any overseas institution, organization, or individual shall be sentenced to imprisonment of not more than five years and a fine or be sentenced to a fine only; or if the circumstances are serious, be sentenced to imprisonment of not less than five years and a fine

(continued)

Before the amendment (effective November 4, 2017)	After the amendment (effective March 1, 2021)
Article 220. When a unit commits the crimes stated in Article 213 through Article 219, it is to be sentenced to a fine; its directly responsible person in charge and other personnel of direct responsibility should be punished in accordance with the stipulations respectively stated in these Articles of this section	**Article 220.** Where an entity commits a crime provided for in Article 213 through Article **219A** of this Section, the entity shall be sentenced to a fine, and its directly liable executive in charge and other directly liable persons shall be punished in accordance with the provisions of the aforesaid articles of this Section respectively

1.6.2 Interpretation (III) of the Supreme People's Court and the Supreme People's Procuratorate of Several Issues Concerning the Specific Application of Law in the Handling of Criminal Cases Involving Infringements upon Intellectual Property Rights

(Interpretation No.10 [2020], SPC, adopted at the 1811th Session of the Judicial Committee of the Supreme People's Court on August 31, 2020 and the 48th Session of the Thirteenth Procuratorial Committee of the Supreme People's Procuratorate on August 21, 2020, and coming into force on September 14, 2020).

For the purposes of legally punishing the crimes of infringements upon intellectual property rights and maintaining the order of socialist market economy, in accordance with the Criminal Law of the People's Republic of China, the Criminal Procedure Law of the People's Republic of China, and other relevant provisions, several issues concerning the specific application of law in the handling of criminal cases involving infringements upon intellectual property rights are hereby interpreted as follows:

Article 1 Any of the following circumstances may be determined as a "trademark identical to a registered trademark" as set forth in Article 213 of the Criminal Law:

(1) Changing the font, letter case, or horizontal or vertical layout of characters of the registered trademark, so that it basically has no difference from the registered trademark.
(2) Changing the space between characters, letters or figures, among others, of the registered trademark, so that it basically has no difference from the registered trademark.
(3) Changing the color of the registered trademark without affecting the distinctive features of the registered trademark.
(4) Adding to the registered trademark the factor lacking distinctive features such as the common name or model of the goods only without affecting the distinctive features of the registered trademark.

(5) Having basically no difference from the three-dimensional mark and graphic element of the stereoscopic registered trademark.
(6) Any other trademark that has basically no difference from the registered trademark or is sufficient to mislead the public.

Article 2 A natural person, a legal person or an unincorporated organization that affixes the signature thereof in a common way to any work or sound recordings set forth in Article 217 of the Criminal Law shall be presumed to be the copyright owner or recording producer and have corresponding rights in relation to such work or sound recordings, unless there is any evidence to the contrary.

In a case involving multiple works or sound recordings and dispersed right holders, if there is any evidence proving that the reproduction involved in the case is illegally published or reproduced for distribution, and the publisher or reproduction distributor fails to provide relevant evidentiary materials proving that it has obtained the approval of the copyright owner or the recording producer, it may be determined as "without the approval of the copyright owner" or "without the approval of the sound recording producer" as provided for in Article 217 of the Criminal Law, except that there is any evidence proving that the right holder has waived the rights thereof, or the copyright of the work involved in the case or rights relating to the sound recordings are not protected by the Copyright Law of China, or the term for the protection of copyright has expired.

Article 3 Stealing any trade secret by such means as illegally reproducing and using without or beyond authorization a computer information system shall be determined as "theft" as provided for in subparagraph (1), paragraph 1 of Article 219 of the Criminal Law.

Where any trade secret of a right holder is obtained by such means as bribery, fraud, and electronic intrusion, such means shall be determined as "other illicit means" set forth in subparagraph (1), paragraph 1 of Article 219 of the Criminal Law.

Article 4 Any act prescribed in Article 219 of the Criminal Law committed under any of the following circumstances shall be determined as "causing heavy loss to the right holder of the trade secret":

(1) The amount of loss caused to the right holder of the trade secret or the amount of illegal income obtained from the infringement upon the trade secret is 300,000 yuan or more.
(2) It directly causes the bankruptcy or closure of the right holder of the trade secret due to great difficulty in operation.
(3) Any other heavy loss is caused to the right holder of the trade secret.

Where the amount of loss caused to the right holder of the trade secret or the amount of illegal income obtained from the infringement upon the trade secret is 2.5 million yuan or more, it shall be determined as "causing particularly serious consequences" as provided for in Article 219 of the Criminal Law.

Article 5 The amount of loss caused by or the amount of illegal income obtained from committing any of the conduct set forth in Article 219 of the Criminal Law may be determined according to the following methods:

(1) Where any trade secret of the right holder obtained by improper means has not been disclosed, used or allowed to be used by any other person, the amount of loss may be determined based on the reasonable royalty of the trade secret.
(2) Where the trade secret of the right holder obtained by improper means is disclosed, used or allowed to be used by any other person, the amount of loss may be determined based on the loss of sales profit caused by the right holder due to infringement, but the amount of loss shall be determined based on the reasonable royalty of the trade secret if it is lower than the reasonable royalty.
(3) Where the possessed trade secret is disclosed, used or allowed to be used by any other person in violation of the agreement or the requirements of the right holder for keeping the trade secret confidential, the amount of loss may be determined based on the loss of the sales profit caused by the right holder due to the infringement.
(4) Where the trade secret is obtained, used or disclosed with clear knowledge that the trade secret is obtained by improper means or in violation of the agreement or the requirements of the right holder on keeping the trade secret confidential, the amount of loss may be determined based on the loss of the sales profit caused by the right holder due to the infringement.
(5) Where any trade secret has been known by the public or lost due to the infringement upon the trade secret, the amount of loss may be determined based on the commercial value of the trade secret. The commercial value of the trade secret may be determined comprehensively based on the research and development cost of the trade secret and the proceeds obtained from the exploitation of the trade secret.
(6) Property or any other property interest obtained from disclosing or permitting any other person to use the trade secret shall be determined as illegal income.

The loss of sales profit caused by the right holder due to the infringement as set forth in subparagraph (2), (3) or (4) of the preceding paragraph may be determined based on the total of decreased sales volume of the right holder due to the infringement multiplied by the reasonable profit of the right holder from each product; if the total of the decreased sales volume cannot be determined, the loss may be determined based on the sales volume of infringing products multiplied by the reasonable profit obtained by the right holder from each product; if neither the total of decreased sales volume of the right holder due to the infringement and the reasonable profit from each product cannot be determined, the loss may be determined based on the sales volume of infringing products multiplied by the reasonable profit of each infringing product. If the trade secret is used for services or any other business activities, the amount of loss may be determined based on the decreased reasonable profit of the right holder due to the infringement.

The remedial expenses incurred to the right holder of a trade secret for the purpose of mitigating the damage to business operation or business plan or restoring the security of the computer information system or any other system shall be included in the loss caused to the right holder of the trade secret.

Article 6 Where a party, a defender, an agent ad litem or a person that is not a party to the case applies in writing to keep confidential the evidence or materials on relevant trade secrets or other business information that needs to be kept confidential in criminal proceedings, necessary confidentiality measures such as organizing participants in proceedings to sign a written confidentiality commitment shall be taken in light of case circumstances.

Whoever violates the requirements of the preceding paragraph regarding confidentiality measures or the confidentiality obligation as provided for by laws and regulations shall assume corresponding liability in accordance with the law. Whoever discloses, uses or allows any other person to use any trade secret accessed or obtained in criminal proceedings without authorization shall be held criminally liable in accordance with the law if it complies with Article 219 of the Criminal Law.

Article 7 Except under special circumstances, the goods bearing counterfeit registered trademarks, illegally produced logos of registered trademarks, reproductions infringing copyright, as well as materials and tools mainly used for manufacturing the goods bearing counterfeit registered trademarks, logos of registered trademarks or infringing reproductions shall be confiscated and destroyed in accordance with the law.

Where any of the aforesaid articles need to be used as evidence in a civil or administrative case, upon application by the right holder, they may be destroyed after the civil or administrative case is concluded or after the evidence is fixed by such methods as sampling and photographing.

Article 8 Whoever falls under any of the following circumstances may be given a heavier punishment as the case may be, to which probation shall generally not apply.

(1) Taking the infringement upon intellectual property rights as the main business.
(2) Infringing upon intellectual property rights once again, which constitutes a crime, after being imposed on an administrative punishment due to the infringement upon intellectual property rights.
(3) Counterfeiting the registered trademark of the goods for emergency rescue and disaster relief or epidemic prevention, among others, during the period of a major natural disaster, accident or disaster, or a public health incident.
(4) Refusing to surrender the illegal income.

Article 9 Whoever falls under any of the following circumstances may be imposed on a lighter punishment as the case may be:

(1) Pleading guilty and accepting punishment.
(2) Obtaining the forgiveness of the right holder.
(3) Showing repentance.
(4) Not disclosing, using or permitting any other person to use the trade secret of the right holder obtained by improper means.

Article 10 Whoever commits a crime of infringement upon intellectual property rights shall be legally imposed on a fine by taking into comprehensive consideration such circumstances as the amount of criminal and illegal income, the amount of illegal operation, the amount of loss caused to a right holder, the quantity of infringing and counterfeit articles and the severity of social harm.

The amount of fine shall generally be determined as not less than one time nor more than five times the amount of illegal income. If the amount of illegal income cannot be ascertained, the amount of fine shall generally be determined as not less than 50% nor more than one time the amount of illegal operation. If neither the amount of illegal income nor the amount of illegal operation can be ascertained, and a sentence of fixed-term imprisonment of not more than three years, criminal detention, public surveillance or a separate fine is imposed, the amount of fine shall generally be determined as not less than 30,000 yuan nor more than one million yuan; and if a sentence of fixed-term imprisonment of not less than three years is imposed, the amount of fine shall generally be determined as not less than 150,000 yuan nor more than five million yuan.

Article 11 For any discrepancies between this Interpretation and judicial interpretations and regulatory documents issued previously before this Interpretation comes into force, this Interpretation shall prevail.

Article 12 This Interpretation shall come into force on September 14, 2020.

1.6.3 Notice by the Supreme People's Procuratorate and the Ministry of Public Security of Issuing the Decision on Amending the Criteria for Launching Formal Investigation into Criminal Cases of Infringement upon Trade Secrets

(Announced at September 17, 2020 by Supreme People's Procuratorate Ministry of Public Security and coming into force on September 17, 2020).

For the purposes of punishing crimes of infringement upon trade secrets in accordance with the law, intensifying the criminal judicial protection of intellectual property rights, and maintaining the economic order of the socialist market, Article 73 Criteria for Launching Formal Investigation into Criminal Cases of Infringement upon Trade Secrets of the Provisions of the Supreme People's Procuratorate and the Ministry of Public Security on the Criteria for Launching Formal Investigation into Criminal Cases under the Jurisdiction of Public Security Organs (II) are amended to read: [Cases of Infringement upon Trade Secrets (Article 219 of the Criminal Law)] Infringement upon a trade secret being suspected of falling under one of the following circumstances shall be subject to formal investigation:

(1) The amount of losses caused to the right holder of a trade secret is more than 300,000 yuan.
(2) The amount of illegal gains from infringement of a trade secret is more than 300,000 yuan.
(3) Bankruptcy and closedown of the right holder of a trade secret due to major operation difficulty which is directly caused by the infringement.
(4) Other circumstances causing major losses to the right holders of trade secrets.

The amount of losses or illegal gains caused as specified in the preceding paragraph may be determined by the following means:

(1) Where the trade secret of a right holder is obtained by the violator by inappropriate means, and is not disclosed, used or allowed to be used by others, the amount of losses may be determined based on the reasonable licensing fees for the trade secret.
(2) Where, after the trade secret of a right holder is obtained by the violator by inappropriate means, it is disclosed, used or allowed to be used by others, the

amount of losses may be determined based on the losses of the right holder's sales profits caused by the infringement, but where the amount of losses is lower than the reasonable licensing fees for the trade secret, it shall be determined based on the reasonable licensing fees.

(3) Where a trade secret obtained is disclosed, used or allowed to be used by others in violation of the agreement and the requirements of the right holder for keeping trade secrets, the amount of losses may be determined based on the losses of the right holder's sales profits due to the infringement.

(4) Where it is known perfectly well that a trade secret is obtained by inappropriate means, or disclosed, used, or allowed to be used in violation of the agreement and the right holder's requirements for the protection of trade secrets, it is still obtained, used or disclosed, the amount of losses may be determined based on the losses of the right holder's sales profits due to the infringement.

(5) Where a trade secret has been known to the public or has been lost due to infringement upon a trade secret, the amount of losses may be determined based on the commercial value of the trade secret. The commercial value of a trade secret may be comprehensively determined based on the research and development costs of the trade secret and the benefits from the implementation of the trade secret.

(6) The property or other property benefits obtained by disclosing or allowing others to use trade secrets shall be deemed illegal gains.

The losses of sales profits caused by the infringement upon a right holder as specified in Items (2), (3) and (4) of the preceding paragraph may be determined by multiplying the total amount of sales reduction caused by the infringement upon the right holder by the reasonable profits of each product of the right holder. Where the total number of sales reductions cannot be determined, it may be determined by multiplying the sales volume of the infringed product by the right holder's reasonable profits per product. And where the right holder's total sales reduction due to infringement and the reasonable profits of each product cannot be determined, it can be determined by multiplying the sales volume of infringed products by the reasonable profits of each infringed product. Where a trade secret is used in other business activities such as services, the amount of losses may be determined based on the reasonable profits of the right holder reduced by the infringement.

The remedial expenses paid by the right holder of a trade secret for reducing the losses of business operation or business plans or restoring the security of computer information systems and other systems shall be included in the losses caused to the right holder of the trade secret.

Open Access This chapter is licensed under the terms of the Creative Commons Attribution 4.0 International License (http://creativecommons.org/licenses/by/4.0/), which permits use, sharing, adaptation, distribution and reproduction in any medium or format, as long as you give appropriate credit to the original author(s) and the source, provide a link to the Creative Commons license and indicate if changes were made.

The images or other third party material in this chapter are included in the chapter's Creative Commons license, unless indicated otherwise in a credit line to the material. If material is not included in the chapter's Creative Commons license and your intended use is not permitted by statutory regulation or exceeds the permitted use, you will need to obtain permission directly from the copyright holder.

Chapter 2
Main Amendments of Germany Patent Act (2021)

Xinmiao Yu and Yuhan Tang

The **Second Act to Simplify and Modernise Patent Law** were promulgated in the Federal Law Gazette (BGBl. I p.3490) on 17 August 2021. The **Act on Further Duties of the German Patent and Trade Mark Office and to Revise the Patent Costs Act** were promulgated in the Federal Law Gazette (BGBl. I p.4074) on 7 September 2021.

The purpose of the **Second Patent Law Modernisation Act** is to simplify and modernise the Patent Act (Patentgesetz) and other IP laws. The amendments relevant to the procedures before the Germany Patent and Trademark Office (DPMA) are contained in several articles. They concern overarching issues in the IP Acts and in the Ordinance Concerning the German Patent and Trade Mark Office (DPMA Verordnung, see A.1) as well as provisions in individual acts and ordinances and in the Act on International Patent Conventions (Gesetz über internationale Patentübereinkommen, see A.2 to A.5). In addition, there are fee amendments (see A.6).

The omnibus act will enter into force on 18 August 2021. Those amendments that require adjustments to the IT systems of the DPMA will enter into force on 1 May 2022. Main changes are as follows:

1. General provisions for all IP procedures
2. Patent procedures and procedures for supplementary protection certificates
3. Utility Model Procedures
4. Trade mark procedures
5. Design procedures
6. Fee provisions
7. Injunctions

X. Yu (✉) · Y. Tang
Shanghai International College of Intellectual Property, Tongji University, Shanghai, China
e-mail: Yuxm@tongji.edu.cn

Patent Act of Germany (English version) can be available on website: https://www.gesezte-im-internet.de/englisch_patg/index.thml, Patent Act of Germany (German version) can be available on website: https://www.gesezte-im-internet.de/patg/

2.1 General Provisions for All IP Procedures

(a) Participation in hearings, proceedings and giving evidence by using image and sound transmission (entry into force: 1 May 2022).

For procedures under the Patent Act, the Utility Model Act (Gebrauchsmustergesetz), the Trade Mark Act (Markengesetz), the Design Act (Designgesetz) and the Semiconductor Protection Act (Halbleiterschutzgesetz), the option of participating in hearings, proceedings, and giving evidence by means of image and sound transmission shall be provided by analogously applying Sect. 128a of the Code of Civil Procedure (Zivilprozessordnung—hearings for oral argument and examinations before the civil courts) (Sect. 46 (1) of the Patent Act, Sect. 17 (2) sentence 6 of the Utility Model Act, Sect. 60 (1) sentence 2 of the Trade Mark Act, Sect. 34a (3) sentence 4 of the Design Act, Sect. 8 (5) of the Semiconductor Protection Act).

Parties can participate in sessions by video conferencing in suitable cases to be decided by the DPMA. It will still be possible to physically be present in order to participate in the sessions on site. These options will be available as soon as the necessary internal technical infrastructure has been established. The DPMA will provide further details in a separate notification.

(b) Uniform rules on public holidays for all DPMA locations (entry into force: 1 May 2022).

All public holidays applicable at at least one of the DPMA locations will be recognised for the purpose of extending a time limit, irrespective of the location where the act required to meet the time limit is actually performed (Sect. 18a of the DPMA Ordinance). The acts and declarations that are subject to a time limit can be performed or made at all three DPMA locations in Munich, Jena and Berlin in order to meet the time limit. In the future, this will eliminate legal uncertainties when calculating a time limit if public holidays that are not uniformly observed throughout Germany fall within that period.

(c) Restriction of the obligation to publish and of the right to inspect files in the case of contents that are obviously contrary to public policy (entry into force: 18 August 2021).

In future, the publication of patent and trade mark applications with obviously morally offensive contents is to be avoided by restricting the obligation to publish (Sect. 32 (2) of the Patent Act, Sect. 33 (3) of the Trade Mark Act). Similarly, the right to inspect files will be excluded across all types of IP rights insofar as the file contains elements that are obviously contrary to public policy or morality (Sect. 31 (3b) of the Patent Act, Sect. 8 (7) of the Utility Model Act, Sect. 62 (4) of the Trade Mark Act, Sect. 22 (3) of the Design Act). This is to prevent the official publication and register database of the DPMA, which is accessible to everyone on the Internet, from being used for the dissemination of contents obviously contrary to public policy or morality. Since the exclusion of publication and inspection is limited to the contents of the files that are contrary to public policy, the interest of the general public in obtaining information is not affected.

2.2 Patent Procedures and Procedures for Supplementary Protection Certificates

(a) Extension of the period for PCT applications to enter the national phase (entry into force: 1 May 2022).

The **period for PCT applications to enter the national phase** will be extended from 30 to 31 months from the filing date or priority date, as the case may be. In future, applicants will have one more month to pay the fee for entry into the national phase at the DPMA and, if applicable, to submit the German translation of the application (Article III Sects. 2.4 and 2.6 of the Act on International Patent Conventions).

(b) Simplifying the change of parties in opposition proceedings (entry into force: 1 May 2022).

The change of parties in opposition proceedings in case of a change in the proprietor will be simplified and streamlined. In future, the person newly entered as right holder in the register may take the place of the former right holder in ongoing opposition proceedings without the consent of the other parties to the proceedings (Sect. 30 (3) sentence 3 of the Patent Act).

(c) Expansion of the examination of obvious deficiencies (entry into force: 18 August 2021).

The examination of obvious deficiencies of a patent application by the Examining Section will be expanded to include the exclusions from patentability under Sect. 2.1a (1) of the Patent Act (human body) and Sect. 2.2a (1) of the Patent Act (plants and animals) (Sect. 42 (2) No. 3 of the Patent Act).

(d) Naming of the inventor (entry into force: 1 May 2022).

It is clarified by law that the inventor may be mentioned by name and an indication of the place in patent publications and in the register. The mention will be omitted completely or with regard to the indication of the place if the inventor designated by the applicant so requests (Sect. 63 (1) of the Patent Act).

(e) Revocation and further processing of supplementary protection certificates (entry into force: 18 August 2021).

In line with existing practice, it is clarified by law that supplementary protection certificates may be revoked upon request of the proprietor under Sect. 64 of the Patent Act and that the procedural option of further processing (Sect. 123a of the Patent Act) also applies to supplementary protection certificates (Sect. 16a (2) of the Patent Act).

2.3 Utility Model Procedures

(a) Simplifying the utility model splitting-off procedure (entry into force: 1 May 2022).

In future, the requirement to file a copy of the patent application or its translation will no longer exist in the utility model splitting-off procedure if these documents have already been filed with the DPMA in the context of applying for a patent (Sect. 2.5 of the Utility Model Act, Sect. 8 of the Utility Model Ordinance [Gebrauchsmusterverordnung]).

(b) Simplifying the utility model cancellation procedure (entry into force: 1 May 2022).

The utility model cancellation procedure will become more efficient (Sect. 17(2) to (5) of the Utility Model Act). In future, a hearing will only take place—similar to the hearing in patent opposition proceedings—if requested by a party or if the DPMA considers it expedient (Sect. 17(2) to (3) of the Utility Model Act). In addition, more flexibility will be introduced to the decision on costs (Sect. 17 (4) of the Utility Model Act). If no decision is made on the merits of the case, a decision on the costs will only be made upon request. If no decision on costs is issued, each party bears their own costs. In future, the Utility Model Division as judicial panel may also determine the value of the matter (Sect. 17(5) of the Utility Model Act).

2.4 Trade Mark Procedures

(a) Harmonisation with the current legal situation of the Madrid system (entry into force: 1 May 2022).

The Trade Mark Act, the Trade Mark Ordinance (Markenverordnung) and the schedule of fees are brought into line with the current legal situation of the Madrid system (Sects. 107 et seq. of the Trade Mark Act, Sect. 25 No. 31, Sects. 43, 45 and 46 (1) of the Trade Mark Ordinance, Part A section III No. 5 of the annex to Sect. 2.2

(1) of the Patent Costs Act). Since 31 October 2015, all members of the Madrid Agreement are also members of the Protocol to the Madrid Agreement. Due to the fact that the Protocol to the Madrid Agreement takes priority over the Madrid Agreement, the international registration of marks is now only governed by the Protocol to the Madrid Agreement. This is taken into account by the amendments.

(b) Clarifying the calculation of the duration of protection in the Trade Mark Act (entry into force: 18 August 2021).

The provisions on the duration of protection in the Trade Mark Act and in the European Union Trade Mark Regulation will be completely harmonised as regards their wording. In order to facilitate the calculation of the time limit, it is clarified by means of the harmonisation that Sect. 47 (1) of the Trade Mark Act – just as the European Union Trade Mark Regulation – refers to a time period that is triggered by an event. The calculation of the duration of protection will not be changed as a result of the amendment.

2.5 Design Procedures

(a) Requirement to hold sessions in design procedures abolished (entry into force: 18 August 2021).

The Design Division will be allowed to take decisions without a session (for example, by way of written procedure) (Sect. 2.6 (3) of the DPMA Ordinance). This places the Design Division on a par with the divisions in other IP proceedings, for which no session is required either.

(b) Ex officio determination of the value of the matter in design procedures (entry into force: 18 August 2021).

In future, it will be possible to determine the value of the matter in design procedures ex officio (Sect. 34a (6) of the Design Act). The purpose is to simplify the procedure and accelerate the subsequent determination of costs.

2.6 Fee Provisions

(a) Fee reduction for joint proprietors or applicants of an IP right (entry into force: 18 August 2021).

In procedures before the DPMA, in which a legal remedy can only be sought by the person in possession of an IP right, the fees will no longer be determined according to the number of proprietors or applicants. For reasons of fee fairness, joint proprietors or applicants are treated as one person for fee purposes (part A Sect. 2.2 of the annex to Sect. 2.2 (1) of the Patent Costs Act). The same fee reduction is granted to joint proprietors or applicants of an affected IP right in appeal proceedings if they jointly file an appeal (part B Sect. 2.1 of the annex to Sect. 2.2 (1) Patent Costs Act).

(b) Due date for payment of annual fees for supplementary protection certificates (entry into force: 1 May 2022).

For determining the due date of payment of the annual fees for supplementary protection certificates, the special circumstances of the individual grant procedures will be taken into account to a greater extent in the interest of the proprietors (Sect. 2.3 (2) sentences 3 and 4 of the Patent Costs Act). This refers in particular to special situations where the supplementary protection certificate is granted only after the IP term has started.

(c) Advance payment of annual fees for supplementary protection certificates (entry into force: 1 May 2022).

In the future, it will be possible to make a legally effective advance payment of the annual fees for supplementary protection certificates more than one year before the due date so as to simplify administrative matters for applicants and the DPMA (Sect. 2.5(2) sentence 3 of the Patent Costs Act).

(d) Fee increase for supplementary protection certificates (entry into force: 1 May 2022).

The annual fees for supplementary protection certificates will be moderately raised given the increased efforts involved in the examination (Nos. 312 210 to 312 261 of the annex to the Patent Costs Act (schedule of fees)). Please refer to the provisions concerning the application of the previous fee rates in certain cases under Sect. 13 of the Patent Costs Act.

(e) Switching back from the "one-class model" to the "three-class model" for the conversion of a European Union trade mark into a national trade mark (entry into force: 1 May 2022).

For the conversion of a European Union trade mark into a national trade mark, what is known as the "three-class model" will be reintroduced into the fee system (part A, section III, No. 5 of the annex to Sect. 2.2 (1) of the Patent Costs Act). Under the up to now applicable "one-class model", the conversion of European Union trade marks into national trade marks results in higher fees compared to a national trade mark application, for which the "three-class model" applies, although the examination effort is basically the same. This will be remedied by the amendment.

2.7 Injunctions

(a) No injunction in case of hardship.

Previously, under §139 of the German Patent Act, an injunction against an infringer was automatic. If the infringement was proven, the court had to grant the injunction, irrespective of the particulars of the case. In recent years, this automatism has come under attack, in particular in patent infringement cases involving complex products, where the grant of an injunction based on a patent on a small component of the product could be particularly damaging to the alleged infringer. To address this, §139 of the German Patent Act now stipulates that:

"The injunction is excluded insofar as it would lead to disproportionate hardship for the infringer or third parties not justified by the exclusive right due to the special circumstances of the individual case and the requirements of good faith. In this case, the infringed party shall be granted appropriate compensation in money. The claim for damages according to paragraph 2 shall remain unaffected."

Accordingly, from now on, the German courts may refuse an injunction in case of "disproportionate hardship for the infringer". There seems to be a consensus among experts that this new remedy should only apply in very exceptional cases.

(b) German nullity Actions—Reducing the injunction gap

Germany is one of the few countries where patents are litigated in parallel at two different courts: at the district court to assess patent infringement, and at the federal patent court to decide on the patent's validity.

This has led to the so-called "injunction gap". The injunction gap is a consequence of the time lag between the infringement and the nullity proceedings: the German district courts are much quicker in deciding on infringement than the federal patent court in deciding on validity.

The injunction gap can be a serious problem for an alleged infringer who may face a situation where they must comply with a cease-and-desist order handed down by the district court while the patent's validity is still being scrutinised by the federal patent court.

To mitigate this problem, the German Patent Act now provides for shorter deadlines in the nullity proceedings at the federal patent court. From now on:

"the patentee must submit his full reply to the nullity action within two months of its notification;"

"the federal patent court should provide its preliminary opinion within six months to the parties and to the district court dealing with the infringement. This six-month deadline is however not mandatory."

(b) Act on Further Duties of the German Patent and Trade Mark Office and to Revise the Patent Costs Act

Increase in annual fees for patents (entry into force: 1 July 2022).

The annual fees for the maintenance of patent applications or patents (Sect. 17 of the Patent Act) will be moderately increased (numbers 312 050 to 312 207 of the annex to the Patent Costs Act (schedule of fees)). The increase takes into account the drop in the fee level caused by inflation since 1999. The change in fees will come into force on 1 July 2022. Please refer to the provisions concerning the application of the previous fee rates in certain cases under Sect. 13 of the Patent Costs Act.

Open Access This chapter is licensed under the terms of the Creative Commons Attribution 4.0 International License (http://creativecommons.org/licenses/by/4.0/), which permits use, sharing, adaptation, distribution and reproduction in any medium or format, as long as you give appropriate credit to the original author(s) and the source, provide a link to the Creative Commons license and indicate if changes were made.

The images or other third party material in this chapter are included in the chapter's Creative Commons license, unless indicated otherwise in a credit line to the material. If material is not included in the chapter's Creative Commons license and your intended use is not permitted by statutory regulation or exceeds the permitted use, you will need to obtain permission directly from the copyright holder.

Chapter 3
Cases

Klaus Bacher, Ann Bartow, Lanqing Ge, Pengfei Huang, and Lu Jin

3.1 Civil Cases on Patent Infringement

3.1.1 Patent Cases from Germany

(1) **The criteria for application of exhaustion of patent right—Case of "Drum Unit" (Case No. X ZR 55/16)**

1.1 Syllabus:
The case illustrates that the patentee's possibilities to avoid exhaustion by tailoring the patent claims are limited. It is generally up to the patentee to define the product for which he claims protection. As long as the patent covers products which are available on the market, the patentee's decision may be relevant for the question of exhaustion. In the current case, the patent also covered a toner cartridge containing a photoelectric drum and a coupling member, and also a laser printer or copier containing such a cartridge. Both products are available on the market. However, replacing the photosensitive drum may not be viewed as remanufacturing such a product. This could give an incentive to claim protection for a product where the

---
Ann Bartow: She is responsible for compiling cases of America.

K. Bacher
Federal Court of Justice of Germany, Karlsruhe, Germany

A. Bartow
University of New Hampshire, New Hampshire, USA

L. Ge (✉)
Shanghai International College of Intellectual Property, Tongji University, Shanghai, China

P. Huang
Shanghai Institute of Quality Inspection and Technical Research (SQI), Shanghai, China

L. Jin
Pudong New District People's Court, Shanghai, China

© Tongji University Press Co. Ltd. 2025
D. Cheng et al. (eds.), *New Progress of Regulations and Judicial Practice of Intellectual Property*, https://doi.org/10.1007/978-981-97-6095-4_3

photosensitive drum forms a major part. Due to the new decision, this strategy only works if this product is also available on the market—which was not the case here.

1.2 Rules:
Directive 2009/125/EG, Patent Act, Sec. 9(2), No. 1
Directive 2009/125/EG

No third-party rights arise from a voluntary agreement in which companies have made commitments to the European Commission to adhere to certain standards for the purpose of environmental protection in order to avoid a compulsory measure under Art. 15 of Directive 2009/125/EC.

Patent Act, Sec. 9(2), No. 1

a) In assessing the question of whether the replacement of parts of an apparatus put into circulation with the permission of the patent holder falls under intended use or represents a new manufacture, the protected product must be considered as a decisive point of reference. This is also the case when the patent holder has put one exemplar of the protected product (here: an image drum unit) into circulation as a component of an object comprising more components (here: a process cartridge).

b) When a patent claim protects a product consisting of several parts and yet the patent holder only puts objects on the market that encompass yet further components, and thus an actual opinion of the relevant public with regard to the protected product cannot be ascertained, the delineation between intended use and new manufacture must be based solely upon whether the technical results of the invention are reflected in precisely the replaced parts (amendment to the decision of 17 July 2012—X ZR 97/11, GRUR 2012, 1118—Palettenbehälter II). Decision of the Federal Supreme Court (Bundesgerichtshof); 24 October 2017.

1.3 Facts:

The plaintiff raises a claim against the defendant for direct patent infringement by the sale of remanufactured toner cartridges for laser printers and similar equipment.

The plaintiff is the proprietor of European patent No.2087407 (patent in suit) granted with effect for the Federal Republic of Germany, which concerns among other things a photosensitive drum unit for an electrophotographic image-forming apparatus. Patent claim No. 1 reads:

An electrophotographic photosensitive drum unit (B) usable with a main assembly of an electrophotographic image forming apparatus, the main assembly including a driving shaft (180) to be driven by a motor, having a rotational force applying portion, wherein said electrophotographic drum unit is dismountable from the main assembly in a dismounting direction substantially perpendicular to an axial direction (L3) of the driving shaft, said electrophotographic drum unit comprising:

i) An electrophotographic photosensitive drum (107) having a photosensitive layer (107b) at a peripheral surface thereof, said electrophotographic photosensitive drum being rotatable about an axis (L1) thereof;

ii) a coupling member (150) rotatable about an axis (L2) thereof, engageable with the driving shaft (180) to receive a rotational force, from the rotational force applying portion, for rotating said electrophotographic photosensitive drum (107) said coupling member is provided at an axial end of said electrophotographic photosensitive drum (107) such that said coupling member (150) is capable of taking a rotational force transmitting angular position substantially co-axial with said axis (L1) of said electrophotographic photosensitive drum (107) for transmitting the rotational force for rotating said electrophotographic photosensitive drum (107) to said electrophotographic photosensitive drum (107) and a disengaging angular position in which said coupling member (150) is inclined away from the axis (11) of said electrophotographic photosensitive drum (107) from said rotational force transmitting angular position for disengagement of the coupling member (150) from the driving shaft (180).

Wherein said electrophotographic drum unit (B) is adapted such that when said electrophotographic drum unit (B) is dismounted from the main assembly in the dismounting direction substantially perpendicular to the axis (L1) of said electrophotographic photosensitive drum (107) said coupling member (150) moves from said rotational force transmitting angular position to said disengaging angular position.

Patent claim 25 places a cartridge under protection encompassing a drum unit with the features from patent claim 1 or one of the sub-claims referring to claim 1; patent claim 29 protects an electrophotographic image-forming apparatus that encompasses a driving shaft and a drum unit with the features from patent claim 1.

The plaintiff produces toner cartridges that include a drum unit with an image drum, a flange and a coupling member (so-called process cartridges), and sells these as original equipment and consumable material for the copying machines and printers it sells. Some of its products are sold by a different supplier under the latter's brand name.

The plaintiff concluded a voluntary agreement with other suppliers ... in which it commits to adhering to certain standards for the purpose of environmental protection. No. 4.4 of the version applying to the case at hand, Version 4 of 3 December 2012, reads:

4.4 Cartridges

For all products placed on the market after 1 January 2012:

4.4.1 Any cartridge produced by or recommended by the OEM for use in the product shall not be designed to prevent its reuse and recycling.

4.4.2 The machine shall not be designed to prevent the use of a non-OEM cartridge. The requirements of paragraph 4.4 shall not be interpreted in such a way that would prevent or limit innovation, development or improvements in design or functionality of the products, cartridges, etc.

Defendant 1 sells in Germany, through defendant 3 among others, recycled process cartridges that can be used in place of the plaintiff's original cartridges. Defendant 2 is the chief executive of defendant 1 and managing director of defendant 3.

For recycling defendant 1 uses used cartridges that were originally put on the market by the plaintiff. In doing so, defendant 1 replaces the expended image drum and, if necessary, the flange as well with new, functionally identical parts that do not stem from the plaintiff. Out of these components and an original coupling member it makes a functional drum unit, which it installs in the used cartridge.

As requested in the statements of claim, which rely on patent claim 1, the district court sentenced the defendants to cease-and-desist, disclosure and rendering of accounts, and sentenced defendants 1 and 3 additionally to destruction and recall, and declared the defendants obligated to pay the plaintiff damage compensation. The defendants' appeal was unsuccessful. With their appeal on the law, which was admitted by the court of appeal, the defendants further pursue their request to dismiss the claim. The plaintiff opposes the appeal.

1.4 Reasoning:
The admissible appeal on the law is well founded and leads to the dismissal of the action.

1. The patent in suit concerns a process cartridge, an electrophotographic image-forming apparatus (hereinafter: "the device") and an electrophotographic photosensitive drum unit.

According to the description of the patent in suit, devices were well known in the prior art in which the image drum is arranged in a removable process cartridge and attached by a projection with a driving shaft. That the driving shaft has to be demounted horizontally away from the cartridge for installation and deinstallation is found to be a disadvantage of this embodiment. Against this background, the patent in suit concerns the technical problem of simplifying the mounting and demounting of the cartridge.

To solve this problem, the patent in suit in patent claim 1 suggests a drum unit whose features can be outlined as reproduced above. The coupling member (150) is of central significance. It facilitates the installation and deinstallation of the cartridge without a horizontal motion of the driving shaft, because it can be pivoted between two different angular positions.

This function is illustrated in Fig. 3.1 of the patent in suit:

The court of appeal rightly arrived at the conclusion that the defence based on the voluntary agreement with other manufacturers of unlawful exercise of a right pursuant to Sec. 242 of the Civil Code is unfounded.

a) The voluntary agreement does not establish any legal positions to the benefit of private third parties. According to No. 7.1 of the agreement, the signatories adopted the commitments provided for therein with vis-à-vis the European Commission. No indications can be gathered from the agreement, that beyond this, third persons should also be granted rights or legal positions. ...

b) In view of this, the court of appeal likewise rightly arrived at the conclusion that the voluntary agreement can establish neither a violation of trust in favour of the defendants, nor any other point of reference for an objection to the assertion of claims arising from a technical property right for devices, cartridges or their components.

From the perspective of a knowledgeable third party there is admittedly the justified expectation that the parties to the agreement will adhere to the commitments made therein, so as to avoid the issuing of compulsory measures by the Commission. At the same time, however, it is clear even to an outside observer that in the case of non-adherence to commitments, the sanctions provided for in the agreement—and

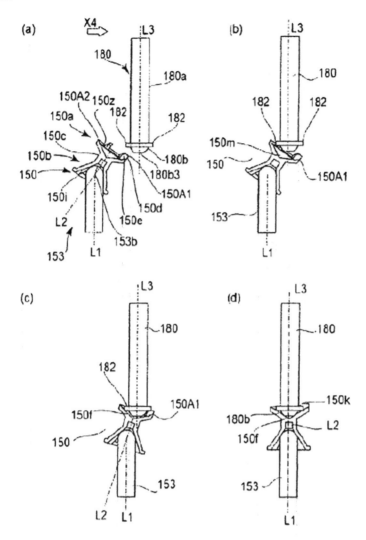

Fig. 3.1 Design figure of "Drum Unit"

if necessary an intervention on the part of the Commission—will settle the matter, and that an enforcement of whatever kind by third parties is not provided for.
2. Contrary to the view of the court of appeal, the defence of exhaustion brought by the defendants is justified.
a) According to the established case law of the Federal Supreme Court, the exclusive right arising from a patent concerning a product is exhausted with respect to such items of the protected product as have been put on the market by or with the permission of the patent holder. The rightful purchasers as well as third-party acquirers following them—including competitors of the patent proprietor—are authorized to

use these items as intended, sell them to third parties or offer them to third parties for one of these purposes [references omitted]. Use as intended includes maintenance and restoration of usability when the functionality or performance of the concrete item is partially or wholly compromised or lost due to wear, damage or for other reasons. Not included in intended use, on the other hand, are all measures resulting in the new manufacture of a product as described by the patent. The exclusive manufacturing authorization of the patent proprietor is not exhausted by the first sale of one item of the product covered by the patent.

b) The court of appeal saw as the decisive point of reference for the assessment of exhaustion, rightly in part, the product protected under patent claim 1.

aa) According to the case law of the Federal Supreme Court, the overall combination is decisive for the delineation between intended use and new manufacture [reference omitted]. This is the product protected according to the main patent claim. In accordance with this principle the Court decided—in a departure from older jurisprudence—that the manufacture of individual parts of a protected product cannot be seen as a direct patent infringement even when these parts are individualized to fulfil a function of the invention. In the installation of individual parts, therefore, the decisive point is whether this is to be seen as a new manufacture of a protected product with all features provided for in the patent claim [reference omitted].

bb) The product protected by virtue of the patent claim forms the decisive point of reference for distinguishing between intended use and new manufacture, even when the patent holder has put an item of it on the market as a component of a more comprehensive object.

(1) As the appeal on the law in part correctly asserts, and as the court of appeal also correctly considered, this question was not relevant for the previous decisions of the Federal Supreme Court on this topic. The Federal Supreme Court did in these decisions always consider the "total apparatus" as the pertinent point of reference [references omitted]. In all these cases, however, the patent protection referred to such a total apparatus, such that the terms "total apparatus" and "protected product" had the same meaning.

(2) For the situation to be evaluated in the case at hand, of the patent holder selling objects that encompass an item of the protected product, the same must be true—independent of whether the total apparatus in its turn is protected by a patent claim of the same or of a different patent.

If the total apparatus is also protected by patent, its being sold by the patent holder does indeed lead to the exhaustion of the respective exclusive right with respect to the entire object. A lawful purchaser is thus entitled to carry out on the total apparatus measures to maintain and restore its usability within the limits of intended use without this constituting an infringement of the patent protecting this product. This has no influence on a coexistent patent protection for individual components of the product, however. The rights to the two protected objects must, rather, be evaluated separately. If a measure with respect to the one object must be considered as intended use, but with respect to the other object as a new manufacture, only the exclusive rights concerning the total apparatus are therefore exhausted, but not those having respect to the component with independent protection.

The same must be true when the total apparatus is not protected by patent. In this situation, a lawful purchaser is free to use the total apparatus in any manner or even to re-manufacture it. From this, however, does not follow the authorization to remanufacture a component that is protected by patent. Putting the total apparatus on the market leads to an exhaustion of the existing exclusive rights in it, even as concerns its individual components. However, whether a measure is to be seen as intended use or as a new manufacture must, even in this situation, be evaluated with respect to the respective protected product.

From the principle established by the Court in another context that the patent holder can assert its exclusive rights one time only, namely, for the first sale of the patent-protected matter [reference omitted], no different assessment arises for the situation to be evaluated in the case at hand.

According to this principle, the patent holder may not reserve the intended use of a product it has itself put on the market on the basis of a patent claim whose subject-matter is exhausted in exactly this intended use, in the style of an instruction manual (BGH GRUR 1998, 130, 132—Handhabungsgerät).

This situation is not given in the case at hand.

The patent claim on which the action is based is indeed directed to the protection of a product that was put on the market with the plaintiff's permission as a component of a total apparatus. The subject matter of this patent claim, however, does not exhaust itself in an intended use of the protected product within the context of the use of the total apparatus. Rather, it encompasses every act of use, irrespective of whether it takes place in the context of the use of a total apparatus put on the market with the plaintiff's permission. Against this background, the new manufacture of such a product without the patent holder's permission is not allowed, even when it serves the intended use of a total apparatus put on the market with the permission of the patent holder.

From the protection regulated in Arts. 34 and 35 TFEU (Treaty on the Functioning of the European Union) of freedom of movement of goods there arises no differing conclusion. ...

For deciding in the case at hand, therefore, it is relevant whether the replacement of the image drum must be seen as a new manufacture of a drum unit in the sense of patent claim 1. Contrary to the view of the court of appeal, here one may not rely on a fictive opinion of the relevant public. Rather, the sole factor is whether the technical results of the invention are reflected in the replaced parts.

According to the case law of the Federal Supreme Court, in principle, what is primarily decisive in delineating the intended use from a new manufacture is whether the measures taken preserve the identity of the concrete item of a product according to the patent which has already been put on the market or amount to the creation of a new item of the product according to the patent.

To assess this question, one must weigh the legitimate interests of the patent holder in the economic use of the invention on the one hand and of the buyer in the unfettered use of the concrete, already sold, patent-embodying product on the other hand, while taking the specific character of the patented product into consideration. This is generally the task of the fact-finding judge [references omitted].

bb) If, however, a measure is, in the view of the public, to be considered a new manufacture, and if it includes the replacement of a part that is essential to the patent claim, according to the case law of this Court, a patent infringement can as a rule not be denied on grounds that the replaced part does not reflect the technical results of the invention. The question of whether the technical results of the invention are reflected precisely in the replaced parts and therefore the replacement of these parts again realizes the technical or economic advantage of the invention, is as a rule only relevant when one must normally expect the part in question to be replaced during the life of the protected product [reference omitted].

An exception must generally be made to the primacy of the opinion of the relevant public, however, when a patent claim protects a product consisting of several parts, but the patent holder only puts objects on the market that include yet further components.
(1) According the case law of the Court, the patent holder can as a rule request the grant of the patent in the embodiment corresponding to the given technical teaching. For this reason the patent holder is free to claim not only a product, but also a process or a use, or to formulate several patent claims of the same category [reference omitted]. For the same reason, the patent holder is always free to decide—provided the claimed object meets the requirements for a patent grant—whether to apply for protection for only individual parts of a more comprehensive product or for the larger product in its entirety.
(2) In the matter of exhaustion, however, it cannot go unconsidered which object is put on the market with the permission of the patent holder.

An opinion of the relevant public, which under the cited principles must always be considered with primacy when delineating between intended use and new manufacture, can only ever be formed with respect to a product that has actually been put on the market in this form. This prerequisite, as ascertained by the court of appeal and as such not contested, in the case at hand, is only fulfilled with respect to printers and process cartridges, but not a drum unit.
(3) Contrary to the view of the court of appeal the delineation between intended use and new manufacture may not in such situations be carried out based on a fictive public opinion defined according to normative criteria. With the delineation, based on public opinion, the legitimate expectations of the purchaser of an economic good put on the market are accounted for. Such expectations are by their nature shaped by the fact that a product is offered on the market in a certain form or configuration. One may not in lieu of them take recourse to fictive expectations that could arise if a different product were on offer. Rather, if the product protected by virtue of the patent claim is not identical with the objects to be had on the market, the result is that public opinion cannot be used as a criterion for distinguishing between new manufacture and intended use.
(4) In the above-mentioned situation, a new manufacture can only be found if the technical results of the invention are reflected precisely in the replaced parts.

According to the case law of the Federal Supreme Court, this criterion serves for arriving at an assessment on the basis of patent law considerations when a new manufacture cannot be ascertained on the basis of public opinion. This requirement is also given in the situation to be assessed in the case at hand—precisely because a public opinion cannot be determined. The criterion in question is also appropriate for this situation, because it relies on patent law considerations and ensures an appropriate balance between the legitimate interests of the patent holder in the economic use of the invention and the legitimate interests of the buyer in the unfettered use of the product on the market.

Against this background, the court of appeal incorrectly viewed the replacement of image drum and flange as a new manufacture of a drum unit.

The question answered in the affirmative by the court of appeal, whether the replacement of the image drum according to the view of the relevant public must be seen as a new manufacture of a drum unit, holds no relevance for deciding the case at hand for the reasons named above. The sole determining factor is whether the technical results of the invention are reflected in the replaced parts—the image drum and flange.

The contested decision does not prove to be correct in the outcome for other reasons. The technical results of the invention are reflected neither in the image drum nor in the flange. ...

According to the case law of the Federal Supreme Court, it can, however, be necessary to see the replacement of a part as a new manufacture also in the case that this part, though not necessarily designed in a special manner as dictated by the protected invention, functions together with a different part designed in accordance with the invention, such that the advantages of the solution given by the invention are realized by the former part. For this it does not suffice, however, that a functional connection be given between the parts in question. Rather, it is additionally necessary that the technical results of the invention are displayed in precisely the replaced part, so that it can be said that the replacement of this part realizes anew the technical or economic advantage of the invention [reference omitted]. These requirements are not given when a replacement part interacts with other parts but in this sense is only the object of an effect intended by the invention that finds its corporeal embodiment solely in the other parts [reference omitted].

In the case at hand, there is a functional connection, as the court of appeal rightly ascertained, because a design of the coupling member in accordance with the invention makes the installation and deinstallation of the drum unit as a component of the process cartridge easier. This effect finds its corporeal embodiment only in the features of the coupling member provided for in feature group 4, however. The image drum is thus in this respect a mere object that, as a component of the process cartridge, takes part in the intended result of the invention without this influencing its function or durability.

In the case that in addition to the image drum the flange is also replaced, the same is true. To the extent that the flange functions together with the coupling member, it is likewise only an object of the result intended by the invention. ...

From the factual statements of the court of appeal it follows for the reasons detailed above that the replacement of the image drum and flange cannot be seen as a new manufacture of a drum unit. Further statements on this issue with relevance for a decision do not come into consideration. Thus the action is clear for dismissal. ...

1.5 Analysis of the Case

Drum Unit (Trommeleinheit)
Federal Court of Justice, 24 October 2017, Case No. X ZR 55/16

In this decision, the Federal Court of Justice refined its case law regarding the conditions for the exhaustion of patent rights.

Essential facts

The plaintiff sued the defendant for infringement of a European patent covering a "drum unit" which is usable with a laser printer or copier. The drum unit consists of a photosensitive drum and a coupling member which can be engaged with a driving shaft within the printer. Usually, such drum units are a part of the toner cartridge, and their life cycle is roughly equal to the time it takes until the cartridge is empty. One essential feature of the patent was the technical design of the coupling member which made it easy to insert the cartridge into the printer and remove it when empty.

The defendant collected and refilled empty cartridges which had originally been put into circulation by the plaintiff. Due to their technical design, the cartridges had to be disassembled completely. Furthermore, the photosensitive drum had to be replaced due to its rather short life cycle. The coupling member and all the other parts could be reused. In the claimant's view, the measures taken by the defendant infringed the patent in suit. The defendant argued that the claimant's patent rights were exhausted because he had sold the original cartridge to the end users.

Relevant questions

Based on the established case law, the case was rather difficult to decide.

According to established case law, the exclusive right arising from a patent concerning a product is exhausted with respect to such items of the protected product as have been put on the market by or with the permission of the patent holder. A rightful user of such an item is entitled to use it as intended. This use includes maintenance and restoration of usability when the functionality or performance of the concrete item is partially or wholly compromised or lost due to wear, damage or for other reasons. Not included are all measures resulting in manufacturing of a new item of the protected product.

In order to distinguish maintenance and restoration from manufacturing of a new product, the Federal Court of Justice had identified two different criteria:

Firstly, whether or not an item has to be considered as newly manufactured depends on the views of the relevant public, i.e. the users buying such products. In general, an item may be considered as being new under this aspect if most of its parts or most of its value has been replaced by spare parts.

Secondly, an item which the relevant public does not consider as being new may nevertheless be new with regard to the question of exhaustion if the replaced parts precisely reflect the technical results of the invention. Under this criterion, even the replacement of a rather small and inexpensive part may infringe the patent if this part has essential significance for using the invention.

The view taken by the Court of Appeal
In the disputed case, the Court of Appeal had decided that the first criteria was met, because the photosensitive drum which had to be replaces was much more expensive than the other parts of the protected drum unit including the coupling member.

The decision of the Federal Court of Justice
The Federal Court of Justice did not share this view, because "drum units" are not available for sale on the market and therefore the views of the relevant public cannot be ascertained. Therefore, it refined its case law by stating that the first criterion is only applicable for products which are available on the market.

Consequently, the Federal Court of Justice had to assess the second criterion. It held that this criterion is not met, because the technical results of the invention are mainly reflected in the coupling member which the defendant does not replace during the refilling process. Therefore, the claim was dismissed.

(2) **How to determine the person skilled in the art in connection with a patent that covers aspects from different fields of technology—Case of "Thermal Energy Management" (Wärmeenergieverwaltung)***

2.1 Syllabus:
The plaintiff filed for the revocation of a patent covering a method for saving thermal energy in buildings with an elevator. The Federal Court of Justice concurred with the Federal Patent Court on the definition of the person skilled in the art. The Court held that the relevant person has knowledge in elevator technology, but that he would at least consult a person with knowledge in air conditioning and ventilation technology on getting aware that questions concerning this field of technology are arising. This condition was met in the case in suit because the problem consisted in ventilating spaces within a building. The decision demonstrates very clearly that the person skilled in the art is generally viewed to have very broad knowledge but that this does not necessarily mean that a combination of features from which by themselves were known in prior art is to be viewed as obvious.

2.2 Rules:
European Patent Convention, Art. 56 Patent Act, Sec. 4

The definition of a person skilled in the art serves to determine a fictive person from whose perspective the patent and the state of the art is to be judged. It therefore cannot rely on considerations regarding interpretation of a patent or creative step.

Decision of the Federal Supreme Court (Bundesgerichtshof); 9 January 2018— Case No. X ZR 14/16.

2.3 Facts:
1. The defendant is the proprietor of European patent No. 1 890 956, granted with effect for the Federal Republic of Germany, which was registered on 24 May 2006 claiming a priority of 13 June 2005 and which concerns a method and system for the management of thermal energy in a building with a shaft for lift facilities. Patent claims 1 and 8, to which thirteen further patent claims refer, read as follows …:

Thermal energy management method in a building (10) comprising a lifting installation (13) with a mobile car (16) in a shaft (14) and a ventilation passage (22) between said shaft (14) and the atmosphere, said method comprising the following steps: the monitoring of at least one state parameter of said lifting installation (13); said monitoring of at least one state parameter comprising the monitoring of the presence of a person in said lifting installation (13) and/or the monitoring of a movement of said car (16) in said shaft (14); the evaluation, in a control unit (32), of the necessity to ventilate said shaft (14) based on these parameters, said control unit (32) ascertaining the necessity to ventilate said shaft (14) when the presence of a person is detected and/or when the movement of said car (16) is detected;

the switching of a closing element (30) associated with said ventilation passage (22) from an open position, wherein the ventilation passage (22) is essentially open, to a close dposition, wherein the ventilation passage (22) is at least partially closed, only when said evaluation indicates that ventilation of said shaft (14) is not required, said closing element (30) being prestressed in its open position.

Thermal energy management system in a building comprising a lifting installation (13) with a mobile car (16) in a shaft (14) and a ventilation passage (22) between said shaft (14) and the atmosphere, said system further comprising:

a closing element (30) associated with said ventilation passage (22), said closing element (30) being mobile between an open position, wherein the ventilation passage (22) is essentially open, and a closed position, wherein the ventilation passage (22) is at least partially closed;

a prestressing means for maintaining, in a passive state, said closing element (30) in its open position; and a control unit (32) controlling the position of said closing element (30), said control unit (32) comprising means for monitoring at least one state parameter of said lifting installation (13) and for evaluating the necessity to ventilate said shaft (14), said control unit (32) only allowing switching of said closing element (30) to a closed position when the evaluation of the necessity to ventilate said shaft (14) indicates that ventilation of said shaft (14) is not required, said means for monitoring at least one state parameter of said lifting installation (13) comprising at least one means for detecting the presence of a person in said lifting installation (13) and/or at least one means for detecting movement of said car (16) in said shaft (14), said control unit (32) concluding to the necessity to ventilate said shaft (14) when the presence of a person is detected and/or when movement of said car (16) is detected.

2. Plaintiff 1 sought a declaration of invalidity of the patent in suit in the scope of patent claims 1 and 8, as far as these provide for determining the presence of a person in the lift system, and the claims making reference thereto, patent claims 2 and 4 through 7, or 9 and 11 through 15, and asserted that the contested subject matter is not patentable and the invention not disclosed so as to allow a person skilled in the art to carry it out. Plaintiff 2 challenged the patent in suit in its entirety on grounds of lack of patentability.

3. The defendant defended the patent in suit, primarily in the granted version, as well as with five auxiliary requests in amended versions.

4. The patent court revoked the patent in suit due to a lack of patentability. This decision is contested by the appeal of the defendant, who further pursues its first-instance requests. The plaintiffs counter the appeal in the scope of their fist-instance requests.

2.4 Reasoning:
The admissible appeal leads to the dismissal of the action. ...
1. The patent court rightly assumed that a skilled person familiar with the development of lifts and the problem posed by the patent in suit was on the date of priority in possession of the knowledge and skills of an engineer for heating, ventilation and air conditioning.

a) On this point the patent court stated that from A4 it follows that a skilled person familiar with the planning of lifts was in 2004 already working on the problem of creating an airtight building envelope for reasons of energy conservation. From this it must be concluded that this expert also dealt with the requirements of shaft ventilation.

b) This assessment is, at least in the outcome, correct.

aa) The questions discussed in detail by the appeal of how to interpret individual features of the patent in suit and whether the subject matter thus understood was made obvious by the state of the art, are in this context irrelevant.

The definition of a person skilled in the art serves precisely to determine a fictive person from whose perspective the patent and the state of the art are to be judged. It therefore cannot rely on considerations on interpreting a patent or on the inventive step.

bb) Correctly in its tendency, the appeal asserts that the definition of a person skilled in the art can depend upon the technical problem the invention serves to solve, and that the technical problem arises from what the invention actually achieves [references omitted]. Under this aspect as well, however, no fault can be found with the contested decision.

According to the view of the appeal, A4 and A3 as the closest prior art reflect the knowledge of a lift systems expert on the date of priority. It speaks in favour of this view that both citations go back to the early days of lift shaft smoke extraction, when stairwell smoke extraction systems were more or less identically transferred to lift systems.

With this, the considerations of the patent court are not called into question, but confirmed.

In this respect the—in any case irrelevant [reference omitted]—question of which citation to consider as the "closest" prior art, can remain open, as can the questions concerning who is addressed by said citations and by whom they were drafted. Simply the fact that they concern the smoke extraction of a part of a building and propose solutions for this problem that were prior knowledge in the smoke extraction of stairwells, at any rate, gave a skilled person familiar with the further development of such systems cause to consult with an engineer for heating, ventilation and air conditioning if that skilled person did not himself possess sufficient knowledge in this field.

cc) Contrary to the view of the appeal, it cannot be deduced from the fact that no solution was disclosed on the date of priority that met both the requirements of the Energy Conservation Ordinance and the requirements of Standards EN 81-1 and EN 81-2 that there was no person skilled in the art who was capable of mastering this task.

If on the date of priority there was in fact no system that met all requirements, and the patent in suit was the first to provide such a solution, this may represent meaningful evidence in favour of confirming patentability. Whether the person skilled in the art had cause to arrive at this solution must, however, be decided according to the criteria required for evaluating the inventive step, but not through the definition of the person skilled in the art. ...

2.5 Analysis of the Case
Thermal Energy Management (Wärmeenergieverwaltung)
Federal Court of Justice, 9 January 2018, Case No. X ZR 14/16

In this decision, the Federal Court of Justice dealt with the question of determining the person skilled in the art in connection with a patent that covers aspects from different fields of technology.

Essential facts

The plaintiff filed for the revocation of a patent covering a method for saving thermal energy in buildings with an elevator.

According to safety regulations in many countries, elevator shafts must be ventilated in order to avoid people suffocating in case of an emergency. This ventilation may lead to the loss of large amounts of energy. To avoid this, the patent in suit suggested to keep the elevator shaft closed with a movable flap during times where there are enough indicators that nobody does use the elevator. For instance, such indicators could be the weight of the elevator booth, the buttons being used for calling the elevator or for prompting it to go to a certain floor, or ultrasonic sensors detecting persons within the booth.

The plaintiff presented prior art where the ventilation of elevator shafts was controlled by a movable flap which could be opened or closed by a manual switch. Additionally he presented documents disclosing air conditioning and ventilation systems which were controlled by automatic sensors which were able to detect the presence of persons within the relevant room. The plaintiff argued that a person skilled in the art who is familiar with elevators would have considered prior art concerning air conditioning and ventilation systems, although this is generally viewed as a different field of technology.

Relevant questions

The Federal Court of Justice had to decide how the relevant person skilled in the art is to be defined if the problem solved by the patent is related to two different fields of technology.

The decision of the Federal Patent Court
The Federal Patent Court revoked the patent. The judges held that the person skilled in the art would have considered solutions from the field of elevator technology and from the field of air conditioning and ventilation technology as well.

The decision of the Federal Court of Justice
The Federal Court of Justice allowed the patentee's appeal and dismissed the revocation action.

However, the Federal Court of Justice concurred with the Federal Patent Court on the definition of the person skilled in the art. The Court held that the relevant person has knowledge in elevator technology, but that he would at least consult a person with knowledge in air conditioning and ventilation technology on getting aware that questions concerning this field of technology are arising. This condition was met in the case in suit because the problem consisted in ventilating spaces within a building.

Nevertheless, the Federal Court of Justice found that even for a person with this broad knowledge it was not obvious to combine elements of sophisticated air conditioning systems with ventilation systems for elevator shafts. The main reason for this was the fact that at the priority date it was generally supposed that ventilation systems for elevators must be active all the time, and neither an expert for elevators nor an expert for air conditioning and ventilation systems was motivated to put this view into question.

Consequences
The decision demonstrates very clearly that the person skilled in the art is generally viewed to have very broad knowledge but that this does not necessarily mean that a combination of features from which by themselves were known in prior art is to be viewed as obvious.

(3) **The conditions for considering a technical solution as obvious without a specific suggestion from prior art—Case of "Baby Crib" (Case No. X ZR 59/16)**

3.1 Syllabus:
The decision shows that the conditions for considering a technical solution as obvious without a specific suggestion from prior art are rather strict. This does not mean that the three criteria listed above can never be met. However, the number of cases where a patent will be revoked based on this criteria might remain rather small. the three criteria are: it must be a general tool or technique which according to the general technical knowledge can be relied on in a number of different use cases; the use of this functionality in the context of the patent must have appeared suitable from an objective point of view; and no special circumstances can be determined that would make its use seem impossible, difficult, or otherwise infeasible.

3.2 Rules:
European Patent Convention, Art. 56 Patent Act, Sec. 4

The fact that a solution that forms a part of the general know-how is in principle suitable can only be sufficient cause to refer to that solution if it is immediately clear to an expert that a technical starting point is given in which the use of the solution in question seems objectively suitable (following Federal Supreme Court, decision of 30 April 2014—X ZR 139/10, 2014 GRUR 647—*Farbversorgungs system*).

Decision of the Federal Supreme Court (Bundesgerichtshof); 27 March 2018—Case No. X ZR 59/16.

3.3 Facts:

(**1**) The defendant is the proprietor of European Patent No. 1 550 387 granted with effect for the Federal Republic of Germany, which was registered on 19 April 2004 claiming a Chinese priority of 2 January 2004 and which concerns a baby crib. Patent claim 1 reads in the language of suit:

(**2**) A baby crib comprising:

a bed frame structure (1) including a plurality of upright tubes (11), each of which has a tube wall (110) defining a receiving hole (111); and having a slit (112) that extends along the length of said tube wall (110) and that is in spatial communication with said receiving hole (111); a fabric member (2) mounted on said bed frame structure (1) to define a surrounding wall around said bed frame structure (1); and a plurality of positioning posts (22) mounted on said fabric member (2) and inserted respectively into said receiving holes (111) in said upright tubes (11), said fabric member (2) being clamped between each of said upright tubes (11) and a corresponding one of said positioning posts (22) and extending outward through said slit (112) in each of said upright tubes (11).

(**3**) The remaining claims refer directly or indirectly back to this patent claim.

(**4**) The plaintiff objected to the patent in suit on grounds that its subject matter was not patentable. The defendant defended the patent in suit as granted and alternatively in limited versions. The Patent Court deemed the patent in suit in the version in alternative claim IV as legally valid and declared all other versions invalid.

(**5**) The defendant contests this decision with the appeal, with which it defends the patent in suit in the version of its first-instance main claim and with five new alternative claims. The plaintiff opposes the appeal.

3.4 Reasoning:

3.4.1 The patent in suit concerns an easy-to-assemble baby crib with a frame and a fabric cover.

(**1**) According to the descriptions in the specifications of the patent in suit, in the state of the art the fabric cover is connected to the frame, on each corner of which upright tubes are arranged. So that the position of the fabric does not shift with respect to the frame, clamps are set on the fabric that are screwed into the tubes and thus fasten the fabric on the frame. The specifications of the patent in suit criticize the time-consuming nature of the assembly. The fabric, it further notes, could tear at the point of attachment. Finally, the visible screw fitting detracts from the appearance of the baby crib.

(**2**) The task of the patent in suit therefore, as laid out in the specifications of the patent in suit, consists in developing a baby crib that is easily and quickly assembled and facilitates a reliable and visually pleasing attachment of the fabric cover to the bed frame (description in para. 5).

(3) As a solution, the patent in suit proposes in claim 1 a crib whose features can be outlined as [in para. 2 above…]. Figure 3.2 shows an example embodiment, where number 1 denotes the frame structure, 2 the fabric cover, 11 the upright tubes and 22 the positioning posts.

(4) On how to read the claim, the Patent Court explained: Its subject matter is a baby crib. The structure of the patent claim in sections with the indications of how the individual components are assembled may induce one to consider these components as corresponding to a logical order of assembly. And yet when considering an assembled baby crib it is irrelevant when the individual components were assembled. A bed frame structure is the structure defining the outer shape of a bed. As the patent in suit explains with respect to the state of the art, the latter is chosen so that an enclosure for the child is determined by the frame structure and a lining member. The upright tubes are a part of the frame structure; and yet it is not limited to them. That the tubes fulfil a function with respect to the stability of the frame structure is not described in the patent in suit.

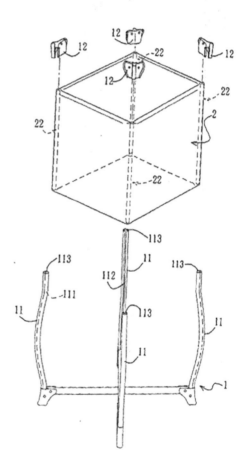

Fig. 3.2 Design figure of baby crib structure

(5) This interpretation of the patent claim only partially stands up to judicial review in the appeal proceeding.

a) According to feature 1, the bed frame structure determines the outer shape of the bed and, together with the fabric member, which forms an enclosure (feature 2), it creates a space to hold the child (description paras. 5, 6, 9). According to the description the bed frame structure is rectangular in shape, displaying four upright tubes which are arranged in the corners (description para. 9, Fig. 3.2).

b) Contrary to the view of the Patent Court only such elements are to be seen as belonging to the frame that fulfil the function of supporting and of forming the bed's substructure.

The English term "structure" does not fully correspond to the meaning of the word "Struktur" in German translation. According to general English usage, it can also be understood to mean an architectural shape or a supporting structure.

From the context of the description it is understood that the "bed frame structure" denotes the supporting structure of the baby crib. The (normally four) positioning posts are "mounted" on the fabric member which in the patent in suit is distinguished from the frame structure (feature 3.1). As their name suggests, they allow this fabric member to be positioned. This in turn is accordingly mounted, via the positioning posts attached to it, on the bed frame (feature 2.1), in that each of the positioning posts is inserted into the receiving holes of one of the tubes of the frame structure (feature 3.2). From this arises the clamping attachment of the fabric member on the frame structure (feature 4.1). Thus an easy-to-assemble baby crib without visible mounting aids is offered, as in order to assemble it one need only insert the fabric member (via the positioning posts) into the tubes of the bed frame (the "supporting structure").

3.4.2 The Patent Court assumed that the subject matter of patent claim 1 was not novel and based this finding essentially on the following reasoning.

The specifications of the Australian utility model 715 883 (Document 9) from which Figs. 1 and 2 here adjacent are taken describe a baby crib with a bed frame structure. It follows from the description that the bed frame structure is made up of an upper frame (10), a lower frame (12) and perpendicular tubes ("corner posts" 20 and "retaining members" 22) located in the corners of the bed (feature 1a). The baby crib thus displays a bed frame structure that contains a number of vertical tubes. The elements described as "retaining members" are tubes cylindrical in shape and arranged perpendicular to the frame with a slit and a receiving hole. A fabric member (14) is mounted on the corner posts (20) and forms a wall surrounding the frame structure. The fabric member is according to the example embodiments arranged such that it is held fast between the corner post (20) and retaining member (22) and extends through the slit in the retaining member.

The Patent Court held that the defendant's objection that the publication shows the corner posts only as a part of the bed frame structure and the retaining members only as clamping elements could not be upheld. According to patent claim 1, the bed frame structure need only contain a number of perpendicular tubes. The claim leaves open, the court explained, whether the bed frame structure contains further components. In that Document 9 calls for mounting a retaining member on a corner post in order to position the fabric member located in between, the baby crib disclosed therein displays a bed frame structure that is made up of the these retaining members and corner posts.

3.4.3 The findings of the Patent Court do not stand up to the objections of the appeal. The subject matter of patent claim 1 is novel; contrary to the view of the Patent Court, it is not disclosed by Document 9.

The Australian utility model 715 883 (Document 9) concerns a retaining member for a baby crib that has a bed frame structure and a fabric side wall. The specifications describe it as long understood that the fabric attached at the lower end of the bed post can wrinkle when it is run (from the outside) across the corner post. Furthermore, the fabric can easily become stretched over time, thus losing tension at the point where it runs across the corner post. To solve these problems Document 9 proposes mounting a retaining member (22) on the corner posts (20) to support the clamping of the fabric side wall of the baby crib and to reduce or cover up creasing in the fabric side wall at the corner posts (Document 9, p. 1 lines 11–15). This retaining member is mounted upright on the bed post and is cylindrical. It has a tube wall and defines a receiving hole. The tube wall of the retaining member in turn displays a slit along its length that is in spatial communication with each receiving hole (Document 9, p. 1 line 24, p. 2 line 4, p. 3 lines 9–12).

Accordingly, the retaining members described as clamping the fabric member in Document 9 are not supporting structural elements of the bed frame structure. According to the description, the retaining members are attached only after the supporting elements are already present and assembled into a frame (Document 9, p. 2 lines 4–7, p. 3 lines 26–28). Therefore, an anticipation of feature group 1 is lacking, as the corner posts belonging to the frame structure have no slit, and the clamped-on retaining members with slits are not a part of the supporting frame structure. Unlike patent claim 1, Document 9 also does not disclose any positioning posts in the sense of feature group 3 that are mounted on the fabric member and inserted into the opening of a tube. Likewise, therefore, feature group 4, which teaches an internal clamping of the fabric side wall between the inner wall of the corner post and the positioning posts ("key slot method"), is not realized.

3.4.4 In its outcome, the judgment of the Patent Court proves not to be correct in other respects as well. The subject matter of the patent in suit is not made obvious by the cited state of the art.

(1) To the extent that the plaintiff asserts that the expert's know-how gave him or her reason to switch the functions of the bed's corner posts and the retaining member in accordance with cited Document 9, this cannot be concurred with.

a) In order to consider the subject matter of an invention as obvious, it is necessary, first, for the expert, with the knowledge and skills gained through training and experience in the field, to have been in the position to develop the invention's solution for the technical problem from the available state of the art. Second, the expert has to have had a reason to take the path of the invention. As a rule, this requires additional impulses, suggestions, information or other occasions going beyond the recognisability of the technical problem [references omitted].

b) No suggestion arose from Document 9 for the expert to redesign the corner posts of the baby crib and to combine it with a mounting of the fabric lining by means of the "key slot method". According to the utility model the fastening of the fabric side wall is achieved by clamping a retaining member from the outside via a corner post of the bed with the fabric member surrounding it in the form of a cuff (para. 21 et seq.). Ideally, the retaining member—insofar like the state of the art described in Document 9—is additionally secured to the fabric with a means of attachment through a hole in the corner post. Contrary to the view of the plaintiff, this gave the expert no reason to, as it were, swap out the functions of the corner posts and the retaining member, so as to give the bed post the further function of holding down the fabric on the inner side. To do so, the expert would have had to deviate from the concept on which Document 9 as well as the more advanced state of the art are based, namely, of running the fabric covering from the outside or by means of a cuff made from the fabric around the corner posts, which are taken as a given because they are prescribed as necessary components of the bed's frame, so as to then attach the fabric covering in as simple and reliable—and visually appealing—a manner as possible.

c) Nor does any other assessment follow from the fact that—as the Patent Court correctly assumed—the expert was familiar with the internal clamping or "key slot method" as such.

The mere fact that the knowledge of a technical matter forms a part of general expert know-how does not yet prove that it was obvious to the expert to make use of this know-how in solving a certain problem [reference omitted]. The very possibility of using the "key slot method" to fix a length of fabric in particular is, contrary to the plaintiff's view, precisely not evidence that the expert had reason to give the bedpost a further function in order to use this technique for fixing the fabric member.

Concerning the lack of a suggestion, this gap cannot even be bridged by the principle recognised in the case law that when a technical solution that is considered as a general technique that can be relied on in a number of use cases by its nature falls within the general know-how of the relevant expert, cause to refer to this solution can already be given when there is no concrete model for using this solution, and yet the use of its functionality in the context at hand appears objectively suitable and no special circumstances can be determined that would make its use seem impossible, difficult or otherwise infeasible [references omitted]. While the documents submitted in the first instance provide evidence that the positioning and fixation of a length of fabric by guiding it into a tube worked into a support and retaining rail was a part of the general know-how as a versatile technique, the fact a solution that forms a part of the general know-how is in principle suitable can only be sufficient cause to refer to that solution if it is immediately clear to an expert that a technical starting point is given in which the use of the solution in question seems objectively suitable. The expert's knowledge of the "key slot method" could only be sufficient cause for using this solution, therefore, if this expert had in mind the general possibility of designing the bedposts themselves as a means of retaining and fixing the fabric covering—that for this purpose must be pulled into place on positioning posts. Only then would the expert have been able to take recourse to the "key slot method" as a general available means to design such a support and retaining apparatus. However, this precondition is lacking considering the examples that arose for the expert from Document 9 and the state of the art described there in the field of fabric-covered baby cribs.

(2) Likewise, accordingly, contrary to the plaintiff's submissions, no suggestion arose for re-designing the corner posts of the bed from US patent specifications No. 5 911 478 (Document 33-5), which use supporting and retaining rails in the shape of sling rails for the backrest and seat of a chair or armchair consisting of a length of fabric. The sling rails are used in addition to the frame elements of the chair and only have the function of supporting, guiding and holding the length of fabric. Therefore, they likewise offer no cause to develop the subject matter of the patent in suit.

(3) The further citations submitted by the plaintiff do not come any closer to the invention than the state of the art evaluated above. They therefore likewise do not make the teaching of patent claim 1 obvious.

(4) Since the further patent claims refer back to patent claim 1, their subject matter is patentable as well. ...

3.5 Analysis of the Case
Baby Crib (Kinderbett)
Federal Court of Justice, 27 March 2018, Case No. X ZR 59/16

This decision deals with the conditions for considering a technical solution as obvious based on common general knowledge although there wasn't a specific inducement to use this solution.

Essential facts
The plaintiff filed for the revocation of a patent covering a portable baby crib consisting of a frame structure and a surrounding cover made of fabric. The cover was made from a single piece of fabric containing four positioning posts. Theses posts could be inserted into upright tubes at each corner of the frame structure, the tubes having slits through which the fabric could extend outward. This allowed the crib to be mounted and unmounted very easily and without any tools.

In the plaintiff's view, the subject matter of the patent was obvious based on an Australian utility model which also covered a baby crib and general common knowledge. The baby crib disclosed in the utility model also consisted of a frame structure and a cover made of a single piece of fabric. However, the fabric was not inserted into the corner tubes, but covered them from the outside. Therefore, the fabric could wrinkle at the lower end of the bed post, allowing the baby to leave the bed unattended. To prevent this, the fabric was fixed with a retaining member at each corner of the bed, which made mounting and unmounting more difficult.

The claimant presented several pieces of prior art where fabric or leather was connected to frame structures by wrapping it around a post and inserting it into a slitted tube. However, there was no specific document suggesting that this technique might be used for fixing a cover made of fabric to a bed frame.

Relevant question
Against this background, the major question was whether using a pole and a slitted tube for connecting a piece of fabric to a frame structure was a general tool provided

by common general knowledge which was obvious to use for the person skilled in the art even without a specific suggestion.

As a rule, the subject matter of an invention can only be considered as obvious if the person skilled in the art was able to develop the protected solution starting from the available state of the art and if he had reason to take the path of the invention. The latter criterion normally requires additional impulses, suggestions, information, or other occasions going beyond the recognizability of the technical problem. However, in some situations a certain solution can be obvious without such a suggestion.

In a former decision, the Federal Court of Justice had developed three conditions which must be met in order to assume that a specific suggestion was not necessary:

- it must be a general tool or technique which according to the general technical knowledge can be relied on in a number of different use cases;
- the use of this functionality in the context of the patent must have appeared suitable from an objective point of view; and
- no special circumstances can be determined that would make its use seem impossible, difficult, or otherwise infeasible.

The decisive question was if these criteria were met in the case at hand.

The view taken by the Federal Patent Court
The Federal Patent Court, which has jurisdiction for revocation cases in the first instance, held the patent invalid. In their view, the retaining members disclosed in the Australian utility model could be viewed as slitted tubes forming a part of the bed frame structure, leading to the consequence that the subject matter of the patent was not novel.

The decision of the Federal Court of Justice

The Federal Court of Justice ruled that the subject matter of the patent is novel because the retaining members disclosed in prior art cannot be viewed as a part of the bed frame structure. Therefore, the question arose whether using a post and a slitted tube instead of a retaining member attached from the outside was obvious based on general common knowledge, i.e. whether the three conditions listed above were met.

The Federal Court of Justice held that the first criterion is met, because the technique of fixing a piece of fabric to a frame structure with a post and a slitted tube was applied in a wide range of use cases.

However, the second criterion was not met in the Court's view. The person skilled in the art not only had to know the technique of fixing a piece of fabric to a frame structure. He also had to realize that he can use the bed posts for this purpose. The latter finding was not obvious from prior art, because separate means had been used to fix the fabric to the bed post.

Consequences
The decision shows that the conditions for considering a technical solution as obvious without a specific suggestion from prior art are rather strict. This does not mean that

the three criteria listed above can never be met. However, the number of cases where a patent will be revoked based on this criteria might remain rather small.

(4) **The methods to define the technical solution as obvious—Case of "Belt Tensioner" (Case No. X ZR 50/16)**

4.1 Syllabus:
In this decision, the Federal Court of Justice clarified that using an approach which a person skilled in the art would have avoided is not sufficient for patentability, if the approach was avoided because of known disadvantages or difficulties and the patent merely accepts these disadvantages or difficulties as inevitable. The decision demonstrates that it is not always sufficient to ask what the person skilled in the art would have done or would not have done, but it may sometimes be essential why he would not have chosen a certain solution.

4.2 Rules:
1. An indication of purpose or function of the claimed device contained in a patent claim regularly expresses the notion that the device must be objectively fit for the indicated purpose or function. The patent claim thus remains a product claim directed to a device with which the purposes or functions named can be realized.
2. It is not sufficient for a finding of patentability that, from the perspective of the prior art, the technical solution proposed by the patent in suit has disadvantages or is difficult to realize if the solution proposed by the inventor accepts these disadvantages or difficulties as inevitable (Confirmation of Federal Supreme Court, decision of 4 June 1996—X ZR49/94, BGHZ 133, 57—*Rauchgasklappe*).

Decision of the Federal Supreme Court (Bundesgerichtshof); 24 April 2018—Case No. X ZR 50/16.

4.3 Facts:
1. The defendant is the registered proprietor of German patent No. 10,2006,026,734 (patent in suit), applied for on 8 June 2006. The patent encompasses five claims. ...
2. The plaintiff asserted that the teaching of the patent in suit was not disclosed in such a manner that a person skilled in the art could carry it out; further, that this teaching was not novel and was not based on an inventive step. ...

4.4. Reasoning:
The admissible appeal is unsuccessful.
4.4.1 The patent in suit concerns a drive train for tensioning safety belts in an automobile.
1. According to the description of the patent in suit, belt tensioner drives known in the prior art feature an electric motor, a gear shaft and an output gear; the latter is coupled to the belt's winding shaft. The electric motor drives the output gear by means of two gear units such that the axle of the motor can be assembled parallel to the belt's winding shaft. The first of these gear units is a crown gear, and the second a worm gear. The patent in suit considers it a disadvantage that the crown gear makes for a hard mesh and, associated with this, considerable noise emission and vibrations.

2. The patent in suit is based on the problem of improving a belt tensioner drive, specifically, of reducing its noise emission when the electric motor is in operation.

3. To solve this problem, patent claim 1 proposes a device with the following features (their numbering follows that of the contested decision):

1. Belt tensioner drive with an electric motor (2), a gear shaft (3) and an output member (4), such that
2. the electric motor (2) powers the gear shaft (3) via a first gear (2d, 3b) And
3. the gear shaft in turn drives the output member (4) via a second gear (3d, 4a).
4. The first gear (2d, 3b) is
a) a 90° deflection gear
b) in the form of a worm gear
5. The second gear (3d, 4a) is
a) a 90° deflection gear in the form of
b1) a worm gear or
b2) a spur gear.
6. The output member (4) is a driven gear whose axial direction runs parallel to the shaft (2c) of the electric motor (2).

The patent in suit shows an example of embodiment in Fig. 1, as follows.

4. Some features are in need of further explanation:

a) The Patent Court sees in feature 1 with the term "belt tensioner drive" an indication of use, according to which the drive is to serve to tighten a safety belt. Whether it thereby ultimately construes patent claim No. 1 as a use claim or an apparatus claim, is not further specified by the Patent Court.

Feature 1 begins with a statement of function, that the subject matter of the patent is a "belt tensioner drive". Indications of purpose and function in an apparatus claim as a rule do not limit the claim's subject matter to the purpose or function indicated. Such statements are not without significance, however. They regularly define the subject matter protected by the patent in the sense that it is formed such that it can be used for the given purpose or fulfil the given function [reference omitted]. When concretising the patent subject matter using the suitability expressed by the statement of purpose or function, the claim directed to a device remains an apparatus claim. Neither the manner in which the device is actually used, nor the use it "serves", is relevant.

In this sense feature 1 concretises the subject matter of the patent to devices that are fit for use as belt tensioners. The subject matter must accordingly be objectively capable of reducing the length of belt that is loose or not in contact with the passenger's body, the "slack", by retracting the belt onto the belt winder.

b) Feature 4 b2 concerns a spur gear in the form of a spur-helical gear. ...

According to the case law of this Court, the patent specification must be read in a meaningful way, and the patent claim, when in doubt, be construed such that no contradictions arise to the embodiments in the description and the drawings [references omitted]. This standard for interpretation is all the more valid when it comes to avoiding contradictions between several features of a patent claim.

According to the statements of the Patent Court, reading feature 4 b2 in the sense of a (typical) spur gear with parallel rotation axes is in contradiction with feature 4a, which implies that the second gear must also be a 90° deflection gear. Furthermore, the Patent Court recognises correctly that the skilled person can also take the term "spur gear" to mean a spur-helical gear if the term "spur gear" is interpreted not in its technically precise meaning, but to include a further, less precise meaning of this term. In this sense, the term "spur gear" as a category also designates a spur-helical gear. These gears exhibit considerable differences to spurgears with parallel axes with respect to their toothing. However, the remaining features the two gear types have in common do justify designating these gears as "spur", their common lexical component [in German, i.e.: *Stirnrad*].

A spur gear with parallel rotation axes cannot be a 90° deflection gear; such function is, however, readily obtainable with a spur-helical gear. Feature 4 b2 is therefore to be understood to cover spur-helical gears not only so as to avoid contradictions within a patent claim, but also based on the principles of a functional interpretation (cf. Federal Supreme Court, decision of 14 June 2016—X ZR 29/15, BGHZ 211, 1, para. 31 et seq.—*Pemetrexed*).

The Patent Court justified the revocation of the patent in suit—to the extent that it is relevant for the appeal proceeding—with the following reasons. ...

With international patent application No. 03/099619 (citation D2) as its starting point, the teaching of the patent in suit ... was obvious. In this citation, a belt(pre) tensioner for safety belts is shown with the features 1, 2, 3, 4a and 4b1, as well as 5a and 7. The apparatus disclosed in D2 differs from the subject matter of the patent in suit in that only the second gear is carried out as a worm gear, whereas for the first deflection gear it proposes a crown gear.

Facing the task of carrying out a belt tensioner drive in a space-saving as well as low-noise and low-vibration manner, the skilled person, defined as an engineer with a degree from a technical college in mechanical engineering and specialised knowledge in developing safety devices for automobile passengers, would have found it obvious to carry out the first gear as a worm gear as well. The skilled person would have known that worm gears are less noise-intensive. The back-to-back assembly of two worm gears was also known to the skilled person from D3, even if this apparatus does not serve to tighten a belt.

4.4.2 This stands up to review in the appeal proceeding.

1. However, the Patent Court wrongly found a fault in the practicability of the teaching of patent claim 1, according to the statements quoted in I 4 b.

The teaching of patent claim 1 in the alternative according to feature 4 b2 (spur gear as the second gear) also covers the embodiment with a spur-helical gear. Such gears can have intersecting rotation axes with a 90° deflection in accordance with feature 4a. The subject matter of the patent claim can therefore also be carried out in this alternative way.

2. The subject matter of patent claim 1 is not patentable, however, because it is not based on an inventive step, at least using as the starting point the prior art documented in D2.

With D2, included in the prior art is a belt-tightening apparatus corresponding to the following Figs. 3.3 and 3.4 of D2, where Fig. 3.3 shows a total side view, and Fig. 3.4 a detail view of the gear shaft (18).

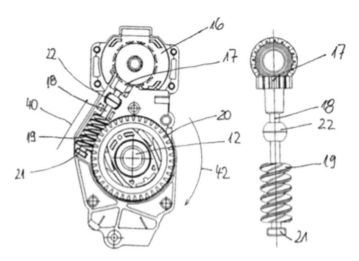

Fig. 3.3 Design figure of total side view

According to the correct statements of the Patent Court, which are not contested by the parties, the example embodiment of D2 displays all features of patent claim 1, with the exception of feature 5b. D2 emphasises that the use of a worm gear as the second gear with a suitable arrangement of the worm gear toothing can effect self-locking, inhibiting a torque emanating from the belt shaft (D2, p. 3, para. 4 through p. 4, para. 1). D2 initially describes the first gear unit between the electric motor and the gear shaft in general terms as a deflection gear with which an especially space-saving design can be realised (D2, p. 5, para. 2). Specifically, a crown gear and a bevel gear are then mentioned as possible forms of carrying out this feature (D2, p. 5, para. 3).

For the skilled person, defined correctly by the Patent Court, there was reason to carry out the first deflection gear shown in D2 as a spur gear, corresponding to feature 5b, as well.

aa) As the patent in suit also mentions, a crown gear has a hard mesh, which causes noises and vibrations (patent in suit, para. 4). Pursuant to the statements of the Patent Court, which in this respect are not contested, the skilled person would have been just as aware of these disadvantageous noise emissions of a crown gear as of the lower noise emissions of other deflection gears, like a worm gear. The skilled person would therefore have had reason, based on general expert knowledge, to think about ways to remedy the noise emissions, taking a different gear unit into consideration.

From D2 itself came the idea to use a (further) worm gear as the first gear unit instead of the crown gear or bevel gear provided for in D2. D2 shows a 90° deflection gear for the first gear unit. Further, it shows as the second gear unit a worm gear with the same 90° deflection. From the two deflection gears there results a parallel arrangement of the electric motor and belt-winding shaft. In order to find a low-noise gear type for the first gear with a 90° deflection, the skilled person would also have

Fig. 3.4 Design figure of detail view of the gear shaft

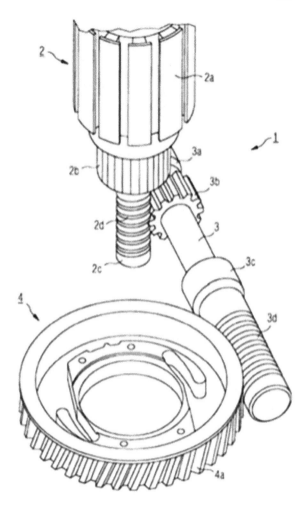

been expected to provide for a worm gear as already shown in D2 for the second gear unit.

Furthermore, D3 shows such an arrangement of two worm gears in a row to have an effect on slack. Even if the retractor for safety belts shown there is not suited for use as a belt tensioner, to the skilled person, D3 nevertheless discloses the principle of using two worm gears as 90° deflection gears so as to achieve a low-noise parallel arrangement of belt-winding shaft and electric motor. On this point, the skilled person understands from D2 that such gears can be used to inhibit a torque emanating from the belt-winding shaft (D2, p. 3, para. 4 through p. 4, para. 1). This, together with the arrangement shown in principle in D3 of an electric motor, two worm gears and a belt-winding shaft, gave the skilled person the knowledge to achieve a safety belt apparatus with the tensioning function. In line with the correct, and thus not challenged, statements of the Patent Court, the skilled person would only have had to reverse the polarity of the electric motor to achieve a different rotational direction and thus achieve belt tension instead of slack.

Consequently, the skilled person had reason to further develop the belt tensioner known from D2 with the goal of reducing noise development, and found suggestions in the prior art on concrete methods to realise such an improvement.

bb) Contrary to the view of the appeal, the obviousness of such an improvement is not precluded by the fact that a second worm gear in the drive train leads to an even greater reduction than that already given by the combination of worm gear and crown gear as presented in the embodiment example in D2. ...

It is not sufficient for a finding of patentability if, from the perspective of the prior art, the technical solution proposed by the patent in suit contains disadvantages or is difficult to realise, but the solutions proposed by the inventor ignore these disadvantages or difficulties and simply accept them as inevitable [references omitted]. Therefore, an inventive step cannot rely on technical difficulties or disadvantages if the patent in suit, as in the case at hand with respect to the greater gear reduction resulting from the second worm gear, does not indicate how to surmount them.

cc) Furthermore, the arguments of the appeal that it was not obvious to construct the belt-winding mechanism known from D2 without an axially movable gear shaft fail to convince. The appeal attempts to base this argument on the fact that D2 shows various examples of embodiment for inhibiting torque from the belt-winding shaft which require movability. Such a movable winding shaft would not be compatible with a worm gear as the first gear unit, however.

D2 does show such examples with a gear shaft that can move in an axial direction. D2 also explains, however, that a self-locking mechanism can only be achieved by a suitable arrangement of the worm gear toothing and a bearing support receiving axial forces, without the gear shaft having to be axially movable to accommodate it (D2, p. 3, para. 4 through p. 4, para. 1). Further, D2 also discloses the possibility of operating the electric motor in a different power range, so that it does not turn, but still checks a torque coming from the drive shaft (D2, p. 7, para. 4). Therefore, D2 is not to be understood to mean that a self-locking operation is only possible with a movable gear shaft.

In addition, the patent in suit gives no indications of how to overcome technical difficulties so as to achieve a self-locking operation with two worm gears arranged one after another in the drive train. If such difficulties or disadvantages with regard to self-locking arise for the skilled person with subject matter described in the patent, the patent in suit accepts and ignores them. As stated above, an inventive step cannot rely on this.

To the extent that the appeal asserts in its submissions that it was more obvious for the skilled person, due to the difficulties in achieving self-locking, to not choose a worm gear as the first gear, instead providing for other measures to reduce noise, this does not preclude obviousness in the patent teaching. If several alternative solutions for a problem are available to the skilled person, more than one of them can be obvious. In this respect it is irrelevant which of the alternative solutions the skilled person would consider first [references omitted]. ...

4.4.3 The auxiliary requests of the defendants are likewise unsuccessful. ...
2. Auxiliary requests Ia through Ic limit the subject matter defined in claim 1 of the granted version with regard to the following further features:

4c1 The second gear unit is made up of the gear shaft, via a worm made of plastic, and the output gear

7a The output gear is equipped with external gear teeth

8 Both gear units are mounted such that they support the self-locking operation of the drive system in the sense of a stiffness in the direction of output.

Auxiliary request Ia is limited by features 4c1 and 7a, and auxiliary request Ib by features 7a and 8. Auxiliary request Ic is limited by all three features, 4c1, 7a and 8.

The Patent Court correctly stated with regard to the version of auxiliary request Ic that a concretising of the subject matter of patent claim 1 with regard to features 4c1 and 8 were obvious to the skilled person from the prior art—especially from D2. Reference is made to these statements. The same is true of auxiliary requests Ia and Ib. Equipping the output gear with external meshing is shown in D2's embodiment examples, which is why in this respect as well no inventive step is given.

3. Auxiliary request II limits the subject matter of auxiliary request Ic by ... further features. ...

The Patent Court also correctly reasoned this subject matter to be obvious from the prior art; reference is made to these statements. ...

4.5 Analysis of the Case
Belt Tensioner (Gurtstraffer)
Federal Court of Justice, 24 April 2018, Case No. X ZR 50/16

In this decision, the Federal Court of Justice clarified that using an approach which a person skilled in the art would have avoided is not sufficient for patentability, if the approach was avoided because of known disadvantages or difficulties and the patent merely accepts these disadvantages or difficulties as inevitable.

1. Essential facts

The plaintiff filed for the revocation of a patent covering a belt tensioner drive consisting of an electric motor and two 90° deflection gears, the first one being a worm gear and the second one either another worm gear or a spur gear. In the claimant's view, the invention was not sufficiently disclosed, because a spur gear in its ordinary form cannot be used to achieve a deflection. Additionally, the claimant argued that the subject matter of the patent was obvious based on an older patent application disclosing a belt tensioner drive with a worm gear and a crown gear.

2. Relevant question

The question which turned out to be relevant in the end was whether a technical solution is obvious based on prior art although a person skilled in the art would have hesitated to choose this option because of known disadvantages.

3. The decision of the Federal Patent Court

The Federal Patent Court revoked the patent for lack of sufficient disclosure with regard to a belt tensioner with a worm gear and a spur gear, and for obviousness with regard to a belt tensioner with two worm gears.

4. The decision of the Federal Court of Justice

The Federal Court of Justice decided otherwise on the issue of sufficient disclosure. According to the ordinary language in the relevant field of technology, a spur gear does not allow a deflection. However, it was common general knowledge that there is a special type of spur gear which is also called spur-helical gear. This type of gear looks similar like a worm gear and allows a 90° deflection. Nevertheless, it does not consist of continuous helical mount, but of a variety of curved spurs, and therefore it is considered as a spur gear.

However, this was only a small victory for the patent holder. The Federal Court of Justice held that the subject matter of the patent in total was obvious based on the already mentioned patent application disclosing a belt tensioner with a worm gear and a crown gear. According to the common general knowledge, using a crown gear as second gear was advantageous, because the motor can run at a comparably low speed. Therefore, a person skilled in the art would not have been strongly inclined to use a worm gear instead, although this allowed reducing noise.

According to the standard test, a technical solution is not obvious if a person skilled in the art would not have considered it as an alternative to solutions known in prior art. However, as the Federal Court of Justice made clear, this rule does not apply, if the only reason a person skilled in the art would have rejected this solution were disadvantages in some regards, and if the patent does no more than accept these disadvantages without obtaining any unexpected advantage. The latter was the case with the patent in suit, because it just accepted having to run the motor at a higher speed for achieving an advantage—less noise—which had also been known in prior art.

5. Consequences

The decision demonstrates that it is not always sufficient to ask what the person skilled in the art would have done or would not have done, but it may sometimes be essential why he would not have chosen a certain solution.

(5) The boundaries of a right to use a patented invention based on prior use—Case of "Protective Covering" (Case No. X ZR 95/18)

5.1 Syllabus:

In this decision, the Federal Court of Justice dealt with the boundaries of a right to use a patented invention based on prior use. With regard to the second question, the Federal Court of Justice decided that a person who used the invention in an indirect way before the priority day, e.g. by providing components ready for manufacturing the patented device or for implementing a patented method, is entitled to use the invention directly, if this is the only reasonable way to use those components. In the case at stake, this condition was met, because the components supplied by the defendant could only be used for manufacturing protective coverings. Therefore, the defendant is also entitled to manufacture such coverings himself.

With regard to the third question, the Court held that the right to use the invention expires if the entitled person has only made arrangements to use the invention before the priority date and gives up these efforts later on. However, if he has already used the invention before the priority date, he stays entitled unless he abandons his right. Depending on the details of the single case, not using the invention for a longer period may be considered as an implied act of abandoning the right. On crucial factor in this regard may be typical product life cycles. In the present case, the right to use the invention has not expired even though the defendant had not used the invention for several years, because protective coverings for large radio systems have a very long life cycle.

5.2 Rules:
Patent Act, Secs. 9, second sentence Nos. 1 and 2, 12(1)
a) The prior user can be banned from modifying the previously used embodiment not only when this interferes for the first time with the subject-matter of the invention protected by the patent, but also when the prior use already corresponds to the teaching of the invention, but the contested embodiment carries it out in a different design or method.
b) The limits of the right based on prior use can be overstepped when the modification realises an additional advantage that was not brought about by the unmodified embodiment. This can be the case when an embodiment is used for the first time which is emphasised due to this additional advantage in a sub-claim or in the patent description.
c) If, on the other hand, two fully equivalent alternatives for a feature are named in a patent claim, the fact that the prior user only used one of these alternatives will as a rule not justify a corresponding limitation of that user's use right. It will likewise have to be assessed if in the patent specifications a modification of the previously used embodiment is disclosed that is an obvious alteration that, from the point of view of the skilled person, is readily compatible with the prior user's possession of the invention at the time of registration or priority.
d) The manufacturer of individual components which technically and economically can only sensibly be assembled to the entire device in accordance with the invention therefore manufactures the entire device even when it does not itself assemble the individual components, but supplies a third party with them, who then assembles them into the protected entire device.
e) The manufacturer of individual components may, under these circumstances, also use a process protected by the patent to manufacture the entire device, as long as the patent claim's instructions for the process teach no more than the only technically and economically sensible assembly.
Decision of the Federal Supreme Court (Bundesgerichtshof); 14 May 2019—Case No. X ZR 95/18

5.3 Facts:
1. The plaintiff is the proprietor of European Patent No. 1 303 003 granted with effect for the Federal Republic of Germany (patent in suit), which was applied for on 12 October 2001 and published on 30 April 2008. The patent in suit concerns

a protective covering for radio-communications equipment as well as a method for fabricating the same.

2. The claims 1 and 17 read as follows:

1. Protective covering (17, 18, 19) for radio systems having components, which in each case comprise an insulation layer (3), in each case a support element (2) connected to the insulation layer being provided at least partly on at least one side of the insulation layer (3), reduction (7) of the thickness of the respective support element (2) being provided at the ends of components (1), characterised in that the spatial region which is formed by the reduction (7) is filled with material of the support element (2) and this material connects adjacent components (1).

17 Method for the fabrication of a protective covering (17, 18, 19) for radio systems, in which components which in each case have an insulation layer (3) and, on at least one side of the insulation layer (3), in each case a support element (2) connected thereto are assembled, the respective support element (2) being produced so as to taper at least towards one end of the respective component (1), characterised in that the material of the support element is applied in the spatial region (15) which is formed by the reduction (7) of the thickness of the respective support element and thus connects adjacent components to one another.

3. The defendant manufactures, among other things, protective coverings for radio systems. From August to November 2004 it erected a spherical radome for the company N. Ltd. in I. (hereinafter: "N.").

4. The defendant invokes a right based on prior use, referring as grounds to several radomes equipped with a protective enclosure and other radio-communications installations, including a spherical radome built to order in 1990–1991 for the Financial Planning Office of B. on H. Hill, near H. (hereinafter "H."). The defendant manufactured the rigid foam segments for this radome and delivered them to the construction site, where they were installed by G. LLC (hereinafter "GE"), the company charged to erect the radome.

5. The plaintiff brought an action against the defendant for injunctive relief, information and rendering of account, destruction and damage compensation on the ground of direct infringement of the patent in suit. ...

5.4 Reasoning:

The admissible appeal on the law remains unsuccessful in substance.

I. The patent in suit concerns protective coverings for radio systems as well as methods for fabricating such protective coverings.

1. According to the description of the patent in suit, radio antennae are in need of protection from the effects of environment and weather conditions, while as a rule the protective enclosures should not reduce the signal intensity of the electromagnetic radiation if possible and thus should only absorb slight amounts of radiation. The known art includes protective enclosures made of rigid polyurethane foam, as shown in supporting part reproduced here.

A drawback to this construction is that, due to the materials needed to provide stability, it has a tendency to crack when exposed to extreme temperature fluctuation, in addition to which ice and snow can collect on its surface, entailing a certain risk of collapse. As the construction components are rather large, their transport and assembly also leads to high costs.

2. In view of this, the patent in suit concerns the technical problem of providing for an improved and easy-to-assemble protective enclosure for radio systems with high stability and favourable absorption characteristics, as well as a method for manufacturing the same.

3. To solve this problem, claim 1 of the patent in suit proposes a device with the following features:

1. The device serves as a protective covering (17, 18, 19) for radio systems.
2. The protective covering (17, 18, 19) consists of (multiple) components (1), each of which comprises
2.1 an insulation layer (3),
2.2 on at least one side of the insulation layer (3) a support element (2) connected at least partly to the insulation layer,
2.3 at the ends of the components (1), reduction (7) of the thickness of the respective support element (2).
3. The spatial region (15) which is formed by the reduction (7)
3.1 is filled with the material of the support element (2) and
3.2 this material connects adjacent components (1).

4. Figure 3.5 reproduced here shows the basic structure of the protective covering using the example of a dome shape (radome). The reduction of thickness (7) provided for in claim 1 and the spatial area (15) formed by it, which is filled with the material of the supporting element (2), which connects adjacent components (1), are shown by way of example in Fig. 3.6, reproduced below. ...

5. This interpretation of patent claim 1, which is not contested by the appeal on the law, raises no legal concerns (Fig. 3.7). It is in accordance with the wording of the claim and the description of the patent in suit. According to this, two adjacent components are to be connected by filling the space between the tapered parts with material of the support element such that even in the connection areas the support element presents a surface that is smooth enough to allow snow and ice to slide off it so as to prevent stress on the protective covering. Another effect to be achieved is that the material in the connection area is as thick as the rest of the component, so that the absorption of the electromagnetic radiation from the radio system is not only

Fig. 3.5 The structure of the protective covering

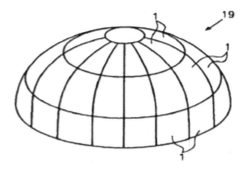

Fig. 3.6 Design figure of connect components

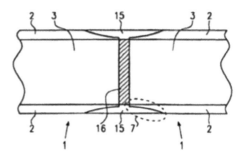

Fig. 3.7 Design figure of the supporting part of protective covering

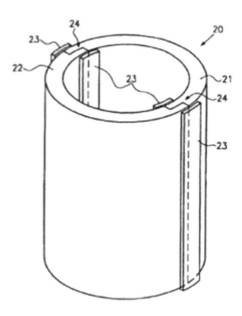

as slight as possible, but also uniform across the entire area of the protective covering in various directions of incoming or outgoing radiation (cf. description, para. 19 et seq. and 41 et seq.). If in the course of assembly on-site material is affixed extending beyond the spatial area formed by the tapering, for instance by overlapping it along the edges of the connected components, this is insignificant at least as long as the invention's intended purpose can be achieved without a practically significant loss. Thus, even such a design meets the requirements of the third set of features at least if ice and snow are unimpeded in sliding off the surface and the uniform absorption of electromagnetic radiation from the radio system by the supporting element, including the connected areas, in various directions of emission and input is not impeded to a practically significant extent.

II. The court of appeal found no infringement of the teaching of the patent in suit, with essentially the following reasoning: …

III. The decision of the court of appeal stands up to legal review.

1. The appeal on the law accepts as favourable the assessment of the court of appeal that the technical teaching of claims 1 and 17 of the patent in suit was carried out by the defendant in that the latter as the construction company offered and assembled radome "N." in I.; here too, no legal error is discernible.

2. The appeal on the law asserts that the court of appeal committed a legal error in holding irrelevant whether in the course of work to assemble radome "H." the laminate aramid fibre strips were inserted edge-to-edge or with overlaps in the transition areas between two components. An insertion of the fibre strips edge-to-edge, as was realised for the protective covering in the assembly of radome "N.", according to the statements of the court of appeal, represents a further development of a previously used embodiment in the transition area that extends beyond the scope of a use right established therewith and interferes with the subject-matter of the protected invention. This argument fails to convince.

a) According to Sec. 9 of the Patent Act, only the patent proprietor or a. party authorised by the proprietor is allowed to use the invention protected by the patent. Other third parties are excluded from such use for the term of the patent. This principle is limited by Sec. 12 of the Patent Act in so far as the effect of the patent does not arise with respect to the party who, on the date of registration, has already made use of the invention in Germany or has made the necessary preparations to do so. This party is allowed to use the invention for the needs of its operation in its own or others' places of operation.

With this limitation, the law intends for reasons of equity to protect a prior user's established legal status that is already present or in preparatory stages, and thereby to prevent the inequitable destruction of values that came into being in a legally valid manner. The patent proprietor should not be able to prevent that party from using the invention who has previously used the protected technical teaching or made concrete preparations for such a use on the basis of an exclusive right that has been established only later or in a legally relevant manner (Federal Supreme Court, decision of 13 November 2001, X ZR 32/99, GRUR 2002, 231, 233 et seq.—*Biegevorrichtung*; decision of 10 September 2009, Xa ZR 18/08, GRUR 2010, 47 para. 16—*Füllstoff*; cf. also on the prior-use right in design law: Federal Supreme Court, decision of 29 June 2017, I ZR 9/16, GRUR 2018, 72 para. 61—*Bettgestell*).

b) In accordance with this legislative purpose, the prior user is limited to such use of that established legal status for which all requirements of an exceptional use were met before the registration or priority date. Further developments beyond the scope of the prior use are not allowed if they interfere with the subject-matter of the protected invention. This Court presumed such an intervention for the case in which the alleged infringing embodiment realises all features of the patent claim, while this was not yet the case with the embodiment previously used due to a lack of one of these features (Federal Supreme Court, decision of 13 November 2001, XZR 32/99, GRUR 2002, 231, 234—*Biegevorrichtung*).

c) Furthermore, an interference with the subject-matter of the patent can also be given when the prior user uses the invention to a greater extent than corresponds to its legal status, or when it uses the invention in a different way than before the registration or priority date. The right of prior use may not be interpreted so narrowly that the prior user can make no economically reasonable use of it. On the other hand, it must be taken into account that the technical teaching of a patent can include alternatives that realise the technical and economic virtues of the invention in quantitatively or qualitatively different ways. In any case, the legal status of the prior user, who has only recognised and used one of these alternatives, does not necessarily justify allowing the prior user access to all these alternatives to the detriment of the patent proprietor. The prior user can therefore be banned from modifying the previously used embodiment even when the technical teaching of the invention is realised by both the prior use and the embodiment used after the registration date, but the latter realises the teaching of the patent claim in a different design or method.

aa) Whether a different form of use in this sense is present must be decided on the standard of the interpreted patent claims under consideration of the description and drawings. Alterations that have no effect on whether and in which manner the technical teaching of a patent claim and its individual features are carried out are irrelevant for the prior-use right. If, on the other hand, at least one feature of the patent claim is carried out in a technically different way than was the case before the registration date, this can exceed the limits of the prior-use right.

Whether this is the case must be decided on the basis of an overall assessment that appropriately balances the interest of the prior user to be able to use the established legal status in an economically sensible way, and the interest of the patent proprietor to only have to accept the use of its proprietary right if the protected technical teaching was actually recognised and implemented by the prior user.

bb) Accordingly, the limits of the prior-use right can be exceeded if the modification realises an additional advantage that was not realised by the non-modified embodiment. This can be the case when an embodiment is used for the first time that is emphasised due to this additional advantage in a sub-claim or in the patent's description.

If, however, two fully equivalent alternatives for a feature are named in a patent claim, the fact that the prior user only used one of these alternatives will as a rule not justify a corresponding limitation of that user's use right. It will likewise have to be assessed if in the patent specifications a modification of the previously used embodiment is disclosed that is an obvious alteration that from the point of view of the skilled person is readily compatible with the prior user's possession of the invention at the time of registration or priority.

Whether and if so under which further requirements the prior user is more over allowed to further develop the prior use in a manner that was obvious to the skilled person based on the prior user's possession of the invention and thus required no inventive step is not in need of a decision in the case at hand (cf. on this Benkard/Scharen, Patent Act, 11th edn. (2015), Sec. 12 para. 22; Bergermann, *Festschrift 80 Jahre Patentgerichtsbarkeit in Düsseldorf* (2016) pp. 51, 59; Busse/ Keukenschrijver, Patent Act, 8th edn. (2016), Sec. 12 para. 43; Keukenschrijver, GRUR 2001, 944, 947; Schulte/Rinken, Patent Act, 10th edn. (2017), Sec. 12 para. 24).

d) According to these principles, the use of the invention in the assembly of radome "N." does not extend beyond the scope of the prior-use right which, according to the statements of the court of appeal, was established by the use made of the invention when manufacturing the protective covering for radome "H." in 1990–1991.

–**aa**) In this respect it must be assumed under the principles governing appeals proceedings in favour of the plaintiff that during the assembly of the protective covering for radome "H." the tapered spaces between adjacent components were laminated with slight overlap on either side, and thus not, according to the court of appeal, as was done with the protective covering for radome "N.", abutting edge-to-edge. Namely, in the factual variant considered by the court of appeal as an alternative that the tapered spaces might also have been laminated edge-to-edge for radome "H." already, the use activities in each case would have been identical and it would thus be clear without a doubt that the later use remained within the factual limits of the right of prior use.

–**bb**) Not only as regards the assembly of the protective covering with its edge-to-edge lamination in the tapered areas between adjacent components, but also when lamination takes place with slight overlap on either side, the teaching of patent claim 1 is carried out in its literal sense.

(**1**) The features 1 to 2.3 were carried out uniformly in both embodiment examples.
(**2**) But also the requirements set by features 3 to 3.2 are met by both embodiments.

As explained, the teaching of the patent in suit does not require solely and exactly that the space created by the tapering be filled with material even with the edge. Rather, this teaching is also realised by embodiments in which material is affixed extending beyond that space, so that slight overlaps are formed on the edges. This is at least the case if ice and snow can slide off the surface unimpeded and the uniform absorption of electromagnetic radiation from the radio system is not impeded to a practically significant extent by the supporting element including the connected areas in various directions of emission and input.

Not only the protective covering as laminated edge-to-edge on radome "N.", but also the protective covering of radome "H.", where the lamination strips were laid with a slight overlap on either side, are in conformity with this. The overlap on the protective covering of radome "H.", namely, according to the findings of the court of appeal which were not contested by the appeal on the law, led to only very slight ridges of significantly less than 1 mm, which "in no way" stood in the way of ice and snow sliding off the surface of the radome, in addition to which the absorption of electromagnetic radiation was not impeded to a practically significant extent. ...

cc) Therefore, an interference with the subject-matter of the protected invention is not given on grounds of the alleged infringing embodiment having realised all features of the patent claim for the first time whereas the previously used embodiment did not yet display all the features. An intervention likewise does not follow from both the prior use and the allegedly infringing use realising all features of the patent claim albeit each in a different embodiment or process. According to the explanations above, this would presuppose that the third set of features was realised in a qualitatively or quantitatively different manner by the modified design carried out by the contested embodiment, which involved filling the space created by the tapering with laminate strips, than in prior use, and in particular was associated with an additional advantage disclosed in the patent specifications. For this finding, however, there is no support, according to the statements of the court of appeal.

From the description of the patent in suit there arises no indication that it would be technically advantageous to fill in the tapered space between two support elements exactly flush with them without allowing even the slightest overlap on either side. In the description it is only indicated that the tapering parts makes it possible to obtain a smooth surface without lumps allowing ice and snow to easily slide off, and to achieve the same thickness of material as in the rest of the component, so that the protective cover's absorption of the electromagnetic radiation from the radio system is fully uniform in various directions of emission and input (para. 19 et seq. and 41 et seq.). Because slight differences in height can never be completely ruled out for an assembly on a construction site, no other useful standard for differentiating more or less advantageous embodiments can be obtained from the patent in suit than that of practically significant effects on the absorption characteristics or whether ice and snow will slide off.

e) Correspondingly, the plaintiff's auxiliary request likewise cannot meet with success, regardless of whether the latter may still be admissibly submitted in the appeal proceeding (cf. on this Federal Supreme Court, decision of 1 April 1998, XII ZR 278/96, NJW 1998, 1857, 1860); in it, the injunctive relief claim based on the wording of patent claims 1 and 17 contains the additional feature "characterised in that the thickness of the layer of material of the supportive element remains uniform across the point of connection between two components".

3. The appeal on the law furthermore asserts that the prior user, which supplied all the components for a device, is not allowed to begin manufacturing the device itself following the registration of the patent even when the assembly of the components on the purchaser's site to the protected entire device was surely predictable in advance and was easy to handle, as the court of appeal presumed in the case of the assembly of the protective covering for radome "H." by the third-party company GE, since all components of it had been delivered in advance by the defendant. This argument likewise is unsuccessful.

a) According to the Court's case law handed down on the then Sec. 6 of the Patent Act of 1968, while a direct infringement of the combination patent may indeed only be found when the form of infringement makes use of the entirety of the combination features, exceptions can still be admitted within narrow limits, if the contested embodiment displays all essential features of the protected invention idea and the only thing it needs to be complete is at most the addition of self-evident parts, so that it is irrelevant if the final act, with no bearing on the inventive step, of putting together the entire device is carried out by third parties (Federal Supreme Court, decision of 10 December 1981, X ZR 70/80, BGHZ 82, 254, 256—*Rigg*). With this the former high-court case law was abandoned, according to which even individual elements of a protected entire device could attain an independent protection if the parts involved were individualised parts in terms of the inventive function (cf. in this respect Federal Supreme Court, decision of 21 November 1958, I ZR 129/57, GRUR 1959, 232, 234—*Förderrinne*). Accordingly, the Court emphasised with regard to Sec. 9, first sentence, No. 1 of the Patent Act (1981) that for differentiating between intended use and (new) manufacture of the protected subject-matter the entire combination is the relevant factor, and that in the manufacture of single parts of a protected product no direct patent infringement can be seen even when these parts are individualised in terms of the inventive function (Federal Supreme Court, decision of 4 May 2004, X ZR 48/03, BGHZ 159, 76, 91—*Flügelradzähler*; decision of 24 October 2017, X ZR 55/16, GRUR 2018, 170 para. 38 et seq.—*Trommeleinheit*).

b) Contrary to the view of the appeal on the law, this does not however mean that the manufacture is limited to the last activity leading directly to the completion of the protected entire device. Rather, the manufacture of the protected product begins as early as the fabrication of essential single parts serving this end (Federal Supreme Court, decision of 20 December 1994, X ZR 56/93, GRUR 1995, 338, 341—*Kleiderbügel*) and includes the entire activity through which the protected product, that is, the entire combination of all features of the patent claim, is brought into being (Benkard/Scharen, Sec. 9 Patent Act, para. 32; Busse/Keukenschrijver, Sec. 9 Patent Act, para. 63; both with further references). Because this overall combination is always the standard for the manufacture of the protected subject-matter, the fabrication of single parts serving the protected product can only be seen as also being the fabrication of the product when its completion represents a result of the actions of the manufacturer of the individual parts. This, when assessing the entire process of manufacture, must be affirmed when the completion of the protected product is clear from the manufacture of its individual parts, or at least can be expected with some certainty. Therefore, the manufacture of individual parts, which can only be technically and economically sensibly assembled into the entire device according to the invention uses the product patent protecting this device directly even when this manufacturer does not itself assemble the parts but supplies a third party with them, who puts them together into the protected entire device (cf. also Düsseldorf Court of Appeal, decision of 17 December 2012—2 W 28/12, juris para. 106; Benkard/Scharen, Sec. 9 Patent Act, para. 32; Chrocziel/Hufnagel, *Festschrift for Tilmann* (2003), 449,451; Giebe, *Festschrift for Schilling* (2007), 143, 162; Kraßer/Ann 7th edn. (2016), Sec. 33, para. 70).

c) Because the requirements of a use activity within the meaning of Sec. 12 of the Patent Act do not go beyond those demanded of a use within the meaning of Sec. 9 of the Patent Act (Federal Supreme Court, decision of 13 March 2003, X ZR100/00, GRUR 2003, 507, 509—*Enalapril*; Benkard/Scharen, Sec. 12 of the Patent Act, para. 11; Busse/Keukenschrijver, Sec. 12 of the Patent Act, para. 23), the manufacture and supply to a third party of the single parts of an entire device, under the above-named circumstances, can therefore also be seen as a direct prior use by the manufacturer of the components.

d) According to these principles, the defendant, who manufactured and delivered all the components for the protective covering of radome "H.", is to be seen as manufacturer of the protective covering according to the patent. That the assembly of the protective covering was carried out by GE does not contradict this. The components of the protective covering delivered by the defendant are not only in accordance with feature 1 and the second set of features, but furthermore, it was only possible to put them together to form a protective covering in a technically and economically sensible manner as provided for in the third set of features, so that it was possible for ice and snow to slide off its surface and the uniform absorption of electromagnetic radiation was not affected to an extent that was practically relevant.

4. Likewise without success is the complaint of the appeal on the law that the defendant is not entitled to a prior-use right on grounds that it began, when assembling radome "N." to use the process protected by patent claim 17 for manufacturing a protective covering for radio systems itself.

a) While it is true that a direct use of the teaching of a process claim cannot be seen in the manufacture and supply of the components for a patent-protected entire device on sole grounds of this delivery, a direct use by the prior user of the method named in the patent must however be allowed, in the case of manufacture and supply of the components for the overall device, according to the above considerations on the direct use of a product claim, when the components supplied by that user can only be technically and economically sensibly assembled by a third party in the manner taught by the process patent, and when the instructions of the patent claim go only so far as to teach this assembly (cf. also Düsseldorf Court of Appeal, GRUR-RR 2001, 201—*Cam-Carpet*). Otherwise, namely, this user would not be able to make any economically sensible use of its prior-use right.

b) As explained above with regard to the direct prior use of the teaching of product claim 1 of the patent in suit, it was technically and economically only sensible for GE to construct the protective covering for radome "H." in such a way that the components provided by the defendant were assembled and connected by attaching the pre-formed strips with material of the supporting element so as to allow ice and snow to slide off the surface, according to features 1 and 2, and not to impinge considerably in practical terms the uniform absorption of electromagnetic radiation. In the teaching to proceed thus, the instructions are exhausted, so that the court of appeal rightly saw the use of the method according to patent claim 17 by the defendant as being covered by its right of prior use.

5. The appeal on the law likewise fails to convince, finally, with the complaint that the court of appeal was not allowed to leave open the question of whether the defendant also used the teaching of the patent in suit in the other projects it cited from the late 1980s and early 1990s; only if the defendant executed other comparable projects in this period, argues the appeal, is the conclusion drawn by the court of appeal, that the prior use alleged by the defendant was not ultimately abandoned, well grounded.

a) A right of prior use does not arise when the prior user ultimately ceases preparations to use the invention before the registration date. If, however, the user has used the subject-matter of the invention in at least one instance, it is not necessary for the creation or the maintenance of the prior-use right for the use to be continued without interruption. In this case, rather, the prior-use right lapses only when the prior user abandons this right (Federal Supreme Court, decision of 7 January 1965, Ia ZR 151/63, GRUR 1965, 411, 413—*Lacktränkeinrichtung*).

b) The court of appeal—without legal error—did not conclude such an abandonment of the prior-use right, which arose in favour of the defendant on grounds of its use activities in the context of erecting radome "H." in 1989, from the fact that almost 10 years passed between the construction of several radomes in the late 1980s and early 1990s and the construction of radome "N.", during which time the defendant did not engage in any activities in this field. Taken by itself, this fact does not represent sufficient indication that the defendant intended to abandon a potential right based on prior use for good. Rather, the court of appeal correctly assumed, in light of the uncontested submission of the defendant that it only failed to be active in shorter intervals because the construction of radomes is a special system for which there was only irregular demand, that an intent to abandon the right did not recognisably arise. Nor can an intent to abandon be deduced offhand from the taking up of production of another protective covering, as cited by the appeal on the law, at least as regards systems like spherical radomes that are not only subject to fluctuating demand but also represent custom orders requiring execution according to the specifications of the client (cf. also Busse/Keukenschrijver, Sec. 12 of the Patent Act, para. 52). ...

5.5 Analysis of the Case
Schutzverkleidung (protective covering)
Federal Court of Justice, 14 May 2019, Case No. X ZR 95/18

In this decision, the Federal Court of Justice dealt with the boundaries of a right to use a patented invention based on prior use.

(a) Essential facts
The plaintiff held a patent for a protective covering that can be used for large radio systems. The defendant manufactures coverings with all the features provided in the patent claim. He contended that he had manufactured and sold all the components necessary for building such coverings already before the priority date. The plaintiff argued that the defendant is using the invention in a different way than he had used it before the priority date and therefore is infringing the patent.

(b) Relevant questions
Section 12 (1) of the German Patent Act states that a patent has no effect against a person who, at the priority date, had already begun to use the invention in Germany, or had made the necessary arrangements to do so.

Against that background, The Federal Court of Justice had to decide

- whether a person who has used the invention in a certain way before the priority date is entitled to use it in a different way after the patent has been granted;
- whether a person who supplied all the components of a patent-protected device to a third person who manufactured such devices before the priority date is entitled to manufacture such devices himself after the patent has been granted;
- whether the right to use an invention based on prior use expires if the entitled person abandons this use for a longer period of time.

(c) The decision of the Court of Appeal
The Court of Appeal dismissed the infringement claims. The appellate judges found that the differences between the way the defendant had used the invention before the

priority date and afterward were not essential and therefore the defendant was still entitled to use the invention.

(d) The decision of the Federal Court of Justice

The Federal Court of Justice dismissed the appeal against the second instance decision.

According to established case law, Sec. 12 (1) does not grant the right to use the invention in every possible way. Based on this principle, the Federal Court of Justice had ruled in an older decision that a person who had used the invention only by equivalent means is not entitled to use it by means falling literally under the patent claim. In the present case, this principle was not relevant, as the defendant had always used the invention with means falling literally under the patent claim. The only thing he changed was the way in which the single components were put together, and the patent claims did not address this detail.

In further developing the principle laid out in the older decision, the Federal Court of Justice held that changes do not affect the right to use the invention if they do not have an effect on whether and in which manner the technical teaching of a patent claim and its individual features are implemented. Such effects may especially occur if the user turns to realise an additional advantage that is emphasized in a sub-claim or in the patent specification. In the case at stake, the defendant did not make use of such advantages. Therefore, he is entitled to use the invention also in the modified way.

With regard to the second question, the Federal Court of Justice decided that a person who used the invention in an indirect way before the priority day, e.g. by providing components ready for manufacturing the patented device or for implementing a patented method, is entitled to use the invention directly, if this is the only reasonable way to use those components. In the case at stake, this condition was met, because the components supplied by the defendant could only be used for manufacturing protective coverings. Therefore, the defendant is also entitled to manufacture such coverings himself.

With regard to the third question, the Court held that the right to use the invention expires if the entitled person has only made arrangements to use the invention before the priority date and gives up these efforts later on. However, if he has already used the invention before the priority date, he stays entitled unless he abandons his right. Depending on the details of the single case, not using the invention for a longer period may be considered as an implied act of abandoning the right. On crucial factor in this regard may be typical product life cycles. In the present case, the right to use the invention has not expired even though the defendant had not used the invention for several years, because protective coverings for large radio systems have a very long life cycle.

(e) Consequences

The decision clarified the limits of a prior-use right in many aspects. However, it will have to be seen how the courts will be able to deal with the crucial question whether a change does have an effect on whether and in which manner the technical teaching of a patent claim and its individual features are implemented.

(6) Requirements for Granting a Compulsory Licence for a Medicinal Product—Case of "Alirocumab"(case No. 2019—X ZB 2/19)

6.1 Syllabus:

In this decision, the Federal Court of Justice dealt with the conditions for granting a compulsory license. The Federal Court of Justice dismissed the plaintiff's appeal against the first instance decision. With regard to the first criterion laid out in Article 24 (1), the Federal Court of Justice referred to its previous decision on this subject which had been issued about one year earlier. There, the Court laid out that the license seeker must have tried over a certain period of time, in a manner appropriate to the situation, to reach an agreement with the patent owner on the grant of a license. The Court held that the plaintiff has not met this requirement, because he gave his license offer very late, offered only a very low license rate and went to court seeking a compulsory license three weeks after that. The plaintiff could have amended this fault by resuming appropriate license negotiations parallel to the court proceedings, but he did not take such measures.

6.2 Rules:

Patent Act, Sec. 24(1)

Official headnotes

a) The extent to which, and the period over which, the licence seeker must seek a licence on reasonable and customary terms also depends on the reaction of the patent owner. Further efforts are usually not required if the patent owner simply refuses to consent to the use of the invention. However, it is not sufficient if the patent owner declares that it will not grant a licence in principle but will consider it under exceptional circumstances.

b) A public interest requiring the grant of a compulsory licence for a medicinal product may be affirmed if significant results of a clinical study according to recognised principles of biostatistics have shown that the active substance of the medicinal product has therapeutic properties in the treatment of serious diseases which are not, or not to the same extent, proven for other products available on the market, in particular that the treatment reduces the risk of the patient dying as a result of the disease, or if such superior properties are proven in another way (continuation of decisions of the Federal Supreme Court, 5 May 2006, X ZR 26/92, BGHZ 131, 247—*Interferongamma*, and 11 July 2017, X ZB 2/17, BGHZ 215, 214—*Raltegravir*). Federal Supreme Court (Bundesgerichtshof), 4 June 2019—X ZB 2/19.

6.3 Facts:

The applicants market the medicinal product Praluent in Germany which contains the active substance alirocumab. This is a monoclonal antibody directed against the protein convertase subtilisin/kexin type 9 (PCSK9). This serine protease is involved in lipid metabolism and impairs the degradation of excessive levels of low-density lipoproteins (LDL cholesterol—LDL-C). An excessive LDL-C value is considered to be one of the main risk factors for atherosclerosis and is usually reduced by the administration of statins. Alirocumab, on the other hand, acts as a PCSK9 inhibitor and thereby (indirectly) reduces LDL cholesterol levels in the blood.

In fat metabolism disorders, a distinction is made between primary disorders, particularly those caused by a hereditary metabolic defect, and. secondary disorders caused by various diseases such as diabetes mellitus or liver disease. Praluent is approved as a 75 mg/ml or 150 mg/ml injection solution in a pre-filled syringe or in a prefilled pen (a tool that automatically inserts the injection needle into the subcutaneous tissue) for the treatment of adults with primary hypercholesterolemia and mixed dyslipidemia (where both cholesterol and triglycerin levels are elevated). On the recommendation of the European Medicines Agency (EMA), the European Commission on 11 March 2019 extended the approval to the treatment of adults with existing atherosclerotic cardiovascular disease to reduce cardiovascular risk by reducing LDL-C levels.

The respondent is the holder of European Patent 2 215 124, filed on 22 August 2008, relating to antigenbinding proteins against PCSK9. The reference to the grant of the patent was published on 24 February 2016. The Opposition Division of the European Patent Office upheld the patent as amended by decision of 30 November 2018; the appeals against this decision have not yet been decided.

The respondent filed a claim inter alia for injunctive relief against. The applicants before the Düsseldorf Regional Court for infringement of the patent at issue. After the proceedings had been suspended in the meantime in the light of the pending opposition proceedings, a hearing for the continuation of the oral proceedings was held before the Regional Court on 30 April 2019.

The respondent markets a medicinal product under the name Repatha containing the antibody Evolocumab, which also acts as a PCSK9 inhibitor. Repatha is also approved for all Praluent indications.

In a written submission dated 12 July 2018, the applicants filed an action for a compulsory licence to the patent at issue and at the same time applied for temporary permission to use the protected invention for the treatment of adultswith primary (heterozygousfamilial and non-familial) hypercholesterolemia or mixed dyslipidemia with the medicinal product Praluent in the four forms of administration mentioned.

The Patent Court rejected the application for an injunction (BPatG, Mitt. 2019, 117). The applicants contest this with their appeal, last extending the requested provisional authorisation in the main application to the further use of the protected invention for the treatment of adults with existing atherosclerotic cardiovascular disease in order to reduce the cardiovascular risk. The applicants also alternatively apply for provisional authorisation to use the invention for the treatment with the drug Praluent of adults with primary (heterozygous familial and non-familial) hypercholesterolemia or mixed dyslipidemia, or adults with existing atherosclerotic cardiovascular disease for the reduction of cardiovascular risk, who

(1) despite a high-intensive statin treatment for up to four weeks with 40 mg or more of atorvastatin daily or 20 mg or more of rosuvastatin daily or the maximum tolerated dose of one of these active substances, have an LDL-C value of 100 mg/dl, and/or

(2) have been hospitalised for myocardial infarction or unstable angina pectoris within four weeks to 12 months prior to commencement of treatment with a PCSK9 inhibitor, and/or
(3) while being treated with Repatha, have an LDL-C value below 25 mg/dl, and/or
(4) have previously taken Praluent 75 mg, and/or
(5) despite treatment with Repatha, have an LDL-C above 70 mg/dl. and/or
(6) cannot continue treatment with Repatha due to side effects, and/or
(7) have discontinued treatment with Repatha due to insufficient LDL-C reduction or because of side effects and for whom treatment with a PCSK9 inhibitor is still indicated.

The respondent defends the Patent Court decision, asks for the auxiliary request to be rejected and, in the alternative, requests that the applicant be ordered to render accounts and provide security.

6.4 Reasoning:
The appeal is admissible, but is unsuccessful on the merits.
The Patent Court essentially gave the following reasons for its decision:

I. The applicants had not within a reasonable period of time endeavoured to obtain consent from the respondent to use the invention on reasonable commercial terms. It was not until the applicants offered to conclude a licence in a lawyer's letter of 20 June 2018 that the applicants could be considered to have made such an effort. The applicants' request for a licence had thus only been made three weeks before the filing of the application for an interim injunction and only slightly more than two months before the oral proceeding. Such a short period was only appropriate in special cases which did not apply in the dispute. The respondent was on the market with its own, directly competing product and had already made clear in proceedings in the USA that it was not willing to grant a licence, or only under special circumstances. The applicants should also not have assumed that they would be able to conclude a licence agreement in a minimum of time because the request for a licence only provided for a very low licence fee of 2% and, in the light of its content and aggressive language, would give rise to the expectation of a generally negative reaction. In addition, the applicants had not explained in more detail why the disputed patent would not prove to be legally valid, although the Opposition Division had taken the opposite position in its interim decision of 13 December 2017.

The applicants had also failed to substantiate that the public interest required the grant of the compulsory licence. There were doubts as to whether Praluent had the alleged therapeutic properties and significantly reduced the mortality risk of the patients treated. The results of the clinical study submitted (the Odyssey Outcomes study) did not prove that the administration of Praluent achieved a significant reduction in the total number of deaths (all-cause mortality) as compared with the placebo control group during the observation period. According to the results of the study, 392 out of 9462 participants in the placebo group died, while in the group of the same size treated with Praluent only 334 and thus 58 fewer patients died. Concerns about the significance of this finding arose, however, from the fact that both with coronary deaths (CHD death) with a P value of 0.38 and with all cardiovascular deaths (CV death) with a P value of 0.15, only a statistically insignificant reduction in deaths had been observed, since $P > 0.05$. Since these non-significant values were included in the P value of 0.026 determined for all-cause mortality, there were concerns as to whether this value, which was below the 5% threshold, was actually significant. These concerns were also shared by both parties' experts, Prof. Dr. P. and Prof. Dr. F.

Ultimately, there was no need to determine the question of Praluent's alleged therapeutic effect. Even assuming that, according to the Odyssey Outcomes study, the overall mortality compared to the control group had generally been reduced by 15% through the administration of alirocumab and by as much as 29% in high-risk patients, the applicants had not substantiated the claim that Praluent had therapeutic properties that Repatha did not possess or did not possess to the same extent. An argument against this was the fact that both the Praluent (Odyssey Outcomes study) and Repatha (Fourier study) studies were designed as placebo-controlled double-blind studies in which the mode of action of the monoclonal antibody contained in the drug was investigated in comparison to a standard therapy with statins. Such studies could not substitute for a direct comparison of the efficacy of the two antibodies, as was the case in an equivalence study in which a uniform patient population received either one or the other antibody as the active substance under a uniform study design.

The main reason was that the patient collectives treated in the aforementioned studies were different. In the patients examined in the Odyssey Outcomes study, the acute coronary syndrome had on average only lasted 2.6 months; whereas, in the Fourier study, the patients' cardiovascular event had on average already occurred 3.3 years previously and thus there was a considerably lower mortality risk. In addition, the studies differed in their study design, so that a direct comparison of the results as well as extrapolations or conversions was not permissible.

Nor was it plausible that there was a public interest in the continued availability of Praluent due to its being available in two different doses and the possibility of administering a significantly lower dose as compared with Repatha, or due to structural differences between the monoclonal antibodies alirocumab and evolocumab. Both antibodies selectively bound to the PSCK9 region that interacted with the extracellular domain of the LDL receptor protein (LDLR), thus preventing a PCSK9-LDLR interaction and an endosomatic degradation of the receptor protein. Although there were structural differences in the antigen binding point, since the respective epitopes overlapped in only two out of 20 amino acids, the applicants had not substantiated any effects on the efficacy or side effects of the antibody.

The same applied to possible patient intolerance reactions or a failure to respond to Repatha. Individual cases in which patients did not respond to Repatha or did so only poorly or showed side effects, while this was not the case when Praluent was administered, did not prove that the difference in the success of the treatment was due to the disadvantageous properties of Repatha as compared to Praluent.

II. This assessment is upheld on review in the appeal proceedings including with respect to the latest version of the main application.

(1) The Patent Court made no error in law in concluding that the applicants had not made sufficient efforts to obtain a contractual licence on reasonable commercial terms.

a) Since the grant of a compulsory licence constitutes a serious interference in the patent owner's fundamental right to freely decide whether and, if so, under what conditions it wishes to allow a third party to use the technical teaching in accordance with the invention (Sec. 9 Patent Act), Sec. 24 of the Patent Act requires not only that the public interest objectively requires the grant of the compulsory licence. The sovereign interference in the exclusive right conferred on the patent owner by the State's granting of the compulsory licence must rather also be necessary because the patent owner has refused the 'milder means' of the contractual grant of permission to use on reasonable terms.

In contrast to previous law, not procedural but substantive, this precondition for the grant of a compulsory licence under patent law does not necessarily have to be satisfied at the time when the compulsory licence action is filed. According to general principles it is sufficient if it is fulfilled at the end of the oral proceeding. However, it follows from the legal requirement that the effort must have been extended over a reasonable period of time, that it is not sufficient if the licence seeker states its willingness to pay an appropriate licence 'at the last minute' during the proceedings. Rather, it must have tried over a certain period of time, in a manner appropriate to the situation, to reach an agreement with the patent owner on the grant of a licence. The period of time and the measures necessary for this are a question for the individual case (decision of the Federal Supreme Court, 11 July 2017, X ZB 2/17, BGHZ 215, 214 para. 19—*Raltegravir*).

The period of time that the licence seeker must allow the patent owner to clarify the question as to whether a licence should be granted and, if so, to negotiate the appropriate terms of a licence, is determined to a large extent by the urgency of the decision on the grant of a contractual licence, but also by the complexity of the decision situation and by whether and at what point the licence seeker provides the patent holder with the information which the latter can reasonably expect before taking a decision on the conclusion of a licence agreement and, if appropriate, its terms.

b) Accordingly, the Patent Court committed no error of law by holding it insufficient that the applicants offered to conclude a licence agreement with the defendant for the first time by letter dated 20 June 2018, although such an offer could have been made at a significantly earlier point in time. This is all the more important, as the Patent Court also rightly assumed, since the only closer details stated in the letter—with the comment that it tended towards being too high rather than too low—were that a (very) low licence fee of 2% was offered for a patented active pharmaceutical ingredient and that this licence fee should only be paid for Praluent products manufactured for marketed in Germany, and since the applicants, without waiting for the reply that the respondent had promised, filed the compulsory licence action only a good three weeks later and filed the application for temporary permission to use with the Patent Court. Under these circumstances, the respondent had no reason to recognise the applicants' letter of 20 June 2018 as a serious attempt to reach a contractual agreement with it on reasonable terms.

Although this did not rule out the possibility that the applicants would meet the requirements of Sec. 24(1) No. 1 Patent Act by the end of the oral proceeding before the Patent Court on 6 September 2018, the situation and the time frame increased the requirements of a reasonable effort in the light of the short time remaining. However, the applicants did not make such reasonable efforts because for their part they failed to reply to the respondent's letter of 24 July 2018 prior to the oral proceeding of 6 September 2018.

A further effort on the part of the applicants would have been unnecessary if the respondent had simply refused to grant a licence in its letter of 24 June 2018 and thus rendered further negotiations futile (cf. Benkard, Rogge and Kober-Dehm, PatG, 11th edn (2015), Sec. 24 para. 13). However, contrary to the applicants' view, such a refusal cannot be inferred from the letter. In the letter, the respondent stated that its fundamental corporate policy was not to grant licences to competitors for the marketing of its own patented product. At the same time, however, it pointed out that an exception could beconsidered if there were extraordinary circumstances and that the existence of such circumstances depended on a review of the applicants' assertion that a compulsory licence actually served the public interest. It justified the need for such a review by arguing that the parties' antibodies blocked the PCSK9-LDLR interaction via the same mechanism and were approved by the European Medicines Agency (EMA) for the treatment of the same diseases and the same patients. No regulatory authority had analysed the data from the Odyssey Outcomes study or even concluded that Praluent offered an advantage over Repatha. It, they respondent, would have expected access to these documents if the applicants were of the opinion that the study data supported their assertion to the contrary. Without such access—which had been ordered in a case in the US, subject to a duty of confidentiality—the claim that Praluent's availability was in the patient's best interest could not be examined.

Accordingly, the applicants cannot be assumed to have made an unsuccessful effort on the grounds that the respondent refused to conclude a licence agreement from the outset. On the contrary, the applicants failed to make sufficient efforts because they only entered into negotiations for the conclusion of a licence agreement at a late stage, making an offer that was not very accommodating in terms of content, and failed to respond to the respondent's reply prior to the oral proceeding before the Patent Court.

c) Nor does the further correspondence between the parties after the oral proceeding before the Patent Court justify a different assessment.

The applicants failed to respond to the respondent's letter of 24 June 2018 until 21 November 2018, i.e. a full two and a half months after the rejection of the application for temporary permission to use and immediately prior to the proceeding before the Opposition Division beginning on 28 November 2018. In this letter, the applicants again explain their submission—which the Patent Court did not consider to be convincing—in the compulsory licence proceedings on the results of the Odyssey Outcomes study, but fail to respond to the defendant's request to make further data available to it, nor do they otherwise improve their licence offer. This reaction was not only clearly too late, but also insufficient in terms of content.

Since a research-based pharmaceutical manufacturer aims to generate an appropriate contribution margin to the total costs of its research and development activities with a patented product, it is often, if not as a rule, in its interest not to grant licences to competitors who want to market a competing product equivalent to its own product. Nevertheless, the grant of a licence is also reasonable, if not even advisable, from its point of view if the competing product has substantially superior characteristics and its availability is therefore not only in the patients' interest but would also justify the granting of a compulsory licence, which the manufacturer can prevent by permitting the use of the protected invention by contract. From the point of view of the patent owner and potential licensor, it is therefore crucial whether the product to be licensed exhibits such characteristics. A 'willing licensee' who makes reasonable efforts to obtain a licence on reasonable and customary terms will acknowledge this interest and provide the patent owner with such information as it can reasonably be expected to provide to verify an alleged superiority of its own product. As is otherwise the case in licence negotiations, the parties will, where appropriate, agree on the confidential treatment of sensitive information, taking due account of both the patent owner's interest in knowledge and the licence seeker's interest in secrecy.

Against this background, it can in any event not be regarded as a reasonable effort where, even after the oral proceeding before the Patent Court, the applicants did not at least enter into a discussion of the respondent's interest in acquiring further information which could possibly—positively or negatively—provide further indications of a significant influence of the administration of Praluent on the mortality risk.

d) Following the oral proceeding before the Opposition Division of the European Patent Office on 30 November 2018, at the end of which the patent at issue was essentially upheld, and the respondent's reply of 19 December 2018, the applicants failed to contact the respondent again until several months later, by letter of 2 April 2019. In this letter, the applicants merely repeated their willingness to conclude a licence agreement, but continued to limit their offer to the German part of the patent at issue and did not increase the 2% licence fee offered for the first time in their letter of 20 June 2018, although the 'massive doubts about the validity' of the patent at issue, with which they had justified this offer of a rather low licence fee, had not been confirmed by the decision of the Opposition Division of the European Patent Office. This cannot be seen as a serious effort on the part of the applicants to conclude a licence agreement, as had already been the case with their previous letters.

(2) Furthermore, the Patent Court was rightly of the opinion that it had not been substantiated that the public interest required the grant of a compulsory licence in the case at issue.

(a) A public interest requiring the grant of a compulsory licence may be affirmed if a medicinal product for the treatment of serious diseases has therapeutic properties which the products available on the market do not possess or do not possess to the same extent, or if its use avoids undesirable side-effects that must be accepted when the other therapeutic products are administered. A compulsory licence, on the other hand, cannot in principle be granted if the public interest can be satisfied with other, essentially equivalent alternative preparations (decision of the Federal Supreme Court, 5 December 1995, X ZR 26/92, BGHZ 131, 247, 254 ff.—*Interferongamma*; BGHZ 215, 214 para. 39—*Raltegravir*).

b) Praluent and the product marketed by the defendant Repatha are based on the same mechanism of action, as the Patent Court set out in more detail and as is not contested in the appeal. The monoclonal antibodies alirocumab and evolocumab each bind selectively to the region of the serine protease PSCK9 that interacts with the extracellular domain of the LDL receptor protein, thus preventing an interaction between the protein convertase and the receptor protein and its endosomatic degradation. This in turn promotes cholesterol degradation and allows a significant reduction in cholesterol levels, which, according to the results of the Fourier study and the Odyssey Outcomes study, reduces the risk of a major adverse cardiovascular event (MACE) such as coronary heart death, heart attack, stroke or unstable angina pectoris by approximately 15%. Since this significant pharmacological effect is achieved by both antibodies, however, it alone cannot justify the public interest in the requested compulsory licence.

c) The Patent Court rightly assumed that the results of the Odyssey Outcomes study did not substantiate the applicants' claim that the administration of Praluent reduced the mortality rate of hypercholesterolemia patients treated with this substance.

aa) It is not disputed that the results of the Odyssey Outcomes study show that numerically fewer patients in the Praluent group suffered coronary heart death or died of a cardiovascular disease than in the control group, but that these results are not statistically significant. Therefore, according to the principles of evidence-based medicine, it cannot be excluded with sufficient certainty that this is a random result, just as it can be chance that, according to the results of the Fourier study (in which the mortality risk was lower due to the chosen observation period), the rate of cardiovascular deaths in the Repatha group was even higher than in the control group.

bb) Against this background, in the appeal proceedings there is no objection to the Patent Court not attaching as much importance to the overall mortality rate shown in the Odyssey Outcomes study, which was numerically lower than that of the control group, as the applicants wanted.

1) It is of essential importance here that the Odyssey Outcomes study examined the achievement of primary and secondary endpoints and that only the coronary and cardiovascular causes of death are counted among the hierarchically upstream secondary endpoints, whereas the total number of deaths (undifferentiated by cause) in the observation period (total mortality) was only considered as a subordinate secondary endpoint. An endpoint in a clinical trial is a (previously determined) efficacy parameter, the achievement of which determines the success of the trial. As the respondent has substantiated, in particular through the statement of Prof. Dr. M. (AG-B7) and the annexes thereto, and at least in principle not disputed by the applicants, the appropriate evaluation of clinical trials with a plurality of predefined endpoints must take into account the risk that a rise in the number of endpoints increases the risk of false-positive conclusions.

In the US Food and Drug Administration (FDA) guidelines, this problem is explained using an example in which with only one endpoint and a threshold value for statistical significance of 0.05 there is a 5% risk of a false positive result, while two endpoints and an individual threshold value for statistical significance of 0.05 have a roughly 10% risk of a false-positive result for one of the two endpoints (cf. FDA, 'Multiple Endpoints in Clinical Trials, Draft Guidance for Industry', January 2017, p. 7, line 258 ff.; Appendix 4 to AG-B7).

This problem of 'multiplicity' can be taken into account by adjusting the threshold value according to the number of endpoints. In the example with two endpoints, this would be a threshold value of 0.025 instead of 0.05 according to the Bonferroni method (cf. on the Bonferroni method and other statistical methods for eliminating the problem of multiplicity: FDA, loc. cit., p. 24 f.). Another approach to solving the problem of multiplicity is a hierarchical test procedure in which a sequence is defined in advance for the endpoints. Unlike, for example, the Bonferroni method, such a hierarchical test procedure does not require a reduction of the threshold value for the P value. Instead, the problem of multiplicity is addressed by the fact that no lower endpoint in the hierarchy is regarded as statistically significant if the significance threshold has not been reached for an endpoint above it (FDA, loc. cit., p. 29 ff. 'The Fixed-Sequence Method'; Statement by M. AG-B7 para. 22 f.).

2) The Odyssey Outcomes study was based on such a hierarchical test procedure. In the presentation of the study results discussed at first instance, the P value of 0.026 for the total mortality rate is therefore referred to as the 'nominal' P value (HE19, slide 33).

This corresponds to the treatment of the secondary endpoint 'all-cause mortality' in the 'Summary of Product Characteristics (SmPC) for Praluent' by the European Medicines Agency (HE-B2). While the EMA, on the basis of the Odyssey Outcomes study, saw this as a significant risk reduction for the primary combined endpoint (summarised as MACE-Plus) consisting of 'death by unstable angina with necessary hospitalisation, ischemia-related coronary revascularisation procedure' (collectively referred to as a CHD event), 'non-fatal myocardial infarction' (MI), 'ischemic stroke' and 'unstable angina', as well as for the risk of a CHD event for the other combined secondary endpoints, severe CHD event, cardiovascular event, and the combined endpoint 'all-cause mortality, non-fatal MI, and non-fatal ischemic stroke', it only states for the secondary endpoint 'all-cause mortality' that 'a reduction of all-cause mortality of even only nominally statistical significance was observed in hierarchical testing'. Accordingly, Table 3 of the summary of the secondary endpoint 'all-cause mortality' with a P value of 0.026, subordinate to the secondary endpoints 'death by CHD' and 'cardiovascular death' with P values of 0.3824 and 0.1528 (and thus more than 0.05), was marked in a footnote as being only 'nominally significant', and the description of the Odyssey Outcomes study states that a reduction of all-cause mortality with 'only' nominally statistical significance was observed in hierarchical testing (HE-B2, S. 17 last paragraph: 'A reduction of all-cause mortality was also observed, with only nominal statistical significance by hierarchical testing [HR 0.85, 95% CI: 0.73, 0.98].').

The statistical evaluation of a significance that is only 'nominal' due to the hierarchy of the endpoints becomes even clearer in the report published in 'The New England Journal of Medicine' by G. G. Schwartz et al. on the Odyssey Outcomes study, in which a footnote in Table 2 states, with regard to the individual secondary endpoints of death due to coronary heart disease, cardiovascular causes and death from any cause, that the widths of the confidence intervals had not been adjusted for multiplicity and therefore the intervals for the endpoints should not be used for causal derivations (G.G. Schwartz et al., 'Alirocumab and Cardiovascular Outcomes after Acute Coronary Syndrome' NEJM 2018, 2097, 2103 [HE-B3], Table 2, footnote §: 'The widths of the confidence intervals for the secondary end points were not adjusted for multiplicity, so the intervals for the outcomes listed below this outcome should not be used to infer definitive treatment effects'). In Table 2, no P values at all are given for the non-significant secondary endpoints of death from coronary heart disease, cardiovascular causes, and death from any cause. In another footnote, this is explained as 'termination of hierarchical analysis in accordance with hierarchical testing plan'.

Finally, other sources are presented in line with this assessment, (Szarek et al., 'Alirocumab Reduces Total Nonfatal Cardiovascular and Fatal Events' Journal of the American College of Cardiology (JACC) 2019, 387, 395 [HE- B6]; Pocock et al., 'Critical Appraisal of the 2018 ACC Scientific Sessions Late-Breaking Trials From a Statistician's Perspective' JACC 2018, 1107, 1108 [AG8]; Genest, 'The Cat Has 9 Lives, Until it Dies' JACC 2019, 397 f. [HE-B10]; Sabatine et al., 'Evolocumab and Clinical Outcomes in Patients with Cardiovascular Disease' NEJM 2017, 1713, 1715: '… significance level 0.05.', 1718 Table 2, footnote *: 'Given the hierarchical nature of the statistical testing, the P values for the primary and key secondary end points should be considered significant, whereas all other P values should be considered exploratory' [AG-B6]).

cc) It is therefore of no consequence that the Patent Court—in a possibly merely misleading wording—spoke of the statistically insignificant P-values for coronary and cardiovascular deaths having 'flowed' into the P-value for all-cause mortality. What is decisive is rather that the nominally significant P-value for all-cause mortality does not provide a sufficiently reliable indication of a causal relationship between the administration of Praluent and a reduction in the overall mortality rate.

The applicants' expert P. also stated, as the Patent Court correctly pointed out, that it was 'somewhat unclear' what caused the reduction of the overall mortality rate in the Praluent group in the Odyssey Outcomes study. Where P.'s expert opinion describes it as 'more likely' than a cause in a previously unknown effect that a number of deaths were incorrectly not classified as cardiovascular (HE-Q39, p. 5), it is not discernible what empirical findings this statement of probability could be based on. It is also to a certain extent in contradiction to the claim in the appeal that it is 'completely plausible' that with high-risk patients Praluent also lowers the mortality not directly caused by cardiovascular disease.

d) Nor did the applicants in any other way substantiate that Praluent has superior characteristics to Repatha in spite of a common mechanism of action and in spite of equal efficacy with regard to the risk of a severe cardiovascular incident.

However, such superior properties of a medicinal product as may require the grant of a compulsory licence do not necessarily have to be proven by statistically significant results of a clinical study according to recognised scientific principles. Rather, evidence of the public interest necessitating the grant of a compulsory licence can in principle also be furnished with any other evidence admissible in court, and the same applies to the substantiation of the urgent public interest required in the proceedings for temporary permission to use. However, superior qualities of Praluent have not been substantiated even if the factual and scientific findings presented are considered in their entirety.

aa) The appeal unsuccessfully objects to the consideration of the hierarchy of endpoints in accordance with the scientific convention as 'formalistic objections' and contests the Patent Court's assessment that the numerical values for coronary heart deaths, cardiovascular deaths or deaths as a whole give a 'coherent picture' because the mortality rate in the Praluent group was always lower compared to the control group. It is obvious that the mere total number of deaths—with no differentiation according to cause of death—would not even make a mortality-lowering effect of Praluent seem plausible if the number of cardiovascular deaths in the patient group concerned were not also below the control group. On the other hand, a nominal significance for the deaths—by definition unspecified with regard to their cause—cannot replace the lack of significance for the cardiovascular and thus disease-specific deaths. Nor is this affected by the fact that the number of incidents in relation to the population as a whole has a reciprocal proportional effect on the P value.

bb) In addition, in the aforementioned work of Szarek et al. in the discussion of the results of the Odyssey Outcomes study, the clinical relevance of the only nominally statistically significant reduction of the overall death rate is justified precisely by the fact that the effect of Praluent is particularly impressive when the total number of fatal and non-fatal cardiovascular incidents (also the title of the work) is considered (HE-B6, p. 394, bottom of right-hand column). From the numerical values it can be deduced that a non-fatal cardiovascular incident is associated with an increased risk of a lethal outcome, which is greater in a second or further incident than in the first, which is why Szarek et al. describe the relationship between non-fatal and fatal events as an important consideration for the interpretation of the data (HE-B6, p. 395 left-hand column). However, if Praluent reduces the risk of death because it reduces the risk of a severe cardiovascular event and therefore also the risk of dying from a second or subsequent such event, it has not been substantiated that it is not the effect of a PSCK9 inhibitor but rather a specific effect of the antibody alirocumab that the antibody evolocumab does not have, that, according to the results of the Fourier study, also significantly reduced the risk of fatal cardiovascular events and non-fatal events (myocardial infarction, stroke, hospital admission due to unstable angina, coronary revascularization) (cf. Sabatine et al., 'Evolocumab and Clinical Outcomes in Patients with Cardiovascular Disease' NEJM 2017, 1713, 1718 Table 2 [Annex HE Q 42]:

'Outcome Primary end point: cardiovascular death, myocardial infarction, stroke, hospitalization for unstable angina or coronar revascularization: Evolocumab 1344 patients (9.8% of patients), placebo 1563 (11.3%); hazard ratio 0.85 (0.79–0.92); P-value <0.001).'

cc) This is not affected by Szarek's statement of 28 May 2019 (HE-B17), in which he compares the deaths in the Odyssey Outcomes study and the Fourier study in the drug group and the placebo group respectively, and comes to the conclusion that the risk of death in the placebo groups of both studies was only minimally different (for Odyssey Outcomes: 14.56 and for Fourier: 14.23 deaths per 1,000 patient years), while the number of deaths in the drug groups was about 17% lower for alirocumab than for evolocumab (for Odyssey Outcomes: 12.36 and for Fourier 14.83 deaths per 1,000 patient years) (HE-B17, para. 10 et seq.). Szarek's conclusion that the significant reduction in all-cause mortality from alirocumab resulting from this comparison would probably not have been observed with evolocumab, even if it had been used instead of alirocumab in the Odyssey Outcomes study, does not take into account the fact that different patient populations were treated in each study (in the Odyssey Outcomes study, acute coronary syndrome had on average occurred only 2.6 months previously, whereas with the patients of the Fourier study this had happened on average 3.3 years previously). Furthermore, the design of the two studies differed, which excludes a direct comparison of the results of both studies, as the Patent Court already correctly held with reference to the applicants' experts C. and P.

dd) The Patent Court also rightly assumed that the applicants had not demonstrated that there was a public interest in the continued availability of Praluent due to its lower dosage compared to Repatha.

1) It took into account that Praluent was administered in the Odyssey Outcomes study in doses of 75 mg or 150 mg and thus in lower doses than Repatha was administered in the Fourier study in which doses of 140 mg or 420 mg were administered. However, Repatha may also be administered at a lower dose using a simple syringe if necessary. In addition, with regard to the sub-study of the Fourier study known as the 'Ebbinghaus study', the question arises whether such a lower dosage is necessary at all, as no undesirable side effects were observed even with LDL-C values of less than 25 mg/dl, which makes a dose reduction in Repatha obsolete.

2) Even if, contrary to the Patent Court's assumption, it may not be possible in practice to administer Repatha reliably in lower doses than is prescribed by the packaging of the medicinal product as a ready-to-use injection solution in the form of a ready-to-use pen, a ready-to-use syringe or a cartridge for an automated mini-dispenser with 140 mg each, this does not alter the fact that the applicants have not substantiated that the administration of Repatha at a dose of 140 mg in a group of patients leads to undesirable side effects which do not occur with Praluent because Praluent is not only available at a dose of 140 mg but also at a dose of 75 mg and can therefore be administered at this lower dose.

In this respect, the applicants argue that some patients treated with Repatha at the 140 mg dose run the risk that the LDL-C value will be lowered below the physiologically normal level of 15 to 20 mg/dl. However, it cannot be determined from their submission how many patients were observed to have LDL-C values lowered below the physiologically normal level after the administration of the drug in a dosage of

140 mg. As also mentioned in the oral proceeding, neither do the applicants' submissions show whether the LDL-C values in the physiological range cannot be stabilised at least by reducing the administration of statin, which is initially administered as part of a standard therapy for acute coronary syndrome to reduce lipids and is also regularly used after the additional administration of a PCSK9 antibody (see P. expert opinion, HE-Q39, p. 3).

In addition, the statements of the applicants' expert P. do not prove that very low LDL-C values lead to increased health risks. Rather it is to be inferred from his expert opinion that very low LDL-C values, even below 10 mg/dl, would have an absolute benefit and could be achieved by the use of PCSK9 antibodies for the first time, although this benefit would, however, be significantly reduced with a very low LDL-cholesterol level. P. further points out that it is not clear whether a very low LDL cholesterol level is associated with other increased risks, such as haemorrhagic strokes, for which there are indications from statin studies. From the data on PCSK9 inhibitors presented so far, there is no sign of this, although the observation time is still too short to be able to make a conclusive statement (HE-Q39, p. 3).

In addition, the hypothesis that a low LDL cholesterol level increases the risk of negative effects on the cognitive abilities of the patients was not confirmed by the Fourier sub-study, the 'Ebbinghaus study', even with 661 patients whose lowest LDL cholesterol level was below 25 mg/dl (Guigliano et al., 'Cognitive Function in a Randomized Trial of Evolocumab' NEJM 2018, 633 Abstract' and 641, right hand column, first paragraph, last sentence; AG 11), as the Patent Court has already pointed out.

ee) Finally, the Patent Court did not err in law in holding that a public interest had not been substantiated even from the point of view of possible incompatibility reactions or a failure to respond to Repatha.

1) Individual cases in which patients had not responded, or only poorly responded, to Repatha or in which side effects had occurred, while this had not been the case with the administration of Praluent, do not, according to the Patent Court's findings, prove that the different treatment success is attributable to disadvantageous characteristics of Repatha which Praluent does not exhibit. Instead, in the cases cited by the applicants, shortcomings in the cooperation of the patients or errors in the administration of the injection were also considered as at least equally possible causes for the different success.

2) The applicants in reply argue that practice has shown that there are patients in whom the LDL-C concentration could not be sufficiently reduced with Repatha or who were obliged to discontinue the treatment due to side effects while the desired success occurred with Praluent or the undesired side effects did not occur. This argument cannot prevail because it does not exclude other causes for the different treatment successes of Repatha and Praluent, which are also possible according to the findings of the Patent Court. In addition, there is a lack of concrete information as to the cases in which the different treatment successes presented by the applicants are supposed to have occurred.

III. Finally, the appeal is also unsuccessful in the auxiliary request.

Irrespective of the question as to whether the auxiliary request can still be submitted for a decision in the appeal proceedings and whether, in particular since it leaves open how the restriction of the use of Praluent to certain groups of patients is to be achieved in the sale of Praluent, it meets the requirement of the certainty of a petition for an injunction under Sec. 99(1) Patent Act in connection with Sec. 253(2) No. 2 Code of Civil Procedure, it is in any case unfounded.

(1) The applicants have not shown that, beyond the provisional permission for use sought in the main application, they have unsuccessfully endeavoured, at least within a reasonable period of time, to obtain a legal licence on reasonable terms with regard to the uses named in the auxiliary request. Therefore, for the reasons stated above, there have also been insufficient efforts to obtain a legal licence in this respect.

(2) Moreover, the applicants have not substantiated that the public interest in the cases named in the auxiliary request requires the grant of a compulsory licence, as can also be seen from the comments on the main petition. Translated from the German by DavidWright, ilb, Austria.

6.5 Analysis of the Case

Alirocumab

Federal Court of Justice, 4 June 2019, Case No. X ZB 2/19

In this decision, the Federal Court of Justice dealt with the conditions for granting a compulsory license. This was the second time that the Federal Court of Justice had to deal with such questions since 2017, but only the fourth time in total in almost forty years.

Essential facts

The defendant holds a patent on proteins binding against an enzyme called PCSK9 (proprotein convertase subtilisin/kexin type 9). He markets a drug called Repatha which is used for treatment of high cholesterol levels, Repatha contains the active substance Evolocumab, which is a PCSK9 inhibitor protected by the patent.

The plaintiff markets a competing product called Praluent containing the active substance Alirocumab, which is another PCSK9 inhibitor. In separate proceedings, the defendant sued for infringement of his patent. In turn, the plaintiff offered to take a license, but only for a license fee which the defendant considered too low. The plaintiff reacted by filing for a compulsory license and a preliminary permission to use the invention. He referred to a study showing—in his view—that the overall percentage of people dying of a cardiovascular disease is lower among patients treated with Praluent then among patients treated with Repatha. However, this difference is not statistically relevant based on the rules on which the study is based.

Relevant questions

Section 24 (1) of the German patent act provides a right to be granted a compulsory license for using a patented invention if the license seeker for a reasonable period of time has unsuccessfully tried to obtain a contractual license under reasonable conditions and if public interest requires the grant of the compulsory license.

In the case at stake, the Federal Court of Justice had to decide on a preliminary basis whether these two conditions were met.

The decision of the Federal Patent Court
The Federal Patent Court dismissed the motion for granting a preliminary permission to use the invention. The found that the plaintiff had not reasonably tried to obtain a contractual license and that granting a compulsory license was not in the public interest, because Praluent/Alirocumab does not have significant advantages over Repatha/Evolocumab.

The decision of the Federal Court of Justice
The Federal Court of Justice dismissed the plaintiff's appeal against the first instance decision. With regard to the first criterion laid out in Article 24 (1), the Federal Court of Justice referred to its previous decision on this subject which had been issued about one year earlier. There, the Court laid out that the license seeker must have tried over a certain period of time, in a manner appropriate to the situation, to reach an agreement with the patent owner on the grant of a licence. The Court held that the plaintiff has not met this requirement, because he gave his license offer very late, offered only a very low license rate and went to court seeking a compulsory license three weeks after that. The plaintiff could have amended this fault by resuming appropriate license negotiations parallel to the court proceedings, but he did not take such measures.

With regard to the second criterion, the Federal Court of Justice also referred to its previous decision. According to this decision, public interest requires the grant of a compulsory license if the license seeker wants to market a product for the treatment of serious diseases having therapeutic properties, which the products available on the market do not possess or do not possess to the same extent. In the Court's view, the study presented by the plaintiff did not offer sufficient evidence that Praluent does have significant advantages compared with Repatha. In particular, the study did not clearly show a lower mortality rate, because the reported difference was not statistically significant according to the rules underlying the study.

Consequences
This decision confirms that getting a compulsory license to use a pharmaceutical invention is very difficult if the patentee or one of his licensees offers a product which also uses the invention, unless the license seeker has clear and strong evidence that his product is significantly better.

3.1.2 Patent Cases from the United States

(1) **Obviousness, Patentable Subject Matter and Judicial Claim Interpretation—KSR INTERNATIONAL CO. v. TELEFLEX INC. ET AL. (No. 04–1350)**

1.1 Syllabus:
SUPREME COURT OF THE UNITED STATES
CERTIORARI TO THE UNITED STATES COURT OF APPEALS FOR THE FEDERAL CIRCUIT
No. 04–1350. Argued November 28, 2006—Decided April 30, 2007

1.2 Facts:
To control a conventional automobile's speed, the driver depresses or releases the gas pedal, which interacts with the throttle via a cable or other mechanical link. Because the pedal's position in the footwell normally cannot be adjusted, a driver wishing to be closer or farther from it must either reposition himself in the seat or move the seat, both of which can be imperfect solutions for smaller drivers in cars with deep footwells. This prompted inventors to design and patent pedals that could be adjusted to change their locations. The Asano patent reveals a support structure whereby, when the pedal location is adjusted, one of the pedal's pivot points stays fixed. Asano is also designed so that the force necessary to depress the pedal is the same regardless of location adjustments. The Redding patent reveals a different, sliding mechanism where both the pedal and the pivot point are adjusted.

In newer cars, computer-controlled throttles do not operate through force transferred from the pedal by a mechanical link, but open and close valves in response to electronic signals. For the computer to know what is happening with the pedal, an electronic sensor must translate the mechanical operation into digital data. Inventors had obtained a number of patents for such sensors. The so-called '936 patent taught that it was preferable to detect the pedal's position in the pedal mechanism, not in the engine, so the patent disclosed a pedal with an electronic sensor on a pivot point in the pedal assembly. The Smith patent taught that to prevent the wires connecting the sensor to the computer from chafing and wearing out, the sensor should be put on a fixed part of the pedal assembly rather than in or on the pedal's footpad. Inventors had also patented self-contained modular sensors, which can be taken off the shelf and attached to any mechanical pedal to allow it to function with a computer-controlled throttle. The '068 patent disclosed one such sensor. Chevrolet also manufactured trucks using modular sensors attached to the pedal support bracket, adjacent to the pedal and engaged with the pivot shaft about which the pedal rotates. Other patents disclose electronic sensors attached to adjustable pedal assemblies. For example, the Rixon patent locates the sensor in the pedal footpad, but is known for wire chafing.

After petitioner KSR developed an adjustable pedal system for cars with cable-actuated throttles and obtained its '976 patent for the design, General Motors Corporation (GMC) chose KSR to supply adjustable pedal systems for trucks using computer-controlled throttles. To make the '976 pedal compatible with the trucks, KSR added a modular sensor to its design. Respondents (Teleflex) hold the exclusive license for the Engelgau patent, claim 4 of which discloses a position-adjustable pedal assembly with an electronic pedal position sensor attached a fixed pivot point. Despite having denied a similar, broader claim, the U. S. Patent and Trademark Office (PTO) had allowed claim 4 because it included the limitation of a fixed pivot position, which distinguished the design from Redding's. Asano was neither included among the Engelgau patent's prior art references nor mentioned in the patent's prosecution, and the PTO did not have before it an adjustable pedal with a fixed pivot point. After learning of KSR's design for GMC, Teleflex sued for infringement, asserting that KSR's pedal system infringed the Engelgau patent's claim 4. KSR countered that claim 4 was invalid under §103 of the Patent Act, which forbids issuance of a patent when "the differences between the subject matter sought to be patented and the prior art are such that the subject matter as a whole would have been obvious at the time the invention was made to a person having ordinary skill in the art."

Graham v. John Deere Co. of Kansas City, 383 U. S. 1, 17–18, set out an objective analysis for applying §103: "[T]he scope and content of the prior art are... determined; differences between the prior art and the claims at issue are... ascertained; and the level of ordinary skill in the pertinent art resolved. Against this background the obviousness or nonobviousness of the subject matter is determined. Such secondary considerations as commercial success, long felt but unsolved needs, failure of others, etc., might be utilized to give light to the circumstances surrounding the origin of the subject matter sought to be patented." While the sequence of these questions might be reordered in any particular case, the factors define the controlling inquiry. However, seeking to resolve the obviousness question with more uniformity and consistency, the Federal Circuit has employed a "teaching, suggestion, or motivation" (TSM) test, under which a patent claim is only proved obvious if the prior art, the problem's nature, or the knowledge of a person having ordinary skill in the art reveals some motivation or suggestion to combine the prior art teachings.

The District Court granted KSR summary judgment. After reviewing pedal design history, the Engelgau patent's scope, and the relevant prior art, the court considered claim 4's validity, applying *Graham*'s framework to determine whether under summary-judgment standards KSR had demonstrated that claim 4 was obvious. The court found "little difference" between the prior art's teachings and claim 4: Asano taught everything contained in the claim except using a sensor to detect the pedal's position and transmit it to a computer controlling the throttle. That additional aspect was revealed in, e.g., the '068 patent and Chevrolet's sensors. The court then held that KSR satisfied the TSM test, reasoning (1) the state of the industry would lead inevitably to combinations of electronic sensors and adjustable pedals, (2) Rixon provided the basis for these developments, and (3) Smith taught a solution to Rixon's chafing problems by positioning the sensor on the pedal's fixed structure, which could lead to the combination of a pedal like Asano with a pedal position sensor.

Reversing, the Federal Circuit ruled the District Court had not applied the TSM test strictly enough, having failed to make findings as to the specific understanding or principle within a skilled artisan's knowledge that would have motivated one with no knowledge of the invention to attach an electronic control to the Asano assembly's support bracket. The Court of Appeals held that the District Court's recourse to the nature of the problem to be solved was insufficient because, unless the prior art references addressed the precise problem that the patentee was trying to solve, the problem would not motivate an inventor to look at those references. The appeals court found that the Asano pedal was designed to ensure that the force required to depress the pedal is the same no matter how the pedal is adjusted, whereas Engelgau sought to provide a simpler, smaller, cheaper adjustable electronic pedal. The Rixon pedal, said the court, suffered from chafing but was not designed to solve that problem and taught nothing helpful to Engelgau's purpose. Smith, in turn, did not relate to adjustable pedals and did not necessarily go to the issue of motivation to attach the electronic control on the pedal assembly's support bracket. So interpreted, the court held, the patents would not have led a person of ordinary skill to put a sensor on an Asano-like pedal. That it might have been obvious to try that combination was likewise irrelevant. Finally, the court held that genuine issues of material fact precluded summary judgment.

1.3 Reasoning:
The Federal Circuit addressed the obviousness question in a narrow, rigid manner that is inconsistent with §103 and this Court's precedents. KSR provided convincing evidence that mounting an available sensor on a fixed pivot point of the Asano pedal was a design step well within the grasp of a person of ordinary skill in the relevant art and that the benefit of doing so would be obvious. Its arguments, and the record, demonstrate that the Engelgau patent's claim 4 is obvious.
1. *Graham* provided an expansive and flexible approach to the obviousness question that is inconsistent with the way the Federal Circuit applied its TSM test here.
a. Neither §103's enactment nor *Graham*'s analysis disturbed the Court's earlier instructions concerning the need for caution in granting a patent based on the combination of elements found in the prior art. See *Great Atlantic & Pacific Tea Co.* v. *Supermarket Equipment Corp.*, 340 U. S. 147, 152. Such a combination of familiar elements according to known methods is likely to be obvious when it does no more than yield predictable results. See, e.g., *United States* v. *Adams*, 383 U. S. 39, 50–52. When a work is available in one field, design incentives and other market forces can prompt variations of it, either in the same field or in another. If a person of ordinary skill in the art can implement a predictable variation, and would see the benefit of doing so, §103 likely bars its patentability. Moreover, if a technique has been used to improve one device, and a person of ordinary skill in the art would recognize that it would improve similar devices in the same way, using the technique is obvious unless its actual application is beyond that person's skill. A court must ask whether the improvement is more than the predictable use of prior-art elements according to their established functions. Following these principles may be difficult if the claimed subject matter involves more than the simple substitution of one known element for another or the mere application of a known technique to a piece of prior art ready for the improvement. To determine whether there was an apparent reason to combine the known elements in the way a patent claims, it will often be necessary to look to interrelated teachings of multiple patents; to the effects of demands known to the design community or present in the marketplace; and to the background knowledge possessed by a person having ordinary skill in the art. To facilitate review, this analysis should be made explicit. But it need not seek out precise teachings directed to the challenged claim's specific subject matter, for a court can consider the inferences and creative steps a person of ordinary skill in the art would employ.
b. The TSM test captures a helpful insight: A patent composed of several elements is not proved obvious merely by demonstrating that each element was, independently, known in the prior art. Although common sense directs caution as to a patent

application claiming as innovation the combination of two known devices according to their established functions, it can be important to identify a reason that would have prompted a person of ordinary skill in the art to combine the elements as the new invention does. Inventions usually rely upon building blocks long since uncovered, and claimed discoveries almost necessarily will be combinations of what, in some sense, is already known. Helpful insights, however, need not become rigid and mandatory formulas. If it is so applied, the TSM test is incompatible with this Court's precedents. The diversity of inventive pursuits and of modern technology counsels against confining the obviousness analysis by a formalistic conception of the words teaching, suggestion, and motivation, or by overemphasizing the importance of published articles and the explicit content of issued patents. In many fields there may be little discussion of obvious techniques or combinations, and market demand, rather than scientific literature, may often drive design trends. Granting patent protection to advances that would occur in the ordinary course without real innovation retards progress and may, for patents combining previously known elements, deprive prior inventions of their value or utility. Since the TSM test was devised, the Federal Circuit doubtless has applied it in accord with these principles in many cases. There is no necessary inconsistency between the test and the *Graham* analysis. But a court errs where, as here, it transforms general principle into a rigid rule limiting the obviousness inquiry.

c. The flaws in the Federal Circuit's analysis relate mostly to its narrow conception of the obviousness inquiry consequent in its application of the TSM test. The Circuit first erred in holding that courts and patent examiners should look only to the problem the patentee was trying to solve. Under the correct analysis, any need or problem known in the field and addressed by the patent can provide a reason for combining the elements in the manner claimed. Second, the appeals court erred in assuming that a person of ordinary skill in the art attempting to solve a problem will be led only to those prior art elements designed to solve the same problem. The court wrongly concluded that because Asano's primary purpose was solving the constant ratio problem, an inventor considering how to put a sensor on an adjustable pedal would have no reason to consider putting it on the Asano pedal. It is common sense that familiar items may have obvious uses beyond their primary purposes, and a person of ordinary skill often will be able to fit the teachings of multiple patents together like pieces of a puzzle. Regardless of Asano's primary purpose, it provided an obvious example of an adjustable pedal with a fixed pivot point, and the prior art was replete with patents indicating that such a point was an ideal mount for a sensor. Third, the court erred in concluding that a patent claim cannot be proved obvious merely by showing that the combination of elements was obvious to try. When there is a design need or market pressure to solve a problem and there are a finite number of identified, predictable solutions, a person of ordinary skill in the art has good reason to pursue the known options within his or her technical grasp. If this leads to the anticipated success, it is likely the product not of innovation but of ordinary skill and common sense. Finally, the court drew the wrong conclusion from the risk of courts and patent examiners falling prey to hindsight bias. Rigid preventative rules that deny recourse to common sense are neither necessary under, nor consistent with, this Court's case law.

2. Application of the foregoing standards demonstrates that claim 4 is obvious.

a. The Court rejects Teleflex's argument that the Asano pivot mechanism's design prevents its combination with a sensor in the manner claim 4 describes. This argument was not raised before the District Court, and it is unclear whether it was raised before the Federal Circuit. Given the significance of the District Court's finding that combining Asano with a pivot-mounted pedal position sensor fell within claim 4's scope, it is apparent that Teleflex would have made clearer challenges if it intended to preserve this claim. Its failure to clearly raise the argument, and the appeals court's silence on the issue, lead this Court to accept the District Court's conclusion.

b. The District Court correctly concluded that when Engelgau designed the claim 4 subject matter, it was obvious to a person of ordinary skill in the art to combine Asano with a pivot-mounted pedal position sensor. There then was a marketplace creating a strong incentive to convert mechanical pedals to electronic pedals, and the prior art taught a number of methods for doing so. The Federal Circuit considered the issue too narrowly by, in effect, asking whether a pedal designer writing on a blank slate would have chosen both Asano and a modular sensor similar to the ones used in the Chevrolet trucks and disclosed in the '068 patent. The proper question was whether a pedal designer of ordinary skill in the art, facing the wide range of needs created by developments in the field, would have seen an obvious benefit to upgrading Asano with a sensor. For such a designer starting with Asano, the question was where to attach the sensor. The '936 patent taught the utility of putting the sensor on the pedal device. Smith, in turn, explained not to put the sensor on the pedal footpad, but instead on the structure. And from Rixon's known wire-chafing problems, and Smith's teaching that the pedal assemblies must not precipitate any motion in the connecting wires, the designer would know to place the sensor on a nonmoving part of the pedal structure. The most obvious such point is a pivot point. The designer, accordingly, would follow Smith in mounting the sensor there. Just as it was possible to begin with the objective to upgrade Asano to work with a computer-controlled throttle, so too was it possible to take an adjustable electronic pedal like Rixon and seek an improvement that would avoid the wire-chafing problem. Teleflex has not shown anything in the prior art that taught away from the use of Asano, nor any secondary factors to dislodge the determination that claim 4 is obvious.

3. The Court disagrees with the Federal Circuit's holding that genuine issues of material fact precluded summary judgment. The ultimate judgment of obviousness is a legal determination. *Graham*, 383 U. S., at 17. Where, as here, the prior art's content, the patent claim's scope, and the level of ordinary skill in the art are not in material dispute and the claim's obviousness is apparent, summary judgment is appropriate. P. 23. 119 Fed. Appx. 282, reversed and remanded.

KENNEDY, J., delivered the opinion for a unanimous Court.
SUPREME COURT OF THE UNITED STATES
No. 04–1350
KSR INTERNATIONAL CO., PETITIONER *v.* TELEFLEX INC. ET AL.
ON WRIT OF CERTIORARI TO THE UNITED STATES COURT OF

APPEALS FOR THE FEDERAL CIRCUIT
[April 30, 2007]
JUSTICE KENNEDY delivered the opinion of the Court.

Teleflex Incorporated and its subsidiary Technology Holding Company—both referred to here as Teleflex—sued KSR International Company for patent infringement. The patent at issue, United States Patent No. 6,237,565 B1, is entitled "Adjustable Pedal Assembly With Electronic Throttle Control." Supplemental App. 1. The patentee is Steven J. Engelgau, and the patent is referred to as "the Engelgau patent." Teleflex holds the exclusive license to the patent.

Claim 4 of the Engelgau patent describes a mechanism for combining an electronic sensor with an adjustable automobile pedal so the pedal's position can be transmitted to a computer that controls the throttle in the vehicle's engine. When Teleflex accused KSR of infringing the Engelgau patent by adding an electronic sensor to one of KSR's previously designed pedals, KSR countered that claim 4 was invalid under the Patent Act, 35 U. S. C. §103, because its subject matter was obvious.

Section 103 forbids issuance of a patent when "the differences between the subject matter sought to be patented and the prior art are such that the subject matter as a whole would have been obvious at the time the invention was made to a person having ordinary skill in the art to which said subject matter pertains."

In *Graham* v. *John Deere Co. of Kansas City*, 383 U. S. 1 (1966), the Court set out a framework for applying the statutory language of §103, language itself based on the logic of the earlier decision in *Hotchkiss* v. *Greenwood*, 11 How. 248 (1851), and its progeny. See 383 U. S., at 15–17. The analysis is objective:

"Under §103, the scope and content of the prior art are to be determined; differences between the prior art and the claims at issue are to be ascertained; and the level of ordinary skill in the pertinent art resolved. Against this background the obviousness or nonobviousness of the subject matter is determined. Such secondary considerations as commercial success, long felt but unsolved needs, failure of others, etc., might be utilized to give light to the circumstances surrounding the origin of the subject matter sought to be patented." *Id.*, at 17–18.

While the sequence of these questions might be reordered in any particular case, the factors continue to define the inquiry that controls. If a court, or patent examiner, conducts this analysis and concludes the claimed subject matter was obvious, the claim is invalid under §103.

Seeking to resolve the question of obviousness with more uniformity and consistency, the Court of Appeals for the Federal Circuit has employed an approach referred to by the parties as the "teaching, suggestion, or motivation" test (TSM test), under which a patent claim is only proved obvious if "some motivation or suggestion to combine the prior art teachings" can be found in the prior art, the nature of the problem, or the knowledge of a person having ordinary skill in the art. See, e.g., *Al-Site Corp.* v. *VSI Int'l, Inc.*, 174 F. 3d 1308, 1323–1324 (CA Fed. 1999). KSR challenges that test, or at least its application in this case. See 119 Fed. Appx. 282, 286–290 (CA Fed. 2005). Because the Court of Appeals addressed the question of obviousness in a manner contrary to §103 and our precedents, we granted certiorari, 547 U. S__(2006). We now reverse.

I
A.

In car engines without computer-controlled throttles, the accelerator pedal interacts with the throttle via cable or other mechanical link. The pedal arm acts as a lever rotating around a pivot point. In a cable-actuated throttle control the rotation caused by pushing down the pedal pulls a cable, which in turn pulls open valves in the carburetor or fuel injection unit. The wider the valves open, the more fuel and air are released, causing combustion to increase and the car to accelerate. When the driver takes his foot off the pedal, the opposite occurs as the cable is released and the valves slide closed.

In the 1990's it became more common to install computers in cars to control engine operation. Computer controlled throttles open and close valves in response to electronic signals, not through force transferred from the pedal by a mechanical link. Constant, delicate adjustments of air and fuel mixture are possible. The computer's rapid processing of factors beyond the pedal's position improves fuel efficiency and engine performance.

For a computer-controlled throttle to respond to a driver's operation of the car, the computer must know what is happening with the pedal. A cable or mechanical link does not suffice for this purpose; at some point, an electronic sensor is necessary to translate the mechanical operation into digital data the computer can understand.

Before discussing sensors further we turn to the mechanical design of the pedal itself. In the traditional design a pedal can be pushed down or released but cannot have its position in the footwell adjusted by sliding the pedal forward or back. As a result, a driver who wishes to be closer or farther from the pedal must either reposition himself in the driver's seat or move the seat in some way. In cars with deep footwells these are imperfect solutions for drivers of smaller stature. To solve the problem, inventors, beginning in the 1970's, designed pedals that could be adjusted to change their location in the footwell. Important for this case are two adjustable pedals disclosed in U. S. Patent Nos. 5,010,782 (filed July 28, 1989) (Asano) and 5,460,061 (filed Sept. 17, 1993) (Redding). The Asano patent reveals a support structure that houses the pedal so that even when the pedal location is adjusted relative to the driver, one of the pedal's pivot points stays fixed. The pedal is also designed so that the force necessary to push the pedal down is the same regardless of adjustments to its location. The Redding patent reveals a different, sliding mechanism where both the pedal and the pivot point are adjusted.

We return to sensors. Well before Engelgau applied for his challenged patent, some inventors had obtained patents involving electronic pedal sensors for computer controlled throttles. These inventions, such as the device disclosed in U. S. Patent No. 5,241,936 (filed Sept. 9, 1991) ('936), taught that it was preferable to detect the pedal's position in the pedal assembly, not in the engine. The '936 patent disclosed a pedal with an electronic sensor on a pivot point in the pedal assembly. U. S. Patent No. 5,063,811 (filed July 9, 1990) (Smith) taught that to prevent the wires connecting the sensor to the computer from chafing and wearing out, and to avoid grime and damage from the driver's foot, the sensor should be put on a fixed part of the pedal assembly rather than in or on the pedal's footpad.

3 Cases

In addition to patents for pedals with integrated sensors inventors obtained patents for self-contained modular sensors. A modular sensor is designed independently of a given pedal so that it can be taken off the shelf and attached to mechanical pedals of various sorts, enabling the pedals to be used in automobiles with computer-controlled throttles. One such sensor was disclosed in U. S. Patent No. 5,385,068 (filed Dec. 18, 1992) ('068). In 1994, Chevrolet manufactured a line of trucks using modular sensors "attached to the pedal support bracket, adjacent to the pedal and engaged with the pivot shaft about which the pedal rotates in operation." 298 F. Supp. 2d 581, 589 (ED Mich. 2003).

The prior art contained patents involving the placement of sensors on adjustable pedals as well. For example, U. S. Patent No. 5,819,593 (filed Aug. 17, 1995) (Rixon) discloses an adjustable pedal assembly with an electronic sensor for detecting the pedal's position. In the Rixon pedal the sensor is located in the pedal footpad. The Rixon pedal was known to suffer from wire chafing when the pedal was depressed and released.

This short account of pedal and sensor technology leads to the instant case.

B.
KSR, a Canadian company, manufactures and supplies auto parts, including pedal systems. Ford Motor Company hired KSR in 1998 to supply an adjustable pedal system for various lines of automobiles with cable-actuated throttle controls. KSR developed an adjustable mechanical pedal for Ford and obtained U. S. Patent No. 6,151,976 (filed July 16, 1999) ('976) for the design. In 2000, KSR was chosen by General Motors Corporation (GMC or GM) to supply adjustable pedal systems for Chevrolet and GMC light trucks that used engines with computer-controlled throttles. To make the '976 pedal compatible with the trucks, KSR merely took that design and added a modular sensor.

Teleflex is a rival to KSR in the design and manufacture of adjustable pedals. As noted, it is the exclusive licensee of the Engelgau patent. Engelgau filed the patent application on August 22, 2000 as a continuation of a previous application for U. S. Patent No. 6,109,241, which was filed on January 26, 1999. He has sworn he invented the patent's subject matter on February 14, 1998. The Engelgau patent discloses an adjustable electronic pedal described in the specification as a "simplified vehicle control pedal assembly that is less expensive, and which uses fewer parts and is easier to package within the vehicle." Engelgau, col. 2, lines 2–5, Supplemental App. 6. Claim 4 of the patent, at issue here, describes:

"A vehicle control pedal apparatus comprising:
a support adapted to be mounted to a vehicle structure;
an adjustable pedal assembly having a pedal arm moveable in for[e] and aft directions with respect to said support;
a pivot for pivotally supporting said adjustable pedal assembly with respect to said support and defining a pivot axis; and
an electronic control attached to said support for controlling a vehicle system;
said apparatus characterized by said electronic control being responsive to said pivot for providing a signal that corresponds to pedal arm position as said pedal arm pivots

about said pivot axis between rest and applied positions wherein the position of said pivot remains constant while said pedal arm moves in fore and aft directions with respect to said pivot." *Id.,* col. 6, lines 17–36, Supplemental App. 8 (diagram numbers omitted).

We agree with the District Court that the claim discloses "a position-adjustable pedal assembly with an electronic pedal position sensor attached to the support member of the pedal assembly. Attaching the sensor to the support member allows the sensor to remain in a fixed position while the driver adjusts the pedal." 298 F. Supp. 2d, at 586–587.

Before issuing the Engelgau patent the U. S. Patent and Trademark Office (PTO) rejected one of the patent claims that was similar to, but broader than, the present claim 4. The claim did not include the requirement that the sensor be placed on a fixed pivot point. The PTO concluded the claim was an obvious combination of the prior art disclosed in Redding and Smith, explaining:

"Since the prior art references are from the field of endeavor, the purpose disclosed... would have been recognized in the pertinent art of Redding. Therefore it would have been obvious... to provide the device of Redding with the... means attached to a support member as taught by Smith." *Id.,* at 595. In other words Redding provided an example of an adjustable pedal and Smith explained how to mount a sensor on a pedal's support structure, and the rejected patent claim merely put these two teachings together.

Although the broader claim was rejected, claim 4 was later allowed because it included the limitation of a fixed pivot point, which distinguished the design from Redding's. *Ibid*. Engelgau had not included Asano among the prior art references, and Asano was not mentioned in the patent's prosecution. Thus, the PTO did not have before it an adjustable pedal with a fixed pivot point. The patent issued on May 29, 2001 and was assigned to Teleflex.

Upon learning of KSR's design for GM, Teleflex sent a warning letter informing KSR that its proposal would violate the Engelgau patent. "Teleflex believes that any supplier of a product that combines an adjustable pedal with an electronic throttle control necessarily employs technology covered by one or more" of Teleflex's patents. *Id.,* at 585. KSR refused to enter a royalty arrangement with Teleflex; so Teleflex sued for infringement, asserting KSR's pedal infringed the Engelgau patent and two other patents. *Ibid.* Teleflex later abandoned its claims regarding the other patents and dedicated the patents to the public. The remaining contention was that KSR's pedal system for GM infringed claim 4 of the Engelgau patent. Teleflex has not argued that the other three claims of the patent are infringed by KSR's pedal, nor has Teleflex argued that the mechanical adjustable pedal designed by KSR for Ford infringed any of its patents.

C.

The District Court granted summary judgment in KSR's favor. After reviewing the pertinent history of pedal design, the scope of the Engelgau patent, and the relevant prior art, the court considered the validity of the contested claim. By direction of 35 U. S. C. §282, an issued patent is presumed valid. The District Court applied

Graham's framework to determine whether under summary judgment standards KSR had overcome the presumption and demonstrated that claim 4 was obvious in light of the prior art in existence when the claimed subject matter was invented. See §102(a).

The District Court determined, in light of the expert testimony and the parties' stipulations, that the level of ordinary skill in pedal design was "an undergraduate degree in mechanical engineering (or an equivalent amount of industry experience) [and] familiarity with pedal control systems for vehicles." 298 F. Supp. 2d, at 590. The court then set forth the relevant prior art, including the patents and pedal designs described above.

Following *Graham*'s direction, the court compared the teachings of the prior art to the claims of Engelgau. It found "little difference." 298 F. Supp. 2d, at 590. Asano taught everything contained in claim 4 except the use of a sensor to detect the pedal's position and transmit it to the computer controlling the throttle. That additional aspect was revealed in sources such as the '068 patent and the sensors used by Chevrolet.

Under the controlling cases from the Court of Appeals for the Federal Circuit, however, the District Court was not permitted to stop there. The court was required also to apply the TSM test. The District Court held KSR had satisfied the test. It reasoned (1) the state of the industry would lead inevitably to combinations of electronic sensors and adjustable pedals, (2) Rixon provided the basis for these developments, and (3) Smith taught a solution to the wire chafing problems in Rixon, namely locating the sensor on the fixed structure of the pedal. This could lead to the combination of Asano, or a pedal like it, with a pedal position sensor.

The conclusion that the Engelgau design was obvious was supported, in the District Court's view, by the PTO's rejection of the broader version of claim 4. Had Engelgau included Asano in his patent application? It reasoned, the PTO would have found claim 4 to be an obvious combination of Asano and Smith, as it had found the broader version an obvious combination of Redding and Smith. As a final matter, the District Court held that the secondary factor of Teleflex's commercial success with pedals based on Engelgau's design did not alter its conclusion. The District Court granted summary judgment for KSR.

With principal reliance on the TSM test, the Court of Appeals reversed. It ruled the District Court had not been strict enough in applying the test, having failed to make "'finding[s] as to the specific understanding or principle within the knowledge of a skilled artisan that would have motivated one with no knowledge of [the] invention'... to attach an electronic control to the support bracket of the Asano assembly." 119 Fed. Appx., at 288 (brackets in original) (quoting *In re Kotzab*, 217 F. 3d 1365, 1371 (CA Fed. 2000)). The Court of Appeals held that the District Court was incorrect that the nature of the problem to be solved satisfied this requirement because unless the "prior art references address[ed] the precise problem that the patentee was trying to solve," the problem would not motivate an inventor to look at those references.

Here, the Court of Appeals found, the Asano pedal was designed to solve the "'constant ratio problem'"—that is, to ensure that the force required to depress the pedal is the same no matter how the pedal is adjusted—whereas Engelgau sought to provide a simpler, smaller, cheaper adjustable electronic pedal. *Ibid.* As for Rixon, the court explained, that pedal suffered from the problem of wire chafing but was not designed to solve it. In the court's view Rixon did not teach anything helpful to Engelgau's purpose. Smith, in turn, did not relate to adjustable pedals and did not "necessarily go to the issue of motivation to attach the electronic control on the support bracket of the pedal assembly." *Ibid.* When the patents were interpreted in this way, the Court of Appeals held, they would not have led a person of ordinary skill to put a sensor on the sort of pedal described in Asano.

That it might have been obvious to try the combination of Asano and a sensor was likewise irrelevant, in the court's view, because "'[o]bvious to try' has long been held not to constitute obviousness." *Id.*, at 289 (quoting *In re Deuel*, 51 F. 3d 1552, 1559 (CA Fed. 1995)).

The Court of Appeals also faulted the District Court's consideration of the PTO's rejection of the broader version of claim 4. The District Court's role, the Court of Appeals explained, was not to speculate regarding what the PTO might have done had the Engelgau patent mentioned Asano. Rather, the court held, the District Court was obliged first to presume that the issued patent was valid and then to render its own independent judgment of obviousness based on a review of the prior art. The fact that the PTO had rejected the broader version of claim 4, the Court of Appeals said, had no place in that analysis.

The Court of Appeals further held that genuine issues of material fact precluded summary judgment. Teleflex had proffered statements from one expert that claim 4 "'was a simple, elegant, and novel combination of features,'" 119 Fed. Appx., at 290, compared to Rixon, and from another expert that claim 4 was nonobvious because, unlike in Rixon, the sensor was mounted on the support bracket rather than the pedal itself. This evidence, the court concluded, sufficed to require a trial.

II
A
We begin by rejecting the rigid approach of the Court of Appeals. Throughout this Court's engagement with the question of obviousness, our cases have set forth an expansive and flexible approach inconsistent with the way the Court of Appeals applied its TSM test here. To be sure, *Graham* recognized the need for "uniformity and definiteness." 383 U. S., at 18. Yet the principles laid down in *Graham* reaffirmed the "functional approach" of *Hotchkiss*, 11 How. 248. See 383 U. S., at 12. To this end, *Graham* set forth a broad inquiry and invited courts, where appropriate, to look at any secondary considerations that would prove instructive. *Id.*, at 17.

Neither the enactment of §103 nor the analysis in *Graham* disturbed this Court's earlier instructions concerning the need for caution in granting a patent based on the combination of elements found in the prior art. For over a half century, the Court has held that a "patent for a combination which only unites old elements with no change in their respective functions... obviously withdraws what is already known into the field of its monopoly and diminishes the resources available to skillful men." *Great Atlantic & Pacific Tea Co.* v. *Supermarket Equipment Corp.*, 340 U. S. 147, 152 (1950). This is a principal reason for declining to allow patents for what is obvious. The combination of familiar elements according to known methods is likely to be obvious when it does no more than yield predictable results. Three cases decided after *Graham* illustrate the application of this doctrine.

In *United States* v. *Adams*, 383 U. S. 39, 40 (1966), a companion case to *Graham*, the Court considered the obviousness of a "wet battery" that varied from prior designs in two ways: It contained water, rather than the acids conventionally employed in storage batteries; and its electrodes were magnesium and cuprous chloride, rather than zinc and silver chloride. The Court recognized that when a patent claims a structure already known in the prior art that is altered by the mere substitution of one element for another known in the field, the combination must do more than yield a predictable result. *383 U. S., at 50–51*. It nevertheless rejected the Government's claim that Adams's battery was obvious. The Court relied upon the corollary principle that when the prior art teaches away from combining certain known elements, discovery of a successful means of combining them is more likely to be nonobvious. *Id.*, at 51–52. When Adams designed his battery, the prior art warned that risks were involved in using the types of electrodes he employed. The fact that the elements worked together in an unexpected and fruitful manner supported the conclusion that Adams's design was not obvious to those skilled in the art.

In *Anderson's-Black Rock, Inc.* v. *Pavement Salvage Co.*, 396 U. S. 57 (1969), the Court elaborated on this approach.

The subject matter of the patent before the Court was a device combining two pre-existing elements: a radiant heat burner and a paving machine. The device, the Court concluded, did not create some new synergy: The radiantheat burner functioned just as a burner was expected to function; and the paving machine did the same. The two in combination did no more than they would in separate, sequential operation. *Id.*, at 60–62. In those circumstances, "while the combination of old elements performed a useful function, it added nothing to the nature and quality of the radiant-heat burner already patented," and the patent failed under §103. *Id.,* at 62 (footnote omitted). Finally, in *Sakraida* v. *AG Pro, Inc.*, 425 U. S. 273 (1976), the Court derived from the precedents the conclusion that when a patent "simply arranges old elements with each performing the same function it had been known to perform" and yields no more than one would expect from such an arrangement, the combination is obvious. *Id.*, at 282.

The principles underlying these cases are instructive when the question is whether a patent claiming the combination of elements of prior art is obvious. When a work is available in one field of endeavor, design incentives and other market forces can prompt variations of it, either in the same field or a different one. If a person of ordinary skill can implement a predictable variation, §103 likely bars its patentability. For the same reason, if a technique has been used to improve one device, and a person of ordinary skill in the art would recognize that it would improve similar devices in the same way, using the technique is obvious unless its actual application is beyond his or her skill. *Sakraida* and *Anderson's-Black Rock* are illustrative—a court must ask whether the improvement is more than the predictable use of prior art elements according to their established functions.

Following these principles may be more difficult in other cases than it is here because the claimed subject matter may involve more than the simple substitution of one known element for another or the mere application of a known technique to a piece of prior art ready for the improvement. Often, it will be necessary for a court to look to interrelated teachings of multiple patents; the effects of demands known to the design community or present in the marketplace; and the background knowledge possessed by a person having ordinary skill in the art, all in order to determine whether there was an apparent reason to combine the known elements in the fashion claimed by the patent at issue. To facilitate review, this analysis should be made explicit. See In re Kahn, 441 F. 3d 977, 988 (CA Fed. 2006) ("[R]ejections on obviousness grounds cannot be sustained by mere conclusory statements; instead, there must be some articulated reasoning with some rational underpinning to support the legal conclusion of obviousness"). As our precedents make clear, however, the analysis need not seek out precise teachings directed to the specific subject matter of the challenged claim, for a court can take account of the inferences and creative steps that a person of ordinary skill in the art would employ.

B

When it first established the requirement of demonstrating a teaching, suggestion, or motivation to combine known elements in order to show that the combination is obvious, the Court of Customs and Patent Appeals captured a helpful insight. See *Application of Bergel, 292 F. 2d 955, 956–957 (1961)*. As is clear from cases such as *Adams*, a patent composed of several elements is not proved obvious merely by demonstrating that each of its elements was, independently, known in the prior art. Although common sense directs one to look with care at a patent application that claims as innovation the combination of two known devices according to their established functions, it can be important to identify a reason that would have prompted a person of ordinary skill in the relevant field to combine the elements in the way the claimed new invention does. This is so because inventions in most, if not all, instances rely upon building blocks long since uncovered, and claimed discoveries almost of necessity will be combinations of what, in some sense, is already known.

Helpful insights, however, need not become rigid and mandatory formulas; and when it is so applied, the TSM test is incompatible with our precedents. The obviousness analysis cannot be confined by a formalistic conception of the words teaching, suggestion, and motivation, or by overemphasis on the importance of published articles and the explicit content of issued patents. The diversity of inventive pursuits and of modern technology counsels against limiting the analysis in this way. In many fields it may be that there is little discussion of obvious techniques or combinations, and it often may be the case that market demand, rather than scientific literature, will drive design trends. Granting patent protection to advances that would occur in the ordinary course without real innovation retards progress and may, in the case of patents combining previously known elements, deprive prior inventions of their value or utility.

In the years since the Court of Customs and Patent Appeals set forth the essence of the TSM test, the Court of Appeals no doubt has applied the test in accord with these principles in many cases. There is no necessary inconsistency between the idea underlying the TSM test and the *Graham* analysis. But when a court transforms the general principle into a rigid rule that limits the obviousness inquiry, as the Court of Appeals did here, it errs.

C

The flaws in the analysis of the Court of Appeals relate for the most part to the court's narrow conception of the obviousness inquiry reflected in its application of the TSM test. In determining whether the subject matter of a patent claim is obvious, neither the particular motivation nor the avowed purpose of the patentee controls. What matters is the objective reach of the claim. If the claim extends to what is obvious, it is invalid under §103. One of the ways in which a patent's subject matter can be proved obvious is by noting that there existed at the time of invention a known problem for which there was an obvious solution encompassed by the patent's claims.

The first error of the Court of Appeals in this case was to foreclose this reasoning by holding that courts and patent examiners should look only to the problem the patentee was trying to solve. *119 Fed. Appx., at 288*. The Court of Appeals failed to recognize that the problem motivating the patentee may be only one of many addressed by the patent's subject matter. The question is not whether the combination was obvious to the patentee but whether the combination was obvious to a person with ordinary skill in the art. Under the correct analysis, any need or problem known in the field of endeavor at the time of invention and addressed by the patent can provide a reason for combining the elements in the manner claimed.

The second error of the Court of Appeals lay in its assumption that a person of ordinary skill attempting to solve a problem will be led only to those elements of prior art designed to solve the same problem. *Ibid.* The primary purpose of Asano was solving the constant ratio problem; so, the court concluded, an inventor considering how to put a sensor on an adjustable pedal would have no reason to consider putting it on the Asano pedal. *Ibid.* Common sense teaches, however, that familiar items may have obvious uses beyond their primary purposes, and in many cases a person of ordinary skill will be able to fit the teachings of multiple patents together like pieces of a puzzle. Regardless of Asano's primary purpose, the design provided an obvious example of an adjustable pedal with a fixed pivot point; and the prior art was replete with patents indicating that a fixed pivot point was an ideal mount for a sensor. The idea that a designer hoping to make an adjustable electronic pedal would ignore Asano because Asano was designed to solve the constant ratio problem makes little sense. A person of ordinary skill is also a person of ordinary creativity, not an automaton.

The same constricted analysis led the Court of Appeals to conclude, in error, that a patent claim cannot be proved obvious merely by showing that the combination of elements was "obvious to try." *Id.*, at 289 (internal quotation marks omitted). When there is a design need or market pressure to solve a problem and there are a finite number of identified, predictable solutions, a person of ordinary skill has good reason to pursue the known options within his or her technical grasp. If this leads to the anticipated success, it is likely the product not of innovation but of ordinary skill and common sense. In that instance the fact that a combination was obvious to try might show that it was obvious under §103.

The Court of Appeals, finally, drew the wrong conclusion from the risk of courts and patent examiners falling prey to hindsight bias. A factfinder should be aware, of course, of the distortion caused by hindsight bias and must be cautious of arguments reliant upon *ex post* reasoning. See *Graham*, 383 U. S., at 36 (warning against a "temptation to read into the prior art the teachings of the invention in issue" and instructing courts to "'guard against slipping into the use of hindsight'" (quoting *Monroe Auto Equipment Co.* v. *Heckethorn Mfg. & Supply Co.*, 332 F. 2d 406, 412 (CA6 1964)). Rigid preventative rules that deny factfinders recourse to common sense, however, are neither necessary under our case law nor consistent with it.

We note the Court of Appeals has since elaborated a broader conception of the TSM test than was applied in the instant matter. See, *e.g., DyStar Textilfarben GmbH & Co. Deutschland KG* v. *C. H. Patrick Co.*, 464 F. 3d 1356, 1367 (2006) ("Our suggestion test is in actuality quite flexible and not only permits, but *requires*, consideration of common knowledge and common sense"); *Alza Corp.* v. *Mylan Labs., Inc.*, 464 F. 3d 1286, 1291 (2006) ("There is flexibility in our obviousness jurisprudence because a motivation may be found *implicitly* in the prior art. We do not have a rigid test that requires an actual teaching to combine…"). Those decisions, of course, are not now before us and do not correct the errors of law made by the Court of Appeals in this case. The extent to which they may describe an analysis more consistent with our earlier precedents and our decision here is a matter for the Court of Appeals to consider in its future cases. What we hold is that the fundamental misunderstandings identified above led the Court of Appeals in this case to apply a test inconsistent with our patent law decisions.

III

When we apply the standards we have explained to the instant facts, claim 4 must be found obvious. We agree with and adopt the District Court's recitation of the relevant prior art and its determination of the level of ordinary skill in the field. As did the District Court, we see little difference between the teachings of Asano and Smith and the adjustable electronic pedal disclosed in claim 4 of the Engelgau patent. A person having ordinary skill in the art could have combined Asano with a pedal position sensor in a fashion encompassed by claim 4, and would have seen the benefits of doing so.

A

Teleflex argues in passing that the Asano pedal cannot be combined with a sensor in the manner described by claim 4 because of the design of Asano's pivot mechanisms. See Brief for Respondents 48–49, and n. 17. Therefore, Teleflex reasons, even if adding a sensor to Asano was obvious, that does not establish that claim 4 encompasses obvious subject matter. This argument was not, however, raised before the District Court. There Teleflex was content to assert only that the problem motivating the invention claimed by the Engelgau patent would not lead to the solution of combining of Asano with a sensor. See Teleflex's Response to KSR's Motion for Summary Judgment of Invalidity in No. 02–74586 (ED Mich.), pp. 18–20, App. 144a–146a. It is also unclear whether the current argument was raised before the Court of Appeals, where Teleflex advanced the nonspecific, conclusory contention that combining Asano with a sensor would not satisfy the limitations of claim 4. See Brief for Plaintiffs-Appellants in No. 04–1152 (CA Fed.), pp. 42–44. Teleflex's own expert declarations, moreover, do not support the point Teleflex now raises. See Declaration of Clark J. Radcliffe, Ph.D., Supplemental App. 204–207; Declaration of Timothy L. Andresen, *id.,* at 208–210. The only statement in either declaration that might bear on the argument is found in the Radcliffe declaration:

"Asano... and Rixon... are complex mechanical linkage-based devices that are expensive to produce and assemble and difficult to package. It is exactly these difficulties with prior art designs that [Engelgau] resolves. The use of an adjustable pedal with a single pivot reflecting pedal position combined with an electronic control mounted between the support and the adjustment assembly at that pivot was a simple, elegant, and novel combination of features in the Engelgau'565 patent." *Id.,* at 206, ¶16.

Read in the context of the declaration as a whole this is best interpreted to mean that Asano could not be used to solve "[t]he problem addressed by Engelgau'565[:] to provide a less expensive, more quickly assembled, and smaller package adjustable pedal assembly with electronic control." *Id.,* at 205, ¶10.

The District Court found that combining Asano with a pivot-mounted pedal position sensor fell within the scope of claim 4. *298 F. Supp. 2d, at 592–593.* Given the significance of that finding to the District Court's judgment, it is apparent that Teleflex would have made clearer challenges to it if it intended to preserve this claim. In light of Teleflex's failure to raise the argument in a clear fashion, and the silence of the Court of Appeals on the issue, we take the District Court's conclusion on the point to be correct.

B

The District Court was correct to conclude that, as of the time Engelgau designed the subject matter in claim 4, it was obvious to a person of ordinary skill to combine Asano with a pivot-mounted pedal position sensor. There then existed a marketplace that created a strong incentive to convert mechanical pedals to electronic pedals, and the prior art taught a number of methods for achieving this advance. The Court of Appeals considered the issue too narrowly by, in effect, asking whether a pedal designer writing on a blank slate would have chosen both Asano and a modular sensor similar to the ones used in the Chevrolet truckline and disclosed in the '068 patent. The District Court employed this narrow inquiry as well, though it reached the correct result nevertheless. The proper question to have asked was whether a pedal designer of ordinary skill, facing the wide range of needs created by developments in the field of endeavor, would have seen a benefit to upgrading Asano with a sensor.

In automotive design, as in many other fields, the interaction of multiple components means that changing one component often requires the others to be modified as well. Technological developments made it clear that engines using computer-controlled throttles would become standard. As a result, designers might have decided to design new pedals from scratch; but they also would have had reason to make pre-existing pedals work with the new engines. Indeed, upgrading its own pre-existing model led KSR to design the pedal now accused of infringing the Engelgau patent.

For a designer starting with Asano, the question was where to attach the sensor. The consequent legal question, then, is whether a pedal designer of ordinary skill starting with Asano would have found it obvious to put the sensor on a fixed pivot point. The prior art discussed above leads us to the conclusion that attaching the sensor where both KSR and Engelgau put it would have been obvious to a person of ordinary skill.

The '936 patent taught the utility of putting the sensor on the pedal device, not in the engine. Smith, in turn, explained to put the sensor not on the pedal's footpad but instead on its support structure. And from the known wire-chafing problems of Rixon, and Smith's teaching that "the pedal assemblies must not precipitate any motion in the connecting wires," Smith, col. 1, lines 35–37, Supplemental App. 274, the designer would know to place the sensor on a nonmoving part of the pedal structure. The most obvious nonmoving point on the structure from which a sensor can easily detect the pedal's position is a pivot point. The designer, accordingly, would follow Smith in mounting the sensor on a pivot, thereby designing an adjustable electronic pedal covered by claim 4.

Just as it was possible to begin with the objective to upgrade Asano to work with a computer-controlled throttle, so too was it possible to take an adjustable electronic pedal like Rixon and seek an improvement that would avoid the wire-chafing problem. Following similar steps to those just explained, a designer would learn from Smith to avoid sensor movement and would come, thereby, to Asano because Asano disclosed an adjustable pedal with a fixed pivot.

Teleflex indirectly argues that the prior art taught away from attaching a sensor to Asano because Asano in its view is bulky, complex, and expensive. The only evidence Teleflex marshals in support of this argument, however, is the Radcliffe declaration, which merely indicates that Asano would not have solved Engelgau's goal of making a small, simple, and inexpensive pedal. What the declaration does not indicate is that Asano was somehow so flawed that there was no reason to upgrade it, or pedals like it, to be compatible with modern engines. Indeed, Teleflex's own declarations refute this conclusion. Dr. Radcliffe states that Rixon suffered from the same bulk and complexity as did Asano. See *id.*, at 206. Teleflex's other expert, however, explained that Rixon was itself designed by adding a sensor to a pre-existing mechanical pedal. See *id.*, at 209. If Rixon's base pedal was not too flawed to upgrade, then Dr. Radcliffe's declaration does not show Asano was either. Teleflex may have made a plausible argument that Asano is inefficient as compared to Engelgau's preferred embodiment, but to judge Asano against Engelgau would be to engage in the very hindsight bias Teleflex rightly urges must be avoided. Accordingly, Teleflex has not shown anything in the prior art that taught away from the use of Asano.

Like the District Court, finally, we conclude Teleflex has shown no secondary factors to dislodge the determination that claim 4 is obvious. Proper application of *Graham* and our other precedents to these facts therefore leads to the conclusion that claim 4 encompassed obvious subject matter. As a result, the claim fails to meet the requirement of §103.

We need not reach the question whether the failure to disclose Asano during the prosecution of Engelgau voids the presumption of validity given to issued patents, for claim 4 is obvious despite the presumption. We nevertheless think it appropriate to note that the rationale underlying the presumption—that the PTO, in its expertise, has approved the claim—seems much diminished here.

IV

A separate ground the Court of Appeals gave for reversing the order for summary judgment was the existence of a dispute over an issue of material fact. We disagree with the Court of Appeals on this point as well. To the extent the court understood the *Graham* approach to exclude the possibility of summary judgment when an expert provides a conclusory affidavit addressing the question of obviousness, it misunderstood the role expert testimony plays in the analysis. In considering summary judgment on that question the district court can and should take into account expert testimony, which may resolve or keep open certain questions of fact. That is not the end of the issue, however. The ultimate judgment of obviousness is a legal determination. Graham, 383 U. S., at 17. Where, as here, the content of the prior art, the scope of the patent claim, and the level of ordinary skill in the art are not in material dispute, and the obviousness of the claim is apparent in light of these factors, summary judgment is appropriate. Nothing in the declarations proffered by Teleflex prevented the District Court from reaching the careful conclusions underlying its order for summary judgment in this case.

We build and create by bringing to the tangible and palpable reality around us new works based on instinct, simple logic, ordinary inferences, extraordinary ideas, and sometimes even genius. These advances, once part of our shared knowledge, define a new threshold from which innovation starts once more. And as progress beginning from higher levels of achievement is expected in the normal course, the results of ordinary innovation are not the subject of exclusive rights under the patent laws. Were it otherwise patents might stifle, rather than promote, the progress of useful arts. *See U. S. Const., Art. I, §8, cl. 8.* These premises led to the bar on patents claiming obvious subject matter established in *Hotchkiss* and codified in §103. Application of the bar must not be confined within a test or formulation too constrained to serve its purpose.

KSR provided convincing evidence that mounting a modular sensor on a fixed pivot point of the Asano pedal was a design step well within the grasp of a person of ordinary skill in the relevant art. Its arguments, and the record, demonstrate that claim 4 of the Engelgau patent is obvious. In rejecting the District Court's rulings, the Court of Appeals analyzed the issue in a narrow, rigid manner inconsistent with §103 and our precedents. The judgment of the Court of Appeals is reversed, and the case remanded for further proceedings consistent with this opinion.

It is so ordered.

1.4 Analysis of the Case

Patent Law: Obviousness, Patentable Subject Matter and Judicial Claim Interpretation

KSR Int'l Co. v. Teleflex Inc., 550 U.S. 398 (2007)

The text of the KSR International v. Teleflex opinion is here:

https://www.supremecourt.gov/opinions/06pdf/04-1350.pdf

In the United States "nonobviousness" is a requirement for patentability, while "obviousness" is a barrier to patentability. Section 105 of the United States Patent Act states:

A patent for a claimed invention may not be obtained, notwithstanding that the claimed invention is not identically disclosed as set forth in Sec. 102, if the differences between the claimed invention and the prior art are such that the claimed invention as a whole would have been obvious before the effective filing date of the claimed invention to a person having ordinary skill in the art to which the claimed invention pertains. Patentability shall not be negated by the manner in which the invention was made.

Even if an invention is not identical to the prior art, it will be denied a patent if the invention is obvious. When USPTO patent examiners deal with issues of obviousness, they will look at a variety of references and may pull one element from one reference and another element of the invention from another reference to see if they can find all the pieces, parts and functionality of the invention in the prior art as a whole. If so, they will conclude that a combination of the prior art references discloses the invention. Alternatively stated, an invention is legally obvious, and therefore not patentable, if it would have been obvious to a person of ordinary skill at the time the patent application is filed. Under the old "first to invent" regime the critical time for determining obviousness was at the time the invention was made. Since the U.S. became a first to file system, however, the critical time for determining obviousness is at the time of filing.

The U.S. Supreme Court's most important ruling on obviousness occurred in 2007, in KSR v. Teleflex. Teleflex sued KSR, alleging that KSR had infringed on its patent for an adjustable gas-pedal system composed of an adjustable accelerator pedal and an electronic throttle control. KSR countered that Teleflex's patent was obvious, and therefore invalid. A federal trial court granted summary judgment for KSR, accepting KSR's argument that the invention was obvious because each of the invention's constituent components existed in previous patents. Anyone with knowledge or experience in the industry, the District Court ruled, would have considered it obvious that the two components could be combined. Teleflex appealed to the Court of Appeals for the Federal Circuit, which reversed the District Court. The Federal Circuit panel found the lower court's analysis incomplete because the District Court had not correctly used the "teaching-suggestion-motivation" test as an analytic tool. Under this test, the party challenging the validity patent needs to identify the specific "teaching, suggestion, or motivation" that would have led a knowledgeable person to combine two or more previously-existing components of the invention in prior patents, publications or existing, publicly known products or processes. KSR appealed to the Supreme Court, arguing that the Circuit Court's "teaching-suggestion-motivation" test conflicted with Supreme Court precedent and that it would allow too many patents of obvious inventions.

The question before the U.S. Supreme Court was whether the Federal Circuit was correct in holding that an invention cannot be held "obvious," and thus unpatentable, without a finding of some "teaching, suggestion, or motivation" that would have led a "person of ordinary skill in the art" to the invention by combining previously-existing ideas. The U.S. Supreme Court's answer was "no."

The U.S. Supreme Court ruled unanimously that the Federal Circuit "analyzed the issue in a narrow, rigid manner inconsistent with [Section 103(a)] and our precedents." Justice Anthony Kennedy wrote the opinion for the Court, which acknowledged that a patent is not necessarily obvious by virtue of being a combination of two previously existing components, and that it can be helpful in such cases for a court to identify a reason that would have motivated a knowledgeable person to combine the components. However, the Court held that the Federal Circuit's "teaching-suggestion-motivation test" was not to be applied as a mandatory rule. This deployment of the test for determining obviousness was too narrow, the Court said, because it only considered teachings on the specific problem the patentee was attempting to solve. Teleflex's gas pedal patent was inspired by previous inventions aimed at different problems. Even though no one had combined the pre-existing adjustable gas pedal and electronic sensor technology in the precise way Teleflex's patent did, the Court held that the existence of the technology would have caused any person of ordinary skill to see the obvious benefit of combining the two. Consequently, Teleflex's patent was obvious and therefore invalid.

Readers interested in the history of the obviousness requirement for patentability in the United States should read a related case, in which the U.S. Supreme Court spoke at length about obviousness: Graham v. John Deere Co., 383 U.S. 1 (1966): https://supreme.justia.com/cases/federal/us/383/1/).

(2) **Requirements of patentable subject matter for software—ALICE CORPORATION PTY. LTD. v. CLS BANK INTERNATIONAL ET AL**

SUPREME COURT OF THE UNITED STATES
CERTIORARI TO THE UNITED STATES COURT OF APPEALS FOR THE FEDERAL CIRCUIT
No. 13–298. Argued March 31, 2014—Decided June 19, 2014

2.1 Syllabus:
Petitioner Alice Corporation is the assignee of several patents that disclose a scheme for mitigating "settlement risk," i.e., the risk that only one party to an agreed-upon financial exchange will satisfy its obligation. In particular, the patent claims are designed to facilitate the exchange of financial obligations between two parties by using a computer system as a third-party intermediary. The patents in suit claim (1) a method for exchanging financial obligations, (2) a computer system configured to carry out the method for exchanging obligations, and (3) a computer-readable medium containing program code for performing the method of exchanging obligations.

Respondents (together, CLS Bank), who operate a global network that facilitates currency transactions, filed suit against petitioner, arguing that the patent claims at issue are invalid, unenforceable, or not infringed. Petitioner counterclaimed, alleging infringement. After *Bilski* v. *Kappos*, 561 U. S. 593, was decided, the District Court held that all of the claims were ineligible for patent protection under 35 U. S. C. §101 because they are directed to an abstract idea. The en banc Federal Circuit affirmed.

2.2 Reasoning:

Because the claims are drawn to a patent-ineligible abstract idea, they are not patent eligible under §101.

(a) The Court has long held that §101, which defines the subject matter eligible for patent protection, contains an implicit exception for "Laws of nature, natural phenomena, and abstract ideas." *Association for Molecular Pathology* v. *Myriad Genetics, Inc.*, 569 U. S. 576, 589,133 S. Ct. 2107, 2116, 186 L.ED.2D 124. In applying the §101 exception, this Court must distinguish patents that claim the "'building blocks'" of human ingenuity, which are ineligible for patent protection, from those that integrate the building blocks into something more, see *Mayo Collaborative Services* v. *Prometheus Laboratories, Inc.*, 566 U. S. 66, 89, 132 S.Ct. 1289, 1303, 182 L.ED.2D 321, thereby "transforming" them into a patent-eligible invention, *id.,* at 72, 132 S.Ct., at 1294. Pp. 2354–2355.

(b) Using this framework, the Court must first determine whether the claims at issue are directed to a patent-ineligible concept. 566 U. S., at 77, 132 S.Ct., at 1296–1297. If so, the Court then asks whether the claim's elements, considered both individually and "as an ordered combination," "transform the nature of the claim" into a patent-eligible application. *Id.,* at 79, 78, 132 S.Ct., at 1297. Pp. 23557–2360.

(1) The claims at issue are directed to a patent-ineligible concept: the abstract idea of intermediated settlement. Under "the longstanding rule that '[a]n idea of itself is not patentable,'" *Gottschalk* v. *Benson*, 409 U. S. 63, 67, this Court has found ineligible patent claims involving an algorithm for converting binary-coded decimal numerals into pure binary form, *id.,* at 71–72; a mathematical formula for computing "alarm limits" in a catalytic conversion process, *Parker* v. *Flook*, 437 U. S. 584, 594–595; and, most recently, a method for hedging against the financial risk of price fluctuations, *Bilski*, 561 U. S, at 599. It follows from these cases, and *Bilski* in particular, that the claims at issue are directed to an abstract idea. On their face, they are drawn to the concept of intermediated settlement, i.e., the use of a third party to mitigate settlement risk. Like the risk hedging in *Bilski*, the concept of intermediated settlement is "'a fundamental economic practice long prevalent in our system of commerce,'" *ibid.,* and the use of a third-party intermediary (or "clearing house") is a building block of the modern economy. Thus, intermediated settlement, like hedging, is an "abstract idea" beyond §101's scope.

(2) Turning to the second step of *Mayo*'s framework: The method claims, which merely require generic computer implementation, fail to transform that abstract idea into a patent-eligible invention.

(i) "Simply appending conventional steps, specified at a high level of generality," to a method already "well known in the art" is not "*enough*" to supply the "'inventive concept'" needed to make this transformation. *Mayo, supra,* at 82, 79, 77, 72, 132 S.Ct., at 1300, 1297, 1294. The introduction of a computer into the claims does not alter the analysis. Neither stating an abstract idea "while adding the words 'apply it,'" *Mayo, supra,* at 72, 132 S.Ct., at 1294, nor limiting the use of an abstract idea "'to a particular technological environment,'" *Bilski, supra,* at 610–611, is enough for patent eligibility. Stating an abstract idea while adding the words "apply it with a computer" simply combines those two steps, with the same deficient result. Wholly generic computer implementation is not generally sort of "additional feature" that provides any "practical assurance that the process is more than a drafting effort designed to monopolize the [abstract idea] itself." *Mayo, supra,* at 77, 132 S.Ct., at 1297. Pp. 2357–2359.

(ii) Here, the representative method claim does no more than simply instruct the practitioner to implement the abstract idea of intermediated settlement on a generic computer. Taking the claim elements separately, the function performed by the computer at each step—creating and maintaining "shadow" accounts, obtaining data, adjusting account balances, and issuing automated instructions—is "purely 'conventional.'" *Mayo,* 566 U. S., at 79, 132 S.Ct., at 1298. Considered "as an ordered combination," these computer components "add nothing... that is not already present when the steps are considered separately." *Ibid.* Viewed as a whole, these method claims simply recite the concept of intermediated settlement as performed by a generic computer. They do not, for example, purport to improve the functioning of the computer itself or effect an improvement in any other technology or technical field. An instruction to apply the abstract idea of intermediated settlement using some unspecified, generic computer is not *"enough"* to transform the abstract idea into a patent-eligible invention. *Id.,* at 77, 132 S.Ct., at 1297. Pp 2359–2360.

(3) Because petitioner's system and media claims add nothing of substance to the underlying abstract idea, they too are patent ineligible under §101. Petitioner conceded below that its media claims rise or fall with its method claims. And the system claims are no different in substance from the method claims. The method claims recite the abstract idea implemented on a generic computer; the system claims recite a handful of generic computer components configured to implement the same idea. This Court has long "warn[ed]... against" interpreting §101 "in ways that make patent eligibility 'depend simply on the draftsman's art.'" *Mayo, supra,* at 72, 132 S.Ct., at 1294. Holding that the system claims are patent eligible would have exactly that result.

717 F. 3d 1269, affirmed.

THOMAS, J., delivered the opinion for a unanimous Court. SOTOMAYOR, J., filed a concurring opinion, in which GINSBURG and BREYER, JJ., joined.

ALICE CORPORATION PTY. LTD., PETITIONER *v.* CLS BANK NTERNATIONAL ET AL.
SUPREME COURT OF THE UNITED STATES
ON WRIT OF CERTIORARI TO THE UNITED STATES COURT OF APPEALS FOR THE FEDERAL CIRCUIT
[June 19, 2014]
JUSTICE THOMAS delivered the opinion of the Court.

The patents at issue in this case disclose a computer implemented scheme for mitigating "settlement risk" (i.e., the risk that only one party to a financial transaction will pay what it owes) by using a third-party intermediary. The question presented is whether these claims are patent eligible under 35 U. S. C. §101, or are instead drawn to a patent-ineligible abstract idea. We hold that the claims at issue are drawn to the abstract idea of intermediated settlement, and that merely requiring generic computer implementation fails to transform that abstract idea into a patent-eligible invention. We therefore affirm the judgment of the United States Court of Appeals for the Federal Circuit.

I

A

Petitioner Alice Corporation is the assignee of several patents that disclose schemes to manage certain forms of financial risk.[1] According to the specification largely shared by the patents, the invention "enables the management of risk relating to specified, yet unknown, future events." App. 248. The specification further explains that the "invention relates to methods and apparatus, including electrical computers and data processing systems applied to financial matters and risk management." *Id.*, at 243.

The claims at issue relate to a computerized scheme for mitigating "settlement risk"—i.e., the risk that only one party to an agreed-upon financial exchange will satisfy its obligation. In particular, the claims are designed to facilitate the exchange of financial obligations between two parties by using a computer system as a third-party intermediary. *Id.*, at 383–384.[2] The intermediary creates "shadow" credit and debit records (i.e., account ledgers) that mirror the balances in the parties' real-world accounts at "exchange institutions" (e.g., banks). The intermediary updates the shadow records in real time as transactions are entered, allowing "only those transactions for which the parties' updated shadow records indicate sufficient resources to satisfy their mutual obligations." *717 F. 3d 1269, 1285 (CA Fed. 2013) (Lourie, J., concurring).* At the end of the day, the intermediary instructs the relevant financial institutions to carry out the "permitted" transactions in accordance with the updated

---

[1] The patents at issue are United States Patent Nos. 5,970,479 the '479 patent), 6,912,510, 7,149,720, and 7,725,375.

[2] The parties agree that claim 33 of the '479 patent is representative of the method claims. Claim 33 recites:

"A method of exchanging obligations as between parties, each party holding a credit record and a debit record with an exchange institution, the credit records and debit records for exchange of predetermined obligations, the method comprising the steps of:

"(a) creating a shadow credit record and a shadow debit record for each stakeholder party to be held independently by a supervisory institution from the exchange institutions;

"(b) obtaining from each exchange institution a start-of-day balance for each shadow credit record and shadow debit record;

"(c) for every transaction resulting in an exchange obligation, the supervisory institution adjusting each respective party's shadow credit record or shadow debit record, allowing only these transactions that do not result in the value of the shadow debit record being less than the value of the shadow credit record at any time, each said adjustment taking place in chronological order, and

"(d) at the end-of-day, the supervisory institution instructing on[e] of the exchange institutions to exchange credits or debits to the credit record and debit record of the respective parties in accordance with the adjustments of the said permitted transactions, the credits and debits being irrevocable, time invariant obligations placed on the exchange institutions." App. 383–384.

shadow records, *ibid.*, thus mitigating the risk that only one party will perform the agreed-upon exchange.

In sum, the patents in suit claim (1) the foregoing method for exchanging obligations (the method claims), (2) a computer system configured to carry out the method for exchanging obligations (the system claims), and (3) a computer-readable medium containing program code for performing the method of exchanging obligations (the media claims). All of the claims are implemented using a computer; the system and media claims expressly recite a computer, and the parties have stipulated that the method claims require a computer as well.

B

Respondents CLS Bank International and CLS Services Ltd. (together, CLS Bank) operate a global network that facilitates currency transactions. In 2007, CLS Bank filed suit against petitioner, seeking a declaratory judgment that the claims at issue are invalid, unenforceable, or not infringed. Petitioner counterclaimed, alleging infringement. Following this Court's decision in *Bilski v. Kappos*, 561 U. S. 593 (2010), the parties filed cross-motions for summary judgment on whether the asserted claims are eligible for patent protection under 35 U. S. C. §101. The District Court held that all of the claims are patent ineligible because they are directed to the abstract idea of "employing a neutral intermediary to facilitate simultaneous exchange of obligations in order to minimize risk." 768 F. Supp. 2d 221, 252 (DC 2011).

A divided panel of the United States Court of Appeals for the Federal Circuit reversed, holding that it was not "manifestly evident" that petitioner's claims are directed to an abstract idea. 685 F. 3d 1341, 1352, 1356 (2012). The Federal Circuit granted rehearing en banc, vacated the panel opinion, and affirmed the judgment of the District Court in a one-paragraph *per curiam* opinion. 717 F. 3d, at 1273. Seven of the ten participating judges agreed that petitioner's method and media claims are patent ineligible. See *id.*, at 1274 (Lourie, J., concurring); *id.*, at 1312–1313 (Rader, C. J., concurring in part and dissenting in part). With respect to petitioner's system claims, the en banc Federal Circuit affirmed the District Court's judgment by an equally divided vote. *Id.*, at 1273. Writing for a five-member plurality, Judge Lourie concluded that all of the claims at issue are patent ineligible. In the plurality's view, under this Court's decision in *Mayo Collaborative Services v. Prometheus Laboratories, Inc.*, 566 U. S. 66 (2012), a court must first "identify the abstract idea represented in the claim," and then determine "whether the balance of the claim adds 'significantly more.'" 717 F. 3d, at 1286. The plurality concluded that petitioner's claims "draw on the abstract idea of reducing settlement risk by effecting trades through a third-party intermediary," and that the use of a computer to maintain, adjust, and reconcile shadow accounts added nothing of substance to that abstract idea. *Ibid.*

Chief Judge Rader concurred in part and dissented in part. In a part of the opinion joined only by Judge Moore, Chief Judge Rader agreed with the plurality that petitioner's method and media claims are drawn to an abstract idea. *Id.*, at 1312–1313. In a part of the opinion joined by Judges Linn, Moore, and O'Malley, Chief Judge Rader would have held that the system claims are patent eligible because they involve computer "hardware" that is "specifically programmed to solve a complex problem." *Id.,* at 1307. Judge Moore wrote a separate opinion dissenting in part, arguing that the system claims are patent eligible. *Id.,* at 1313–1314. Judge Newman filed an opinion concurring in part and dissenting in part, arguing that all of petitioner's claims are patent eligible. *Id.,* at 1327. Judges Linn and O'Malley filed a separate dissenting opinion reaching that same conclusion. *Ibid.*

We granted certiorari, 571 U. S. 1090, 134 S.Ct. 734, 187 L.Ed.2d 590 (2013), and now affirm.

II

Section 101 of the Patent Act defines the subject matter eligible for patent protection. It provides:

"Whoever invents or discovers any new and useful process, machine, manufacture, or composition of matter, or any new and useful improvement thereof, may obtain a patent therefor, subject to the conditions and requirements of this title." 35 U. S. C. §101.

"We have long held that this provision contains an important implicit exception: Laws of nature, natural phenomena, and abstract ideas are not patentable." *Association for Molecular Pathology* v. *Myriad Genetics, Inc.,* 569 U. S. 576, 589, 133 S.Ct. 2107, 2116, 186 L.Ed.2d 124 (2013) (slip op., at 11) (internal quotation marks and brackets omitted). We have interpreted §101 and its predecessors in light of this exception for more than 150 years. *Bilski, supra,* at 601–602; see also *O'Reilly* v. *Morse,* 15 How. 62, 112–120 (1854); *Le Roy* v. *Tatham,* 14 How. 156, 174–175 (1853).

We have described the concern that drives this exclusionary principle as one of pre-emption. See, e.g., *Bilski, supra,* at 611–612 (upholding the patent "would preempt use of this approach in all fields, and would effectively grant a monopoly over an abstract idea"). Laws of nature, natural phenomena, and abstract ideas are " the basic tools of scientific and technological work." *Myriad, supra,* at 589, 133 S.Ct., at 2116. "Monopolization of those tools through the grant of a patent might tend to impede innovation more than it would tend to promote it," thereby thwarting the primary object of the patent laws. *Mayo, supra,* at 71 132, S.Ct., at 1293; see U. S. Const., Art. I, §8, cl. 8 (Congress "shall have Power... To promote the Progress of Science and useful Arts"). We have "repeatedly emphasized this... concern that patent law not inhibit further discovery by improperly tying up the future use of" these building blocks of human ingenuity. *Mayo, supra,* at 85, 132 S.Ct., at 1301 (citing *Morse, supra,* at 113). At the same time, we tread carefully in construing this exclusionary principle lest it swallow all of patent law. *Mayo,* 566 U. S., at 66 (slip op., at 2). At some level, "all inventions... embody, use, reflect, rest upon, or apply laws of nature, natural phenomena, or abstract ideas." *Ibid.* Thus, an invention is not rendered ineligible for patent simply because it involves an abstract concept. See *Diamond* v. *Diehr,* 450 U. S. 175, 187 (1981). "Applications" of such concepts "'to a new and useful end,'" we have said, remain eligible for patent protection. *Gottschalk* v. *Benson,* 409 U. S. 63, 67 (1972). Accordingly, in applying the §101 exception, we must distinguish between patents that claim the "building blocks" of human ingenuity and those that integrate the building blocks into something more, *Mayo*, 566 U. S., at 89, 132 S.Ct., at 1303, thereby "transforming" them into a patent-eligible invention, *id.*, at 72, 132 S.Ct., at 1294. The former "would risk disproportionately tying up the use of the underlying" ideas, *id.*, at 73, 132 S.Ct., at 1294, and are therefore ineligible for patent protection. The latter pose no comparable risk of pre-emption, and therefore remain eligible for the monopoly granted under our patent laws.

III

In *Mayo Collaborative Services* v. *Prometheus Laboratories, Inc.*, 566 U. S. 66 (2012), we set forth a framework for distinguishing patents that claim laws of nature, natural phenomena, and abstract ideas from those that claim patent-eligible applications of those concepts. First, we determine whether the claims at issue are directed to one of those patent-ineligible concepts. *Id.*, at 77, 132 S.Ct., at 1296–1297. If so, we then ask, "what else is there in the claims before us?" *Id.*, at 78, 132 S.Ct., at 1297. To answer that question, we consider the elements of each claim both individually and "as an ordered combination" to determine whether the additional elements "transform the nature of the claim" into a patent-eligible application. *Id.*, at 79, 78, 132 S.Ct., at 1298. We have described step two of this analysis as a search for an "'inventive concept'"—i.e., an element or combination of elements that is "sufficient to ensure that the patent in practice amounts to significantly more than a patent upon the ineligible concept itself." *Id.*, at 72–73, 132 S.Ct., at 1294.[3]

A

We must first determine whether the claims at issue are directed to a patent-ineligible concept. We conclude that they are: These claims are drawn to the abstract idea of intermediated settlement.

The "abstract ideas" category embodies "the longstanding rule that 'an idea of itself is not patentable.'" *Benson, supra*, at 67 (quoting *Rubber-Tip Pencil Co.* v. *Howard*, 20 Wall. 498, 507 (1874)); see also *Le Roy, supra*, at 175 ("A principle, in the abstract, is a fundamental truth; an original cause; a motive; these cannot be patented, as no one can claim in either of them an exclusive right"). In *Benson*, for example, this Court rejected as ineligible patent claims involving an algorithm for converting binary coded decimal numerals into pure binary form, holding that the claimed patent was "in practical effect... a patent on the algorithm itself." 409 U. S., at 71–72. And in *Parker* v. *Flook*, 437 U. S. 584, 594–595 (1978), we held that a mathematical formula for computing "alarm limits" in a catalytic conversion process was also a patent ineligible abstract idea.

We most recently addressed the category of abstract ideas in *Bilski* v. *Kappos*, 561 U. S. 593 (2010). The claims at issue in *Bilski* described a method for hedging against the financial risk of price fluctuations. Claim 1 recited a series of steps for hedging risk, including: (1) initiating a series of financial transactions between providers and

---

[3] Because the approach we made explicit in *Mayo* considers all claim elements, both individually and in combination, it is consistent with the general rule that patent claims "must be considered as a whole." *Diamond* v. *Diehr*, 450 U. S. 175, 188 (1981); see *Parker* v. *Flood*, 437 U. S. 584, 594 (1978) ("Our approach . . . is . . . not at all inconsistent with the view that a patent claim must be considered as a whole").

consumers of a commodity; (2) identifying market participants that have a counterrisk for the same commodity; and (3) initiating a series of transactions between those market participants and the commodity provider to balance the risk position of the first series of consumer transactions. *Id.,* at 599. Claim 4 "put the concept articulated in claim 1 into a simple mathematical formula." *Ibid.* The remaining claims were drawn to examples of hedging in commodities and energy markets.

"All members of the Court agreed" that the patent at issue in *Bilski* claimed an "abstract idea." *Id.,* at 609; see also *id.,* at 619 (Stevens, J., concurring in judgment). Specifically, the claims described "the basic concept of hedging, or protecting against risk." *Id.,* at 611. The Court explained that "Hedging is a fundamental economic practice long prevalent in our system of commerce and taught in any introductory finance class." *Ibid.* "The concept of hedging" as recited by the claims in suit was therefore a patent-ineligible "abstract idea, just like the algorithms at issue in *Benson* and *Flook.*" *Ibid.* It follows from our prior cases, and *Bilski* in particular, that the claims at issue here are directed to an abstract idea. Petitioner's claims involve a method of exchanging financial obligations between two parties using a thirdparty intermediary to mitigate settlement risk. The intermediary creates and updates "shadow" records to reflect the value of each party's actual accounts held at "exchange institutions," thereby permitting only those transactions for which the parties have sufficient resources. At the end of each day, the intermediary issues irrevocable instructions to the exchange institutions to carry out the permitted transactions.

On their face, the claims before us are drawn to the concept of intermediated settlement, i.e., the use of a third party to mitigate settlement risk. Like the risk hedging in *Bilski,* the concept of intermediated settlement is "a fundamental economic practice long prevalent in our system of commerce." *Ibid.*; see, e.g., Emery, Speculation on the Stock and Produce Exchanges of the United States, in 7 Studies in History, Economics and Public Law 283, 346–356 (1896) (discussing the use of a "clearing-house" as an intermediary to reduce settlement risk). The use of a third-party intermediary (or "clearing house") is also a building block of the modern economy. See, e.g., Yadav, The Problematic Case of Clearinghouses in Complex Markets, 101 Geo. L. J. 387, 406–412 (2013); J. Hull, Risk Management and Financial Institutions 103–104 (3d ed. 2012). Thus, intermediated settlement, like hedging, is an "abstract idea" beyond the scope of §101.

Petitioner acknowledges that its claims describe intermediated settlement, see Brief for Petitioner 4, but rejects the conclusion that its claims recite an "abstract idea." Drawing on the presence of mathematical formulas in some of our abstract-ideas precedents, petitioner contends that the abstract-ideas category is confined to "preexisting, fundamental truths" that "exist in principle apart from any human action.'" *Id.,* at 23, 26 (quoting *Mayo,* 566 U. S., at 66).

Bilski belies petitioner's assertion. The concept of risk hedging we identified as an abstract idea in that case cannot be described as a "preexisting, fundamental truth." The patent in *Bilski* simply involved a "series of steps instructing how to hedge risk." 561 U. S., at 599. Although hedging is a longstanding commercial practice, *id.,* at 599, it is a method of organizing human activity, not a "truth" about the natural world "that has always existed," Brief for Petitioner 22 (quoting *Flook, supra,* at 593, n. 15).

One of the claims in *Bilski* reduced hedging to a mathematical formula, but the Court did not assign any special significance to that fact, much less the sort of talismanic significance petitioner claims. Instead, the Court grounded its conclusion that all of the claims at issue were abstract ideas in the understanding that risk hedging was a "fundamental economic practice." 561 U. S., at 611.

In any event, we need not labor to delimit the precise contours of the "abstract ideas" category in this case. It is enough to recognize that there is no meaningful distinction between the concept of risk hedging in *Bilski* and the concept of intermediated settlement at issue here. Both are squarely within the realm of "abstract ideas" as we have used that term.

B

Because the claims at issue are directed to the abstract idea of intermediated settlement, we turn to the second step in *Mayo*'s framework. We conclude that the method claims, which merely require generic computer implementation, fail to transform that abstract idea into a patenteligible invention.

1. At *Mayo* step two, we must examine the elements of the claim to determine whether it contains an "inventive concept" sufficient to "transform" the claimed abstract idea into a patent-eligible application. 566 U. S., at 66 (slip op., at 3, 11). A claim that recites an abstract idea must include "additional features" to ensure "that the claim is more than a drafting effort designed to monopolize the abstract idea." *Id.,* at 77, 132 S.Ct., at 1297. *Mayo* made clear that transformation into a patent-eligible application requires "more than simply stating the abstract idea while adding the words 'apply it.'" *Id.,* at 72, 132 S.Ct., at 1294.

Mayo itself is instructive. The patents at issue in *Mayo* claimed a method for measuring metabolites in the bloodstream in order to calibrate the appropriate dosage of thiopurine drugs in the treatment of autoimmune diseases. *Id.,* at 73–75, 132 S.Ct., at 1294–1296. The respondent in that case contended that the claimed method was a patenteligible application of natural laws that describe the relationship between the concentration of certain metabolites and the likelihood that the drug dosage will be harmful or ineffective. But methods for determining metabolite levels were already "well known in the art," and the process at issue amounted to "nothing significantly more than an instruction to doctors to apply the applicable laws when treating their patients." *Id.,* at 79, 132 S.Ct., at 1298. "Simply appending conventional steps, specified at a high level of generality," was not "*enough*" to supply an "inventive concept." *Id.,* at 82, 77, 72, 132 S.Ct., at 1300, 1297, 1294. The introduction of a computer into the claims does not alter the analysis at *Mayo* step two. In *Benson,* for example, we considered a patent that claimed an algorithm implemented on "a general-purpose digital computer." 409 U. S., at 64. Because the algorithm was an abstract idea, see *supra,* at 8, the claim had to supply a "new and useful" application of the idea in order to be patent eligible. 409 U. S., at 67. But the computer implementation did not supply the necessary inventive concept; the process could be "carried out in existing computers long in use." *Ibid.* We accordingly "held that simply implementing a mathematical principle on a physical machine, namely a computer, is not a patentable application of that principle." *Mayo, supra,* at 84, 132 S.Ct., at 1301.

Flook is to the same effect. There, we examined a computerized method for using a mathematical formula to adjust alarm limits for certain operating conditions (e.g., temperature and pressure) that could signal inefficiency or danger in a catalytic conversion process. 437 U. S., at 585–586. Once again, the formula itself was an abstract idea, see *supra,* at 8, and the computer implementation was purely conventional. 437 U. S., at 594 (noting that the "use of computers for 'automatic monitoring alarming'" was "well known"). In holding that the process was patent ineligible, we rejected the argument that "implementing a principle in some specific fashion" will "automatically fall within the patentable subject matter of §101." *Id.,* at 593. Thus, "*Flook* stands for the proposition that the prohibition against patenting abstract ideas cannot be circumvented by attempting to limit the use of the idea to a particular technological environment." *Bilski,* 561 U. S., at 610–611 (internal quotation marks omitted).

In *Diehr,* 450 U. S. 175, by contrast, we held that a computer-implemented process for curing rubber was patent eligible, but not because it involved a computer. The claim employed a "well-known" mathematical equation, but it used that equation in a process designed to solve a technological problem in "conventional industry practice." *Id.,* at 177, 178. The invention in *Diehr* used a "thermocouple" to record constant temperature measurements inside the rubber mold—something "the industry had not been able to obtain." *Id.,* at 178, and n. 3. The temperature measurements were then fed into a computer, which repeatedly recalculated the remaining cure time by using the mathematical equation. *Id.,* at 178–179. These additional steps, we recently explained, "transformed the process into an inventive application of the formula." *Mayo, supra,* at 81, 132 S.Ct., at 1299. In other words, the claims in *Diehr* were patent eligible because they improved an existing technological process, not because they were implemented on a computer.

These cases demonstrate that the mere recitation of a generic computer cannot transform a patent-ineligible abstract idea into a patent-eligible invention. Stating an abstract idea "while adding the words 'apply it'" is not enough for patent eligibility. *Mayo, supra,* at 72, 132 S.Ct., at 1294. Nor is limiting the use of an abstract idea "to a particular technological environment." *Bilski, supra,* at 610–611. Stating an abstract idea while adding the words "apply it with a computer" simply combines those two steps, with the same deficient result. Thus, if a patent's recitation of a computer amounts to a mere instruction to "implement" an abstract idea "on... a computer," *Mayo, supra,* at 84, 132 S.Ct., at 1301, that addition cannot impart patent eligibility. This conclusion accords with the preemption concern that undergirds our §101 jurisprudence. Given the ubiquity of computers, see 717 F. 3d, at 1286 (Lourie, J., concurring), wholly generic computer implementation is not generally the sort of "additional feature" that provides any "practical assurance that the process is more than a drafting effort designed to monopolize the abstract idea itself." *Mayo,* 566 U. S., at 77, 132 S.Ct., at 1297.

The fact that a computer "necessarily exists in the physical, rather than purely conceptual, realm," Brief for Petitioner 39, is beside the point. There is no dispute that a computer is a tangible system (in §101 terms, a "machine"), or that many computer-implemented claims are formally addressed to patent-eligible subject matter. But if that were the end of the §101 inquiry, an applicant could claim any principle of the physical or social sciences by reciting a computer system configured to implement the relevant concept. Such a result would make the determination of patent eligibility "depend simply on the draftsman's art," *Flook, supra,* at 593, thereby eviscerating the rule that "'Laws of nature, natural phenomena, and abstract ideas are not patentable,'" *Myriad,* 569 U. S., at 589, 133 S.Ct., at 2116.

2. The representative method claim in this case recites the following steps: (1) "creating" shadow records for each counterparty to a transaction; (2) "obtaining" start-of-day balances based on the parties' real-world accounts at exchange institutions; (3) "adjusting" the shadow records as transactions are entered, allowing only those transactions for which the parties have sufficient resources; and (4) issuing irrevocable end-of-day instructions to the exchange institutions to carry out the permitted transactions. See n.2, *supra.* Petitioner principally contends that the claims are patent eligible because these steps "require a substantial and meaningful role for the computer." Brief for Petitioner 48. As stipulated, the claimed method requires the use of a computer to create electronic records, track multiple transactions, and issue simultaneous instructions; in other words, "the computer is itself the intermediary." *Ibid.* (emphasis deleted).

In light of the foregoing, see *supra,* at 11–14, the relevant question is whether the claims here do more than simply instruct the practitioner to implement the abstract idea of intermediated settlement on a generic computer. They do not.

Taking the claim elements separately, the function performed by the computer at each step of the process is "purely conventional." *Mayo, supra,* at 79, 132 S.Ct., 1298 (internal quotation marks omitted). Using a computer to create and maintain "shadow" accounts amounts to electronic recordkeeping—one of the most basic functions of a computer. See, e.g., *Benson,* 409 U. S., at 65 (noting that a computer "operates... upon both new and previously stored data"). The same is true with respect to the use of a computer to obtain data, adjust account balances, and issue automated instructions; all of these computer functions are "well-understood, routine, conventional activities" previously known to the industry. *Mayo,* 566 U. S., at 73, 132 S.Ct., at 1294. In short, each step does no more than require a generic computer to perform generic computer functions.

Considered "as an ordered combination," the computer components of petitioner's method "add nothing... that is not already present when the steps are considered separately." *Id.,* at 79, 132 S.Ct., at 1298. Viewed as a whole, petitioner's method claims simply recite the concept of intermediated settlement as performed by a generic computer. See 717 F. 3d, at 1286 (Lourie, J., concurring) (noting that the representative method claim "lacks *any* express language to define the computer's participation"). The method claims do not, for example, purport to improve the functioning of the computer itself. See *ibid.* ("There is no specific or limiting recitation of... improved computer technology..."); Brief for United States as *Amicus Curiae* 28–30. Nor do they effect an improvement in any other technology or technical field. See, e.g., *Diehr,* 450 U. S., at 177–178. Instead, the claims at issue amount to "nothing significantly more" than an instruction to apply the abstract idea of intermediated settlement using some unspecified, generic computer. *Mayo,* 566 U. S., at 79, 132

S.Ct., at 1298. Under our precedents, that is not *"enough"* to transform an abstract idea into a patent-eligible invention. *Id.,* at 77, 132 S.Ct., at 1297.

C

Petitioner's claims to a computer system and a computer readable medium fail for substantially the same reasons. Petitioner conceded below that its media claims rise or fall with its method claims. En Banc Response Brief for Defendant-Appellant in No. 11–1301 (CA Fed.) p. 50, n. 3. As to its system claims, petitioner emphasizes that those claims recite "specific hardware" configured to perform "specific computerized functions." Brief for Petitioner 53. But what petitioner characterizes as specific hardware—a "data processing system" with a "communications controller" and "data storage unit," for example, see App. 954, 958, 1257—is purely functional and generic. Nearly every computer will include a "communications controller" and "data storage unit" capable of performing the basic calculation, storage, and transmission functions required by the method claims. See 717 F. 3d, at 1290 (Lourie, J., concurring). As a result, none of the hardware recited by the system claims "offers a meaningful limitation beyond generally linking 'the use of the method to a particular technological environment,' that is, implementation via computers." *Id.,* at 1291 (quoting *Bilski,* 561 U. S., at 610–611).

Put another way, the system claims are no different from the method claims in substance. The method claims recite the abstract idea implemented on a generic computer; the system claims recite a handful of generic computer components configured to implement the same idea. This Court has long "warned… against" interpreting §101 "in ways that make patent eligibility 'depend simply on the draftsman's art.'" *Mayo, supra,* at 72, 132 S.Ct., at 1294 (quoting *Flook,* 437 U. S., at 593); see *id.,* at 590 ("The concept of patentable subject matter under §101 is not 'like a nose of wax which may be turned and twisted in any direction…'"). Holding that the system claims are patent eligible would have exactly that result.

Because petitioner's system and media claims add nothing of substance to the underlying abstract idea, we hold that they too are patent ineligible under §101. For the foregoing reasons, the judgment of the Court of Appeals for the Federal Circuit is affirmed.

It is so ordered.

2.3 Analysis of the Case

Alice Corp. v. CLS Bank International, 573 U.S. 208 (2014).

The text of Alice Corp. v. CLS Bank is available here:

https://www.supremecourt.gov/opinions/13pdf/13-298_7lh8.pdf

Alice Corporation (Alice) is an Australian company that held several issued patents having to do with a computerized trading platform that facilitated financial transactions in which a third party settles obligations between two others to eliminate settlement risk. Settlement risk is the risk to each party in an exchange that only one party will pay its obligation. Alice's patents address that risk by using the third party as the guarantor.

CLS Bank International (CLS) sued Alice and sought a declaratory judgment of non-infringement and invalidity of the several patent claims. Alice counter sued and claimed infringement. CLS moved for summary judgment by arguing that any possible infringement could not have occurred in the United States and that Alice's claims were drawn from ineligible subject matter. The trial court held that Alice's patents were invalid because they were directed at an abstract idea and that those claims could preempt the use of the abstract concept of a neutral intermediary to facilitate exchange and eliminate risk. The U.S. Court of Appeals for the Federal Circuit affirmed. On appeal the U.S. Supreme Court addressed the question of whether claims regarding computer-implemented inventions—including systems, machines, processes, and items of manufacture—were patent-eligible subject matter. Justice Clarence Thomas wrote the opinion for the unanimous Court. The Court held that patent law should not restrain abstract ideas that are the "building blocks of human ingenuity" and held all of Alice's claims ineligible for patent protection. Because using a third party to eliminate settlement risk is a fundamental and prevalent practice, it is essentially a building block of the modern economy. The Court held that Alice's claims did no more than require a generic computer to implement this abstract idea of intermediated settlement by performing generic computer functions, which is not enough to transform an abstract idea into a patent-eligible invention.

Justice Sonia M. Sotomayor wrote a concurring opinion in which she argued that any claim that merely describes a method of doing business should not be patentable. In this case, Justice Sotomayor agreed that the method claims at issue pertained to an abstract idea and implementing those claims on a computer was not enough to transform that idea into patentable subject matter. Although the Alice opinion did not mention software as such, this case is widely considered applicable to software patents and patents on software for business methods.

A full understanding of the current state of Sec. 101 "Subject Matter" U.S. Supreme Court jurisprudence requires familiarity with two related cases:

a. Bilski v. Kappos, 561 U.S. 593 (2010)

https://www.supremecourt.gov/opinions/09pdf/08-964.pdf

In Bilski v. Kappos, applicants were denied a patent by the Patent and Trademark Office (PTO) for claims pertaining to a process of managing risk in commodities trading. The PTO examiner concluded that the invention was not patentable subject matter within the meaning of 35 U.S.C. Sec. 101. The Board of Patent Appeals and Interferences affirmed the decision. On appeal, the U.S. Court of Appeals for the Federal Circuit affirmed. The Federal Circuit relied on Supreme Court precedent stating that an invention is patentable if: "1) it is tied to a particular machine or apparatus, or 2) it transforms a particular article into a different state or thing." Reasoning from this, it held that the applicants' invention clearly failed this test (the machine-or-transformation test) and therefore did not constitute patentable subject matter.

On appeal the U.S. Supreme Court addressed two questions: Whether the Federal Circuit was correct to use the machine-or-transformation test in determining patentable subject matter, and whether the machine-or-transformation test prevents patent protection for business methods in a way that contradicts congressional intent that patents protect "methods of doing or conducting business." The Supreme Court affirmed the Federal Circuit, holding that the applicants' claimed invention was not patent eligible, but also held that the machine-or-transformation test should not be the sole test for determining eligibility.

b. Mayo v. Prometheus, 566 U.S. 66 (2012):

https://www.supremecourt.gov/opinions/11pdf/10-1150.pdf

Prometheus Laboratories Inc. patented steps of testing for proper dosages of drug treatments used to treat gastrointestinal diseases like Crohn's disease, and sued the Mayo Clinic when it attempted to use its own, similar test. The District Court invalidated the patents, holding that the patent could not cover the body's reaction to drugs. The U.S. Court of Appeals for the Federal Circuit reversed, and the U.S. Supreme Court reversed again. In a 9-0 decision, Justice Stephen J. Breyer wrote the unanimous opinion holding that the processes involved in the disputed test are unpatentable laws of nature, and the "steps" Prometheus had added to its patent application were merely instructions to apply the laws of nature.

(3) **Who are the better suited to find the acquired meaning of patent terms: jurors of judges—Case of MARKMAN et al. v. WESTVIEW INSTRUMENTS, INC., et al.**

517 U.S. 370 (1996)
OCTOBER TERM, 1995
certiorari to the united states court of appeals for the federal circuit
No. 95–26.Argued January 8, 1996—Decided April 23, 1996

3.1 Syllabus:
Petitioner Markman owns the patent to a system that tracks clothing through the drycleaning process using a keyboard and data processor to generate transaction records, including a bar code readable by optical detectors. According to the patent's claim, the portion of the patent document that defines the patentee's rights, Markman's product can "maintain an inventory total" and "detect and localize spurious additions to inventory." The product of respondent Westview Instruments, Inc., also uses a keyboard and processor and lists dry-cleaning charges on bar-coded tickets that can be read by optical detectors. In this infringement suit, after hearing an expert witness testify about the meaning of the claim's language, the jury found that Westview's product had infringed Markman's patent. The District Court nevertheless directed a verdict for Westview on the ground that its device is unable to track "inventory" as that term is used in the claim. The Court of Appeals affirmed, holding the interpretation of claim terms to be the exclusive province of the court and the Seventh Amendment to be consistent with that conclusion.

3.2 Reasoning:
The construction of a patent, including terms of art within its claim, is exclusively within the province of the court.
(a) The Seventh Amendment right of trial by jury is the right which existed under the English common law when the Amendment was adopted. *Baltimore & Carolina Line, Inc. v. Redman,* 295 U. S. 654, 657. Thus, the Court asks, first, whether infringement

cases either were tried at law at the time of the founding or are at least analogous to a cause of action that was. There is no dispute that infringement cases today must be tried before a jury, as their predecessors were more than two centuries ago. This conclusion raises a second question: whether the particular trial issue (here a patent claim's construction) is necessarily a jury issue. This question is answered by comparing the modern practice to historical sources. Where there is no exact antecedent in the common law, the modern practice should be compared to earlier practices whose allocation to court or jury is known, and the best analogy that can be drawn between an old and the new must be sought.

(b) There is no direct antecedent of modern claim construction in the historical sources. The closest 18th-century analogue to modern claim construction seems to have been the construction of patent specifications describing the invention. Early patent cases from England and this Court show that judges, not juries, construed specification terms. No authority from this period supports Markman's contention that even if judges were charged with construing most patent terms, the art of defining terms of art in a specification fell within the jury's province.

(c) Since evidence of common-law practice at the time of the framing does not entail application of the Seventh Amendment's jury guarantee to the construction of the claim document, this Court must look elsewhere to characterize this determination of meaning in order to allocate it as between judge or jury. Existing precedent, the relative interpretive skills of judges and juries, and statutory policy considerations all favor allocating construction issues to the court. As the former patent practitioner, Justice Curtis, explained, the first issue in a patent case, construing the patent, is a question of law, to be determined by the court. The second issue, whether infringement occurred, is a question of fact for a jury. *Winans* v. *Denmead,* 15 How. 330, 338. Contrary to Markman's contention, *Bischoff* v. *Wethered,* 9 Wall. 812, and *Tucker* v. *Spalding,* 13 Wall. 453, neither indicate that 19th-century juries resolved the meaning of patent terms of art nor undercut Justice Curtis's authority. Functional considerations also favor having judges define patent terms of art. A judge, from his training and discipline, is more likely to give proper interpretation to highly technical patents than a jury and is in a better position to ascertain whether an expert's proposed definition fully comports with the instrument as a whole. Finally, the need for uniformity in the treatment of a given patent favors allocation of construction issues to the court. 52 F. 3d 967, affirmed. Souter, J., delivered the opinion for a unanimous Court.

MARKMAN et al. v. WESTVIEW INSTRUMENTS, INC., et al.

517 U.S. 370 (1996)

OCTOBER TERM, 1995

William B. Mallin argued the cause for petitioners. With him on the briefs were Timothy P. Ryan, Timothy S. Coon, Lewis F. Gould, Jr., and Stephan P. Gribok.

Frank H. Griffin III argued the cause for respondents. With him on the brief were *Peter A. Vogt* and *Polly M.Shaffe.*[4]

Justice Souter delivered the opinion of the Court.

---

[4] *Jeffrey Robert White, Pamela A. Liapakis,* and *Joseph W. Cotchett* filed a brief for the Association of Trial Lawyers of America as *amicus curiae* urging reversal.

The question here is whether the interpretation of a so called patent claim, the portion of the patent document that defines the scope of the patentee's rights, is a matter of law reserved entirely for the court, or subject to a Seventh Amendment guarantee that a jury will determine the meaning of any disputed term of art about which expert testimony is offered. We hold that the construction of a patent, including terms of art within its claim, is exclusively within the province of the court.

I

The Constitution empowers Congress "to promote the Progress of Science and useful Arts, by securing for limited Times to Authors and Inventors the exclusive Right to their respective Writings and Discoveries." Art. I, §8, cl. 8. Congress first exercised this authority in 1790, when it provided for the issuance of "letters patent," Act of Apr. 10, 1790, ch. 7, §1, 1 Stat. 109, which, like their modern counterparts, granted inventors "the right to exclude others from making, using, offering for sale, selling, or importing the patented invention," in exchange for full disclosure of an invention, H. Schwartz, Patent Law and Practice 1, 33 (2d ed. 1995). It has long been understood that a patent must describe the exact scope of an invention and its manufacture to "secure to the patentee all to which he is entitled, and to apprise the public of what is still open to them." *McClain* v. *Ortmayer,* 141 U. S. 419, 424 (1891). Under the modern American system, these objectives are served by two distinct elements of a patent document. First, it contains a specification describing the invention "in such full, clear, concise, and exact terms as to enable any person skilled in the art... to make and use the same." 35 U. S. C. §112; see also 3 E. Lipscomb, Walker on Patents §10:1, pp. 183–184 (3d ed. 1985) (Lipscomb) (listing the requirements for a specification). Second, a patent includes one or more "claims," which "particularly point out and distinctly claim the subject matter which the applicant regards as his invention." 35 U. S. C. §112. "A claim covers and secures a process, a machine, a manufacture, a composition of matter, or a design, but never the function or result of either, nor the scientific explanation of their operation." 6 Lipscomb §21:17, at 315– 316. The claim "defines the scope of a patent grant," 3 *id.,* §11:1, at 280, and functions to forbid not only exact copies of an invention, but products that go to

---

Briefs of amici curiae urging affirmance were filed for the American Intellectual Property Law Association by Don W. Martens, Charles L. Gholz, R. Carl Moy, Roger W. Parkhurst, Joseph R. Re, Paul A. Stewart, and Harold C. Wegner; for the Federal Circuit Bar Association by David H. T. Kane and Rudolph P. Hofmann; for the Dallas-Fort Worth Intellectual Property Law Association; for Honeywell, Inc., by Richard G. Taranto and David L. Shapiro; for Intellectual Property Owners by Rex E. Lee, Carter G. Phillips, Mark E. Haddad, and Constantine L. Trela; for Matsushita Electric Corp. of America et al. by Morton Amster and Joel E. Lutzker; for United States Surgical Corp. by John G. Kester, J. Alan Galbraith, William E. McDaniels, Arthur R. Miller, Thomas R. Bremer, and John C. Andres; for John T. Roberts, pro se; and for Douglas W. Wyatt by Mr. Wyatt, pro se, Paul M. Janicke, and John R. Kirk, Jr.

Briefs of *amici curiae* were filed for Airtouch Communications, Inc., by *Allan N. Littman* and *Robert P. Taylor;* for the American Automobile Manufacturers Association by *Charles W. Bradley, Stanley L. Amberg, Phillip D. Brady,* and *Andrew D. Koblenz;* for the American Board of Trial Advocates by *Robert G. Vial;* for Exxon Corp. et al. by *Donald B. Craven, Gerald Goldman, James P. Tuite,* and *James R. Lovelace;* and for Litton Systems, Inc., by *Laurence H. Tribe, Jonathan S. Massey,* and *Kenneth J. Chesebro.*

"the heart of an invention but avoids the literal language of the claim by making a noncritical change," Schwartz, *supra,* at 82.[5] In this opinion, the word "claim" is used only in this sense peculiar to patent law.

Characteristically, patent lawsuits charge what is known as infringement, Schwartz, *supra,* at 75, and rest on allegations that the defendant "without authority ma[de], use[d] or [sold the] patented invention, within the United States during the term of the patent therefor...." 35 U. S. C. §271(a). Victory in an infringement suit requires a finding that the patent claim "covers the alleged infringer's product or process," which in turn necessitates a determination of "what the words in the claim mean." Schwartz, *supra,* at 80; see also 3 Lipscomb §11:2, at 288–290.

Petitioner in this infringement suit, Markman, owns United States Reissue Patent No. 33,054 for his "Inventory Control and Reporting System for Drycleaning Stores." The patent describes a system that can monitor and report the status, location, and movement of clothing in a drycleaning establishment. The Markman system consists of a keyboard and data processor to generate written records for each transaction, including a bar code readable by optical detectors operated by employees, who log the progress of clothing through the dry-cleaning process. Respondent Westview's product also includes a keyboard and processor, and it lists charges for the dry-cleaning services on bar-coded tickets that can be read by portable optical detectors.

Markman brought an infringement suit against Westview and Althon Enterprises, an operator of dry-cleaning establishments using Westview's products (collectively, Westview). Westview responded that Markman's patent is not infringed by its system because the latter functions merely to record an inventory of receivables by tracking invoices and transaction totals, rather than to record and track an inventory of articles of clothing. Part of the dispute hinged upon the meaning of the word "inventory," a term found in Markman's independent claim 1, which states that Markman's product can "maintain an inventory total" and "detect and localize spurious additions to inventory." The case was tried before a jury, which heard, among others, a witness produced by Markman who testified about the meaning of the claim language.

After the jury compared the patent to Westview's device, it found an infringement of Markman's independent claim 1 and dependent claim 10.[6] The District Court nevertheless granted Westview's deferred motion for judgment as a matter of law, one of its reasons being that the term "inventory" in Markman's patent encompasses "both cash inventory and the actual physical inventory of articles of clothing." 772 F. Supp. 1535, 1537–1538 (ED Pa. 1991). Under the trial court's construction of the patent, the production, sale, or use of a tracking system for dry cleaners would not infringe Markman's patent unless the product was capable of tracking articles

---

[5] Thus, for example, a claim for a ceiling fan with three blades attached to a solid rod connected to a motor would not only cover fans that take precisely this form, but would also cover a similar fan that includes some additional feature, e.g., such a fan with a cord or switch for turning it on and off, and may cover a product deviating from the core design in some noncritical way, e.g., a three-bladed ceiling fan with blades attached to a hollow rod connected to a motor. H. Schwartz, Patent Law and Practice 81–82 (ad ed. 1995).

[6] Dependent claim 10 specifies that, in the invention of claim 1, the input device is an alpha-numeric keyboard in which single keys may be used to enter the attributes of the items in question.

of clothing throughout the cleaning process and generating reports about their status and location. Since Westview's system cannot do these things, the District Court directed a verdict on the ground that Westview's device does not have the "means to maintain an inventory total" and thus cannot "'detect and localize spurious additions to inventory as well as spurious deletions therefrom,'" as required by claim 1. *Id.,* at 1537.

Markman appealed, arguing it was error for the District Court to substitute its construction of the disputed claim term 'inventory' for the construction the jury had presumably given it. The United States Court of Appeals for the Federal Circuit affirmed, holding the interpretation of claim terms to be the exclusive province of the court and the Seventh Amendment to be consistent with that conclusion. 52 F. 3d 967 (1995). Markman sought our review on each point, and we granted certiorari. 515 U. S. 1192 (1995). We now affirm.

II

The Seventh Amendment provides that "in Suits at common law, where the value in controversy shall exceed twenty dollars, the right of trial by jury shall be preserved...." U. S. Const., Amdt. 7. Since Justice Story's day, *United States* v. *Wonson,* 28 F. Cas. 745, 750 (No. 16,750) (CC Mass. 1812), we have understood that "the right of trial by jury thus preserved is the right which existed under the English common law when the Amendment was adopted." *Baltimore & Carolina Line, Inc.* v. *Redman,* 295 U. S. 654, 657 (1935). In keeping with our longstanding adherence to this "historical test," Wolfram, The Constitutional History of the Seventh Amendment, 57 Minn. L. Rev. 639, 640–643 (1973), we ask, first, whether we are dealing with a cause of action that either was tried at law at the time of the founding or is at least analogous to one that was, see, e.g., *Tull* v. *United States,* 481 U. S. 412, 417 (1987). If the action in question belongs in the law category, we then ask whether the particular trial decision must fall to the jury in order to preserve the substance of the common-law right as it existed in 1791. See *infra,* at 377–378.[7]

A

As to the first issue, going to the character of the cause of action, "the form of our analysis is familiar. 'First we compare the statutory action to 18th-century actions brought in the courts of England prior to the merger of the courts of law and equity.'" *Granfinanciera, S. A.* v. *Nordberg,* 492 U. S. 33, 42 (1989) (citation omitted). Equally familiar is the descent of today's patent infringement action from the infringement actions tried at law in the eighteenth century, and there is no dispute that infringement cases today must be tried to a jury, as their predecessors were more than two centuries ago. See, e.g., *Bramah* v. *Hardcastle,* 1 Carp. P. C. 168 (K. B. 1789).

B

This conclusion raises the second question, whether a particular issue occurring within a jury trial (here the construction of a patent claim) is itself necessarily a jury

---

[7] Our formulations of the historical test do not deal with the possibility of conflict between actual English common-law practice and American assumptions about what that practice was, or between English and American practices at the relevant time. No such complications arise in this case.

issue, the guarantee being essential to preserve the right to a jury's resolution of the ultimate dispute. In some instances the answer to this second question may be easy because of clear historical evidence that the very subsidiary question was so regarded under the English practice of leaving the issue for a jury. But when, as here, the old practice provides no clear answer, see *infra,* at 378–380, we are forced to make a judgment about the scope of the Seventh Amendment guarantee without the benefit of any foolproof test.

The Court has repeatedly said that the answer to the second question "must depend on whether the jury must shoulder this responsibility *as necessary to preserve the 'substance of the common-law right of trial by jury.'" Tull* v. *United States, supra,* at 426 (emphasis added) (quoting *Colgrove* v. *Battin,* 413 U. S. 149, 157 (1973)); see also *Baltimore & Carolina Line, supra,* at 657. "Only those incidents which are regarded as fundamental, as inherent in and of the essence of the system of trial by jury, are placed beyond the reach of the legislature." *Tull* v. *United States, supra,* at 426 (citations omitted); see also *Galloway* v. *United States,* 319 U. S. 372, 392 (1943).

The "substance of the common-law right" is, however, a pretty blunt instrument for drawing distinctions. We have tried to sharpen it, to be sure, by reference to the distinction between substance and procedure. See *Baltimore & Carolina Line, supra,* at 657; see also *Galloway* v. *United States, supra,* at 390–391; *Ex parte Peterson,* 253 U. S. 300, 309 (1920); *Walker* v. *New Mexico & Southern Pacific R. Co.,* 165 U. S. 593, 596 (1897); but see *Sun Oil Co.* v. *Wortman,* 486 U. S. 717, 727 (1988). We have also spoken of the line as one between issues of fact and law. See *Baltimore & Carolina Line, supra,* at 657; see also *Ex parte Peterson, supra,* at 310; *Walker* v. *New Mexico & Southern Pacific R. Co., supra,* at 597; but see *Pullman-Standard* v. *Swint,* 456 U. S. 273, 288 (1982).

But the sounder course, when available, is to classify a mongrel practice (like construing a term of art following receipt of evidence) by using the historical method, much as we do in characterizing the suits and actions within which they arise. Where there is no exact antecedent, the best hope lies in comparing the modern practice to earlier ones whose allocation to court or jury we do know, cf. *Baltimore & Carolina Line, supra,* at 659, 660; *Dimick* v. *Schiedt,* 293 U. S. 474, 477, 482 (1935), seeking the best analogy we can draw between an old and the new, see *Tull* v. *United States, supra,* at 420–421 (we must search the English common law for "appropriate analogies" rather than a "precisely analogous common-law cause of action").

C

"Prior to 1790 nothing in the nature of a claim had appeared either in British patent practice or in that of the American states," Lutz, Evolution of the Claims of U. S. Patents, 20 J. Pat. Off. Soc. 134 (1938), and we have accordingly found no direct antecedent of modern claim construction in the historical sources. Claim practice did not achieve statutory recognition until the passage of the Act of July 4, 1836, ch. 357, §6, 5 Stat. 119, and inclusion of a claim did not become a statutory requirement until 1870, Act of July 8, 1870, ch. 230, §26, 16 Stat. 201; see 1 A. Deller, Patent Claims §4, p. 9 (2d ed. 1971). Although, as one historian has observed, as early as 1850 "judges were... beginning to express more frequently the idea that in seeking to ascertain the invention 'claimed' in a patent the inquiry should be limited to interpreting the summary, or 'claim,'" Lutz, *supra,* at 145, "the idea that the claim is just as important if not more important than the description and drawings did not develop until the Act of 1870 or thereabouts." Deller, *supra,* §4, at 9.

At the time relevant for Seventh Amendment analogies, in contrast, it was the specification, itself a relatively new development, H. Dutton, The Patent System and Inventive Activity During the Industrial Revolution, 1750–1852, pp. 75–76 (1984), that represented the key to the patent. Thus, patent litigation in that early period was typified by so-called novelty actions, testing whether "any essential part of the patent had been disclosed to the public before," *Huddart* v. *Grimshaw,* Dav. Pat. Cas. 265, 298 (K. B. 1803), and "enablement" cases, in which juries were asked to determine whether the specification described the invention well enough to allow members of the appropriate trade to reproduce it, see, e.g., *Arkwright* v. *Nightingale,* Dav. Pat. Cas. 37, 60 (C. P. 1785).

The closest 18th-century analogue of modern claim construction seems, then, to have been the construction of specifications, and as to that function the mere smattering of patent cases that we have from this period shows no established jury practice sufficient to support an argument by analogy that today's construction of a claim should be a guaranteed jury issue. Few of the case reports even touch upon the proper interpretation of disputed terms in the specifications at issue, see, e.g., *Bramah* v. *Hardcastle,* 1 Carp. P. C. 168 (K. B. 1789); *King* v. *Else,* 1 Carp. P. C. 103, Dav. Pat. Cas. 144 (K. B. 1785); *Dollond's Case,* 1 Carp. P. C. 28 (C. P. 1758); *Administrators of Calthorp* v. *Waymans,* 3 Keb. 710, 84 Eng. Rep. 966 (K. B. 1676), and none demonstrates that the definition of such a term was determined by the jury.[8] This absence of an established practice should not surprise us, given the primitive state of jury patent practice at the end of the eighteenth century, when juries were still new to the field. Although by 1791 more than a century had passed since the enactment of the Statute of Monopolies, which provided that the validity of any monopoly should be determined in accordance with the common law, patent litigation had remained

---

[8] Marksman relies heavily upon Justice Buller's notes of Lord Mansfield's instructions in *Larded* v. *Johnson* (K. B. 1778), in 1 J. Oldham, The Mansfield Manuscripts and the Growth of English Law in the Eighteenth Century 748 (1992). *Larded* was an enablement case about the invention of stucco, in which a defendant asserted that the patent was invalid because it did not fully describe the appropriate method for producing the substance. Even setting aside concerns about the accuracy of the summary of the jury instructions provided for this case from outside the established reports, see 1 Oldham, *supra,* at 752, n. 11, it does not show that juries construed disputed terms in a patent. From its ambiguous references, e.g., 1 Oldham, *supra,* at 756 ("[Lord Mansfield] left to the jury 1st, on all objections made to exactness, certainty and propriety of the Specification, & whether any workman could make it by [the Specification]"), we cannot infer the existence of an established practice, cf. *Galloway* v. *United States,* 319 U. S. 372, 392 (1943) (expressing concern regarding the "uncertainty and the variety of conclusions which follows from an effort at purely historical accuracy"), especially when, as here, the inference is undermined by evidence that judges, rather than jurors, ordinarily construed written documents at the time. See *infra,* at 381–383.

Before the turn of the century, "no more than twenty-two [reported] cases came before the superior courts of London." H. Dutton, The Patent System and Inventive Activity During the Industrial Revolution, 1750– 1852, p. 71 (1984).

within the jurisdiction of the Privy Council until 1752 and hence without the option of a jury trial. E. Walterscheid, Early Evolution of the United States Patent Law: Antecedents (Part 3), 77 J. Pat. & Tm. Off. Soc. 771, 771–776 (1995). Indeed, the state of patent law in the common-law courts before 1800 led one historian to observe that "the reported cases are destitute of any decision of importance.... At the end of the eighteenth century, therefore, the Common Law Judges were left to pick up the threads of the principles of law without the aid of recent and reliable precedents." Hulme, On the Consideration of the Patent Grant, Past and Present, 13 L. Q. Rev. 313, 318 (1897). Earlier writers expressed similar discouragement at patent law's amorphous character,[9] and, as late as the 1830's, English commentators were irked by enduring confusion in the field. See Dutton, *supra*, at 69–70.

Markman seeks to supply what the early case reports lack in so many words by relying on decisions like *Turner* v. *Winter*, 1 T. R. 602, 99 Eng. Rep. 1274 (K. B. 1787), and *Arkwright* v. *Nightingale*, Dav. Pat. Cas. 37 (C. P. 1785), to argue that the 18th-century juries must have acted as definers of patent terms just to reach the verdicts we know they rendered in patent cases turning on enablement or novelty. But the conclusion simply does not follow. There is no more reason to infer that juries supplied plenary interpretation of written instruments in patent litigation than in other cases implicating the meaning of documentary terms, and we do know that in other kinds of cases during this period judges, not juries, ordinarily construed written documents.[10] The probability that the judges were doing the same thing in the patent litigation of the time is confirmed by the fact that as soon as the English reports did begin to describe the construction of patent documents, they show the judges construing the terms of the specifications. See *Bovill* v. *Moore,* Dav. Pat. Cas. 361, 399, 404 (C. P. 1816) (judge submits question of novelty to the jury only after explaining some of the language and "stating in what terms the specification runs"); cf. *Russell* v. *Cowley & Dixon,* Webs. Pat. Cas. 457, 467–470 (Exch. 1834) (construing the terms of the specification in reviewing a verdict); *Haworth* v. *Hardcastle,* Webs. Pat. Cas. 480, 484–485 (1834) (same). This evidence is in fact buttressed by cases from this Court; when they first reveal actual practice, the practice revealed

---

[9] See, e.g., *Bolton and Watt* v. *Bull,* 2 H. Bl. 463, 491, 126 Eng. Rep. 651, 665 (C. P. 1795) (Eyre, C. J.) ("Patent rights are no where that I can find accurately discussed in our books"); Dutton, *supra* n. 4, at 70–71 (quoting Abraham Weston as saying "it may with truth be said that the [Law] Books are silent on the subject [of patents] and furnish no clue to go by, in agitating the Question What is the Law of Patents?").

[10] See, e.g., Devlin, Jury Trial of Complex Cases: English Practice at the Time of the Seventh Amendment, 80 Colum. L. Rev. 43, 75 (1980); Weiner, The Civil Jury Trial and the Law-Fact Distinction, 54 Calif. L. Rev. 1867, 1932 (1966). For example, one historian observed that it was generally the practice of judges in the late 18th century "to keep the construction of writings *out of the jury's hands* and reserve it for themselves," a "safeguard" designed to prevent a jury from "constru[ing] or refin[ing] it at pleasure." 9 J. Wigmore, Evidence §2461, p. 194 (J. Chadbourn rev. ed. 1981) (emphasis in original; internal quotation marks omitted). The absence of any established practice supporting Markman's view is also shown by the disagreement between Justices Willis and Buller, reported in *Macbeath* v. *Haldimand,* 1 T. R. 173, 180–182, 99 Eng. Rep. 1036, 1040–1041 (K. B. 1786), as to whether juries could ever construe written documents when their meaning was disputed.

is of the judge construing the patent. See, e.g., *Winans* v. *New York & Erie R. Co.,* 21 How. 88, 100 (1859); *Winans* v. *Denmead,* 15 How. 330, 338 (1854); *Hogg* v. *Emerson,* 6 How. 437, 484 (1848); cf. *Parker* v. *Hulme,* 18 F. Cas. 1138 (No. 10,740) (CC ED Pa. 1849). These indications of our patent practice are the more impressive for being all of a piece with what we know about the analogous contemporary practice of interpreting terms within a land patent, where it fell to the judge, not the jury, to construe the words.[11]

D

Losing, then, on the contention that juries generally had interpretive responsibilities during the eighteenth century, Markman seeks a different anchor for analogy in the more modest contention that even if judges were charged with construing most terms in the patent, the art of defining terms of art employed in a specification fell within the province of the jury. Again, however, Markman has no authority from the period in question, but relies instead on the later case of *Neilson* v. *Harford,* Webs. Pat. Cas. 328 (Exch. 1841). There, an exchange between the judge and the lawyers indicated that although the construction of a patent was ordinarily for the court, *id.,* at 349 (Alderson, B.), judges should "leave the question of words of art to the jury," *id.,* at 350 (Alderson, B.); see also *id.,* at 370 (judgment of the court); *Hill* v. *Evans,* 4 De. G. F. & J. 288, 293–294, 45 Eng. Rep. 1195, 1197 (Ch. 1862). Without, however, in any way disparaging the weight to which Baron Alderson's view is entitled, the most we can say is that an English report more than 70 years after the time that concerns us indicates an exception to what probably had been occurring earlier.[12] In place of Markman's inference that this exceptional practice existed in 1791 there is at best only a possibility that it did, and for anything more than a possibility we have found no scholarly authority.

III

Since evidence of common-law practice at the time of the framing does not entail application of the Seventh Amendment's jury guarantee to the construction of the claim document, we must look elsewhere to characterize this determination of meaning in order to allocate it as between court or jury. We accordingly consult

---

[11] As we noted in *Brown* v. *Huger,* 21 How. 305, 318 (1859):

"With regard to the second part of this objection, that which claims for the jury the construction of the patent, we remark that the patent itself must be taken as evidence of its meaning; that, like other written instruments, it must be interpreted as a whole . . . and the legal deductions drawn therefrom must be conformable with the scope and purpose of the entire document. This construction and these deductions we hold to be within the exclusive province of the court."

[12] In explaining that judges generally construed all terms in a written document at the end of the eighteenth century, one historian observed that "[i]nterpretation by local usage for example (today the plainest case of legitimate deviation from the normal standard) was still but making its way." 9 Wigmore, Evidence §2461, at 195; see also *id.,* at 195, and n. 6 (providing examples of this practice). We need not in any event consider here whether our conclusion that the Seventh Amendment does not require terms of art in patent claims to be submitted to the jury supports a similar result in other types of cases.

existing precedent[13] and consider both the relative interpretive skills of judges and juries and the statutory policies that ought to be furthered by the allocation.

A

The two elements of a simple patent case, construing the patent and determining whether infringement occurred, were characterized by the former patent practitioner, Justice Curtis.[14] "The first is a question of law, to be determined by the court, construing the letters-patent, and the description of the invention and specification of claim annexed to them. The second is a question of fact, to be submitted to a jury." *Winans* v. *Denmead, supra,* at 338; see *Winans* v. *New York & Erie R. Co., supra,* at 100; *Hogg* v. *Emerson, supra,* at 484; cf. *Parker* v. *Hulme, supra,* at 1140.

In arguing for a different allocation of responsibility for the first question, Markman relies primarily on two cases, *Bischoff* v. *Wethered,* 9 Wall. 812 (1870), and *Tucker* v. *Spalding,* 13 Wall. 453 (1872). These are said to show that evidence of the meaning of patent terms was offered to 19thcentury juries, and thus to imply that the meaning of a documentary term was a jury issue whenever it was subject to evidentiary proof. That is not what Markman's cases show, however.

In order to resolve the *Bischoff* suit implicating the construction of rival patents, we considered "whether the court below was bound to compare the two specifications, and to instruct the jury, as a matter of law, whether the inventions therein described were, or were not, identical." 9 Wall., at 813 (statement of the case). We said it was not bound to do that, on the ground that investing the court with so dispositive a role would improperly eliminate the jury's function in answering the ultimate question of infringement. On that ultimate issue, expert testimony had been admitted on "the nature of the various mechanisms or manufactures described in the different patents produced, and as to the identity or diversity between them." *Id.,* at 814. Although the jury's consideration of that expert testimony in resolving the question of infringement was said to impinge upon the well established principle "that it is the province of the court, and not the jury, to construe the meaning of documentary evidence," *id.,* at 815, we decided that it was not so. We said:

"The specifications... profess to describe mechanisms and complicated machinery, chemical compositions and other manufactured products, which have their existence *in pais,* outside of the documents themselves; and which are commonly described by terms of the art or mystery to which they respectively belong; and these descriptions and terms of art often require peculiar knowledge and education to understand them aright.... Indeed, the whole subject-matter of a patent is an embodied conception outside of the patent itself.... This outward embodiment of the terms

---

[13] Because we conclude that our precedent supports classifying the question as one for the court, we need not decide either the extent to which the Seventh Amendment can be said to have crystallized a law/fact distinction, cf. *Ex parte Peterson,* 253 U. S. 300, 310 (1920); *Walker* v. *New Mexico & Southern Pacific R. Co.,* 165 U. S. 593, 597 (1897), or whether post 1791 precedent classifying an issue as one of fact would trigger the protections of the Seventh Amendment if (unlike this case) there were no more specific reason for decision.

[14] See 1 A Memoir of Benjamin Robbins Curtis, L. L. D., 84 (B. Curtis ed. 1879); cf. *O'Reilly* v. *Morse,* 15 How. 62, 63 (1854) (noting his involvement in a patent case).

contained in the patent is the thing invented, and is to be properly sought, like the explanation of all latent ambiguities arising from the description of external things, by evidence *in pais*." *Ibid.*

Bischoff does not then, as Markman contends, hold that the use of expert testimony about the meaning of terms of art requires the judge to submit the question of their construction to the jury. It is instead a case in which the Court drew a line between issues of document interpretation and product identification, and held that expert testimony was properly presented to the jury on the latter, ultimate issue, whether the physical objects produced by the patent were identical. The Court did not see the decision as bearing upon the appropriate treatment of disputed terms. As the opinion emphasized, the Court's "view of the case is not intended to, and does not, trench upon the doctrine that the construction of written instruments is the province of the court alone. *It is not the construction of the instrument, but the character of the thing invented, which is sought in questions of identity and diversity of inventions.*" *Id.,* at 816 (emphasis added). *Tucker,* the second case proffered by Markman, is to the same effect. Its reasoning rested expressly on *Bischoff,* and it just as clearly noted that in addressing the ultimate issue of mixed fact and law, it was for the court to "lay down to the jury the law which should govern them." *Tucker, supra,* at 455.[15]

If the line drawn in these two opinions is a fine one, it is one that the Court has drawn repeatedly in explaining the respective roles of the jury and judge in patent cases, and one understood by commentators writing in the aftermath of the cases Markman cites. Walker, for example, read *Bischoff* as holding that the question of novelty is not decided by a construction of the prior patent, "but depends rather upon the outward embodiment of the terms contained in the prior patent; and that such outward embodiment is to be properly sought, like the explanation of latent ambiguities arising from the description of external things, by evidence *in pais.*" A. Walker, Patent Laws §75, p. 68 (3d ed. 1895). He also emphasized in the same treatise that matters of claim construction, even those aided by expert testimony, are questions for the court:

"Questions of construction are questions of law for the judge, not questions of fact for the jury. As it cannot be expected, however, that judges will always possess the requisite knowledge of the meaning of the terms of art or science used in letters patent, it often becomes necessary that they should avail themselves of the light furnished by experts relevant to the significance of such words and phrases. The judges are not, however, obliged to blindly follow such testimony." *Id.,* §189, at 173 (footnotes omitted).

Virtually the same description of the court's use of evidence in its interpretive role was set out in another contemporary treatise:

(Exch. 1841), which we discuss, *supra,* at 383, and, whether or not he agreed with *Neilson,* he stated, "but I do not proceed upon this ground." 29 F. Cas., at 325. [13]

---

[15] We are also unpersuaded by petitioner's heavy reliance upon the decision of Justice Story on circuit in *Washburn* v. *Gould,* 29 F. Cas. 312 (No. 17,214) (CC Mass. 1844). Although he wrote that "the jury are to judge of the meaning of words of art, and technical phrases," *id.,* at 325, he did so in describing the decision in *Neilson* v. *Harford,* Webs. Pat. Cas. 328.

See, e.g., *Coupe* v. *Royer,* 155 U. S. 565, 579–580 (1895); *Silsby* v. *Foote,* 14 How. 218, 226 (1853); *Hogg* v. *Emerson,* 6 How. 437, 484 (1848); cf. *Brown* v. *Piper,* 91 U. S. 37, 41 (1875); *Winans* v. *New York & Erie R. Co.,* 21 How. 88, 100 (1859); cf. also *U. S. Industrial Chemicals, Inc.* v. *Carbide & Carbon Chemicals Corp.,* 315 U. S. 668, 678 (1942).

"The duty of interpreting letters-patent has been committed to the courts. A patent is a legal instrument, to be construed, like other legal instruments, according to its tenor.... Where technical terms are used, or where the qualities of substances or operations mentioned or any similar data necessary to the comprehension of the language of the patent are unknown to the judge, the testimony of witnesses may be received upon these subjects, and any other means of information be employed. *But in the actual interpretation of the patent the court proceeds upon its own responsibility, as an arbiter of the law, giving to the patent its true and final character and force.*" 2 W. Robinson, Law of Patents §732, pp. 481–483 (1890) (emphasis added; footnotes omitted).

In sum, neither *Bischoff* nor *Tucker* indicates that juries resolved the meaning of terms of art in construing a patent, and neither case undercuts Justice Curtis's authority.

B

Where history and precedent provide no clear answers, functional considerations also play their part in the choice between judge and jury to define terms of art. We said in *Miller* v. *Fenton,* 474 U. S. 104, 114 (1985), that when an issue "falls somewhere between a pristine legal standard and a simple historical fact, the fact/law distinction at times has turned on a determination that, as a matter of the sound administration of justice, one judicial actor is better positioned than another to decide the issue in question." So it turns out here, for judges, not juries, are the better suited to find the acquired meaning of patent terms.

The construction of written instruments is one of those things that judges often do and are likely to do better than jurors unburdened by training in exegesis. Patent construction in particular "is a special occupation, requiring, like all others, special training and practice. The judge, from his training and discipline, is more likely to give a proper interpretation to such instruments than a jury; and he is, therefore, more likely to be right, in performing such a duty, than a jury can be expected to be." *Parker* v. *Hulme,* 18 F. Cas., at 1140. Such was the understanding nearly a century and a half ago, and there is no reason to weigh the respective strengths of judge and jury differently in relation to the modern claim; quite the contrary, for "the claims of patents have become highly technical in many respects as the result of special doctrines relating to the proper form and scope of claims that have been developed by the courts and the Patent Office." Woodward, Definiteness and Particularity in Patent Claims, 46 Mich. L. Rev. 755, 765 (1948).

Markman would trump these considerations with his argument that a jury should decide a question of meaning peculiar to a trade or profession simply because the question is a subject of testimony requiring credibility determinations, which are the jury's forte. It is, of course, true that credibility judgments have to be made about the experts who testify in patent cases, and in theory there could be a case in which a simple credibility judgment would suffice to choose between experts whose testimony was equally consistent with a patent's internal logic. But our own experience with document construction leaves us doubtful that trial courts will run into many cases like that. In the main, we expect, any credibility determinations will be subsumed within the necessarily sophisticated analysis of the whole document, required by the standard construction rule that a term can be defined only in a way that comports with the instrument as a whole. See *Bates* v. *Coe,* 98 U. S. 31, 38 (1878); 6 Lipscomb §21:40, at 393; 2 Robinson, *supra,* §734, at 484; Woodward, *supra,* at 765; cf. *U. S. Industrial Chemicals, Inc.* v. *Carbide & Carbon Chemicals Co.,* 315 U. S. 668, 678 (1942); cf. 6 Lipscomb §21:40, at 393. Thus, in these cases a jury's capabilities to evaluate demeanor, cf. *Miller, supra,* at 114, 117, to sense the "mainsprings of human conduct," *Commissioner* v. *Duberstein,* 363 U. S. 278, 289 (1960), or to reflect community standards, *United States* v. *McConney,* 728 F. 2d 1195, 1204 (CA9 1984) (en banc), are much less significant than a trained ability to evaluate the testimony in relation to the overall structure of the patent. The decisionmaker vested with the task of construing the patent is in the better position to ascertain whether an expert's proposed definition fully comports with the specification and claims and so will preserve the patent's internal coherence. We accordingly think there is sufficient reason to treat construction of terms of art like many other responsibilities that we cede to a judge in the normal course of trial, notwithstanding its evidentiary underpinnings.

C

Finally, we see the importance of uniformity in the treatment of a given patent as an independent reason to allocate all issues of construction to the court. As we noted in *General Elec. Co.* v. *Wabash Appliance Corp.,* 304 U. S. 364, 369 (1938), "the limits of a patent must be known for the protection of the patentee, the encouragement of the inventive genius of others and the assurance that the subject of the patent will be dedicated ultimately to the public." Otherwise, a "zone of uncertainty which enterprise and experimentation may enter only at the risk of infringement claims would discourage invention only a little less than unequivocal foreclosure of the field," *United Carbon Co.* v. *Binney & Smith Co.,* 317 U. S. 228, 236 (1942), and "the public would be deprived of rights supposed to belong to it, without being clearly told what it is that limits these rights." *Merrill* v. *Yeomans,* 94 U. S. 568, 573 (1877). It was just for the sake of such desirable uniformity that Congress created the Court of Appeals for the Federal Circuit as an exclusive appellate court for patent cases, H. R. Rep. No. 97–312, pp. 20–23 (1981), observing that increased uniformity would "strengthen the United States patent system in such a way as to foster technological growth and industrial innovation." *Id.,* at 20.

Uniformity would, however, be ill served by submitting issues of document construction to juries. Making them jury issues would not, to be sure, necessarily leave evidentiary questions of meaning wide open in every new court in which a patent might be litigated, for principles of issue preclusion would ordinarily foster uniformity. Cf. *BlonderTongue Laboratories, Inc.* v. *University of Ill. Foundation,*

402 U. S. 313 (1971). But whereas issue preclusion could not be asserted against new and independent infringement defendants even within a given jurisdiction, treating interpretive issues as purely legal will promote (though it will not guarantee) intra-jurisdictional certainty through the application of *stare decisis* on those questions not yet subject to interjurisdictional uniformity under the authority of the single appeals court.

Accordingly, we hold that the interpretation of the word "inventory" in this case is an issue for the judge, not the jury, and affirm the decision of the Court of Appeals for the Federal Circuit.

It is so ordered.

3.3 Analysis of the Case

Markman v. Westview Instruments, Inc., 517 U.S. 370 (1996).

The text of Markman v. Westview Instruments is available here:

https://supreme.justia.com/cases/federal/us/517/370/

Herbert Markman held the patent to a system that tracks clothing through the dry-cleaning process using a keyboard and data processor to generate transaction records, including a bar code readable by optical detectors. According to the patent claims, Markman's invention could "maintain an inventory total" and "detect and localize spurious additions to inventory." Westview Instruments, Inc.'s competing product also used a keyboard and processor and listed dry-cleaning charges on bar-coded tickets that could be read by optical detectors. In an infringement suit, after hearing an expert witness testify about the meaning of the claim's language, a jury found that Westview's product had infringed Markman's patent. However, the District Court directed a verdict for Westview on the ground that its device was unable to track "inventory" as that term was used in the claim. In affirming, the Court of Appeals for the Federal Circuit held that the interpretation of claim terms is the exclusive province of the court and that the Seventh Amendment right to a jury trial was consistent with that conclusion.

In patent litigation the judge and the jury have very different responsibilities. In a typical jury trial case, the jury is tasked with finding the facts, while the judge's job is to interpret the law. On appeal, the U.S. Supreme Court addressed the question of whether the interpretation of a patent's claim, the portion of the patent document that defines the scope of the patentee's rights, was a matter of fact to be decided by jurors, or a matter of law to be decided by the judge(s). In a unanimous decision authored by Justice David H. Souter, the Court held that the construction of a patent, including terms of art within its claim, is exclusively within the province of the court. Justice Souter wrote that "judges, not juries, are the better suited to find the acquired meaning of patent terms."

This case had a profound effect on patent litigation in the United States. Now, before validity or infringement issues are litigated, the trial court convenes a "Markman Hearing." A Markman Hearing is a proceeding through which a judge determines the meaning of the words comprising relevant patent claims, for the purposes of the trial. This is called claim construction. There are two types of evidence that might be heard in a Markman hearing: intrinsic and extrinsic. Intrinsic evidence is evidence that is related to the case under litigation for patent infringement. Examples of intrinsic evidence in a Markman hearing include a patent application summary, and correspondence between patent applicant and patent examiner to help to show the thinking of the inventor in why she used the terms that she did and the given definitions of key words. Extrinsic evidence is any evidence that is used in a claim construction case that is not directly related to the patent under litigation. Examples of extrinsic evidence in a Markman hearing include standard dictionary definitions for non-technical words, and an IEEE dictionary or encyclopedia for technical terms. The Supreme Court did not define a specific process for a Markman Hearing that must be followed to decide claim construction, and different courts have developed different processes over the years.

3.1.3 Patent Cases from the China

(1) **Requirements for defining malicious lawsuit of intellectual property—Tan Fawen v. Shenzhen Tencent Computer System Co., Ltd.**

1.1 Case Judgement   Court: Guangdong High People's Court
Case No.: No. 407 [2019]
Judgment Date: 10–06-2019

Cause of action: the liability for damages caused by maliciously bringing an intellectual property action.

Appellant (defendant in the first instance): Tan Fawen, male, born on May 9, 1980, Han nationality, living in Futian District, Shenzhen City, Guangdong Province.

Authorized litigation agent: Zhu Qiuhui, lawyer of Guangdong Yuzi Law Firm.

Appellee (plaintiff in the first instance): Shenzhen Tencent Computer System Co., Ltd., domiciled at 5-10th Floor, FIYTA Building, Gaoxin South 1st Road, High-tech Zone, Nanshan District, Shenzhen, Guangdong Province.

Legal representative: Ma Huateng, chairman of the company.

Authorized litigation agent: Wang Zhengze, male, employee of the company.

Authorized litigation agent: Wang Chengen, lawyer of Beijing Yingke (Shenzhen) Law Firm.

The appellant Tan Fawen appealed to this Court against a civil judgment (No. 632[2007], First Instance, Civil Judgement, Guangdong, No. 3) made by Shenzhen Intermediate People's Court of Guangdong Province for disputes with the appellee Shenzhen Tencent Computer System Co., Ltd. (hereinafter referred to as Tencent Company) over the liability for damages caused by maliciously bringing an intellectual property action. After filing the case on March 8, 2019, this court organized a collegiate bench to hear the case. Now the hearing has been concluded.

Tan Fawen appealed to this court to request: to revoke the first-instance judgment and dismiss Tencent Company's pleading. The facts and reasons are as follows: (1) When defining the facts, the first-instance judgment made a long story to beautify Tencent's image, without mentioning the lack of social responsibility of Tencent

Company. It can be indicated that the court of first instance lost its justice. (2) The court of first instance confirmed the facts through the mediation (No. 348 and No. 349[2011]) and mediation transcripts made by Futian District People's Court of Shenzhen City, indicating that Tan Fawen violated the law "maliciously". Moreover, in those two cases mentioned above, Tan Fawen's commitment to withdraw his patent for design, a speaker (Xzeit mini penguin-shaped) with a patent number of ZL20083025×××× 0.6. (hereinafter referred to as the patent involved) in the mediation transcripts was not included in the mediation. It was reasonable for Tan Fawen to believe that this part of the content was not approved by the court, which means Tan Fawen still has rights over the patent involved. Tencent Company knew that Tan Fawen enjoyed the right, but it did not apply for invalidation of the involved patent. Instead, it waited until Tan Fawen sued, indicating that Tencent Company was malicious. (3) The litigation expense paid by Tencent Company in this case was only 59,000 yuan, but the judgement of first instance ordered Tan Fawen to compensated for a maximum price of 500,000 yuan, which was an abuse of judicial discretion.

Tencent Company defended that the judgment of first instance was clear in fact finding and in application of law. Meanwhile, it requested to reject the appeal and maintain the original judgment. The reasons are as follows: (1) Tan Fawen misunderstood the provisions of judicial interpretation on self confession during the mediation process. The facts recognized by the parties in the mediation of the case can continue to be applied to subsequent litigation. Tan Fawen should perform his commitment made in the mediation transcripts. (2) The amount of compensation in the judgment of first instance isn't too high. Tencent Company had paid attorney fees, fees of application for invalidation, and travel expenses for this case. This case caused the loss of Tencent Company's available profits and brought negative effect to the goodwill of Tencent's Company. There is no abuse of judicial discretion regarding the compensation in the original judgment.

Tencent Company filed a lawsuit to the court of first instance and request: 1. to order Tan Fawen to compensate Tencent Company for all kinds of expenses caused by bringing an intellectual property action maliciously, including attorney fees, travel expenses, loss of goodwill, expected benefits, etc. The total economic loss was 2 million yuan; 2. to order Tan Fawen to bear reasonable expenses paid by Tencent Company to defend itself in the lawsuit, including attorney fees and notarization fees, etc.; 3. to order Tan Fawen to apologize to Tencent Company for its malicious litigation on the prominent position of the homepage of websites such as Sina.com (××), Sohu (××) and Netease (××), and on the first pages of newspapers such as "*Legal Daily*" and "*China Intellectual Property News*", as well as eliminate negative impact. Specific content shall be reviewed and approved by the court; 4. All costs of litigation in this case shall be borne by Tan Fawen. During the process of litigation, Tencent Company changed its request as follows: 1. to order Tan Fawen to compensate Tencent Company all kinds of expenses caused by bringing an intellectual property action maliciously, including attorney fees, travel expenses, loss of goodwill, expected benefits, etc. and other reasonable expenses paid by Tencent Company to defend itself in the lawsuit, including attorney fees and notarization fees, etc. It all adds up to be 2 million yuan; 2. to order Tan Fawen to apologize to Tencent

Company for its malicious litigation on the prominent position of the homepage of websites such as Sina.com (××), Sohu (××) and Netease (××), and on the first pages of newspapers such as "*Legal Daily*" and "*China Intellectual Property News*", as well as eliminate negative impact. Specific content shall be reviewed and approved by the court; 3. All costs of litigation in this case shall be borne by Tan Fawen.

The court of first instance found the following facts:
1. The rights and history of the QQ Penguin's image involved in this case
The copyright registration certificate issued by the Radio and Television Administration of Guangdong Province shows that the name of the work is "the second work of the Tencent QQ Picture Series—QQ Penguin" LOGO series of fine art works. The copyright owner is Tencent Company. The work was completed on August 15, 2000. The registration date is June 20, 2001, and the number of copyright registration certificate is 19-2001-F-486.

The copyright registration certificate issued by the Radio and Television Administration of Guangdong Province shows that the name of the work is "the forth of the Tencent QQ Picture Series—QQ Penguin" series of fine art works about daily life. The copyright owner is Tencent Company. The work was completed on August 15, 2000. The registration date is June 20, 2001, and the number of copyright registration certificate is 19-2001-F-488.

No. 1915548 trademark, the registrant is Tencent Technology (Shenzhen) Co., Ltd. The goods/services on which the trademark is approved to be used belongs to category 9, including floppy disks, computer peripherals, telephones, computers, cameras (photography), computer floppy disks (for recording), CDs, glasses, cartoons, and entertainment devices used in conjunction with TV sets. The period of registration is from December 7, 2002 to December 6, 2022.

On January 1, 2010, a " Certificate of Trademark License" issued by Tencent Technology (Shenzhen) Co., Ltd. Stated that: Tencent Technology (Shenzhen) Co., Ltd. licensed all trademarks under its name to Tencent Company (licensee) for free, and the licensee can re-license and enjoy the right to deal with affairs about trademark infringement on its own. The license will maintain valid until the licensor withdraws this license.

According to the information in the commercial registration, the legal representative of Tencent Company and Tencent Technology (Shenzhen) Co., Ltd. is Ma Huateng, and Ren Yuxin serves as the director of both companies.

No. 4557 (2017) notarization of Yantian District in Shenzhen City records: On June 15, 2017, Tencent Company's authorized agent Cui Linan applied to the Yantian Notary Public Office of Shenzhen city in Guangdong Province for evidence preservation. Cui Linan, Tencent Company's authorized agent, searched the web for propaganda introductions about QQ under the supervision of the notary Mei and the notary assistant Peng. The details are as follows:

The page of Sogou Encyclopedia (××) shows: QQ is an instant messaging software launched by Tencent Company in 1999… QQ has covered multiple mainstream platforms such as Windows, Android, IOS, and is currently the most widely used communication software in China. In the news about name changing, it is described that except for its business name, the logo of Tencent QQ has not been changed.

It maintains to be a little penguin. By 2000, Tencent Company's OICQ has basically occupied nearly 100% of China's online instant messaging market, becoming the dominant player in the instant messaging industry in China. In January 2001, Tencent Company ranked top three in China. In February 2001, online users of Tencent QQ successfully exceeded the threshold of 1 million, and the number of registered users has increased to 20 million. In September 2003, the number of registered QQ users rose to 200 million. In April 2004, the number of registered users of QQ reached a new peak, breaking 300 million; in May, it ranked fourth in the "Top 100 Shenzhen Software Companies in 2003"; in July, it ranked 25th among the "Top 100 Private Enterprises in Guangdong Province in 2003"; In August, Simultaneously online users of QQ games exceeded 620,000, making it the largest casual game portal in China; in September, it ranked 29th in the "Top 100 Taxpayers in the National Private Enterprises in 2003"; in October, Tencent Company was Rated as one of Chinese "largest website by market value"; on October 22, in the just-concluded "2004 China Top 100 Commercial Websites" survey, Tencent ranked first in votes, ahead of portals such as Sina, Sohu, and NetEase; In December, Tencent Company ranked 17th among the "Top 500 High-Tech Asia–Pacific Regions in 2004" and was selected as one of the "Top 50 Shenzhen Private Enterprises in 2003". In May 2005, Tencent Company ranked 25th in the "Top 100 Companies with the Largest Scale of China's Software Industry in 2005". In June 2008, QQ simultaneously online users exceeded 40 million, with nearly 800 million registered users. In September 2008, it launched value-added business and attractive souvenir of a doll whose image was QQ penguin. In 2011, the number of simultaneously online users of Tencent QQ exceeded 140 million. According to the description of QQ members, since its birth, Tencent has solidified its brand on the image of a lovely penguin and has been accumulating positive energy.

On May 30, 2016, Jiang Hongchang published the article *"During a period of 17 years, the evolution of the image of QQ penguin has also been a history of Internet development"*. The article is an interview with Dai Yongyu, the design director of Tencent ISUX (Internet Social User Experience), which records: QQ Penguin is probably the most well-known image in the Internet industry, and it has accompanied many people in the whole process of "touching the Internet". What you may not have noticed is that this penguin is already 17 years old; During the period of 17 years, its image has changed 5 times, from the thin lifelike penguin, the fat penguin with a red scarf, the silhouette penguin, to the flat, neutral penguin at present, each change represents a new design trend, and even reflects different development stages of the Internet. In 2000, we asked an outsourcing team to redesign this image. In Chinese people's impression, fat represents joy, such as Maitreya Buddha. This change was very successful, and a red scarf was added, which immediately became a hit. The fat penguin in 2000 is actually asymmetrical. If you look closely, you will find that it is a bit crooked. Looking back now, it will be funny. In 2006, we made the penguin more symmetrical, neater, and more like a logo. In addition, the penguin in 2000 was flat, without gradual change or texture. In 2006, we added the effect of the three-dimensional texture of the shiny crystal. This was mainly led by Apple.

iPhone hadn't been launched at the time, but the three-dimensional crystal texture on the Mac system was very popular.

On March 6, 2014, Tengniu.com published an article titled *"Reviewing the evolutionary history of OICQ to QQ when QQ is 15 years old"*. The content of the page records: Interface of OICQ software installation program made by Tencent Technology (Shenzhen) Co., Ltd. shows the image of the QQ penguin, the version date is December 1, 2000.

On April 20, 2014, MaNong.com published an article titled *"The 15-year evolutionary history of QQ."* The content of the page records: QQ in 2000 has begun to take shape, and it seems that it has evolved to WindowsXP. The little penguin has got fatter. The installation interface shows that the interface of QQ program installation had already included the image of a little penguin in 2000.

On June 8, 2017, Xinhua News Agency published an article entitled *"U.S. Media: Tencent Company Becomes the First Chinese Brand among the Top 10 BrandZ Global Brand List"*. The content of the page records: U.S. Media said that on June 6, the world's largest communications group WPP released the 2017 BrandZ Global Top 100 Most Valuable Brands list in London, UK. Tencent Company ranked 8th, becoming the first Chinese company to enter the top ten list. In the previously released 2017 BrandZ Top 100 Most Valuable Chinese Brands list, Tencent ranked first and won the title of "Most Valuable Chinese Brand" for the third consecutive year.

On January 27, 2015, Xinhuanet published the article "BrandZ Top 100 Most Valuable Chinese Brands in 2015". The content of the page stated: "In the field of technology, Tencent Company ranked top on the list with a brand value of US$66.077 billion."

2. The fact of accusing Tan Fawen of maliciously filing an intellectual property lawsuit by Tencent Company

Files No. 348 and 349 of Futian District People's Court of Shenzhen City (2011) (hereinafter referred to as Case No. 348 and 349) records: On November 10, 2008, Aowei Technology (Shenzhen) Co., Ltd. registered in Hong Kong, the registration information shows that Tan Fawen is a shareholder and director of the company. Aowei Technology (Shenzhen) Co., Ltd.'s company website and leaflets show the speakers with the "" image. On December 6, 2010, Tencent Company commissioned an agent to purchase 30 Penguin speakers from Tan Fawen through the QQ chatting tool (QQ number $36\times\times\times19$), and paid 850 yuan to his personal account. On March 9, 2011, Tencent Company and Tencent Technology (Shenzhen) Co., Ltd. instituted an action in the Futian District People's Court of Shenzhen City as QQ mini speakers sold by Tan Fawen and Aowei Technology (Shenzhen) Co., Ltd. had infringed their copyright and trademark rights. On May 23, 2011, both parties reached an agreement on those two cases. The main contents are: 1. Tan Fawen immediately stopped selling the infringing product QQ Penguin speakers under his own name or in the name of Aowei Technology (Shenzhen) Co., Ltd.; 2. Tan Fawen paid 25,000 yuan to Tencent and Tencent Technology (Shenzhen) Co., Ltd. respectively. According to the transcript of the mediation, Tan Fawen stated during the mediation process that: "I applied to the State Intellectual Property Office for a design patent for a speaker (Xzeit mini penguin) on December 23, 2008. I promise to withdraw the application within one month." Based on this, Tencent Company claims that Tan Fawen is familiar with Tencent Company's QQ image of a Penguin. He also knows that Tencent Company has copyright and trademark right over the image. Tan Fawen infringed Tencent Company's copyright by selling and promising to sell speakers of QQ Penguin through his registered company in Hong Kong. He maliciously applied for a design patent for the speaker which has the image of QQ Penguin, and concealed the fact that the design patent has been authorized and published during the process of mediation, and refused to fulfill the promise of "withdrawing the application". His subjective malice was obvious. Tan Fawen recognizes the authenticity of the evidence, but he believes that facts accepted by the parties by compromise for the purpose of reaching an reconciliation agreement or a settlement agreement shall not be regarded as basis adverse thereto in the subsequent lawsuits.

Patent searching information offered by State Intellectual Property Office patent shows that: On December 23, 2008, Tan Fawen applied to the State Intellectual Property Office for a patent on design named "speaker (Xzeit mini penguin)", which was authorized on January 13, 2010, and the patent number is ZL20083025×××.6. The picture shown in the patent certificate is consistent with the appearance of the picture of the alleged infringing product in Case No. 348 and 349. The patentee paid annual patent fees on December 8, 2011, December 14, 2012, February 21, 2014, April 16, 2015, and December 31, 2015.

On February 25, 2016, Tan Fawen filed a lawsuit in the court of first instance (Case No. 236 (2016) Guangdong 03, First Instance, Civil Judgment, hereinafter referred to as Case No. 236), alleging that Tencent Company and Shenzhen Zhongke Ruicheng Intelligent Technology Co., Ltd. (hereinafter referred to as Zhongke Company) infringed its patent design named "speaker (Xzeit mini penguin type)", whose patent number was ZL20083025××. And Tan Fawen requested the court to confirm the infringement by Tencent and Zhongke and order them to pay the royalties for 900,000 yuan.

On March 21, 2016, Tencent Company requested the Patent Re-examination Board of the State Intellectual Property Office (Hereinafter referred to as the Patent Re-examination Board) for invalidation based on the copyright registration certificate of "the second work of the Tencent QQ Picture Series—QQ Penguin LOGO series" and No. 1915548 trademark registration certificate. After reviewing, the Patent Re-examination Board found that: the prior work represented the penguin whose prototype was an animal as a cartoon image by using the technique of anthropomorphic. The shape of the cartoon penguin constitutes the original and creative expression of the work. The image of the cartoon penguin of the patented product in this case is highly consistent with that in the prior work in terms of technique of expression and elements of design. Although the image of cartoon penguin in the involved patent is slightly different from that of the prior work, it did not deviate from the original creation expressed in the prior work. Essentially, it copied the results of intellectual creation of the prior work and reproduced the artistic beauty of the prior work. As the patentee did not provide evidence to prove that his design of the image of cartoon penguin was independently completed, the work displayed in the involved patent was substantially similar to the prior works. In view of the fact that the patentee used a design that is substantially similar to the prior work in the involved patent without the copyright owner's permission, its implementation will damage the relevant legal rights or rights and interests of the prior copyright owner. The involved patent conflicts with the prior copyright, and it violates Article 23 of the Patent Law. Therefore, the Patent Reexamination Board issued the No. 29537 Invalidation Request Examination Decision, announcing that the rights on the design patent numbered 200830254103.6 were all invalid. On August 5, 2016, the court of first instance ruled to dismiss Tan Fawen's prosecution. Based on this, Tencent Company asserted that Tan Fa Wen filed a lawsuit in the court and refused to avoid the damage causing to Tencent Company although he could have chosen to avoid while he knew clearly that his design patent numbered ZL20083025×××.6 named "speaker (Xzeit mini penguin)" could not be granted patent right and his requests would not be supported by the court. His action is malicious, and this the malicious lawsuit has caused damage to Tencent Company.

3. The facts regarding the amount of compensation requested by Tencent Company Tencent Company claims that Tan Fawen should compensate for economic losses and the reasonable costs for defending. The total amount adds up to be 2 million yuan. Tencent Company submits the following evidence to prove:

1. On April 26, 2016, Tencent Company signed a "Civil Agency Contract" with Guangzhou Sanhuan Huihua Law Firm, agreeing to entrust it to deal with the litigation and invalidation of case No. 236 filed by Tan Fawen. The amount is 35,000 yuan, and an invoice is attached.
2. On March 20, 2017, Tencent signed a "Civil Agency Contract" with Beijing Yingke (Shenzhen) Law Firm, entrusting it to handle litigation matters in this case. The attorney fee is 20,000 yuan. An invoice with the corresponding amount is attached.
3. Tencent Company paid a notarization fee of RMB 4,000 for this case.

In addition, Tencent Company believes that due to Case No. 236, Zhongke Company has terminated their cooperation which caused damage to Tencent Company. When determining the amount of compensation, the court shall take the factors mentioned above into consideration.

The court of first instance held that this case was a dispute over the liability for damages caused by maliciously bringing an intellectual property action. According to the arguments of both parties, dispute in this case focus on: 1. Whether Tan Fawen's suing Tencent company for infringing his right on design patent constitutes a malicious lawsuit; 2. The issue of legal liability.

Regarding the first focus of dispute, Whether Tan Fawen's suing Tencent company for infringing his right on design patent constitutes a malicious lawsuit.

The principle of good faith is the basic criterion that all participants in the market should follow. On the one hand, it encourages and supports people to accumulate social wealth and create social value through honest labor. It also protects the property rights formed on this basis, as well as the freedom and rights to control the property rights for the sake of legal and legitimate purposes; On the one hand, it also requires people to pay attention to credit and honesty in the market activities, to avoid cheating, and to pursue their own interests without harming others' legitimate interests, the public interests of the society and the market order. Civil litigation activities should also follow the principle of good faith. On the one hand, it guarantees that the parties have the right to exercise and dispose of their own civil rights and litigation rights within the scope provided by law; on the other hand, it requires the parties to exercise their own rights in good faith and prudence without harming public interest and others' rights. Any behavior that violates the purpose and spirit of the law, aiming at harming the legitimate rights and interests of others, maliciously obtaining and exercising rights, and disrupting the fair competition in the market will be an abuse of rights, and its related claims should not be protected and supported by the law.

The so-called malicious litigation usually refers to a lawfully and factually unfounded lawsuit initiated by a party for the purpose of obtaining illegal or illegitimate benefits, causing the counterparty to suffer losses in the litigation. Malicious litigation is essentially a tort. Specifically, its behavior appears to be abusing of rights rather than exercising rights properly. It aims to obtain illegal or improper benefits as well as to cause the counterparty to suffer damage in the litigation, rather than to relieve the rights granted by the law. According to *General Principles of the Civil Law of the People's Republic of China* and *Tort Law of the People's Republic of China,* malicious litigation should have four elements, including subjective fault, act of infringement, consequences of damage, casual relationship between infringement and damage. That means, if a certain litigation belongs to a malicious lawsuit, the following constitutive requirements should be met: 1. A party made a certain request by filing an intellectual property lawsuit; 2. The requesting party has subjective malice; 3. There is actual damage; 4. There is a causal relationship between the act of maliciously bringing an intellectual property action and the results of damage.

Regarding the above-mentioned element 1, "a party made a certain request" usually means that the party who makes the request has taken advantage of the litigation rights granted by the law to initiate an intellectual property lawsuit, and has dragged the other party into the litigation, making the other party fall into a disadvantaged position. In this case, Tan Fawen sued Tencent Company in Case No. 236, requesting confirmation of Tencent Company's infringement and payment of patent royalties, His action has dragged Tencent Company into the litigation of patent infringement, and he has completed the act of filing specific litigation requests.

Regarding the above-mentioned element 2, malice means that the party who makes the request exercises the right of litigation improperly with an intention to cause damage to the other party's property or reputation, which violates the purpose of legislation although he knows clearly that the request lacks justified reasons. Article 4 of the *"General Principles of the Civil Law of the People's Republic of China"* stipulates that in civil activities, the principles of voluntariness, fairness, making compensation for equal value, honesty and credibility shall be observed. In this case, according to the files of cases No. 348 and 349, Tan Fawen knew clearly that Tencent had prior copyright over the art works of QQ Penguin involved in the case, and the work had been used in advance. However, he still applied for a design patent that is basically consistent with the image of QQ Penguin and obtained authorization as system of design patents in China has no substantive examination. Such application violates the principle of good faith and it is malicious. Tan Fawen knew that the acquisition of his patent right was not substantively justified. The patent right was obtained improperly. He intended to obtain illegal benefits of in market competition, so he exercised his right in an obviously malicious way. Tan Fawen argued that Tencent Company's art work was flat, while the design patent involved in this case was three-dimensional. Those two works did not constitute a conflict of rights and there was no subjective malice. The court of first instance held that the expression pf Tencent Company's art works and that of the patent applied by Tan Fawen were substantially the same. They were both images of QQ Penguin although the forms were different. The court of first instance rejected to accept Tan Fawen's argument which stated that those two works did not constitute a conflict of rights and there was no subjective malice as this argument lack the support of law and facts. Moreover, during the mediation process of Cases No. 348 and 349, Tan Fawen was also aware that the patent involved was basically the same as the art works of Tencent Company who had the copyright, and he made a clear promise to withdraw the patent involved. After the mediation, Tan Fawen not only failed to fulfill his promise, but also continued to pay the annual fee of the patent. Then he even claimed that Tencent Company had infringed his patent right, with the intention of causing damage to Tencent Company's property or reputation. His subjective maliciousness was obvious and the circumstance was execrable. Tan Fawen argued that facts accepted by the parties by compromise for the purpose of reaching an reconciliation agreement or a settlement agreement shall not be regarded as basis adverse thereto in the subsequent lawsuits. In this regard, the court of first instance held that Article 107 of the "*Interpretation of the Supreme People's Court on the Application of the Civil Procedure Law of the People's Republic of China*" stipulates: "In lawsuits, facts accepted by the parties by compromise for the purpose of reaching an reconciliation agreement or a settlement agreement shall not be regarded as basis adverse thereto in the subsequent lawsuits, except as otherwise specified by laws or agreed by the parties." This article mainly provides that during the process of mediation or settlement, admission of the facts can not apply to the rules of self-admission. The purpose is to ensure that one party's recognition of the facts in a certain case due to mediation or settlement will not have adverse effect on subsequent litigation, so as to encourage the parties to resolve disputes through settlement. This provision applies to situations in which the parties wish but fail to reach a mediation agreement or a settlement agreement during the litigation process of the same case. Under this circumstance, facts accepted by the parties by compromise for the purpose of reaching a reconciliation agreement or a settlement agreement shall not be regarded as basis adverse thereto in the subsequent lawsuits. On the one hand, this article does not exclude all the facts accepted by the parties by compromise for the purpose of reaching an reconciliation agreement or a settlement agreement from the possibility of being used as a basis for determining facts in subsequent litigation or another litigation; on the other hand, it does not prohibit the mediation agreement or settlement agreement reached to be used as documentary evidence in another litigation. Regarding the probative force of such evidence, the principles followed by the people's courts during judging have no difference from other evidence. They should all be reviewed in a comprehensive and objective manner in accordance with legal procedures. The possibility of facts should be reviewed comprehensively based on other evidence submitted by the parties, together with relevant facts. Therefore, if a party wants to overturn the facts proved by the mediation agreement or the settlement agreement, he shall bear the burden of proof by providing corresponding evidence. This case about is a dispute between Tencent Company and Tan Fawen over liability for damages caused by maliciously bringing an intellectual property action. It is a different litigation from case No. 348 and 349 of trademark infringement and copyright dispute. The Mediation Record can be used as documentary evidence in this case. Tan Fawen's defence lacks legal basis, and the court of first instance rejected to accept the defence.

Regarding the above-mentioned element 3, there is actual harm caused to the other party in the litigation of intellectual property. In this case, Tencent Company paid attorney fee, notarization fee, and production fee in response to the patent infringement lawsuit filed in Case No. 236, which actually caused economic losses to Tencent Company.

Regarding the above-mentioned element 4, there is a causal relationship between the tort and the damage, that is, the consequences of damage such as the reduction of social reputation and the loss of property are all caused by the opposing party's abuse of litigation rights. In this case, taking the complexity of the patent disputes into account, Tencent Company hired an agent to respond to the lawsuit in order to protect its legitimate rights and interests. This is in line with common sense. The attorney fee it has paid is necessary. The notarization fee, production fee, travel expenses paid for collecting evidence are also necessary. The above fees are of course related to the patent infringement lawsuit maliciously initiated by Tan Fawen.

Regarding the second focus of the dispute, the issue of legal liability. As mentioned above, Tan Fawen maliciously filed a lawsuit of patent infringement against Tencent Company although he knew his request lacked justified basis. His lawsuit has caused economic losses to Tencent Company. According to Article 15 of *Tort Law of the People's Republic of China*, it shall bear civil liability for damages. Regarding the amount of compensation, the court of first instance comprehensively considered the following factors: First, Tan Fawen knew clearly that Tencent Company had copyright on the image of QQ Penguin involved in the case and the right to exploit it in advance. But he still took advantage of the fact that applications of design patent in China do not require substantive examination and applied for patent right in a bad will. His subjective malice is obvious; secondly, after the mediation of case No. 348 and 349, Tan Fawen still abused the right of litigation to file a design patent infringement lawsuit against Tencent Company. The subjective malice was obvious and the circumstance was execrable; thirdly, during the period when the case is heard, Tan Fawen could not provide a reasonable explanation for his malicious lawsuits on infringement of intellectual property. Instead, he insisted that he exercised his rights in accordance with the law on the grounds that his patent authorization was not illegal. His subjective maliciousness of covering up the substantive infringement by legitimate form was obvious. It violates the principle of good faith; fourthly, the reasonable expenses paid by Tencent Company in response to the lawsuit. The court of first instance determined that Tan Fawen should compensate Tencent Company for economic losses and reasonable expenses paid for defence for a total amount of 500,000 yuan.

Since Tencent Company did not provide evidence to prove that Tan Fawen's actions had affected its goodwill and the economic compensation was sufficient to make up for Tencent Company's losses, the court of first instance did not support Tencent Company's litigation request to ask Tan Fawen to publicly apologize on relevant websites and newspapers to eliminate the impact.

In summary, in accordance with Article 4 of the "General Principles of the Civil Law of the People's Republic of China", Article 6 Paragraph 1 and Article 15 of the "Tort Liability Law of the People's Republic of China", and Article 64 of the "Civil Procedure Law of the People's Republic of China", the court of first instance make the judgment as follows: 1. Tan Fawen compensates Tencent Company for economic losses and reasonable expenses for a total amount of 500,000 yuan within ten days from the effective date of the judgment; 2. Rejects Tencent Company's other claims. If Tan Fawen fails to perform the obligation within the period specified in the judgment, he will pay double interest for the debt for the period of deferred performance in accordance with Article 253 of the Civil Procedure Law of the People's Republic of China. The acceptance fee of first instance was 22,800 yuan, which was borne by Tan Fawen.

In the second instance, neither party submitted new evidence.

The facts ascertained by the court of first instance are true and confirmed by this court in accordance with the law.

This court also find out the following facts:

1. The certificate of design patent and No. 29537 Invalidation Request Examination Decision issued by the Patent Re-examination Board showed that Tan Fawen hired a patent agency, Shenzhen Qiming Patent Agency, to apply for the patent involved, and appointed a lawyer to attend the oral hearing during the invalidation procedure, etc. The civil ruling of Case No. 236 shows that Tan Fawen appointed a lawyer as an agent in the patent litigation involved.
2. According to case file No. 236, Tan Fawen argued in the complaint that Tencent Company and Zhongke Company had produced and sold Penguin speakers similar to the patents involved in several large online stores in China without his permission. The speakers were available as early as 2013. It was sold online in August 2014, and the sales was more than 1,000 per month. As a result, he requested the court to order Tencent Company and Zhongke Company to stop the infringement, and order Tencent Company and Zhongke Company to pay the royalties for 18 months, from August 2014 to January 2016. The royalties sums up to be 900,000 yuan. According to the transcript of the trial, Tan Fawen submitted the exhibits he purchased in court. The outer packaging and the front marked "Little QQ + Smart Personal Companion", the lower right corner of the box marked "produced by Tencent Company", and the bottom left corner

marked "jointly produced by Tencent Zhongke Ruicheng", "Manufacturer: Shenzhen Zhongke Ruicheng Intelligent Technology Co., Ltd.", and "Copyright by Tencent". Both Tan Fawen and Tencent Company confirmed this fact.
3. Tencent Company paid the fee for invalidation request of 1,500 yuan to the International Intellectual Property Office for invalidation of the patent involved on March 18, 2016.

This court believes that this case is a dispute over damages caused by maliciously bringing an intellectual property action. According to Tan Fawen's appeal and reasons, the focus of disputes between the parties in the second instance is:
1. Whether Tan Fawen should bear the civil liability for maliciously filed an intellectual property lawsuit; 2. Whether the amount of compensation determined in the first instance judgment is reasonable.
1. Regarding whether Tan Fawen should bear the civil liability for maliciously filed intellectual property litigation

The second paragraph of Article 106 of the "*General Principles of the Civil Law of the People's Republic of China*" stipulates: "Citizens and Legal Persons who Breach a Contract or fail to fulfil other obligations shall bear civil Liability." Article 6 of the *Tort Law of the People's Republic of China* stipulates: "One who is at fault for infringement upon a civil right or interest of another person shall be subject to the tort liability." In essence, bringing an intellectual property action maliciously is an act of tort. In this case, Tan Fawen filed the case No. 236 with the court of first instance on February 25, 2016, arguing that Tencent Company and Zhongke Company's production and sales of Penguin speakers similar to the patent involved infringed his patent rights, and appealed to the court to order Tencent Company to pay the royalties for 900,000 yuan. To determine whether Tan Fawen's act was fault or not and whether he should bear civil liability to Tencent Company, an analysis should be made based on whether the act constituted a tort.

First of all, as to whether Tan Fawen has any fault in filing the case No. 236. According to Article 13 of the *Civil Procedure Law of the People's Republic of China*, In civil procedures, the principle of good faith shall be adhered to. The parties shall exercise the litigation rights granted by the law in good faith in accordance with the law, and shall not violate the principle of good faith or maliciously use the litigation procedures to achieve the purpose of harming the rights and interests of others and seeking illegal benefits. When analyzing the basis of rights in case No. 236 filed by Tan Fawen, according to Article 23 of the "*Patent Law of the People's Republic of China*" *(amended in 2000)*: Any design for which a patent right is granted shall not be identical with or similar to any design which, before the date of filing, has been publicly disclosed in publications in our country or abroad or has been publicly used in our country, nor shall it be in conflict with the prior lawful right of anyone else. Tencent Company designed the image of QQ Penguin in 2000 and obtained the copyright registration certificate of "QQ Penguin" series and the trademark right on trademark "". Since 2000, the image of QQ Penguin has been used as the image and trademark of Tencent Company's instant messaging software. The image of the penguin has a high reputation. Tan Fawen applied to the State

Intellectual Property Office for a design patent on "speaker (Xzeit mini penguin)" on December 23, 2008, and was authorized on January 13, 2010. The patent is similar to Tencent Company's image of QQ penguin. Tan Fawen took advantage of the system of design patents without substantive examination to apply for a design patent on the image of QQ Penguin on which others have already had prior rights. The patent right involved lacked a legitimate basis of right. As for Tan Fawen's subjective state, on December 6, 2010, Tencent Company and Tencent Technology (Shenzhen) Co., Ltd. filed case No. 348 and 349 against Futian District People's Court of Shenzhen City as Tan Fawen infringed on the copyright and trademark rights of the QQ Penguin image by selling speakers with a ""' image and provided evidence such as the copyright and trademark rights certificates of QQ Penguin image owned by Tencent Company and Tencent Technology (Shenzhen) Co., Ltd. Tan Fawen reached a settlement with Tencent Company and other parties in those two cases and agreed to cease the infringement and compensate for the losses. It can be indicated that Tan Fawen had known that Tencent Company had prior rights on the image of QQ Penguin before filing the No. 236 case and its patented products infringed Tencent's intellectual property rights. In the complaint of case No. 236, Tan Fawen also admitted that Tencent Company's speaker with QQ Penguin image was similar to the design patent involved. Therefore, Tan Fawen knows subjectively that his design patent lacks the legitimate basis of rights. Tan Fawen appealed that the mediation transcripts of case No. 348 and 349 regarding Tan Fawen's commitment to withdraw the patent involved were not included in the mediation statement. Tan Fawen had enough reason to believe that this part of the content was not supported by the court. Therefore, Tan Fawen had legitimate rights on the patent involved. The court of first instance judged that Tan Fawen was subjectively malicious based on the mediation statement and mediation transcripts. Such judgement is improper. In this regard, this court believes that when Tan Fawen hired a patent agency and attorney when applying for the involved patent and filing the No. 236 case, so he has the ability to judge whether his design patent meets requirements of authorization stipulated by the law. He admitted it in the settlement and he also promised to stop infringing on the rights of Tencent Company. Tan Fawen believes that his claim that he has legitimate rights on the patent involved lacks factual and legal basis. The facts that Tan Fawen reached a settlement with Tencent Company in case No. 348 and 349 exist objectively, and the mediation statement can be used as a basis for determining the facts of this case. Even without considering Tan Fawen's commitment to withdraw the patent involved in the mediation transcript, the evidence in this case is sufficient to determine that Tan Fawen was subjectively aware of Tencent Company's prior rights and he knew the patents involved lacked legal basis. As for Tan Fawen's behavior of filing a litigation, Tan Fawen sued Tencent Company for infringement of the patent involved even though he knew that Tencent Company had prior rights on the image of QQ Penguin and the patents involved did not have the basis of legitimate rights. After the patent invalidation procedure was filed by Tencent Company, he continued to participate in the invalidation procedure and the litigation procedure of case No. 236. In the above procedures, Tan Fawen entrusted professional attorneys to participate in the relevant procedures, and he was able to foresee the results of his actions. He exercised the rights of litigation maliciously and had an intention to damage the rights and interests of others. In summary, Tan Fawen's act in filing the No. 236 case violated the principle of good faith. It was subjective and malicious, and was at fault.

Secondly, regarding whether Tan Fawen's filing of case No. 236 infringed on the civil rights of others. In this case, Tan Fawen sued Tencent Company by filing an intellectual property lawsuit and requested a compensation of 900,000 yuan. In response to the lawsuit brought by Tan Fawen, Tencent Company hired an attorney to appear in court and declare invalidation of the patent involved. As a result, Tencent Company has suffered loss of property. Moreover, Tan Fawen's litigation has adversely affected Zhongke Company's manufacture and sales of speakers with the image of QQ Penguin authorized by Tencent Company. Therefore, Tan Fawen's behavior directly infringed Tencent Company's civil rights.

Considering Tan Fawen's basis of right for filing Case No. 236, his ability to judge the patents involved, his performance in actions related to litigation and the reasons for defense, this court determined that Tan Fawen was aware that his litigation request lacked a legitimate basis, but he still filed the lawsuit improperly. His action violates the principle of good faith and is subjectively malicious, harming the legitimate rights and interests of Tencent Company. It belongs to malicious initiation of intellectual property lawsuits. In accordance with Article 6 of the "*Tort Law of the People's Republic of China*", "One who is at fault for infringement upon a civil right or interest of another person shall be subject to the tort liability." and Article 47 of the "*Patent Law of the People's Republic of China*" "the patentee shall compensate the damages it has maliciously caused to any other person", Tan Fawen shall bear the civil liability on damages.

2. Regarding whether the amount of compensation determined in the first-instance judgment is reasonable

Tencent Company claims that the losses it suffered include the reasonable expenses to defend itself paid due to the No. 236 case, the invalidation procedure and the litigation in this case, the loss of profits of royalties that Tencent Company was unable to requested from Zhongke Company due to the malicious litigation, and the damage of goodwill suffered by Tencent Company. Tencent Company request the court to determine the amount of compensation. Tan Fawen appealed that Tencent Company had paid only 59,000 yuan for litigation, and the amount of compensation determined in the first instance was too high. In this regard, this court believes that losses caused to others due to the malice of the patentee should include direct losses and indirect losses. When the specific amount of loss cannot be determined, the amount of compensation shall be determined based on the circumstances of the infringement and the degree of maliciousness. In this case, first of all, Tencent Company has submitted evidence to prove that it has paid 60,500 yuan of reasonable expenses such as attorney fees in case No. 236, fees of invalidation request, attorney fees in the first instance, and notarization fees and preservation fees. This part of the loss was incurred in response to malicious litigation. This court supports the above mentioned expenses. Tencent Company also claimed that it had paid travel expenses and attorney fees for the second instance. This part of the expenditure is reasonable and necessary, and it has actually occurred. However, as Tencent Company did not submit any relevant evidence, this part of the loss will be supported by this court at its discretion. Secondly, Tencent Company claimed that it had terminated its cooperation with Zhongke Company due to malicious litigation and suffered a loss of gains such as royalties. In case No. 236, both Tan Fawen and Tencent Company recognized the cooperation between Tencent Company and Zhongke Company, but Tencent Company did not submit evidence to prove the amount of royalties or loss of available benefits. According to business practices, cooperation between Tencent Company and Zhongke Company will undoubtedly be affected to some extent by malicious litigation. This circumstances can be used as factor for reference when determining the amount of compensation. Thirdly, Tencent Company claims that its goodwill has been harmed due to malicious litigation. Given that the first instance did not support this part of the loss, and Tencent Company did not file an appeal, this court will not support Tencent Company's claim. Based on the aforementioned losses suffered by Tencent Company due to malicious litigation, and considering the high popularity of the image of QQ Penguin, Tan Fawen applied for a patent right maliciously although he knew that this application lacked legitimate basis. After mediation of Case No. 348 and 349, Tan Fawen abused litigation right to bring an intellectual property action maliciously, asking Tencent Company to pay for royalties of 900,000 yuan. It obviously violates the principle of good faith, the subjective maliciousness is obvious, and the circumstances are vile. This court believes that the judgment by court of first instance which ordered Tan Fawen to compensate Tencent Company 500,000 yuan for economic losses and reasonable expenses for defending has sufficient factual and legal basis. It shall be maintained in accordance with the law.

In summary, Tan Fawen's request can't be established and is rejected by this court. The facts ascertained in the judgment of first instance were clear and the applicable law was correct, and this court maintained it in accordance with the law. In accordance with the first paragraph of Article 170 of *the Civil Procedure Law of the People's Republic of China*, the judgment is made as follows:

(1) The appeal was rejected and the original judgment was upheld.
(2) The acceptance fee of the second instance was 8,800 yuan, which should be borne by Tan Fawen.

This decision shall be final.
Chief Judge: Wang Jing
Judge: Deng Yanhui
Judge: Zheng Ying
Agent Judge: Zhang Suliu
Clerk: Liang Yingxin
10.06.2019

1.2 Analysis of the Case

1. Facts

On November 10, 2008, Aowei Technology (Shenzhen) Co., Ltd. was registered in Hong Kong, and Tan Fawen was a shareholder and director of the company. Aowei Technology (Shenzhen) Co., Ltd.'s company website and leaflets show speakers with the image of "Penguin". On March 9, 2011, Tencent and Tencent Technology (Shenzhen) Co., Ltd. reported to the Futian District People's Court of Shenzhen City that the QQ mini speakers sold by Tan Fawen and Aowei Technology (Shenzhen) Co., Ltd. infringed their copyright and trademark rights and so file a lawsuit. On May 23, 2011, the two parties reached a settlement agreement on the two cases. The main contents are: 1. Tan Fawen immediately stopped selling the infringing product QQ Penguin speakers under his own name or in the name of Aowei Technology (Shenzhen) Co., Ltd.; 2. Tan Fawen paid 25,000 yuan in compensation to Tencent Technology (Shenzhen) Co., Ltd. respectively. Tan Fawen stated during the mediation process: "I applied to the State Intellectual Property Office for a design patent for the speaker on December 23, 2008, and I promise to withdraw the aforementioned design patent application to the State Intellectual Property Office within one month."

On December 23, 2008, Tan Fawen applied to the State Intellectual Property Office for a penguin design patent, which was authorized on January 13, 2010. The picture shown in the patent certificate is consistent with the appearance of the picture of the alleged infringing product. The patentees paid annual patent fees on December 8, 2011, December 14, 2012, February 21, 2014, April 16, 2015, and December 31, 2015.

On February 25, 2016, Tan Fawen filed a lawsuit in the court of first instance on the grounds that Tencent and Shenzhen Zhongke Ruicheng Intelligent Technology Co., Ltd. infringed their design patents, requesting confirmation of the infringement by Tencent and Zhongke and making an order of 900,000 yuan for the use of patents. On March 21, 2016, Tencent submitted an invalidation request to the Patent Reexamination Board of the State Intellectual Property Office (hereinafter referred to as the Patent Reexamination Board).

In view of the fact that the patentee used a design that is substantially similar to the prior work in the involved patent without the copyright owner's permission, its implementation will damage the relevant legal rights or rights of the prior copyright owner. The copyright conflicts and does not comply with the provisions of Article 23 of the Patent Law. Therefore, the Patent Reexamination Board issued a written decision No. 29537 on request for invalidation.

On August 5, 2016, the court of first instance ruled to dismiss Tan Fawen's prosecution. Based on this, Tencent asserted that Tan Fawen was aware that his design patent did not meet the conditions for granting patent rights, and his litigation request could not be supported by the court, he filed a lawsuit with the court, and he could choose to stop for many times, but still refused to make any actions that can avoid continuing to cause losses to Tencent, He is subjective and intentional, and cause corresponding losses to Tencent due to malicious litigation.

The court of first instance judged: 1. Tan Fawen compensated Tencent for economic losses and reasonable expenses of 500,000 yuan within ten days from the effective date of the judgment; 2. Dismissed other claims of Tencent.

2. Focus of dispute:
1) Whether it constituted a malicious lawsuit for Tan Fawen to sue Tencent for infringement of its design patents? 2) What is the legal liability?

3) Legal rules and their application
3. Legal rules involved
The second paragraph of Article 106 of the "General Principles of the Civil Law of the People's Republic of China": Citizens and legal persons who infringe upon state and collective property due to their fault, or infringe on the property or personal life of others, shall bear civil liability.

Article 4 of the "General Principles of the Civil Law of the People's Republic of China": civil activities shall follow the principles of voluntariness, fairness, compensation for equal value, and good faith.

According to Article 13 of the Civil Procedure Law of the People's Republic of China: civil litigation shall follow the principle of good faith.

According to Article 253 of the "Civil Procedure Law of the People's Republic of China": the interest on debts during the period of delayed performance shall be doubled.

Article 6 of the Tort Liability Law of the People's Republic of China: The perpetrator shall bear the tort liability for infringement of the civil rights and interests of others due to his fault.

Article 15 of the Tort Liability Law of the People's Republic of China: civil liability for damages shall be assumed.

Article 23 of the "Patent Law of the People's Republic of China" (amended in 2000): the design granted a patent right shall be different from the design published in domestic and foreign publications or publicly used in China before the date of application. It is not similar and must not conflict with the legal rights obtained by others in the first place.

Article 107 of the "Interpretation of the Supreme People's Court on the Application of the Civil Procedure Law of the People's Republic of China": In litigation, the facts recognized by the parties in order to reach a mediation agreement or a settlement shall not be used in subsequent litigation as a basis for its disadvantage, unless the law provides otherwise or the parties agree.

4. Reasoning
Malicious filing of intellectual property lawsuits is essentially an infringement. The case clarified the essentials for judging malicious infringement, that is, whether the perpetrator was at fault, and whether the litigation filed by the party infringed the civil rights of others. Regarding the issue of whether there was any fault in Tan Fawen's case No. 236.

When Tan Fawen applied for the patent involved and filed the No. 236 case, he hired patent agencies and lawyers. He has the ability to judge whether his design patent meets the authorization requirements stipulated by the law, and he admitted in the settlement and promised to stop infringing on Tencent. Tan Fawen believes that his claim that the patent in question has legal rights lacks factual and legal basis. From the analysis of Tan Fawen's litigation behavior, Tan Fawen still sued Tencent for infringement of the patent in the case even though he knew that Tencent had prior rights to the image of QQ Penguin and that the patents involved in the case did not have the basis of legal rights. After the patent invalidation procedure was filed, he continued to participate in the invalidation procedure. In the above procedures, Tan Fawen entrusted professional lawyers to participate in the relevant procedures, and he was able to foresee the results of his actions, and the actions were not exercised in good faith. He has the intention to damage the rights and interests of others. In summary, Tan Fawen's act in filing the No. 236 case violated the principle of good faith. It was malicious action, and was at fault.

5. Conclusions and Enlightenment

Tan Fawen's behavior began with malicious litigation and should bear corresponding civil liabilities. How to judge whether a litigation act is malicious? The so-called malicious litigation usually refers to a unlawfully and infactually founded lawsuit filed by a party for the purpose of obtaining illegal or illegitimate benefits, and causes the counterparty to suffer losses in the litigation. Malicious litigation is essentially a tort, and its behavior is manifested as an abuse of rights rather than a proper exercise of rights. Its purpose is to obtain illegal or improper benefits, and at the same time cause the counterparty to suffer damages in the litigation, rather than to provide relief to the rights granted by the law. According to the General Principles of my country's Civil Law and the relevant provisions of the Tort Liability Law, malicious litigation should have four elements: subjective fault, infringement action, damage consequences, and causal relationship between infringement and damage consequences. That is to say, to determine that a certain specific litigation is a malicious initiation of an intellectual property lawsuit, the following constituent elements should be satisfied:

1) One of the parties filed a certain request by way of filing an intellectual property lawsuit.

It usually refers to the fact that the party making the request with the litigation rights granted by the law to initiate an intellectual property lawsuit and has dragged the other party into the litigation procedure, putting the other party in a disadvantageous position.

2) The requesting party has subjective malice. The so-called bad faith refers to the fact that a party making a request knows that its request lacks justified reasons and improperly exercises litigation rights contrary to the purpose when the rights were established, with the intention of causing damage to the other party's property or reputation.

3) There are actual damage consequences. Cause actual damage to the other party in an intellectual property lawsuit.

4) There is a causal relationship between the act of the requesting party to initiate an intellectual property lawsuit and the consequences of damage. That is to say, the damage consequences such as the reduction of social reputation and the loss of property are all caused by the abuse of litigation rights by the opposing party.

(2) **How to identify functional features in patent litigation?—Valeo Systems D'essuyange v. Xiamen Lukasi Automobile Parts Co., Ltd.**

2.1 Case Judgement Court: The Supreme People's Court
Case No.: No. 2 (2019)
Judgement Date: 27.03.2019
Cause of action: Infringement upon Invention Patent

Appellant (defendant in the first instance): Xiamen Lukasi Automobile Parts Co., Ltd. Domicile: Siming Park, Tongan Industrial Concentration Zone, Tongan District, Xiamen City, Fujian Province, People's Republic of China.

Legal representative: Chen Shaoqiang, general manager of the company.

Authorized litigation agent: Chen Qinghua, lawyer of Fujian Tianheng United Law Firm.

Authorized litigation agent: Zhang Chen, lawyer of Fujian Tianheng United Law Firm.

Appellant (defendant in the first instance): Xiamen Fuke Automobile Parts Co., Ltd. Domicile: Siming Park, Tongan Industrial Concentration Zone, Xiamen City, Fujian Province, People's Republic of China.

Legal representative: Wang Shuwu, chairman of the company.

Authorized litigation agent: Chen Qinghua, lawyer of Fujian Tianheng United Law Firm.

Authorized litigation agent: Zhang Chen, lawyer of Fujian Tianheng United Law Firm.

Appellee (plaintiff in the first instance): Valeo Systems D'essuyange (Valeo Systèmes d'Essuyage). Domicile: Rue Louis Lormand 78320 La Verrière, France.

Authorized Representative: Murielle Khairallah, Director of Intellectual Property of the company.

Authorized litigation agent: Lin Yi, lawyer of Shanghai Fangda Law Firm.

Autorized litigation agent: Liao Tingting, lawyer of Shanghai Fangda Law Firm.

Defendant in the first instance: Chen Shaoqiang, male, born on March 27, 1975, Han nationality, living in Xiamen City, Fujian Province, People's Republic of China.

In the cases of disputes over infringement upon patents for invention (Appellant Xiamen Lukasi Automobile Parts Co., Ltd. (hereinafter referred to as Lukasi Company), Xiamen Fuke Automobile Parts Co., Ltd. (hereinafter referred to as Fuke Company) v. appellee VALEO SYSTEMES D'ESSUYAGE (hereinafter referred to as VALEO) and the defendant in the original trial Chen Shaoqiang), Lukasi Company and Fuke Company refused to accept the civil judgment (No. 859 [2016], First, Civil Judgement, 73, Shanghai) made by the Shanghai Intellectual Property Court on January 22, 2019 on the confirmation of the infringement and the suspension of the infringement and appealed to the Supreme People's Court. After filing the case on February 15, 2019, the court legally formed a collegiate panel consisting of five persons and held an open trial of this case on March 27, 2019. Chen Qinghua and Zhang Chen (attorneys of the appellant Lukasi Company and Fuke Company), Lin Yi and Liao Tingting (attorneys of the appellee VALEO) attended the trial. Chen Shaoqiang, the defendant in the original trial was summoned by the court, but he refused to appear in court without justified reasons. The court heard the trial by default according to law. So far, the trial of this case has been concluded.

Lukasi Company and Fuke Company appealed to the court to: Revoke the original judgment and reject VALEO's claim to immediately suspense the infringement of the patent right referring to the invention titled "Connectors and corresponding connecting devices for wipers of motor vehicles" with a patent number ZL200610160549.(hereinafter referred to as the involved patent). Main facts and reasons are as follows:

(1) The first instance judgment affirmed that the alleged infringing product can be used under the condition described in claim 1 of the involved patent that "A connector for a wiper, which is used to ensure the connection and articulation between an arm of a wiper and a component of the brush body of a wiper". Such affirmation is wrong. 1. The arm of the wiper of the alleged infringing product was connected to the connector, and the connector was jointed with the brush body by a hinge. There was neither direct contact nor hinge joint between the arm and the brush body. 2. VALEO's claim that the arm of the wiper of the alleged infringing product and the component of the brush body are jointed with each other indirectly through a connector isn't correct. This interpretation violates the principle that the claims should be interpreted literally in the first place. Besides, it cannot be indicated from the specification that they are jointed indirectly with each other. The parent document of the involved patent does not disclose that the connector is used to ensure the indirect joint between the arm and the component of brush body. Thus, such claim cannot be set up based on a divisional application.

(2) The first instance judgment was wrong in the determination that the involved patent claims did not restrict the arm of the wiper to be a "standard arm of the wiper". In this case, a person skilled in the art can be informed clearly and reasonably that the protected object must use a standard arm and a standard connector after reading the patent claims and specifications involved. In other words, the width of the arm must be compatible with the locking element of the connector. Otherwise the elastic element cannot lock the connector. The alleged infringing product doesn't necessarily commercially apply to the condition defined by claim 1 in the involved patent, and it can apply to non-standard wiper arms. The alleged infringing product is also provided with a horizontal baffle (model S950) or a pair of intermediate protrusions connected with each other (model S850, S851) in the front of the safety buckle. When the safety buckle is closed, the horizontal baffle or protrusions will be positioned in front of the wiper arm to block it from moving forward and getting out of the elastic element. The alleged infringing product doesn't fall into the protection scope of claim 1.

(3) The first instance judgment was wrong in the affirmation that the alleged infringing product had the technical feature that "the (elastic) element locks the connector at the embedded position in the front end of the wiper arm". 1. "The (elastic) element locks the connector at the embedded position in the front end of the wiper arm" and "the safety buckle extends to the locking element (i.e. The elastic element) to prevent the locking element from deforming and to lock the connector." The term "lock" used above should be equivalent. The elastic element of the alleged infringing product can only "locate" the connector at the embedded position in the front end of the wiper

arm, but cannot "lock" the connector; the connector can only be locked when the safety buckle is closed. 2. The above affirmation of the first instance judgment was based on the premise that the accused infringing product applies to a standard arm and a standard connector of the wiper. When the accused infringing product applies to a non-standard wiper arm, it will be impossible for the elastic element to "lock" the connector in the embedded position in the front end of the wiper arm.

(4) The first instance judgment affirmed that only the description of paragraph [0056] of the involved patent specification should be considered to restrict the functional technical feature that "used to prevent the locking element from deforming and lock the connector". Such affirmation is wrong. The above function can be achieved only through the method described in paragraph [0056] of the patent specification. That is to extend to the locking element. Therefore, the indispensable technical feature for achieving this function request the inner surface of the vertical side of the safety buckle (number 77 in the attached picture) to extend along the (parallel) outer surface of the locking element to prevent the locking element from deforming laterally outside the connector. According to number 77 in the attached picture, the inner surface of the safety buckle has a pair of protrusions parallel to the vertical side of the safety buckle.

(5) The first instance judgment was wrong in the affirmation that the safety buckle of the alleged infringing product extended to the locking element when it was closed. As for the involved patent, the first instance judgment adopted the concept that the safety buckle is located in the front, and part of the safety buckle (inner surface) extends along the outer surface of the claw; As for the alleged infringing product, the first instance judgment adopted the concept that part (the front part) of the safety buckle is located in the front and part (two sides) of it is parallel to the claw. Obviously, the safety buckle of the alleged infringing product does not extend to the locking element as a whole, but encloses the locking element; either does it extend to the locking element in part, but extends vertically to the locking element. The method to compare used by the first instance judgement was wrong, which expanded the scope of protection of the involved patent right.

(6) The first instance judgment affirmed that the technical method of the alleged infringing product "restricting the locking element from elastic opening by using the vertical protrusion of the safety buckle which is located on the surface of the inner sides of the safety buckle and the claw which is perpendicular to the locking element." and the technical method of the patent involved "directly restricting the locking element through the claw which is parallel to the locking element and is located on the inner surface of the safety buckle" are basically the same, and their function and effects are also the same. Such affirmation is wrong. 1. The safety buckle of the patent involved faces the locking element as a whole, and part (protrusion on the inner surface) of the safety buckle extends parallel to the lock, while the safety buckle of the alleged infringing product which contains the locking element is entirely closed, and part (protrusion on the inner surface of the front part) of the safety buckle extends vertically to the lock. The technical methods used above are not basically the same. 2. The effect of the alleged infringing product whose safety buckle contains the locking element and can be closed as a whole is obviously better than that of the

involved patent whose safety buckle is located in front of the locking element as a whole; The effect of the alleged infringing product which extends vertically to the lock is significantly better than that of the involved patent which extend parallel to the lock. The above-mentioned distinguishing features can only be discovered through creative work by ordinary skilled person in the art when the alleged infringement occurs.

(7) The first instance judgment made an error in the affirmation that Lukasi Company and Fuke Company jointly committed the act of manufacturing the alleged infringing product.

During the trial of the second instance, Lukasi Company and Fuke Company clearly waived the aforementioned grounds for appeal (7).

VALEO argued that: Lukasi Company and Fuke Company's grounds for appealing that the alleged infringing product did not fall into the protection scope of claim 1 of the involved patent cannot be established.

(1) Regarding the features of condition for using that "a connector of a wiper, which is used to ensure the connection and articulation between an arm of the wiper and a component of the brush body of the wiper". 1. According to the claims literally, the connection and articulation between the arm and the component of the brush body is achieved by an independent part, which is the connector. So there is obviously no need for the arm and the component of the brush body to connect with each other directly. 2. The above literal meaning has been verified by the examples in specification of the involved patent. 3. The description of the technical feature of the connector used for connection and articulation in the parent document of the involved patent is completely consistent with the above description in the specification of the involved patent. As the alleged infringing product also connect the arm and the component of brush body through the connector, it has the above-mentioned features of condition for using.

(2) Regarding the technical feature that "and including at least one elastically deformable element which locks the connector at the embedded position in the front end of the arm of the wiper". 1. Claim 1, the specification and the files of examination of the involved patent do not restrict the technical solution to be applied only for "standard arms of wiper". 2. The alleged infringing product can be used under the condition defined in claim 1, which is also approved by Lukasi Company and Fuke Company. Moreover, the condition restricted in claim 1 is the only reasonable commercial use of the alleged infringing product. The claims of Lukasi Company and Fuke Company that the alleged infringing products can be used for non-standard wiper arms with smaller widths lack basis. According to the introduction of the product by Lukasi Company and Fuke Company, the minimum widths of the wiper's arm for models S850, S851 and S950 are 7.8, 7.8 and 8.7 mm respectively. After measurement, the width of the locking claw of the connector of the alleged infringing product does not exceed 7 mm. Therefore, in actual applications, the alleged infringing product cannot be used for wiper's arms with a width less than the inner diameter of the locking element. In addition, if the wiper's arm is not wide enough, it will inevitably shake after installation, resulting in uneven wiping. This kind of unstable installation obviously needs to be avoided commercially and technically.

(3) Regarding the technical feature that "the connector is locked at the embedded position of the wiper's arm by a safety buckle". 1. According to the introduction of the alleged infringing products by Lukasi Company and Fuke Company, the size of the connector and that of arm are matched with each other, and the connector can be locked in the embedded position of the arm by a safety buckle. 2. Consumers will only buy wipers that match their own models of vehicles, and the connector can certainly be locked in the embedded position of the arm by a safety buckle.

(4) Regarding the technical feature that "the safety buckle extends to the locking element to prevent elastic deformation of the locking element and lock the connector". 1. Regarding the question of whether the safety buckle is faced to the connector as a whole or partly. The shape of the safety buckle is not an indispensable technical feature for realizing the locking function. Whether the safety buckle faces the connector as a whole or partly, as long as a part of the safety buckle extends to the locking element, the locking function can be realized and the technical characteristic mentioned above is included. 2. Regarding the side of the inner surface. An indispensable technical feature for realizing the above-mentioned locking function is that the safety buckle extends to the locking element. On the premise of satisfying this indispensable technical feature, the specific shape of the inner surface side of the safety buckle does not affect the realization of the locking function. In addition, regardless of whether the inside of the safety buckle extends vertically or parallel to the locking element, as long as it overlaps with the locking element in space, it can be prevented from being deformed. Vertical extension and parallel extension belong to the same technical solution. 3. Regarding the baffle at the front end. At the front end of the connector, the alleged infringing product is additionally provided with a baffle or a pair of protrusions connected with each other in the middle. This additional technical feature cannot change the result of infringement. Moreover, the alleged infringing product is practically impossible to be used for a wiper's arm with a small width.

In summary, VALEO requested to dismiss the appeal and uphold the original judgment. At the same time, in view of new evidence which can prove that the alleged infringement is still going on, VALEO requested this court to support its application to order Lukasi Company and Fuke Company to immediately cease the infringement of the involved patent right.

VALEO brought a suit to the court of first instance and request to order Lukasi Company, Fuke Company and Chen Shaoqiang to immediately cease the infringement, that is, to order Lucas Company and Fuke Company to immediately cease manufacturing, selling and promising to sell the alleged infringing products, and to order Chen Shaoqiang to Immediately stop manufacturing and selling the alleged infringing products; to order Lukasi Company, Fuke Company and Chen Shaoqiang to destroy the alleged infringing products that have been manufactured, as well as the equipment, molds, drawings and other related physical objects and materials used to manufacture the alleged infringing products; to order Lukasi Company, Fuke Company and Chen Shaoqiang to pay compensation (temporarily calculated) of 5 million yuan and other reasonable expenses for stopping infringement activities (temporarily calculated) of 1 million yuan; to order Lukasi Company, Fuke Company and Chen Shaoqiang to pay for all litigation fees and preservation fees in this case jointly. In the process of the first instance trial, VALEO requested the court of the first instance to confirm that the three types of the wipers of the alleged infringing products S850, S851, and S950 fall within the scope of protection in claims 1–10 of the involved patent, and to judge Lukasi Company, Fuke Company and Chen Shaoqiang to immediately stop infringing on the involved patent right in advance.

The court of first instance found the following facts: VALEO is the patentee of the involved patent for invention named the "connector of motor vehicle wiper and the corresponding connecting device", and the patent is still under protection. The claims of the patent are: "1. A wiper's connector, which is used to ensure the connection and articulation between the wiper's arm and a component of the wiper's brush body. The connector is longitudinally embedded into the front end of the wiper's arm from back to the front, which is bent longitudinally backward into a U shape, including at least one elastically deformable element-the element locks the connector in the embedded position on the front end of the wiper's arm, including two longitudinally vertical sides, the sides are arranged to be accommodated between the two side wings of the component of wiper's brush body; the connector is characterized in that the connector is locked in an embedded position in the wiper's arm by a safety buckle which is flexibly installed between a closed position and an open position. In the closed position, the safety buckle extends toward the locking element. It is designed to prevent elastic deformation of the locking element and to lock the connector. Meanwhile, the open position can release the connector from the wiper's arm. 2. The wiper's connector mentioned in claim 1 is characterized in that the safety buckle is flexibly installed relative to the component of the wiper's brush body. 3. The connector of the wiper mentioned in claim 2 is characterized in that the safety buckle is hingedly installed relative to the component of the wiper's brush body. 4. The connector of the wiper mentioned in claim 3 is characterized in that the safety buckle is hingedly installed around a vertical axis of the wiper's brush body. 5. The connector of the wiper mentioned in claim 4 is characterized in that the hinging axis of the safety buckle is located on the longitudinal front end of the side wing of the component. 6. The connector of the wiper mentioned in claim 2–5 is characterized in that it can keep the safety buckle closed by an elastic structure which can fit the connector in shape. 7. The connector of the wiper mentioned in claim 1–5 is characterized in that the locking element is a claw. The claw extends forward from the longitudinal front end on one side of the connector freely and longitudinally, and its free end has a shape of oblique or beak which extends laterally into the connector. It extends toward the front surface of the longitudinal front end of the wiper's arm when the connector is located in the embedded position. 8. The wiper's connector mentioned in claim 7 is characterized in that the safety buckle forms a protective cover which extends toward the outer surface of the free end of the locking claw of the connector in the closed position. 9. The wiper mentioned in claim 1–5 is characterized in that the safety buckle can prevent the locking claw from deforming laterally to the outside of the connector in order to ensure that the connector does not fall out of the front end of the wiper's arm. 10. A connecting device, connecting the component of a wiper's brush body and a wiper's arm, is characterized in that it comprises a connector described as any one of claims 1–9 and a component inserted on the wiper's brush body."

It is stated in paragraph [0006] in the specification of the involved patent that "The locking position of the connector is generally secured by an elastically deformable element. However, the wiper's brush body may be violently pushed under an impact. The locking element will deform for lack of strength. As a result, it can no longer guarantee its locking function, which may cause the connector to accidentally come out. Due to the same reason, the wiper's brush body may be separated from and the wiper's arm." Paragraph [0011] states, "The object of this invention is therefore to provide a device for fixing the connector to a part of the wiper's brush body, which can lock the connector in the position of installation. It can also install any type of wiper on a standard arm and a standard connector". Paragraph [0055] records, "The buckle is a plastic-pouring hollow element in the shape of a cover. It rotates around a vertical axis of the component, and it is also flexibly installed between a closed position and an open position. In the open position, the buckle can lock the connector in the embedded position in the hook-shaped end shown in Fig. 2. In the open position, it can release the connector". Paragraph [0056] states, "The locking of the connector is ensured by the inner surface of the vertical side of the buckle, which extends along the outer surface of the claw. Therefore, the buckle can prevent the claw from deforming laterally to the outside of the connector so that the connector cannot move out from the hook-shaped end."

In this case, the alleged infringing products are three types of wipers for vehicle, whose model names are S850, S851 and S950, consisting of brush body, connector and safety buckle. Wherein, the connector is hingedly installed on the base of the wiper's main body. The connector can connect the wiper's arm and brush body. After connection, the wiper's arm can rotate together with the connector around a horizontal axis on the base of the brush body. The connector has two protruding or extending sides located between the two side wings of the base of the brush body. They can form a pair of elastically deformable elements. The end of the elastic element is laterally bent (model S850, S851) or raised (model S950) into the connector, so that the bent part in front of the wiper's arm can be locked and fixed at the position of connection and assembly, that is, the embedded position. There is a safety buckle above the connector. The rear part of the safety buckle is installed on the wiper's base through a hinge, and it can rotate around a horizontal axis determined by the hinge point to close or open. The connector ensures that the safety buckle remains in the closed position through an elastic structure whose shape can fit the buckle. The inner surfaces of the two side walls of the safety belt buckle are provided with a pair of protrusions perpendicular to the side walls. When the seat belt buckle is in the closed position, the front part of the seat belt buckle is located in front of the elastic element, which receives and closes the elastic element. There is a pair of protrusions on the inner surface of two sides of the buckle, vertical to the sides. When the safety buckle is located in closing position, the front part of the safety buckle will be located in front of the locking element and include the locking element. Those protrusions are correspond to the outer surface of the elastic element and restrict its elastic opening, in order to lock it and prevent the wiper's arm from getting out. The alleged infringing product is also provided with a horizontal baffle (model S950) or a pair of intermediate protrusions connected with each other (model S850, S851) in the front of the safety buckle. When the safety buckle is closed, the horizontal baffle or protrusions will be positioned in front of the wiper's arm.

The court of first instance held that: in this case, it is possible judge in advance as to whether the alleged infringing product falls within the protection scope of claims 1–10 of the involved patent, and supports VALEO's request for a partial judgment in advance. All parties confirm that the alleged infringing product has the additional technical features in claims 2, 3, 6–10 of the involved patent. The main dispute is whether the alleged infringing product has the three technical features in claim 1 additional technical features in claim 4 and 5.

(1) Regarding whether the alleged infringing product has the technical feature of "a connector of a wiper, which is used to ensure the connection and articulation between an arm of the wiper and a component of the brush body of the wiper" in claim 1 of the involved patent. The court of first instance held that the above-mentioned technical features described the using conditions of the involved patent. The claims of the involved patent did not restrict the wiper's arm to be a "standard wiper arm". The alleged infringing product is a wiper for vehicle, which is connected to the wiper's arm through a connector. The wiper arm's can rotate with the connector around the horizontal axis on the base of the wiper's brush body. The method of connection should be determined as hinging. The alleged infringing product can be used under the condition restricted by claim 1, and it has the feature of condition.

(2) Regarding whether the alleged infringing product has technical feature in claim 1 of the involved patent that "and includes at least one elastically deformable element which locks the connector into the embedded position on the front end of the wiper's arm." The court of first instance held that a pair of inward bend (model S850, S851) or protrusion (model S950) on the end of the elastic elements of the alleged infringing product can snap in the curved part located in the front of the wiper's arm, thereby limiting the assembly connection position That is, the embedded position is not easy to take out under small external force. It should be considered that the elastic element can lock the connector in the embedded position in the front end of the wiper arm, and has the above-mentioned technical features of the involved patent.

(3) Regarding whether the alleged infringing product has the technical feature in claim 1 of the involved patent that "the connector is locked in the embedded position in the wiper's arm by a safety buckle... In the closed position, the safety buckle extends towards the locking element to prevent elastic deformation of the locking element and to lock the connector". The court of first instance held that the above technical features only disclosed the relationship about direction and position between the safety buckle and the locking element (the elastic element). Such relationship about direction is not sufficient to prevent the elastic deformation of the locking element. Ordinary person skilled in art cannot directly and clearly ascertain the technical method to realize the function of "preventing the elastic deformation of the locking element and locking the connector" just by reading the claims. So the above technical features belong to functional features. Only the technical feature described in paragraph [0056] of the specification of the involved patent that "the locking of the connector is ensured by

the inner surface of the vertical side of the buckle, and the inner surface extends along the outer surface of the claw. Therefore, the buckle prevents the claw from deforming laterally to the outside of the connector so that the connector cannot be released from the hook-shaped end" is an indispensable technical feature to realize this function. This part of the content should be used to restrict the functional technical features. When the safety buckle of the involved patent is closed, it is located directly in front of a pair of locking elements and faces the locking element as a whole; the locking of the connector is ensured by the inner surface of the vertical side of the safety buckle which fits the outer surface of the locking element. It extends along the outer surface of the claw of the locking element, restricting the locking element from laterally deforming outside the connector, so as to lock the connector. Although the safety buckle of the alleged infringing product is not directly located in front of a pair of locking elements in the closed position, its front part contains and encloses the locking element, and the front part of the safety buckle is also directly located in front of the locking element. The two sides of the safety buckle are also parallel to the two claws of the locking element. It can be regarded that the safety buckle extends toward the locking element. On the inner surfaces of two sides of the safety buckle of the alleged infringing product, there is a pair of protrusions perpendicular to the side. When the safety buckle is located in the closed position, the position of the protrusions corresponds to the outer surface of the claw of the locking element and restricts its elastically opening, so that the connector can be locked. Both the alleged infringing product and the involved patent use the surface outside the claw of the locking element corresponding to two vertical sides of the safety buckle to prevent the claw from deforming laterally to the outside of the connector. The technical means used by both the alleged infringing product and the involved patent are basically the same. They are also same in the effect of locking and preventing locking element from elastically deforming. Ordinary persons skilled in art can think of this technical solution without creative work when the alleged infringement occurs. Therefore, the alleged infringing product has equivalent technical features with that of the involved patent.

(4) Regarding whether the alleged infringing product has the additional technical features mentioned in claims 4 and 5 of the involved patent. The court of first instance held that the corresponding technical features of the alleged infringing product were neither the same nor equivalent to the additional technical features in claims 4 and 5 of the involved patent. It did not include the additional technical features in claims 4 and 5 of the involved patent. In summary, the alleged infringing product falls within the scope of protection in claims 1–3 and 6–10 of the involved patent, but does not fall within the scope of protection in claims 4 and 5 of the involved patent. Lukasi Company and Fuke Company carried out the act of selling, promising to sell and jointly manufacturing the alleged infringing products. They should bear the civil liability to cease the infringement. However, the existing evidence in this case cannot prove that Chen Shaoqiang manufactured and sold the alleged infringing products.

To sum up, the court of first instance judged that: Lukasi Company and Fuke Company should immediately stopped infringing on the patent right of the invention involved in the case from the date of this judgment.

During the second instance of this court, both parties legally submitted evidence concerning the appeal request. This court organized both parties to conduct evidence exchange and cross-examination. Lukasi Company and Fuke Company submitted two evidence: Evidence 1, "China Automotive Industry Standard·Type and Size of Electric Wipers for Windshield of Automobiles (QC/T46-92)" is submitted to prove that the hook-shaped arm of the wiper has two widths of 9 and 7 mm (error 0–0.1 mm), other types and sizes are allowed when there are special requirements, which shall be negotiated by both parties; Evidence 2, the US patent with patent number US005611103A and its Chinese translation version, are submitted to prove that the previous connector cannot accommodate hook-shaped wiper's arms of different sizes. The function of the US patent is to accommodate three wiper's arms of different widths, which proves that the involved patent can only accommodate one wiper's arm whose width is compatible with that of the locking element of the connector. However, the alleged infringing product can accommodate the wiper's arm whose width does not match that of the locking element of the connector. VALEO issued a cross-examination opinion on the two pieces of evidence, and VALEO recognized the authenticity of the evidence, but denied the relevance of the evidence. VALEO hold that those evidence cannot prove the claims of Lukasi Company and Fuke Company. Regarding the above-mentioned evidence submitted by Lukasi Company and Fuke Company, considering VALEO's opinions in cross-examination, this court made the following certification: The authenticity of Evidence 1 and Evidence 2 can be confirmed, but they lack sufficient relevance to the interpretation of the claims in this case and the judgment of infringement. So they cannot be accepted.

VALEO submitted two notarizations: Hudong Zhengjing Zi No. 2263 and No. 2340 (2019) issued by Shanghai Oriental Notary Public Office to prove that after the original judgment was made, "CARALL Jingdong self-employed Flagship Store" is still selling the alleged infringing products. Lukasi Company and Fuke Company recognized the authenticity of the two notarizations, and confirmed that the product attached to the notarization was the S851 model product, the alleged infringing product in this case. At the same time, Lukasi Company and Fuke Company claimed that they had ceased manufacturing and selling of the alleged infringing products. The S851 model product is exclusively provided for JD.com, and the products purchased by VALEO this time should be commodity stocks of JD.com. VALEO recognized that the S851 model product accused of infringement in this case was exclusively provided for JD.com, and also recognized that "carall flagship store" on T Mall had stopped sales of the accused product. Regarding the above-mentioned evidence submitted by VALEO, combined with the cross-examination opinions of Lukasi Company and Fuke Company, this court makes the following certification: Lukasi Company and Fuke Company have no objection to the authenticity of the two notarizations, and the facts proved by the evidence are relevant to this case and shall be adopted.

This court found that the facts ascertained by the court of first instance are true.
This court also found out:
(1) Regarding the specification of the involved patent, paragraph [0043] states that "the lever ensures that the connector is hingedly installed on the wiper's brush body around the horizontal axis 'T1'". Paragraph [0044] states, "After the connector is

embedded on the lever, the wiper's arm will be installed on this small component according to a well-known design, that is to embed the hook-shaped end onto the framework of the connector from front to back. The surface of the parallel side of the lever is located between side plates of the connector". Figures 1 and 3 in the specification clearly show the connection and articulation between the wiper's arm and a part of the wiper brush body through the connector.

(2) Regarding the alleged infringing products and acts of tort. "FAQ about the Wiper" printed on the packaging of the model S851 product which is accused of infringement in this case stated that "the wiper should be replaced if vibration occurs." Lukasi Company and Fuke Company have ceased selling alleged infringing products in "Carall Flagship Store" on T Mall platform. During the second instance, The alleged infringing product of the model S851 bought by VALEO from "Carl CARALL Jingdong Self-operated Flagship Store" is exclusively provided for JD.com. The act of purchasing has been proved by notarization. So JD.com is still selling the alleged infringing product of the model S851 in a self-operating manner.

(3) Regarding opinions of assistant expert. During the trial of the second instance, VALEO requested Tian Weichao, director of Asia R&D Center for VALEO's wiper to appear in court as an expert assistant. He expressed opinions on the factors that need to be considered in the product design of wipers for vehicles. Lukasi Company and Fuke Company asked Tian Weichao several questions. Tian Weichao hold that safety and compliance are two important considerations when designing wipers for vehicles. In terms of safety, the product design must ensure that the components of wiper include firm connection between the wiper's arm and the connector. When the wiper's arm does not fit the connector, it will shake, which may affect wiping and threaten the safety of driving. Tian Weichao's opinions are objective and reasonable. Lukasi Company and Fuke Company have not suspect the reasonableness of Tian Weichao's opinions. This court will consider those opinions when evaluating relevant issues.

(4) Regarding the application for behavior protection during litigation. During the first instance trial of this case, VALEO filed an application to the court of first instance to order Lukasi Company, Fuke Company and Chen Shaoqiang to cease the infringement of the involved patent rights, and to provide a cash guarantee of 1 million yuan. VALEO's application for behavior protection in the lawsuit has not yet been processed by the court of first instance. During the second instance, VALEO insisted on ordering Lukasi Company and Fuke Company to stop the infringement of the involved patent rights involved in the lawsuit. This court decide to support the application.

The Supreme People's Court held:

I. Whether the technical feature "A connector for a wiper, which is used to ensure the connection and articulation between an arm of a wiper and a component of the brush body of a wiper" is a functional feature, and whether the alleged infringing product has the above-mentioned feature.

First, whether the above technical feature is a functional feature. A functional feature refers to a technical feature that defines the structure, component, step, condition or their relationships, etc., through its function or effect in the invention creation, instead of directly defining the structure, component, step, condition or their relationships, etc., of the technical proposal of the invention. No technical feature that has defined or implied a specific structure, component, step, condition or their relationships, etc., of the technical proposal of the invention may, even if it simultaneously defines the function or effect achieved by it, be identified as a functional feature referred to in Article 8 of the Interpretation of the Supreme People's Court on Several Issues Concerning the Application of Laws in the Trial of Cases in Relation to Disputes over Infringement of Patent Rights (II) in principle and be used for infringement comparison as a functional feature. The above-mentioned technical feature actually defines the directional relationship between the safety buckle and the locking element and implies a specific structure—"the safety buckle extends facing the said locking element", and the role of such direction and structure is "for preventing the elastic deformation of the said locking element and locking the said connector". In light of this directional and structural relationship, based on the specification and the attached drawings of the patent involved, especially the record in Paragraph [0056] of the specification that "the locking of the connector is guaranteed by the inner surface of the vertical side wall of the buckle, which extends along the outer surface of the claw; therefore, the buckle prevents the claw from being deformed laterally towards the outside of the connector, so that the connector cannot be released from the hook-shaped end", general technicians in this field can understand that "the safety buckle extends facing the said locking element", and when the distance between the extension and the outer surface of the locking element is small enough, it can achieve the effect of preventing the elastic deformation of the locking element and locking of the connector. It can be seen that the above-mentioned technical feature is characterized by defining both the specific direction and structure and the function thereof, and only through combined understanding of the direction and structure as well as the function thereof can the specific contents of such direction and structure be clearly determined. Although such technical feature of "direction or structure + functional description" contains the description of functions, it is still a directional or structural feature essentially, rather than a functional feature in the sense as prescribed in Article 8 of the Interpretation of the Supreme People's Court on Several Issues Concerning the Application of Laws in the Trial of Cases in Relation to Disputes over Infringement of Patent Rights (II).

Second, whether the alleged infringing product has the above-mentioned technical feature. The above-mentioned technical feature of patent claim 1 involved not only defines the directional and structural relationship between the safety buckle and the locking element, but also describes the function of the safety buckle, which plays a role of definition in determining the directional and structural relationship between the safety buckle and the locking element. The above-mentioned technical feature is actually not a functional feature, and its definition of the directional and structural relationship and of function shall all be taken into consideration in the identification of infringement. In this case, the inner surface of two side walls of the safety buckle of the alleged infringing product is set with a pair of protrusions perpendicular to the side walls. When the safety buckle is in the off position, the protrusions in the side walls thereof face the outer surface of the elastic element, achieving the effects of restricting the deformation and expansion of the elastic element, locking the elastic element, and preventing the wiper arm from coming out of the elastic element. That the protrusions perpendicular to the side walls on inner surface of the two side walls of the safety buckle face the outer surface of the elastic element when the safety buckle of the alleged infringing product is in the off position belongs to a form where "the said safety buckle extends facing the said locking element" referred to in patent claim 1 involved, and can also achieve the function of "preventing the elastic deformation of the said locking element and locking of the said connector". Therefore, the alleged infringing product has the above-mentioned technical feature and falls within the protection scope of patent claim 1 involved. On the basis of identifying the above-mentioned feature as a functional feature, the court of first instance identified that the alleged infringing product had the technical feature equivalent to the above-mentioned feature, and despite the deviation in the comparison method and conclusion, it did not affect the infringement identification and judgment result in this case.

II. Specific Handling of the Application for Act Preservation in this Case

The special circumstance required to be taken into consideration in this case is that although the court of first instance had made a pre-judgment ordering cessation of the infringement of the patent right involved, it did not come into effect, and the patentee continued to insist on its application for act preservation in the proceedings of the first instance court. At this point, the people's court of second instance may respectively handle the application for act preservation to stop the infringement of a patent right by taking into consideration the following circumstances: where the patentee files an application for act preservation where the circumstance is urgent or may cause other damage, the people's court of second instance shall, if it is impossible to make a final judgment within the time limit for handling the application for act preservation, handle the application for act preservation separately and legally make a ruling in a timely manner; if the conditions for act preservation are met, it shall take preservation measures without delay. At that time, as the judgment of first instance has identified that the infringement is established, the people's court of second instance may examine the application for act preservation based on the case facts without necessarily requiring the provision of a guarantee. The people's court of second instance may, if it is able to make a final judgment within the time limit for handling the application for act preservation, make a judgment in a timely manner and reject the application for act preservation. In this case, Valeo Company insisted on its application for in-lawsuit act preservation that Lukasi Company and Fuke Company shall be ordered to stop their infringement of the patent right involved, but the evidence submitted by it was not sufficient to prove the occurrence of any emergency that caused damage to it, and moreover, the Supreme People's Court had already made a judgment in court, which had already come into effect, so it was no longer necessary to make a separate ruling on act preservation to order to stop the infringement of the patent right involved. Valeo Company's application for in-lawsuit act preservation was not upheld.

In summary, the appeal request of Lukasi Company and Fuke Company cannot be established and is rejected by this court. The facts ascertained in the judgment of first

instance were clear. Although the applicable law regarding the determination of the functional features is flawed, it does not affect the result of the case. In accordance of the Article 59 of the Patent Law of the People's Republic of China, Article 8 of Interpretations of the Supreme People's Court on Issues Concerning the Application of Law in the Trial of Patent Infringement Dispute Cases (II), the first paragraph of Article 170 of the Civil Procedure Law of the People's Republic of China, Article 340 Interpretation of the Supreme People's Court on the Application of the Civil Procedure Law of the People's Republic of China, the judgment is made as follows:
(1) The appeal was rejected and the original judgment was upheld.
(2) The acceptance fee of the second instance was 500 yuan, which should be borne by Lukasi company and Fuke Company.

This decision shall be final.
Chief Judge: Luo Dongchuan
Judge: Wang Chuang
Judge: Zhu Li
Judge: Ren Xiao Lan
Judge Assistant: Liao Jibo
27.09.2019
Technical Investigator: Ding Lei
Clerk: Li Wei

2.2 Analysis of the Case

1. Basic Case

Valeo Cleaning System Company (VALEO SYSTEMES D'ESSUYAGE, hereinafter referred to as Valeo Company) is the patentee of the Chinese invention patent No. ZL200610160549.2, entitled "Connectors and corresponding connecting devices for wipers of motor vehicles". Valeo filed a lawsuit with the Shanghai Intellectual Property Court in 2016, claiming that Xiamen Lucas Auto Parts Co., Ltd. (hereinafter referred to as Lucas Company) and Xiamen Fuke Auto Parts Co., Ltd. (hereinafter referred to as Fuke Company) were unauthorized Manufacturing, selling, and promising to sell, the wiper products manufactured and sold by Chen Shaoqiang fall into the scope of its patent protection, requesting an order for Lucas, Fuke, and Chen Shaoqiang to stop infringement, compensation for losses and reasonable expenses for stopping infringement, temporarily totaling 6 million Yuan damages. Later, Valeo applied to the court to make a partial judgment and found that Lucas, Fuke and Chen Shaoqiang constituted infringement and ordered them to stop the infringement.

In addition, Valeo also filed an application for temporary behavior preservation (also known as a temporary injunction), requesting the court to rule Lucas, Fuke and Chen Shaoqiang to immediately stop the infringement. The Shanghai Intellectual Property Court made a partial judgment on January 22, 2019, determined that Lucas and Fuke Company constituted infringement and ordered them to stop the infringement, and therefore did not deal with the application for temporary injunction. Lucas and Fuke dissatisfied with some of the above judgments, and appealed to the Supreme People's Court, requesting to revoke the judgment, and the judgment was changed to dismiss Valeo's request to stop the infringement. After review, the Supreme People's Court upheld the first-instance judgment.

2. Focus of controversy:
(1) How to identify functional features?
(2) How does the court of second instance deal with the interim injunction applied by the party in the first instance procedure?

3. Related rules:
Article 59 of the "Patent Law of the People's Republic of China": The scope of protection of a patent right for an invention or utility model shall be subject to the content of the claim. The description and drawings may be used to interpret the content of the claim. The protection scope of the design patent right is based on the design of the product shown in the picture or photo, and the brief description can be used to explain the design of the product represented by the picture or photo.

"The Supreme People's Court Interpretation on Several Issues Concerning the Application of Law in the Trial of Patent Infringement Cases (2)" Article 8: Functional features refer to the structure, composition, steps, conditions or the relationship between them, etc., through the invention The technical features that define the functions or effects in the creation, except that those of ordinary skill in the art can directly and clearly determine the specific implementation manners to achieve the above functions or effects only by reading the claims. Compared with the technical features that are indispensable for realizing the functions or effects mentioned in the preceding paragraph, the corresponding technical features of the alleged infringing technical solution are basically the same means to achieve the same function and achieve the same effect, and If a person of ordinary skill in the art can associate it without creative work when the alleged infringement occurs, the people's court shall determine that the corresponding technical feature is the same or equivalent to the functional feature.

4. Application of law and its results:
The collegiate panel held that the alleged infringing product had all the technical features of the patent rights in the case and fell within the scope of protection of the patent rights in the case. The actions of Lucas Company and Fuke Company constituted infringement and should bear the legal liability to stop the infringement. Temporary injunctions have unique value. When part of the judgment ordering to stop the infringement has not yet taken effect, the temporary injunction can have the effect of timely enforcement and can more fully protect the interests of the patentee. In view of the judgment of this case in court, the judgment of this case immediately became legally effective, and the provisional injunction ruling is no longer necessary in this case. Therefore, the application for a temporary injunction filed by the French company Valeo is not supported.

The judgment of this case discussed for the first time the relationship between the partial judgment system to stop the infringement and the temporary injunction system, clarified the unique value of the temporary injunction when the partial judgment to stop the infringement has not yet taken effect, and clarified the applicable conditions when the two systems coexist. The rules will have guiding significance for the adjudication mechanism of innovative technology-related intellectual property cases, the enhancement of judicial protection of intellectual property rights, and the reduction of rights protection costs.

(3) **How to define the obvious error and implicit technical features of patent documents in litigation—Wuxi Guowei Ceramic Electric Appliances Co., Ltd. and Jiang Guoping v. Changshu Linzhi Electric Heating Components Co., Ltd. and Suning.com Group Co., Ltd.**

3.1 Case Judgement   Court: The Supreme People's Court
Case No.: No. 111 [2018]
Judgment Date: 06–26-2018
Cause of action: Infringement upon Utility Model Patent

Retrial applicant (plaintiff in the first instance, appellant in the second instance): Wuxi Guowei Ceramic Appliance Co., Ltd. Address: Tongshu West Road, Dingshu Town, Yixing City, Jiangsu Province.

Legal representative: Jiang Guoping, general manager of the company.

Retrial applicant (plaintiff in the first instance, appellant in the second instance): Jiang Guoping, male, born on May 21, 1955, Han nationality, living in Yixing City, Jiangsu Province.

Co-authorized litigation agent of the two retrial applicants: Bai Shangchun, male, born on April 23, 1962, Han nationality, patent attorney of Nanjing Sugao Patent and Trademark Office, living in Nanjing, Jiangsu Province.

Co-appointed litigation agent of the two retrial applicants: Kang Yanwen, lawyer of Jiangsu Su Gao Law Firm.

Respondent (defendant in the first instance, appellant in the second instance): the respondent Changshu Linzhi Electric Heating Components Co., Ltd. Address: No. 88, Tonglin Road, Hi-tech Park, Economic and Technological Development Zone, Changshu City, Jiangsu Province.

Legal representative: He Zhengan, chairman of the company.

Respondent (defendant in the first instance, appellee in the second instance): Suning.com Group Co., Ltd. (formerly Suning Yunshang Group Co., Ltd.). Domicile: Floor 1–5, Jinshan Building, No. 8 Shanxi Road, Nanjing City, Jiangsu Province.

Legal representative: Zhang Jindong, chairman of the company.

Authorized litigation agent: Zheng Fangyan, female, employee of the company.

Retrial applicants Wuxi Guowei Ceramic Electric Appliances Co., Ltd. (hereinafter referred to as Guowei Company), Jiang Guoping and the respondent Changshu Linzhi Electric Heating Components Co., Ltd. (hereinafter referred to as Linzhi Company), the respondent Suning.com Group Co., Ltd. (hereinafter referred to as Suning Company) in case of dispute over infringement upon a utility-model patent, not accepted the Jiangsu Higher People's Court (2016) Su Min Final No.105 Civil Judgment, and petitioned to this court for retrial. This court made a civil ruling (2017) Supreme People's Court Min Shen No. 2638 on December 21, 2017 and directly retried the case. The Court formed a collegial bench in accordance with the law, assigned Wang Dong as a technical investigator to participate in the litigation activities of the case, and held a public hearing of the case. Jiang Guoping himself, Guowei Company and Jiang Guoping jointly entrusted litigation agents Bai Shangchun, Kang

Yanwen, Suning company entrusted litigation agent Zheng Fangyan to participate in the lawsuit. Linzhi company summoned by the court summons, refused to appear in court without justifiable reasons, the court conducted a trial in absentia in accordance with the law. The case has now been closed.

Guowei Company and Jiang Guoping petitioned to this court for retrial and claimed that the facts found in the second-instance judgement were unclear and the application of the laws was wrong. This case complies with Article 200, Item 6 of the Civil Procedure Law of the People's Republic of China and the court shall conduct a retrial. Main reasons are as follows: (1) The introduction of "implicit technical features" in the second-instance judgment violated the principle of comprehensive coverage, narrowed the scope of protection of patent claim 2 of Guowei Company and Jiang Guoping in this case, so it lacked legal basis. (2) The second-instance judgment errored in interpreting the patent claim 2 in this case. In the patent claim 2, it describes "the heat-dissipating aluminum strips (11) are pasted on the left and right sides of the heat-conducting aluminum tube (1) in the heating core (10)", however, the "left and right sides" should be a clerical error. The only interpretation of this claim should be that the heat dissipation aluminum strips are pasted on the "upper and lower surfaces" of the heat-conducting aluminum tube in the heating core. However, "the upper and lower surfaces of the heat-conducting aluminum tube in the patent claim 2 should have grooves, and the function of the grooves is to ensure that the width of the upper and lower surfaces is consistent with the width of the heat-dissipating aluminum strips" is not the premise of above explanation. The functions of grooves on the left and right sides of the heat-conducting aluminum tube differ from ones on the upper and lower surfaces, and there is no necessary connection between them. Based on above reasons, Guowei Company and Jiang Guoping claimed: 1. Revoke the Civil Judgment of the Jiangsu Higher People's Court ((2016) Su Ming Final No. 105) ; 2. Confirm Linzhi Company's infringement and support all the claims of Guowei Company and Jiang Guoping in the first instance, which claims Linzhi Company should compensate Guowei Company and Jiang Guoping 15 million yuan including economic loss and reasonable expenses; 3. Linzhi Company shall bear all the litigation expenses of this case.

Linzhi Company claimed that Guowei Company and Jiang Guoping's petition for retrial is not justified and should be rejected. Main reasons are as follows: I. The patent claim 2 of has the implicit technical feature that there are grooves on the upper and lower surfaces. The "heat-conducting aluminum tube (1)" in the patent claim 2 and the "heat-conducting aluminum tube (1)" in claim 1 use the same identification, and they are exactly the same. Therefore, there is a reference relationship between claim 2 and claim 1 essentially. Combined with the description of the grooves (4) in the patent description, it can be sure that the "heat-conducting aluminum tube (1)" of claim 2 has grooves on the upper and lower surfaces. Besides, according to the description and examples of the advantages of the utility model patent in the description, the grooves on the left and right sides and the upper and lower surfaces of the heat-conducting aluminum tube must exist at the same time, and they depend on each other. There is an implicit technical feature in claim 2 that the "heat-conducting aluminum tube (1)" has grooves on the upper and lower surfaces. II. It is not a clerical error in the patent claim 2 that the heat-dissipating aluminum strips are pasted on the "left and right sides" of the heat-conducting aluminum tube in the heating core. According to the description, it is only a preferred solution, not the only solution, to stick the heat-dissipating aluminum strips on the upper and lower surfaces of the heat-conducting aluminum tube in the heating core. Moreover, there is no possible that the heat-dissipating aluminum strips cannot be pasted in a semicircular groove. It is easier for heat dissipation when the heat-dissipating aluminum strips are pasted on a bigger surface of the heating core. It is heat-conducting aluminum tube and its contact surface with the heating core that determine which place to paste the heat-dissipating aluminum strips. III. The alleged infringing products in this case did not fall into the scope of protection of patent claim 2. The alleged infringing products in this case is neither the same nor equivalent to multiple technical features of claim 2. The heat-conducting aluminum tubes of the alleged infringing products have no grooves on the upper and lower surfaces; the side grooves of the heat-conducting aluminum tube are not semicircular shape and are formed before being pressed, which are different from the corresponding technical features of the patent claim 2 in terms of technics and effect. Its heat sink is not glued but fixed by wedge grooves, which is not installed on the left and right sides of the heat-conducting aluminum tube, and its width is also smaller than that of the heat-conducting aluminum tube.

Guowei Company and Jiang Guoping instituted an action in Nanjing Intermediate People's Court, Jiangsu Province (the court of first instance), and claimed that: 1. Linzhi Company stopped the infringement immediately and destroyed the infringing products; Suning Company stopped selling the air conditioning machine containing the alleged infringing products; 2. Linzhi Company compensated Guowei Company and Jiang Guoping for economic losses and reasonable expenses totaling 15 million yuan; 3. Linzhi Company bears all litigation expenses.

The court of first instance found the following main facts:

1. The rights of Guowei Company and Jiang Guoping

Jiang Guoping applied to the National Intellectual Property Administration for a utility model patent for "a heat-conducting aluminum tube for a PTC heater and a PTC heater" on September 8, 2009. On June 2, 2010, the National Intellectual Property Administration granted him a utility model patent. The patent number is ZL200920230829.5 (the patent in this case). On June 23, 2010, Jiang Guoping signed a license contract with Guowei Company to authorize Guowei Company to exploit the patent exclusively. The contract is valid until the expiration date of the patent, and it is agreed that Guowei Company has the right to use litigation rights individually or collectively with Guowei Company.

In the first instance, Linzhi Company filed a request for invalidation to the Patent Reexamination Board of the National Intellectual Property Administration, and the Patent Reexamination Board of the National Intellectual Property Administration made the No. 24085 review decision on the request for invalidation on October 9, 2014 (hereinafter referred to as Decision No. 24085), declared that the patent rights was partially invalid. Claim 1 that maintains validity is: a heat-conducting aluminum tube for a PTC heater, the heat-conducting aluminum tube (1) has a cavity

(2) at both ends, and it is: there are grooves(4) on the upper and lower surfaces of the heat-conducting aluminum. The thickness of the aluminum tube wall (3) is 0–1.5 mm. Claim 2: a PTC heater, containing a heating core (10) and a heat-dissipating aluminum strip (11), characterized in that: the heating core (10) consists of a ceramic PTC heating element (5), an insulating ceramic sheet (6), the conductive electrode (7) and the insulating layer (8) pass through the back cavity of the heat-conducting aluminum tube (1) and then formed by pressing; the heat-dissipating aluminum strip (11) is pasted on the left and right sides of heat-conducting aluminum tube (1) in the heating core (10); after being pressed, the heat-conducting aluminum tube will form semicircular grooves (9) on the left and right sides respectively. Guowei Company and Jiang Guoping made it clear that the scope of their rights is the claim 2 which remains valid after invalidation review.

2. Linzhi Company and Suning Company and their alleged infringement

On October 18, 2013, Yuan Junhuan, a notary from the Notary Office of Yixing City, Jiangsu Province, and Xu Mingming, a notary worker, joined Guowei Company, Yue Qing, Jiang Guoping's authorized agents, and Wu Jie came to Suning Appliance Store on Middle Street, Lishui District, Nanjing City, Jiangsu Province. The agent Yue Qing picked up one TCL, Hisense and Midea air conditioner (including indoor unit and outdoor unit) in the electrical appliance store and obtained 3 the Jiangsu VAT special invoices and deduction corresponding to each air conditioner on the spot. The total price of TCL air conditioner is 1,699 yuan, Hisense is 2,799 yuan, and Midea is 2,299 yuan. After the delivery, the above-mentioned person brought the air conditioners and invoices to the notary office of Yixing City. In the parking lot of the notary office, the air-conditioning maintenance staff disassembled the air-conditioning indoor unit. The notary Yuan Junhuan seals the dismantled PTC heater and affixes the seal of the notary office. Yuan Junhuan took a total of 36 photos of the above delivery site, the delivered goods and the site where the air conditioner was disassembled. The above-mentioned process was carried out under the supervision of notary Yuan Junhuan and notary staff Xu Jianping. The Notary Office of Yixing City, Jiangsu Province issued a notarization certificate (2013) Xiyizheng Jingneizi No. 2592. Linzhi Company confirmed that the PTC heaters in air conditioners such as TCL purchased by notarized were the products it sold.

Comparing the alleged infringing products with the patent in this case. Guowei Company and Jiang Guoping believe that the "left and right sides" in claim 2 "the heat-dissipating aluminum strip (11) is pasted on the left and right sides of the heat-conducting aluminum tube (1) in the heating core (10)" is a clerical error. It can be seen from the description and drawings that it should be "upper and lower sides". There are grooves on the left and right sides of the alleged infringing products, and the alleged infringing products have a process of suppression. The claim does not limit that only left and right suppression falls into the scope of protection. At the same time, even if the left and right sides are slightly recessed before the suppression, it will not affect the alleged infringing products falling into the scope of protection. The grooves on the left and right sides are used to absorb the excess extension during the pressing process and make the products' structure more compact, and the shape is not very important. The alleged infringing products also contain the other technical features of claim 2, which fall into the scope of patent protection.

Linzhi Company claims: 1. It disagrees with the claim that there are clerical errors in the claims. The scope of patent protection in this case shall be subject to the content of claims. As long as the content of claims can express their meaning clearly, there is no necessity to cite the description and examples of explanation. Moreover, paragraph 0008 of the description also states clearly that it is "left and right sides", the description gives a preferred technical solution, and the drawings show the preferred solution, so Guowei Company and Jiang Guoping's claim of clerical errors cannot be established. 2. The grooves on the left and right sides of the alleged infringing products were formed in advance. There is a clear gap between the left and right sides of the aluminum tube and the heating core. The middle part of the upper and lower surfaces in contact with the heating core is raised slightly. Therefore, the heating position should be at the four corners of the aluminum tube, the purpose is to compact the upper and lower surfaces of the aluminum tube and the heating core to make them more closely to fit, not to form semicircular grooves. The role of the grooves in the alleged infringing products is different from the semicircular grooves' in the patent. And the grooves in the alleged infringing products are consistent with the technical features disclosed in the utility model patent documents of the patent number 200620034186.3. 3. The alleged infringing products are not semicircular grooves, and the grooves have various shapes such as U-shaped, V-shaped, and W-shaped. Therefore, the alleged infringing products did not fall into the scope of patent protection in claim 2 claimed by Guowei Company and Jiang Guoping.

Linzhi Company recognized that the aluminum tube and the heating core in the aluminum tube are close to each other and there is a suppression process, but what suppressed in the alleged infringing products are four corners of the aluminum tube.

Both parties agreed that the structure of the PTC heater obtained by the court of first instance from Linzhi Company, TCL Air Conditioner (Zhongshan) Co., Ltd., and Hisense (Shandong) Air Conditioning Co., Ltd. during the evidence preservation was basically the same as the above products.

3. The defense of Linzhi Company

Linzhi Company believes that the utility model patent documents with the patent number 200620034186.3 disclose the technical features of the alleged infringing products that the grooves of the alleged infringing products are pre-formed. Using the existing technology does not constitutes an infringement. At the same time, in order to maintain the validity of the patent in this case, Guowei Company and Jiang Guoping emphasized that the suppression of the grooves is the technical feature of the patent while the infringing products do not include this technical feature.

Guowei Company and Jiang Guoping believe that, first of all, the 200620034186.3 utility model patent has been compared in Decision No. 24085, and there is a clear conclusion to maintain the patent effective. Secondly, the "U"-shaped grooves disclosed in the 200620034186.3 utility model patent has not been suppressed, which is different from the semicircular grooves formed by the patent in this case.

4. Other identified circumstances

Guowei Company and Jiang Guoping confirmed that Linzhi Company sold the alleged infringing products up to 160 million yuan. According to: (1) the investigation transcript made by the court of first instance to Guangdong Midea Refrigeration Equipment Co., Ltd., a list of material codes issued by Guangdong Midea Refrigeration Equipment Co., Ltd. and the supply agreement with Linzhi Company; (2) Investigation transcript, material code list, copy of contract, etc. from the court of first instance to TCL Air Conditioner (Zhongshan) Co., Ltd.; (3) A copy of the statement issued by the Purchasing Department of Hisense (Zhejiang) Air Conditioning Co., Ltd.; (4) Investigation transcript, power of attorney, investigation order reply letter, summary sheet, certificate (2015) Yang You Zheng Min Nei Zi No. 992 and the physical objects made by the company and Jiang Guoping's agent. Linzhi Company claims that the product models in the two material code lists are different from the actual product models of the alleged infringing products and cannot be considered the same as the product structure in this case; the authenticity, legality and relevance of the explanation issued by Hisense (Zhejiang) Air Conditioning Co., Ltd. cannot be recognized, and the description does not tell what product is being supplied, which is not relevant to this case; only the names of Liu Zhongkai and Zhao Sheng are signed on the summary sheet, without the company seal and the signature of the legal representative, which will not be recognized, and whether the products on the summary sheet fall into the scope of patent protection cannot be reflected.

Guowei Company and Jiang Guoping also provided the "Report on the 2014 Corporate Information Disclosure and Attestation of Wuxi Guowei Ceramic Appliance Co., Ltd." issued by Yixing Zhengda Tax Office. Guowei Company and Jiang Guoping argued that the report confirmed the profit margin of the patent products produced by Guowei Company in this case was more than 30%. Given the sales of Linzhi Company, the amount of compensation claimed by Linzhi Company was reasonable. Linzhi Company disagreed with the authenticity, legality and relevance of the report.

In order to prove that the alleged infringing products it sold had a legal source, Suning provided the contract and invoice for its purchase of TCL air conditioners. Since Guowei Company, Jiang Guoping and Linzhi Company recognized the authenticity of the evidence and the purpose of proof, the fact that the alleged infringing products sold by Suning Company had a legal source was confirmed.

The court of first instance held that: (1) The interpretation of patent claim 2 in this case. In patent claim 2, the "left and right sides" in "the heat-dissipating aluminum strip (11) is pasted on the left and right sides of the heat-conducting aluminum tube (1) in the heating core (10)" is a clerical error and should be the "upper and lower sides". (2) The alleged infringing products in this case fall within the scope of protection of patent claim 2. The grooves on the infringing products in this case were further deformed after being pressed, which absorbed the extension of the aluminum tube in the width direction during the pressing process inevitably to make the structure of products more compact, which reflects the technical characteristics of the patent claim 2. Whether the grooves on the left and right sides of the alleged infringing products belong to semicircular grooves strictly does not affect the creative function of the heat-conducting aluminum tube to clamp the heating elements to improve the heat dissipation performance. Therefore, the alleged infringing products in this case fall into the scope of protection of patent claim 2. (3) Regarding the assumption of civil liability. Linzhi Company should stop the infringement immediately and destroy the infringing products, and Suning Company should stop selling the air conditioning machine containing the infringing products immediately. Given the evidence submitted by Guowei Company and Jiang Guoping could not prove that all the products sold by Linzhi Company were the alleged infringing products, it could not prove the profit obtained by Linzhi Company, and the evidence provided by Guowei Company and Jiang Guoping could not prove their losses due to Linzhi Company produced and sold infringing products. Therefore, the compensation amount should be based on the scope of compensation claimed by Guowei Company and Jiang Guoping, the general sales price of PTC heater products, profit margin, Linzhi Company's sales time, the nature of the infringement, and the expenses to stop the infringement. The specific compensation should be one million yuan. In summary, according to the provisions of Article 11, Paragraph 1, Article 59, Paragraph 1, and Article 65 of the Patent Law of the People's Republic of China, the court of first instance made following judgments: 1. Linzhi Company stopped producing and selling infringing products which infringed Guowei Company and Jiang Guoping's patent immediately, and destroyed the stock infringing products immediately; 2. Suning Company stopped selling the air conditioning machines that infringed the patent; 3. Linzhi Company shall compensate Guowei Company and Jiang Guoping's economic losses and reasonable expenses totaled one million yuan within ten days after the judgment became effective; 4. The other claims of Guowei Company and Jiang Guoping were rejected. The litigation expenses of 111,800 yuan shall be borne by Linzhi Company.

Guowei Company, Jiang Guoping and Linzhi Company were all dissatisfied and appealed to the Jiangsu Higher People's Court (the court of second instance). Guowei Company and Jiang Guoping requested the court to revoke the third item of the first instance judgment, and the sentence shall be changed to that Linzhi Company should compensate Guowei Company and Jiang Guoping for economic losses and reasonable expenses of 15 million yuan; Linzhi Company shall bear the litigation expenses of the first and second instances. The main facts and reasons are as follows: The first-instance judgment calculated the amount of infringement compensation without enough reasons. It did not analyze and explain the relevant evidence materials related to the infringing products in detail. It rejected believing and supporting the evidence provided by Guowei Company and Jiang Guoping and their claims based on these without convincing and sufficient reason.

Linzhi Company requested to revoke the judgment of the first instance, and dismiss the claims of Guowei Company and Jiang Guoping, and Guowei Company and Jiang Guoping should bear the litigation expenses of the first and second instance of this case. Main facts and reasons are as follows: I. There are many differences between the alleged infringing products and the patent in this case: 1. The upper and lower surfaces of the heat-conducting aluminum tube of the alleged infringing products did not have the grooves (4) that was extended to offset the pressing as ones in the patent claim 1.

2. The alleged infringing products did not have the heat-conducting aluminum tube (1) described in claim 2 of the patent. 3. The heat-dissipating aluminum strips of the alleged infringing product were fixed on the upper and lower surfaces by brazing or wedge grooves on the heat-conducting aluminum tube instead of the left and right sides as described in claim 2. 4. The grooves on the left and right sides of the alleged infringing products were not formed after pressing, but were formed before pressing, and the shapes of the grooves was inverted "人", and "U"-shaped, which are different from the semicircular shape in the patent no matter in time of shaping or the functions. 5. Patent claim 2 has the implicit technical feature that the width of the heat-conducting aluminum tube is the same as the width of the heat-dissipating aluminum strip. But they are different in the alleged infringing products. II. The first-instance judgment determined that the "heat-dissipating aluminum strips pasted on the left and right sides of the heat-conducting aluminum tube" in claim 2 of the patent was a clerical error, and facts identification was wrong. III. The analysis of the effects of the first-instance judgment on the grooves on the upper and lower surfaces and the semicircular grooves on the left and right sides is inconsistent with the description, which is an error in fact determination. IV. The first-instance judgment to confuse the "squeezing" of the alleged infringing products with the "suppression" in claim 2 is an error in finding facts. V. The first-instance judgment held that Linzhi's defense of existing technology was not in accordance with the facts. Linzhi Company cited evidence 5 in the invalidation decision in the first instance to prove that the U-shaped groove of the alleged infringing products was different from the semicircular grooves of the patent in this case, which was a defense of non-infringement. VI. In the invalidation procedure, the patentee of the patent made a limited interpretation of the patent claims in this case, that is, emphasized the difference and advantages of the semicircular grooves of the patent and the U-shaped grooves of the existing technology, which was adopted by the Patent Reexamination Board of the National Intellectual Property Administration. In this case, the principle of estoppel shall be applied, and the semicircular grooves of the patent in this case shall be interpreted consistent with the statement made by the patentee in the invalidation procedure. According to this interpretation, the U-shaped grooves of the alleged infringing products are inconsistent with the technical feature of the semicircular grooves of the patent in this case.

The court of second instance also found that: the upper and lower surfaces of the heat-conducting aluminum tube of the alleged infringing products were smooth, and a pair of inwardly closing flashes were provided on the left and right sides of the upper and lower surfaces, so that the upper and lower parts of the cross section of the heat-conducting aluminum tube form a dovetail groove. The flashes on both sides clamp the sides of the heat-dissipating aluminum strip, so that the heat-dissipating aluminum strips are fixed and close to the upper and lower surfaces of the heat-conducting aluminum tube. The grooves on the left and right sides of the alleged infringing products are inverted "人"-shaped grooves and "U"-shaped grooves. The width of the heat- dissipation aluminum strips are narrower than the width of the heat-conduction aluminum tube.

The Patent Reexamination Board of the National Intellectual Property Administration made Decision No. 24085 on October 9, 2014. Regarding the issue that the heat-dissipating aluminum strips are pasted on the left and right sides of the heat-conducting aluminum tube described in claim 2 of the patent, the decision is that: "According to the current limitation of claim 2, the left and right sides of the heat-conducting aluminum tube form semi-circular grooves after being pressed. It cannot form a plane, and the heat-dissipating aluminum strip cannot be pasted in a semicircular groove; that is, the above-mentioned technical features of claim 2 are obviously inconsistent. According to paragraph 0006 of the patent description, the upper and the lower surface of the heat-conducting aluminum tube in the PTC heater are provided with grooves. Paragraph 0007 records that the heat-conducting aluminum tube forms semicircular grooves on the left and right sides after being pressed. Paragraph 0010 describes the grooves on the surface of the aluminum tube and the semi-circular grooves on the side of the heating core offset the extension of the aluminum tube in the width direction, ensuring that the width of aluminum tube in the heating core after pressing is consistent with the width of the heat-dissipation strips. It can be seen that the semi-circular grooves on the left and right sides are for clamping and heating to ensure that the width of the upper and lower surfaces is consistent with the width of the heat-dissipation strips, it can be seen that the heat-dissipation strips should obviously be pasted on the upper and lower surfaces of the heat-conducting aluminum tube instead of the left and right sides. Figure 4 of this patent description can also support this conclusion. That is, according to the description, the obvious contradictory feature in claim 2 can be uniquely and correctly understood, which should be "a heat-dissipating aluminum strip pasted on the upper and lower surfaces of the heat-conducting aluminum tube in the heating core". The scope of protection of claim 2 can be clarified, and the following comments on invitation shall be subject to this scope of protection".

The court of second instance held that: I. The interpretation of the patent claims in this case. Guowei Company and Jiang Guoping asserted that the "left and right sides" in claim 2 "the heat-dissipating aluminum strip (11) is pasted on the left and right sides of the heat-conducting aluminum tube (1) in the heating core (10)" is a clerical error, which should be understood as "upper and lower surfaces". Decision No. 24085, combined with the relevant content of the patent description, determined that "according to the description, the obvious contradictory features in claim 2 can be uniquely and correctly understood, and it should be "a heat-dissipating aluminum strip pasted on the upper and lower surfaces of the heat-conducting aluminum tube in the heating core." This determination shall be the basis for the interpretation of Claim 2. The basis for reinterpreting the ambiguous content in the claims must be strictly limited to the scope of the claims, description and drawings. Moreover, in the process of argumentation for clarification or errata interpretation, those related technical features cited in the claims, descriptions and drawings as the prerequisites and intermediate conditions of the argument shall be regarded as implicit technical features. It has an effect on limiting the claims after clarification or correction. In this case, Decision No. 24085 made an errata interpretation of the position of the heat-dissipating aluminum strip in claim 2 that: "The semi-circular grooves on the left and right sides are used to clamp the heating core, and the grooves on the upper and lower surface of the aluminum tube are used to ensure that the width of the upper and lower surfaces is consistent with the width of the heat sink, and made a determination: "Based on this, it is clear that the heat sink should be pasted on the upper and lower surfaces of the heat-conducting aluminum tube instead of the left and right sides." Therefore, No. 24085 decided to determine the text description of the "left and right side" of the heat-dissipating aluminum strip in the patent claim 2 as a clerical error and correct it as "upper and lower surfaces". The precondition of above determination is that there must be grooves on the upper and lower surfaces of the heat-conducting aluminum tube in patent claim 2, and the function of the grooves is to ensure that the width of the upper and lower surfaces is consistent with the width of the heat-dissipation aluminum strip. If there is no such prerequisite, the correction of the "left and right sides" in the patent claim to "upper and lower surfaces" will lack a basis for argumentation. Therefore, although the patent claim 2 does not have the technical feature of "there are grooves on the upper and lower surfaces of the heat-conducting aluminum tube", it is due to the process of errata interpretation of the ambiguity of the text in claim 2." There are grooves on the upper and lower surfaces of the heat-conducting aluminum tube" and its function are used as a prerequisite for the demonstration. Therefore, it should be regarded as the implicit technical feature of claim 2, which should be considered its function of limitation to the scope of protection of claim 2. II. The technical comparison between the alleged infringing products and the patent right in this case. Although the patent claim 2 does not limit the presence of grooves on the upper and lower surfaces of the heat-conducting aluminum tube directly, due to the errata interpretation, the limitation function of the technical feature "there are grooves on the upper and lower surfaces of the heat-conducting aluminum tube respectively" must be considered. Because there are no grooves on the upper and lower surfaces of the heat-conducting aluminum tube of the alleged infringing products, and the grooves in the patent are not dispensable, it has the effect of "guaranteeing that the width of the upper and lower surfaces is consistent with the width of the heat sink". Therefore, the alleged infringing products lack the technical features implied in the patent claim 2 in this case: there also are grooves on the upper and lower surfaces of the heat-conducting aluminum tube, and the groove is to ensure that the width of the upper and lower surfaces is consistent with the width of the heat-dissipating aluminum strip. Therefore, according to the "full coverage principle", the alleged infringing products do not fall into the scope of protection of the patent claim 2 in this case. According to Article 7 of the Interpretation of the Supreme People's Court on Several Issues Concerning the Application of Law in the Trial of Patent Infringement Disputes, Article 4 of the Interpretation of the Supreme People's Court on Several Issues in the Application of Law in the Trial of Patent Infringement Dispute Cases (2), and Article 170, paragraph 1, item(2) of the Civil Procedure Law of the People's Republic of China, the court of second instance decided as follows: 1. Revoke the Civil Judgment of Nanjing Intermediate People's Court (2013) Ning Zhi Min Chu Zi No. 510; 2. Dismissed all claims of Guowei Company and Jiang Guoping. The litigation expenses of the first instance and the second instance are RMB 111,800 respectively, which shall be borne by Guowei Company and Jiang Guoping.

The retrial court found that: Guowei Company and Jiang Guoping filed a lawsuit with the court of first instance on November 20, 2013. They initially requested the court to judge Linzhi Company, TCL Air Conditioner (Zhongshan) Co., Ltd., and Suning Company to compensate for their economic losses of 1.05 million yuan jointly. On May 29, 2014, Guowei Company and Jiang Guoping withdrew the lawsuit against TCL Air Conditioner (Zhongshan) Co., Ltd. On August 28, 2015, Guowei Company and Jiang Guoping changed their litigation claim to Linzhi Company compensate their economic losses of 15 million yuan (including necessary investigation and evidence collection costs). During the first instance, according to the investigation order issued by the court of first instance, the agents of Guowei Company and Jiang Guoping went to Hisense (Shandong) Air Conditioning Co., Ltd. to investigate, and obtained the power of attorney issued by Hisense (Shandong) Air Conditioning Co., Ltd., the reply letter to the investigation order, and the summary tables, and electric heating samples, etc. Among them, the power of attorney was stamped with the seal of Hisense (Shandong) Air Conditioning Co., Ltd., which entrusted Liu Zhongkai and Zhao Sheng as the authorized agents of Hisense (Shandong) Air Conditioning Co., Ltd. and its authority included providing evidence or materials on behalf of Hisense. The reply letter to the investigation order was signed by Liu Zhongkai and Zhao Sheng, and its main content was 1407131, 1396701, 1422806, 1466479, 1496503, 149504, 1498572, 1819629, 1340556 and other nine types of ceramic PTC electric heaters supplied by Linzhi Company. There was no difference between the different models in the aluminum tube structure of the heating element. The summary table summarized the quantity and amount of nine types of electric heaters supplied by Linzhi Company to Hisense Pingdu, Huzhou, Shunde, and Jiangmen during 2011 to 2015 (among which, the amount of Pingdu base was 70,494,578.19 yuan and the amount of Huzhou base was 55,260,602.34 yuan including tax, the amount of Shunde base was 6,758,667.99 yuan and the amount of Jiangmen base was 129,828.75 yuan excluding tax), the total quantity was 558,588 pieces, and the total amount was about 132,643,677 yuan. In addition, according to the material codes and purchase quantities obtained by the court of first instance from Guangdong Midea Refrigeration Equipment Co., Ltd., Linzhi Company provided 302,499 heaters to Guangdong Midea Refrigeration Equipment Co., Ltd. from January 1, 2010 to November 28, 2013. The total amount was 4,138,570 yuan (the unit price did not indicate whether it includes tax). According to the statement issued by the Purchasing Department of Hisense (Zhejiang) Air Conditioning Co., Ltd., Linzhi Company supplied products of 24,374,094-yuan (including tax) to the Purchasing Department of Hisense (Zhejiang) Air Conditioning Co., Ltd. from January 1, 2012 to December 31, 2013. According to the supply list obtained by the court of first instance from the procurement department of the TCL air-conditioning division, Linzhi Company began to supply the procurement department of the TCL air-conditioning division in March 2012. By November 2013, the total supply amount was 8.43 million yuan (tax included). However, the aforementioned evidence provided by Guangdong Midea Refrigeration Equipment Co., Ltd., Hisense (Zhejiang) Air Conditioning Co., Ltd. Purchasing Department, and TCL Air Conditioning Division Purchasing Department did not indicate clearly whether the total involved supply amount was the amount of the alleged infringing products in this case. In the first trial on June 19, 2014, Linzhi Company stated that the profit margin of its products was about 10–15%. According to the company's products sales profit calculation table attached to the "Report on the 2014 Corporate Information Disclosure and Assurance of Wuxi Guowei Ceramic Appliance Co., Ltd." issued by Zhengda Tax Accountants Office in Yixing City, Jiangsu Province, among the 12 products of Guowei Company, the lowest sales profit margin was 16.54%, and the highest sales profit margin was 32.04%.

On August 21, 2014, the Patent Reexamination Board of the National Intellectual Property Administration conducted an oral hearing on Linzhi's request for invalidation of the patent in this case. On page 5 of the oral trial record form that day, the patentee's statement was recorded as follows: "The groove of Evidence 5 was different from the grooves of this patent. The U, W, and V-shaped grooves in the claims 3 and 4 of Evidence 5 were for fixing, while the function of this patent was to offset the extension of the width of the aluminum tube. Example 2 on page 4 of the description in Evidence 5 described the formation of the V-shaped groove. The V-shaped groove was formed before pressing. In the grooves of this patent, the heat-conducting aluminum tube would only form a groove after being pressed. The grooves in Evidence 5 were formed before pressing. The grooves on the left and right sides were formed after being pressed in this patent." In the statement of opinions submitted to the Patent Reexamination Board of the National Intellectual Property Administration, the patentee in this case also made a similar statement.

On September 28, 2014, the Patent Reexamination Board of the National Intellectual Property Administration made Decision No. 24085. Page 11 of the decision states: "Evidence 5 discloses a sealed positive temperature coefficient thermistor heater, including heating elements and motor terminals 4, the accommodating cavity 1 and the finned heat sink 11, the accommodating cavity 1 and the finned heat sink are an integral structure and are integrally processed from aluminum profiles. The finned heat sink is located on the outer surface of the housing cavity and heat elements is located in the cavity of the accommodating cavity 1. On two opposite sides of the accommodating cavity, a V-shaped groove is arranged along the axial direction of the accommodating cavity, and the bottom edge of the V-shaped groove is recessed into the cavity. The side surface of the V-shaped groove and the side surface of the finned heat sink are perpendicular to each other. Through the plastic forming method, the containing cavity is processed in the direction perpendicular to the surface of the V groove using a stamping die, which makes the containing cavity deform and shrink to the inside, and the force is continuously adjustable to ensure good and close contact between the two metal electrode plates 6 and each PTC thermistor 8 (temperature coefficient thermistor), and good contact with the accommodating cavity, to improve heat transfer efficiency and heating performance. In order to compress the heating element in the accommodating cavity evenly, a pressing groove for recessing the accommodating cavity is arranged on the edge of the accommodating cavity. The edges of the cavity refer to the four edges of a rectangular body; the V-shaped groove can also be a U-shaped groove. Therefore, Evidence 5 disclosed the feature of making the U-shaped groove, that is, a semi-circular groove on the sides of the aluminum tube in the PTC heater. However, in Evidence 5, this groove is not used to absorb the widthwise extension of the aluminum tube during the pressing process. Since the finned heat sink and the accommodating cavity are an integrated structure, the operation of pressing the accommodating cavity from the upper and lower surfaces from which the finned heat sink is scooped out cannot be realized. Therefore, in the structure of evidence 5, it is necessary to provide a U-shaped groove before pressing the aluminum tube to provide a continuously adjustable pressing force, so that the U-shaped groove is moved up and down after the heating element is introduced into the containing cavity. Squeezing makes it provide an up and down pressing force to evenly compress the heating elements in the cavity. In this patent, the semicircular grooves on the left and right sides of the aluminum tube are formed after being pressed. Therefore, when the heating element is introduced into the aluminum tube, the semicircular groove may not be formed temporarily or slightly recessed. Thereby it is smoother and safer, and will not be scratched; and after the semi-circular groove is formed after pressing, the gap between the aluminum tube and the heating element is smaller, thereby eliminating the hidden danger of loose fittings; and setting the semicircular groove can make the width of the upper and lower surfaces of the aluminum tube after being pressed consistent with the width of the heat dissipation strip completely. None of these technical effects can be achieved by the U-shaped groove structure of Evidence 5. Therefore, the U-shaped groove of Evidence 5 cannot be equivalent to the 'semicircular groove' of this patent."

Paragraph 0010 on page 2 of the patent description of this case records the beneficial effects of the present invention, including: the technical solution of the present invention makes the product structure more compact; the components are more firmly bonded after being pressed, and the thermal conductivity is improved; the matching gap between the fittings in the cavity and the inner wall of the aluminum tube side is reduced, which eliminates the safety hazards of loose fittings caused by external forces and the jitter of the whole machine and improves the reliability of the product; the product structure is reasonable, the production is simple, and the installation and maintenance are convenient and safe to use.

The retrial court held that, based on the retrial applicants' application for retrial and the facts of the case, the focus of the case at the retrial stage is: whether the interpretation of the patent claim 2 in the second-instance judgment is correct; whether the alleged infringing products fall into the scope of protection of patent claim 2; the assumption of civil liability for tort in this case. Therefore, the analysis is as follows:

1. Whether the interpretation of claim 2 of the patent in the second-instance judgment is correct.

This question includes two interrelated aspects: on the one hand, whether the statement that the heat-dissipating aluminum strips are pasted on the "left and right sides" of the heat-conducting aluminum tube in the heating core in claim 2 is an obvious error that can be corrected; on the other hand, whether claim 2 should have the implicit technical feature of "there are grooves on the upper and lower surfaces of the heat-conducting aluminum tube respectively".

First of all, whether the description that the heat-dissipating aluminum strips are pasted on the "left and right sides" of the heat-conducting aluminum tube in the heating core in claim 2 is an obvious error that can be corrected. Article 4 of the "Interpretation of the Supreme People's Court on Several Issues Concerning the Application of Law in the Trial of Patent Infringement Dispute Cases (2)" states: "When the grammar, words, punctuation, graphics, symbols, etc. in the claims, descriptions and drawings are ambiguous, if a person of ordinary skill in the art can obtain the only understanding by reading the claims, the descriptions and the drawings, the people's court shall make a determination based on the only understanding." Referring to this provision, the obvious errors that can be corrected require two conditions: One is that a person of ordinary skill in the art can recognize that there are ambiguities or errors in the description of the patent application documents or the drawings; The other is that the person of ordinary skill in the art can obtain the only understanding to resolve the ambiguity or the error by reading the claims, descriptions and drawings. In this case, Guowei Company and Jiang Guoping asserted that the "left and right sides" of "the heat-dissipating aluminum strips (11) are pasted on the left and right sides of the heat-conducting aluminum tube (1) in the heating core (10)" in claim 2 is a clerical error, which should be understood as "upper and lower surfaces". As to whether this proposition can be established, our analysis is as follows: Firstly, according to the technical solution described in claim 2, after the heat-conducting aluminum tube is pressed, a semicircular groove is formed on the left and right sides instead of a plane. Because the role of the heat-dissipation aluminum strips are to conduct the heat of the heating core, even if the heat-dissipation aluminum strip can be pasted in a semicircular groove, this pasting method does not conform to the basic principle of heat dissipation and conduction obviously, and it cannot be effective. Therefore, a person of ordinary skill in the art can realize that there is an error in pasting the heat-dissipating aluminum strip on the left and right sides of the heat-conducting aluminum tube. Secondly, the record in paragraph 0008 of the patent description of this case further highlights this error and gives hints to resolve the error. Paragraph 0008 of the description of the patent states: "The heat-dissipating aluminum strips are pasted on the left and right sides of the heat-conducting aluminum tube in the heating core; ... In order to meet the safety requirements of split air conditioners with small installation space, it is preferable to use a row of corrugated heat-dissipating aluminum strips pasted on the upper and lower surfaces of the heat-conducting aluminum tube in the heating core respectively." Above description is based on the fact that the heat-dissipating aluminum strips are pasted on the left and right sides of the heat-conducting aluminum tube in the heating core. However, the pasting position of the heat-dissipating aluminum strips are expressed as "on the upper and lower surfaces of the heat-conducting aluminum tube in the heating core" in the preferable solution. This record not only hints that claim 2 has an error in the pasting position of the heat-dissipating aluminum strip, but also gives hints on the correct solution. Finally, paragraph 0021 of the patent description and its drawings further give the only answer to the error. Paragraph 0021 of the patent description in this case states: "The heater shown in Fig. 4 is composed of a corrugated heat sink with the same width as the surface of the heating core 10 on the upper and lower surfaces provided with grooves." At the same time, Figs. 4 and 6 show that the heat-dissipating aluminum strips are pasted on the upper and lower surfaces of the heat-conducting aluminum tube in the heating core. Therefore, the heat-dissipating aluminum strips should be pasted on the upper and lower surfaces of the heat-conducting aluminum tube obviously instead of the left and right sides. In the patent claim 2 of this case, "left and right sides" of "the heat-dissipating aluminum strip (11) is pasted on left and right sides of the heat-conducting aluminum tube (1) in the heating core (10)." is indeed a clerical error of the "upper and lower surfaces", which is an obvious error that can be corrected.

Secondly, whether claim 2 should have the implicit technical feature that "there are grooves on the upper and lower surfaces of the heat-conducting aluminum tube respectively, and the function of the grooves is to ensure that the width of the upper and lower surfaces is consistent with the width of the heat-dissipating aluminum strip." The second-instance judgment held that the prerequisite for determining the "left and right sides" as a clerical error of the "upper and lower surfaces" is: There are grooves on the upper and lower surfaces of the heat-conducting aluminum tube in patent claim 2, and the function of the grooves is to ensure that the width of the upper and lower surfaces is consistent with the width of the heat-dissipating aluminum strip. If there is no such prerequisite, the correction of the "left and right sides" to the "upper and lower surface" in the patent claim 2 will lack of argumentation basis. Therefore, although the patent claim 2 in this case does not have the technical feature of "there are grooves on the upper and lower surfaces of the heat-conducting aluminum tube respectively", it should be regarded as the implicit technical feature of claim 2, which has the function of limiting the scope of protection of claim 2. This court believes that the so-called implied technical features in the second-instance judgment actually introduced content that was not clearly recorded in the claims as a precondition for corrections when interpreting the meaning of the technical features of the claims. Introducing the content that is not recorded in the claims clearly should be particularly cautious when interpreting claims as this introduction will limit the scope of protection of the claims generally. Specific to this case, whether "there are grooves on the upper and lower surfaces of the heat-conducting aluminum tube, which is to ensure that the width of the upper and lower surfaces is consistent with the width of the heat-dissipating aluminum strips" is the premise of determining that the "left and right sides" is the typo of the "upper and lower surfaces", which should be corrected, about the position of pasting heat-dissipating aluminum strip in the patent claim 2. First of all, based on the aforementioned statement that the heat-dissipating aluminum strips are pasted on the "left and right sides" of the heat-conducting aluminum tube in the heating core in the patent claim 2, it is an obvious error that can be corrected. There are grooves on the upper and lower surfaces of the heat-conducting aluminum tube is not a premise to identify and correct this obvious error. Secondly, the grooves on the upper and lower surfaces of the heat-conducting aluminum tube in claim 1 and the semicircular grooves formed on the left and right sides of the heat-conducting aluminum tube in claim 2 have different functions, and they are not directly related. In this case, paragraph 0006 of the patent description records that there are grooves on the upper and lower surfaces of the heat-conducting aluminum tube of the PTC heater respectively; paragraph 0007 records that the semicircle grooves will form on the left and right sides of the heat-conducting aluminum tube after being pressed; Paragraph 0010 records that the grooves on the surface of the aluminum tube and the semicircular groove on the side of the aluminum tube heating core offset the extension in the width direction of the aluminum tube, ensuring the width of the heat-conducting aluminum tube in the heating core is the same as the width of the heat-dissipation aluminum after being pressed. It can be seen that the semicircular grooves on the left and right sides of the heat-conducting aluminum tube are used to clamp the heating core, and the grooves on the upper and lower surfaces are used to ensure that the width of the upper and lower surfaces after being pressed is consistent with the width of the heat sink. Therefore, the semicircular grooves on the left and right sides of the heat-conducting aluminum tube and the grooves on the upper and lower surfaces of the aluminum tube play different roles, and there is no synergy between the two, and neither of them is based on the existence of each other. Finally, Decision No. 24085 did not presuppose the existence of grooves on the upper and lower surfaces of the heat-conducting aluminum tube when correcting the obvious error of claim 2. Decision No. 24085 made an errata interpretation of the position of the heat-dissipating aluminum strips in claim 2 that: "According to the current limitation of claim 2, the left and right sides of the heat-conducting aluminum tube are formed with semicircular grooves after being pressed and cannot be formed a flat surface, the heat-dissipating aluminum strip cannot be pasted in a semicircular groove, that is, the description of above-mentioned feature of claim 2 is obviously inconsistent." Therefore, the reason for the clerical error in claim 2 in Decision No. 24085 is only "After the heat-conduction aluminum tube is pressed, semicircular grooves are formed on the left and right sides and cannot form a flat surface." While there is no necessary connection of whether the upper and lower surfaces of the heat-conducting aluminum tube are provided with grooves. Therefore, the second-instance judgment found that the patent claim 2 in this case implies a technical feature that "There are grooves on the upper and lower surfaces of the heat-conducting aluminum tube respectively, and the function of the grooves is to ensure that the width of the upper and lower surfaces is consistent with the width of the heat-dissipating aluminum strip", which lacks factual basis.

In summary, the second-instance judgment made an error regarding the scope of protection of patent claim 2 in this case. Guowei Company and Jiang Guoping's application for retrial is justified and should be supported.

2. Whether the alleged infringing products fall into the scope of protection of patent claim 2

The patent claim 2 in this case can be divided into the following technical features: a PTC heater (feature A), including a heating core (feature B) and a heat-dissipating aluminum strip (feature C); the heating core is made of ceramic PTC heating elements and insulating ceramic sheet, the conductive electrode and the insulating layer pass through the back cavity of the heat-conducting aluminum tube and then pressed to form (feature D); the heat-dissipating aluminum strips are pasted on the left and right sides of the heat-conducting aluminum tube in the heating core (feature E); After being pressed, semicircular grooves (feature F) are formed on the left and right sides of the heat-conducting aluminum tube respectively.

Based on the defenses raised by Linzhi Company during the original trial, it believes that the alleged infringing products have the following technical characteristics different from the patent claim 2 of this case: there is no groove on the upper and lower surfaces of the heat-conducting aluminum tube of the alleged infringing products, while there are grooves on the upper and lower surfaces of the heat-conducting aluminum tube in the patent claim 2 (distinguishing feature 1); the heat-dissipating aluminum strips of the alleged infringing products are fixed on the upper and lower surfaces by brazing or wedge grooves on the heat-conducting aluminum tube, while the heat-dissipating aluminum strips are pasted on the left and right sides of the heat-conducting aluminum tube in the patent claim 2 (distinguishing feature 2); the grooves on the left and right sides of the alleged infringing products are not formed after being pressed, but have been formed before pressing, and the shapes of the grooves are inverted "人" and U-shaped, compared with the semicircular groove in claim 2 of the patent, their formation time, shape and function are all different (distinguishing feature 3); The width of the heat-conducting aluminum tube is different from the width of the heat-dissipating strips in the alleged infringing products, and claim 2 of the patent in this case has the implicit technical feature that "the width of the heat-conducting aluminum tube and the heat-dissipating aluminum bar are the same" (distinguishing feature 4). In addition, Linzhi Company also maintains that the principle of estoppel should be applied in this case. The patentee has made a limited interpretation of the patent claims in the invalidation procedure, which emphasizes the difference and advantages of the semicircular grooves of the patent compared with the existing technologies, which were adopted by the Patent Reexamination Board of the National Intellectual Property Administration. The U-shaped grooves of the alleged infringing products were inconsistent with the semicircular groove of the patent in this case. The so-called distinguishing feature 1, 2, and 4 of Linzhi Company are related to the interpretation of patent claim 2; the so-called distinguishing feature 3 is related to the estoppel principle it advocates. Therefore, our court makes following analysis:

First of all, the so-called distinguishing characteristics 1 and 4 by Linzhi Company. Distinguishing feature 1 that "There are no grooves on the upper and lower surfaces of the heat-conducting aluminum tube of the alleged infringing products" and the distinguishing feature 4 that "The width of the heat-conducting aluminum tube of the alleged infringing products is inconsistent with the width of the heat-dissipating aluminum strip" are both related to the "implicit technical features" of patent claim 2 introduced by the second instance judgment. As mentioned earlier, the second-instance judgment found that the patent claim 2 in this case implies a technical feature that "There are grooves on the upper and lower surfaces of the heat-conducting aluminum tube respectively, and the function of the grooves is to ensure that the width of the upper and lower surfaces is consistent with the width of the heat-dissipating aluminum strips", which lacks factual basis. The patent claim 2 of this case does not imply the above technical feature. Therefore, the so-called distinguishing features 1 and 4 by Linzhi Company are not the difference between the technical solution of the alleged infringing products and claim 2 of this case.

Secondly, regarding the so-called distinguishing feature 2 by Linzhi Company. The second distinguishing feature "The heat-dissipating aluminum strips of the alleged infringing products are fixed on the upper and lower surfaces by brazing or by wedge grooves on the heat-conducting aluminum tube", which is related to the feature E of patent claim 2 that "The heat-dissipating aluminum strips are pasted on the left and right sides of the heat-conducting aluminum tube in the heating core." As mentioned above, the "left and right sides" in claim 2 is indeed a clerical error of the "upper and lower surfaces", which should be corrected to "upper and lower surfaces". Therefore, the so-called distinguishing feature by Linzhi Company is only in the fixing method of the heat-dissipating aluminum strips of the alleged infringing products, that is, the heat-dissipating aluminum strips of the alleged infringing products are fixed on the upper and lower surfaces by brazing or wedge grooves on the heat-conducting aluminum tube. And in the feature E of patent claim 2, the heat-dissipating aluminum strips are "pasted" on the upper and lower surfaces of the heat-conducting aluminum tube. This issue involves the interpretation of "pasted" in the feature E of patent claim 2. The interpretation of patent claims must be understood from the perspective of those skilled in the art and combined with the information given in the description. The purpose of this patent is to provide a thermally conductive aluminum tube of a PTC heater with a lower cost and a more reasonable structure and a PTC heater with better thermal conductivity and better insulation performance according to the description of the purpose of the patent. In order to achieve this purpose, those skilled in the art can understand that the heat-dissipating aluminum strips are "pasted" on the upper and lower surfaces of the heat-conducting aluminum tube in feature E is to make the heating core and the aluminum strips fit fully to ensure that the heat of the heating core can pass out by the heat-dissipating aluminum strips efficiently. Therefore, "pasted" here should be understood as "fitting". As for the way to achieve the fitting between the heating core and the heat-dissipating aluminum strips, there is no strict limitation, and it can be welding, wedge fixing, or other means such as adhesive. It can be seen that the feature of the alleged infringing products that "the heat-dissipating aluminum strips are fixed on the upper and lower surfaces by brazing or through the wedge grooves on the heat-conducting aluminum tube" is the same as the feature E of claim 2 in this case that "The mentioned heat-dissipating aluminum strips are pasted on the upper and lower surfaces of the heat-conducting aluminum tube in the heating core."

Thirdly, regarding the so-called distinguishing feature 3 by Linzhi Company and the application of the principle of estoppel. Above points are related to the feature F of claim 2 that "The heat-conducting aluminum tube will form semicircular grooves on the left and right sides after being pressed respectively". Linzhi Company claimed that the grooves on the left and right sides of the alleged infringing products had been formed before being pressed, not after being pressed, and the shape of grooves was an inverted "人" or "U". Compared with the semicircular grooves, the forming time, shape and function are all different. First of all, regarding the explanation of the feature F of claim 2. According to the patent description, "the heat-conducting aluminum tube is formed with semicircular grooves on the left and right sides after being pressed" is to offset the extension of the heat-conducting aluminum tube in the width direction during pressing, and to ensure that the fitting gap between the internal fittings of the thermally conductive aluminum tube cavity and the inner wall of the aluminum tube side is reduced, making the structure of products more compact. Therefore, the semicircular groove in the feature F needs a pressing process, and the deformation in the inward direction occurs during the pressing process, which is formed after being pressed. As for whether there are grooves on the left and right sides of the heat-conducting aluminum tube and the shape of the grooves before being pressed, which are not limited in the feature F of claim 2. Secondly, regarding the formation time and function of the grooves on the left and right sides of the alleged infringing products. According to Linzhi's statement in the original trial, the grooves on the left and right sides of the alleged infringing products were pre-formed, but the four corners of the heat-conducting aluminum tube need to be pressed, which makes the grooves further deformed to compress the upper and lower surfaces of the aluminum tube and the heating core to make them more fit. It can be seen that even if the grooves on the left and right sides of the alleged infringing products are pre-formed, there is still a pressing process, and the grooves will deform inwardly during the pressing process, which absorbs the width direction extension of the aluminum tube during the pressing process. This is the same as the function of the semicircular grooves in the feature F of claim 2 of this case. Moreover, there is no limitation on whether there are grooves on the left and right sides of the heat-conducting aluminum tube before being pressed in the feature F of claim 2. Besides, regarding the shape of the grooves on the left and right sides of the alleged infringing products. The shape of the grooves on the left and right sides of the alleged infringing products are inverted "人" or "U". As mentioned above, the main function of the "semicircular grooves" on the left and right sides of the heat-conducting aluminum tube after being pressed in the feature F of claim 2 is to offset the extension of the heat-conducting aluminum tube in the width direction during pressing to make the structure of the products more compact. The inverted "人"-shaped grooves or "U"-shaped grooves on the left and right sides of the alleged infringing products also deformed during the pressing process, absorbing the width of the aluminum tube during the pressing process, making the product structure more compact. It can be seen that the inverted "人"-shaped grooves or "U"-shaped grooves on the left and right sides of the alleged infringing products have the same function as the "semicircular grooves" in feature F and achieve the same effect. At the same time, the inverted "人"-shaped grooves or the "U"-shaped grooves and the semicircular grooves are all inwardly recessed to absorb the width direction extension of the aluminum tube during the pressing process. The methods are basically the same, which can be thought by those of ordinary skill in the art without creative work. Therefore, the alleged infringing products have equivalent features to the feature F of claim 2 that "There will form the semicircular grooves on the left and right sides of the heat-conducting aluminum tube after being pressed". Finally, regarding the application of the so-called estoppel principle by Linzhi Company. According to the facts ascertained by this court, during the patent invalidation process in this case, the patentee claimed that the grooves of the patent in this case have different function from the grooves of Evidence 5. In Evidence 5, the function of the "U", "W" and "V" shaped grooves are to fix the component, while the function of the semicircular grooves of the patent is to offset the extension of the aluminum tube in the width direction; the grooves of the patent are formed after the heat-conducting aluminum tube is pressed, while the V-shaped grooves of Evidence 5 are formed before the pressing. The above-mentioned claims of different function were recognized by Decision No. 24085. Regarding the patentee's claim that the above-mentioned grooves in the patent were formed after being pressed, while the V-shaped grooves of Evidence 5 were formed before the suppression, Decision No. 24085 believes that since the solution of Evidence 5 cannot realize the pressing operation of the accommodating cavity from the upper and lower surfaces of the finned fins, the structure of Evidence 5 needs to set a "U" groove before pressing the aluminum tube to provide continuous adjustable pressing force, and the patent in this case can temporarily not form a semicircular groove or just a slight depression when the heating element is introduced into the aluminum tube. The semi-circular grooves on the left and right sides of the aluminum tube are formed after being pressed. It can be seen that although the patentee emphasized the role and formation time of the semicircular grooves on the left and right sides of the heat-conducting aluminum tube of the patent during the process of patent invalidation, it did not rule out the existence of specific-shaped grooves on the left and right sides of the heat-conducting aluminum tube before being pressed completely. At the same time, Decision No. 24085 affirms that the left and right sides of the heat-conducting aluminum tube in the patent can be slightly recessed before being pressed. Therefore, the patentee's statement in the invalidation procedure did not abandon the technical solution that there are grooves of specific shapes on the left and right sides of the heat-conducting aluminum tube before being pressed. Decision No. 24085 further affirmed that the patent in this case includes the technical solution that there are grooves of specific shapes on the left and right sides of the heat-conducting aluminum tube before being pressed. The statement made by the patentee during the invalidation procedure did not lead to the so-called legal effect of estoppel.

Except for the above-mentioned reasons, Linzhi Company did not raise other differences between the alleged infringing products and the patents claim 2 in this case. The court found that the alleged infringing products had other technical features of claim 2 in this case.

In summary, the alleged infringing products in this case have the same or equivalent technical features as the patent claim 2 in this case and fall within the scope of protection of the patent claim 2.

3. The civil liability for tort in this case

Since the alleged infringing products fall into the scope of protection of patent claim 2, according to the litigation requests of Guowei Company and Jiang Guoping, the respondent Linzhi Company and Suning Company shall bear corresponding civil liabilities. Regarding the specific manner of assuming civil liability, combined with the claims of Guowei Company and Jiang Guoping, the analysis and judgment are as follows:

Firstly, the litigation request to stop infringing. The alleged infringing products fall within the scope of protection of patent claim 2 in this case, and Linzhi Company and Suning Company should bear the civil liability for stopping the infringement. Stopping producing and selling infringing products is one of the necessary measures to stop the infringement. Regarding Guowei Company and Jiang Guoping's request to order Linzhi Company to stop producing and selling the alleged infringing products immediately, and Suning Company stopped selling the air conditioning machine containing the infringing products immediately, this court supports it. If Linzhi Company has the infringing products at present, it should be destroyed to prevent the infringing products from entering the sales channel. This court supports Guowei Company and Jiang Guoping's lawsuit requesting Linzhi Company to destroy infringing products.

Secondly, the litigation request for compensation for losses and reasonable expenses of stopping the infringement. Guowei Company and Jiang Guoping requested to order Linzhi Company to pay compensation for economic losses and reasonable expenses of stopping the infringement total 15 million yuan. Guowei Company and Jiang Guoping claimed that the damages in this case should be calculated based on Linzhi Company's interests of infringing. The calculation method is: Linzhi Company's total sales amount of infringing products is 169,556,341 yuan multiplied by 15% of the infringing products profit margin, resulting in an infringement profit of approximately 25.43 million yuan. Accordingly, Guowei Company and Jiang Guoping believe that the amount of compensation claimed by them is reasonable. In this regard, our analysis is as follows:

First of all, regarding the reasonableness of the calculation method of compensation claimed by Guowei Company and Jiang Guoping. 1. regarding the total sales amount of the infringing products of Linzhi Company claimed by Guowei Company and Jiang Guoping. Guowei Company and Jiang Guoping claimed that the total sales amount of Linzhi Company's infringing products was 169,556,341 yuan. This amount includes the amount to Guangdong Midea Refrigeration Equipment Co., Ltd., Hisense (Zhejiang) Air Conditioning Co., Ltd. Purchasing Department, Hisense (Shandong) Air Conditioning Co., Ltd., and TCL Air Conditioning Division Purchasing Department supplied by Linzhi Company, while the evidence provided by the Guangdong Midea Refrigeration Equipment Co., Ltd., the procurement department of Hisense (Zhejiang) Air Conditioning Co., Ltd. and the procurement department of TCL Air Conditioning Division did not show that the supply amount involved was all the supply amount of the alleged infringing products in this case. At the same time, the total sales amount of the product includes both the tax-included amount (for example, the amount of Hisense Pingdu base and Huzhou base is tax-included) and the non-tax-included amount (for example, the amount of Hisense Shunde base and Jiangmen base is not including tax). Therefore, the total sales amount of Linzhi Company's infringing products claimed by Guowei Company and Jiang Guoping is not accurate. 2. regarding the calculation method of compensation claimed by Guowei Company and Jiang Guoping. Guowei Company and Jiang Guoping claimed that the total sales amount of infringing products should be multiplied by the profit margin of infringing products as the method of calculating compensation. The total sales amount of the infringing products multiplied by the profit margin of the infringing products is the sales profit of the infringing products, which is not the profit made by the infringer due to the infringement for sure. The reason is that in addition to the use of technical solutions of the patents, the profit source of the alleged infringing products may come from other patents or other components. Therefore, it is necessary to consider the contribution of the patent in this case to the profit of the infringing products. Given above point, this court will consider the calculation method of compensation proposed by Guowei Company and Jiang Guoping after excluding the influence of the above-mentioned unreasonable factors.

Secondly, the calculation of the total sales amount of Linzhi's infringing products. Guowei Company and Jiang Guoping submitted evidence of the quantity and amount of goods supplied by Linzhi Company to Guangdong Midea Refrigeration Equipment Co., Ltd., Hisense (Zhejiang) Air Conditioning Co., Ltd. Purchasing Department, Hisense (Shandong) Air Conditioning Co., Ltd. and TCL Air Conditioning Division Purchasing Department. 1. Evidence regarding Linzhi's supply to Guangdong Midea Refrigeration Equipment Co., Ltd., Hisense (Zhejiang) Air Conditioning Co., Ltd. Purchasing Department and TCL Air Conditioning Division Purchasing Department. Although the Linzhi Company's supply evidence issued by Guangdong Midea Refrigeration Equipment Co., Ltd. and TCL's Air Conditioning Division's Purchasing Department recorded the material code, it is still difficult to determine the proportion of the alleged infringing products based on the code. The evidence issued by the Purchasing Department of Hisense (Zhejiang) Air Conditioning Co., Ltd. only recorded the amount of supply, and it is also difficult to determine the proportion of the alleged infringing products. Therefore, it is difficult for this court to use these three evidences as the basis for calculating the amount of compensation. For these three evidences, this court will determine the amount of compensation in accordance with the method of statutory compensations. 2. Evidence regarding Linzhi Company's supply to Hisense (Shandong) Air Conditioning Co., Ltd. Hisense (Shandong) Air Conditioning Co., Ltd. not only provided evidence of the supply quantity and amount of the nine models supplied by Linzhi Company, but also provided physical evidence of the related seven models, and clearly stated that there is no difference between all 9 models in aluminum tube structure in the heating object. Since Linzhi Company did not provide evidence to the contrary, this court presumed that the quantity and sales number of products supplied by Linzhi Company provided by Hisense (Shandong) Air Conditioning Co., Ltd. were the quantity and sales amount of the infringing products in this case. According to the evidence provided by Hisense (Shandong) Air Conditioning Co., Ltd., Linzhi Company supplied nine types of electric heaters to Hisense Pingdu, Huzhou, Shunde, and Jiangmen from 2011 to 2015, of which the total supply amount of Pingdu and Huzhou bases is 125,755,180.53 yuan (tax included), and the total supply amount of Shunde and Jiangmen bases is 6,688,496.74 yuan (excluding tax). Since the total sales amount of the products supplied by Linzhi Company provided by Hisense (Shandong) Air Conditioning Co., Ltd. includes both the tax-included amount of Hisense Pingdu Base and Huzhou Base, and the non-tax-included amount of Hisense Shunde Base and Jiangmen Base, the tax-included amount of Hisense Pingdu Base and Huzhou Base should be converted into non-tax-included amount. According to Article 2 of the Interim Regulations on Value-Added Tax of the People's Republic of China (implemented on January 1, 2009), as a manufacturing and processing enterprise, Linzhi Company shall pay a VAT rate of 17%. After deducting the corresponding value-added tax, the total sales amount (excluding tax) of the infringing products sold by Linzhi Company to Hisense (Shandong) Air Conditioning Co., Ltd. was about 114,371,557 yuan.

Again, regarding Linzhi's profit margin for selling infringing products. Linzhi Company stated in the first instance of this case that the profit margin of its products is about 10–15%. According to the "Report on the 2014 Corporate Information Disclosure and Attestation of Wuxi Guowei Ceramic Appliance Co., Ltd." issued by Zhengda Tax Accountant Office of Yixing City, Jiangsu Province, among the 12 products of Guowei Company, the lowest sales profit margin is 16.54%, and the highest sales profit margin is 32.04%. Given the highest profit margin claimed by Linzhi Company and the lowest profit margin claimed by Guowei Company, this court has determined that the profit margin of the alleged infringing products is 15%.

Finally, regarding the contribution of the patent to the profit of the infringing products. According to the record of the beneficial effects of the invention in the patent description, the beneficial effects related to the technical solution of the patent claim 2 of this case include a more compact product structure, a firmer combination of various accessories after pressing, improved thermal conductivity, and reduced security hazards of loosening accessories, improved reliability of products and costs of production, etc. Therefore, the patent in this case has played an important role in the market attractiveness of Linzhi's PTC heater. At the same time, given that it is the semicircular grooves on the left and right sides of the heat-conducting aluminum tube after being pressed in patent claim 2 that realize above beneficial effects, while there are other components in the PTC heater. So, it is inappropriate to attribute all profits to the patent in this case. In the case that Linzhi Company refused to participate in the trial without justifiable reasons, this court determined that the contribution of the patent to the profit of Linzhi Company's infringing products was 50%.

Based on the above analysis, this court calculates the profit acquired by Linzhi Company through the infringement during the process of selling the alleged infringing products to Hisense (Shandong) Air Conditioning Co., Ltd. as follows: 114,371,557 yuan × 15% × 50% = 8 57,7 86,7 yuan.

Thirdly, regarding the calculation of compensation for Linzhi's supply of goods to Guangdong Midea Refrigeration Equipment Co., Ltd., Hisense (Zhejiang) Air Conditioning Co., Ltd. Purchasing Department and TCL Air Conditioning Division Purchasing Department. As mentioned earlier, since the existing evidence is insufficient to prove the proportion of the alleged infringing products in the total sales of Linzhi Company to the above three units, it is difficult to determine the losses of Guowei Company and Jiang Guoping, and the benefits acquired by Linzhi Company through the infringement. And there is no reasonable patent license fee for reference. This court will determine the damage compensation for Linzhi Company's sales of the alleged infringing products to the above three units in accordance with the statutory compensations amount. Given that the patent in this case is a utility model patent, Linzhi Company is engaged in the production and sales of the alleged infringing products, and the scale is large, this court decided that Linzhi Company shall compensate the patentees Guowei Company and Jiang Guoping for economic losses of 800,000 yuan due to its infringement that it sold the alleged infringing products to Guangdong Midea Refrigeration Equipment Co., Ltd. and the Purchasing Department of Hisense (Zhejiang) Air Conditioning Co., Ltd. and the Ministry and Purchasing Department of the TCL Air Conditioning Co., Ltd.

Fourthly, regarding reasonable expenses for stopping infringement. During the first instance of this case, Guowei Company and Jiang Guoping purchased three air conditioners notarized to obtain the alleged infringing products in this case. The total price of TCL air conditioner was 1,699 yuan, the total price of Hisense air conditioner was 2,799 yuan, and the total price of Midea air conditioner was 2,299 yuan. A total of 6,797 yuan. In addition to the above-mentioned evidence collection fees confirmed by the corresponding invoices, Guowei Company and Jiang Guoping did not provide corresponding bills to prove the expenses of their entrusted notarization, entrusted investigation and collection of evidence, and entrusted lawyers to participate in the litigation of this case. Nevertheless, considering the actual situation of the case, it is reasonable and necessary for Guowei Company and Jiang Guoping to entrust notarization, investigation and evidence collection, and to entrust lawyers to participate in the litigation of this case. Since these behaviors had taken place, corresponding expenses would occur inevitably. This court will support for notarization fees, investigation and evidence collection fees, and attorney fees as appropriate. Based on the circumstances of this case, this court determined that Linzhi Company should compensate the patentees for reasonable expenses of 60 thousand yuan to stop the infringement.

In summary, the interpretation of the second-instance judgment regarding the scope of protection of patent claim 2 was improper. On this basis, it was determined that the alleged infringing products did not fall within the scope of protection of patent claim 2. The judgment was wrong and should be corrected. Although the judgment of the first-instance that Linzhi Company constituted an infringement of the patent in this case was correct, it applied statutory compensations to calculate the amount of compensation when part of evidence could prove the benefits acquired by the infringer through the infringement, which made errors in applying the law and should be corrected. According to Article 207 Paragraph 1 and Article 170 Paragraph 1 (2) of the Civil Procedure Law of the People's Republic of China, and Article 11 Paragraph 1, Article 59 Paragraph 1, and Article 65 Paragraph 1 of the Patent Law of the People's Republic of China, the judgment is as follows:

1. Revoke the Civil Judgment No. 105 Su Min Zhong (2016) of Jiangsu Higher People's Court;

2. Uphold the first, second and fourth items of the Civil Judgment No. 51 Ning Zhi Min Chu Zi (2013) of Nanjing Intermediate People's Court, Jiangsu Province;

3. Change the third item of the Civil Judgment No. 510 Ning Zhi Min Chu Zi (2013) of Nanjing Intermediate People's Court, Jiangsu Province to "Changshu Linzhi Electric

Heating Device Co., Ltd. shall compensate Wuxi Guowei Ceramic Appliance Co., Ltd. and Jiang Guoping's economic losses 9,377,867 yuan, and reasonable expenses for stopping the infringement 60,000 yuan, totaling 9,437,867 yuan within ten days after this judgment becomes effective."

If the obligation to pay money is not fulfilled within the period specified in the judgment, the interest on the debt during the delayed performance period shall be doubled in accordance with Article 253 of the Civil Procedure Law of the People's Republic of China.

The litigation expenses of the first and second instances are respectively 111,800 yuan, which shall be borne by Changshu Linzhi Electric Heating Devices Co., Ltd. This decision is final.

Judge: Zhu Li
Judge: Mao Lihua
Judge: Tong Shu
June 26, 2018
Judge Assistant: Zhang Bo
Clerk: Liu Fangfang

3.2 Analysis of the Case

1. Facts

Jiang Guoping is the patentee of the utility model patent titled "A heat-conducting aluminum tube for PTC heater" (the patent in this case). Wuxi Guowei Ceramic Appliance Co., Ltd. (referred to as Guowei Company) is the exclusive licensee of the patent in this case. Guowei Company and Jiang Guoping filed a lawsuit on the grounds that the air-conditioning PTC heater produced and sold by Changshu Linzhi Electric Heating Device Co., Ltd. (Linzhi Company) infringed its patent rights, demanding to stop the infringement, and compensate them for economic losses and reasonable expenses totaling 15 million. Yuan. The Nanjing Intermediate People's Court of Jiangsu Province held that the alleged infringing product fell within the scope of the patent claim 2 of this case, and ruled Linzhi Company and others to stop the infringement, and determined Linzhi Company to compensate Guowei Company and Jiang Guoping for economic losses and reasonable expenses totaling 1 million Yuan. Guowei Company, Jiang Guoping and Linzhi Company refused to accept and filed appeals respectively. The Jiangsu High People's Court held that the alleged infringing product lacked the implicit technical features of patent claim 2 in this case and did not fall into the protection scope of patent claim 2. The judgment was then revoked and the claims of Guowei Company and Jiang Guoping were dismissed. Guowei Company and Jiang Guoping were dissatisfied and applied to the Supreme People's Court for a retrial. The Supreme People's Court ruled that the case should be brought to trial. The Supreme People's Court held that the interpretation of the scope of protection of patent claim 2 in the second instance judgment was improper, and the alleged infringing product fell into the scope of protection of patent claim 2 in this case. It was then decided to revoke the second-instance judgment and change the amount of economic losses totaling 9.37 million yuan.

2. The focus of the dispute

The first is whether the statement that the heat-dissipating aluminum strip is pasted on the "left and right sides" of the heat-conducting aluminum tube in the heating core in claim 2 of this case is an obvious error that can be corrected; the second is whether claim 2 should have implicit technical feature of "grooves on the lower surface." The third is the issue of infringement liability.

3. Focus of disputes

What is Obvious mistake?

Article 4 of the "Interpretation of the Supreme People's Court on Several Issues Concerning the Application of Law in the Trial of Patent Infringement Disputes (2)" stipulates: "There are ambiguities in the grammar, words, punctuation, graphics, and symbols in the claims, descriptions and drawings. However, if a person of ordinary skill in the art can obtain the only understanding by reading the claims, the description and the drawings, the people's court shall make a determination based on the only understanding."

Referring to this provision, the obvious mistakes that can be corrected require two conditions: One is that a person of ordinary skill in the art can recognize that there are ambiguities or errors in the description of the patent application document or the drawings; second, the person of ordinary skill in the art can obtain the only understanding to solve the ambiguity by reading the claims, the description and the drawings.

What is implied technical features?

The so-called implied technical features in the second-instance judgment actually introduced content that was not clearly recorded in the claims as a precondition for corrections when interpreting the meaning of the technical features of the claims. Since the introduction of content that is not clearly recorded in the claims will generally further limit the scope of protection of the claims, in the process of claim interpretation, the introduction of content that is not clearly recorded in the claims should be particularly cautious.

3. The conclusion and its enlightenment

The retrial judgment in this case has innovated the infringement damages determination mechanism, which is typical and guiding in the determination of damages. The evidence that can reflect the sales amount of the alleged infringing product, the total sales amount, profit rate, and contribution of the infringing product can be used to calculate the damages; For the evidence that cannot reflect the specific sales amount of the accused infringing product, determining the amount of damage compensation sould be in accordance with statutory compensation. Reasonable use of evidence rules, economic analysis methods and other methods in this case fully considered factors such as the contribution of the patents involved in the case to the profit of the accused infringing product. The final judgment was revised to compensate the right holder for economic losses and reasonable expenses of nearly 9.5 million yuan, and the judicial decision made efforts to achieve the coordination and proportionality between compensation for infringement damages and the market value of intellectual property rights, which fully reflects the judicial policy of strictly protecting intellectual property rights, and effectively guarantees that the right holders receive full compensation.

3.2 Civil Cases on Copyright Infringement

3.2.1 Copyright Cases from United States

(1) **The definition and application of Transformative Use Doctrine in copyright litigation—CAMPBELL, aka SKYYWALKER, et al. v. ACUFF ROSE MUSIC, INC.**

United States v. Detroit Lumber Co., 200 U.S. 321, 337.
SUPREME COURT OF THE UNITED STATES
certiorari to the united states court of appeals for the sixth circuit
No. 92–1292. Argued November 9, 1993 – Decided March 7, 1994

1.1 Syllabus
Respondent Acuff Rose Music, Inc., filed suit against petitioners, the members of the rap music group 2 Live Crew and their record company, claiming that 2 Live Crew's song, "Pretty Woman," infringed Acuff Rose's copyright in Roy Orbison's rock ballad, "Oh Pretty Woman." The District Court granted summary judgment for 2 Live Crew, holding that its song was a parody that made fair use of the original song. See Copyright Act of 1976, 17 U.S.C. § 107. The Court of Appeals reversed and remanded, holding that the commercial nature of the parody rendered it presumptively unfair under the first of four factors relevant under §107; that, by taking the "heart" of the original and making it the "heart" of a new work, 2 Live Crew had, qualitatively, taken too much under the third §107 factor; and that market harm for purposes of the fourth §107 factor had been established by a presumption attaching to commercial uses.

1.2 Reasoning:
Live Crew's commercial parody may be a fair use within the meaning of §107. Pp. 4–25.
(a) Section 107, which provides that "the fair use of a copyrighted work… for purposes such as criticism [or] comment… is not an infringement…," continues the common law tradition of fair use adjudication and requires case by case analysis rather than bright line rules. The statutory examples of permissible uses provide only general guidance. The four statutory factors are to be explored and weighed together in light of copyright's purpose of promoting science and the arts. Pp. 4–8.
(b) Parody, like other comment and criticism, may claim fair use. Under the first of the four §107 factors, "the purpose and character of the use, including whether such use

is of a commercial nature...," the enquiry focuses on whether the new work merely supersedes the objects of the original creation, or whether and to what extent it is "transformative," altering the original with new expression, meaning, or message. The more transformative the new work, the less will be the significance of other factors, like commercialism, that may weigh against a finding of fair use. The heart of any parodist's claim to quote from existing material is the use of some elements of a prior author's composition to create a new one that, at least in part, comments on that author's work. But that tells courts little about where to draw the line. Thus, like other uses, parody has to work its way through the relevant factors. Pp. 8–12.

(c) The Court of Appeals properly assumed that 2 Live Crew's song contains parody commenting on and criticizing the original work, but erred in giving virtually dispositive weight to the commercial nature of that parody by way of a presumption, ostensibly culled from *Sony Corp. of America* v. *Universal City Studios, Inc.,* 464 U.S. 417, 451, that "every commercial use of copyrighted material is presumptively... unfair...." The statute makes clear that a work's commercial nature is only one element of the first factor enquiry into its purpose and character, and *Sony* itself called for no hard evidentiary presumption. The Court of Appeals's rule runs counter to *Sony* and to the long common law tradition of fair use adjudication. Pp. 12–16.

(d) The second §107 factor, "the nature of the copyrighted work," is not much help in resolving this and other parody cases, since parodies almost invariably copy publicly known, expressive works, like the Orbison song here. Pp. 16–17.

(e) The Court of Appeals erred in holding that, as a matter of law, 2 Live Crew copied excessively from the Orbison original under the third §107 factor, which asks whether "the amount and substantiality of the portion used in relation to the copyrighted work as a whole" are reasonable in relation to the copying's purpose. Even if 2 Live Crew's copying of the original's first line of lyrics and characteristic opening bass riff may be said to go to the original's "heart," that heart is what most readily conjures up the song for parody, and it is the heart at which parody takes aim. Moreover, 2 Live Crew thereafter departed markedly from the Orbison lyrics and produced otherwise distinctive music. As to the lyrics, the copying was not excessive in relation to the song's parodic purpose. As to the music, this Court expresses no opinion whether repetition of the bass riff is excessive copying, but remands to permit evaluation of the amount taken, in light of thesong's parodic purpose and character, its transformative elements, and considerations of the potential for market substitution. Pp. 17–20.

(f) The Court of Appeals erred in resolving the fourth §107 factor, "the effect of the use upon the potential market for or value of the copyrighted work," by presuming, in reliance on *Sony, supra,* at 451, the likelihood of significant market harm based on 2 Live Crew's use for commercial gain. No "presumption" or inference of market harm that might find support in *Sony* is applicable to a case involving something beyond mere duplication for commercial purposes. The cognizable harm is market substitution, not any harm from criticism. As to parody pure and simple, it is unlikely that the work will act as a substitute for the original, since the two works usually serve different market functions. The fourth factor requires courts also to consider the potential market for derivative works. See, e.g., *Harper & Row, supra,* at 568. If the later work has cognizable substitution effects in protectable markets for derivative

works, the law will look beyond the criticism to the work's other elements. 2 Live Crew's song comprises not only parody but also rap music. The absence of evidence or affidavits addressing the effect of 2 Live Crew's song on the derivative market for a nonparody, rap version of "Oh, Pretty Woman" disentitled 2 Live Crew, as the proponent of the affirmative defense of fair use, to summary judgment. Pp. 20–25.
972 F. 2d 1429, reversed and remanded.
Souter, J., delivered the opinion for a unanimous Court. Kennedy, J., filed a concurring opinion.
SUPREME COURT OF THE UNITED STATES
No. 92-1292.
LUTHER R. CAMPBELL aka LUKE SKYYWALKER, et al., PETITIONERS v. ACUFF ROSE MUSIC, INC.
on writ of certiorari to the united states court of appeals for the sixth circuit
[March 7, 1994]
Justice Souter delivered the opinion of the Court.

In 1964, Roy Orbison and William Dees wrote a rock ballad called "Oh, Pretty Woman" and assigned their rights in it to respondent Acuff Rose Music, Inc. See Appendix A, *infra*, at 26. Acuff Rose registered the song for copyright protection.

Petitioners Luther R. Campbell, Christopher Wongwon, Mark Ross, and David Hobbs, are collectively known as 2 Live Crew, a popular rap music group.[n.1] In 1989, Campbell wrote a song entitled "Pretty Woman," which he later described in an affidavit as intended, "through comical lyrics, to satirize the original work...." App. to Pet. for Cert. 80a. On July 5, 1989, 2 Live Crew's manager informed Acuff Rose that 2 Live Crew had written a parody of "Oh, Pretty Woman," that they would afford all credit for ownership and authorship of the original song to Acuff Rose, Dees, and Orbison, and that they were willing to pay a fee for the use they wished to make of it. Enclosed with the letter were a copy of the lyrics and a recording of 2 Live Crew's song. See Appendix B, *infra*, at 27. Acuff Rose's agent refused permission, stating that "I am aware of the success enjoyed by 'The 2 Live Crews', but I must inform you that we cannot permit the use of a parody of 'Oh, Pretty Woman.'" App. to Pet. for Cert. 85a. Nonetheless, in June or July 1989,[n.2] 2 Live Crew released records, cassette tapes, and compact discs of "Pretty Woman" in a collection of songs entitled "As Clean As They Wanna Be." The albums and compact discs identify the authors of "Pretty Woman" as Orbison and Dees and its publisher as Acuff Rose.

Almost a year later, after nearly a quarter of a millioncopies of the recording had been sold, Acuff Rose sued 2 Live Crew and its record company, Luke Skyywalker Records, for copyright infringement. The District Court granted summary judgment for 2 Live Crew,[n.3] reasoning that the commercial purpose of 2 Live Crew's song was no bar to fair use; that 2 Live Crew's version was a parody, which "quickly degenerates into a play on words, substituting predictable lyrics with shocking ones" to show "how bland and banal the Orbison song" is; that 2 Live Crew had taken no more than was necessary to "conjure up" the original in order to parody it; and that it was "extremely unlikely that 2 Live Crew's song could adversely affect the market for the original." 754 F. Supp. 1150, 1154–1155, 1157–1158 (MD Tenn. 1991). The

District Court weighed these factors and held that 2 Live Crew's song made fair use of Orbison's original. *Id.*, at 1158–1159.

The Court of Appeals for the Sixth Circuit reversed and remanded. 972 F. 2d 1429, 1439 (1992). Although it assumed for the purpose of its opinion that 2 Live Crew's song was a parody of the Orbison original, the Court of Appeals thought the District Court had put too little emphasis on the fact that "every commercial use... is presumptively... unfair," *Sony Corp. of America* v. *Universal City Studios, Inc.*, 464 U.S. 417, 451 (1984), and it held that "the admittedly commercial nature" of the parody "requires the conclusion" that the first of four factors relevant under the statute weighs against a finding of fair use. 972 F. 2d, at 1435, 1437. Next, the Court of Appeals determined that, by "taking the heart of the original and making it the heart of a new work," 2 Live Crew had, qualitatively, taken too much. *Id.*, at 1438. Finally, after noting that the effect on the potential market for the original (and the market for derivative works) is "undoubtedly the single most important element of fair use," *Harper & Row, Publishers, Inc.* v. *Nation Enterprises*, 471 U.S. 539, 566 (1985), the Court of Appeals faulted the District Court for "refusing to indulge the presumption" that "harm for purposes of the fair use analysis has been established by the presumption attaching to commercial uses." 972 F. 2d, at 1438–1439. In sum, the court concluded that its "blatantly commercial purpose... prevents this parody from being a fair use." *Id.*, at 1439.

We granted certiorari, to determine whether 2 Live Crew's commercial parody could be a fair use.

It is uncontested here that 2 Live Crew's song would be an infringement of Acuff Rose's rights in "Oh, Pretty Woman," under the Copyright Act of 1976, 17 U.S.C. § 106 (1988 ed. and Supp. IV), but for a finding of fair use through parody.[n.4] From the infancy of copyright protection, some opportunity for fair use of copyrighted materials has been thought necessary to fulfill copyright's very purpose, "to promote the Progress of Science and useful Arts...." U. S. Const., Art. I, § 8, cl. 8.[n.5] For as Justice Story explained, "in truth, in literature, in science and in art, there are, and can be, few, if any, things which in an abstract sense, are strictly new and original throughout. Every book in literature, science and art, borrows, and must necessarily borrow, and use much which was well known and used before." *Emerson* v. *Davies*, 8 F. Cas. 615, 619 (No. 4,436) (CCD Mass. 1845). Similarly, Lord Ellenborough expressed the inherent tension in the need simultaneously to protect copyrighted material and to allow others to build upon it when he wrote, "while I shall think myself bound to secure every man in the enjoyment of his copy right, one must not put manacles upon science." *Carey* v. *Kearsley*, 4 Esp. 168, 170, 170 Eng. Rep. 679, 681 (K.B. 1803). In copyright cases brought under the Statute of Anne of 1710, [n.6] English courts held that in some instances "fair abridgements" would not infringe an author's rights, see W. Patry, The Fair Use Privilege in Copyright Law 6-17 (1985) (hereinafter Patry); Leval, Toward a Fair Use Standard, 103 Harv. L. Rev. 1105, 1105 (1990) (hereinafter Leval), and although the First Congress enacted our initial copyright statute, Act of May 31, 1790, 1 Stat. 124, without any explicit reference to "fair use," as it later came to be known,[n.7] the doctrine was recognized by the American courts nonetheless.

In *Folsom v. Marsh*, Justice Story distilled the essence of law and methodology from the earlier cases: "look to the nature and objects of the selections made, the quantity and value of the materials used, and the degree in which the use may prejudice the sale, or diminish the profits, or supersede the objects, of the original work." 9 F. Cas. 342, 348 (No. 4,901) (CCD Mass. 1841). Thus expressed, fair use remained exclusively judge made doctrine until the passage of the 1976 Copyright Act, in which Story's summary is discernible:[n.8]

"§ 107. Limitations on exclusive rights: Fair use

%Notwithstanding the provisions of Sects. 106 and 106A, the fair use of a copyrighted work, including such use by reproduction in copies or phonorecords or by any other means specified by that section, for purposes such as criticism, comment, news reporting, teaching (including multiple copies for classroom use), scholarship, or research, is not an infringement of copyright. In determining whether the use made of a work in any particular case is a fair use the factors to be considered shall include:

(1) the purpose and character of the use, including whether such use is of a commercial nature or is for nonprofit educational purposes;
(2) the nature of the copyrighted work;
(3) the amount and substantiality of the portion used in relation to the copyrighted work as a whole; and
(4) the effect of the use upon the potential market for or value of the copyrighted work.

The fact that a work is unpublished shall not itself bar a finding of fair use if such finding is made upon consideration of all the above factors." 17 U.S.C. § 107 (1988 ed. and Supp. IV).

Congress meant § 107 "to restate the present judicial doctrine of fair use, not to change, narrow, or enlarge it in any way" and intended that courts continue the common law tradition of fair use adjudication. H. R. Rep. No. 94-1476, p. 66 (1976) (hereinafter House Report); S. Rep. No. 94-473, p. 62 (1975) (hereinafter Senate Report). The fair use doctrine thus "permits and requires courts to avoid rigid application of the copyright statute when, on occasion, it would stifle the very creativity which that law is designed to foster." *Stewart v. Abend*, 495 U.S. 207, 236 (1990) (internal quotation marks and citation omitted).

The task is not to be simplified with bright line rules, for the statute, like the doctrine it recognizes, calls for case by case analysis. *Harper & Row*, 471 U. S., at 560; *Sony*, 464 U. S., at 448, and n. 31; House Report, pp. 65–66; Senate Report, pp. 62. The text employs the terms "including" and "such as" in the preamble paragraph to indicate the "illustrative and not limitative" function of the examples given, § 101; see *Harper & Row, supra*, at 561, which thus provide only general guidance about the sorts of copying that courts and Congress most commonly had found to be fair uses.[n.9] Nor may the four statutory factors be treated in isolation, one from another. All are to be explored, and the results weighed together, in light of the purposes of copyright. See Leval 1110-1111; Patry & Perlmutter, Fair Use Misconstrued: Profit, Presumptions, and Parody, 11 Cardozo Arts & Ent. L. J. 667, 685–687 (1993) (hereinafter Patry & Perlmutter).[n.10]

The first factor in a fair use enquiry is "the purpose and character of the use, including whether such use is of a commercial nature or is for nonprofit educational purposes." § 107(1). This factor draws on Justice Story's formulation, "the nature and objects of the selections made." *Folsom* v. *Marsh*, 9 F. Cas., at 348. The enquiry here may be guided by the examples given in the preamble to § 107, looking to whether the use is for criticism, or comment, or news reporting, and the like, see § 107. The central purpose of this investigation is to see, in Justice Story's words, whether the new work merely "supersedes the objects" of the original creation, *Folsom* v. *Marsh, supra*, at 348; accord, *Harper & Row, supra*, at 562 ("supplanting" the original), or instead adds something new, with a further purpose or different character, altering the first with new expression, meaning, or message; it asks, in other words, whether and to what extent the new work is "transformative." Leval 1111. Although such transformative use is not absolutely necessary for a finding of fair use, *Sony, supra*, at 455, n. 40,[n.11] the goal of copyright, to promote science and the arts, is generally furthered by the creation of transformative works. Such works thus lie at the heart of the fair use doctrine's guarantee of breathing space within the confines of copyright, see, e.g., *Sony, supra*, at 478–480 (Blackmun, J., dissenting), and the more transformative the new work, the less will be the significance of other factors, like commercialism, that may weigh against a finding of fair use.

This Court has only once before even considered whether parody may be fair use, and that time issued no opinion because of the Court's equal division. *Benny* v. *Loew's Inc.*, 239 F. 2d 532 (CA9 1956), aff'd *sub nom. Columbia Broadcasting System, Inc.* v. *Loew's Inc.*, 356 U.S. 43 (1958). Suffice it to say now that parody has an obvious claim to transformative value, as Acuff Rose itself does not deny. Like less ostensibly humorous forms of criticism, it can provide social benefit, by shedding light on an earlier work, and, in the process, creating a new one. We thus line up with the courts that have held that parody, like other comment or criticism, may claim fair use under § 107. See, e.g., *Fisher* v. *Dees*, 794 F. 2d 432 (CA9 1986) ("When Sonny Sniffs Glue," a parody of "When Sunny Gets Blue," is fair use); *Elsmere Music, Inc.* v. *National Broadcasting Co.*, 482 F. Supp. 741 (SDNY), aff'd, 623 F. 2d 252 (CA2 1980) ("I Love Sodom," a "Saturday Night Live" television parody of "I Love New York" is fair use); see also House Report, p. 65; Senate Report, p. 61 ("Use in a parody of some of the content of the work parodied" may be fair use).

The germ of parody lies in the definition of the Greek *parodeia*, quoted in Judge Nelson's Court of Appeals dissent, as "a song sung alongside another." 972 F. 2d, at 1440, quoting 7 Encyclopedia Britannica 768 (15th ed. 1975). Modern dictionaries accordingly describe a parody as a "literary or artistic work that imitates the characteristic style of an author or a work for comic effect or ridicule,"[n.12] or as a "composition in prose or verse in which the characteristic turns of thought and phrase in an author or class of authors are imitated in such a way as to make them appear ridiculous."[n.13] For the purposes of copyright law, the nub of the definitions and the heart of any parodist's claim to quote from existing material is the use of some elements of a prior author's composition to create a new one that, at least in part, comments on that author's works. See, e.g., *Fisher* v. *Dees, supra*, at 437; *MCA, Inc.* v. *Wilson*, 677 F. 2d 180, 185 (CA2 1981). If, on the contrary, the commentary has no critical bearing on the substance or style of the original composition, which the alleged infringer merely uses to get attention or to avoid the drudgery in working up something fresh, the claim to fairness in borrowing from another's work diminishes accordingly (if it does not vanish), and other factors, like the extent of its commerciality, loom larger.[n.14] Parody needs to mimic an original to make its point, and so has some claim to use the creation of its victim's (or collective victims') imagination, whereas satire can stand on its own two feet and so requires justification for the very act of borrowing.[n.15] See *Ibid.*; Bisceglia, Parody and Copyright Protection: Turning the Balancing Act Into a Juggling Act, in ASCAP, Copyright Law Symposium, No. 34, p. 25 (1987).

The fact that parody can claim legitimacy for some appropriation does not, of course, tell either parodist or judge much about where to draw the line. Like a book review quoting the copyrighted material criticized, parody may or may not be fair use, and petitioner's suggestion that any parodic use is presumptively fair has no more justification in law or fact than the equally hopeful claim that any use for news reporting should be presumed fair, see *Harper & Row*, 471 U. S., at 561. The Act has no hint of an evidentiary preference for parodists over their victims, and no workable presumption for parody could take account of the fact that parody often shades into satire when society is lampooned through its creative artifacts, or that a work may contain both parodic and non parodic elements. Accordingly, parody, like any other use, has to work its way through the relevant factors, and be judged case by case, in light of the ends of the copyright law.

Here, the District Court held, and the Court of Appeals assumed, that 2 Live Crew's "Pretty Woman" contains parody, commenting on and criticizing the original work, whatever it may have to say about society at large. As the District Court remarked, the words of 2 Live Crew's song copy the original's first line, but then "quickly degenerate into a play on words, substituting predictable lyrics with shocking ones... that derisively demonstrate how bland and banal the Orbison song seems to them." 754 F. Supp., at 1155 (footnote omitted). Judge Nelson, dissenting below, came to the same conclusion, that the 2 Live Crew song "was clearly intended to ridicule the white bread original" and "reminds us that sexual congress with nameless streetwalkers is not necessarily the stuff of romance and is not necessarily without its consequences. The singers (there are several) have the same thing on their minds as did the lonely man with the nasal voice, but here there is no hint of wine and roses." 972 F. 2d, at 1442. Although the majority below had difficulty discerning any criticism of the original in 2 Live Crew's song, it assumed for purposes of its opinion that there was some. *Id.*, at 1435–1436, and n. 8.

We have less difficulty in finding that critical element in 2 Live Crew's song than the Court of Appeals did, although having found it we will not take the further step of evaluating its quality. The threshold questions when fair use is raised in defense of parody is whether a parodic character may reasonably be perceived.[n.16] Whether, going beyond that, parody is in good taste or bad does not and should not matter to fair use. As Justice Holmes explained, "it would be a dangerous undertaking for persons trained only to the law to constitute themselves final judges of the worth of a work, outside of the narrowest and most obvious limits. At the one extreme some works of genius would be sure to miss appreciation. Their very novelty would make them repulsive until the public had learned the new language in which their author spoke." *Bleistein* v. *Donaldson Lithographing Co.*, 188 U.S. 239, 251 (1903) (circus posters have copyright protection); cf. *Yankee Publishing Inc.* v. *News America Publishing, Inc.*, 809 F. Supp. 267, 280 (SDNY 1992) (Leval, J.) ("First Amendment protections do not apply only to those who speak clearly, whose jokes are funny, and whose parodies succeed") (trademark case).

While we might not assign a high rank to the parodic element here, we think it fair to say that 2 Live Crew's song reasonably could be perceived as commenting on the original or criticizing it to some degree. 2 Live Crew juxtaposes the romantic musings of a man whose fantasy comes true, with degrading taunts, a bawdy demand for sex, and a sigh of relief from paternal responsibility. The later words can be taken as a comment on the naivete of the original of an earlier day, as a rejection of its sentiment that ignores the ugliness of street life and the debasement that it signifies. It is this joinder of reference and ridicule that marks off the author's choice of parody from the other types of comment and criticism that traditionally have had a claim to fair use protection as transformative works.[n.17]

The Court of Appeals, however, immediately cut short the enquiry into 2 Live Crew's fair use claim by confining its treatment of the first factor essentially to one relevant fact, the commercial nature of the use. The court then inflated the significance of this fact by applying a presumption ostensibly culled from *Sony*, that "every commercial use of copyrighted material is presumptively… unfair…" *Sony*, 464 U. S., at 451. In giving virtually dispositive weight to the commercial nature of the parody, the Court of Appeals erred.

The language of the statute makes clear that the commercial or nonprofit educational purpose of a work is only one element of the first factor enquiry into its purpose and character. Section 107(1) uses the term "including" to begin the dependent clause referring to commercial use, and the main clause speaks of a broader investigation into "purpose and character." As we explained in *Harper & Row*, Congress resisted attempts to narrow the ambit of this traditional enquiry by adopting categories of presumptively fair use, and it urged courts to preserve the breadth of their traditionally ample view of the universe of relevant evidence. 471 U. S., at 561; House Report, p. 66. Accordingly, the mere fact that a use is educational and not for profit does not insulate it from a finding of infringement, any more than the commercial character of a use bars a finding of fairness. If, indeed, commerciality carried presumptive force against a finding of fairness, the presumption would swallow nearly all of the illustrative uses listed in the preamble paragraph of § 107, including news reporting, comment, criticism, teaching, scholarship, and research, since these activities "are generally conducted for profit in this country." *Harper & Row, supra*, at 592 (Brennan, J., dissenting). Congress could not have intended such a rule, which certainly is not inferable from the common law cases, arising as they did from the world of letters in which Samuel Johnson could pronounce that "no man but a blockhead ever wrote, except for money." 3 Boswell's Life of Johnson 19 (G. Hill ed. 1934).

Sony itself called for no hard evidentiary presumption. There, we emphasized the need for a "sensitive balancing of interests," 464 U. S., at 455, n. 40, noted that

Congress had "eschewed a rigid, bright line approach to fair use," *id.*, at 449, n. 31, and stated that the commercial or nonprofit educational character of a work is "not conclusive," *id.*, at 448–449, but rather a fact to be "weighed along with others in fair use decisions." *Id.*, at 449, n. 32 (quoting House Report, p. 66). The Court of Appeals's elevation of one sentence from *Sony* to a per se rule thus runs as much counter to *Sony* itself as to the long common law tradition of fair use adjudication. Rather, as we explained in *Harper & Row*, *Sony* stands for the proposition that the "fact that a publication was commercial as opposed to nonprofit is a separate factor that tends to weigh against a finding of fair use." 471 U. S., at 562. But that is all, and the fact that even the force of that tendency will vary with the context is a further reason against elevating commerciality to hard presumptive significance. The use, for example, of a copyrighted work to advertise a product, even in a parody, will be entitled to less indulgence under the first factor of the fair use enquiry, than the sale of a parody for its own sake, let alone one performed a single time by students in school. See generally Patry & Perlmutter 679–680; *Fisher* v. *Dees*, 794 F. 2d, at 437; *Maxtone Graham* v. *Burtchaell*, 803 F. 2d 1253, 1262 (CA2 1986); *Sega Enterprises Ltd.* v. *Accolade, Inc.*, 977 F. 2d 1510, 1522 (CA9 1992).[n.18]

The second statutory factor, "the nature of the copyrighted work," § 107(2), draws on Justice Story's expression, the "value of the materials used." *Folsom* v. *Marsh*, 9 F. Cas., at 348. This factor calls for recognition that some works are closer to the core of intended copyright protection than others, with the consequence that fair use is more difficult to establish when the former works are copied. See, e.g., *Stewart* v. *Abend*, 495 U. S., at 237–238 (contrasting fictional short story with factual works); *Harper & Row*, 471 U. S., at 563–564 (contrasting soon to be published memoir with published speech); *Sony*, 464 U. S., at 455, n. 40 (contrasting motion pictures with news broadcasts); *Feist*, 499 U. S., 348–351 (contrasting creative works with bare factual compilations); 3 M. Nimmer & D. Nimmer, Nimmer on Copyright § 13.05[A][2] (1993) (hereinafter Nimmer); Leval 1116. We agree with both the District Court and the Court of Appeals that the Orbison original's creative expression for public dissemination falls within the core of the copyright's protective purposes. 754 F. Supp., at 1155–1156; 972 F. 2d, at 1437. This fact, however, is not much help in this case, or ever likely to help much in separating the fair use sheep from the infringing goats in a parody case, since parodies almost invariably copy publicly known, expressive works.

The third factor asks whether "the amount and substantiality of the portion used in relation to the copyrighted work as a whole," § 107(3) (or, in Justice Story's words, "the quantity and value of the materials used," *Folsom* v. *Marsh, supra*, at 348) are reasonable in relation to the purpose of the copying. Here, attention turns to the persuasiveness of a parodist's justification for the particular copying done, and the enquiry will harken back to the first of the statutory factors, for, as in prior cases, we recognize that the extent of permissible copying varies with the purpose and character of the use. See *Sony*, 464 U. S., at 449–450 (reproduction of entire work "does not have its ordinary effect of militating against a finding of fair use" as to home videotaping of television programs); *Harper & Row*, 471 U. S., at 564 ("Even substantial quotations might qualify as fair use in a review of a published work or a news account of a speech" but not in a scoop of a soon to be published memoir). The facts bearing on this factor will also tend to address the fourth, by revealing the degree to which the parody may serve as a market substitute for the original or potentially licensed derivatives. See Leval 1123.

The District Court considered the song's parodic purpose in finding that 2 Live Crew had not helped themselves over much. 754 F. Supp., at 1156–1157. The Court of Appeals disagreed, stating that "while it may not be inappropriate to find that no more was taken than necessary, the copying was qualitatively substantial.... We conclude that taking the heart of the original and making it the heart of a new work was to purloin a substantial portion of the essence of the original." 972 F. 2d, at 1438.

The Court of Appeals is of course correct that this factor calls for thought not only about the quantity of the materials used, but about their quality and importance, too. In *Harper & Row*, for example, the Nation had taken only some 300 words out of President Ford's memoirs, but we signalled the significance of the quotations in finding them to amount to "the heart of the book," the part most likely to be newsworthy and important in licensing serialization. 471 U. S., at 564–566, 568 (internal quotation marks omitted). We also agree with the Court of Appeals that whether "a substantial portion of the infringing work was copied verbatim" from the copyrighted work is a relevant question, see *id.*, at 565, for it may reveal a dearth of transformative character or purpose under the first factor, or a greater likelihood of market harm under the fourth; a work composed primarily of an original, particularly its heart, with little added or changed, is more likely to be a merely superseding use, fulfilling demand for the original.

Where we part company with the court below is in applying these guides to parody, and in particular to parody in the song before us. Parody presents a difficult case. Parody's humor, or in any event its comment, necessarily springs from recognizable allusion to its object through distorted imitation. Its art lies in the tension between a known original and its parodic twin. When parody takes aim at a particular original work, the parody must be able to "conjure up" at least enough of that original to make the object of its critical wit recognizable. See, e.g., *Elsmere Music*, 623 F. 2d, at 253, n. 1; *Fisher v. Dees*, 794 F. 2d, at 438–439. What makes for this recognition is quotation of the original's most distinctive or memorable features, which the parodist can be sure the audience will know. Once enough has been taken to assure identification, how much more is reasonable will depend, say, on the extent to which the song's overriding purpose and character is to parody the original or, in contrast, the likelihood that the parody may serve as a market substitute for the original. But using some characteristic features cannot be avoided.

We think the Court of Appeals was insufficiently appreciative of parody's need for the recognizable sight or sound when it ruled 2 Live Crew's use unreasonable as a matter of law. It is true, of course, that 2 Live Crew copied the characteristic opening bass riff (or musical phrase) of the original, and true that the words of the first line copy the Orbison lyrics. But if quotation of the opening riff and the first line may be said to go to the "heart" of the original, the heart is also what most readily conjures up the song for parody, and it is the heart at which parody takes aim. Copying does not become excessive in relation to parodic purpose merely because the portion taken was the original's heart. If 2 Live Crew had copied a significantly less memorable part of the original, it is difficult to see how its parodic character would have come through. See *Fisher v. Dees*, 794 F. 2d, at 439.

This is not, of course, to say that anyone who calls himself a parodist can skim the cream and get away scot free. In parody, as in news reporting, see *Harper & Row, supra*, context is everything, and the question of fairness asks what else the parodist did besides go to the heart of the original. It is significant that 2 Live Crew not only copied the first line of the original, but thereafter departed markedly from the Orbison lyrics for its own ends. 2 Live Crew not only copied the bass riff and repeated it,[n.19] but also produced otherwise distinctive sounds, interposing "scraper" noise, overlaying the music with solos in different keys, and altering the drum beat. See 754 F. Supp., at 1155. This is not a case, then, where "a substantial portion" of the parody itself is composed of a "verbatim" copying of the original. It is not, that is, a case where the parody is so insubstantial, as compared to the copying, that the third factor must be resolved as a matter of law against the parodists.

Suffice it to say here that, as to the lyrics, we think the Court of Appeals correctly suggested that "no more was taken than necessary," 972 F. 2d, at 1438, but just for that reason, we fail to see how the copying can be excessive in relation to its parodic purpose, even if the portion taken is the original's "heart." As to the music, we express no opinion whether repetition of the bass riff is excessive copying, and we remand to permit evaluation of the amount taken, in light of the song's parodic purpose and character, its transformative elements, and considerations of the potential for market substitution sketched more fully below.

The fourth fair use factor is "the effect of the use upon the potential market for or value of the copyrighted work." § 107(4). It requires courts to consider not only the extent of market harm caused by the particular actions of the alleged infringer, but also "whether unrestricted and widespread conduct of the sort engaged in by the defendant... would result in a substantially adverse impact on the potential market" for the original. Nimmer § 13.05[A][4], p. 13-102.61 (footnote omitted); accord *Harper & Row*, 471 U. S., at 569; Senate Report, p. 65; *Folsom v. Marsh*, 9 F. Cas., at 349. The enquiry "must take account not only of harm to the original but also of harm to the market for derivative works." *Harper & Row, supra*, at 568.

Since fair use is an affirmative defense,[n.20] its proponent would have difficulty carrying the burden of demonstrating fair use without favorable evidence about relevant markets.[n.21] In moving for summary judgment, 2 Live Crew left themselves at just such a disadvantage when they failed to address the effect on the market for rap derivatives, and confined themselves to uncontroverted submissions that there was no likely effect on the market for the original. They did not, however, thereby subject themselves to the evidentiary presumption applied by the Court of Appeals. In assessing the likelihood of significant market harm, the Court of Appeals quoted from language in *Sony* that "if the intended use is for commercial gain, that likelihood may be presumed. But if it is for a noncommercial purpose, the likelihood must be demonstrated.'" 972 F. 2d, at 1438, quoting *Sony*, 464 U. S., at 451. The court reasoned that because "the use of the copyrighted work is wholly commercial,... we presume a likelihood of future harm to Acuff Rose exists." 972 F. 2d, at 1438. In so doing, the court resolved the fourth factor against 2 Live Crew, just as it had the first, by applying a presumption about the effect of commercial use, a presumption which as applied here we hold to be error.

No "presumption" or inference of market harm that might find support in *Sony* is applicable to a case involving something beyond mere duplication for commercial purposes. *Sony*'s discussion of a presumption contrasts a context of verbatim copying of the original in its entirety for commercial purposes, with the non commercial context of *Sony* itself (home copying of television programming). In the former circumstances, what *Sony* said simply makes common sense: when a commercial use amounts to mere duplication of the entirety of an original, it clearly "supersedes the objects," *Folsom* v. *Marsh*, 9 F. Cas., at 348, of the original and serves as a market replacement for it, making it likely that cognizable market harm to the original will occur. *Sony,* 464 U. S., at 451. But when, on the contrary, the second use is transformative, market substitution is at least less certain, and market harm may not be so readily inferred. Indeed, as to parody pure and simple, it is more likely that the new work will not affect the market for the original in a way cognizable under this factor, that is, by acting as a substitute for it ("supersed[ing] [its] objects"). See Leval 1125; Patry & Perlmutter 692, 697–698. This is so because the parody and the original usually serve different market functions. Bisceglia, ASCAP, Copyright Law Symposium, No. 34, p. 23.

We do not, of course, suggest that a parody may not harm the market at all, but when a lethal parody, like a scathing theater review, kills demand for the original, it does not produce a harm cognizable under the Copyright Act. Because "parody may quite legitimately aim at garroting the original, destroying it commercially as well as artistically," B. Kaplan, An Unhurried View of Copyright 69 (1967), the role of the courts is to distinguish between "biting criticism that merely suppresses demand and copyright infringement, which usurps it." *Fisher* v. *Dees*, 794 F. 2d, at 438.

This distinction between potentially remediable displacement and unremediable disparagement is reflected in the rule that there is no protectable derivative market for criticism. The market for potential derivative uses includes only those that creators of original works would in general develop or license others to develop. Yet the unlikelihood that creators of imaginative works will license critical reviews or lampoons of their own productions removes such uses from the very notion of a potential licensing market. "People ask… for criticism, but they only want praise." S. Maugham, Of Human Bondage 241 (Penguin ed. 1992). Thus, to the extent that the opinion below may be read to have considered harm to the market for parodies of "Oh, Pretty Woman," see 972 F. 2d, at 1439, the court erred. Accord, *Fisher* v. *Dees*, 794 F. 2d, at 437; Leval 1125; Patry & Perlmutter 688–691.[n.22]

In explaining why the law recognizes no derivative market for critical works, including parody, we have, of course, been speaking of the later work as if it had nothing but a critical aspect (i.e., "parody pure and simple," *supra*, at 22). But the later work may have a more complex character, with effects not only in the arena of criticism but also in protectable markets for derivative works, too. In that sort of case, the law looks beyond the criticism to the other elements of the work, as it does here. 2 Live Crew's song comprises not only parody but also rap music, and the derivative market for rap music is a proper focus of enquiry, see *Harper & Row,* 471 U. S., at 568; Nimmer § 13.05[B]. Evidence of substantial harm to it would weigh against a finding of fair use,[n.23] because the licensing of derivatives is an important economic incentive to the creation of originals. See 17 U.S.C. § 106(2) (copyright owner has rights to derivative works). Of course, the only harm to derivatives that need concern us, as discussed above, is the harm of market substitution. The fact that a parody may impair the market for derivative uses by the very effectiveness of its critical commentary is no more relevant under copyright than the like threat to the original market.[n.24]

Although 2 Live Crew submitted uncontroverted affidavits on the question of market harm to the original, neither they, nor Acuff Rose, introduced evidence or affidavits addressing the likely effect of 2 Live Crew's parodic rap song on the market for a non parody, rap version of "Oh, Pretty Woman." And while Acuff Rose would have us find evidence of a rap market in the very facts that 2 Live Crew recorded a rap parody of "Oh, Pretty Woman" and another rap group sought a license to record a rap derivative, there was no evidence that a potential rap market was harmed in any way by 2 Live Crew's parody, rap version. The fact that 2 Live Crew's parody sold as part of a collection of rap songs says very little about the parody's effect on a market for a rap version of the original, either of the music alone or of the music with its lyrics. The District Court essentially passed on this issue, observing that Acuff Rose is free to record "whatever version of the original it desires," 754 F. Supp., at 1158; the Court of Appeals went the other way by erroneous presumption. Contrary to each treatment, it is impossible to deal with the fourth factor except by recognizing that a silent record on an important factor bearing on fair use disentitled the proponent of the defense, 2 Live Crew, to summary judgment. The evidentiary hole will doubtless be plugged on remand.

It was error for the Court of Appeals to conclude that the commercial nature of 2 Live Crew's parody of "Oh, Pretty Woman" rendered it presumptively unfair. No such evidentiary presumption is available to address either the first factor, the character and purpose of the use, or the fourth, market harm, in determining whether a transformative use, such as parody, is a fair one. The court also erred in holding that 2 Live Crew had necessarily copied excessively from the Orbison original, considering the parodic purpose of the use. We therefore reverse the judgment of the Court of Appeals and remand for further proceedings consistent with this opinion.

It is so ordered.

Appendix A

"Oh, Pretty Woman" by Roy Orbison and William Dees
Pretty Woman, walking down the street,
Pretty Woman, the kind I like to meet,
Pretty Woman, I don't believe you,
You're not the truth,
No one could look as good as you
Mercy

Pretty Woman, won't you pardon me,
Pretty Woman, I couldn't help but see,
Pretty Woman, that you look lovely as can be
Are you lonely just like me?
Pretty Woman, stop a while,
Pretty Woman, talk a while,
Pretty Woman give your smile to me
Pretty woman, yeah, yeah, yeah
Pretty Woman, look my way,
Pretty Woman, say you'll stay with me
'Cause I need you, I'll treat you right
Come to me baby, Be mine tonight
Pretty Woman, don't walk on by,
Pretty Woman, don't make me cry,
Pretty Woman, don't walk away,
Hey, O. K.
If that's the way it must be, O. K.
I guess I'll go on home, it's late
There'll be tomorrow night, but wait!
What do I see
Is she walking back to me?
Yeah, she's walking back to me!
Oh, Pretty Woman.

Appendix B

"Pretty Woman" as Recorded by 2 Live Crew
Pretty woman walkin' down the street
Pretty woman girl you look so sweet
Pretty woman you bring me down to that knee
Pretty woman you make me wanna beg please
Oh, pretty woman
Big hairy woman you need to shave that stuff
Big hairy woman you know I bet it's tough
Big hairy woman all that hair it ain't legit
'Cause you look like 'Cousin It'
Big hairy woman
Bald headed woman girl your hair won't grow
Bald headed woman you got a teeny weeny afro
Bald headed woman you know your hair could look nice
Bald headed woman first you got to roll it with rice
Bald headed woman here, let me get this hunk of biz for ya
Ya know what I'm saying you look better than rice a roni

Oh bald headed woman
Big hairy woman come on in
And don't forget your bald headed friend
Hey pretty woman let the boys
Jump in
Two timin' woman girl you know you ain't right
Two timin' woman you's out with my boy last night
Two timin' woman that takes a load off my mind
Two timin' woman now I know the baby ain't mine
Oh, two timin' woman
Oh pretty woman

Notes

1 Rap has been defined as a "style of black American popular music consisting of improvised rhymes performed to a rhythmic accompaniment." The Norton/Grove Concise Encyclopedia of Music 613 (1988). 2 Live Crew plays "[b]ass music," a regional, hip hop style of rap from the Liberty City area of Miami, Florida. Brief for Petitioners 34.

2 The parties argue about the timing. 2 Live Crew contends that the album was released on July 15, and the District Court so held. 754 F. Supp. 1150, 1152 (MD Tenn. 1991). The Court of Appeals states that Campbell's affidavit puts the release date in June, and chooses that date. 972 F. 2d 1429, 1432 (CA6 1992). We find the timing of the request irrelevant for purposes of this enquiry. See n. 18, *infra*, discussing good faith.

3 2 Live Crew's motion to dismiss was converted to a motion for summary judgment. Acuff Rose defended against the motion, but filed no cross motion.

4 Section 106 provides in part:

"Subject to Sects. 107 through 120, the owner of copyright under this title has the exclusive rights to do and to authorize any of the following:

"(1) to reproduce the copyrighted work in copies or phonorecords;"

"(2) to prepare derivative works based upon the copyrighted work;"

"(3) to distribute copies or phonorecords of the copyrighted work to the public by sale or other transfer of ownership, or by rental, lease, or lending . . . ."

A derivative work is defined as one "based upon one or more preexisting works, such as a translation, musical arrangement, dramatization, fictionalization, motion picture version, sound recording, art reproduction, abridgment, condensation, or any other form in which a work may be recast, transformed, or adapted. A work consisting of editorial revisions, annotations, elaborations, or other modifications which, as a whole, represent an original work of authorship, is a 'derivative work.'" 17 U.S.C. § 101.

2 Live Crew concedes that it is not entitled to a compulsorylicense under § 115 because its arrangement changes "the basic melody or fundamental character" of the original. § 115(a)(2).

5 The exclusion of facts and ideas from copyright protection serves that goal as well. See § 102(b) ("In no case does copyright protection for an original work of authorship extend to any idea, procedure, process, system, method of operation, concept, principle, or discovery…"); *Feist Publications* v. *Rural Telephone Service Co.*, 499 U.S. 340, 359 (1991) ("[F]acts contained in existing works may be freely copied"); *Harper & Row, Publishers, Inc.* v. *Nation Enterprises*, 471 U.S. 539, 547 (1985) (copyright owner's rights exclude facts and ideas, and fair use).

6 An Act for the Encouragement of Learning, 8 Anne, ch. 19.

7 Patry 27, citing *Lawrence* v. *Dana*, 15 F. Cas. 26, 60 (No. 8,136) (CCD Mass. 1869).

8 Leval 1105. For a historical account of the development of the fair use doctrine, see Patry 1–64.

9 See Senate Report, p. 62 ("[W]hether a use referred to in the first sentence of Sec. 107 is a fair use in a particular case will depend upon the application of the determinative factors").

10 Because the fair use enquiry often requires close questions of judgment as to the extent of permissible borrowing in cases involving parodies (or other critical works), courts may also wish to bear in mind that the goals of the copyright law, "to stimulate the creation and publication of edifying matter," Leval 1134, are not always best served by automatically granting injunctive relief when parodists are found to have gone beyond the bounds of fair use. See 17 U.S.C. § 502(a) (court "*may…grant… injunctions on such terms as it may deem reasonable to prevent or restrain infringement*") (emphasis added); Leval 1132 (while in the "vast majority of cases, [an injunctive] remedy is justified because most infringements are simple piracy," such cases are "worlds apart from many of those raising reasonable contentions of fair use" where "there may be a strong public interest in the publication of the secondary work [and] the copyright owner's interest may be adequately protected by an award of damages for whatever infringement is found"); *Abend* v. *MCA, Inc.*, 863 F. 2d 1465, 1479 (CA9 1988) (finding "special circumstances" that would cause "great injustice" to defendants and "public injury" were injunction to issue), aff'd *sub nom. Stewart* v. *Abend*, 495 U.S. 207 (1990).

11 The obvious statutory exception to this focus on transformative uses is the straight reproduction of multiple copies for classroom distribution.

12 The American Heritage Dictionary 1317 (3d ed. 1992).

13 11 The Oxford English Dictionary 247 (2d ed. 1989).

14 A parody that more loosely targets an original than the parody presented here may still be sufficiently aimed at an original work to come within our analysis of parody. If a parody whose wide dissemination in the market runs the risk of serving as a substitute for the original or licensed derivatives (see *infra*, discussing factor four), it is more incumbent on one claiming fair use to establish the extent of transformation and the parody's critical relationship to the original. By contrast, when there is little or no risk of market substitution, whether because of the large extent of transformation of the earlier work, the new work's minimal distribution in the market, the small extent to which it borrows from an original, or other factors, taking parodic aim at an original is a less critical factor in the analysis, and looser forms of parody may

be found to be fair use, as may satire with lesser justification for the borrowing than would otherwise be required.

15 Satire has been defined as a work "in which prevalent follies or vices are assailed with ridicule," 14 The Oxford English Dictionary 500 (2d ed. 1989), or are "attacked through irony, derision, or wit," The American Heritage Dictionary 1604 (3d ed. 1992).

16 The only further judgment, indeed, that a court may pass on a work goes to an assessment of whether the parodic element is slight or great, and the copying small or extensive in relation to the parodic element, for a work with slight parodic element and extensive copying will be more likely to merely "supersede the objects" of the original.

17 We note in passing that 2 Live Crew need not label its whole album, or even this song, a parody in order to claim fair use protection, nor should 2 Live Crew be penalized for this being its first parodic essay. Parody serves its goals whether labeled or not, and there is no reason to require parody to state the obvious, (or even the reasonably perceived). See Patry & Perlmutter 716–717.

18 Finally, regardless of the weight one might place on the alleged infringer's state of mind, compare *Harper & Row*, 471 U. S., at 562 (fair use presupposes good faith and fair dealing) (quotation marks omitted), with *Folsom* v. *Marsh*, 9 F. Cas. 342, 349 (No. 4,901) (CCD Mass. 1841) (good faith does not bar a finding of infringement); Leval 1126–1127 (good faith irrelevant to fair use analysis), we reject Acuff Rose's argument that 2 Live Crew's request for permission to use the original should be weighed against a finding of fair use. Even if good faith were central to fair use, 2 Live Crew's actions do not necessarily suggest that they believed their version was not fair use; the offer may simply have been made in a good faith effort to avoid this litigation. If the use is otherwise fair, then no permission need be sought or granted. Thus, being denied permission to use a work does not weigh against a finding of fair use. See *Fisher* v. *Dees*, 794 F. 2d 432, 437 (CA9 1986).

19 This may serve to heighten the comic effect of the parody, as one witness stated, App. 32a, Affidavit of Oscar Brand; see also *Elsmere Music, Inc.* v. *National Broadcasting Co.*, 482 F. Supp. 741, 747 (SDNY 1980) (repetition of "I Love Sodom"), or serve to dazzle with the original's music, as Acuff Rose now contends.

20 *Harper & Row*, 471 U. S., at 561; H. R. Rep. No. 102–836, p. 3, n. 3 (1992).

21 Even favorable evidence, without more, is no guarantee of fairness. Judge Leval gives the example of the film producer's appropriation of a composer's previously unknown song that turns the song into a commercial success; the boon to the song does not make the film's simple copying fair. Leval 1124, n. 84. This factor, no less than the other three, may be addressed only through a "sensitive balancing of interests." *Sony*, 464 U. S., at 455, n. 40. Market harm is a matter of degree, and the importance of this factor will vary, not only with the amount of harm, but also with the relative strength of the showing on the other factors.

22 We express no opinion as to the derivative markets for works using elements of an original as vehicles for satire or amusement, making no comment on the original or criticism of it.

23 See Nimmer § 13.05[A][4], p. 13–102.61 ("a substantially adverse impact on the potential market"); Leval 1125 ("reasonably substantial" harm); Patry & Perlmutter 697–698 (same).

24 In some cases it may be difficult to determine whence the harm flows. In such cases, the other fair use factors may provide some indicia of the likely source of the harm. A work whose overriding purpose and character is parodic and whose borrowing is slight in relation to its parody will be far less likely to cause cognizable harm than a work with little parodic content and much copying.

1.3 Analysis of the Case

Campbell v. Acuff-Rose Music, Inc., 510 U.S. 569 (1994)

The text of Campbell v. Acuff-Rose is available here:
https://www.law.cornell.edu/supct/html/92-1292.ZS.html

The band 2 Live Crew—Luke (Luther Campbell, named defendant), Fresh Kid Ice, Mr. Mixx and Brother Marquis—composed a song called "Pretty Woman," a parodic rap version of Roy Orbison's rock ballad, "Oh, Pretty Woman." Desiring to both release the song commercially and avoid a lawsuit, the band's manager's asked Acuff-Rose Music for a license to use Orbison's tune as a basis for its parody. Acuff-Rose Music refused, but 2 Live Crew produced and released the parody anyway.

About a year later, after nearly a quarter of a million copies of the song had been sold, Acuff-Rose sued 2 Live Crew and its record company, Luke Skyywalker Records, for copyright infringement. The trial court granted summary judgment for 2 Live Crew, holding that the song was a parody which made fair use of expressive components of the original song. It was therefore non-infringing under § 107 of the Copyright Act of 1976. Section 107 features a four-pronged test intended as a probative tool for ascertaining whether an unauthorized use is fair by analyzing:

1. The purpose and character of the use, including whether such use is of a commercial nature or is for nonprofit educational purposes;
2. the nature of the copyrighted work;
3. the amount and substantiality of the portion used in relation to the copyrighted work as a whole; and
4. the effect of the use upon the potential market for or value of the copyrighted work.

The Sixth Circuit Court of Appeals disagreed and reversed, holding that the commercial nature of the parody rendered it presumptively unfair under the first factor of the four factor test found in § 107. The Court of Appeals believed (incorrectly, as it turns out) that the U.S. Supreme Court had held that unauthorized commercial uses of copyrighted works were presumptively unfair, in Sony Corp. of America v. Universal City Studios, Inc., 464 U.S. 417 (1984). The Court of Appeals also held that 2 Live Crew had taken the "heart" of Orbison's song, and that Acuff-Rose Music had suffered market harms as a result.

Campbell successfully appealed the case up to the U.S. Supreme Court, which then faced the question of whether 2 Live Crew's commercial parody of Roy Orbison's "Oh, Pretty Woman" was a fair use within the meaning of § 107 of the Copyright Act of 1976. And in a unanimous opinion delivered by Justice David H. Souter, the Court held that a parody's commercial character is only one element to be weighed in a fair use enquiry, and that insufficient consideration was given to the nature of parody in weighing the degree of copying. Criticizing the Ninth Circuit's focus on commercial use being presumptively unfair, Souter wrote: "If, indeed, commerciality carried presumptive force against a finding of fairness, the presumption would swallow nearly all of the uses" Congress intended to authorize.

Justice Souter noted that the four parts of the Sec. 107 fair use test could not "be treated in isolation, one from another," but were to "be explored and the results weighed together, in light of the purposes of copyright." He wrote, "Parody needs to mimic an original to make its point, and so has some claim to use the creation of its victim's (or collective victims') imagination ...," and that while a given parody may not be in good taste, that "does not and should not matter to fair use."

The Court concluded that 2 Live Crew had taken only enough from the original song to make it a recognizable and successful parody. The Court also emphasized the importance of freedom of expression with respect to creative works. It held that the prime directive of Copyright is to incentivize new works, not squelch them. Because 2 Live Crew had used some of the protectable elements of Orbison's ballad to creative a popular and original new song, the use was fair. The Court called this a "transformative use," one that uses an existing original work to create a new expressive work, thereby "promot[ing] the progress of Science and the Useful Arts" (quoting U.S. Const. art. I, § 8, cl. 8). As both U.S. Supreme Court precedent and the legislative history underlying Sec. 107 attest, the fair use doctrine is intended to facilitate unauthorized uses of copyrighted work for free speech related purposes such as criticism, commentary, scholarship, and news reporting, all listed in the preamble to § 107 of the Copyright Act of 1976.

More than 20 years have passed since this Court articulated the transformative use test in Campbell v. Acuff-Rose Music. The intervening period has seen an unprecedented and dramatic shift in the ways in which fair use facilitates new uses and adaptations of existing copyrighted works by virtue of what is now called the Transformative Use Doctrine.

(2) **How to define the contributory infringement of copyright: application of SONY RULE METRO-GOLDWYN-MAYER STUDIOS INC. V.GROKSTER, LTD.**

SUPREME COURT OF THE UNITED STATES
METRO-GOLDWYN-MAYER STUDIOS INC. et al. *v.* GROKSTER, LTD., et al.
OCTOBER TERM, 2004
certiorari to the united states court of appeals for the ninth circuit
No. 04–480. Argued March 29, 2005—Decided June 27, 2005.

2.1 Syllabus

Respondent companies distribute free software that allows computer users to share electronic files through peer-to-peer networks, so called because the computers communicate directly with each other, not through central servers. Although such networks can be used to share any type of digital file, recipients of respondents' software have mostly used them to share copyrighted music and video files without authorization. Seeking damages and an injunction, a group of movie studios and other copyright holders (hereinafter MGM) sued respondents for their users' copyright infringements, alleging that respondents knowingly and intentionally distributed their software to enable users to infringe copyrighted works in violation of the Copyright Act.

Discovery revealed that billions of files are shared across peer-to-peer networks each month. Respondents are aware that users employ their software primarily to download copyrighted files, although the decentralized networks do not reveal which files are copied, and when. Respondents have sometimes learned about the infringement directly when users have e-mailed questions regarding copyrighted works, and respondents have replied with guidance. Respondents are not merely passive recipients of information about infringement. The record is replete with evidence that when they began to distribute their free software, each of them clearly voiced the objective that recipients use the software to download copyrighted works and took active steps to encourage infringement. After the notorious file-sharing service, Napster, was sued by copyright holders for facilitating copyright infringement, both respondents promoted and marketed themselves as Napster alternatives. They receive no revenue from users, but, instead, generate income by selling advertising space, then streaming the advertising to their users. As the number of users increases, advertising opportunities are worth more. There is no evidence that either respondent made an effort to filter copyrighted material from users' downloads or otherwise to impede the sharing of copyrighted files.

While acknowledging that respondents' users had directly infringed MGM's copyrights, the District Court nonetheless granted respondents summary judgment as to liability arising from distribution of their software. The Ninth Circuit affirmed. It read *Sony Corp. of America* v. *Universal City Studios, Inc.*, 464 U. S. 417, as holding that the distribution of a commercial product capable of substantial noninfringing uses could not give rise to contributory liability for infringement unless the distributor had actual knowledge of specific instances of infringement and failed to act on that knowledge. Because the appeals court found respondents' software to be capable of substantial noninfringing uses and because respondents had no actual knowledge of infringement owing to the software's decentralized architecture, the court held that they were not liable. It also held that they did not materially contribute to their users' infringement because the users themselves searched for, retrieved, and stored the infringing files, with no involvement by respondents beyond providing the software in the first place. Finally, the court held that respondents could not be held liable under a vicarious infringement theory because they did not monitor or control the software's use, had no agreed-upon right or current ability to supervise its use, and had no independent duty to police infringement.

2.2 Reasoning:
One who distributes a device with the object of promoting its use to infringe copyright, as shown by clear expression or other affirmative steps taken to foster infringement,

going beyond mere distribution with knowledge of third-party action, is liable for the resulting acts of infringement by third parties using the device, regardless of the device's lawful uses.

(a) The tension between the competing values of supporting creativity through copyright protection and promoting technological innovation by limiting infringement liability is the subject of this case. Despite off setting considerations, the argument for imposing indirect liability here is powerful, given the number of infringing downloads that occur daily using respondents' software. When a widely shared product is used to commit infringement, it may be impossible to enforce rights in the protected work effectively against all direct infringers, so that the only practical alternative is to go against the device's distributor for secondary liability on a theory of contributory or vicarious infringement. One infringes contributorily by intentionally inducing or encouraging direct infringement, and infringes vicariously by profiting from direct infringement while declining to exercise the right to stop or limit it. Although "[t]he Copyright Act does not expressly render anyone liable for [another's] infringement," *Sony*, 464 U. S., at 434, these secondary liability doctrines emerged from common law principles and are well established in the law, e.g., *id.*, at 486.

(b) *Sony* addressed a claim that secondary liability for infringement can arise from the very distribution of a commercial product. There, copyright holders sued Sony, the manufacturer of videocassette recorders, claiming that it was contributorily liable for the infringement that occurred when VCR owners taped copyrighted programs. The evidence showed that the VCR's principal use was "time-shifting," i.e., taping a program for later viewing at a more convenient time, which the Court found to be a fair, noninfringing use. 464 U. S., at 423–424. Moreover, there was no evidence that Sony had desired to bring about taping in violation of copyright or taken active steps to increase its profits from unlawful taping. *Id.*, at 438. On those facts, the only conceivable basis for liability was on a theory of contributory infringement through distribution of a product. *Id.*, at 439. Because the VCR was "capable of commercially significant noninfringing uses," the Court held that Sony was not liable. *Id.*, at 442. This theory reflected patent law's traditional staple article of commerce doctrine that distribution of a component of a patented device will not violate the patent if it is suitable for use in other ways. 35 U. S. C §271(c). The doctrine absolves the equivocal conduct of selling an item with lawful and unlawful uses and limits liability to instances of more acute fault. In this case, the Ninth Circuit misread *Sony* to mean that when a product is capable of substantial lawful use, the producer cannot be held contributorily liable for third parties' infringing use of it, even when an actual purpose to cause infringing use is shown, unless the distributors had specific knowledge of infringement at a time when they contributed to the infringement and failed to act upon that information. *Sony* did not displace other secondary liability theories. Pp. 13–17.

(c) Nothing in *Sony* requires courts to ignore evidence of intent to promote infringement if such evidence exists. It was never meant to foreclose rules of fault-based liability derived from the common law. 464 U. S., at 439. Where evidence goes beyond a product's characteristics or the knowledge that it may be put to infringing uses, and shows statements or actions directed to promoting infringement, *Sony*'s staple-article rule will not preclude liability. At common law a copyright or patent defendant who "not only expected but invoked [infringing use] by advertisement" was liable for infringement. *Kalem Co.* v. *Harper Brothers*, 222 U. S. 55, 62–63. The rule on inducement of infringement as developed in the early cases is no different today. Evidence of active steps taken to encourage direct infringement, such as advertising an infringing use or instructing how to engage in an infringing use, shows an affirmative intent that the product be used to infringe, and overcomes the law's reluctance to find liability when a defendant merely sells a commercial product suitable for some lawful use. A rule that premises liability on purposeful, culpable expression and conduct does nothing to compromise legitimate commerce or discourage innovation having a lawful promise. Pp. 17–20.

(d) On the record presented, respondents' unlawful objective is unmistakable. The classic instance of inducement is by advertisement or solicitation that broadcasts a message designed to stimulate others to commit violations. MGM argues persuasively that such a message is shown here. Three features of the evidence of intent are particularly notable. First, each of the respondents showed itself to be aiming to satisfy a known source of demand for copyright infringement, the market comprising former Napster users. Respondents' efforts to supply services to former Napster users indicate a principal, if not exclusive, intent to bring about infringement. Second, neither respondent attempted to develop filtering tools or other mechanisms to diminish the infringing activity using their software. While the Ninth Circuit treated that failure as irrelevant because respondents lacked an independent duty to monitor their users' activity, this evidence underscores their intentional facilitation of their users' infringement. Third, respondents make money by selling advertising space, then by directing ads to the screens of computers employing their software. The more their software is used, the more ads are sent out and the greater the advertising revenue. Since the extent of the software's use determines the gain to the distributors, the commercial sense of their enterprise turns on high-volume use, which the record shows is infringing. This evidence alone would not justify an inference of unlawful intent, but its import is clear in the entire record's context. Pp. 20–23.

(e) In addition to intent to bring about infringement and distribution of a device suitable for infringing use, the inducement theory requires evidence of actual infringement by recipients of the device, the software in this case. There is evidence of such infringement on a gigantic scale. Because substantial evidence supports MGM on all elements, summary judgment for respondents was error. On remand, reconsideration of MGM's summary judgment motion will be in order. Pp. 23–24.

380 F. 3d 1154, vacated and remanded.

Souter, J., delivered the opinion for a unanimous Court. Ginsburg, J., filed a concurring opinion, in which Rehnquist, C. J., and Kennedy, J., joined. Breyer, J., filed a concurring opinion, in which Stevens and O'Connor, JJ., joined.

OPINION OF THE COURT
METRO-GOLDWYN-MAYER STUDIOS INC. V.GROKSTER, LTD.
545 U. S. ____ (2005)
SUPREME COURT OF THE UNITED STATES

NO. 04-480
METRO-GOLDWYN-MAYER STUDIOS INC., et al., PETITIONERS v. GROKSTER, LTD., et al.
on writ of certiorari to the united states court of appeals for the ninth circuit
[June 27, 2005]
Justice Souter delivered the opinion of the Court.

The question is under what circumstances the distributor of a product capable of both lawful and unlawful use is liable for acts of copyright infringement by third parties using the product. We hold that one who distributes a device with the object of promoting its use to infringe copyright, as shown by clear expression or other affirmative steps taken to foster infringement, is liable for the resulting acts of infringement by third parties.

I

A

Respondents, Grokster, Ltd., and StreamCast Networks, Inc., defendants in the trial court, distribute free software products that allow computer users to share electronic files through peer-to-peer networks, so called because users' computers communicate directly with each other, not through central servers. The advantage of peer-to-peer networks over information networks of other types shows up in their substantial and growing popularity. Because they need no central computer server to mediate the exchange of information or files among users, the high-bandwidth communications capacity for a server may be dispensed with, and the need for costly server storage space is eliminated. Since copies of a file (particularly a popular one) are available on many users' computers, file requests and retrievals may be faster than on other types of networks, and since file exchanges do not travel through a server, communications can take place between any computers that remain connected to the network without risk that a glitch in the server will disable the network in its entirety. Given these benefits in security, cost, and efficiency, peer-to-peer networks are employed to store and distribute electronic files by universities, government agencies, corporations, and libraries, among others.[Footnote 1].

Other users of peer-to-peer networks include individual recipients of Grokster's and StreamCast's software, and although the networks that they enjoy through using the software can be used to share any type of digital file, they have prominently employed those networks in sharing copyrighted music and video files without authorization. A group of copyright holders (MGM for short, but including motion picture studios, recording companies, songwriters, and music publishers) sued Grokster and StreamCast for their users' copyright infringements, alleging that they knowingly and intentionally distributed their software to enable users to reproduce and distribute the copyrighted works in violation of the Copyright Act, 17 U. S. C. §101 *et seq.* (2000 ed. and Supp. II).[Footnote 2] MGM sought damages and an injunction.

Discovery during the litigation revealed the way the software worked, the business aims of each defendant company, and the predilections of the users. Grokster's eponymous software employs what is known as FastTrack technology, a protocol developed by others and licensed to Grokster. StreamCast distributes a very similar product except that its software, called Morpheus, relies on what is known as Gnutella technology.[Footnote 3] A user who downloads and installs either software possesses the protocol to send requests for files directly to the computers of others using software compatible with FastTrack or Gnutella. On the FastTrack network opened by the Grokster software, the user's request goes to a computer given an indexing capacity by the software and designated a supernode, or to some other computer with comparable power and capacity to collect temporary indexes of the files available on the computers of users connected to it. The supernode (or indexing computer) searches its own index and may communicate the search request to other supernodes. If the file is found, the supernode discloses its location to the computer requesting it, and the requesting user can download the file directly from the computer located. The copied file is placed in a designated sharing folder on the requesting user's computer, where it is available for other users to download in turn, along with any other file in that folder.

In the Gnutella network made available by Morpheus, the process is mostly the same, except that in some versions of the Gnutella protocol there are no supernodes. In these versions, peer computers using the protocol communicate directly with each other. When a user enters a search request into the Morpheus software, it sends the request to computers connected with it, which in turn pass the request along to other connected peers. The search results are communicated to the requesting computer, and the user can download desired files directly from peers' computers. As this description indicates, Grokster and StreamCast use no servers to intercept the content of the search requests or to mediate the file transfers conducted by users of the software, there being no central point through which the substance of the communications passes in either direction.[Footnote 4]

Although Grokster and StreamCast do not therefore know when particular files are copied, a few searches using their software would show what is available on the networks the software reaches. MGM commissioned a statistician to conduct a systematic search, and his study showed that nearly 90% of the files available for download on the FastTrack system were copyrighted works.[Footnote 5] Grokster and StreamCast dispute this figure, raising methodological problems and arguing that free copying even of copyrighted works may be authorized by the rightholders. They also argue that potential noninfringing uses of their software are significant in kind, even if infrequent in practice. Some musical performers, for example, have gained new audiences by distributing their copyrighted works for free across peer-to-peer networks, and some distributors of unprotected content have used peer-to-peer networks to disseminate files, Shakespeare being an example. Indeed, StreamCast has given Morpheus users the opportunity to download the briefs in this very case, though their popularity has not been quantified.

As for quantification, the parties' anecdotal and statistical evidence entered thus far to show the content available on the FastTrack and Gnutella networks does not say much about which files are actually downloaded by users, and no one can say how often the software is used to obtain copies of unprotected material. But MGM's evidence gives reason to think that the vast majority of users' downloads are acts of infringement, and because well over 100 million copies of the software in question are known to have been downloaded, and billions of files are shared across the FastTrack and Gnutella networks each month, the probable scope of copyright infringement is staggering.

Grokster and StreamCast concede the infringement in most downloads, Brief for Respondents 10, n. 6, and it is uncontested that they are aware that users employ their software primarily to download copyrighted files, even if the decentralized FastTrack and Gnutella networks fail to reveal which files are being copied, and when. From time to time, moreover, the companies have learned about their users' infringement directly, as from users who have sent e-mail to each company with questions about playing copyrighted movies they had downloaded, to whom the companies have responded with guidance.[Footnote 6] App. 559–563, 808–816, 939–954. And MGM notified the companies of 8 million copyrighted files that could be obtained using their software.

Grokster and StreamCast are not, however, merely passive recipients of information about infringing use. The record is replete with evidence that from the moment Grokster and StreamCast began to distribute their free software, each one clearly voiced the objective that recipients use it to download copyrighted works, and each took active steps to encourage infringement.

After the notorious file-sharing service, Napster, was sued by copyright holders for facilitation of copyright infringement, *A & M Records, Inc.* v. *Napster, Inc.*, 114 F. Supp. 2d 896 (ND Cal. 2000), aff'd in part, rev'd in part, 239 F. 3d 1004 (CA9 2001), StreamCast gave away a software program of a kind known as OpenNap, designed as compatible with the Napster program and open to Napster users for downloading files from other Napster and OpenNap users' computers. Evidence indicates that "[i]t was always [StreamCast's] intent to use [its OpenNap network] to be able to capture email addresses of [its] initial target market so that [it] could promote [its] StreamCast Morpheus interface to them," App. 861; indeed, the OpenNap program was engineered "'to leverage Napster's 50 million user base,'" *id.*, at 746.

StreamCast monitored both the number of users downloading its OpenNap program and the number of music files they downloaded. *Id.*, at 859, 863, 866. It also used the resulting OpenNap network to distribute copies of the Morpheus software and to encourage users to adopt it. *Id.*, at 861, 867, 1039. Internal company documents indicate that StreamCast hoped to attract large numbers of former Napster users if that company was shut down by court order or otherwise, and that StreamCast planned to be the next Napster. *Id.*, at 861. A kit developed by StreamCast to be delivered to advertisers, for example, contained press articles about StreamCast's potential to capture former Napster users, *id.*, at 568–572, and it introduced itself to some potential advertisers as a company "which is similar to what Napster was," *id.*, at 884. It broadcast banner advertisements to users of other Napster-compatible software, urging them to adopt its OpenNap. *Id.*, at 586. An internal e-mail from a company executive stated: "'We have put this network in place so that when Napster pulls the plug on their free service ... or if the Court orders them shut down prior to that ... we will be positioned to capture the flood of their 32 million users that will be actively looking for an alternative.'" *Id.*, at 588–589, 861.

Thus, StreamCast developed promotional materials to market its service as the best Napster alternative. One proposed advertisement read: "Napster Inc. has announced that it will soon begin charging you a fee. That's if the courts don't order it shut down first. What will you do to get around it?" *Id.*, at 897. Another proposed ad touted StreamCast's software as the "#1 alternative to Napster" and asked "[w]hen the lights went off at Napster ... where did the users go?" *Id.*, at 836 (ellipsis in original).[Footnote 7] StreamCast even planned to flaunt the illegal uses of its software; when it launched the OpenNap network, the chief technology officer of the company averred that "[t]he goal is to get in trouble with the law and get sued. It's the best way to get in the new[s]." *Id.*, at 916.

The evidence that Grokster sought to capture the market of former Napster users is sparser but revealing, for Grokster launched its own OpenNap system called Swaptor and inserted digital codes into its Web site so that computer users using Web search engines to look for "Napster" or "[f]ree filesharing" would be directed to the Grokster Web site, where they could download the Grokster software. *Id.*, at 992–993. And Grokster's name is an apparent derivative of Napster.

StreamCast's executives monitored the number of songs by certain commercial artists available on their networks, and an internal communication indicates they aimed to have a larger number of copyrighted songs available on their networks than other file-sharing networks. *Id.*, at 868. The point, of course, would be to attract users of a mind to infringe, just as it would be with their promotional materials developed showing copyrighted songs as examples of the kinds of files available through Morpheus. *Id.*, at 848. Morpheus in fact allowed users to search specifically for "Top 40" songs, *id.*, at 735, which were inevitably copyrighted. Similarly, Grokster sent users a newsletter promoting its ability to provide particular, popular copyrighted materials. Brief for Motion Picture Studio and Recording Company Petitioners 7–8.

In addition to this evidence of express promotion, marketing, and intent to promote further, the business models employed by Grokster and StreamCast confirm that their principal object was use of their software to download copyrighted works. Grokster and StreamCast receive no revenue from users, who obtain the software itself for nothing. Instead, both companies generate income by selling advertising space, and they stream the advertising to Grokster and Morpheus users while they are employing the programs. As the number of users of each program increases, advertising opportunities become worth more. Cf. App. 539, 804. While there is doubtless some demand for free Shakespeare, the evidence shows that substantive volume is a function of free access to copyrighted work. Users seeking Top 40 songs, for example, or the latest release by Modest Mouse, are certain to be far more numerous than those seeking a free Decameron, and Grokster and StreamCast translated that demand into dollars.

Finally, there is no evidence that either company made an effort to filter copyrighted material from users' downloads or otherwise impede the sharing of copyrighted files. Although Grokster appears to have sent e-mails warning users about infringing content when it received threatening notice from the copyright holders, it never blocked anyone from continuing to use its software to share copyrighted files. *Id.*, at 75–76. StreamCast not only rejected another company's offer of help to monitor infringement, *id.*, at 928–929, but blocked the Internet Protocol addresses of entities it believed were trying to engage in such monitoring on its networks, *id.*, at 917–922.

B

After discovery, the parties on each side of the case cross-moved for summary judgment. The District Court limited its consideration to the asserted liability of Grokster and StreamCast for distributing the current versions of their software, leaving aside whether either was liable "for damages arising from *past* versions of their software, or from other past activities." 259 F. Supp. 2d 1029, 1033 (CD Cal. 2003). The District Court held that those who used the Grokster and Morpheus software to download copyrighted media files directly infringed MGM's copyrights, a conclusion not contested on appeal, but the court nonetheless granted summary judgment in favor of Grokster and StreamCast as to any liability arising from distribution of the then current versions of their software. Distributing that software gave rise to no liability in the court's view, because its use did not provide the distributors with actual knowledge of specific acts of infringement. Case No. CV 01 08541 SVW (PJWx) (CD Cal., June 18, 2003), App. 1213.

The Court of Appeals affirmed. 380 F. 3d 1154 (CA9 2004). In the court's analysis, a defendant was liable as a contributory infringer when it had knowledge of direct infringement and materially contributed to the infringement. But the court read *Sony Corp. of America* v. *Universal City Studios, Inc.*, 464 U. S. 417 (1984), as holding that distribution of a commercial product capable of substantial noninfringing uses could not give rise to contributory liability for infringement unless the distributor had actual knowledge of specific instances of infringement and failed to act on that knowledge. The fact that the software was capable of substantial noninfringing uses in the Ninth Circuit's view meant that Grokster and StreamCast were not liable, because they had no such actual knowledge, owing to the decentralized architecture of their software. The court also held that Grokster and StreamCast did not materially contribute to their users' infringement because it was the users themselves who searched for, retrieved, and stored the infringing files, with no involvement by the defendants beyond providing the software in the first place.

The Ninth Circuit also considered whether Grokster and StreamCast could be liable under a theory of vicarious infringement. The court held against liability because the defendants did not monitor or control the use of the software, had no agreed-upon right or current ability to supervise its use, and had no independent duty to police infringement. We granted certiorari. 543 U. S. ___ (2004).

II

A

MGM and many of the *amici* fault the Court of Appeals's holding for upsetting a sound balance between the respective values of supporting creative pursuits through copyright protection and promoting innovation in new communication technologies by limiting the incidence of liability for copyright infringement. The more artistic protection is favored, the more technological innovation may be discouraged; the administration of copyright law is an exercise in managing the trade-off. See *Sony*

Corp. v. *Universal City Studios, supra*, at 442; see generally Ginsburg, Copyright and Control Over New Technologies of Dissemination, 101 Colum. L. Rev. 1613 (2001); Lichtman & Landes, Indirect Liability for Copyright Infringement: An Economic Perspective, 16 Harv. J. L. & Tech. 395 (2003).

The tension between the two values is the subject of this case, with its claim that digital distribution of copyrighted material threatens copyright holders as never before, because every copy is identical to the original, copying is easy, and many people (especially the young) use file-sharing software to download copyrighted works. This very breadth of the software's use may well draw the public directly into the debate over copyright policy, Peters, Brace Memorial Lecture: Copyright Enters the Public Domain, 51 J. Copyright Soc. 701, 705–717 (2004) (address by Register of Copyrights), and the indications are that the ease of copying songs or movies using software like Grokster's and Napster's is fostering disdain for copyright protection, Wu, When Code Isn't Law, 89 Va. L. Rev. 679, 724–726 (2003). As the case has been presented to us, these fears are said to be offset by the different concern that imposing liability, not only on infringers but on distributors of software based on its potential for unlawful use, could limit further development of beneficial technologies. See, e.g., Lemley & Reese, Reducing Digital Copyright Infringement Without Restricting Innovation, 56 Stan. L. Rev. 1345, 1386–1390 (2004); Brief for Innovation Scholars and Economists as *Amici Curiae* 15–20; Brief for Emerging Technology Companies as *Amici Curiae* 19–25; Brief for Intel Corporation as *Amicus Curiae* 20–22.[Footnote 8].

The argument for imposing indirect liability in this case is, however, a powerful one, given the number of infringing downloads that occur every day using StreamCast's and Grokster's software. When a widely shared service or product is used to commit infringement, it may be impossible to enforce rights in the protected work effectively against all direct infringers, the only practical alternative being to go against the distributor of the copying device for secondary liability on a theory of contributory or vicarious infringement. See *In re Aimster Copyright Litigation*, 334 F. 3d 643, 645–646 (CA7 2003).

One infringes contributorily by intentionally inducing or encouraging direct infringement, see *Gershwin Pub. Corp.* v. *Columbia Artists Management, Inc.*, 443 F. 2d 1159, 1162 (CA2 1971), and infringes vicariously by profiting from direct infringement while declining to exercise a right to stop or limit it, *Shapiro, Bernstein & Co.* v. *H. L. Green Co.*, 316 F. 2d 304, 307 (CA2 1963).[Footnote 9] Although "[t]he Copyright Act does not expressly render anyone liable for infringement committed by another," *Sony Corp.* v. *Universal City Studios,*464 U. S., at 434, these doctrines of secondary liability emerged from common law principles and are well established in the law, *id.*, at 486 (Blackmun, J., dissenting); *Kalem Co.* v. *Harper Brothers*, 222 U. S. 55, 62–63 (1911); *Gershwin Pub. Corp.* v. *Columbia Artists Management, supra*, at 1162; 3 M. Nimmer & D. Nimmer, Copyright, §12.04[A] (2005).

B

Despite the currency of these principles of secondary liability, this Court has dealt with secondary copyright infringement in only one recent case, and because MGM has tailored its principal claim to our opinion there, a look at our earlier holding is in order. In *Sony Corp. v. Universal City Studios, supra,* this Court addressed a claim that secondary liability for infringement can arise from the very distribution of a commercial product. There, the product, novel at the time, was what we know today as the videocassette recorder or VCR. Copyright holders sued Sony as the manufacturer, claiming it was contributorily liable for infringement that occurred when VCR owners taped copyrighted programs because it supplied the means used to infringe, and it had constructive knowledge that infringement would occur. At the trial on the merits, the evidence showed that the principal use of the VCR was for "'time-shifting,'" or taping a program for later viewing at a more convenient time, which the Court found to be a fair, not an infringing, use. *Id.,* at 423–424. There was no evidence that Sony had expressed an object of bringing about taping in violation of copyright or had taken active steps to increase its profits from unlawful taping. *Id.,* at 438. Although Sony's advertisements urged consumers to buy the VCR to "'record favorite shows'" or "'build a library'" of recorded programs, *id.,* at 459 (Blackmun, J., dissenting), neither of these uses was necessarily infringing, *id.,* at 424, 454–455.

On those facts, with no evidence of stated or indicated intent to promote infringing uses, the only conceivable basis for imposing liability was on a theory of contributory infringement arising from its sale of VCRs to consumers with knowledge that some would use them to infringe. *Id.,* at 439. But because the VCR was "capable of commercially significant noninfringing uses," we held the manufacturer could not be faulted solely on the basis of its distribution. *Id.,* at 442.

This analysis reflected patent law's traditional staple article of commerce doctrine, now codified, that distribution of a component of a patented device will not violate the patent if it is suitable for use in other ways. 35 U. S. C. §271(c); *Aro Mfg. Co. v. Convertible Top Replacement Co.,* 377 U. S. 476, 485 (1964) (noting codification of cases); *id.,* at 486, n. 6 (same). The doctrine was devised to identify instances in which it may be presumed from distribution of an article in commerce that the distributor intended the article to be used to infringe another's patent, and so may justly be held liable for that infringement. "One who makes and sells articles which are only adapted to be used in a patented combination will be presumed to intend the natural consequences of his acts; he will be presumed to intend that they shall be used in the combination of the patent." *New York Scaffolding Co. v. Whitney,* 224 F. 452, 459 (CA8 1915); see also *James Heekin Co. v. Baker,* 138 F. 63, 66 (CA8 1905); *Canda v. Michigan Malleable Iron Co.,* 124 F. 486, 489 (CA6 1903); *Thomson-Houston Electric Co. v. Ohio Brass Co.,* 80 F. 712, 720–721 (CA6 1897); *Red Jacket Mfg. Co. v. Davis,* 82 F. 432, 439 (CA7 1897); *Holly v. Vergennes Machine Co.,* 4 F. 74, 82 (CC Vt. 1880); *Renwick v. Pond,* 20 F. Cas. 536, 541 (No. 11,702) (CC SDNY 1872).

In sum, where an article is "good for nothing else" but infringement, *Canda v. Michigan Malleable Iron Co., supra,* at 489, there is no legitimate public interest in its unlicensed availability, and there is no injustice in presuming or imputing an intent to infringe, see *Henry v. A. B. Dick Co.*, 224 U. S. 1, 48 (1912), overruled on other grounds, *Motion Picture Patents Co. v. Universal Film Mfg. Co.*, 243 U. S. 502 (1917). Conversely, the doctrine absolves the equivocal conduct of selling an item with substantial lawful as well as unlawful uses, and limits liability to instances of more acute fault than the mere understanding that some of one's products will be misused. It leaves breathing room for innovation and a vigorous commerce. See *Sony Corp. v. Universal City Studios, supra*, at 442; *Dawson Chemical Co. v. Rohm & Haas Co.*, 448 U. S. 176, 221 (1980); *Henry v. A. B. Dick Co., supra*, at 48.

The parties and many of the *amici* in this case think the key to resolving it is the *Sony* rule and, in particular, what it means for a product to be "capable of commercially significant noninfringing uses." *Sony Corp. v. Universal City Studios, supra*, at 442. MGM advances the argument that granting summary judgment to Grokster and StreamCast as to their current activities gave too much weight to the value of innovative technology, and too little to the copyrights infringed by users of their software, given that 90% of works available on one of the networks was shown to be copyrighted. Assuming the remaining 10% to be its noninfringing use, MGM says this should not qualify as "substantial," and the Court should quantify Sony to the extent of holding that a product used "principally" for infringement does not qualify. See Brief for Motion Picture Studio and Recording Company Petitioners 31. As mentioned before, Grokster and StreamCast reply by citing evidence that their software can be used to reproduce public domain works, and they point to copyright holders who actually encourage copying. Even if infringement is the principal practice with their software today, they argue, the noninfringing uses are significant and will grow.

We agree with MGM that the Court of Appeals misapplied *Sony*, which it read as limiting secondary liability quite beyond the circumstances to which the case applied. *Sony* barred secondary liability based on presuming or imputing intent to cause infringement solely from the design or distribution of a product capable of substantial lawful use, which the distributor knows is in fact used for infringement. The Ninth Circuit has read *Sony*'s limitation to mean that whenever a product is capable of substantial lawful use, the producer can never be held contributorily liable for third parties' infringing use of it; it read the rule as being this broad, even when an actual purpose to cause infringing use is shown by evidence independent of design and distribution of the product, unless the distributors had "specific knowledge of infringement at a time at which they contributed to the infringement, and failed to act upon that information." 380 F. 3d, at 1162 (internal quotation marks and alterations omitted). Because the Circuit found the StreamCast and Grokster software capable of substantial lawful use, it concluded on the basis of its reading of *Sony* that neither company could be held liable, since there was no showing that their software, being without any central server, afforded them knowledge of specific unlawful uses.

This view of *Sony*, however, was error, converting the case from one about liability resting on imputed intent to one about liability on any theory. Because *Sony* did not displace other theories of secondary liability, and because we find below that it was error to grant summary judgment to the companies on MGM's inducement claim, we do not revisit *Sony* further, as MGM requests, to add a more quantified description of the point of balance between protection and commerce when liability rests solely on distribution with knowledge that unlawful use will occur. It is enough to note that the Ninth Circuit's judgment rested on an erroneous understanding of *Sony* and to leave further consideration of the *Sony* rule for a day when that may be required.

C

Sony's rule limits imputing culpable intent as a matter of law from the characteristics or uses of a distributed product. But nothing in *Sony* requires courts to ignore evidence of intent if there is such evidence, and the case was never meant to foreclose rules of fault-based liability derived from the common law.[Footnote 10] *Sony Corp. v. Universal City Studios*, 464 U. S., at 439 ("If vicarious liability is to be imposed on Sony in this case, it must rest on the fact that it has sold equipment with constructive knowledge" of the potential for infringement). Thus, where evidence goes beyond a product's characteristics or the knowledge that it may be put to infringing uses, and shows statements or actions directed to promoting infringement, *Sony*'s staple-article rule will not preclude liability.

The classic case of direct evidence of unlawful purpose occurs when one induces commission of infringement by another, or "entic[es] or persuad[es] another" to infringe, Black's Law Dictionary 790 (8th ed. 2004), as by advertising. Thus at common law a copyright or patent defendant who "not only expected but invoked [infringing use] by advertisement" was liable for infringement "on principles recognized in every part of the law." *Kalem Co. v. Harper Brothers*, 222 U. S., at 62–63 (copyright infringement). See also *Henry v. A. B. Dick Co.*, 224 U. S., at 48–49 (contributory liability for patent infringement may be found where a good's "most conspicuous use is one which will coöperate in an infringement when sale to such user is invoked by advertisement" of the infringing use); *Thomson-Houston Electric Co. v. Kelsey Electric R. Specialty Co.*, 75 F. 1005, 1007–1008 (CA2 1896) (relying on advertisements and displays to find defendant's "willingness ... to aid other persons in any attempts which they may be disposed to make towards [patent] infringement"); *Rumford Chemical Works v. Hecker*, 20 F. Cas. 1342, 1346 (No. 12,133) (CC N. J. 1876) (demonstrations of infringing activity along with "avowals of the [infringing] purpose and use for which it was made" supported liability for patent infringement).

The rule on inducement of infringement as developed in the early cases is no different today.[Footnote 11] Evidence of "active steps ... taken to encourage direct infringement," *Oak Industries, Inc. v. Zenith Electronics Corp.*, 697 F. Supp. 988, 992 (ND Ill. 1988), such as advertising an infringing use or instructing how to engage in an infringing use, show an affirmative intent that the product be used to infringe, and a showing that infringement was encouraged overcomes the law's reluctance to find liability when a defendant merely sells a commercial product suitable for some lawful use, see, e.g., *Water Technologies Corp. v. Calco, Ltd.*, 850 F. 2d 660, 668 (CA Fed. 1988) (liability for inducement where one "actively and knowingly aid[s] and abet[s] another's direct infringement" (emphasis omitted)); *Fromberg, Inc. v. Thornhill*, 315 F. 2d 407, 412–413 (CA5 1963) (demonstrations by sales staff of infringing uses supported liability for inducement); *Haworth Inc.* v. *Herman Miller Inc.*, 37 USPQ 2d 1080, 1090 (WD Mich. 1994) (evidence that defendant "demonstrate[d] and recommend[ed] infringing configurations" of its product could support inducement liability); *Sims* v. *Mack Trucks, Inc.*, 459 F. Supp. 1198, 1215 (ED Pa. 1978) (finding inducement where the use "depicted by the defendant in its promotional film and brochures infringes the ... patent"), overruled on other grounds, 608 F. 2d 87 (CA3 1979). Cf. W. Keeton, D. Dobbs, R. Keeton, & D. Owen, Prosser and Keeton on Law of Torts 37 (5th ed. 1984) ("There is a definite tendency to impose greater responsibility upon a defendant whose conduct was intended to do harm, or was morally wrong").

For the same reasons that *Sony* took the staple-article doctrine of patent law as a model for its copyright safe-harbor rule, the inducement rule, too, is a sensible one for copyright. We adopt it here, holding that one who distributes a device with the object of promoting its use to infringe copyright, as shown by clear expression or other affirmative steps taken to foster infringement, is liable for the resulting acts of infringement by third parties. We are, of course, mindful of the need to keep from trenching on regular commerce or discouraging the development of technologies with lawful and unlawful potential. Accordingly, just as *Sony* did not find intentional inducement despite the knowledge of the VCR manufacturer that its device could be used to infringe, 464 U. S., at 439, n. 19, mere knowledge of infringing potential or of actual infringing uses would not be enough here to subject a distributor to liability. Nor would ordinary acts incident to product distribution, such as offering customers technical support or product updates, support liability in themselves. The inducement rule, instead, premises liability on purposeful, culpable expression and conduct, and thus does nothing to compromise legitimate commerce or discourage innovation having a lawful promise.

III

A

The only apparent question about treating MGM's evidence as sufficient to withstand summary judgment under the theory of inducement goes to the need on MGM's part to adduce evidence that StreamCast and Grokster communicated an inducing message to their software users. The classic instance of inducement is by advertisement or solicitation that broadcasts a message designed to stimulate others to commit violations. MGM claims that such a message is shown here. It is undisputed that StreamCast beamed onto the computer screens of users of Napster-compatible programs ads urging the adoption of its OpenNap program, which was designed, as its name implied, to invite the custom of patrons of Napster, then under attack in the courts for facilitating massive infringement. Those who accepted StreamCast's OpenNap program were offered software to perform the same services, which a factfinder could conclude would readily have been understood in the Napster market as the ability to download copyrighted music files. Grokster distributed an electronic newsletter containing links to articles promoting its software's ability to access popular copyrighted music. And anyone whose Napster or free file-sharing searches turned up a link to Grokster would have understood Grokster to be offering the same file-sharing ability as Napster, and to the same people who probably used Napster for infringing downloads; that would also have been the understanding of anyone offered Grokster's suggestively named Swaptor software, its version of OpenNap. And both companies communicated a clear message by responding affirmatively to requests for help in locating and playing copyrighted materials.

In StreamCast's case, of course, the evidence just described was supplemented by other unequivocal indications of unlawful purpose in the internal communications and advertising designs aimed at Napster users ("When the lights went off at Napster ... where did the users go?" App. 836 (ellipsis in original)). Whether the messages were communicated is not to the point on this record. The function of the message in the theory of inducement is to prove by a defendant's own statements that his unlawful purpose disqualifies him from claiming protection (and incidentally to point to actual violators likely to be found among those who hear or read the message). See *supra*, at 17–19. Proving that a message was sent out, then, is the preeminent but not exclusive way of showing that active steps were taken with the purpose of bringing about infringing acts, and of showing that infringing acts took place by using the device distributed. Here, the summary judgment record is replete with other evidence that Grokster and StreamCast, unlike the manufacturer and distributor in *Sony*, acted with a purpose to cause copyright violations by use of software suitable for illegal use. See *supra*, at 6–9.

Three features of this evidence of intent are particularly notable. First, each company showed itself to be aiming to satisfy a known source of demand for copyright infringement, the market comprising former Napster users. StreamCast's internal documents made constant reference to Napster, it initially distributed its Morpheus software through an OpenNap program compatible with Napster, it advertised its OpenNap program to Napster users, and its Morpheus software functions as Napster did except that it could be used to distribute more kinds of files, including copyrighted movies and software programs. Grokster's name is apparently derived from Napster, it too initially offered an OpenNap program, its software's function is likewise comparable to Napster's, and it attempted to divert queries for Napster onto its own Web site. Grokster and StreamCast's efforts to supply services to former Napster users, deprived of a mechanism to copy and distribute what were overwhelmingly infringing files, indicate a principal, if not exclusive, intent on the part of each to bring about infringement.

Second, this evidence of unlawful objective is given added significance by MGM's showing that neither company attempted to develop filtering tools or other mechanisms to diminish the infringing activity using their software. While the Ninth Circuit treated the defendants' failure to develop such tools as irrelevant because they lacked an independent duty to monitor their users' activity, we think this evidence underscores Grokster's and StreamCast's intentional facilitation of their users' infringement.[Footnote 12].

Third, there is a further complement to the direct evidence of unlawful objective. It is useful to recall that StreamCast and Grokster make money by selling advertising space, by directing ads to the screens of computers employing their software. As the record shows, the more the software is used, the more ads are sent out and the greater the advertising revenue becomes. Since the extent of the software's use determines the gain to the distributors, the commercial sense of their enterprise turns on high-volume use, which the record shows is infringing.[Footnote 13] This evidence alone would not justify an inference of unlawful intent, but viewed in the context of the entire record its import is clear.

The unlawful objective is unmistakable.

B

In addition to intent to bring about infringement and distribution of a device suitable for infringing use, the inducement theory of course requires evidence of actual infringement by recipients of the device, the software in this case. As the account of the facts indicates, there is evidence of infringement on a gigantic scale, and there is no serious issue of the adequacy of MGM's showing on this point in order to survive the companies' summary judgment requests. Although an exact calculation of infringing use, as a basis for a claim of damages, is subject to dispute, there is no question that the summary judgment evidence is at least adequate to entitle MGM to go forward with claims for damages and equitable relief.

* * *

In sum, this case is significantly different from *Sony* and reliance on that case to rule in favor of StreamCast and Grokster was error. *Sony* dealt with a claim of liability based solely on distributing a product with alternative lawful and unlawful uses, with knowledge that some users would follow the unlawful course. The case struck a balance between the interests of protection and innovation by holding that the product's capability of substantial lawful employment should bar the imputation of fault and consequent secondary liability for the unlawful acts of others.

MGM's evidence in this case most obviously addresses a different basis of liability for distributing a product open to alternative uses. Here, evidence of the distributors' words and deeds going beyond distribution as such shows a purpose to cause and profit from third-party acts of copyright infringement. If liability for inducing infringement is ultimately found, it will not be on the basis of presuming or imputing fault, but from inferring a patently illegal objective from statements and actions showing what that objective was.

There is substantial evidence in MGM's favor on all elements of inducement, and summary judgment in favor of Grokster and StreamCast was error. On remand, reconsideration of MGM's motion for summary judgment will be in order.

The judgment of the Court of Appeals is vacated, and the case is remanded for further proceedings consistent with this opinion.

It is so ordered.

Footnote 1

Peer-to-peer networks have disadvantages as well. Searches on peer-to-peer networks may not reach and uncover all available files because search requests may not be transmitted to every computer on the network. There may be redundant copies of popular files. The creator of the software has no incentive to minimize storage or bandwidth consumption, the costs of which are borne by every user of the network. Most relevant here, it is more difficult to control the content of files available for retrieval and the behavior of users.

Footnote 2

The studios and recording companies and the songwriters and music publishers filed separate suits against the defendants that were consolidated by the District Court.

Footnote 3

Subsequent versions of Morpheus, released after the record was made in this case, apparently rely not on Gnutella but on a technology called Neonet. These developments are not before us.

Footnote 4

There is some evidence that both Grokster and StreamCast previously operated supernodes, which compiled indexes of files available on all of the nodes connected to them. This evidence, pertaining to previous versions of the defendants' software, is not before us and would not affect our conclusions in any event.

Footnote 5

By comparison, evidence introduced by the plaintiffs in *A & M Records, Inc.* v. *Napster, Inc.*, 239 F. 3d 1004 (CA9 2001), showed that 87% of files available on the Napster filesharing network were copyrighted, *id.*, at 1013.

Footnote 6

The Grokster founder contends that in answering these e-mails he often did not read them fully. App. 77, 769.

Footnote 7

The record makes clear that StreamCast developed these promotional materials but not whether it released them to the public. Even if these advertisements were not released to the public and do not show encouragement to infringe, they illuminate StreamCast's purposes.

Footnote 8

The mutual exclusivity of these values should not be overstated, however. On the one hand technological innovators, including those writing filesharing computer programs, may wish for effective copyright protections for their work. See, e.g., Wu, When Code Isn't Law, 89 Va. L. Rev. 679, 750 (2003). (StreamCast itself was urged by an associate to "get [its] technology written down and [its intellectual property] protected." App. 866.) On the other hand the widespread distribution of creative works through improved technologies may enable the synthesis of new works or generate audiences for emerging artists. See *Eldred* v. *Ashcroft*, 537 U. S. 186, 223–226 (2003) (Stevens, J., dissenting); Van Houweling, Distributive Values in Copyright, 83 Texas L. Rev. 1535, 1539–1540, 1562–1564 (2005); Brief for Sovereign Artists et al. as *Amici Curiae* 11.

Footnote 9

We stated in *Sony Corp. of America* v. *Universal City Studios, Inc.*, 464 U. S. 417 (1984), that " 'the lines between direct infringement, contributory infringement and vicarious liability are not clearly drawn' .... [R]easoned analysis of [the *Sony* plaintiffs' contributory infringement claim] necessarily entails consideration of arguments and case law which may also be forwarded under the other labels, and indeed the parties ... rely upon such arguments and authority in support of their respective positions on the issue of contributory infringement," *id.*, at 435, n. 17 (quoting *Universal City Studios, Inc.* v. *Sony Corp.*, 480 F. Supp. 429, 457–458 (CD Cal. 1979)). In the present case MGM has argued a vicarious liability theory, which allows imposition of liability when the defendant profits directly from the infringement and has a right and ability to supervise the direct infringer, even if the defendant initially lacks knowledge of the infringement. See, e.g., *Shapiro, Bernstein & Co.* v. *H. L. Green Co.*, 316 F. 2d 304, 308 (CA2 1963); *Dreamland Ball Room, Inc.* v. *Shapiro, Bernstein & Co.*, 36 F. 2d 354, 355 (CA7 1929). Because we resolve the case based on an inducement theory, there is no need to analyze separately MGM's vicarious liability theory.

Footnote 10

Nor does the Patent Act's exemption from liability for those who distribute a staple article of commerce, 35 U. S. C. §271(c), extend to those who induce patent infringement, §271(b).

Footnote 11

Inducement has been codified in patent law. *Ibid.*

Footnote 12

Of course, in the absence of other evidence of intent, a court would be unable to find contributory infringement liability merely based on a failure to take affirmative steps to prevent infringement, if the device otherwise was capable of substantial noninfringing uses. Such a holding would tread too close to the *Sony* safe harbor.

Footnote 13

Grokster and StreamCast contend that any theory of liability based on their conduct is not properly before this Court because the rulings in the trial and appellate courts dealt only with the present versions of their software, not "past acts ... that allegedly encouraged infringement or assisted ... known acts of infringement." Brief for Respondents 14; see also *id.*, at 34. This contention misapprehends the basis for their potential liability. It is not only that encouraging a particular consumer to infringe a copyright can give rise to secondary liability for the infringement that results. Inducement liability goes beyond that, and the distribution of a product can itself give rise to liability where evidence shows that the distributor intended and encouraged the product to be used to infringe. In such a case, the culpable act is not merely the encouragement of infringement but also the distribution of the tool intended for infringing use. See *Kalem Co. v. Harper Brothers*, 222 U. S. 55, 62–63 (1911); *Cable/Home Communication Corp. v. Network Productions, Inc.*, 902 F. 2d 829, 846 (CA11 1990); *A & M Records, Inc. v. Abdallah*, 948 F. Supp. 1449, 1456 (CD Cal. 1996).

2.3 Analysis of the Case
MGM Studios, Inc. v. Grokster, Ltd., 545 U.S. 913 (2005).
The text of MGM v. Grokster is available here:
https://supreme.justia.com/cases/federal/us/545/913/

This dispute involved innovative file sharing technologies, and assertive efforts by large scale copyright holders to control their distribution and use through copyright law. A full understanding of MGM v. Grokster requires beginning with an earlier, related case: Sony v. Universal Studios; Sony Corp. of America v. Universal City Studios, Inc., 464 U.S. 417 (1984): https://supreme.justia.com/cases/federal/us/464/417/. Sony Corporation of America manufactured and sold "Betamax" home video tape recorders (VTRs). Universal City Studios owned the copyrights to television programs broadcast on public airwaves. Universal sued Sony for copyright infringement, alleging that because consumers used Sony's Betamax to record unauthorized copies of Universal's copyrighted works, Sony was liable for the copyright infringement allegedly committed by those consumers, in violation of the Copyright Act. This theory of secondary (or third party) liability for copyright infringement was borrowed from the U.S. Patent Act and patent litigation jurisprudence, and was not expressly articulated in the Copyright Act. Universal asserted that because Sony contributed to the infringement by supplying the machines that made the unauthorized copies, Sony could be held liable for "contributory infringement."

Universal sought monetary damages, an equitable accounting of profits, and an injunction against the manufacturing and marketing of Sony Betamax VTRs. The trial court denied all relief, holding that the noncommercial home use recording of material broadcast over the public airwaves was a fair use of copyrighted works and did not constitute copyright infringement. The court also concluded that Sony could not be held liable as a contributory infringer even if the home use of a VTR was considered an infringing use.

The Ninth Circuit Court of Appeals reversed, holding Sony liable for contributory infringement because the Betamax allowed consumers to make infringing (rather than fair use) copies of shows that were broadcast on television. On appeal, the U.S. Supreme Court faced the question of whether Sony's sale of "Betamax" video tape recorders to the general public constituted contributory infringement of televised copyrighted materials that were non-permissively recorded by consumers. But they never really reached an answer. Instead, once the majority concluded that home taping by consumers constituted fair use within the meaning of Sec. 107 of the Copyright Act, there no longer was any copyright infringement that the Sony Betamax had contributed to. In a 5–4 opinion delivered by Justice John Paul Stevens, the Court concluded that a substantial number of copyright holders who license their works for free public broadcasts would not object to having their broadcasts time-shifted by private viewers and that Universal failed to show that time-shifting would cause non-minimal harm to the potential market for, or the value of, their copyrighted works. Justice Stevens wrote: "**the sale of copying equipment…does not constitute contributory infringement if the product is widely used for legitimate, unobjectionable purposes, or, indeed, is merely capable of substantial noninfringing uses.**" These bolded words became known as the "Sony Test" (or Sony Rule) even though they were merely dicta. The Sony Test gave lower courts a framework with which to analyze whether the distribution of new copying technologies should be enjoined or restricted because of the infringement risks they posed to copyrighted works.

As the Internet developed as a distribution network, Grokster and other companies distributed free software that allowed computer users to share electronic files through peer-to-peer networks. Within these networks, users can share digital files directly between their computers, without the use of a central server or directory. Users employed the software primarily to download copyrighted files, file-sharing which the software companies knew about and encouraged. The companies profited from advertising revenue since they streamed ads to the software users. A group of movie studios and other copyright holders sued and alleged that Grokster and the other companies violated the Copyright Act by intentionally distributing software to enable users to infringe copyrighted works.

The trial court ruled for Grokster, reasoning that the software distribution companies were not liable for copyright violations stemming from their software, which could have been used lawfully because they met the Sony Test. Grokster was being widely used for legitimate, unobjectionable purposes, and was clearly capable of substantial non-infringing uses. The Ninth Circuit Court of Appeals affirmed. But the U.S. Supreme Court had an unpleasant surprise in store for Grokster.

The Supreme Court took up the question of whether companies that distributed file-sharing software, and encouraged and profited from direct copyright infringement, which was facilitated by the use of the software, could be contributorily liable for the infringement. The unanimous opinion was, "yes." In an opinion written by Justice David Souter, the Court held that companies that distributed software, and promoted that software's ability to infringe copyrights, were liable for the resulting acts of infringement by consumers. The Court held that although the Copyright Act did not expressly make any party liable for another's infringing acts, secondary liability doctrines as described in the Sony Betamax case were applicable in the context of copyright law. The Grokster software in this case was widely distributed and used to infringe copyrights on a scale that would have made it immensely difficult for copyright holders to deal one by one with individual infringers. The Court concluded that the "only practical alternative" was to allow copyright holders to sue software distributors under secondary liability doctrines. Grokser and the other software companies were ultimately held liable for encouraging and profiting from the direct infringement by users of the software. The Court took great pains to announce that the Sony Test was still in effect and had not been overruled. Most observers, however, believe that this case hollowed out the Sony Test and tipped the uneasy balance between technology companies and the copyright industries decidedly in favor of copyright holders.

(3) **Whether the retroactively extending the duration of copyrights violate the constitution—ELDRED ET AL. v. ASHCROFT, ATTORNEY GENERAL**

OCTOBER TERM, 2002
CERTIORARI TO THE UNITED STATES COURT OF APPEALS FOR THE DISTRICT OF COLUMBIA CIRCUIT
No. 01-618. Argued October 9, 2002-Decided January 15, 2003

3.1 Syllabus
The Copyright and Patent Clause, U. S. Const., Art. I, § 8, cl. 8, provides as to copyrights: "Congress shall have Power ... to promote the Progress of Science ... by securing [to Authors] for limited Times ... the exclusive Right to their ... Writings." In the 1998 Copyright Term Extension Act (CTEA), Congress enlarged the duration of copyrights by 20 years: Under the 1976 Copyright Act (1976 Act), copyright protection generally lasted from a work's creation until 50 years after the author's death; under the CTEA, most copyrights now run from creation until 70 years after the author's death, 17 U. S. C. § 302(a). As in the case of prior copyright extensions, principally in 1831, 1909, and 1976, Congress provided for application of the enlarged terms to existing and future copyrights alike.

Petitioners, whose products or services build on copyrighted works that have gone into the public domain, brought this suit seeking a determination that the CTEA fails constitutional review under both the Copyright Clause's "limited Times" prescription and the First Amendment's free speech guarantee. Petitioners do not challenge the CTEA's "life-plus-70-years" timespan itself. They maintain that Congress went awry not with respect to newly created works, but in enlarging the term for published works with existing copyrights. The "limited Time" in effect when a copyright is secured, petitioners urge, becomes the constitutional boundary, a clear line beyond the power of Congress to extend. As to the First Amendment, petitioners contend that the CTEA is a content-neutral regulation of speech that fails inspection under the heightened judicial scrutiny appropriate for such regulations. The District Court entered judgment on the pleadings for the Attorney General (respondent here), holding that the CTEA does not violate the Copyright Clause's "limited Times" restriction because the CTEA's terms, though longer than the 1976 Act's terms, are still limited, not perpetual, and therefore fit within Congress' discretion. The court also held that there are no First Amendment rights to use the copyrighted works of others. The District of Columbia Circuit affirmed. In that court's unanimous view, *Harper & Row, Publishers, Inc. v. Nation Enterprises,* 471 U. S. 539, foreclosed petitioners' First Amendment challenge to the CTEA. The appeals court reasoned that copyright does not impermissibly restrict free speech, for it grants the author an exclusive right only to the specific form of expression; it does not shield any idea or fact contained in the copyrighted work, and it allows for "fair use" even of the expression itself. A majority of the court also rejected petitioners' Copyright Clause claim. The court ruled that Circuit precedent precluded petitioners' plea for interpretation of the "limited Times" prescription with a view to the Clause's preambular statement of purpose:

"To promote the Progress of Science." The court found nothing in the constitutional text or history to suggest that a term of years for a copyright is not a "limited Time" if it may later be extended for another "limited Time." Recounting that the First Congress made the 1790 Copyright Act applicable to existing copyrights arising under state copyright laws, the court held that that construction by contemporaries of the Constitution's formation merited almost conclusive weight under *Burrow-Giles Lithographic Co. v. Sarony,* 111 U. S. 53, 57. As early as *McClurg v. Kingsland,* 1 How. 202, the Court of Appeals recognized, this Court made it plain that the Copyright Clause permits Congress to amplify an existing patent's terms. The court added that this Court has been similarly deferential to Congress' judgment regarding copyright. E.g., *Sony Corp. of America v. Universal City Studios, Inc.,* 464 U. S. 417. Concerning petitioners' assertion that Congress could evade the limitation on its authority by stringing together an unlimited number of "limited Times," the court stated that such legislative misbehavior clearly was not before it. Rather, the court emphasized, the CTEA matched the baseline term for United States copyrights with the European Union term in order to meet contemporary circumstances.

3.2 Reasoning:
In placing existing and future copyrights in parity in the CTEA, Congress acted within its authority and did not transgress constitutional limitations.

1. The CTEA's extension of existing copyrights does not exceed Congress' power under the Copyright Clause.
(a) Guided by text, history, and precedent, this Court cannot agree with petitioners that extending the duration of existing copyrights is categorically beyond Congress' Copyright Clause authority. Although conceding that the CTEA's baseline term of life plus 70 years qualifies as a "limited Time" as applied to future copyrights, petitioners contend that existing copyrights extended to endure for that same term are not "limited." In petitioners' view, a time prescription, once set, becomes forever "fixed" or "inalterable." The word "limited," however, does not convey a meaning so constricted. At the time of the Framing, "limited" meant what it means today: confined within certain bounds, restrained, or circumscribed. Thus understood, a timespan appropriately "limited" as applied to future copyrights does not automatically cease to be "limited" when applied to existing copyrights. To comprehend the scope of Congress' Copyright Clause power, "a page of history is worth a volume of logic." *New York Trust Co. v. Eisner,* 256 U. S. 345, 349. History reveals an unbroken congressional practice of granting to authors of works with existing copyrights the benefit of term extensions so that all under copyright protection will be governed evenhandedly under the same regime. Moreover, because the Clause empowering Congress to confer copyrights also authorizes patents, the Court's inquiry is significantly informed by the fact that early Congresses extended the duration of numerous individual patents as well as copyrights. Lower courts saw no "limited Times" impediment to such extensions. Further, although this Court never before has had occasion

to decide whether extending existing copyrights complies with the "limited Times" prescription, the Court has found no constitutional barrier to the legislative expansion of existing patents. See, e.g., *McClurg*, 1 How., at 206. Congress' consistent historical practice reflects a judgment that an author who sold his work a week before should not be placed in a worse situation than the author who sold his work the day after enactment of a copyright extension. The CTEA follows this historical practice by keeping the 1976 Act's duration provisions largely in place and simply adding 20 years to each of them.

The CTEA is a rational exercise of the legislative authority conferred by the Copyright Clause. On this point, the Court defers substantially to Congress. *Sony*, 464 U. S., at 429. The CTEA reflects judgments of a kind Congress typically makes, judgments the Court cannot dismiss as outside the Legislature's domain. A key factor in the CTEA's passage was a 1993 European Union (EU) directive instructing EU members to establish a baseline copyright term of life plus 70 years and to deny this longer term to the works of any non-EU country whose laws did not secure the same extended term. By extending the baseline United States copyright term, Congress sought to ensure that American authors would receive the same copyright protection in Europe as their European counterparts. The CTEA may also provide greater incentive for American and other authors to create and disseminate their work in the United States. Additionally, Congress passed the CTEA in light of demographic, economic, and technological changes, and rationally credited projections that longer terms would encourage copyright holders to invest in the restoration and public distribution of their works.

(b) Petitioners' Copyright Clause arguments, which rely on several novel readings of the Clause, are unpersuasive.

(1) Nothing before this Court warrants construction of the CTEA's 20-year term extension as a congressional attempt to evade or override the "limited Times" constraint. Critically, petitioners fail to show how the CTEA crosses a constitutionally significant threshold with respect to "limited Times" that the 1831, 1909, and 1976 Acts did not. Those earlier Acts did not create perpetual copyrights, and neither does the CTEA.

(2) Petitioners' dominant series of arguments, premised on the proposition that Congress may not extend an existing copyright absent new consideration from the author, are unavailing. The first such contention, that the CTEA's extension of existing copyrights overlooks the requirement of "originality," incorrectly relies on *Feist Publications, Inc. v. Rural Telephone Service Co.*, 499 U. S. 340, 345, 359. That case did not touch on the duration of copyright protection. Rather, it addressed only the core question of copyright ability. Explaining the originality requirement, *Feist* trained on the Copyright Clause words "Authors" and "Writings," id., at 346–347, and did not construe the "limited Times" prescription, as to which the originality requirement has no bearing. Also unavailing is petitioners' second argument, that the CTEA's extension of existing copyrights fails to "promote the Progress of Science" because it does not stimulate the creation of new works, but merely adds value to works already created. The justifications that motivated Congress to enact the CTEA, set forth *supra*, provide a rational basis for concluding that the CTEA

"promote[s] the Progress of Science." Moreover, Congress' unbroken practice since the founding generation of applying new definitions or adjustments of the copyright term to both future works and existing works overwhelms petitioners' argument. Also rejected is petitioners' third contention, that the CTEA's extension of existing copyrights without demanding additional consideration ignores copyright's *quid pro quo*, whereby Congress grants the author of an original work an "exclusive Right" for a "limited Time" in exchange for a dedication to the public thereafter. Given Congress' consistent placement of existing copyright holders in parity with future holders, the author of a work created in the last 170 years would reasonably comprehend, as the protection offered her, a copyright not only for the time in place when protection is gained, but also for any renewal or extension legislated during that time. *Sears, Roebuck & Co.* v. *Stiffel Co.,* 376 U. S. 225, 229, and *Bonito Boats, Inc.* v. *Thunder Craft Boats, Inc.,* 489 U. S. 141, 146, both of which involved the federal patent regime, are not to the contrary, since neither concerned the extension of a patent's duration nor suggested that such an extension might be constitutionally infirm. Furthermore, given crucial distinctions between patents and copyrights, one cannot extract from language in the Court's patent decisions-language not trained on a grant's duration-genuine support for petitioners' *quid pro quo* argument. Patents and copyrights do not entail the same exchange, since immediate disclosure is not the objective of, but is *exacted from,* the patentee, whereas disclosure is the desired objective of the author seeking copyright protection. Moreover, while copyright gives the holder no monopoly on any knowledge, fact, or idea, the grant of a patent prevents full use by others of the inventor's knowledge.

(3) The "congruence and proportionality" standard of review described in cases evaluating exercises of Congress' power under § 5 of the Fourteenth Amendment has never been applied outside the § 5 context. It does not hold sway for judicial review of legislation enacted, as copyright laws are, pursuant to Article I authorization. Section 5 authorizes Congress to "enforce" commands contained in and incorporated into the Fourteenth Amendment. The Copyright Clause, in contrast, empowers Congress to *define* the scope of the substantive right. See *Sony,* 464 U. S., at 429. Judicial deference to such congressional definition is "but a corollary to the grant to Congress of any Article I power." *Graham* v. *John Deere Co. of Kansas City,* 383 U. S. 1, 6. It would be no more appropriate for this Court to subject the CTEA to "congruence and proportionality" review than it would be to hold the Act unconstitutional per se.

2. The CTEA's extension of existing and future copyrights does not violate the First Amendment.

That Amendment and the Copyright Clause were adopted close in time. This proximity indicates the Framers' view that copyright's limited monopolies are compatible with free speech principles. In addition, copyright law contains built-in First Amendment accommodations. See *Harper & Row,* 471 U. S., at 560. First, 17 U. S. C. § 102(b), which makes only expression, not ideas, eligible for copyright protection, strikes a definitional balance between the First Amendment and copyright law by permitting free communication of facts while still protecting an author's expression.

Harper & Row, 471 U. S., at 556. Second, the "fair use" defense codified at § 107 allows the public to use not only facts and ideas contained in a copyrighted work, but also expression itself for limited purposes. "Fair use" thereby affords considerable latitude for scholarship and comment, id., at 560, and even for parody, see *Campbell* v. *Acuff-Rose Music, Inc., 510* U. S. 569. The CTEA itself supplements these traditional First Amendment safeguards in two prescriptions: The first allows libraries and similar institutions to reproduce and distribute copies of certain published works for scholarly purposes during the last 20 years of any copyright term, if the work is not already being exploited commercially and further copies are unavailable at a reasonable price, § 108(h); the second exempts small businesses from having to pay performance royalties on music played from licensed radio, television, and similar facilities, § 1l0(5)(B). Finally, petitioners' reliance on *Turner Broadcasting System, Inc.* v. *FCC,* 512 U. S. 622, 641, is misplaced. *Turner Broadcasting* involved a statute requiring cable television operators to carry and transmit broadcast stations through their proprietary cable systems. The CTEA, in contrast, does not oblige anyone to reproduce another's speech against the carrier's will. Instead, it protects authors' original expression from unrestricted exploitation. The First Amendment securely protects the freedom to make—or decline to make—one's own speech; it bears less heavily when speakers assert the right to make other people's speeches. When, as in this case, Congress has not altered the traditional contours of copyright protection, further First Amendment scrutiny is unnecessary. See, e.g., *Harper & Row, 471* U. S., at 560. Pp. 218–222.

239 F.3d 372, affirmed.

ELDRED ET AL. v. ASHCROFT, ATTORNEY GENERAL
CERTIORARI TO THE UNITED STATES COURT OF APPEALS FOR THE DISTRICT OF COLUMBIA CIRCUIT
No. 01-618. Argued October 9, 2002-Decided January 15, 2003
OCTOBER TERM, 2002

GINSBURG, J., delivered the opinion of the Court, in which REHNQUIST, C. J., and O'CONNOR, SCALIA, KENNEDY, SOUTER, and THOMAS, JJ., joined. STEVENS, J., post, p. 222, and BREYER, J., post, p. 242, filed dissenting opinions.

Lawrence Lessig argued the cause for petitioners. With him on the briefs were Kathleen M. Sullivan, Alan B. Morrison, Edward Lee, Charles Fried, Geoffrey S. Stewart, Donald B. Ayer, Robert P. Ducatman, Daniel H. Bromberg, Charles R. Nesson, and Jonathan L. Zittrain.

Solicitor General Olson argued the cause for respondent.

With him on the brief were Assistant Attorney General McCallum, Deputy Solicitor General Wallace, Jeffrey A. Lamken, William Kanter, and John S. Koppel.*

*Briefs of amici curiae urging reversal were filed for the American Association of Law Libraries et al. by Arnold P. Lutzker and Carl H. Settlemyer III; for the College Art Association et al. by Jeffrey P. Cunard and Bruce P. Keller; for the Eagle Forum Education and Legal Defense Fund et al. by Karen Tripp and Phyllis Schlafiy; for the Free Software Foundation by Eben M oglen; for Intellectual Property Law Professors by Jonathan Weinberg; for the Internet Archive et al. by Deirdre K. Mulli.

JUSTICE GINSBURG delivered the opinion of the Court. This case concerns the authority the Constitution assigns to Congress to prescribe the duration of copyrights. The Copyright and Patent Clause of the Constitution, Art. I, § 8, cl. 8, provides as to copyrights: "Congress shall have gan, Mark A. Lemley, and Steven M. Harris; and for Jack M. Balkin et al. by Burt Neuborne.

Briefs of amici curiae urging affirmance were filed for the American Intellectual Property Law Association by Baila H. Celedonia, Mark E. Haddad, and Roger W Parkhurst; for the American Society of Composers, Authors and Publishers et al. by Carey R. Ramos, Peter L. Felcher, Drew S. Days III, Beth S. Brinkmann, and Paul Goldstein; for Amsong, Inc., by Dorothy M. Weber; for AOL Time Warner, Inc., by Kenneth W Starr, Richard A. Cordray, Daryl Joseffer, Paul T. Cappuccio, Edward J. Weiss, and Shira Perlmutter; for the Association of American Publishers et al. by Charles S. Sims and Jon A. Baumgarten; for the Bureau of National Mfairs, Inc., et al. by Paul Bender and Michael R. Klipper; for the Directors Guild of America et al. by George H. Cohen, Leon Dayan, and Laurence Gold; for Dr. Seuss Enterprises, L. P., et al. by Karl ZoBell, Nancy O. Dix, Cathy Ann Bencivengo, Randall E. Kay, and Herbert B. Cheyette; for the Intellectual Property Owners Association by Charles D. Ossola and Ronald E. Myrick; for the International Coalition for Copyright Protection by Eric Lieberman; for the Motion Picture Association of America, Inc., by Seth P. Waxman, Randolph D. Moss, Edward C. DuMont, Neil M. Richards, and Simon Barsky; for the Recording Artists Coalition by Thomas G. Corcoran, Jr.; for the Recording Industry Association of America by Donald B. Verrilli, Jr., Thomas J. Perrelli, William M. Hohengarten, Matthew J. Oppenheim, and Stanley Pierre-Louis; for the Songwriters Guild of America by Floyd Abrams and Joel Kurtzberg; for Jack Beeson et al. by I. Fred Koenigsberg and Gaela K. Gehring Flores; for Senator Orrin G. Hatch by Thomas R. Lee; for Edward Samuels, pro se; and for Representative F. James Sensenbrenner, Jr., et al. by Arthur B. Culvahouse, Jr., and Robert M. Schwartz.

Briefs of amici curiae were filed for Hal Roach Studios et al. by H. Jefferson Powell and David Lange; for Intel Corp. by James M. Burger; for the Nashville Songwriters Association International by Stephen K. Rush; for the New York Intellectual Property Law Association by Bruce M. Wexler and Peter Saxon; for the National Writers Union et al. by Peter Jaszi; for the Progressive Intellectual Property Law Association et al. by Michael H. Davis; for George A. Akerlof et al. by Roy T. Englert, Jr.; for Tyler T. Ochoa et al. by Mr. Ochoa; and for Malla Pollack, pro se.

Power ... [t]o promote the Progress of Science ... by securing [to Authors] for limited Times ... the exclusive Right to their ... Writings." In 1998, in the measure here under inspection, Congress enlarged the duration of copyrights by 20 years. Copyright Term Extension Act (CTEA), Pub. L. 105–298, §§ 102(b) and (d), 112 Stat. 2827–2828 (amending 17 U. S. C. §§ 302, 304). As in the case of prior extensions, principally in 1831, 1909, and 1976, Congress provided for application of the enlarged terms to existing and future copyrights alike.

Petitioners are individuals and businesses whose products or services build on copyrighted works that have gone into the public domain. They seek a determination that the CTEA fails constitutional review under both the Copyright Clause's "limited

Times" prescription and the First Amendment's free speech guarantee. Under the 1976 Copyright Act, copyright protection generally lasted from the work's creation until 50 years after the author's death. Pub. L. 94553, § 302(a), 90 Stat. 2572 (1976 Act). Under the CTEA, most copyrights now run from creation until 70 years after the author's death. 17 U. S. C. § 302(a). Petitioners do not challenge the "life-plus-70-years" timespan itself. "Whether 50 years is enough, or 70 years too much," they acknowledge, "is not a judgment meet for this Court." Brief for Petitioners 14.1 Congress went awry, petitioners maintain, not with respect to newly created works, but in enlarging the term for published works with existing copyrights. The "limited Tim[e]" in effect when a copyright is secured, petitioners urge, becomes the constitutional boundary, a clear line beyond the power of Congress to extend. See ibid. As to the First Amendment, petitioners contend that the CTEA is a content-neutral regulation of speech that fails inspection.

JUSTICE BREYER'S dissent is not similarly restrained. He makes no effort meaningfully to distinguish existing copyrights from future grants. See, e.g., post, at 242–243, 254–260, 264–266. Under his reasoning, the CTEA's 20-year extension is globally unconstitutional under the heightened judicial scrutiny appropriate for such regulations.

In accord with the District Court and the Court of Appeals, we reject petitioners' challenges to the CTEA. In that 1998 legislation, as in all previous copyright term extensions, Congress placed existing and future copyrights in parity. In prescribing that alignment, we hold, Congress acted within its authority and did not transgress constitutional limitations.

IA
We evaluate petitioners' challenge to the constitutionality of the CTEA against the backdrop of Congress' previous exercises of its authority under the Copyright Clause. The Nation's first copyright statute, enacted in 1790, provided a federal copyright term of 14 years from the date of publication, renewable for an additional 14 years if the author survived the first term. Act of May 31, 1790, ch. 15, § 1, 1 Stat. 124 (1790 Act). The 1790 Act's renewable 14-year term applied to existing works (i.e., works already published and works created but not yet published) and future works alike. Ibid. Congress expanded the federal copyright term to 42 years in 1831 (28 years from publication, renewable for an additional 14 years), and to 56 years in 1909 (28 years from publication, renewable for an additional 28 years). Act of Feb. 3, 1831, ch. 16, §§ 1, 16, 4 Stat. 436, 439 (1831 Act); Act of Mar. 4, 1909, ch. 320, §§ 23–24, 35 Stat. 1080–1081 (1909 Act). Both times, Congress applied the new copyright term to existing and future works, 1831 Act §§ 1, 16; 1909 Act §§ 23–24; to qualify for the 1831 extension, an existing work had to be in its initial copyright term at the time the Act became effective, 1831 Act §§ 1, 16.

In 1976, Congress altered the method for computing federal copyright terms. 1976 Act §§ 302–304. For works created by identified natural persons, the 1976 Act provided that federal copyright protection would run from the work's creation, not-as in the 1790, 1831, and 1909 Acts-its publication; protection would last until 50 years after the author's death. § 302(a). In these respects, the 1976 Act aligned United

States copyright terms with the then-dominant international standard adopted under the Berne Convention for the Protection of Literary and Artistic Works. See H. R. Rep. No. 94-1476, p. 135 (1976). For anonymous works, pseudonymous works, and works made for hire, the 1976 Act provided a term of 75 years from publication or 100 years from creation, whichever expired first. § 302(c).

These new copyright terms, the 1976 Act instructed, governed all works not published by its effective date of January 1, 1978, regardless of when the works were created. §§ 302,303. For published works with existing copyrights as of that date, the 1976 Act granted a copyright term of 75 years from the date of publication, §§ 304(a) and (b), a 19-year increase over the 56-year term applicable under the 1909 Act.

The measure at issue here, the CTEA, installed the fourth major duration extension of federal copyrights. 2 Retaining the general structure of the 1976 Act, the CTEA enlarges the terms of all existing and future copyrights by 20 years. For works created by identified natural persons, the term now lasts from creation until 70 years after the author's.

2 Asserting that the last several decades have seen a proliferation of copyright legislation in departure from Congress' traditional pace of legislative amendment in this area, petitioners cite nine statutes passed between 1962 and 1974, each of which incrementally extended existing copyrights for brief periods. See Pub. L. 87-668, 76 Stat. 555; Pub. L. 89-142, 79 Stat. 581; Pub. L. 90-141, 81 Stat. 464; Pub. L. 90-416, 82 Stat. 397; Pub. L. 91-147, 83 Stat. 360; Pub. L. 91-555, 84 Stat. 1441; Pub. L. 92-170, 85 Stat. 490; Pub. L. 92-566, 86 Stat. 1181; Pub. L. 93-573, Title I, 88 Stat. 1873. As respondent (Attorney General Ashcroft) points out, however, these statutes were all temporary placeholders subsumed into the systemic changes effected by the 1976 Act. Brief for Respondent 9 death. 17 U. S. C. § 302(a). This standard harmonizes the baseline United States copyright term with the term adopted by the European Union in 1993. See Council Directive 93/98/EEC of 29 October 1993 Harmonizing the Term of Protection of Copyright and Certain Related Rights, 1993 Official J. Eur. Corns. (L 290), p. 9 (EU Council Directive 93/ 98). For anonymous works, pseudonymous works, and works made for hire, the term is 95 years from publication or 120 years from creation, whichever expires first. 17 U. S. C. § 302(c). Paralleling the 1976 Act, the CTEA applies these new terms to all works not published by January 1, 1978. §§ 302(a), 303(a). For works published before 1978 with existing copyrights as of the CTEA's effective date, the CTEA extends the term to 95 years from publication. §§ 304(a) and (b). Thus, in common with the 1831, 1909, and 1976 Acts, the CTEA's new terms apply to both future and existing copyrights.3

B
Petitioners' suit challenges the CTEA's constitutionality under both the Copyright Clause and the First Amendment. On cross-motions for judgment on the pleadings, the District Court entered judgment for the Attorney General (respondent here). 74 F. Supp. 2d 1 (DC 1999). The court held that the CTEA does not violate the "limited Times" restriction of the Copyright Clause because the CTEA's terms, though 3 Petitioners argue that the 1790 Act must be distinguished from the later Acts on the

ground that it covered existing works but did not extend existing copyrights. Reply Brief 3–7. The parties disagree on the question whether the 1790 Act's copyright term should be regarded in part as compensation for the loss of any then existing state- or common-law copyright protections. See Brief for Petitioners 28–30; Brief for Respondent 17, n. 9; Reply Brief 3–7. Without resolving that dispute, we underscore that the First Congress clearly did confer copyright protection on works that had already been created longer than the 1976 Act's terms, are still limited, not perpetual, and therefore fit within Congress' discretion. Id., at 3. The court also held that "there are no First Amendment rights to use the copyrighted works of others." Ibid.

The Court of Appeals for the District of Columbia Circuit affirmed. 239 F.3d 372 (2001). In that court's unanimous view, Harper & Row, Publishers, Inc. v. Nation Enterprises, 471 U. S. 539 (1985), foreclosed petitioners' First Amendment challenge to the CTEA. 239 F. 3d, at 375. Copyright, the court reasoned, does not impermissibly restrict free speech, for it grants the author an exclusive right only to the specific form of expression; it does not shield any idea or fact contained in the copyrighted work, and it allows for "fair use" even of the expression itself. Id., at 375–376.

A majority of the Court of Appeals also upheld the CTEA against petitioners' contention that the measure exceeds Congress' power under the Copyright Clause. Specifically, the court rejected petitioners' plea for interpretation of the "limited Times" prescription not discretely but with a view to the "preambular statement of purpose" contained in the Copyright Clause: "To promote the Progress of Science." Id., at 377–378. Circuit precedent, Schnapper v. Foley, 667 F. 2d 102 (CADC 1981), the court determined, precluded that plea. In this regard, the court took into account petitioners' acknowledgment that the preamble itself places no substantive limit on Congress' legislative power. 239 F. 3d, at 378.

The appeals court found nothing in the constitutional text or its history to suggest that "a term of years for a copyright is not a 'limited Time' if it may later be extended for another 'limited Time.'" Id., at 379. The court recounted that "the First Congress made the Copyright Act of 1790 applicable to subsisting copyrights arising under the copyright laws of the several states." Ibid. That construction of Congress' authority under the Copyright Clause "by [those] contemporary with [the Constitution's] formation," the court said, merited "very great" and in this case "almost conclusive" weight. Ibid. (quoting Burrow-Giles Lithographic Co. v. Sarony, 111 U. S. 53, 57 (1884)). As early as McClurg v. Kingsland, 1 How. 202 (1843), the Court of Appeals added, this Court had made it "plain" that the same Clause permits Congress to "amplify the terms of an existing patent." 239 F. 3d, at 380. The appeals court recognized that this Court has been similarly deferential to the judgment of Congress in the realm of copyright. Ibid. (citing Sony Corp. of America v. Universal City Studios, Inc., 464 U. S. 417 (1984); Stewart v. Abend, 495 U. S. 207 (1990)).

Concerning petitioners' assertion that Congress might evade the limitation on its authority by stringing together "an unlimited number of 'limited Times,'" the Court of Appeals stated that such legislative misbehavior "clearly is not the situation before us." 239 F. 3d, at 379. Rather, the court noted, the CTEA "matches" the baseline term for "United States copyrights [with] the terms of copyrights granted by the European Union." Ibid. "[I]n an era of multinational publishers and instantaneous electronic transmission," the court said, "harmonization in this regard has obvious practical benefits" and is "a 'necessary and proper' measure to meet contemporary circumstances rather than a step on the way to making copyrights perpetual." Ibid.

Judge Sentelle dissented in part. He concluded that Congress lacks power under the Copyright Clause to expand the copyright terms of existing works. Id., at 380–384. The Court of Appeals subsequently denied rehearing and rehearing en banco 255 F.3d 849 (2001).

We granted certiorari to address two questions: whether the CTEA's extension of existing copyrights exceeds Congress' power under the Copyright Clause; and whether the CTEA's extension of existing and future copyrights violates the First Amendment. 534 U. S. 1126 and 1160 (2002). We now answer those two questions in the negative and affirm.

IIA

We address first the determination of the courts below that Congress has authority under the Copyright Clause to extend the terms of existing copyrights. Text, history, and precedent, we conclude, confirm that the Copyright Clause empowers Congress to prescribe "limited Times" for copyright protection and to secure the same level and duration of protection for all copyright holders, present and future.

The CTEA's baseline term of life plus 70 years, petitioners concede, qualifies as a "limited Tim[e]" as applied to future copyrights.[16] Petitioners contend, however, that existing copyrights extended to endure for that same term are not "limited." Petitioners' argument essentially reads into the text of the Copyright Clause the command that a time prescription, once set, becomes forever "fixed" or "inalterable." The word "limited," however, does not convey a meaning so constricted. At the time of the Framing, that word meant what it means today: "confine[d] within certain bounds," "restrain[ed]," or "circumscribe[d]." S. Johnson, A Dictionary of the English Language (7th ed. 1785); see T. Sheridan, A Complete Dictionary of the English Language (6th ed. 1796) ("confine[d] within certain bounds"); Webster's Third New International Dictionary 1312 (1976) ("confined within limits"; "restricted in extent, number, or duration"). Thus understood, a timespan appropriately "limited" as applied to future copyrights does not automatically cease to be "limited" when applied to existing copyrights. And as we observe, infra, at 209–210, there is no cause to suspect that a purpose to evade the "limited Times" prescription prompted Congress to adopt the CTEA.

To comprehend the scope of Congress' power under the Copyright Clause, "a page of history is worth a volume of logic." New York Trust Co. v. Eisner, 256 U. S. 345, 349 (1921) (Holmes, J.). History reveals an unbroken congressional practice of granting to authors of works with existing copyrights the benefit of term extensions so that all under copyright protection will be governed evenhandedly under the same regime. As earlier recounted, see supra, at 194, the First Congress accorded the

---

[16] We note again that JUSTICE BREYER makes no such concession. See supra, at 193, n. 1. He does not train his fire, as petitioners do, on Congress' choice to place existing and future copyrights in parity. Moving beyond the bounds of the parties' presentations, and with abundant policy arguments but precious little support from precedent, he would condemn Congress' entire product as irrational.

protections of the Nation's first federal copyright statute to existing and future works alike. 1790 Act § 1.[17] Since then, Congress has regularly applied.

JUSTICE STEVENS stresses the rejection of a proposed amendment to the Statute of Anne that would have extended the term of existing copyrights, and reports that opponents of the extension feared it would perpetuate the monopoly position enjoyed by English booksellers. Post, at 232233, and n. 9. But the English Parliament confronted a situation that never existed in the United States. Through the late seventeenth century, a government-sanctioned printing monopoly was held by the Stationers' Company, "the ancient London guild of printers and booksellers." M. Rose, Authors and Owners: The Invention of Copyright 4 (1993); see L. Patterson, Copyright in Historical Perspective ch. 3 (1968). Although duration extensions to both existing and future copyrights. 1831 Act §§ 1, 16; 1909 Act §§ 23–24; 1976 Act §§ 302–303; 17 U. S. C. §§ 302–304.[18]

Because the Clause empowering Congress to confer copyrights also authorizes patents, congressional practice with respect to patents informs our inquiry. We count it significant that early Congresses extended the duration of numerous individual patents as well as copyrights. See, e.g., Act of Jan. 7, 1808, ch. 6, 6 Stat. 70 (patent); Act of Mar. 3, 1809, ch. 35, 6 Stat. 80 (patent); Act of Feb. 7, 1815, ch. 36, 6 Stat. 147 (patent); Act of May 24, 1828, ch. 145, 6 Stat. 389 (copyright); Act of Feb. 11, 1830, ch. 13, 6 Stat. 403 (copyright); that legal monopoly ended in 1695, concerns about monopolistic practices remained, and the 18th-century English Parliament was resistant to any enhancement of booksellers' and publishers' entrenched position. See Rose, supra, at 52–56. In this country, in contrast, competition among publishers, printers, and booksellers was "intens[e]" at the time of the founding, and "there was not even a rough analog to the Stationers' Company on the horizon." Nachbar, Constructing Copyright's Mythology, 6 Green Bag 2d 37, 45 (2002). The Framers guarded against the future accumulation of monopoly power in booksellers and

---

[17] This approach comported with English practice at the time. The Statute of Anne, 1710,8 Ann. c. 19, provided copyright protection to books not yet composed or published, books already composed but not yet published, and books already composed and published. See ibid. ("[T]he author of any book or books already composed, and not printed and published, or that shall hereafter be composed, and his assignee or assigns, shall have the sole liberty of printing and reprinting such book and books for the term of fourteen years, to commence from the day of the first publishing the same, and no longer."); ibid. ("[T]he author of any book or books already printed ... or the bookseller or booksellers, printer or printers, or other person or persons, who hath or have purchased or acquired the copy or copies of any book or books, in order to print or reprint the same, shall have the sole right and liberty of printing such book and books for the term of one and twenty years, to commence from the said tenth day of April, and no longer.").

[18] Moreover, the precise duration of a federal copyright has never been fixed at the time of the initial grant. The 1790 Act provided a federal copyright term of 14 years from the work's publication, renewable for an additional 14 years if the author survived and applied for an additional term. § 1. Congress retained that approach in subsequent statutes. See Stewart v. Abend, 495 U. S. 207,217 (1990) ("Since the earliest copyright statute in this country, the copyright term of ownership has been split between an original term and a renewal term."). Similarly, under the method for measuring copyright terms established by the 1976 Act and retained by the CTEA, the baseline copyright term is measured in part by the life of the author, rendering its duration indeterminate at the time of the grant. See 1976 Act § 302(a); 17 U. S. C. § 302(a).

publishers by authorizing Congress to vest copyrights only in "Authors." JUSTICE STEVENS does not even attempt to explain how Parliament's response to England's experience with a publishing monopoly may be construed to impose a constitutional limitation on Congress' power to extend copyrights granted to "Authors." see generally Ochoa, Patent and Copyright Term Extension and the Constitution: A Historical Perspective, 49 J. Copyright Soc. 19 (2001). The courts saw no "limited Times" impediment to such extensions; renewed or extended terms were upheld in the early days, for example, by Chief Justice Marshall and Justice Story sitting as circuit justices. See Evans v. Jordan, 8 F. Cas. 872, 874 (No. 4,564) (CC Va. 1813) (Marshall, J.) ("Th[e] construction of the constitution which admits the renewal of a patent, is not controverted. A renewed patent … confers the same rights, with an original."), aff'd, 9 Cranch 199 (1815); Blanchard v. Sprague, 3 F. Cas. 648,650 (No. 1,518) (CC Mass. 1839) (Story, J.) ("I never have entertained any doubt of the constitutional authority of congress" to enact a 14-year patent extension that "operates retrospectively"); see also Evans v. Robinson, 8 F. Cas. 886, 888 (No. 4,571) (CC Md. 1813) (Congresses "have the exclusive right … to limit the times for which a patent right shall be granted, and are not restrained from renewing a patent or prolonging" it.).[19]

Further, although prior to the instant case this Court did not have occasion to decide whether extending the duration of existing copyrights complies with the "limited Times" prescription, the Court has found no constitutional barrier to the legislative expansion of existing patents.[20] McClurg v. Kingsland, 1 How. 202 (1843), is the pathsetting precedent. The patentee in that case was unprotected under the law in force when the patent issued because he had allowed his employer briefly to practice the invention before he obtained the patent. Only upon enactment, two years later, of an exemption for such allowances did the patent become valid, retroactive to the time it issued. McClurg upheld retroactive application of the new law. The Court explained that the legal regime governing a particular patent "depend[s] on the law as it stood at the emanation of the patent, together with such changes as have been

---

[19] JUSTICE STEVENS would sweep away these decisions, asserting that Graham v. John Deere Co. of Kansas City, 383 U. S. 1 (1966), "flatly contradicts" them. Post, at 237. Nothing but wishful thinking underpins that assertion. The controversy in Graham involved no patent extension. Graham addressed an invention's very eligibility for patent protection, and spent no words on Congress' power to enlarge a patent's duration.

[20] JUSTICE STEVENS recites words from Sears, Roebuck & Co. v. Stiffel Co., 376 U. S. 225 (1964), supporting the uncontroversial proposition that a State may not "extend the life of a patent beyond its expiration date," id., at 231, then boldly asserts that for the same reasons Congress may not do so either. See post, at 222, 226. But Sears placed no reins on Congress' authority to extend a patent's life. The full sentence in Sears, from which JUSTICE STEVENS extracts words, reads: "Obviously a State could not consistently with the Supremacy Clause of the Constitution, extend the life of a patent beyond its expiration date or give a patent on an article which lacked the level of invention required for federal patents." 376 U. S., at 231. The point insistently made in Sears is no more and no less than this: States may not enact measures inconsistent with the federal patent laws. Ibid. ("[A] State cannot encroach upon the federal patent laws directly … [and] cannot … give protection of a kind that clashes with the objectives of the federal patent laws."). A decision thus rooted in the Supremacy Clause cannot be turned around to shrink congressional choices.

since made; for though they may be retrospective in their operation, that is not a sound objection to their validity." Id., at 206.[21] Neither is it a sound.

Also unavailing is JUSTICE STEVENS' appeal to language found in a private letter written by James Madison. Post, at 230, n. 6; see also dissenting opinion of BREYER, J., post, at 246–247, 260, 261. Respondent points to a better "demonstrat[ion]," post, at 226, n. 3 (STEVENS, J., dissenting), of Madison's and other Framers' understanding of the scope of Congress' power to extend patents: "[T]hen-President Thomas Jefferson-the first administrator of the patent system, and perhaps the Founder with the narrowest view of the copyright and patent powers-signed the 1808 and 1809 patent term extensions into law; ... James Madison, who drafted the Constitution's 'limited Times' language, issued the extended patents under those laws as Secretary of State; and ... Madison as President signed another patent term extension in 1815." Brief for Respondent 15.

Congress' consistent historical practice of applying newly enacted copyright terms to future and existing copyrights reflects a judgment stated concisely by Representative Huntington at the time of the 1831 Act: "[J]ustice, policy, and equity alike forb[id]" that an "author who had sold his [work] a week ago, be placed in a worse situation than the author who should sell his work the day after the passing of [the] act." 7 Congo Deb. 424 (1831); accord, Symposium, The Constitutionality of Copyright Term Extension, 18 Cardozo Arts & Ent. L. J. 651, 694 (2000) (Prof. Miller) ("[S]ince 1790, it has indeed been Congress's policy that the author of yesterday's work should not get a lesser reward than the author of tomorrow's work just because Congress passed a statute lengthening the term today."). The CTEA follows this historical practice by keeping the duration provisions of the 1976 Act largely in place and simply adding 20 years to each of them. Guided by text, history, and precedent, we cannot agree with petitioners' submission that extending the duration of existing copyrights is categorically beyond Congress' authority under the Copyright Clause.

Satisfied that the CTEA complies with the "limited Times" prescription, we turn now to whether it is a rational exercise of the legislative authority conferred by the Copyright Clause. On that point, we defer substantially to Congress such change. To the contrary, as JUSTICE STEVENS acknowledges, McClurg held that use of an invention by the patentee's employer did not invalidate the inventor's 1834 patent, "even if it might have had that effect prior to the amendment of the patent statute in 1836." Post, at 239. In other words, McClurg evaluated the patentee's rights not simply in light of the patent law in force at the time the patent issued, but also in light of "such changes as had been since made." 1 How. at 206. It is thus inescapably plain that McClurg upheld the application of expanded patent protection to an existing patent. Sony, 464 U. S., at 429 ("It is Congress that has been assigned the task of

---

[21] JUSTICE STEVENS reads McClurg to convey that "Congress cannot change the bargain between the public and the patentee in a way that disadvantages the patentee." Post, at 239. But McClurg concerned no objection to the validity of a copyright term extension, enacted pursuant to the same constitutional grant of authority, that the enlarged term covers existing copyrights.

defining the scope of the limited monopoly that should be granted to authors ... in order to give the public appropriate access to their work product.").[22]

The CTEA reflects judgments of a kind Congress typically makes, judgments we cannot dismiss as outside the Legislature's domain. As respondent describes, see Brief for Respondent 37–38, a key factor in the CTEA's passage was a 1993 European Union (EU) directive instructing EU members to establish a copyright term of life plus 70 years. EU Council Directive 93/98, Art. 1(1), p. 11; see 144 Congo Rec. S12377-S12378 (daily ed. Oct. 12, 1998) (statement of Sen. Hatch). Consistent with the Berne Convention, the EU directed its members to deny this longer term to the works of any non-EU country whose laws did not secure the same extended term. See Berne Conv. Art. 7(8); P. Goldstein, International Copyright § 5.3, p. 239 (2001). By extending the baseline United States copyright term to life plus 70 years, Congress sought to ensure that American authors would receive the same copyright protection in Europe as their European counterparts.[23] The CTEA may also provide greater incentive for American and other authors to create and disseminate their work in the United States. See Perlmutter, Participation in the International Copyright System as a Means to Promote the Progress of Science and Useful Arts, 36 Loyola (LA) L. Rev. 323, 330 (2002) ("[M]atching thee] level of [copyright] protection in the United States [to that in the EU] can ensure stronger protection for U. S. works abroad and avoid competitive disadvantages vis-a-vis foreign rightholders."); see also id., at 332 (the United States could not "playa leadership role" in the give-and-take evolution of the international copyright system, indeed it would "lose all flexibility," "if the

---

[22] JUSTICE BREYER would adopt a heightened, three-part test for the constitutionality of copyright enactments. Post, at 245. He would invalidate the CTEA as irrational in part because, in his view, harmonizing the United States and European Union baseline copyright terms "apparent[ly]" fails to achieve "significant" uniformity. Post, at 264. But see infra this page and 206. The novelty of the "rational basis" approach he presents is plain. Cf. Board of Trustees of Univ. of Ala. v. Garrett, 531 U. S. 356, 383 (2001) (BREYER, J., dissenting) ("Rational-basis review with its presumptions favoring constitutionality—is 'a paradigm of judicial restraint.'" (quoting FCC v. Beach Communications, Inc., 508 U. S. 307, 314 (1993))). Rather than subjecting Congress' legislative choices in the copyright area to heightened judicial scrutiny, we have stressed that "it is not our role to alter the delicate balance Congress has labored to achieve." Stewart v. Abend, 495 U. S., at 230; see Sony Corp. of America v. Universal City Studios, Inc., 464 U. S. 417, 429 (1984). Congress' exercise of its Copyright Clause authority must be rational, but JUSTICE BREYER'S stringent version of rationality is unknown to our literary property jurisprudence.

[23] Responding to an inquiry whether copyrights could be extended "forever," Register of Copyrights Marybeth Peters emphasized the dominant reason for the CTEA: "There certainly are proponents of perpetual copyright: We heard that in our proceeding on term extension. The Songwriters Guild suggested a perpetual term. However, our Constitution says limited times, but there really isn't a very good indication on what limited times is. The reason why you're going to life-plus-70 today is because Europe has gone that way ...." Copyright Term, Film Labeling, and Film Preservation Legislation: Hearings on H. R. 989 et al. before the Subcommittee on Courts and Intellectual Property of the House Committee on the Judiciary, 104th Cong., 1st Sess., 230 (1995) (hereinafter House Hearings).

only way to promote the progress of science were to provide incentives to create new works").[24]

In addition to international concerns,[25] Congress passed the CTEA in light of demographic, economic, and technological changes, Brief for Respondent 25–26, 33, and nn. 23 and 24,[26] and rationally credited projections that longer terms would encourage copyright holders to invest in the restoration and public distribution of their works, id., at 34–37; see H. R. Rep. No. 105–452, p. 4 (1998) (term extension "provide[s] copyright owners generally with the incentive to restore older works and further disseminate them to the public").[27]

In sum, we find that the CTEA is a rational enactment; we are not at liberty to second-guess congressional determinations and policy judgments of this order, however debatable or arguably unwise they may be. Accordingly, we cannot conclude that the CTEA-which continues the unbroken congressional practice of treating future and existing copyrights in parity for term extension purposes-is an impermissible exercise of Congress' power under the Copyright Clause.

B

Petitioners' Copyright Clause arguments rely on several novel readings of the Clause. We next address these arguments and explain why we find them unpersuasive.

---

[24] The author of the law review article cited in text, Shira Perlmutter, currently a vice president of AOL Time Warner, was at the time of the CTEA's enactment Associate Register for Policy and International Mfairs, United States Copyright Office.

[25] See also Austin, Does the Copyright Clause Mandate Isolationism? 26 Colum. J. L. & Arts 17, 59 (2002) (cautioning against "an isolationist reading of the Copyright Clause that is in tension with ... America's international copyright relations over the last hundred or so years").

[26] Members of Congress expressed the view that, as a result of increases in human longevity and in parents' average age when their children are born, the pre-CTEA term did not adequately secure "the right to profit from licensing one's work during one's lifetime and to take pride and comfort in knowing that one's children-and perhaps their children-might also benefit from one's posthumous popularity." 141 Congo Rec. 6553 (1995) (statement of Sen. Feinstein); see 144 Congo Rec. S12377 (daily ed. Oct. 12, 1998) (statement of Sen. Hatch) ("Among the main developments [compelling reconsideration of the 1976 Act's term] is the effect of demographic trends, such as increasing longevity and the trend toward rearing children later in life, on the effectiveness of the life-plus-50 term to provide adequate protection for American creators and their heirs."). Also cited was "the failure of the U. S. copyright term to keep pace with the substantially increased commercial life of copyrighted works resulting from the rapid growth in communications media." Ibid. (statement of Sen. Hatch); cf. Sony, 464 U. S., at 430-431 ("From its beginning, the law of copyright has developed in response to significant changes in technology .... [A]s new developments have occurred in this country, it has been the Congress that has fashioned the new rules that new technology made necessary.").

[27] JUSTICE BREYER urges that the economic incentives accompanying copyright term extension are too insignificant to "mov[e]" any author with a "rational economic perspective." Post, at 255; see post, at 254-257. Calibrating rational economic incentives, however, like "fashion[ing] ... new rules [in light of] new technology," Sony, 464 U. S., at 431, is a task primarily for Congress, not the courts. Congress heard testimony from a number of prominent artists; each expressed the belief that the copyright system's assurance offair compensation for themselves and their heirs was an incentive to create. See, e.g., House Hearings 233-239 (statement of Quincy Jones); Copyright Term Extension Act of 1995: Hearing before the Senate Committee on the Judiciary, 104th Cong., 1st Sess., 55–56 (1995).

1

Petitioners contend that even if the CTEA's 20-year term extension is literally a "limited Tim[e]," permitting Congress to extend existing copyrights allows it to evade the "limited Times" constraint by creating effectively perpetual copyrights through repeated extensions. We disagree (statement of Bob Dylan); id., at 56–57 (statement of Don Henley); id., at 57 (statement of Carlos Santana). We would not take Congress to task for crediting this evidence which, as JUSTICE BREYER acknowledges, reflects general "propositions about the value of incentives" that are "undeniably true." Post, at 255.

Congress also heard testimony from Register of Copyrights Marybeth Peters and others regarding the economic incentives created by the CTEA. According to the Register, extending the copyright for existing works "could ... provide additional income that would finance the production and publication of new works." House Hearings 158. "Authors would not be able to continue to create," the Register explained, "unless they earned income on their finished works. The public benefits not only from an author's original work but also from his or her further creations. Although this truism may be illustrated in many ways, one of the best examples is Noah Webster[,] who supported his entire family from the earnings on his speller and grammar during the twenty years he took to complete his dictionary." Id., at 165.

As the Court of Appeals observed, a regime of perpetual copyrights "clearly is not the situation before us." 239 F. 3d, at 379. Nothing before this Court warrants construction of the CTEA's 20-year term extension as a congressional attempt to evade or override the "limited Times" constraint.[28] Critically, we again emphasize, petitioners fail to show how the CTEA crosses a constitutionally significant threshold

---

[28] JUSTICE BREYER agrees that "Congress did not intend to act unconstitutionally" when it enacted the CTEA, post, at 256, yet in his very next breath, he seems to make just that accusation, ibid. What else is one to glean from his selection of scattered statements from individual Members of Congress? He does not identify any statement in the statutory text that installs a perpetual copyright, for there is none. But even if the statutory text were sufficiently ambiguous to warrant recourse to legislative history, JUSTICE BREYER'S selections are not the sort to which this Court accords high value: "In surveying legislative history we have repeatedly stated that the authoritative source for finding the Legislature's intent lies in the Committee Reports on the bill, which 'represen[t] the considered and collective understanding of those [Members of Congress] involved in drafting and studying proposed legislation.'" Garcia v. United States, 469 U. S. 70, 76 (1984) (quoting Zuber v. Allen, 396 U. S. 168, 186 (1969)). The House and Senate Reports accompanying the CTEA reflect no purpose to make copyright a forever thing. Notably, the Senate Report expressly acknowledged that the Constitution "clearly precludes Congress from granting unlimited protection for copyrighted works," S. Rep. No. 104-315, p. 11 (1996), and disclaimed any intent to contravene that prohibition, ibid. Members of Congress instrumental in the CTEA's passage spoke to similar effect. See, e.g., 144 Congo Rec. H1458 (daily ed. Mar. 25, 1998) (statement of Rep. Coble) (observing that "copyright protection should be for a limited time only" and that "[p]erpetual protection does not benefit society"). JUSTICE BREYER nevertheless insists that the "economic effect" of the CTEA is to make the copyright term "virtually perpetual." Post, at 243. Relying on formulas and assumptions provided in an amicus brief supporting petitioners, he stresses that the CTEA creates a copyright term worth 99.8% of the value of a perpetual copyright. Post, at 254–256. If JUSTICE BREYER'S calculations were a basis for holding the CTEA unconstitutional, then the 1976 Act would surely fall as well, for-under the same assumptions he indulges-the term set by that Act secures 99.4% of the value of a perpetual term. See Brief for George A. Akerlof et al. as Amici Curiae 6, n. 6

with respect to "limited Times" that the 1831, 1909, and 1976 Acts did not. See supra, at 194–196; Austin, supra n. 13, at 56 ("If extending copyright protection to works already in existence is constitutionally suspect," so is "extending the protections of U. S. copyright law to works by foreign authors that had already been created and even first published when the federal rights attached."). Those earlier Acts did not create perpetual copyrights, and neither does the CTEA.[29]

2

Petitioners dominantly advance a series of arguments all premised on the proposition that Congress may not extend an existing copyright absent new consideration from the author. They pursue this main theme under three headings. Petitioners contend that the CTEA' extension of existing copyrights (1) overlooks the requirement of "originality," (2) fails to "promote the Progress of Science," and (3) ignores copyright's quid pro quo.

Acts might be suspect. JUSTICE BREYER several times places the Founding Fathers on his side. See, e.g., post, at 246–247, 260, 261. It is doubtful, however, that those architects of our Nation, in framing the "limited Times" prescription, thought in terms of the calculator rather than the calendar.

Petitioners' "originality" argument draws on Feist Publications, Inc. v. Rural Telephone Service Co., 499 U. S. 340 (1991). In Feist, we observed that "[t]he sine qua non of copyright is originality," id., at 345, and held that copyright protection is unavailable to "a narrow category of works in which the creative spark is utterly lacking or so trivial as to be virtually nonexistent," id., at 359. Relying on Feist, petitioners urge that even if a work is sufficiently "original" to qualify for copyright protection in the first instance, any extension of the copyright's duration is impermissible because, once published, a work is no longer original.

Feist, however, did not touch on the duration of copyright protection. Rather, the decision addressed the core question of copyrightability, i. e., the "creative spark" a work must have to be eligible for copyright protection at all. Explaining the originality requirement, Feist trained on the Copyright Clause words "Authors" and "Writings." Id., at 346–347. The decision did not construe the "limited Times" for which a work may be protected, and the originality requirement has no bearing on that prescription.

(describing the relevant formula). Indeed, on that analysis even the "limited" character of the 1909 (97.7%) and 1831 (94.1%).

[29] Respondent notes that the CTEA's life-plus-70-years baseline term is expected to produce an average copyright duration of 95 years, and that this term "resembles some other long-accepted durational practices in the law, such as 99-year leases of real property and bequests within the rule against perpetuities." Brieffor Respondent 27, n. 18. Whether such referents mark the outer boundary of "limited Times" is not before us today. JUSTICE BREYER suggests that the CTEA's baseline term extends beyond that typically permitted by the traditional rule against perpetuities. Post, at 256–257. The traditional common-law rule looks to lives in being plus 21 years. Under that rule, the period before a bequest vests could easily equal or exceed the anticipated average copyright term under the CTEA. If, for example, the vesting period on a deed were defined with reference to the life of an infant, the sum of the measuring life plus 21 years could commonly add up to 95 years.

More forcibly, petitioners contend that the CTEA's extension of existing copyrights does not "promote the Progress of Science" as contemplated by the preambular language of the Copyright Clause. Art. I, § 8, cl. 8. To sustain this objection, petitioners do not argue that the Clause's preamble is an independently enforceable limit on Congress' power. See 239 F. 3d, at 378 (Petitioners acknowledge that "the preamble of the Copyright Clause is not a substantive limit on Congress' legislative power." (internal quotation marks omitted)). Rather, they maintain that the preambular language identifies the sole end to which Congress may legislate; accordingly, they conclude, the meaning of "limited Times" must be "determined in light of that specified end." Brief for Petitioners 19. The CTEA's extension of existing copyrights categorically fails to "promote the Progress of Science," petitioners argue, because it does not stimulate the creation of new works but merely adds value to works already created.

As petitioners point out, we have described the Copyright Clause as "both a grant of power and a limitation," Graham v. John Deere Co. of Kansas City, 383 U. S. 1, 5 (1966), and have said that "[t]he primary objective of copyright" is "to promote the Progress of Science," Feist, 499 U. S., at 349. The "constitutional command," we have recognized, is that Congress, to the extent it enacts copyright laws at all, create a "system" that "promote the Progress of Science." Graham, 383 U. S., at 6.[30]

We have also stressed, however, that it is generally for Congress, not the courts, to decide how best to pursue the Copyright Clause's objectives. See Stewart v. Abend, 495 U. S., at 230 ("Th[e] evolution of the duration of copyright protection tellingly illustrates the difficulties Congress faces .... [I]t is not our role to alter the delicate balance Congress has labored to achieve."); Sony, 464 U. S., at 429 ("[I]t is Congress that has been assigned the task of defining the scope of [rights] that should be granted to authors or to inventors in order to give the public appropriate access to their work product."); Graham, 383 U. S., at 6 ("Within the limits of the constitutional grant, the Congress may, of course, implement the stated purpose of the Framers by selecting the policy which in its judgment best effectuates the constitutional aim."). The justifications we earlier set out for Congress' enactment of the CTEA, supra, at

---

[30] JUSTICE STEVENS' characterization of reward to the author as "a secondary consideration" of copyright law, post, at 227, n. 4 (internal quotation marks omitted), understates the relationship between such rewards and the "Progress of Science." As we have explained, "[t]he economic philosophy behind the [Copyright] [C]lause ... is the conviction that encouragement of individual effort by personal gain is the best way to advance public welfare through the talents of authors and inventors." Mazer v. Stein, 347 U. S. 201, 219 (1954). Accordingly, "copyright law celebrates the profit motive, recognizing that the incentive to profit from the exploitation of copyrights will redound to the public benefit by resulting in the proliferation of knowledge .... The profit motive is the engine that ensures the progress of science." American Geophysical Union v. Texaco Inc., 802 F. Supp. 1, 27 (SDNY 1992), aff'd, 60 F.3d 913 (CA2 1994). Rewarding authors for their creative labor and "promot[ing] ... Progress" are thus complementary; as James Madison observed, in copyright "[t]he public good fully coincides ... with the claims of individuals." The Federalist No. 43, p. 272 (C. Rossiter ed. 1961). JUSTICE BREYER'S assertion that "copyright statutes must serve public, not private, ends," post, at 247, similarly misses the mark. The two ends are not mutually exclusive; copyright law serves public ends by providing individuals with an incentive to pursue private ones.

205–207, provide a rational basis for the conclusion that the CTEA "promote[s] the Progress of Science."

On the issue of copyright duration, Congress, from the start, has routinely applied new definitions or adjustments of the copyright term to both future works and existing works not yet in the public domain.19[31] Such consistent congressional practice is entitled to "very great weight, and when it is remembered that the rights thus established have not been disputed during a period of [over two] centur[ies], it is almost conclusive." Burrow-Giles Lithographic Co. v. Sarony, 111 U. S., at 57. Indeed, "[t]his Court has repeatedly laid down the principle that a contemporaneous legislative exposition of the Constitution when the founders of our Government and framers of our Constitution were actively participating in public affairs, acquiesced in for a long term of years, fixes the construction to be given [the Constitution's] provisions." Myers v. United States, 272 U. S. 52, 175 (1926). Congress' unbroken practice since the founding generation thus overwhelms petitioners' argument that the CTEA's extension of existing copyrights fails per se to "promote the Progress of Science."[32]

Closely related to petitioners' preambular argument, or a variant of it, is their assertion that the Copyright Clause "imbeds a quid pro quo." Brief for Petitioners 23. They contend, in this regard, that Congress may grant to an "Autho[r]" an "exclusive Right" for a "limited Tim[e]," but only in exchange for a "Writin[g]." Congress' power to confer copyright protection, petitioners argue, is thus contingent upon an exchange: The author of an original work receives an "exclusive Right" for a "limited Tim[e]" in exchange for a dedication to the public thereafter. Extending an existing copyright without demanding additional consideration, petitioners maintain, bestows an unpaid-for benefit on copyright holders and their heirs, in violation of the quid pro quo requirement.

We can demur to petitioners' description of the Copyright Clause as a grant of legislative authority empowering Congress "to secure a bargain-this for that." Id., at 16; see Mazer v. Stein, 347 U. S. 201, 219 (1954) ("The economic philosophy behind the clause empowering Congress to grant patents and copyrights is the conviction that encouragement of individual effort by personal gain is the best way to advance public welfare through the talents of authors and inventors in 'Science and useful Arts.'"). But the legislative evolution earlier recalled demonstrates what the bargain

---

[31] As we have noted, see supra, at 196, n. 3, petitioners seek to distinguish the 1790 Act from those that followed. They argue that by requiring authors seeking its protection to surrender whatever rights they had under state law, the 1790 Act enhanced uniformity and certainty and thus "promote[d] ... Progress." See Brief for Petitioners 28–31. This account of the 1790 Act simply confirms, however, that the First Congress understood it could "promote ... Progress" by extending copyright protection to existing works. Every subsequent adjustment of copyright's duration, including the CTEA, reflects a similar understanding..

[32] JUSTICE STEVENS, post, at 235, refers to the "legislative veto" held unconstitutional in INS v. Chadha, 462 U. S. 919 (1983), and observes that we reached that decision despite its impact on federal laws geared to our "contemporary political system," id., at 967 (White, J., dissenting). Placing existing works in parity with future works for copyright purposes, in contrast, is not a similarly pragmatic endeavor responsive to modern times. It is a measure of the kind Congress has enacted under its Patent and Copyright Clause authority since the founding generation. See supra, at 194–196.

entails. Given the consistent placement of existing copyright holders in parity with future holders, the author of a work created in the last 170 years would reasonably comprehend, as the "this" offered her, a copyright not only for the time in place when protection is gained, but also for any renewal or extension legislated during that time.[33] Congress could rationally seek to "promote ... Progress" by including in every copyright statute an express guarantee that authors would receive the benefit of any later legislative extension of the copyright term. Nothing in the Copyright Clause bars Congress from creating the same incentive by adopting the same position as a matter of unbroken practice. See Brief for Respondent 31–32.

Neither Sears, Roebuck & Co. v. Stiffel Co., 376 U. S. 225 (1964), nor Bonito Boats, Inc. v. Thunder Craft Boats, Inc., 489 U. S. 141 (1989), is to the contrary. In both cases, we invalidated the application of certain state laws as inconsistent with the federal patent regime. Sears, 376 U. S., at 231233; Bonito, 489 U. S., at 152. Describing Congress' constitutional authority to confer patents, Bonito Boats noted:

"The Patent Clause itself reflects a balance between the need to encourage innovation and the avoidance of monopolies which stifle competition without any concomitant advance in the 'Progress of Science and useful Arts.'" Id., at 146.

Sears similarly stated that "[p]atents are not given as favors ... but are meant to encourage invention by rewarding the inventor with the right, limited to a term of years fixed by the patent, to exclude others from the use of his invention." 376 U. S., at 229. Neither case concerned the extension of a patent's duration. Nor did either suggest that such an extension might be constitutionally infirm. Rather, Bonito Boats reiterated the Court's unclouded understanding: "It is for Congress to determine if the present system" effectuates the goals of the Copyright and Patent Clause. 489 U. S., at 168. And as we have documented, see supra, at 201–204, Congress has many times sought to effectuate those goals by extending existing patents.

We note, furthermore, that patents and copyrights do not entail the same exchange, and that our references to a quid pro quo typically appear in the patent context. See, e.g., J. E. M. Ag Supply, Inc. v. Pioneer Hi-Bred International, Inc., 534 U. S. 124, 142 (2001) ("The disclosure required by the Patent Act is 'the quid pro quo of the right to exclude.'" (quoting Kewanee Oil Co. v. Bicron Corp., 416 U. S. 470, 484 (1974))); Bonito Boats, 489 U. S., at 161 ("the quid pro quo of substantial creative effort required by the federal [patent] statute"); Brenner v. Manson, 383 U. S. 519, 534 (1966) ("The basic quid pro quo ... for granting a patent monopoly is the benefit derived by the public from an invention with substantial utility."); Pennock

---

[33] Standard copyright assignment agreements reflect this expectation.

See, e.g., A. Kohn & B. Kohn, Music Licensing 471 (3d ed. 1992–2002) (short form copyright assignment for musical composition, under which assignor conveys all rights to the work, "including the copyrights and proprietary rights therein and in any and all versions of said musical composition(s), and any renewals and extensions thereof (whether presently available or subsequently available as a result of intervening legislation)" (emphasis added)); 5 M. Nimmer & D. Nimmer, Copyright §21.11[B], p. 21-305 (2002) (short form copyright assignment under which assignor conveys all assets relating to the work, "including without limitation, copyrights and renewals and/or extensions thereof"); 6 id., § 30.04[B][1], p. 30-325 (form composer-producer agreement under which composer "assigns to Producer all rights (copyrights, rights under copyright and otherwise, whether now or hereafter known) and all renewals and extensions (as may now or hereafter exist)").

v. Dialogue, 2 Pet. 1, 23 (1829) (If an invention is already commonly known and used when the patent is sought, "there might be sound reason for presuming, that the legislature did not intend to grant an exclusive right," given the absence of a "quid pro quo."). This is understandable, given that immediate disclosure is not the objective of, but is exacted from, the patentee. It is the price paid for the exclusivity secured. See J. E. M. Ag Supply, 534 U. S., at 142. For the author seeking copyright protection, in contrast, disclosure is the desired objective, not something exacted from the author in exchange for the copyright. Indeed, since the 1976 Act, copyright has run from creation, not publication. See 1976 Act § 302(a); 17 U. S. C. § 302(a).

Further distinguishing the two kinds of intellectual property, copyright gives the holder no monopoly on any knowledge. A reader of an author's writing may make full use of any fact or idea she acquires from her reading. See § 102(b). The grant of a patent, on the other hand, does prevent full use by others of the inventor's knowledge. See Brief for Respondent 22; Alfred Bell & Co. v. Catalda Fine Arts, 191 F. 2d 99, 103, n. 16 (CA2 1951) (The monopoly granted by a copyright "is not a monopoly of knowledge. The grant of a patent does prevent full use being made of knowledge, but the reader of a book is not by the copyright laws prevented from making full use of any information he may acquire from his reading." (quoting W. Copinger, Law of Copyright 2 (7th ed. 1936))). In light of these distinctions, one cannot extract from language in our patent decisions-language not trained on a grant's duration-genuine support for petitioners' bold view. Accordingly, we reject the proposition that a quid pro quo requirement stops Congress from expanding copyright's term in a manner that puts existing and future copyrights in parity.[34] As an alternative to their various arguments that extending existing copyrights violates the Copyright Clause per se, petitioners urge heightened judicial review of such extensions to ensure that they appropriately pursue the purposes of the Clause. See Brief for Petitioners 31–32. Specifically, petitioners ask us to apply the "congruence and proportionality" standard described in cases evaluating exercises of Congress' power under § 5 of the Fourteenth Amendment. See, e.g., City of Boerne v. Flores, 521 U. S. 507 (1997). But we have never applied that standard outside the § 5 context; it does not hold sway for judicial review of legislation enacted, as copyright laws are, pursuant to Article I authorization.

Section 5 authorizes Congress to enforce commands contained in and incorporated into the Fourteenth Amendment. Arndt. 14, § 5 ("The Congress shall have power to enforce, by appropriate legislation, the provisions of this article." (emphasis added)). The Copyright Clause, in contrast, empowers Congress to define the scope of the substantive right. See Sony, 464 U. S., at 429. Judicial deference to such congressional definition is "but a corollary to the grant to Congress of any Article I power." Graham, 383 U. S., at 6. It would be no more appropriate for us to subject the CTEA to

---

[34] The fact that patent and copyright involve different exchanges does not, of course, mean that we may not be guided in our "limited Times" analysis by Congress' repeated extensions of existing patents. See supra, at 201–204. If patent's quid pro quo is more exacting than copyright's, then Congress' repeated extension of existing patents without constitutional objection suggests even more strongly that similar legislation with respect to copyrights is constitutionally permissible.

"congruence and proportionality" review under the Copyright Clause than it would be for us to hold the Act unconstitutional per se.

For the several reasons stated, we find no Copyright Clause impediment to the CTEA's extension of existing copyrights.

III

Petitioners separately argue that the CTEA is a contentneutral regulation of speech that fails heightened judicial review under the First Amendment.[35] 23 We reject petitioners' plea for imposition of uncommonly strict scrutiny on a copyright scheme that incorporates its own speech-protective purposes and safeguards. The Copyright Clause and First Amendment were adopted close in time. This proximity indicates that, in the Framers' view, copyright's limited monopolies are compatible with free speech principles. Indeed, copyright's purpose is to promote the creation and publication of free expression. As Harper & Row observed: "[T]he Framers intended copyright itself to be the engine of free expression. By establishing a marketable right to the use of one's expression, copyright supplies the economic incentive to create and disseminate ideas." 471 U. S., at 558.

In addition to spurring the creation and publication of new expression, copyright law contains built-in First Amendment accommodations. See id., at 560. First, it distinguishes between ideas and expression and makes only the latter eligible for copyright protection. Specifically, 17 U. S. C. § 102(b) provides: "In no case does copyright protection for an original work of authorship extend to any idea, procedure, process, system, method of operation, concept, principle, or discovery, regardless of the form in which it is described, explained, illustrated, or embodied in such work." As we said in Harper & Row, this "idea/expression dichotomy strike[s] a definitional balance between the First Amendment and the Copyright Act by permitting free communication of facts while still protecting an author's expression." 471 U. S., at 556 (internal quotation marks omitted). Due to this distinction, every idea, theory, and fact in a copyrighted work becomes instantly available for public exploitation at the moment of publication. See Feist, 499 U. S., at 349–350.

Second, the "fair use" defense allows the public to use not only facts and ideas contained in a copyrighted work, but also expression itself in certain circumstances. Codified at 17 U. S. C. § 107, the defense provides: "The fair use of a copyrighted work, including such use by reproduction in copies ..., for purposes such as criticism, comment, news reporting, teaching (including multiple copies for classroom use), scholarship, or research, is not an infringement of copyright." The fair use defense affords considerable "latitude for scholarship and comment," Harper & Row, 471 U. S., at 560, and even for parody, see Campbell v. Acuff-Rose Music, Inc., 510 U. S.

---

[35] Petitioners originally framed this argument as implicating the CTEA's extension of both existing and future copyrights. See Pet. for Cert. i. Now, however, they train on the CTEA's extension of existing copyrights and urge against consideration of the CTEA's First Amendment validity as applied to future copyrights. See Brief for Petitioners 39–48; Reply Brief 16–17; Tr. of Oral Arg. 11–13. We therefore consider petitioners' argument as so limited. We note, however, that petitioners do not explain how their First Amendment argument is moored to the prospective/retrospective line they urge us to draw, nor do they say whether or how their free speech argument applies to copyright duration but not to other aspects of copyright protection, notably scope.

569 (1994) (rap group's musical parody of Roy Orbison's "Oh, Pretty Woman" may be fair use).

The CTEA itself supplements these traditional First Amendment safeguards. First, it allows libraries, archives, and similar institutions to "reproduce" and "distribute, display, or perform in facsimile or digital form" copies of certain published works "during the last 20 years of any term of copyright ... for purposes of preservation, scholarship, or research" if the work is not already being exploited commercially and further copies are unavailable at a reasonable price. 17 U. S. C. § 108(h); see Brief for Respondent 36. Second, Title II of the CTEA, known as the Fairness in Music Licensing Act of 1998, exempts small businesses, restaurants, and like entities from having to pay performance royalties on music played from licensed radio, television, and similar facilities. 17 U. S. C. § 110(5)(B); see Brief for Representative F. James Sensenbrenner, Jr., et al. as Amici Curiae 5–6, n. 3.

Finally, the case petitioners principally rely upon for their First Amendment argument, Turner Broadcasting System, Inc. v. FCC, 512 U. S. 622 (1994), bears little on copyright. The statute at issue in Turner required cable operators to carry and transmit broadcast stations through their proprietary cable systems. Those "must-carry" provisions, we explained, implicated "the heart of the First Amendment," namely, "the principle that each person should decide for himself or herself the ideas and beliefs deserving of expression, consideration, and adherence." Id., at 641.

The CTEA, in contrast, does not oblige anyone to reproduce another's speech against the carrier's will. Instead, it protects authors' original expression from unrestricted exploitation. Protection of that order does not raise the free speech concerns present when the government compels or burdens the communication of particular facts or ideas. The First Amendment securely protects the freedom to make or decline to make-one's own speech; it bears less heavily when speakers assert the right to make other people's speeches. To the extent such assertions raise First Amendment concerns, copyright's built-in free speech safeguards are generally adequate to address them. We recognize that the D. C. Circuit spoke too broadly when it declared copyrights "categorically immune from challenges under the First Amendment." 239 F. 3d, at 375. But when, as in this case, Congress has not altered the traditional contours of copyright protection, further First Amendment scrutiny is unnecessary. See Harper & Row, 471 U. S., at 560; cf. San Francisco Arts & Athletics, Inc. v. United States Olympic Comm., 483 U. S. 522 (1987).[36]

If petitioners' vision of the Copyright Clause held sway, it would do more than render the CTEA's duration extensions unconstitutional as to existing works. Indeed, petitioners' assertion that the provisions of the CTEA are not severable would make the CTEA's enlarged terms invalid even as to tomorrow's work. The 1976 Act's time

---

[36] We are not persuaded by petitioners' attempt to distinguish Harper & Row on the ground that it involved an infringement suit rather than a declaratory action of the kind here presented. As respondent observes, the same legal question can arise in either posture. See Brief for Respondent 42. In both postures, it is appropriate to construe copyright's internal safeguards to accommodate First Amendment concerns. Cf. United States v. X-Citement Video, Inc., 513 U. S. 64, 78 (1994) ("It is ... incumbent upon us to read the statute to eliminate [serious constitutional] doubts so long as such a reading is not plainly contrary to the intent of Congress.").

extensions, which set the pattern that the CTEA followed, would be vulnerable as well.

As we read the Framers' instruction, the Copyright Clause empowers Congress to determine the intellectual property regimes that, overall, in that body's judgment, will serve the ends of the Clause. See Graham, 383 U. S., at 6 (Congress may "implement the stated purpose of the Framers by selecting the policy which in its judgment best effectuates the constitutional aim." (emphasis added)). Beneath the facade of their inventive constitutional interpretation, petitioners forcefully urge that Congress pursued very bad policy in prescribing the CTEA's long terms. The wisdom of Congress' action, however, is not within our province to second-guess. Satisfied that the legislation before us remains inside the domain the Constitution assigns to the First Branch, we affirm the judgment of the Court of Appeals.

It is so ordered.

JUSTICE STEVENS, dissenting.

Writing for a unanimous Court in 1964, Justice Black stated that it is obvious that a State could not "extend the life of a patent beyond its expiration date," Sears, Roebuck & Co. v. Stiffel Co., 376 U. S. 225, 231 (1964).[37] As I shall explain, the reasons why a State may not extend the life of a patent apply to Congress as well. If Congress may not expand the scope of a patent monopoly, it also may not extend the life of a copyright beyond its expiration date. Accordingly, insofar as the 1998 Sonny Bono Copyright Term Extension Act, 112 Stat. 2827, purported to extend the life of unexpired copyrights, it is invalid. Because the majority's contrary conclusion rests on the mistaken premise that this Court has virtually no role in reviewing congressional grants of monopoly privileges to authors, inventors, and their successors, I respectfully dissent.

I

The authority to issue copyrights stems from the same Clause in the Constitution that created the patent power. It provides:

"Congress shall have Power ... To promote the Progress of Science and useful Arts, by securing for limited Times to Authors and Inventors the exclusive Right to their respective Writings and Discoveries." Art. I, § 8, cl. 8.

It is well settled that the Clause is "both a grant of power and a limitation" and that Congress "may not overreach the restraints imposed by the stated constitutional purpose." Graham v. John Deere Co. of Kansas City, 383 U. S. 1, 5–6 (1966). As we have made clear in the patent context, that purpose has two dimensions. Most

---

[37] Justice Harlan wrote a brief concurrence, but did not disagree with this statement. Justice Black's statement echoed a portion of Attorney General Wirt's argument in Gibbons v. Ogden, 9 Wheat. 1, 171 (1824):

"The law of Congress declares, that all inventors of useful improvements throughout the United States, shall be entitled to the exclusive right in their discoveries for fourteen years only. The law of New-York declares, that this inventor shall be entitled to the exclusive use of his discovery for thirty years, and as much longer as the State shall permit. The law of Congress, by limiting the exclusive right to fourteen years, in effect declares, that after the expiration of that time, the discovery shall be the common right of the whole people of the United States."

obviously the grant of exclusive rights to their respective writings and discoveries is intended to encourage the creativity of "Authors and Inventors." But the requirement that those exclusive grants be for "limited Times" serves the ultimate purpose of promoting the "Progress of Science and useful Arts" by guaranteeing that those innovations will enter the public domain as soon as the period of exclusivity expires:

"Once the patent issues, it is strictly construed, United States v. Masonite Corp., 316 U. S. 265, 280 (1942), it cannot be used to secure any monopoly beyond that contained in the patent, Morton Salt Co. v. G. S. Suppiger Co., 314 U. S. 488, 492 (1942), ... and especially relevant here, when the patent expires the monopoly created by it expires, too, and the right to make the article-including the right to make it in precisely the shape it carried when patented-passes to the public. Kellogg Co. v. National Biscuit Co., 305 U. S. 111, 120–122 (1938); Singer Mfg. Co. v. June Mfg. Co., 163 U. S. 169, 185 (1896)." Sears, Roebuck & Co., 376 U. S., at 230.

It is that ultimate purpose that explains why a patent may not issue unless it discloses the invention in such detail that one skilled in the art may copy it. See, e.g., Grant v. Raymond, 6 Pet. 218, 247 (1832) (Marshall, C. J.) ("The third section [of the 1793 Act] requires, as preliminary to a patent, a correct specification and description of the thing discovered. This is necessary in order to give the public, after the privilege shall expire, the advantage for which the privilege is allowed, and is the foundation of the power to issue the patent"). Complete disclosure as a precondition to the issuance of a patent is part of the quid pro quo that justifies the limited monopoly for the inventor as consideration for full and immediate access by the public when the limited time expires.[38]

Almost two centuries ago the Court plainly stated that public access to inventions at the earliest possible date was the essential purpose of the Clause:

"While one great object was, by holding out a reasonable reward to inventors and giving them an exclusive right to their inventions for a limited period, to stimulate the efforts of genius; the main object was 'to promote the progress of science and useful arts;' and this could be done best, by giving the public at large a right to make, construct, use, and vend the thing invented, at as early a period as possible, having a due regard to the rights of the inventor. If an inventor should be permitted to hold back from the knowledge of the public the secrets of his invention; if he should for a long period of years retain the monopoly, and make, and sell his invention publicly, and thus gather the whole profits of it, relying upon his superior skill and knowledge of the structure; and then, and then only, when the danger of competition should force him to secure the exclusive right, he should be allowed to take out a patent, and thus exclude the public from any farther use than what should be derived under it during his fourteen years; it would materially retard the progress of science and the useful

---

[38] Attorney General Wirt made this precise point in his argument in Gibbons v. Ogden, 9 Wheat., at 175: "The limitation is not for the advantage of the inventor, but of society at large, which is to take the benefit of the invention after the period of limitation has expired. The patentee pays a duty on his patent, which is an effective source of revenue to the United States. It is virtually a contract between each patentee and the people of the United States, by which the time of exclusive and secure enjoyment is limited, and then the benefit of the discovery results to the public".

arts, and give a premium to those, who should be least prompt to communicate their discoveries." Pennock v. Dialogue, 2 Pet. 1, 18 (1829).

Pennock held that an inventor could not extend the period of patent protection by postponing his application for the patent while exploiting the invention commercially. As we recently explained, "implicit in the Patent Clause itself" is the understanding "that free exploitation of ideas will be the rule, to which the protection of a federal patent is the exception. Moreover, the ultimate goal of the patent system is to bring new designs and technologies into the public domain through disclosure." Bonito Boats, Inc. v. Thunder Craft Boats, Inc., 489 U. S. 141, 151 (1989).

The issuance of a patent is appropriately regarded as a quid pro quo-the grant of a limited right for the inventor's disclosure and subsequent contribution to the public domain. See, e.g., Pfaff v. Wells Electronics, Inc., 525 U. S. 55, 63 (1998) ("[T]he patent system represents a carefully crafted bargain that encourages both the creation and the public disclosure of new and useful advances in technology, in return for an exclusive monopoly for a limited period of time"). It would be manifestly unfair if, after issuing a patent, the Government as a representative of the public sought to modify the bargain by shortening the term of the patent in order to accelerate public access to the invention. The fairness considerations that underlie the constitutional protections against ex post facto laws and laws impairing the obligation of contracts would presumably disable Congress from making such a retroactive change in the public's bargain with an inventor without providing compensation for the taking. Those same considerations should protect members of the public who make plans to exploit an invention as soon as it enters the public domain from a retroactive modification of the bargain that extends the term of the patent monopoly. As I discuss below, the few historical exceptions to this rule do not undermine the constitutional analysis. For quite plainly, the limitations "implicit in the Patent Clause itself," 489 U. S., at 151, adequately explain why neither a State nor Congress may "extend the life of a patent beyond its expiration date," Sears, Roebuck & Co., 376 U. S., at 231.3.[39]

Neither the purpose of encouraging new inventions nor the overriding interest in advancing progress by adding knowledge to the public domain is served by retroactively increasing the inventor's compensation for a completed invention and frustrating the legitimate expectations of members of the public who want to make use of it in a free market. Because those twin purposes provide the only avenue

---

[39] The Court acknowledges that this proposition is "un controversial" today, see ante, at 202, n. 8, but overlooks the fact that it was highly controversial in the early 1800's. See n. 11, infra. The Court assumes that the Sears holding rested entirely on the pre-emptive effect of congressional statutes even though the opinion itself, like the opinions in Graham v. John Deere Co. of Kansas City, 383 U. S. 1 (1966), and Bonito Boats, Inc. v. Thunder Craft Boats, Inc., 489 U. S. 141 (1989), also relied on the pre-emptive effect of the constitutional provision. That at least some of the Framers recognized that the Constitution itself imposed a limitation even before Congress acted is demonstrated by Madison's letter, quoted in n. 6, infra. in conferring the monopoly lie in the general benefits derived by the public from the labors of authors. "It is said that reward to the author or artist serves to induce release to the public of the products of his creative genius." 334 U. S., at 158.

for congressional action under the Copyright/Patent Clause of the Constitution, any other action is manifestly unconstitutional.

II

We have recognized that these twin purposes of encouraging new works and adding to the public domain apply to copyrights as well as patents. Thus, with regard to copyrights on motion pictures, we have clearly identified the overriding interest in the "release to the public of the products of [the author's] creative genius." United States v. Paramount Pictures, Inc., 334 U. S. 131, 158 (1948).[40] And, as with patents, we have emphasized that the overriding purpose of providing a reward for authors' creative activity is to motivate that activity and "to allow the public access to the products of their genius after the limited period of exclusive control has expired." Sony Corp. of America v. Universal City Studios, Inc., 464 U. S. 417, 429 (1984). Ex post facto extensions of copyrights result in a gratuitous transfer of wealth from the public to authors, publishers, and their successors in interest. Such retroactive extensions do not even arguably serve either of the purposes of the Copyright/Patent Clause. The reasons why such extensions of the patent monopoly are unconstitutional apply to copyrights as well.

Respondent, however, advances four arguments in support of the constitutionality of such retroactive extensions: (1) The first Copyright Act enacted shortly after the Constitution was ratified applied to works that had already been produced; (2) later Congresses have repeatedly authorized extensions of copyrights and patents; (3) such extensions promote the useful arts by giving copyright holders an incentive to preserve and restore certain valuable motion pictures; and (4) as a matter of equity, whenever Congress provides a longer term as an incentive to the creation of new works by authors, it should provide an equivalent reward to the owners of all unexpired copyrights. None of these arguments is persuasive.

III

Congress first enacted legislation under the Copyright!
Patent Clause in 1790 when it passed bills creating federal patent and copyright protection. Because the content of that first legislation, the debate that accompanied it, and the differences between the initial versions and the bills that ultimately passed provide strong evidence of early Congresses' understanding of the constitutional limits of the Copyright/Patent Clause, I examine both the initial copyright and patent statutes.

Congress first considered intellectual property statutes in its inaugural session in 1789. The bill debated, House Resolution 10—"a bill to promote the progress of science and useful arts, by securing to authors and inventors the exclusive right to their respective writings and discoveries," Documentary History of First Federal Congress of the United States 94 (L. de Pauw, C. Bickford, & L. Hauptman eds. 1977)

---

[40] "The copyright law, like the patent statutes, makes reward to the owner a secondary consideration. In Fox Film Corp. v. Doyal, 286 U. S. 123, 127, Chief Justice Hughes spoke as follows respecting the copyright monopoly granted by Congress," The sole interest of the United States and the primary object.

(hereinafter Documentary History)—provided both copyright and patent protection for similar terms.5[41] The first Congress did not pass H. R. 10, though a similar version was reintroduced in the second Congress in 1790. After minimal debate, however, the House of Representatives began consideration of two separate bills, one covering patents and the other copyrights. Because, as the majority recognizes, "congressional practice with respect to patents informs our inquiry," ante, at 201, I consider the history of both patent and copyright legislation.

The Patent Act

What eventually became the Patent Act of 1790 had its genesis in House Resolution 41, introduced on February 16, 1790. That resolution differed from H. R. 10 in one important respect. Whereas H. R. 10 would have extended patent protection to only those inventions that were "not before known or used," H. R. 41, by contrast, added the phrase "within the United States" to that limitation and expressly authorized patent protection for "any person, who shall after the passing of this act, first import into the United States ... any ... device ... not before used or known in the said States." Documentary History 1626–1632. This change would have authorized patents of importation, providing United States patent protection for inventions already in use elsewhere. This change, however, was short lived and was removed by a floor amendment on March 5, 1789. Walterscheid 125. Though exact records of the floor debate are lost, correspondence from House Members indicate that doubts about the constitutionality of such a provision led to its removal. Representative Thomas Fitzsimmons wrote to a leading industrialist that day stating that the section "'allowing to Importers, was left out, the Constitutional power being Questionable.'" Id., at 126 (quoting Letter from Rep. Thomas Fitzsimmons to Tench Coxe (Mar. 5, 1790)). James Madison himself recognized this constitutional limitation on patents of importation, flatly stating that the constitution "forbids patents for that purpose." 13 Papers of James Madison 128 (C. Hobson & R. Rutland eds. 1981) (reprinting letter to Tench Coxe (Mar. 28, 1790)).[42]

The final version of the 1790 Patent Act, 1 Stat. 109, did not contain the geographic qualifier and thus did not provide for patents of importation. This statutory omission, coupled with the contemporaneous statements by legislators, provides strong evidence that Congress recognized significant limitations on their constitutional

---

[41] A copy of this bill specifically identified has not been found, though strong support exists for considering a bill from that session as H. R. 10. See E. Walterscheid, To Promote the Progress of Useful Arts: American Patent Law and Administration, 1798–1836, pp. 87–88 (1998) (hereinafter Walterscheid). This bill is reprinted in 4 Documentary History 513–519.

[42] "Your idea of appropriating a district of territory to the encouragement of imported inventions is new and worthy of consideration. I can not but apprehend however that the clause in the constitution which forbids patents for that purpose will lie equally in the way of your expedient. Congress seem to be tied down to the single mode of encouraging inventions by granting the exclusive benefit of them for a limited time, and therefore to have no more power to give a further encouragement out of a fund of land than a fund of money. This fetter on the National Legislature tho' an unfortunate one, was a deliberate one. The Latitude of authority now wished for was strongly urged and expressly rejected." Madison's description of the Copyright/Patent Clause as a "fetter on the National Legislature" is fully consistent with this Court's opinion in Graham.

authority under the Copyright/Patent Clause to extend protection to a class of intellectual properties. This recognition of a categorical constitutional limitation is fundamentally at odds with the majority's reading of Article I, § 8, to provide essentially no limit on congressional action under the Clause. If early congressional practice does, indeed, inform our analysis, as it should, then the majority's judicial excision of these constitutional limits cannot be correct.

The Copyright Act
Congress also passed the first Copyright Act, 1 Stat. 124, in 1790. At that time there were a number of maps, charts, and books that had already been printed, some of which were copyrighted under state laws and some of which were arguably entitled to perpetual protection under the common law. The federal statute applied to those works as well as to new works. In some cases the application of the new federal rule reduced the pre-existing protections, and in others it may have increased the protection.[43] What is significant is that the statute provided a general rule creating new federal rights that supplanted the diverse state rights that previously existed. It did not extend or attach to any of those pre-existing state and common-law rights: "That congress, in passing the act of 1790, did not legislate in reference to existing rights, appears clear." Wheaton v. Peters, 8 Pet. 591, 661 (1834); see also Fox Film Corp. v. Doyal, 286 U. S. 123, 127 (1932) ("As this Court has repeatedly said, the Congress did not sanction an existing right but created a new one"). Congress set in place a federal structure governing certain types of intellectual property for the new Republic. That Congress exercised its unquestionable constitutional authority to create a new federal system securing rights for authors and inventors in 1790 does not provide support for the proposition that Congress can extend pre-existing federal protections retroactively.

Respondent places great weight on this first congressional action, arguing that it proves that "Congress thus unquestionably understood that it had authority to apply a new, more favorable copyright term to existing works." Brief for Respondent 12–13. That understanding, however, is not relevant to the question presented by this case-whether "Congress has the power under the Copyright Clause to extend retroactively the term of existing copyrights?"[44] Precisely put, the question presented by this case does not even implicate the 1790 Act, for that Act created, rather than extended,

---

[43] Importantly, even this first Act required a quid pro quo in order to receive federal copyright protection. In order to receive protection under the Act, the author was first required to register the work: "That no person shall be entitled to the benefit of this act, in cases where any map, chart, book or books, hath or have been already printed and published, unless he shall first deposit, and in all other cases, unless he shall before publication deposit a printed copy of the title of such map, chart, book or books, in the clerk's office of the district court where the author or proprietor shall reside." § 3, 1 Stat. 124. This registration requirement in federal district court-a requirement obviously not required under the various state laws protecting written works-further illustrates that the 1790 Act created new rights, rather than extending existing rights.

[44] Respondent's reformulation of the questions presented by this case confuses this basic distinction. We granted certiorari to consider the question: "Did the D. C. Circuit err in holding that Congress has the power under the Copyright Clause to extend retroactively the term of existing copyrights?" Respondent's reformulation of the first question presented—"'Whether the 20-year extension of the terms of all unexpired copyrights ... violates the Copyright Clause of the Constitution insofar as it

copyright protection. That this law applied to works already in existence says nothing about the First Congress' conception of its power to extend this newly created federal right.

Moreover, Members of Congress in 1790 were well aware of the distinction between the creation of new copyright regimes and the extension of existing copyrights. The 1790 Act was patterned, in many ways, after the Statute of Anne enacted in England in 1710. 8 Ann., c. 19; see Fred Fisher Music Co. v. M. Witmark & Sons, 318 U. S. 643, 647–648 (1943). The English statute, in addition to providing authors with copyrights on new works for a term of 14 years renewable for another 14-year term, also replaced the booksellers' claimed perpetual rights in existing works with a single 21-year term. In 1735, the booksellers proposed an amendment that would have extended the terms of existing copyrights until 1756, but the amendment was defeated. Opponents of the amendment had argued that if the bill were to pass, it would "in Effect be establishing a perpetual Monopoly ... only to increase the private Gain of the Booksellers ...."[45] The authors of the federal statute that used the Statute of Anne as a model were familiar with this history. Accordingly, this Court should be especially wary of relying on Congress' creation of a new system to support the proposition that Congress unquestionably understood that it had constitutional authority to extend existing copyrights.

IV

Since the creation of federal patent and copyright protection in 1790, Congress has passed a variety of legislation, both providing specific relief for individual authors and inventors as well as changing the general statutes conferring patent and copyright privileges. Some of the changes did indeed, as the majority describes, extend existing protections retroactively. Other changes, however, did not do so. A more complete and comprehensive look at the history of congressional action under the Copyright/Patent Clause demonstrates that history, in this case, does not provide the "'volume of logic,'" ante, at 200, necessary to sustain the Sonny Bono Act's constitutionality.

Congress, aside from changing the process of applying for a patent in the 1793 Patent Act, did not significantly alter the basic patent and copyright systems for the next 40 years. During this time, however, Congress did consider many private bills. Respondent seeks support from "Congress's historical practice of using its Copyright and Patent Clause authority to extend the terms of individual patents and copyrights." Brief for Respondent 13. Carefully read, however, these private bills do not support respondent's historical gloss, but rather significantly undermine the historical claim.

---

applies to works in existence when it took effect"—significantly changes the substance of inquiry by changing the focus from the federal statute at issue to irrelevant common-law protections. Brieffor Respondent I. Indeed, this reformulation violated this Court's Rule 24(1)(a), which states that "the brief [on the merits] may not raise additional questions or change the substance of the questions already presented in" the petition for certiorari.

[45] "A LETTER to a MEMBER of Parliament concerning the Bill now depending ... for making more effectual an Act in the 8th Year of the Reign of Queen Anne, entituled, An Act for the Encouragement of Learning, by ... Vesting the Copies of Printed Books in the Authors or Purchasers." Document reproduced in Goldsmiths'-Kress Library of Economic Literature, Segment I: Printed Books Through 1800, Microfilm No. 7300 (reel 460).

The first example relied upon by respondent, the extension of Oliver Evans' patent in 1808, ch. 13, 6 Stat. 70, demonstrates the pitfalls of relying on an incomplete historical analysis. Evans, an inventor who had developed several improvements in milling flour, received the third federal patent on January 7, 1791. See Federico, Patent Trials of Oliver Evans, 27 J. Pat. Off. Soc. 586, 590 (1945). Under the 14-year term provided by the 1790 Patent Act, this patent was to expire on January 7, 1805. Claiming that 14 years had not provided him a sufficient time to realize income from his invention and that the net profits were spent developing improvements on the steam engine, Evans first sought an extension of his patent in December 1804. Id., at 598; 14 Annals of Congo 1002 (1805). Unsuccessful in 1804, he tried again in 1805, and yet again in 1806, to persuade Congress to pass his private bill. Undaunted, Evans tried one last time to revive his expired patent after receiving an adverse judgment in an infringement action. See Evans v. Chambers, 8 F. Cas. 837 (No. 4,555) (CC Pa. 1807). This time, his effort at private legislation was successful, and Congress passed a bill extending his patent for 14 years. See An Act for the relief of Oliver Evans, 6 Stat. 70. This legislation, passed January 21, 1808, restored a patent monopoly for an invention that had been in the public domain for over four years. As such, this Act unquestionably exceeded Congress' authority under the Copyright/Patent Clause: "The Congress in the exercise of the patent power may not overreach the restraints imposed by the stated constitutional purpose .... Congress may not authorize the issuance of patents whose effects are to remove existent knowledge from the public domain, or to restrict free access to materials already available." Graham, 383 U. S., at 5–6 (emphasis added).

This extension of patent protection to an expired patent was not an isolated incident. Congress passed private bills either directly extending patents or allowing otherwise untimely applicants to apply for patent extensions for approximately 75 patents between 1790 and 1875. Of these 75 patents, at least 56 had already fallen into the public domain.10[46] The fact that this repeated practice was patently unconstitutional completely undermines the majority's reliance on this history as "significant." Ante, at 201.

Copyright legislation has a similar history. The federal Copyright Act was first amended in 1831. That amendment, like later amendments, not only authorized a longer term for new works, but also extended the terms of unexpired copyrights. Respondent argues that that historical practice effectively establishes the constitutionality of retroactive extensions of unexpired copyrights. Of course, the practice buttressess the presumption of validity that attaches to every Act of Congress. But, as our decision in INS v. Chadha, 462 U. S. 919 (1983), demonstrates, the fact that Congress has repeatedly acted on a mistaken interpretation of the Constitution does

---

[46] See, e.g., ch. 74, 6 Stat. 458 (patent had expired for three months); ch. 113, 6 Stat. 467 (patent had expired for over two years); ch. 213, 6 Stat. 589 (patent had expired for five months); ch. 158, 9 Stat. 734 (patent had expired for over two years); ch. 72, 14 Stat. 621 (patent had expired nearly four years); ch. 175, 15 Stat. 461 (patent had expired for over two years); ch. 15, 16 Stat. 613 (patent had expired for six years); ch. 317, 16 Stat. 659 (patent had expired for nearly four years); ch. 439, 17 Stat. 689 (patent had expired for over two years).

not qualify our duty to invalidate an unconstitutional practice when it is finally challenged in an appropriate case. As Justice White pointed out in his dissent in Chadha, that case sounded the "death knell for nearly 200 other statutory provisions" in which Congress had exercised a "'legislative veto.'" Id., at 967. Regardless of the effect of unconstitutional enactments of Congress, the scope of "'the constitutional power of Congress ... is ultimately a judicial rather than a legislative question, and can be settled finally only by this Court.'" United States v. Morrison, 529 U. S. 598, 614 (2000) (quoting Heart of Atlanta Motel, Inc. v. United States, 379 U. S. 241, 273 (1964) (Black, J., concurring)). For, as this Court has long recognized, "[i]t is obviously correct that no one acquires a vested or protected right in violation of the Constitution by long use, even when that span of time covers our entire national existence." Walz v. Tax Comm'n of City of New York, 397 U. S. 664, 678 (1970).

It would be particularly unwise to attach constitutional significance to the 1831 amendment because of the very different legal landscape against which it was enacted. Congress based its authority to pass the amendment on grounds shortly thereafter declared improper by the Court. The Judiciary Committee Report prepared for the House of Representatives asserted that "an author has an exclusive and perpetual right, in preference to any other, to the fruits of his labor." 7 Congo Deb., App., p. cxx (1831). The floor debate echoed this same sentiment. See, e.g., id., at 424 (statement of Mr. Verplanck (rejecting the idea that copyright involved "an implied contract existing between an author and the public" for "there was no contract; the work of an author was the result of his own labor" and copyright was "merely a legal provision for the protection of a natural right")). This sweat-of-the-brow view of copyright, however, was emphatically rejected by this Court in 1834 in Wheaton v. Peters, 8 Pet., at 661 ("Congress, then, by this act, instead of sanctioning an existing right, as contended for, created it"). No presumption of validity should attach to a statutory enactment that relied on a shortly thereafter discredited interpretation of the basis for congressional power.[47]

In 1861, Congress amended the term of patents, from a 14-year term plus opportunity for 7-year extension to a flat 17 years with no extension permitted. Act of Mar. 2, 1861, ch. 88, § 16, 12 Stat. 249. This change was not retroactive, but rather only applied to "all patents hereafter granted." Ibid. To be sure, Congress, at many times in its history, has retroactively extended the terms of existing copyrights and patents. This history, however, reveals a much more heterogeneous practice than

---

[47] In the period before our decision in Wheaton, the pre-emptive effect of the Patent/Copyright Clause was also a matter of serious debate within the legal profession. Indeed, in their argument in this Court in Gibbons v. Ogden, 9 Wheat., at 44-61, 141-157, the defenders of New York's grant of a 30-year monopoly on the passenger trade between New Jersey and Manhattan argued that the Clause actually should be interpreted as confirming the State's authority to grant monopoly privileges that supplemented any federal grant. That argument is, of course, flatly inconsistent with our recent unanimous decision in Bonito Boats, Inc. v. Thunder Craft Boats, Inc., 489 U. S. 141 (1989). Although Attorney General Wirt had urged the Court to endorse our present interpretation of the Clause, its implicit limitations were unsettled when the 1831 Copyright Act was passed.

respondent contends. It is replete with actions that were unquestionably unconstitutional. Though relevant, the history is not dispositive of the constitutionality of the Sonny Bono Act.

The general presumption that historic practice illuminates the constitutionality of congressional action is not controlling in this case. That presumption is strongest when the earliest acts of Congress are considered, for the overlap of identity between those who created the Constitution and those who first constituted Congress provides "contemporaneous and weighty evidence" of the Constitution's "true meaning." Wisconsin v. Pelican Ins. Co., 127 U. S. 265, 297 (1888). But that strong presumption does not attach to congressional action in 1831, because no member of the 1831 Congress had been a delegate to the framing convention 44 years earlier.

Moreover, judicial opinions relied upon by the majority interpreting early legislative enactments have either been implicitly overruled or do not support the proposition claimed. Graham flatly contradicts the cases relied on by the majority and respondent for support that "renewed or extended terms were upheld in the early days." Ante, at 202.12 Evans v. Jordan, 8 F. Cas. 872, 874 (No. 4,564) (CC Va. 1813) (Marshall, J.); Evans v. Robinson, 8 F. Cas. 886, 888 (No. 4,571) (CC Md. 1813); and Blanchard v. Sprague, 3 F. Cas. 648, 650 (No. 1,518) (CC Mass. 1839) (Story, J.), all held that private bills passed by Congress extending previously expired patents were valid. Evans v. Jordan and Evans v. Robinson both considered Oliver Evans' private bill discussed above while Blanchard involved ch. 213, 6 Stat. 589, which extended Thomas Blanchard's patent after it had been in the public domain for five months. Irrespective of what circuit courts held "in the early days," ante, at 202, such holdings have been implicitly overruled by Graham and, therefore, provide no support for respondent in the present constitutional inquiry.

The majority's reliance on the other patent case it cites is similarly misplaced. Contrary to the suggestion in the Court's opinion, McClurg v. Kingsland, 1 How. 202 (1843), did not involve the "legislative expansion" of an existing patent. Ante, at 202. The question in that case was whether the former employer of the inventor, one James Harley, could be held liable as an infringer for continuing to use the process that Harley had invented in 1834 when he was in its employ. The Court first held that the employer's use of the process before the patent issued was not a public use that would invalidate the patent, even if it might have had that effect prior to the amendment of the patent statute in 1836. 1 How., at 206–208. The Court then disposed of the case on the ground that a statute enacted in 1839 protected the alleged infringer's right to continue to use the process after the patent issued. Id., at 209–211. Our opinion said nothing about the power of Congress to extend the life of an issued patent. It did note that Congress has plenary power to legislate on the subject of patents provided "that they do not take away the rights of property in existing patents." Id., at 206. The fact that Congress cannot change the bargain between the public and the patentee in a way that disadvantages the patentee is, of course, fully consistent with the view that it cannot enlarge the patent monopoly to the detriment of the public after a patent has issued.

The history of retroactive extensions of existing and expired copyrights and patents, though relevant, is not conclusive of the constitutionality of the Sonny Bono

Act. The fact that the Court has not previously passed upon the constitutionality of retroactive copyright extensions does not insulate the present extension from constitutional challenge.

V

Respondent also argues that the Act promotes the useful arts by providing incentives to restore old movies. For at least three reasons, the interest in preserving perishable copies of old copyrighted films does not justify a wholesale extension of existing copyrights. First, such restoration and preservation will not even arguably promote any new works by authors or inventors. And, of course, any original expression in the restoration and preservation of movies will receive new copyright protection.[48] Second, however strong the justification for preserving such works may be, that justification applies equally to works whose copyrights have already expired. Yet no one seriously contends that the Copyright/Patent Clause would authorize the grant of monopoly privileges for works already in the public domain solely to encourage their restoration. Finally, even if this concern with aging movies would permit congressional protection, the remedy offered-a blanket extension of all copyrights-simply bears no relationship to the alleged harm.

VI

Finally, respondent relies on concerns of equity to justify the retroactive extension. If Congress concludes that a longer period of exclusivity is necessary in order to provide an adequate incentive to authors to produce new works, respondent seems to believe that simple fairness requires that the same lengthened period be provided to authors whose works have already been completed and copyrighted. This is a classic non sequitur. The reason for increasing the inducement to create something new simply does not apply to an already-created work. To the contrary, the equity argument actually provides strong support for petitioners. Members of the public were entitled to rely on a promised access to copyrighted or patented works at the expiration of the terms specified when the exclusive privileges were granted. On the other hand, authors will receive the full benefit of the exclusive terms that were promised as an inducement to their creativity, and have no equitable claim to increased compensation for doing nothing more.

One must indulge in two untenable assumptions to find support in the equitable argument offered by respondent that the public interest in free access to copyrighted works is entirely worthless and that authors, as a class, should receive a windfall solely based on completed creative activity. Indeed, Congress has apparently indulged in those assumptions for under the series of extensions to copyrights, with the exception

---

[48] Indeed, the Lodging of the Motion Picture Association of America, Inc., as Amicus Curiae illustrates the significant creative work involved in releasing these classics. The Casablanca Digital Video Disc (DVD) contains a "documentary You Must Remember This, hosted by Lauren Bacall and featuring recently unearthed outtakes" and an "[a]ll-new introduction by Lauren Bacall." Disc cover text. Similarly, the Citizen Kane DVD includes "[t]wo feature-length audio commentaries: one by film critic Roger Ebert and the other by director/Welles biographer Peter Bogdanovich" and a "gallery of storyboards, rare photos, alternate ad campaigns, studio correspondence, call sheets and other memorabilia" in addition to a 2-hour documentary. Disc cover text.

of works which required renewal and which were not renewed, no copyrighted work created in the past 80 years has entered the public domain or will do so until 2019. But as our cases repeatedly and consistently emphasize, ultimate public access is the overriding purpose of the constitutional provision. See, e.g., Sony Corp., 464 U. S., at 429. Ex post facto extensions of existing copyrights, unsupported by any consideration of the public interest, frustrate the central purpose of the Clause.

VII

The express grant of a perpetual copyright would unquestionably violate the textual requirement that the authors' exclusive rights be only "for limited Times." Whether the extraordinary length of the grants authorized by the 1998 Act are invalid because they are the functional equivalent of perpetual copyrights is a question that need not be answered in this case because the question presented by the certiorari petition merely challenges Congress' power to extend retroactively the terms of existing copyrights. Accordingly, there is no need to determine whether the deference that is normally given to congressional policy judgments may save from judicial review its decision respecting the appropriate length of the term.[49] 14 It is important to note, however, that a categorical rule prohibiting retroactive extensions would effectively preclude perpetual copyrights. More importantly, as the House of Lords recognized when it refused to amend the Statute of Anne in 1735, unless the Clause is construed to embody such a categorical rule, Congress may extend existing monopoly privileges ad infinitum under the majority's analysis.

By failing to protect the public interest in free access to the products of inventive and artistic genius-indeed, by virtually ignoring the central purpose of the Copyright/Patent Clause-the Court has quitclaimed to Congress its principal responsibility in this area of the law. Fairly read, the Court has stated that Congress' actions under the Copyright/Patent Clause are, for all intents and purposes, judicially unreviewable. That result cannot be squared with the basic tenets of our constitutional structure. It is not hyperbole to recall the trenchant words of Chief Justice John Marshall:

"It is emphatically the province and duty of the judicial department to say what the law is." Marbury v. Madison, 1 Cranch 137, 177 (1803). We should discharge that responsibility as we did in Chadha.

I respectfully dissent.

JUSTICE BREYER, dissenting.

The Constitution's Copyright Clause grants Congress the power to "promote the Progress of Science ... by securing for limited Times to Authors ... the exclusive Right to their respective Writings." Art. I, § 8, cl. 8 (emphasis added). The statute before us, the 1998 Sonny Bono Copyright Term Extension Act, extends the term of most existing copyrights ("We have recognized, in a number of contexts, the legitimacy of protecting reasonable reliance on prior law even when that requires

---

[49] Similarly, the validity of earlier retroactive extensions of copyright protection is not at issue in this case. To decide the question now presented, we need not consider whether the reliance and expectation interests that have been established by prior extensions passed years ago would alter the result. Cf. Heckler v. Mathews, 465 U. S. 728, 746 (1984).

allowing an unconstitutional statute to remain in effect for a limited period of time"). Those interests are not at issue now, because the act under review in this case was passed only four years ago and has been under challenge in court since shortly after its enactment to 95 years and that of many new copyrights to 70 years after the author's death. The economic effect of this 20-year extension—the longest blanket extension since the Nation's founding—is to make the copyright term not limited, but virtually perpetual. Its primary legal effect is to grant the extended term not to authors, but to their heirs, estates, or corporate successors. And most importantly, its practical effect is not to promote, but to inhibit, the progress of "Science"—by which word the Framers meant learning or knowledge, E. Walterscheid, The Nature of the Intellectual Property Clause: A Study in Historical Perspective 125–126 (2002).

The majority believes these conclusions rest upon practical judgments that at most suggest the statute is unwise, not that it is unconstitutional. Legal distinctions, however, are often matters of degree. Panhandle Oil Co. v. Mississippi ex rel. Knox, 277 U. S. 218, 223 (1928) (Holmes, J., dissenting), overruled in part by Alabama v. King & Boozer, 314 U. S. 1, 8–9 (1941); accord, Walz v. Tax Comm'n of City of New York, 397 U. S. 664, 678–679 (1970). And in this case the failings of degree are so serious that they amount to failings of constitutional kind. Although the Copyright Clause grants broad legislative power to Congress, that grant has limits. And in my view this statute falls outside them.

I

The "monopoly privileges" that the Copyright Clause confers "are neither unlimited nor primarily designed to provide a special private benefit." Sony Corp. of America v. Universal City Studios, Inc., 464 U. S. 417, 429 (1984); cf. Graham v. John Deere Co. of Kansas City, 383 U. S. 1, 5 (1966). This Court has made clear that the Clause's limitations are judicially enforceable. E.g., Trade-Mark Cases, 100 U. S. 82, 93–94 (1879). And, in assessing this statute for that purpose, I would take into account the fact that the Constitution is a single document, that it contains both a Copyright Clause and a First Amendment, and that the two are related.

The Copyright Clause and the First Amendment seek related objectives-the creation and dissemination of information. When working in tandem, these provisions mutually reinforce each other, the first serving as an "engine of free expression," Harper & Row, Publishers, Inc. v. Nation Enterprises, 471 U. S. 539, 558 (1985), the second assuring that government throws up no obstacle to its dissemination. At the same time, a particular statute that exceeds proper Copyright Clause bounds may set Clause and Amendment at cross-purposes, thereby depriving the public of the speech related benefits that the Founders, through both, have promised.

Consequently, I would review plausible claims that a copyright statute seriously, and unjustifiably, restricts the dissemination of speech somewhat more carefully than reference to this Court's traditional Copyright Clause jurisprudence might suggest, cf. ante, at 204–205, and n. 10. There is no need in this case to characterize that review as a search for "'congruence and proportionality,'" ante, at 218, or as some other variation of what this Court has called "intermediate scrutiny," e.g., San Francisco Arts & Athletics, Inc. v. United States Olympic Comm., 483 U. S. 522, 536–537

(1987) (applying intermediate scrutiny to a variant of normal trademark protection). Cf. Nixon v. Shrink Missouri Government PAC, 528 U. S. 377, 402–403 (2000) (BREYER, J., concurring) (test of proportionality between burdens and benefits "where a law significantly implicates competing constitutionally protected interests"). Rather, it is necessary only to recognize that this statute involves not pure economic regulation, but regulation of expression, and what may count as rational where economic regulation is at issue is not necessarily rational where we focus on expression—in a Nation constitutionally dedicated to the free dissemination of speech, information, learning, and culture. In this sense only, and where line-drawing among constitutional interests is at issue, I would look harder than does the majority at the statute's rationality—though less hard than precedent might justify, see, e.g., Cleburne v. Cleburne Living Center, Inc., 473 U. S. 432, 446–450 (1985); Plyler v. Doe, 457 U. S. 202, 223–224 (1982); Department of Agriculture v. Moreno, 413 U. S. 528, 534–538 (1973).

Thus, I would find that the statute lacks the constitutionally necessary rational support (1) if the significant benefits that it bestows are private, not public; (2) if it threatens seriously to undermine the expressive values that the Copyright Clause embodies; and (3) if it cannot find justification in any significant Clause-related objective. Where, after examination of the statute, it becomes difficult, if not impossible, even to dispute these characterizations, Congress' "choice is clearly wrong." Helvering v. Davis, 301 U. S. 619, 640 (1937).

II A

Because we must examine the relevant statutory effects in light of the Copyright Clause's own purposes, we should begin by reviewing the basic objectives of that Clause. The Clause authorizes a "tax on readers for the purpose of giving a bounty to writers." 56 Parl. Deb. (3d Ser.) (1841) 341, 350 (Lord Macaulay). Why? What constitutional purposes does the "bounty" serve?

The Constitution itself describes the basic Clause objective as one of "promot[ing] the Progress of Science," i. e., knowledge and learning. The Clause exists not to "provide a special private benefit," Sony, supra, at 429, but "to stimulate artistic creativity for the general public good," Twentieth Century Music Corp. v. Aiken, 422 U. S. 151, 156 (1975). It does so by "motivat[ing] the creative activity of authors" through "the provision of a special reward." Sony, supra, at 429. The "reward" is a means, not an end. And that is why the copyright term is limited. It is limited so that its beneficiaries—the public—"will not be permanently deprived of the fruits of an artist's labors." Stewart v. Abend, 495 U. S. 207, 228 (1990).

That is how the Court previously has described the Clause's objectives. See also Mazer v. Stein, 347 U. S. 201, 219 (1954) ("[C]opyright law ... makes reward to the owner a secondary consideration" (internal quotation marks omitted)); Sony, 464 U. S., at 429 ("[L]imited grant" is "intended ... to allow the public access to the products of [authors'] genius after the limited period of exclusive control has expired"); Harper & Row, supra, at 545 (Copyright is "intended to increase and not to impede the harvest of knowledge"). But cf. ante, at 212, n. 18. And, in doing so, the Court simply has reiterated the views of the Founders.

Madison, like Jefferson and others in the founding generation, warned against the dangers of monopolies. See, e.g., Monopolies. Perpetuities. Corporations. Ecclesiastical Endowments. in J. Madison, Writings 756 (J. Rakove ed. 1999) (hereinafter Madison on Monopolies); Letter from Thomas Jefferson to James Madison (July 31, 1788), in 13 Papers of Thomas Jefferson 443 (J. Boyd ed. 1956) (hereinafter Papers of Thomas Jefferson) (arguing against even copyright monopolies); 2 Annals of Congo 1917 (1791) (statement of Rep. Jackson in the First Congress, Feb. 1791) ("What was it drove our forefathers to this country? Was it not the ecclesiastical corporations and perpetual monopolies of England and Scotland?"). Madison noted that the Constitution had "limited them to two cases, the authors of Books, and of useful inventions." Madison on Monopolies 756. He thought that in those two cases monopoly is justified because it amounts to "compensation for" an actual community "benefit" and because the monopoly is "temporary" the term originally being 14 years (once renewable). Ibid. Madison concluded that "under that limitation a sufficient recompence and encouragement may be given." Ibid. But he warned in general that monopolies must be "guarded with strictness agst abuse." Ibid.

Many Members of the Legislative Branch have expressed themselves similarly. Those who wrote the House Report on the landmark Copyright Act of 1909, for example, said that copyright was not designed "primarily" to "benefit" the "author" or "any particular class of citizens, however worthy." H. R. Rep. No. 2222, 60th Cong., 2d Sess., 6–7 (1909). Rather, under the Constitution, copyright was designed "primarily for the benefit of the public," for "the benefit of the great body of people, in that it will stimulate writing and invention." Id., at 7. And were a copyright statute not "believed, in fact, to accomplish" the basic constitutional objective of advancing learning, that statute "would be beyond the power of Congress" to enact. Id., at 6–7. Similarly, those who wrote the House Report on legislation that implemented the Berne Convention for the Protection of Literary and Artistic Works said that "[t]he constitutional purpose of copyright is to facilitate the flow of ideas in the interest of learning." H. R. Rep. No. 100–609, p. 22 (1988) (internal quotation marks omitted). They added:

"Under the U. S. Constitution, the primary objective of copyright law is not to reward the author, but rather to secure for the public the benefits derived from the authors' labors. By giving authors an incentive to create, the public benefits in two ways: when the original expression is created and ... when the limited term ... expires and the creation is added to the public domain." Id., at 17.

For present purposes, then, we should take the following as well established: that copyright statutes must serve public, not private, ends; that they must seek "to promote the Progress" of knowledge and learning; and that they must do so both by creating incentives for authors to produce and by removing the related restrictions on dissemination after expiration of a copyright's "limited Tim[e]"—a time that (like "a limited monarch") is "restrain[ed]" and "circumscribe[d]," "not [left] at large," 2 S. Johnson, A Dictionary of the English Language 1151 (4th rev. ed. 1773). I would examine the statute's effects in light of these well established constitutional purposes.

B

This statute, like virtually every copyright statute, imposes upon the public certain expression-related costs in the form of (1) royalties that may be higher than necessary to evoke creation of the relevant work, and (2) a requirement that one seeking to reproduce a copyrighted work must obtain the copyright holder's permission. The first of these costs translates into higher prices that will potentially restrict a work's dissemination. The second means search costs that themselves may prevent reproduction even where the author has no objection. Although these costs are, in a sense, inevitable concomitants of copyright protection, there are special reasons for thinking them especially serious here.

First, the present statute primarily benefits the holders of existing copyrights, i. e., copyrights on works already created. And a Congressional Research Service (CRS) study prepared for Congress indicates that the added royaltyrelated sum that the law will transfer to existing copyright holders is large. E. Rappaport, CRS Report for Congress, Copyright Term Extension: Estimating the Economic Values (1998) (hereinafter CRS Report). In conjunction with official figures on copyright renewals, the CRS Report indicates that only about 2% of copyrights between 55 and 75 years old retain commercial value—i. e., still generate royalties after that time. Brief for Petitioners 7 (estimate, uncontested by respondent, based on data from the CRS, Census Bureau, and Library of Congress). But books, songs, and movies of that vintage still earn about $400 million per year in royalties. CRS Report 8, 12, 15. Hence, (despite declining consumer interest in any given work over time) one might conservatively estimate that 20 extra years of copyright protection will mean the transfer of several billion extra royalty dollars to holders of existing copyrights-copyrights that, together, already will have earned many billions of dollars in royalty "reward." See id., at 16.

The extra royalty payments will not come from thin air.

Rather, they ultimately come from those who wish to read or see or hear those classic books or films or recordings that have survived. Even the $500,000 that United Airlines has had to pay for the right to play George Gershwin's 1924 classic Rhapsody in Blue represents a cost of doing business, potentially reflected in the ticket prices of those who fly. See Ganzel, Copyright or Copywrong? 39 Training 36, 42 (Dec. 2002). Further, the likely amounts of extra royalty payments are large enough to suggest that unnecessarily high prices will unnecessarily restrict distribution of classic works (or lead to disobedience of the law)-not just in theory but in practice. Cf. CRS Report 3 ("[N]ew, cheaper editions can be expected when works come out of copyright"); Brief for College Art Association et al. as Amici Curiae 24 (One year after expiration of copyright on Willa Cather's My Antonia, seven new editions appeared at prices ranging from $2 to $24); Ganzel, supra, at 40–41, 44 (describing later abandoned plans to charge individual Girl Scout camps $257 to $1,439 annually for a license to sing songs such as God Bless America around a campfire).

A second, equally important, cause for concern arises out of the fact that copyright extension imposes a "permissions" requirement—not only upon potential users of "classic" works that still retain commercial value, but also upon potential users of any other work still in copyright. Again using CRS estimates, one can estimate that, by 2018, the number of such works 75 years of age or older will be about 350,000. See Brief for Petitioners 7. Because the Copyright Act of 1976 abolished the requirement that an owner must renew a copyright, such still-in-copyright works (of little or no commercial value) will eventually number in the millions. See Pub. L. 94–553, §§ 302–304,90 Stat. 2572–2576; U. S. Dept. of Commerce, Bureau of Census, Statistical History of the United States: From Colonial Times to the Present 956 (1976) (hereinafter Statistical History).

The potential users of such works include not only movie buffs and aging jazz fans, but also historians, scholars, teachers, writers, artists, database operators, and researchers of all kinds-those who want to make the past accessible for their own use or for that of others. The permissions requirement can inhibit their ability to accomplish that task. Indeed, in an age where computer-accessible databases promise to facilitate research and learning, the permissions requirement can stand as a significant obstacle to realization of that technological hope.

The reason is that the permissions requirement can inhibit or prevent the use of old works (particularly those without commercial value): (1) because it may prove expensive to track down or to contract with the copyright holder, (2) because the holder may prove impossible to find, or (3) because the holder when found may deny permission either outright or through misinformed efforts to bargain. The CRS, for example, has found that the cost of seeking permission "can be prohibitive." CRS Report 4. And amici, along with petitioners, provide examples of the kinds of significant harm at issue.

Thus, the American Association of Law Libraries points out that the clearance process associated with creating an electronic archive, Documenting the American South, "consumed approximately a dozen man-hours" per work. Brief for American Association of Law Libraries et al. as Amici Curiae 20. The College Art Association says that the costs of obtaining permission for use of single images, short excerpts, and other short works can become prohibitively high; it describes the abandonment of efforts to include, e.g., campaign songs, film excerpts, and documents exposing "horrors of the chain gang" in historical works or archives; and it points to examples in which copyright holders in effect have used their control of copyright to try to control the content of historical or cultural works. Brief for College Art Association et al. as Amici Curiae 7–13. The National Writers Union provides similar examples. Brief for National Writers Union et al. as Amici Curiae 25–27. Petitioners point to music fees that may prevent youth or community orchestras, or church choirs, from performing early 20th-century music. Brief for Petitioners 3–5; see also App. 16–17 (Copyright extension caused abandonment of plans to sell sheet music of Maurice Ravel's Alborada Del Gracioso). Amici for petitioners describe how electronic databases tend to avoid adding to their collections works whose copyright holders may prove difficult to contact, see, e.g., Arms, Getting the Picture: Observations from the Library of Congress on Providing Online Access to Pictorial Images, 48 Library Trends 379, 405 (1999) (describing how this tendency applies to the Library of Congress' own digital archives).

As I have said, to some extent costs of this kind accompany any copyright law, regardless of the length of the copyright term. But to extend that term, preventing works from the 1920's and 1930's from falling into the public domain, will dramatically increase the size of the costs just as perversely—the likely benefits from protection diminish. See infra, at 254–256. The older the work, the less likely it retains commercial value, and the harder it will likely prove to find the current copyright holder. The older the work, the more likely it will prove useful to the historian, artist, or teacher. The older the work, the less likely it is that a sense of authors' rights can justify a copyright holder's decision not to permit reproduction, for the more likely it is that the copyright holder making the decision is not the work's creator, but, say, a corporation or a great-grandchild whom the work's creator never knew. Similarly, the costs of obtaining permission, now perhaps ranging in the millions of dollars, will multiply as the number of holders of affected copyrights increases from several hundred thousand to several million. See supra, at 249–250. The costs to the users of nonprofit databases, now numbering in the low millions, will multiply as the use of those computer-assisted databases becomes more prevalent. See, e.g., Brief for Internet Archive et al. as Amici Curiae 2, 21, and n. 37 (describing nonprofit Project Gutenberg). And the qualitative costs to education, learning, and research will multiply as our children become ever more dependent for the content of their knowledge upon computer-accessible databases-thereby condemning that which is not so accessible, say, the cultural content of early 20th-century history, to a kind of intellectual purgatory from which it will not easily emerge.

The majority finds my description of these permissions related harms overstated in light of Congress' inclusion of a statutory exemption, which, during the last 20 years of a copyright term, exempts "facsimile or digital" reproduction by a "library or archives" "for purposes of preservation, scholarship, or research," 17 U. S. C. § 108(h). Ante, at 220. This exemption, however, applies only where the copy is made for the special listed purposes; it simply permits a library (not any other subsequent users) to make "a copy" for those purposes; it covers only "published" works not "subject to normal commercial exploitation" and not obtainable, apparently not even as a used copy, at a "reasonable price"; and it insists that the library assure itself through "reasonable investigation" that these conditions have been met. § 108(h). What database proprietor can rely on so limited an exemption-particularly when the phrase "reasonable investigation" is so open-ended and particularly if the database has commercial, as well as noncommercial, aspects?

The majority also invokes the "fair use" exception, and it notes that copyright law itself is restricted to protection of a work's expression, not its substantive content. Ante, at 219–220. N either the exception nor the restriction, however, would necessarily help those who wish to obtain from electronic databases material that is not there-say, teachers wishing their students to see albums of Depression Era photographs, to read the recorded words of those who actually lived under slavery, or to contrast, say, Gary Cooper's heroic portrayal of Sergeant York with filmed reality from the battlefield of Verdun. Such harm, and more, see supra, at 248252, will occur despite the 1998 Act's exemptions and despite the other "First Amendment safeguards" in which the majority places its trust, ante, at 219–220.

I should add that the Motion Picture Association of America also finds my concerns overstated, at least with respect to films, because the extension will sometimes make it profitable to reissue old films, saving them from extinction. Brief for Motion Picture Association of America, Inc., as Amicus Curiae 14–24. Other film preservationists note, however, that only a small minority of the many films, particularly silent films, from the 1920's and 1930's have been preserved. 1 Report of the Librarian of Congress, Film Preservation 1993, pp. 3–4 (Half of all pre-1950 feature films and more than 80% of all such pre-1929 films have already been lost); cf. Brief for Hal Roach Studios et al. as Amici Curiae 18 (Out of 1,200 Twenties Era silent films still under copyright, 63 are now available on digital video disc). They seek to preserve the remainder. See, e.g., Brief for Internet Archive et al. as Amici Curiae 22 (Nonprofit database digitized 1,001 public-domain films, releasing them online without charge); 1 Film Preservation 1993, supra, at 23 (reporting well over 200,000 titles held in public archives). And they tell us that copyright extension will impede preservation by forbidding the reproduction of films within their own or within other public collections. Brief for Hal Roach Studios et al. as Amici Curiae 10–21; see also Brief for Internet Archive et al. as Amici Curiae 16–29; Brief for American Association of Law Libraries et al. as Amici Curiae 26–27. Because this subsection concerns only costs, not countervailing benefits, I shall simply note here that, with respect to films as with respect to other works, extension does cause substantial harm to efforts to preserve and to disseminate works that were created long ago. And I shall turn to the second half of the equation: Could Congress reasonably have found that the extension's toll-related and permissions related harms are justified by extension's countervailing preservationist incentives or in other ways?

C

What copyright-related benefits might justify the statute's extension of copyright protection? First, no one could reasonably conclude that copyright's traditional economic rationale applies here. The extension will not act as an economic spur encouraging authors to create new works. See Mazer, 347 U. S., at 219 (The "economic philosophy" of the Copyright Clause is to "advance public welfare" by "encouraging] individual effort" through "personal gain"); see also ante, at 212, n. 18 ("[C]opyright law serves public ends by providing individuals with an incentive to pursue private ones"). No potential author can reasonably believe that he has more than a tiny chance of writing a classic that will survive commercially long enough for the copyright extension to matter. After all, if, after 55 to 75 years, only 2% of all copyrights retain commercial value, the percentage surviving after 75 years or more (a typical pre-extension copyright term)—must be far smaller. See supra, at 248; CRS Report 7 (estimating that, even after copyright renewal, about 3.8% of copyrighted books go out of print each year). And any remaining monetary incentive is diminished dramatically by the fact that the relevant royalties will not arrive until 75 years or more into the future, when, not the author, but distant heirs, or shareholders in a successor corporation, will receive them. Using assumptions about the time value of money provided us by a group of economists (including five Nobel prize winners), Brief for George A. Akerlof et al. as Amici Curiae 5–7, it seems fair to say that, for example, a 1% likelihood of earning $100 annually for 20 years, starting 75 years into the future, is worth less than seven cents today. See id., App. 3a; see also CRS Report 5. See generally Appendix, Part A, infra.

What potential Shakespeare, Wharton, or Hemingway would be moved by such a sum? What monetarily motivated Melville would not realize that he could do better for his grandchildren by putting a few dollars into an interest bearing bank account? The Court itself finds no evidence to the contrary. It refers to testimony before Congress (1) that the copyright system's incentives encourage creation, and (2) (referring to Noah Webster) that income earned from one work can help support an artist who "'continue[s] to create.'" Ante, at 208, n. 15. But the first of these amounts to no more than a set of undeniably true propositions about the value of incentives in general. And the applicability of the second to this Act is mysterious. How will extension help today's Noah Webster create new works 50 years after his death? Or is that hypothetical Webster supposed to support himself with the extension's present discounted value, i.e., a few pennies? Or (to change the metaphor) is the argument that Dumas fils would have written more books had Dumas pere's Three Musketeers earned more royalties?

Regardless, even if this cited testimony were meant more specifically to tell Congress that somehow, somewhere, some potential author might be moved by the thought of greatgrandchildren receiving copyright royalties a century hence, so might some potential author also be moved by the thought of royalties being paid for two centuries, five centuries, 1,000 years, "'til the End of Time." And from a rational economic perspective the time difference among these periods makes no real difference. The present extension will produce a copyright period of protection that, even under conservative assumptions, is worth more than 99.8% of protection in perpetuity (more than 99.99% for a songwriter like Irving Berlin and a song like Alexander's Ragtime Band). See Appendix, Part A, infra. The lack of a practically meaningful distinction from an author's ex ante perspective between (a) the statute's extended terms and (b) an infinite term makes this latest extension difficult to square with the Constitution's insistence on "limited Times." Cf. Tr. of Oral Arg. 34 (Solicitor General's related concession).

I am not certain why the Court considers it relevant in this respect that "[n]othing ... warrants construction of the [1998 Act's] 20-year term extension as a congressional attempt to evade or override the 'limited Times' constraint." Ante, at 209. Of course Congress did not intend to act unconstitutionally. But it may have sought to test the Constitution's limits. After all, the statute was named after a Member of Congress, who, the legislative history records, "wanted the term of copyright protection to last forever." 144 Congo Rec. H9952 (daily ed. Oct. 7, 1998) (statement of Rep. Mary Bono). See also Copyright Term, Film Labeling, and Film Preservation Legislation: Hearings on H. R. 989 et al. before the Subcommittee on Courts and Intellectual Property of the House Judiciary Committee, 104th Cong., 1st Sess., 94 (1995) (hereinafter House Hearings) (statement of Rep. Sonny Bono) (questioning why copyrights should ever expire); ibid. (statement of Rep. Berman) ("I guess we could ... just make a permanent moratorium on the expiration of copyrights"); id., at 230 (statement of Rep. Hoke) ("Why 70 years? Why not forever?

Why not 150 years?"); cf. ibid. (statement of the Register of Copyrights) (In Copyright Office proceedings, "[t]he Songwriters Guild suggested a perpetual term"); id., at 234 (statement of Quincy Jones) ("I'm particularly fascinated with Representative Hoke's statement .... [W]hy not forever?"); id., at 277 (statement of Quincy Jones) ("If we can start with 70, add 20, it would be a good start"). And the statute ended up creating a term so long that (were the vesting of 19th-century real property at issue) it would typically violate the traditional rule against perpetuities. See 10 R. Powell, Real Property §§ 71.02[2]-[3], p. 71-11 (M. Wolf ed. 2002) (traditional rule that estate must vest, if at all, within lives in being plus 21 years); cf. id., § 71.03, at 71-15 (modern statutory perpetuity term of 90 years, 5 years shorter than 95-year copyright terms).

In any event, the incentive-related numbers are far too small for Congress to have concluded rationally, even with respect to new works, that the extension's economic incentive effect could justify the serious expression-related harms earlier described. See Part II-B, supra. And, of course, in respect to works already created-the source of many of the harms previously described-the statute creates no economic incentive at all. See ante, at 226–227 (STEVENS, J., dissenting).

Second, the Court relies heavily for justification upon international uniformity of terms. Ante, at 196, 205–206. Although it can be helpful to look to international norms and legal experience in understanding American law, cf. Printz v. United States, 521 U. S. 898, 977 (1997) (BREYER, J., dissenting), in this case the justification based upon foreign rules is surprisingly weak. Those who claim that significant copyright-related benefits flow from greater international uniformity of terms point to the fact that the nations of the European Union have adopted a system of copyright terms uniform among themselves. And the extension before this Court implements a term of life plus 70 years that appears to conform with the European standard. But how does "uniformity" help to justify this statute?

Despite appearances, the statute does not create a uniform American-European term with respect to the lion's share of the economically significant works that it affects-all works made "for hire" and all existing works created prior to 1978. See Appendix, Part B, infra. With respect to those works the American statute produces an extended term of 95 years while comparable European rights in "for hire" works last for periods that vary from 50 to 70 years to life plus 70 years. Compare 17 U. S. C. §§ 302(c), 304(a)–(b), with Council Directive 93/98/EEC of 29 October 1993 Harmonizing the Term of Protection of Copyright and Certain Related Rights, Arts. 1–3, 1993 Official J. Eur. Corns. (L 290), pp. 11–12 (hereinafter EU Council Directive 93/98). Neither does the statute create uniformity with respect to anonymous or pseudonymous works. Compare 17 U. S. C. §§ 302(c), 304(a)–(b), with EU Council Directive 93/98, Art. 1, p. 11.

The statute does produce uniformity with respect to copyrights in new, post-1977 works attributed to natural persons. Compare 17 U. S. C. § 302(a) with EU Council Directive 93/98, Art. 1(1), p. 11. But these works constitute only a subset (likely a minority) of works that retain commercial value after 75 years. See Appendix, Part B, infra. And the fact that uniformity comes so late, if at all, means that bringing

American law into conformity with this particular aspect of European law will neither encourage creation nor benefit the long-dead author in any other important way.

What benefit, then, might this partial future uniformity achieve? The majority refers to "greater incentive for American and other authors to create and disseminate their work in the United States," and cites a law review article suggesting a need to "'avoid competitive disadvantages.'" Ante, at 206. The Solicitor General elaborates on this theme, postulating that because uncorrected disuniformity would permit Europe, not the United States, to hold out the prospect of protection lasting for "life plus 70 years" (instead of "life plus 50 years"), a potential author might decide to publish initially in Europe, delaying American publication. Brief for Respondent 38. And the statute, by creating a uniformly longer term, corrects for the disincentive that this disuniformity might otherwise produce.

That disincentive, however, could not possibly bring about serious harm of the sort that the Court, the Solicitor General, or the law review author fears. For one thing, it is unclear just who will be hurt and how, should American publication come second—for the Berne Convention still offers full protection as long as a second publication is delayed by 30 days. See Berne Conv. Arts. 3(4), 5(4). For another, few, if any, potential authors would turn a "where to publish" decision upon this particular difference in the length of the copyright term. As we have seen, the present commercial value of any such difference amounts at most to comparative pennies. See supra, at 254–256. And a commercial decision that turned upon such a difference would have had to have rested previously upon a knife edge so fine as to be invisible. A rational legislature could not give major weight to an invisible, likely nonexistent incentive-related effect.

But if there is no incentive-related benefit, what is the benefit of the future uniformity that the statute only partially achieves? Unlike the Copyright Act of 1976, this statute does not constitute part of an American effort to conform to an important international treaty like the Berne Convention. See H. R. Rep. No. 94-1476, pp. 135–136 (1976) (The 1976 Act's life-plus-50 term was "required for adherence to the Berne Convention"); S. Rep. No. 94-473, p. 118 (1975) (same). Nor does European acceptance of the longer term seem to reflect more than special European institutional considerations, i.e., the needs of, and the international politics surrounding, the development of the European Union. House Hearings 230 (statement of the Register of Copyrights); id., at 396–398 (statement of J. Reichman). European and American copyright law have long coexisted despite important differences, including Europe's traditional respect for authors' "moral rights" and the absence in Europe of constitutional restraints that restrict copyrights to "limited Times." See, e.g., Kwall, Copyright and the Moral Right:

Is an American Marriage Possible? 38 Vand. L. Rev. 1–3 (1985) (moral rights); House Hearings 187 (testimony of the Register of Copyrights) ("limited [T]imes"). In sum, the partial, future uniformity that the 1998 Act promises cannot reasonably be said to justify extension of the copyright term for new works. And concerns with uniformity cannot possibly justify the extension of the new term to older works, for the statute there creates no uniformity at all.

Third, several publishers and filmmakers argue that the statute provides incentives to those who act as publishers to republish and to redistribute older copyrighted works. This claim cannot justify this statute, however, because the rationale is inconsistent with the basic purpose of the Copyright Clause—as understood by the Framers and by this Court. The Clause assumes an initial grant of monopoly, designed primarily to encourage creation, followed by termination of the monopoly grant in order to promote dissemination of already—created works. It assumes that it is the disappearance of the monopoly grant, not its perpetuation, that will, on balance, promote the dissemination of works already in existence. This view of the Clause does not deny the empirical possibility that grant of a copyright monopoly to the heirs or successors of a long-dead author could on occasion help publishers resurrect the work, say, of a long-lost Shakespeare. But it does deny Congress the Copyright Clause power to base its actions primarily upon that empirical possibility-lest copyright grants become perpetual, lest on balance they restrict dissemination, lest too often they seek to bestow benefits that are solely retroactive.

This view of the Clause finds strong support in the writings of Madison, in the antimonopoly environment in which the Framers wrote the Clause, and in the history of the Clause's English antecedent, the Statute of Anne—a statute which sought to break up a publishers' monopoly by offering, as an alternative, an author's monopoly of limited duration. See Patterson, Understanding the Copyright Clause, 47 J. Copyright Soc. 365, 379 (2000) (Statute of Anne); L. Patterson, Copyright in Historical Perspective 144–147 (1968) (same); Madison on Monopolies 756–757; Papers of Thomas Jefferson 442–443; The Constitutional Convention and the Formation of the Union 334, 338 (W. Solberg 2d ed. 1990); see also supra, at 246–247.

This view finds virtually conclusive support in the Court's own precedents. See Sony, 464 U. S., at 429 (The Copyright Clause is "intended ... to allow the public access ... after the limited period of exclusive control"); Stewart, 495 U. S., at 228 (The copyright term is limited to avoid "permanently depriv[ing]" the public of "the fruits of an artist's labors"); see also supra, at 245–246.

This view also finds textual support in the Copyright Clause's word "limited." Cf. J. Story, Commentaries on the Constitution § 558, p. 402 (R. Rotunda & J. Nowak eds. 1987) (The Copyright Clause benefits the public in part because it "admit[s] the people at large, after a short interval, to the full possession and enjoyment of all writings ... without restraint" (emphasis added)). It finds added textual support in the word "Authors," which is difficult to reconcile with a rationale that rests entirely upon incentives given to publishers perhaps long after the death of the work's creator. Cf. Feist Publications, Inc. v. Rural Telephone Service Co., 499 U. S. 340, 346–347 (1991).

It finds empirical support in sources that underscore the wisdom of the Framers' judgment. See CRS Report 3 ("[N]ew, cheaper editions can be expected when works come out of copyright"); see also Part II-B, supra. And it draws logical support from the endlessly self-perpetuating nature of the publishers' claim and the difficulty of finding any kind of logical stopping place were this Court to accept such a uniquely publisher-related rationale. (Would it justify continuing to extend copyrights indefinitely, say, for those granted to F. Scott Fitzgerald or his lesser known contemporaries? Would it not, in principle, justify continued protection of the works of Shakespeare, Melville, Mozart, or perhaps Salieri, Mozart's currently less popular contemporary?

Could it justify yet further extension of the copyright on the song Happy Birthday to You (melody first published in 1893, song copyrighted after litigation in 1935), still in effect and currently owned by a subsidiary of AOL Time Warner? See Profitable "Happy Birthday," Times of London, Aug. 5, 2000, p. 6.)

Given this support, it is difficult to accept the conflicting rationale that the publishers advance, namely, that extension, rather than limitation, of the grant will, by rewarding publishers with a form of monopoly, promote, rather than retard, the dissemination of works already in existence. Indeed, given these considerations, this rationale seems constitutionally perverse-unable, constitutionally speaking, to justify the blanket extension here at issue. Cf. ante, at 239240 (STEVENS, J., dissenting).

Fourth, the statute's legislative history suggests another possible justification. That history refers frequently to the financial assistance the statute will bring the entertainment industry, particularly through the promotion of exports. See, e.g., S. Rep. No. 104-315, p. 3 (1996) ("The purpose of the bill is to ensure adequate copyright protection for American works in foreign nations and the continued economic benefits of a healthy surplus balance of trade"); 144 Congo Rec., at H9951 (statement of Rep. Foley) (noting "the importance of this issue to America's creative community," "[w]hether it is Sony, BMI, Disney," or other companies). I recognize that Congress has sometimes found that suppression of competition will help Americans sell abroad-though it has simultaneously taken care to protect American buyers from higher domestic prices. See, e.g., Webb-Pomerene Act (Export Trade), 40 Stat. 516, as amended, 15 U. S. C. §§ 61–65; see also IA P. Areeda & H. Hovenkamp, Antitrust Law ~ 251a, pp. 134–137 (2d ed. 2000) (criticizing export cartels). In doing so, however, Congress has exercised its commerce, not its copyright, power. I can find nothing in the Copyright Clause that would authorize Congress to enhance the copyright grant's monopoly power, likely leading to higher prices both at home and abroad, solely in order to produce higher foreign earnings. That objective is not a copyright objective. Nor, standing alone, is it related to any other objective more closely tied to the Clause itself. Neither can higher corporate profits alone justify the grant's enhancement. The Clause seeks public, not private, benefits.

Finally, the Court mentions as possible justifications "demographic, economic, and technological changes"—by which the Court apparently means the facts that today people communicate with the help of modern technology, live longer, and have children at a later age. Ante, at 206–207, and n. 14. The first fact seems to argue not for, but instead against, extension. See Part II-B, supra. The second fact seems already corrected for by the 1976 Act's life-plus-50 term, which automatically grows with lifespans. Cf. Department of Health and Human Services, Centers for Disease Control and Prevention, Deaths: Final Data for 2000 (2002) (Table 8) (reporting a 4-year increase in expected lifespan between 1976 and 1998). And the third fact— that adults are having children later in life—is a makeweight at best, providing no explanation of why the 1976 Act's term of 50 years after an author's death—a longer term than was available to authors themselves for most of our Nation's history—is an insufficient potential bequest. The weakness of these final rationales simply underscores the conclusion that emerges from consideration of earlier attempts at justification: There is no legitimate, serious copyright-related justification for this statute.

III

The Court is concerned that our holding in this case not inhibit the broad decision making leeway that the Copyright Clause grants Congress. Ante, at 204–205, 208, 222. It is concerned about the implications of to day's decision for the Copyright Act of 1976—an Act that changed copyright's basic term from 56 years (assuming renewal) to life of the author plus 50 years, ante, at 194–195. Ante, at 222. It is concerned about having to determine just how many years of copyright is too many—a determination that it fears would require it to find the "right" constitutional number, a task for which the Court is not well suited. See ibid.; but cf. ante, at 210, n. 17.

I share the Court's initial concern, about intrusion upon the decision making authority of Congress. See ante, at 205, n. 10. But I do not believe it intrudes upon that authority to find the statute unconstitutional on the basis of (1) a legal analysis of the Copyright Clause's objectives, see supra, at 245–248, 260–263; (2) the total implausibility of any incentive effect, see supra, at 254–257; and (3) the statute's apparent failure to provide significant international uniformity, see supra, at 257–260. Nor does it intrude upon congressional authority to consider rationality in light of the expressive values underlying the Copyright Clause, related as it is to the First Amendment, and given the constitutional importance of correctly drawing the relevant Clause/Amendment boundary. Supra, at 243–245. We cannot avoid the need to examine the statute carefully by saying that "Congress has not altered the traditional contours of copyright protection," ante, at 221, for the sentence points to the question, rather than the answer. Nor should we avoid that examination here. That degree of judicial vigilance—at the far outer boundaries of the Clause—is warranted if we are to avoid the monopolies and consequent restrictions of expression that the Clause, read consistently with the First Amendment, seeks to preclude. And that vigilance is all the more necessary in a new century that will see intellectual property rights and the forms of expression that underlie them play an ever more important role in the Nation's economy and the lives of its citizens.

I do not share the Court's concern that my view of the 1998 Act could automatically doom the 1976 Act. Unlike the present statute, the 1976 Act thoroughly revised copyright law and enabled the United States to join the Berne Convention—an international treaty that requires the 1976 Act's basic life-plus-50 term as a condition for substantive protections from a copyright's very inception, Berne Conv. Art. 7(1). Consequently, the balance of copyright-related harms and benefits there is far less one sided. The same is true of the 1909 and 1831 Acts, which, in any event, provided for maximum terms of 56 years or 42 years while requiring renewal after 28 years, with most copyrighted works falling into the public domain after that 28-year period, well before the putative maximum terms had elapsed. See ante, at 194; Statistical History 956–957. Regardless, the law provides means to protect those who have reasonably relied upon prior copyright statutes. See Heckler v. Mathews, 465 U. S. 728, 746 (1984). And, in any event, we are not here considering, and we need not consider, the constitutionality of other copyright statutes.

Neither do I share the Court's aversion to line-drawing in this case. Even if it is difficult to draw a single clear bright line, the Court could easily decide (as I would decide) that this particular statute simply goes too far. And such examples—of what goes too far—sometimes offer better constitutional guidance than more absolute-sounding rules. In any event, "this Court sits" in part to decide when a statute exceeds a constitutional boundary. See Panhandle Oil, 277 U. S., at 223 (Holmes, J., dissenting). In my view, "[t]ext, history, and precedent," ante, at 199, support both the need to draw lines in general and the need to draw the line here short of this statute. See supra, at 242–248, 260–263. But see ante, at 199, n. 4.

Finally, the Court complains that I have not "restrained" my argument or "train[ed] my] fire, as petitioners do, on Congress' choice to place existing and future copyrights in parity." Ante, at 193, n. 1, and 199, n. 4. The reason that I have not so limited my argument is my willingness to accept, for purposes of this opinion, the Court's understanding that, for reasons of "[j]ustice, policy, and equity"—as well as established historical practice—it is not "categorically beyond Congress' authority" to "exten[d] the duration of existing copyrights" to achieve such parity. Ante, at 204 (internal quotation marks omitted). I have accepted this view, however, only for argument's sake-putting to the side, for the present, JUSTICE STEVENS' persuasive arguments to the contrary, ante, at 226–242 (dissenting opinion). And I make this assumption only to emphasize the lack of rational justification for the present statute. A desire for "parity" between A (old copyrights) and B (new copyrights) cannot justify extending A when there is no rational justification for extending B. At the very least (if I put aside my rationality characterization), to ask B to support A here is like asking Tom Thumb to support Paul Bunyan's ox. Where the case for extending new copyrights is itself so weak, what "justice," what "policy," what "equity" can warrant the tolls and barriers that extension of existing copyrights imposes?

IV

This statute will cause serious expression-related harm.

It will likely restrict traditional dissemination of copyrighted works. It will likely inhibit new forms of dissemination through the use of new technology. It threatens to interfere with efforts to preserve our Nation's historical and cultural heritage and efforts to use that heritage, say, to educate our Nation's children. It is easy to understand how the statute might benefit the private financial interests of corporations or heirs who own existing copyrights. But I cannot find any constitutionally legitimate, copyright-related way in which the statute will benefit the public. Indeed, in respect to existing works, the serious public harm and the virtually nonexistent public benefit could not be more clear.

I have set forth the analysis upon which I rest these judgments. This analysis leads inexorably to the conclusion that the statute cannot be understood rationally to advance a constitutionally legitimate interest. The statute falls outside the scope of legislative power that the Copyright Clause, read in light of the First Amendment, grants to Congress. I would hold the statute unconstitutional.

I respectfully dissent.

APPENDIX TO OPINION OF BREYER, J.

A

The text's estimates of the economic value of 1998 Act copyrights relative to the economic value of a perpetual copyright, supra, at 255–256, as well as the incremental value of a 20-year extension of a 75-year term, supra, at 254255, rest upon the conservative future value and discount rate assumptions set forth in the brief of economist amici. Brief for George A. Akerlof et al. as Amici Curiae 5–7. Under these assumptions, if an author expects to live 30 years after writing a book, the copyright extension (by increasing the copyright term from "life of the author plus 50 years" to "life of the author plus 70 years") increases the author's expected income from that book—i.e., the economic incentive to write-by no more than about 0.33%. Id., at 6.

The text assumes that the extension creates a term of 95 years (the term corresponding to works made for hire and for all existing pre-1978 copyrights). Under the economists' conservative assumptions, the value of a 95-year copyright is slightly more than 99.8% of the value of a perpetual copyright. See also Tr. of Oral Arg. 50 (Petitioners' statement of the 99.8% figure). If a "life plus 70" term applies, and if an author lives 78 years after creation of a work (as with Irving Berlin and Alexander's Ragtime Band), the same assumptions yield a figure of 99.996%.

The most unrealistically conservative aspect of these assumptions, i.e., the aspect most unrealistically favorable to the majority, is the assumption of a constant future income stream. In fact, as noted in the text, supra, at 248, uncontested data indicate that no author could rationally expect that a stream of copyright royalties will be constant forever. Indeed, only about 2% of copyrights can be expected to retain commercial value at the end of 55 to 75 years. Ibid. Thus, in the overwhelming majority of cases, the ultimate value of the extension to copyright holders will be zero, and the economic difference between the extended copyright and a perpetual copyright will be zero.

Nonetheless, there remains a small 2% or so chance that a given work will remain profitable. The CRS Report suggests a way to take account of both that likelihood and the related "decay" in a work's commercial viability: Find the annual decay rate that corresponds to the percentage of works that become commercially unavailable in any given year, and then discount the revenue for each successive year accordingly. See CRS Report 7. Following this approach, if one estimates, conservatively, that a full 2% of all works survives at the end of 75 years, the corresponding annual decay rate is about 5%. I instead (and again conservatively) use the 3.8% decay rate the CRS has applied in the case of books whose copyrights were renewed between 1950 and 1970. Ibid. U sing this 3.8% decay rate and the economist amici's proposed 7% discount rate, the value of a 95-year copyright is more realistically estimated not as 99.8%, but as 99.996% of the value of a perpetual copyright. The comparable "Irving Berlin" figure is 99.99999%. (With a 5% decay rate, the figures are 99.999% and

99.999998%, respectively.) Even these figures seem likely to be underestimates in the sense that they assume that, if a work is still commercially available, it earns as much as it did in a year shortly after its creation.

B
Conclusions regarding the economic significance of "works made for hire" are judgmental because statistical information about the ratio of "for hire" works to all works is scarce. Cf. Community for Creative Non-Violence v. Reid, 490 U. S. 730, 737–738, n. 4 (1989). But we know that, as of 1955, copyrights on "for hire" works accounted for 40% of newly registered copyrights. Varmer, Works Made for Hire and on Commission, Study No. 13, in Copyright Law Revision Studies Nos. 1–19, prepared for the Subcommittee on Patents, Trademarks, and Copyrights of the Senate Committee on the Judiciary, 86th Cong., 2d Sess., 139, n. 49 (Comm. Print 1960). We also know that copyrights on works typically made for hire-feature-Iength movies-were renewed, and since the 1930's apparently have remained commercially viable, at a higher than average rate. CRS Report 13–14. Further, we know that "harmonization" looks to benefit United States exports, see, e.g., H. R. Rep. No. 105–452, p. 4 (1998), and that films and sound recordings account for the dominant share of export revenues earned by new copyrighted works of potential lasting commercial value (i.e., works other than computer software), S. Siwek, Copyright Industries in the U. S. Economy: The 2002 Report 17. It also appears generally accepted that, in these categories, "for hire" works predominate. E.g., House Hearings 176 (testimony of the Register of Copyrights) ("[A]udiovisual works are generally works made for hire"). Taken together, these circumstances support the conclusion in the text that the extension fails to create uniformity where it would appear to be most important-pre-1978 copyrighted works nearing the end of their pre-extension terms, and works made for hire.

3.3 Analysis of the Case
Eldred v. Ashcroft, 537 U.S. 186 (2003)
The text of Eldred v. Ashcroft is available here:
https://supreme.justia.com/cases/federal/us/537/186/

Under the Copyright and Patent Clause of the U.S. Constitution, Article 1, Sec. 8, "Congress shall have Power...to promote the Progress of Science...by securing [to Authors] for limited Times...the exclusive Right to their...Writings." In the 1998 Sony Bono Copyright Term Extension Act (CTEA), Congress extended the duration of copyrights by 20 years, both proscriptively and retroactively. This meant that going forward, existing copyrights would have their terms extended by twenty years. New copyrights would now run from creation until 70 years after the author's death. Petitioners, whose products or services were built upon copyrighted works that have entered the public domain, argued that the CTEA violates both the Copyright Clause's "limited Times" prescription and the First Amendment's free speech guarantee. They also argued that Congress could not constitutionally extend the copyright term for published works, because the goal of the Copyright Act is to incentivize the creation of new works. Existing works did not need addition incentives, and many of their human authors were deceased, meaning they would not be creating new works no matter how lengthy or lucrative the copyright term became. Works that entered the public domain when their copyrights expired could be fodder for new authors and new creative works. The 20-year copyright term extension would mean that virtually no older works would fall into the public domain for a twenty-year period.

Both the trial court and the District of Columbia Circuit Court of Appeals disagreed with petitioners, ultimately requiring the U.S. Supreme Court to address two questions: Did the 1998 Copyright Term Extension Act's extension of the term of protection for existing copyrights exceed Congress's power under the Copyright Clause in the U.S. Constitution? And did the CTEA's extension of existing and future copyrights violate the First Amendment?

In a 7-2 opinion written by Justice Ruth Bader Ginsburg, the Court held that Congress acted within its authority and did not transgress constitutional limitations in placing existing and future copyrights in parity in the CTEA. Disagreeing with the argument that a copyright term once set is fixed, the majority found that the CTEA "continues the unbroken congressional practice of treating future and existing copyrights in parity for term extension purposes," and is a permissible exercise of Congress's power under the Copyright Clause, even if it might be a dumb idea for policy reasons. Moreover, the Court held that the CTEA's extension of existing and future copyrights did not violate the First Amendment, even though for free expression related policy reasons it might not be a great idea either. Congress had acted within its constitutionally ordained powers. One somewhat unexpected takeaway from the majority's discussion is a clear statement by the Court that the U.S. Congress can make ill-advised copyright laws without violating the U.S. Constitution.

Justices John Paul Stevens and Stephen G. Breyer emphatically dissented, arguing that the CTEA amounted to a grant of perpetual copyright that undermined public interests. Justice Stevens wrote:

"Writing for a unanimous Court in 1964, Justice Black stated that it is obvious that a State could not "extend the life of a patent beyond its expiration date." As I shall explain, the reasons why a State may not extend the life of a patent apply to Congress as well. If Congress may not expand the scope of a patent monopoly, it also may not extend the life of a copyright beyond its expiration date. Accordingly, insofar as the 1998 Sonny Bono Copyright Term Extension Act, 112 Stat. 2827, purported to extend the life of unexpired copyrights, it is invalid. Because the majority's contrary conclusion rests on the mistaken premise that this Court has virtually no role in reviewing congressional grants of monopoly privileges to authors, inventors, and their successors, I respectfully dissent."

(4) **How to protect the separatable works in the useful articles—STAR ATHLETICA, L.L.C. v. case of VARSITY BRANDS, INC. ET AL.**

SUPREME COURT OF THE UNITED STATES
CERTIORARI TO THE UNITED STATES COURT OF APPEALS FOR THE SIXTH CIRCUIT
No. 15–866. Argued October 31, 2016—Decided March 22, 2017

4.1 Syllabus

The Copyright Act of 1976 makes "pictorial, graphic, or sculptural features" of the "design of a useful article" eligible for copyright protection as artistic works if those features "can be identified separately from, and are capable of existing independently of, the utilitarian aspects of the article." 17 U. S. C. §101.

Respondents have more than 200 copyright registrations for two dimensional designs—consisting of various lines, chevrons, and colorful shapes—appearing on the surface of the cheerleading uniforms that they design, make, and sell. They sued petitioner, who also markets cheerleading uniforms, for copyright infringement. The District Court granted petitioner summary judgment, holding that the designs could not be conceptually or physically separated from the uniforms and were therefore ineligible for copyright protection. In reversing, the Sixth Circuit concluded that the graphics could be "identified separately" and were "capable of existing independently" of the uniforms under §101.

4.2 Reasoning

A feature incorporated into the design of a useful article is eligible for copyright protection only if the feature (1) can be perceived as a two- or three-dimensional work of art separate from the useful article, and (2) would qualify as a protectable pictorial, graphic, or sculptural work—either on its own or fixed in some other tangible medium of expression—if it were imagined separately from the useful article into which it is incorporated. That test is satisfied here. Pp. 3–17.

(a) Separability analysis is necessary in this case. Respondents claim that two-dimensional surface decorations are always separable, even without resorting to a §101 analysis, because they are "*on* a useful article" rather than "*designs of* a useful article." But this argument is inconsistent with §101's text. "[P]ictorial" and "graphic" denote two-dimensional features such as pictures, paintings, or drawings. Thus, by providing protection for "pictorial, graphical, and sculptural works" incorporated into the "design of a useful article," §101 necessarily contemplates that such a design can include two dimensional features. This Court will not adjudicate in the first instance the Government's distinct argument against applying separability analysis, which was neither raised below nor advanced here by any party.

(b) Whether a feature incorporated into a useful article "can be identified separately from," and is "capable of existing independently of," the article's "utilitarian aspects" is a matter of "statutory interpretation." *Mazer* v. *Stein*, 347 U. S. 201, 214. Pp. 6–10.

(1) Section 101's separate-identification requirement is met if the decisionmaker is able to look at the useful article and spot some two- or three-dimensional element that appears to have pictorial, graphic, or sculptural qualities. To satisfy the independent-existence requirement, the feature must be able to exist as its own pictorial, graphic, or sculptural work once it is imagined apart from the useful article. If the feature could not exist as a pictorial, graphic, or sculptural work on its own, it is simply one of the article's utilitarian aspects. And to qualify as a pictorial, graphic, or sculptural work on its own, the feature cannot be a useful article or "[a]n article that is normally a part of a useful article," §101. Neither could one claim a copyright in a useful article by creating a replica of it in another medium.

(2) The statute as a whole confirms this interpretation. Section 101, which protects art first fixed in the medium of a useful article, is essentially the mirror image of §113(a), which protects art first fixed in a medium other than a useful article and subsequently applied to a useful article. Together, these provisions make clear that copyright protection extends to pictorial, graphic, and sculptural works regardless of whether they were created as freestanding art or as features of useful articles.

(3) This interpretation is also consistent with the Copyright Act's history. In *Mazer*, a case decided under the 1909 Copyright Act, the Court held that respondents owned a copyright in a statuette created for use as a lamp base. In so holding, the Court approved a Copyright Office regulation extending protection to works of art that might also serve a useful purpose and held that it was irrelevant to the copyright inquiry whether the statuette was initially created as a freestanding sculpture or as a lamp base. Soon after, the Copyright Office enacted a regulation implementing *Mazer*'s holding that anticipated the language of §101, thereby introducing the modern separability test to copyright law. Congress essentially lifted the language from those post-*Mazer* regulations and placed it in §101 of the 1976 Act.

(c) Applying the proper test here, the surface decorations on the cheerleading uniforms are separable and therefore eligible for copyright protection. First, the decorations can be identified as features having pictorial, graphic, or sculptural qualities. Second, if those decorations were separated from the uniforms and applied in another medium, they would qualify as two-dimensional works of art under §101. Imaginatively removing the decorations from the uniforms and applying them in another medium also would not replicate the uniform itself.

The dissent argues that the decorations are ineligible for copyright protection because, when imaginatively extracted, they form a picture of a cheerleading uniform. Petitioner similarly claims that the decorations cannot be copyrighted because, even when extracted from the useful article, they retain the outline of a cheerleading uniform. But this is not a bar to copyright. Just as two-dimensional fine art correlates to the shape of the canvas on which it is painted, twodimensional applied art correlates to the contours of the article on which it is applied. The only feature of respondents' cheerleading uniform eligible for a copyright is the two-dimensional applied art on the surface of the uniforms. Respondents may prohibit the reproduction only of the surface designs on a uniform or in any other medium of expression. Respondents have no right to prevent anyone from manufacturing a cheerleading uniform that is identical in shape, cut, or dimensions to the uniforms at issue here.

(d) None of the objections raised by petitioner or the Government is meritorious.

(1) Petitioner and the Government focus on the relative utility of the plain white uniform that would remain if the designs were physically removed from the uniform. But the separability inquiry focuses on the extracted feature and not on any aspects of the useful article remaining after the imaginary extraction. The statute does not require the imagined remainder to be a fully functioning useful article at all. Nor can an artistic feature that would be eligible for copyright protection on its own lose that protection simply because it was first created as a feature of the design of a useful article, even if it makes that article more useful. This has been the rule since *Mazer*, and it is consistent with the statute's explicit protection of "applied art." In rejecting

petitioner's view, the Court necessarily abandons the distinction between "physical" and "conceptual" separability adopted by some courts and commentators.

(2) Petitioner also suggests incorporating two "objective" components into the test—one requiring consideration of evidence of the creator's design methods, purposes, and reasons, and one looking to the feature's marketability. The Court declines to incorporate these components because neither is grounded in the statute's text.

(3) Finally, petitioner claims that protecting surface decorations is inconsistent with Congress' intent to entirely exclude industrial design from copyright. But Congress has given limited copyright protection to certain features of industrial design. Approaching the statute with presumptive hostility toward protection for industrial design would undermine that choice. In any event, the test adopted here does not render the underlying uniform eligible for copyright protection.

799 F. 3d 468, affirmed.

THOMAS, J., delivered the opinion of the Court, in which R OBERTS, C. J., and A LITO, S OTOMAYOR, and K AGAN, JJ., joined. G INSBURG, J., filed an opinion concurring in the judgment. BREYER, J., filed a dissenting opinion, in which KENNEDY, J., joined.

STAR ATHLETICA, L. L. C., PETITIONER v. VARSITY BRANDS, INC., ET AL
SUPREME COURT OF THE UNITED STATES
No. 15–866
ON WRIT OF CERTIORARI TO THE UNITED STATES COURT OF APPEALS FOR THE
SIXTH CIRCUIT
[March 22, 2017]
JUSTICE THOMAS delivered the opinion of the Court.

Congress has provided copyright protection for original works of art, but not for industrial designs. The line between art and industrial design, however, is often difficult to draw. This is particularly true when an industrial design incorporates artistic elements. Congress has afforded limited protection for these artistic elements by providing that "pictorial, graphic, or sculptural features" of the "design of a useful article" are eligible for copyright protection as artistic works if those features "can be identified separately from, and are capable of existing independently of, the utilitarian aspects of the article." 17 U. S. C. §101.

We granted certiorari to resolve widespread disagreement over the proper test for implementing §101's separate-identification and independent-existence requirements. 578 U. S. ___ (2016). We hold that a feature incorporated into the design of a useful article is eligible for copyright protection only if the feature (1) can be perceived as a two- or three-dimensional work of art separate from the useful article and (2) would qualify as a protectable pictorial, graphic, or sculptural work—either on its own or fixed in some other tangible medium of expression—if it were imagined separately from the useful article into which it is incorporated. Because that test is satisfied in this case, we affirm.

I

Respondents Varsity Brands, Inc., Varsity Spirit Corporation, and Varsity Spirit Fashions and Supplies, Inc., design, make, and sell cheerleading uniforms. Respondents have obtained or acquired more than 200 U. S. copyright registrations for two-dimensional designs appearing on the surface of their uniforms and other garments. These designs are primarily "combinations, positionings, and arrangements of elements" that include "chevrons…, lines, curves, stripes, angles, diagonals, inverted [chevrons], coloring, and shapes." App. 237. At issue in this case are Designs 299A, 299B, 074, 078, and 0815. See Appendix, *infra.*

Petitioner Star Athletica, L. L. C., also markets and sells cheerleading uniforms. Respondents sued petitioner for infringing their copyrights in the five designs. The District Court entered summary judgment for petitioner on respondents' copyright claims on the ground that the designs did not qualify as protectable pictorial, graphic, or sculptural works. It reasoned that the designs served the useful, or "utilitarian," function of identifying the garments as "cheerleading uniforms" and therefore could not be "physically or conceptually" separated under §101 "from the utilitarian function" of the uniform. 2014 WL 819422, *8–*9 (WD Tenn., Mar. 1, 2014).

The Court of Appeals for the Sixth Circuit reversed. 799 F. 3d 468, 471 (2015). In its view, the "graphic designs" were "separately identifiable" because the designs "and a blank cheerleading uniform can appear 'side by side'—one as a graphic design, and one as a cheerleading uniform." *Id.,* at 491 (quoting Compendium of U. S. Copyright Office Practices §924.2(B) (3d ed. 2014) (Compendium)). And it determined that the designs were "'capable of existing independently'" because they could be incorporated onto the surface of different types of garments, or hung on the wall and framed as art. 799 F. 3d, at 491, 492.

Judge McKeague dissented. He would have held that, because "identifying the wearer as a cheerleader" is a utilitarian function of a cheerleading uniform and the surface designs were "integral to" achieving that function, the designs were inseparable from the uniforms. *Id.,* at 495–496.

II

The first element of a copyright-infringement claim is "ownership of a valid copyright." *Feist Publications, Inc.* v. *Rural Telephone Service Co.,* 499 U. S. 340, 361 (1991). A valid copyright extends only to copyrightable subject matter. See 4 M. Nimmer & D. Nimmer, Copyright §13.01[A] (2010) (Nimmer). The Copyright Act of 1976 defines copyrightable subject matter as "original works of authorship fixed in any tangible medium of expression." 17 U. S. C. §102(a).

"Works of authorship" include "pictorial, graphic, and sculptural works," §102(a)(5), which the statute defines to include "two-dimensional and three-dimensional works of fine, graphic, and applied art, photographs, prints and art reproductions, maps, globes, charts, diagrams, models, and technical drawings, including architectural plans," §101. And a work of authorship is "'fixed' in a tangible medium of expression when it[is] embodi[ed] in a" "material objec[t]… from which the work can be perceived, reproduced, or otherwise communicated." *Ibid.* (definitions of "fixed" and "copies").

The Copyright Act also establishes a special rule for copyrighting a pictorial, graphic, or sculptural work incorporated into a "useful article," which is defined as "an article having an intrinsic utilitarian function that is not merely to portray the appearance of the article or to convey information." *Ibid.* The statute does not protect useful articles as such. Rather, "the design of a useful article" is "considered a pictorial, graphical, or sculptural work only if, and only to the extent that, such design incorporates pictorial, graphic, or sculptural features that can be identified separately from, and are capable of existing independently of, the utilitarian aspects of the article." *Ibid.*

Courts, the Copyright Office, and commentators have described the analysis undertaken to determine whether a feature can be separately identified from, and exist independently of, a useful article as "separability." In this case, our task is to determine whether the arrangements of lines, chevrons, and colorful shapes appearing on the surface of respondents' cheerleading uniforms are eligible for copyright protection as separable features of the design of those cheerleading uniforms.

A

As an initial matter, we must address whether separability analysis is necessary in this case.

1

Respondents argue that "[s]eparability is only implicated when a [pictorial, graphic, or sculptural] work is the 'design of a useful article.'" Brief for Respondents 25. They contend that the surface decorations in this case are "twodimensional graphic designs that appear *on* useful articles," but are not themselves designs *of* useful articles. *Id.*, at 52. Consequently, the surface decorations are protected two-dimensional works of graphic art without regard to any separability analysis under §101. *Ibid.*; see 2 W. Patry, Copyright §3:151, p. 3–485 (2016) (Patry) ("Courts looking at two-dimensional design claims should not apply the separability analysis regardless of the threedimensional form that design is embodied in"). Under this theory, two-dimensional artistic features on the surface of useful articles are "inherently separable." Brief for Respondents 26.

This argument is inconsistent with the text of §101. The statute requires separability analysis for any "pictorial, graphic, or sculptural features" incorporated into the "design of a useful article." "Design" refers here to "the combination" of "details" or "features" that "go to make up" the useful article. 3 Oxford English Dictionary 244 (def. 7, first listing) (1933) (OED). Furthermore, the words "pictorial" and "graphic" include, in this context, twodimensional features such as pictures, paintings, or drawings. See 4 *id.*, at 359 (defining "[g]raphic" to mean "[o]f or pertaining to drawing or painting"); 7 *id.*, at 830 (defining "[p]ictorial" to mean "of or pertaining to painting or drawing"). And the statute expressly defines "[p]ictorial, graphical, and sculptural works" to include "two dimensional… works of… art." §101. The statute thus provides that the "design of a useful article" can include two-dimensional "pictorial" and "graphic" features, and separability analysis applies to those features just as it does to three-dimensional "sculptural" features.

2

The United States makes a related but distinct argument against applying separability analysis in this case, which respondents do not and have not advanced. As part of their copyright registrations for the designs in this case, respondents deposited with the Copyright Office drawings and photographs depicting the designs incorporated onto cheerleading uniforms. App. 213–219; Appendix, *infra*. The Government argues that, assuming the other statutory requirements were met, respondents obtained a copyright in the deposited drawings and photographs and have simply reproduced those copyrighted works on the surface of a useful article, as they would have the exclusive right to do under the Copyright Act. See Brief for United States as *Amicus Curiae* 14–15, 17–22. Accordingly, the Government urges, separability analysis is unnecessary on the record in this case. We generally do not entertain arguments that were not raised below and that are not advanced in this Court by any party, *Burwell v. Hobby Lobby Stores, Inc.*, 573 U. S. ___, ___ (2014), because "[i]t is not the Court's usual practice to adjudicate either legal or predicate factual questions in the first instance," *CRST Van Expedited, Inc. v. EEOC*, 578 U. S. ___, ___ (2016) (slip op., at 16). We decline to depart from our usual practice here.

B

We must now decide when a feature incorporated into a useful article "can be identified separately from" and is "capable of existing independently of" "the utilitarian aspects" of the article. This is not a free-ranging search for the best copyright policy, but rather "depends solely on statutory interpretation." *Mazer v. Stein*, 347 U. S. 201, 214 (1954). "The controlling principle in this case is the basic and unexceptional rule that courts must give effect to the clear meaning of statutes as written." *Estate of Cowart v. Nicklos Drilling Co.*, 505 U. S. 469, 476 (1992). We thus begin and end our inquiry with the text, giving each word its "ordinary, contemporary, common meaning." *Walters v. Metropolitan Ed. Enterprises, Inc.*, 519 U. S. 202, 207 (1997) (internal quotation marks omitted). We do not, however, limit this inquiry to the text of §101 in isolation. "[I]nterpretation of a phrase of uncertain reach is not confined to a single sentence when the text of the whole statute gives instruction as to its meaning." *Maracich v. Spears*, 570 U. S. ___, ___ (2013) (slip op., at 15).

We thus "look to the provisions of the whole law" to determine §101's meaning. *United States v. Heirs of Boisdoré*, 8 How. 113, 122 (1849).

1

The statute provides that a "pictorial, graphic, or sculptural featur[e]" incorporated into the "design of a useful article" is eligible for copyright protection if it (1) "can be identified separately from," and (2) is "capable of existing independently of, the utilitarian aspects of the article." §101. The first requirement—separate identification—is not onerous. The decisionmaker need only be able to look at the useful article and spot some two- or threedimensional element that appears to have pictorial, graphic, or sculptural qualities. See 2 Patry §3:146, at 3–474 to 3–475.

The independent-existence requirement is ordinarily more difficult to satisfy. The decisionmaker must determine that the separately identified feature has the capacity to exist apart from the utilitarian aspects of the article. See 2 OED 88 (def. 5) (defining "[c]apable" of as "[h]aving the needful capacity, power, or fitness for"). In other words, the feature must be able to exist as its own pictorial, graphic, or sculptural work as defined in §101 once it is imagined apart from the useful article. If the feature is not capable of existing as a pictorial, graphic, or sculptural work once separated from the useful article, then it was not a pictorial, graphic, or sculptural feature of that article, but rather one of its utilitarian aspects.

Of course, to qualify as a pictorial, graphic, or sculptural work on its own, the feature cannot itself be a useful article or "[a]n article that is normally a part of a useful article" (which is itself considered a useful article). §101. Nor could someone claim a copyright in a useful article merely by creating a replica of that article in some other medium—for example, a cardboard model of a car. Although the replica could itself be copyrightable, it would not give rise to any rights in the useful article that inspired it.

2

The statute as a whole confirms our interpretation. The Copyright Act provides "the owner of [a] copyright" with the "exclusive righ[t]... to reproduce the copyrighted work in copies." §106(1). The statute clarifies that this right "includes the right to reproduce the [copyrighted] work in or on any kind of article, whether useful or otherwise." §113(a). Section 101 is, in essence, the mirror image of §113(a). Whereas §113(a) protects a work of authorship first fixed in some tangible medium other than a useful article and subsequently applied to a useful article, §101 protects art first fixed in the medium of a useful article. The two provisions make clear that copyright protection extends to pictorial, graphic, and sculptural works regardless of whether they were created as freestanding art or as features of useful articles. The ultimate separability question, then, is whether the feature for which copyright protection is claimed would have been eligible for copyright protection as a pictorial, graphic, or sculptural work had it originally been fixed in some tangible medium other than a useful article before being applied to a useful article.

3

This interpretation is also consistent with the history of the Copyright Act. In *Mazer*, a case decided under the 1909 Copyright Act, the respondents copyrighted a statuette depicting a dancer. The statuette was intended for use as a lamp base, "with electric wiring, sockets and lamp shades attached." 347 U. S., at 202. Copies of the statuette were sold both as lamp bases and separately as statuettes. *Id.,* at 203. The petitioners copied the statuette and sold lamps with the statuette as the base. They defended against the respondents' infringement suit by arguing that the respondents did not have a copyright in a statuette intended for use as a lamp base. *Id.,* at 204–205. Two of *Mazer*'s holdings are relevant here. First, the Court held that the respondents owned a copyright in the statuette even though it was intended for use as a lamp base. See *id.,* at 214. In doing so, the Court approved the Copyright Office's regulation extending copyright protection to works of art that might also serve a useful purpose. See *ibid.* (approving 37 CFR §202.8(a) (1949) (protecting "works of artistic craftsmanship, in so far as their form but not their mechanical or utilitarian aspects are concerned")).

Second, the Court held that it was irrelevant to the copyright inquiry whether the statuette was initially created as a freestanding sculpture or as a lamp base. 347 U. S., at 218–219 ("Nor do we think the subsequent registration of a work of art published as an element in a manufactured article, is a misuse of copyright. This is not different from the registration of a statuette and its later embodiment in an industrial article"). *Mazer* thus interpreted the 1909 Act consistently with the rule discussed above: If a design would have been copyrightable as a standalone pictorial, graphic, or sculptural work, it is copyrightable if created first as part of a useful article. Shortly thereafter, the Copyright Office enacted a regulation implementing the holdings of *Mazer*. See 1 Nimmer §2 A.08[B][1][b] (2016). As amended, the regulation introduced the modern separability test to copyright law:

"If the sole intrinsic function of an article is its utility, the fact that the article is unique and attractively shaped will not qualify it as a work of art. However, if the shape of a utilitarian article incorporates features, such as artistic sculpture, carving, or pictorial representation, which can be identified separately and are capable of existing independently as a work of art, such features will be eligible for registration." 37 CFR §202.10(c) (1960) (punctuation altered).

Congress essentially lifted the language governing protection for the design of a useful article directly from the post-*Mazer* regulations and placed it into §101 of the 1976 Act. Consistent with *Mazer*, the approach we outline today interprets §§101 and 113 in a way that would afford copyright protection to the statuette in *Mazer* regardless of whether it was first created as a standalone sculptural work or as the base of the lamp. See 347 U. S., at 218–219.

C

In sum, a feature of the design of a useful article is eligible for copyright if, when identified and imagined apart from the useful article, it would qualify as a pictorial, graphic, or sculptural work either on its own or when fixed in some other tangible medium.

Applying this test to the surface decorations on the cheerleading uniforms is straightforward. First, one can identify the decorations as features having pictorial, graphic, or sculptural qualities. Second, if the arrangement of colors, shapes, stripes, and chevrons on the surface of the cheerleading uniforms were separated from the uniform and applied in another medium—for example, on a painter's canvas—they would qualify as "two-dimensional... works of... art," §101. And imaginatively removing the surface decorations from the uniforms and applying them in another medium would not replicate the uniform itself. Indeed, respondents have applied the designs in this case to other media of expression—different types of clothing—without replicating the uniform. See App. 273–279. The decorations are therefore separable from the uniforms and eligible for copyright protection.[50]

---

[50] We do not today hold that the surface decorations are copyrightable. We express no opinion on whether these works are sufficiently original to qualify for copyright protection, see *Feist Publications, Inc.* v. *Rural Telephone Service Co.*, 499 U. S. 340, 358–359 (1991), or on whether any other prerequisite of a valid copyright has been satisfied.

The dissent argues that the designs are not separable because imaginatively removing them from the uniforms and placing them in some other medium of expression—a canvas, for example—would create "pictures of cheerleader uniforms." *Post*, at 10 (opinion of BREYER, J.). Petitioner similarly argues that the decorations cannot be copyrighted because, even when extracted from the useful article, they retain the outline of a cheerleading uniform. Brief for Petitioner 48–49.

This is not a bar to copyright. Just as two-dimensional fine art corresponds to the shape of the canvas on which it is painted, two-dimensional applied art correlates to the contours of the article on which it is applied. A fresco painted on a wall, ceiling panel, or dome would not lose copyright protection, for example, simply because it was designed to track the dimensions of the surface on which it was painted. Or consider, for example, a design etched or painted on the surface of a guitar. If that entire design is imaginatively removed from the guitar's surface and placed on an album cover, it would still resemble the shape of a guitar. But the image on the cover does not "replicate" the guitar as a useful article. Rather, the design is a two-dimensional work of art that corresponds to the shape of the useful article to which it was applied. The statute protects that work of art whether it is first drawn on the album cover and then applied to the guitar's surface, or vice versa. Failing to protect that art would create an anomaly: It would extend protection to two-dimensional designs that cover a part of a useful article but would not protect the same design if it covered the entire article. The statute does not support that distinction, nor can it be reconciled with the dissent's recognition that "artwork printed on a t-shirt" could be protected. *Post*, at 4 (internal quotation marks omitted).

To be clear, the only feature of the cheerleading uniform eligible for a copyright in this case is the two-dimensional work of art fixed in the tangible medium of the uniform fabric. Even if respondents ultimately succeed in establishing a valid copyright in the surface decorations at issue here, respondents have no right to prohibit any person from manufacturing a cheerleading uniform of identical shape, cut, and dimensions to the ones on which the decorations in this case appear. They may prohibit only the reproduction of the surface designs in any tangible medium of expression—a uniform or otherwise.[51]

---

[51] The dissent suggests that our test would lead to the copyrighting of shovels. *Post*, at 7; Appendix to opinion of BREYER, J., Fig. 4, post. But a shovel, like a cheerleading uniform, even if displayed in an art gallery, is "an article having an intrinsic utilitarian function that is not merely to portray the appearance of the article or to convey information." 17 U. S. C. §101. It therefore cannot be copyrighted. A drawing of a shovel could, of course, be copyrighted. And, if the shovel included any artistic features that could be perceived as art apart from the shovel, and which would qualify as protectable pictorial, graphic, or sculptural works on their own or in another medium, they too could be copyrighted. But a shovel as a shovel cannot.

D

Petitioner and the Government raise several objections to the approach we announce today. None is meritorious.

1

Petitioner first argues that our reading of the statute is missing an important step. It contends that a feature may exist independently only if it can stand alone as a copyrightable work *and* if the useful article from which it was extracted would remain equally useful. In other words, copyright extends only to "solely artistic" features of useful articles. Brief for Petitioner 33. According to petitioner, if a feature of a useful article "advance[s] the utility of the article," *id.*, at 38, then it is categorically beyond the scope of copyright, *id.*, at 33. The designs here are not protected, it argues, because they are necessary to two of the uniforms' "inherent, essential, or natural functions"—identifying the wearer as a cheerleader and enhancing the wearer's physical appearance. *Id.*, at 38, 48; Reply Brief 2, 16. Because the uniforms would not be equally useful without the designs, petitioner contends that the designs are inseparable from the "utilitarian aspects" of the uniform. Brief for Petitioner 50.

The Government raises a similar argument, although it reaches a different result. It suggests that the appropriate test is whether the useful article with the artistic feature removed would "remai[n] *similarly* useful." Brief for United States as *Amicus Curiae* 29 (emphasis added). In the view of the United States, however, a plain white cheerleading uniform is "similarly useful" to uniforms with respondents' designs. *Id.*, at 27–28.

The debate over the relative utility of a plain white cheerleading uniform is unnecessary. The focus of the separability inquiry is on the extracted feature and not on any aspects of the useful article that remain after the imaginary extraction. The statute does not require the decisionmaker to imagine a fully functioning useful article without the artistic feature. Instead, it requires that the separated feature qualify as a nonuseful pictorial, graphic, or sculptural work on its own.

Of course, because the removed feature may not be a useful article—as it would then not qualify as a pictorial, graphic, or sculptural work—there necessarily would be some aspects of the original useful article "left behind" if the feature were conceptually removed. But the statute does not require the imagined remainder to be a fully functioning useful article at all, much less an equally useful one. Indeed, such a requirement would deprive the *Mazer* statuette of protection had it been created first as a lamp base rather than as a statuette. Without the base, the "lamp" would be just a shade, bulb, and wires. The statute does not require that we imagine a nonartistic replacement for the removed feature to determine whether that *feature* is capable of an independent existence.

Petitioner's argument follows from its flawed view that the statute protects only "solely artistic" features that have no effect whatsoever on a useful article's utilitarian function. This view is inconsistent with the statutory text. The statute expressly protects two- and three-dimensional "applied art." §101. "Applied art" is art "employed in the decoration, design, or execution of useful objects," Webster's Third New International Dictionary 105 (1976) (emphasis added), or "those arts or crafts that have a *primarily utilitarian function*, or... the designs and decorations used in these arts," Random House Dictionary 73 (1966) (emphasis added); see also 1 OED 576 (2d ed. 1989) (defining "applied" as "[p]ut to practical use"). An artistic feature that would be eligible for copyright protection on its own cannot lose that protection simply because it was first created as a feature of the design of a useful article, even if it makes that article more useful. Indeed, this has been the rule since *Mazer*. In holding that the statuette was protected, the Court emphasized that the 1909 Act abandoned any "distinctions between purely aesthetic articles and useful works of art." 347 U. S., at 211. Congress did not enact such a distinction in the 1976 Act. Were we to accept petitioner's argument that the only protectable features are those that play absolutely no role in an article's function, we would effectively abrogate the rule of *Mazer* and read "applied art" out of the statute.

Because we reject the view that a useful article must remain after the artistic feature has been imaginatively separated from the article, we necessarily abandon the distinction between "physical" and "conceptual" separability, which some courts and commentators have adopted based on the Copyright Act's legislative history. See H. R. Rep. No. 94–1476, p. 55 (1976). According to this view, a feature is *physically* separable from the underlying useful article if it can "be physically separated from the article by ordinary means while leaving the utilitarian aspects of the article completely intact."

Compendium §924.2(A); see also *Chosun Int'l, Inc. v. Chrisha Creations, Ltd.*, 413 F. 3d 324, 329 (CA2 2005). *Conceptual* separability applies if the feature physically could not be removed from the useful article by ordinary means. See Compendium §924.2(B); but see 1 P. Goldstein, Copyright §2.5.3, p. 2:77 (3d ed. 2016) (explaining that the lower courts have been unable to agree on a single conceptual separability test); 2 Patry §§3:140–3:144.40 (surveying the various approaches in the lower courts).

The statutory text indicates that separability is a conceptual undertaking. Because separability does not require the underlying useful article to remain, the physical-conceptual distinction is unnecessary.

2

Petitioner next argues that we should incorporate two "objective" components, Reply Brief 9, into our test to provide guidance to the lower courts: (1) "whether the design elements can be identified as reflecting the designer's artistic judgment exercised independently of functional influence," Brief for Petitioner 34 (emphasis deleted and internal quotation marks omitted), and (2) whether "there is [a] substantial likelihood that the pictorial, graphic, or sculptural feature would still be marketable to some significant segment of the community without its utilitarian function," *id.,* at 35 (emphasis deleted and internal quotation marks omitted).

We reject this argument because neither consideration is grounded in the text of the statute. The first would require the decisionmaker to consider evidence of the creator's design methods, purposes, and reasons. *Id.,* at 48. The statute's text makes clear, however, that our inquiry is limited to how the article and feature are perceived, not how or why they were designed. See *Brandir Int'l, Inc. v. Cascade Pacific Lumber*

Co., 834 F. 2d 1142, 1152 (CA2 1987) (Winter, J., concurring in part and dissenting in part) (The statute "expressly states that the legal test is how the final article is perceived, not how it was developed through various stages").

The same is true of marketability. Nothing in the statute suggests that copyrightability depends on market surveys. Moreover, asking whether some segment of the market would be interested in a given work threatens to prize popular art over other forms, or to substitute judicial aesthetic preferences for the policy choices embodied in the Copyright Act. See *Bleistein* v. *Donaldson Lithographing Co.*, 188 U. S. 239, 251 (1903) ("It would be a dangerous undertaking for persons trained only to the law to constitute themselves final judges of the worth of pictorial illustrations, outside of the narrowest and most obvious limits").

3

Finally, petitioner argues that allowing the surface decorations to qualify as a "work of authorship" is inconsistent with Congress' intent to entirely exclude industrial design from copyright. Petitioner notes that Congress refused to pass a provision that would have provided limited copyright protection for industrial designs, including clothing, when it enacted the 1976 Act, see *id.,* at 9–11 (citing S. 22, Tit. II, 94th Cong., 2d Sess., 122 Cong. Rec. 3856–3859 (1976)), and that it has enacted laws protecting designs for specific useful articles—semiconductor chips and boat hulls, see 17 U. S. C. §§901–914, 1301–1332—while declining to enact other industrial design statutes, Brief for Petitioner 29, 43. From this history of failed legislation petitioner reasons that Congress intends to channel intellectual property claims for industrial design into design patents. It therefore urges us to approach this question with a presumption against copyrightability. *Id.,* at 27.

We do not share petitioner's concern. As an initial matter, "[c]ongressional inaction lacks persuasive significance" in most circumstances. *Pension Benefit Guaranty Corporation* v. *LTV Corp.*, 496 U. S. 633, 650 (1990) (internal quotation marks omitted). Moreover, we have long held that design patent and copyright are not mutually exclusive. See *Mazer*, 347 U. S., at 217. Congress has provided for limited copyright protection for certain features of industrial design, and approaching the statute with presumptive hostility toward protection for industrial design would undermine Congress' choice. In any event, as explained above, our test does not render the shape, cut, and physical dimensions of the cheerleading uniforms eligible for copyright protection.

III

We hold that an artistic feature of the design of a useful article is eligible for copyright protection if the feature (1) can be perceived as a two- or three-dimensional work of art separate from the useful article and (2) would qualify as a protectable pictorial, graphic, or sculptural work either on its own or in some other medium if imagined separately from the useful article. Because the designs on the surface of respondents' cheerleading uniforms in this case satisfy these requirements, the judgment of the Court of Appeals is affirmed.

It is so ordered.

3 Cases

Design 299A   Design 299B   Design 074   Design 078   Design 0815

APPENDIX TO OPINION OF THE COURT

SUPREME COURT OF THE UNITED STATES
No. 15–866
STAR ATHLETICA, L. L. C., PETITIONER v. VARSITY BRANDS, INC., ET AL
ON WRIT OF CERTIORARI TO THE UNITED STATES COURT OF APPEALS FOR THE SIXTH CIRCUIT
[March 22, 2017]
JUSTICE GINSBURG, concurring in the judgment.

I concur in the Court's judgment but not in its opinion. Unlike the majority, I would not take up in this case the separability test appropriate under 17 U. S. C. §101.[52] Consideration of that test is unwarranted because the designs at issue are not designs *of* useful articles. Instead, the designs are themselves copyrightable pictorial or graphic works *reproduced on* useful articles.[53]

A pictorial, graphic, or sculptural work (PGS work) is copyrightable. §102(a)(5). PGS works include "two-dimensional and three-dimensional works of fine, graphic, and applied art." §101. Key to this case, a copyright in a standalone PGS work "includes the right to reproduce the work in or on any kind of article, whether useful or otherwise." §113(a). Because the owner of a copyright in a pre-existing PGS work may exclude a would-be infringer from reproducing that work on a useful article, there is no need to engage in any separability inquiry to resolve the instant petition.

---

[52] Courts "have struggled mightily to formulate a test" for the separability analysis. 799 F. 3d 468, 484 (CA6 2015); see 2 W. Patry, Copyright §3:136, p. 3–420 (2016) (noting "widespread interpretative disarray" over the separability test); Ginsburg, "Courts Have Twisted Themselves into Knots": U. S. Copyright Protection for Applied Art, 40 Colum. J. L. & Arts 1, 2 (2016) ("The 'separability' test . . . has resisted coherent application . . . ."); 1 M. Nimmer & D. Nimmer, Copyright §2A.08[B][6], p. 2A–84 (2016) (separability is a "perennially tangled aspect of copyright doctrine").

[53] Like the Court, I express no opinion on whether the designs otherwise meet the requirements for copyrightable subject matter. See *ante*, at 11, n. 1; 17 U. S. C. §102(a) ("Copyright protection subsists, in accordance with this title, in original works of authorship fixed in any tangible medium of expression, now known or later developed, from which they can be perceived, reproduced, or otherwise communicated."). In view of the dissent's assertion that Varsity's designs are "plainly unoriginal," *post*, at 11, however, I note this Court's recognition that "the requisite level of creativity [for copyrightability] is extremely low; even a slight amount will suffice," *Feist Publications, Inc.* v. *Rural Telephone Service Co.*, 499 U. S. 340, 345 (1991); see *Atari Games Corp.* v. *Oman*, 979 F. 2d 242 (CADC 1992).

The designs here in controversy are standalone pictorial and graphic works that respondents Varsity Brands, Inc., et al. (Varsity) reproduce on cheerleading uniforms. Varsity's designs first appeared as pictorial and graphic works that Varsity's design team sketched on paper. App. 281. Varsity then sought copyright protection for those two-dimensional designs, not for cheerleading costumes; its registration statements claimed "2-Dimensional artwork" and "fabric design (artwork)." Appendix, *infra*, at 4–7, 9–10, 12–14. Varsity next reproduced its two-dimensional graphic designs on cheerleading uniforms, also on other garments, including T-shirts and jackets. See, e.g., App. 274, 276.[54]

In short, Varsity's designs are not themselves useful articles meet for separability determination under §101; they are standalone PGS works that may gain copyright protection as such, including the exclusive right to reproduce the designs on useful articles.[55]

SUPREME COURT OF THE UNITED STATES
No. 15–866
STAR ATHLETICA, L. L. C., PETITIONER *v.* VARSITY BRANDS, INC., ET AL
ON WRIT OF CERTIORARI TO THE UNITED STATES COURT OF APPEALS FOR THE SIXTH CIRCUIT
[March 22, 2017]

JUSTICE BREYER, with whom JUSTICE KENNEDY joins, dissenting.

I agree with much in the Court's opinion. But I do not agree that the designs that Varsity Brands, Inc., submitted to the Copyright Office are eligible for copyright protection. Even applying the majority's test, the designs *cannot* "be perceived as... two- or three-dimensional work[s] of art separate from the useful article." *Ante*, at 1. Look at the designs that Varsity submitted to the Copyright Office. See Appendix to opinion of the Court, *ante*. You will see only pictures of cheerleader uniforms. And

---

[54] That Varsity's designs can be placed on jackets or T-shirts without replicating a cheerleader's uniform supports their qualification as fabric designs. The dissent acknowledges that fabric designs are copyrightable, but maintains that Varsity's designs do not count because Varsity's submissions depict clothing, not fabric designs. *Post*, at 10–11. But registrants claiming copyrightable designs may submit drawings or photos of those designs as they appear on useful articles.

See Compendium of U. S. Copyright Office Practices §1506 (3d ed. 2014) ("To register a copyrightable design that has been applied to the back of a useful article, such as a chair, the applicant may submit drawings of the design as it appears on the chair[.]"), online at https://www.copyright.gov/comp3/docs/compendium.pdf (as last visited Mar. 8, 2017). And, as noted in text, Varsity's registration statements claimed "2-Dimensional artwork" and "fabric design (artwork)." Appendix, *infra*, at 4–7, 9–10, 12–14.

The dissent also acknowledges that artwork printed on a T-shirt is copyrightable. *Post*, at 4. Varsity's colored shapes and patterns can be, and indeed are, printed on T-shirts. See, e.g., App. 274. Assuming Varsity's designs meet the other requirements for copyrightable subject matter, they would fit comfortably within the Copyright Office guidance featured by the dissent. See *post*, at 4 (citing Compendium of U. S. Copyright Office Practices, *supra*, §924.2(B).

[55] The majority declines to address this route to decision because, it says, Varsity has not advanced it. *Ante*, at 5–6. I read Varsity's brief differently. See Brief for Respondents 25 (explaining that the Copy right Act "expressly provides that PGS designs do not lose their protection when they appear 'in or on' a useful article," quoting §113(a)); *id.*, at 52 (disclaiming the need for separability analysis because the designs are themselves PGS works).

cheerleader uniforms are useful articles. A picture of the relevant design features, whether separately "perceived" on paper or in the imagination, is a picture of, and thereby "replicate[s]," the underlying useful article of which they are a part. *Ante,* at 1, 10. Hence the design features that Varsity seeks to protect are not "capable of existing independently o[f] the utilitarian aspects of the article." 17 U. S. C. §101.

I

The relevant statutory provision says that the "design of a useful article" is copyrightable "only if, and only to the extent that, such design incorporates pictorial, graphic, or sculptural features that can be identified separately from, and are capable of existing independently of, the utilitarian aspects of the article." *Ibid.* But what, we must ask, do the words "identified separately" mean? Just when is a design separate from the "utilitarian aspect of the [useful] article?" The most direct, helpful aspect of the Court's opinion answers this question by stating:

"Nor could someone claim a copyright in a useful article merely by creating a replica of that article in some other medium—for example, a cardboard model of a car. Although the replica could itself be copyrightable, it would not give rise to any rights in the useful article that inspired it." *Ante,* at 7–8.

Exactly so. These words help explain the Court's statement that a copyrightable work of art must be "perceived as a two- or three-dimensional work of art separate from the useful article." *Ante,* at 1, 17. They help clarify the concept of separateness. Cf. 1 M. Nimmer & D. Nimmer, Nimmer on Copyright §2A.08[A][1] (2016) (Nimmer) (describing courts' difficulty in applying that concept). They are consistent with Congress' own expressed intent. 17 U. S. C. §101; H. R. Rep. No. 94–1476, pp. 55, 105 (1976).

(H. R. Rep.). And they reflect long held views of the Copyright Office. See Compendium of U. S. Copyright Office Practices §924.2(B) (3d ed. 2014), online at
http://www.copyright.gov/comp3/docs/compendium.pdf (as last visited Mar. 7, 2017) (Compendium).

Consider, for example, the explanation that the House Report for the Copyright Act of 1976 provides. It says:

"Unless the shape of an automobile, airplane, ladies' dress, food processor, television set, or any other industrial product contains some element that, *physically or conceptually*, can be identified as separable from the utilitarian aspects of that article, the design would not be copyrighted...." H. R. Rep., at 55 (emphasis added).

These words suggest two exercises, one physical, one mental. Can the design features (the picture, the graphic, the sculpture) be physically removed from the article (and considered separately), all the while leaving the fully functioning utilitarian object in place? If not, can one nonetheless conceive of the design features separately without replicating a picture of the utilitarian object? If the answer to either of these questions is "yes," then the design is eligible for copyright protection. Otherwise, it is not. The abstract nature of these questions makes them sound difficult to apply. But with the Court's words in mind, the difficulty tends to disappear.

An example will help. Imagine a lamp with a circular marble base, a vertical 10-inch-tall brass rod (containing wires) inserted off center on the base, a light bulb fixture emerging from the top of the brass rod, and a lampshade sitting on top. In front of the brass rod a porcelain Siamese cat sits on the base facing outward. Obviously, the Siamese cat is *physically separate* from the lamp, as it could be easily removed while leaving both cat and lamp intact. And, assuming it otherwise qualifies, the designed cat is eligible for copyright protection.

Now suppose there is no long brass rod; instead, the cat sits in the middle of the base and the wires run up through the cat to the bulbs. The cat is not physically separate from the lamp, as the reality of the lamp's construction is such that an effort to physically separate the cat and lamp will destroy both cat and lamp. The two are integrated into a single functional object, like the similar configuration of the ballet dancer statuettes that formed the lamp bases at issue in *Mazer* v. *Stein*, 347 U. S. 201 (1954). But we can easily imagine the cat on its own, as did Congress when conceptualizing the ballet dancer. See H. R. Rep., at 55 (the statuette in *Mazer* was "incorporated into a product without losing its ability to exist independently as a work of art"). In doing so, we do not create a mental picture of a lamp (or, in the Court's words, a "replica" of the lamp), which is a useful article. We simply perceive the cat separately, as a small cat figurine that could be a copyrightable design work standing alone that does not replicate the lamp. Hence the cat is conceptually *separate* from the utilitarian article that is the lamp. The pair of lamps pictured at Fig. 3.8a, b in the Appendix to this opinion illustrate this principle.

Case law, particularly case law that Congress and the Copyright Office have considered, reflects the same approach. Congress cited examples of copyrightable design works, including "a carving on the back of a chair" and "a floral relief design on silver flatware." H. R. Rep., at 55. Copyright Office guidance on copyrightable designs in useful articles include "an engraving on a vase," "[a]rtwork printed on a t-shirt," "[a] colorful pattern decorating the surface of a shopping bag," "[a] drawing on the surface of wallpaper," and "[a] floral relief decorating the handle of a spoon." Compendium §924.2(B). Courts have found copyrightable matter in a plaster ballet dancer statuette encasing the lamp's electric cords and forming its base, see *Mazer*,

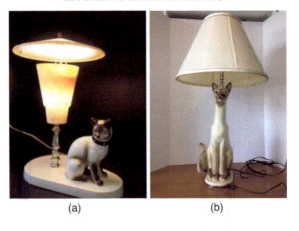

Fig. 3.8 The pair of lamps picture used to illustrate principle

APPENDIX TO OPINION OF BREYER, J.

(a)   (b)

supra, as well as carvings engraved onto furniture, see *Universal Furniture Int'l, Inc. v. Collezione Europa USA, Inc.*, 618 F. 3d 417, 431–435 (CA4 2010) (*per curiam*), and designs on laminated floor tiles, see *Home Legend, LLC* v. *Mannington Mills, Inc.*, 784 F. 3d 1404, 1412–1413 (CA11 2015). See generally Brief for Intellectual Property Professors as *Amici Curiae*.

By way of contrast, Van Gogh's painting of a pair of old shoes, though beautifully executed and copyrightable as a painting, would not qualify for a shoe design copyright. See Appendix, Fig. 3.9, *infra*; 17 U. S. C. §§113(a)–(b). Courts have similarly denied copyright protection to objects that begin as three-dimensional designs, such as measuring spoons shaped like heart-tipped arrows, *Bonazoli* v. *R. S. V. P. Int'l, Inc.*, 353 F. Supp. 2d 218, 226–227 (RI 2005); candleholders shaped like sailboats, *Design Ideas, Ltd.* v. *Yankee Candle Co.*, 889 F. Supp. 2d 1119, 1128 (CD Ill. 2012); and wire spokes on a wheel cover, *Norris Industries, Inc.* v. *International Tel. & Tel. Corp.*, 696 F. 2d 918, 922–924 (CA11 1983). None of these de signs could qualify for copyright protection that would prevent others from selling spoons, candleholders, or wheel covers with the same design. Why not? Because in each case the design is not separable from the utilitarian aspects of the object to which it relates. The designs cannot be physically separated because they themselves make up the shape of the spoon, candleholders, or wheel covers of which they are a part. And spoons, candlehold ers, and wheel covers are useful objects, as are the old shoes depicted in Van Gogh's painting. More importantly, one cannot easily imagine or otherwise conceptualize the design of the spoons or the candleholders or the shoes *without that picture, or image, or replica being a picture of spoons, or candleholders, or wheel covers, or shoes*. The designs necessarily bring along the underlying utilitarian object. Hence each design is not conceptually separable from the physical useful object.

APPENDIX TO OPINION OF BREYER, J.

Fig. 3.9 The oil painting of Van Gogh's "shoes"

The upshot is that one could copyright the floral design on a soupspoon but one could not copyright the shape of the spoon itself, no matter how beautiful, artistic, or esthetically pleasing that shape might be: A picture of the shape of the spoon is also a picture of a spoon; the picture of a floral design is not. See Compendium §924.2(B). To repeat: A separable design feature must be "capable of existing independently" of the useful article as a separate artistic work that is not itself the useful article. If the claimed feature could be extracted without replicating the useful article of which it is a part, and the result would be a copyrightable artistic work standing alone, then there is a separable design. But if extracting the claimed features would necessarily bring along the underlying useful article, the design is not separable from the useful article. In many or most cases, to decide whether a design or artistic feature of a useful article is conceptually separate from the article itself, it is enough to imagine the feature on its own and ask, "Have I created a picture of a (useful part of a) useful article?" If so, the design is not separable from the useful article. If not, it is.

In referring to imagined pictures and the like, I am not speaking technically. I am simply trying to explain an intuitive idea of what separation is about, as well as how I understand the majority's opinion. So understood, the opinion puts design copyrights in their rightful place. The law has long recognized that drawings or photographs of real-world objects are copyrightable as drawings or photographs, but the copyright does not give protection against others making the underlying useful objects. See, e.g., *Burrow-Giles Lithographic Co.* v. *Sarony*, 111 U. S. 53 (1884). That is why a copyright on Van Gogh's painting would prevent others from reproducing that painting, but it would not prevent others from reproducing and selling the comfortable old shoes that the painting depicts. Indeed, the purpose of §113(b) was to ensure that "'copyright in a pictorial, graphic, or sculptural work, portraying a useful article as such, does not extend to the manufacture of the useful article itself.'" H. R. Rep., at 105.

II

To ask this kind of simple question—does the design picture the useful article?—will not provide an answer in every case, for there will be cases where it is difficult to say whether a picture of the design is, or is not, also a picture of the useful article. But the question will avoid courts focusing primarily upon what I believe is an unhelpful feature of the inquiry, namely, whether the design can be imagined as a "two- or three-dimensional work of art." *Ante*, at 1, 17. That is because virtually any industrial design can be thought of separately as a "work of art": Just imagine a frame surrounding the design, or its being placed in a gallery. Consider Marcel Duchamp's "readymades" series, the functional mass-produced objects he designated as art. See Appendix, Fig. 3.10, infra. What is there in the world that, viewed through an esthetic lens, cannot be seen as a good, bad, or indifferent work of art? What design features could not be imaginatively reproduced on a painter's canvas? Indeed, great industrial design may well include design that is inseparable from the useful article—where, as Frank Lloyd Wright put it, "form and function are one." F. Wright, An Autobiography 146 (1943) (reprint 2005). Where they are one, the de signer may be able to obtain 15 years of protection through a design patent. 35 U. S. C. §§171, 173; see also

Fig. 3.10 Marcel Duchamp "In advance of the broken arm"

APPENDIX TO OPINION OF BREYER, J.

McKenna & Strandburg, Progress and Competition in Design, 17 Stan. Tech. L. Rev. 1, 48–51 (2013). But, if they are one, Congress did not intend a century or more of copyright protection.

III

The conceptual approach that I have described reflects Congress' answer to a problem that is primarily practical and economic. Years ago, Lord Macaulay drew attention to the problem when he described copyright in books as a "tax on readers for the purpose of giving a bounty to writers." 56 Parl. Deb. (3d Ser.) (1841) 341, 350. He called attention to the main benefit of copyright protection, which is to provide an incentive to produce copyrightable works and thereby "promote the Progress of Science and useful Arts." U. S. Const., Art. I, §8, cl. 8. But Macaulay also made clear that copyright protection imposes costs. Those costs include the higher prices that can accompany the grant of a copyright monopoly. They also can include (for those wishing to display, sell, or perform a design, film, work of art, or piece of music, for example) the costs of discovering whether there are previous copyrights, of contacting copyright holders, and of securing permission to copy. *Eldred* v. *Ashcroft*, 537 U. S. 186, 248–252 (2003) (BREYER, J., dissenting). Sometimes, as Thomas Jefferson wrote to James Madison, costs can outweigh "the benefit even of limited monopolies." Letter from Thomas Jefferson to James Madison (July 31, 1788), in 13 Papers of Thomas Jefferson 443 (J. Boyd ed. 1956) (Jefferson Letter). And that is particularly true in light of the fact that Congress has extended the "limited Times" of protection, U. S. Const., Art. I, §8, cl. 8, from the "14 years" of Jefferson's day to potentially more than a century today. Jefferson Letter 443; see also *Eldred, supra,* at 246–252 (opinion of BREYER, J.).

The Constitution grants Congress primary responsibility for assessing comparative costs and benefits and drawing copyright's statutory lines. Courts must respect those lines and not grant copyright protection where Congress has decided not to do so. And it is clear that Congress has not extended broad copyright protection to the fashion design industry. See, e.g., 1 Nimmer §2A.08[H][3][c] (describing how Congress rejected proposals for fashion design protection within the 1976 Act and has rejected every proposed bill to this effect since then); *Esquire, Inc.* v. *Ringer*, 591 F. 2d 796, 800, n. 12 (CADC 1978) (observing that at the time of the 1976 Copyright Act, Congress had rejected every one of the approximately 70 design protection bills that had been introduced since 1914); e.g., H. R. 5055, 109th Cong., 2d Sess.: "To Amend title 17, United States Code, to provide protection for fashion design" (introduced Mar. 30, 2006; unenacted). Congress has left "statutory... protection... largely unavailable for dress designs." 1 Nimmer §2A.08[H][3][a]; Raustiala & Sprigman, The Piracy Paradox: Innovation and Intellectual Property in Fashion Design, 92 Va. L. Rev. 1687, 1698–1705 (2006).

Congress' decision not to grant full copyright protection to the fashion industry has not left the industry without protection. Patent design protection is available. 35 U. S. C. §§171, 173. A maker of clothing can obtain trademark protection under the Lanham Act for signature features of the clothing. 15 U. S. C. §1051 et *seq.* And a designer who creates an original textile design can receive copyright protection for that pattern as placed, for example, on a bolt of cloth, or anything made with that cloth. E.g., Compendium §924.3(A)(1). "[T]his [type of] claim... is generally made by the fabric producer rather than the garment or costume designer," and is "ordinarily made when the two-dimensional design is applied to the textile fabric and before the garment is cut from the fabric." 56 Fed. Reg. 56531 (1991).

The fashion industry has thrived against this backdrop, and designers have contributed immeasurably to artistic and personal self-expression through clothing. But a decision by this Court to grant protection to the design of a garment would grant the designer protection that Congress refused to provide. It would risk increased prices and unforeseeable disruption in the clothing industry, which in the United States alone encompasses nearly $370 billion in annual spending and 1.8 million jobs. Brief for Council of Fashion Designers of America, Inc., as *Amicus Curiae* 3–4 (citing U. S. Congress, Joint Economic Committee, The New Economy of Fashion 1 (2016)). That is why I believe it important to emphasize those parts of the Court's opinion that limit the scope of its interpretation. That language, as I have said, makes clear that one may not "claim a copyright in a useful article merely by creating a replica of that article in some other medium," which "would not give rise to any rights in the useful article that inspired it." *Ante,* at 7–8.

IV

If we ask the "separateness" question correctly, the answer here is not difficult to find. The majority's opinion, in its appendix, depicts the cheerleader dress designs that Varsity submitted to the Copyright Office. Can the design features in Varsity's pictures exist separately from the utilitarian aspects of a dress? Can we extract those features as copyrightable design works standing alone, without bringing along, via picture or design, the dresses of which they constitute a part?

Consider designs 074, 078, and 0815. They certainly look like cheerleader uniforms. That is to say, they look like pictures of cheerleader uniforms, just like Van Gogh's old shoes look like shoes. I do not see how one could see them otherwise. Designs 299A and 2999B present slightly closer questions. They omit some of the dresslike context that the other designs possess. But the necklines, the sleeves, and the cut of the skirt suggest that they too are pictures of dresses. Looking at all five of Varsity's pictures, I do not see how one could conceptualize the design features in a way that does not picture, not just artistic designs, but dresses as well.

Where I to accept the majority's invitation to "imaginatively remov[e]" the chevrons and stripes *as they are arranged* on the neckline, waistline, sleeves, and skirt of each uniform, and apply them on a "painter's canvas," *ante*, at 10, that painting would be of a cheerleader's dress. The esthetic elements on which Varsity seeks protection exist only as part of the uniform design—there is nothing to separate out but for dress-shaped lines that replicate the cut and style of the uniforms. Hence, each design is not physically separate, nor is it conceptually separate, from the useful article it depicts, namely, a cheerleader's dress. They cannot be copyrighted.

Varsity, of course, could have sought a design patent for its designs. Or, it could have sought a copyright on a textile design, even one with a similar theme of chevrons and lines.

But that is not the nature of Varsity's copyright claim.

It has instead claimed ownership of the particular "'treatment and arrangement'" of the chevrons and lines of the design as they appear at the neckline, waist, skirt, sleeves, and overall cut of each uniform. Brief for Respondents 50. The majority imagines that Varsity submitted something different—that is, only the surface decorations of chevrons and stripes, as in a textile design. As the majority sees it, Varsity's copyright claim would be the same had it submitted a plain rectangular space depicting chevrons and stripes, like swaths from a bolt of fabric. But considered on their own, the simple stripes are plainly unoriginal. Varsity, then, seeks to do indirectly what it cannot do directly: bring along the design and cut of the dresses by seeking to protect surface decorations whose "treatment and arrangement" are *coextensive with that design and cut*. As Varsity would have it, it would prevent its competitors from making useful three-dimensional cheerleader uniforms by submitting plainly unoriginal chevrons and stripes as cut and arranged on a useful article. But with that cut and arrangement, the resulting pictures on which Varsity seeks protection do not simply depict designs. They depict clothing. They depict the useful articles of which the designs are inextricable parts. And Varsity cannot obtain copyright protection that would give them the power to prevent others from making those useful uniforms, any more than Van Gogh can copyright comfortable old shoes by painting their likeness.

I fear that, in looking past the three-dimensional design inherent in Varsity's claim by treating it as if it were no more than a design for a bolt of cloth, the majority has lost sight of its own important limiting principle. One may not "claim a copyright in a useful article merely by creating a replica of that article in some other medium," such as in a picture. *Ante,* at 7. That is to say, one cannot obtain a copyright that would give its holder "any rights in the useful article that inspired it." *Ante,* at 8. With respect, I dissent.

4.3 Analysis of the Case

Star Athletica, LLC v. Varsity Brands, Inc., 580 U.S. ___ (2017); 137 S. Ct. 1002 (2017).

The text of Star Athletica v. Varsity Brands is available here: https://www.supremecourt.gov/opinions/16pdf/15-866_0971.pdf

[Cheerleader uniforms at the heart of the case. Image credit: U.S. Supreme Court, Appendix to the Opinion in Star Athletica, LLC v. Varsity Brands, Inc.]

Varsity Brands, Inc. (Varsity Brands) designs and manufactures clothing and accessories for use in various athletic activities, particularly cheerleading. Varsity Brands applied for and received copyright registrations for design features incorporated into several cheerleading costumes. When a competitor, Star Athletica, LLC (Star), began advertising similar looking cheerleading concepts for sale. Varsity sued Star and alleged, among other claims, that Star violated the Copyright Act by infringing its original designs. Star asserted counterclaims, including one that alleged that Varsity had made fraudulent representations to the Copyright Office because the designs at issue were not copyrightable.

Star argued that Varsity did not have valid copyrights because the designs were for "useful articles," and the designs could not be separated from the cheerleading uniforms themselves. Varsity countered that the designs were separable and nonfunctional, and therefore the copyrights were valid and had been infringed. The trial court granted summary judgment for Star and held that the designs were integral to the functionality of the cheerleading uniforms. The U.S. Court of Appeals for the Sixth Circuit reversed and held that the Copyright Act allows graphic features of a design to be copyright protected even when those designs are not separable from a "useful article." On appeal, the Supreme Court was tasked with articulating the appropriate test to determine whether a feature of a "useful article" is copyrightable under the Copyright Act. Justice Clarence Thomas authored the opinion of the 6–2 majority.

A design feature of a useful article is copyrightable if it can be perceived as a two- or three-dimensional artwork that is separable from the useful article and if it would be a protectable pictorial, graphic, or sculptural work on its own, or if applied to another medium, such as a canvas. In Sec. 101 the U.S. Copyright Act explains: "Pictorial, graphic, and sculptural works" include two-dimensional and three-dimensional works of fine, graphic, and applied art, photographs, prints and art reproductions, maps, globes, charts, diagrams, models, and technical drawings, including architectural plans. Such works shall include works of artistic craftsmanship insofar as their form but not their mechanical or utilitarian aspects are concerned; the design of a useful article, as defined in this section, shall be considered a pictorial, graphic, or sculptural work only if, and only to the extent that, such design incorporates pictorial, graphic, or sculptural features that can be identified separately from, and are capable of existing independently of, the utilitarian aspects of the article."

The Court noted that, in addition to the pertinent words of the Copyright Act and its legislative history, there were precedential cases which had established the basic principal that to be independently copyrightable, a design element of a useful article must be able to be identified separately from the article and be capable of existing separately from the article. The Court cited the text of Sec. 101 and the Copyright Act as a whole, noting that Secs. 101, 106, and 113(a) provided copyright protection for pictorial, graphic and sculptural works regardless of whether they are fixed first as part of a useful article, or as stand-alone works. Justice Thomas asserted that this interpretation was consistent with the history of the Copyright Act because it did not overrule Mazer v. Stein, 347 U.S. 201 (1954), the U.S. Supreme Court opinion that informed the statute's relevant text, and was cited in its legislative history. In Mazer v. Stein, decided under the precursor Copyright Act of 1909, the Court addressed the copyrightability of statuettes—male and female dancing figures made of semivitreous china—used as bases for fully equipped electric lamps were copyrightable, even though the lamps themselves were utilitarian mass-produced items.

Drawing a line between protectable art and non-protectable useful articles is necessary because the Copyright Act does not protect useful articles such as cheerleading uniforms or other "article[s] having an intrinsic utilitarian function that is not merely to portray the appearance of the article or to convey information." The Court observed that the Copyright Act "establishes a special rule for copyrighting a pictorial, graphic, or sculptural work incorporated into a 'useful article,'" which limits protection to the "pictorial, graphic, or sculptural features that can be identified separately from, and are capable of existing independently of, the utilitarian aspects of the [useful] article."

To "give effect to the clear meaning of the statute as written," the Court held that "a feature incorporated into the design of a useful article is eligible for copyright protection only if the feature (1) can be perceived as a two- or three-dimensional work of art separate from the useful article and (2) would qualify as a protectable pictorial, graphic, or sculptural work—either on its own or fixed in some other tangible medium of expression—if it were imagined separately from the useful article into which it is incorporated." The first inquiry, whether a design element is separately identifiable, is relatively straightforward; the second inquiry, the independent existence question, is generally more difficult both to explain and to satisfy.

After articulating this test the Court applied this test to the disputed cheerleader uniform design features and held that Varsity Brands' graphic designs—various arrangements of colored stripes, chevrons, geometric shapes and lines—could be imagined separately from the cheerleading uniforms (useful articles) on which they were applied, and were eligible for copyright protection. Since the stripes, chevrons, shapes, and lines were separately perceivable, the first prong was satisfied. The second prong was met because the stripes, chevrons, shapes and lines, when "applied in another medium," would be two-dimensional works of art that "would not replicate the uniform itself."

In her concurring opinion, Justice Ruth Bader Ginsburg wrote that separability analysis was unnecessary in this case because the designs are themselves copyrightable and are merely reproduced on useful articles. Justice Stephen G. Breyer, however, wrote a dissent in which he argued that although he agreed with the majority opinion's analysis of the test that the statute required, the designs at issue in this case failed the test. He asserted that a feature is not separable from the useful article if it cannot be extracted without necessarily replicating the useful article in another medium. Because the designs in this case could only be represented as pictures, and therefore replicas, of the uniforms, in his opinion they were not capable of existing independently of the useful article. Therefore, the disputed design elements failed the second prong of the articulated separability test.

3.2.2 Copyright Cases from China

(1) **The requirements of copyrightablity of short vedio and its protect conditions—Beijing Weibo Vision Technology Co., Ltd. v. Baidu Online Network Technology (Beijing) Co., Ltd. Etc.**

1.1 Case Judgement Beijing Internet Court
Case number: (2018) Beijing 0491 Minchu No. 1
26-12-2018
The cause of action: copyright infringement

The parties:
The plaintiff: Beijing Weibo Vision Technology Co., Ltd.
The defendant: Baidu Online Network Technology (Beijing) Co., Ltd.
The defendant: Baidu Netcom Technology Co., Ltd.

The plaintiff claimed:
1. Order the two defendants to immediately stop infringing on the plaintiff's copyright and stop providing online playback and download services of the alleged infringing short video; 2. Order the two defendants to publish a statement in a prominent position on the homepage of Baidu.com website (www.baidu.com) and the homepage of Huopai video client for 24 consecutive hours within three days from the effective date of the judgment to eliminate the impact; 3. Order the two defendants to compensate the plaintiff for economic losses of 1 million yuan and reasonable expenses of 50,000 yuan.

Facts and reasons:
The Douyin short video website and mobile phone software (collectively known as the Douyin platform) are original short video sharing platforms legally owned and operated by the plaintiff. "Black Face V" is a well-known big "V" user on the Douyin platform. With its imaginative and uniquely designed characters and video works, it is deeply loved by users on the Douyin platform. It has attracted 26.37 million

followers and each of its works has a high number of clicks and likes. On May 12, 2018, the "5.12, I want to say to you" short video released on the Douyin platform (hereinafter referred to as the "I want to say to you" short video) was independently created and uploaded by "Black Face V". This short video is a comprehensive work of design, arrangement, editing, and performance within 13 s, fully expressing the memory of the tenth anniversary of the Wenchuan earthquake. As soon as the work was released, it was widely praised by netizens with more than 2.8 million likes and it became a work created in a similar way to filming movies (hereinafter referred to as works created in a way similar to cinematography.

With the legal authorization of "Black Face V", the plaintiff enjoys the exclusive right of information network dissemination worldwide and the exclusive right to defend the rights in the name of the plaintiff for the "I want to say to you" short video.

Baidu Online Company is the developer of the Android system of the Huopai video mobile phone software and Baidu Netcom Company is the developer of the iOS system of the Huopai video mobile phone software. The two defendants jointly provide users with the download, installation, operation, update, maintenance and promotion of the Huopai video mobile phone software. Without the permission of the plaintiff, the two defendants disseminated the short video of "I want to say to you" on the Huopai video and provided downloading and sharing services, thereby attracting a large number of Internet users to browse and watch on the Huopai video, which infringed the information network dissemination right of "I want to tell you" short video. At the same time, the accused infringing short video did not display the watermark of Douyin and the user ID. The two defendants must have implemented the act of removing the above watermark, and there was intention to destroy the plaintiff's relevant technical measures. This behavior also constituted an infringement of the plaintiff's right to spread information on the Internet. The above two actions of the two defendants caused great economic losses to the plaintiff and affected the plaintiff's reputation. We urge the court to support all the plaintiff's claims. During the litigation, the plaintiff recognized that the short video accused of infringement had been deleted, and gave up the lawsuit request of "request to order the two defendants to immediately stop the infringement of the plaintiff's copyright and stop providing online playback and download services of the short video accused of infringing."

The two defendants jointly argued that:
they do not agree with the claims of plaintiff and shall not bear the legal responsibility requested by the plaintiff. The reasons are as follows: 1. "I want to tell you" short video is not original and does not constitute a work protected by copyright law. The ideas expressed in this short video are not different from other users who imitate gesture dance and upload short videos. It is not original ands fail to meet the high requirements for originality of works created in a way similar to cinematography. The video is only 13-s long and has a small creative space. The main materials are all from the demonstration videos of the party media platform and there are few independent creative factors; there is no choice or screening in the shooting of the materials and the selection and arrangement of the shooting pictures; It is difficult to use software to process the image of characters in a way to form a high degree

of originality of works created in a way similar to cinematography there are a large number of short videos similar to or the same as the "I want to tell you" short video on the Internet; The person participating in the performance is not the original right holder himself.

2. The plaintiff and the defendant are not eligible. The licensor claimed by the plaintiff is not the author or right holder of the "I want to tell you" short video so the plaintiff does not have the basis of right to sue the two defendants; the defendant, Baidu Netcom company, is responsible for operating the mobile phone software for Huopai small videos, and the defendant Baidu Online company is only the registered developer of the software, so the Baidu Online company is not a qualified defendant in this case.

3. The defendant, Baidu Netcom company, shall not bear the legal responsibility requested by the plaintiff: (1) The mobile phone software of Huopai Video only provides information storage space services and the short videos on it are uploaded by netizens themselves. The alleged infringing short video is uploaded by the registered user ID451670. (2) Baidu.Netcom company clearly stated in the user agreement that users should not upload content that infringes on the intellectual property or other rights of others and also informed the right holders of the methods and channels for complaints. Baidu Netcom company has fulfilled the prompting and management obligations stipulated by the law in accordance with the law; (3) After receiving the valid complaint from the plaintiff, Baidu Netcom company has promptly deleted it. There was no fault and it should not bear civil liability.

4. The plaintiff's claims lacked factual and legal basis. The plaintiff's alleged economic loss of 1 million was estimated based on the amount of broadcasts, reposts and likes on the Douyin platform. These data are operable by the plaintiff and the claim on economic losses lacks authenticity; The method of assuming responsibility for eliminating the impact does not apply to infringement of property rights, and its request to publish a statement to eliminate the impact has no legal basis. In summary, the court is requested to dismiss all claims of the plaintiff in accordance with the law. The court believes that based on the facts ascertained, the dispute point in this case is:

1. Whether Weibo Vision Company and Baidu Online Company are the eligible subjects in this case; 2. Whether the "I want to tell you" short video constitutes the work created in a way similar to cinematography; 3. Whether the defendants infringe on the "I want to talk to you" short video.

Whether Weibo Vision Company and Baidu Online Company are eligible subjects in this case

1) Whether the plaintiff is a qualified subject in the case

In this case, the plaintiff claimed that Xie, an outsider in the case, was the producer of the "I want to tell you" short video. With Xie's authorization, the plaintiff obtained the right of information network dissemination of the "I want to tell you" short video. The two defendants did not recognize Xie as the original right holder, so this case needs to first examine whether Xie is the original right holder.

According to the Article 11 of Copyright Law, except otherwise provided in this Law, the copyright in a work shall belong to its author. The author of a work is the citizen who has created the work. Where a work is created according to the intention and under the supervision and responsibility of a legal entity or another organization, such legal entity or organization shall be the author of the work. The citizen, legal entity or organization whose name is affixed to a work shall, without the contrary proof, be the author of the work.

Short video refers to the video content that is played on various new Internet media platforms and is suitable for viewing on the move. The time varies from a few seconds to a few minutes. Generally, there will be no specially produced signature or ownership statement in the video. Therefore, when a producer uploads a short video to the corresponding platform, it will automatically mark "@Video Maker" in the corner of the short video, which can be regarded as a signature for the short video. According to the signature presumption rules of the Copyright Law, if there is no evidence to the contrary, it should be presumed that the signature is the producer of the short video and enjoys the copyright to the short video.

In this case, the "I want to tell you" short video is marked with "@Black Face V" in the corner. If the short video constitutes a work, it can be inferred that the producer of the "I want to tell you" short video is "Black Face V". If the signature is not the real name, the party claiming the right shall bear the burden of proof that there is a true correspondence between the signature and the author's identity. For works published on the Internet, where the author's signature is not his real name, and the party claiming the right can prove that there is a true correspondence between the signature and the author by logging in to the account, etc., he can also be presumed to be the author. Because "Black Face V" is not the real name of the producer, if the plaintiff claims that Xie is the producer, he should bear the burden of proof that there is a true correspondence between "Black Face V" and Xie. The notarial certificate submitted by the plaintiff showed that Xie had logged into the aforementioned "Black Face V" account of Toutiao mobile phone software and Douyin short video mobile phone software by entering the mobile phone number registered in the background and the corresponding verification code. The above evidence can presume that Xie is the producer of the "I want to tell you" short video.

The two defendants believed that the owner of the mobile phone number used when registering the "Black Face V" account was Lei. Therefore, the producer should be Lei. Considering that Lei had mailed a confidential application signed by Xie to the Court, the plaintiff arranged for Xie and Lei to be interviewed according to the requirements of the Court. According to the statements made by Xie and Lei when they were interviewed online, Lei and Xie agreed that the mobile phone number belonged to Lei but was used by Xie; they agreed that the "Black Face V" account involved in the case was registered and used by Xie and the "I want to tell you" short video was shot and produced by Xie. Considering that the "separation of man and machine" in real life exists objectively and the two defendants have no evidence to deny the above statement. The defendants' claim is untenable.

Therefore, according to the authorization confirmation issued by Xie, the plaintiff obtained the exclusive right to use and protect the right of information network dissemination of the short video produced by Xie during the period from January 1, 2018 to January 1, 2019. The plaintiff has a direct interest in this case. According to Article 119 Paragraph 1 of the Civil Procedure Law of the People's Republic of China, the plaintiff has the right to initiate a lawsuit in this case.

2) Whether Baidu Online Company is a Qualified Defendant.
The operator of the mobile phone software shall be identified based on the registration information of the application store and the operator stated in the information marked in the mobile phone software. If the registration information of the application store and the information marked in the mobile phone software are inconsistent, the two may be deemed to be joint operators. In this case, the Android system of the Huopai Video mobile phone software only showed that the developer was Baidu Online and did not display the information of other business entities such as the operator. The Baidu Online company should be recognized as the operator. Baidu Online denied that it was the operator of the system. The two defendants explained that the country has a limit on the number of mobile phone software under each subject account, so the Android system of the Huopai video mobile phone software is registered under Baidu Online. The Court believes that, firstly, the two defendants' evasion of administrative supervision cannot be an effective defense; secondly, the disclosure of rights holder information on relevant software is not only based on the management requirements of law enforcement agencies, but also has the significance of promising the public to bear relevant civil liabilities. The public's trust based on the above publicity should be protected; thirdly, although the two defendants claimed that the operator is Baidu Netcom company has stated in the user agreement of Huopai Video mobile phone software, the relevant clauses are not effective for third parties outside the contract. In addition, even if the two defendants explained that Baidu Online had loaned relevant enterprise qualifications to Baidu Netcom company it should also assume joint and several liabilities with Baidu Netcom company. In summary, this court determined that Baidu Online Company was a qualified defendant in this case.

2. Whether the "I want to tell you" short video constitutes work created in a way similar to cinematography.
According to Article 2 of Regulation for the Implementation of the Copyright Law of the People's Republic of China, the term "works" as referred to in the Copyright Law means intellectual creations with originality in the literary, artistic or scientific domain, insofar as they can be reproduced in a tangible form. Article 4(11) clarifies that "cinematographic works and works created by a process analogous to cinematography" means works which are recorded on some material, consisting of a series of images, with or without accompanying sound, and which can be projected with the aid of suitable devices or communicated by other means. In this case, the "I want to tell you" short video clearly meets these formal requirements.

The plaintiff claimed that the "I want to tell you" short video constituted the work created in a way similar to cinematography, and the defendant believed that the short video did not have the originality required by works created in a way similar to cinematography. Whether "I want to tell you" short video belongs to a work created in a way similar to cinematography, the key lies in the judgment of its originality. According to the Article 15 of Interpretation of the Supreme People's Court Concerning the Application of Laws in the Trial of Civil Disputes over Copyright, With regards to a work created by different authors on the basis of a same topic, the authors shall enjoy independent copyright if the expression of the work is completed independently and is creative. According to the above regulations, the work with originality should meet two requirements: 1. Whether it is completed by the author independently; 2. Whether it is "creative".

1) the determination of "independent completion"
In this case, the producer responded to the initiative of the Party media platform and People's Daily, with the theme of "Remember the disaster, Pay tribute to rebirth, Use your own strength, and move forward courageously", with the basic elements of gesture dance, accompanying sound and light and dark changes in the demonstration videos on the party media platform and People's Daily, a short video of "I want to tell you" was created by combining software technology and taking pictures downloaded from the Internet as basic materials. Therefore, to determine whether the "I want to tell you" short video meets the requirements of "independent completion", it should be based on whether there is an objectively identifiable difference between the short video and the above-mentioned demonstration videos and network pictures. The same theme does not affect the determination of whether the short video "I want to tell you" is independently completed.

According to the facts ascertained, the demonstration videos on the Party media platform and the People's Daily and the pictures downloaded from the Internet are originally independent elements that have nothing to do with each other. "Black Face V" combines the above elements to produce the "I want to tell you" short video, which is different from the former two which can be objectively identified. This short video is also quite different from the short videos produced by other users on the Douyin platform who participated in the same topic and there is no evidence to prove that the same or similar short video content exists before the short video is released on Douyin platform. Therefore, the short video "I want to tell you" is determined to be created independently by the producer.

2) the determination of "creativeness"
Regarding the standard of creativity, in the process of formation and development, it is always connected with the social environment and industry characteristics and developed and improved according to the actual social environment and the characteristics of various types of works. With the popularization of mobile smart terminals and the development of software development technology, since 2016, a large number of mobile short video applications have come out intensively, short video content entrepreneurs have shown explosive growth and the short video industry has ushered in a period of rapid development. Short videos integrate text, pictures, voice and video content to meet the diverse expression and communication needs of users intuitively and three-dimensionally. In this context, defining the creative standards of short video works has important practical significance to ensure the normal and orderly dissemination of short videos, promote cultural prosperity and create social

wealth. Judicial trials should adopt a cautious and positive attitude and properly use creative discretion standards to facilitate the development and growth of emerging industries.

Short video is a new type of video format with the characteristics of low creation threshold, short recording time, clear theme, strong sociality and interaction and easy dissemination. The above characteristics generally simplify the short video production process and the producers are mostly individuals or small teams. The creation and dissemination of short videos contributes to the diversified expression of the public and the prosperity of culture. Therefore, when judging whether short videos meet the requirements of creativity, the creation height should not be exacting. As long as it can reflect the individual expression of the producer, it can be considered creative.

When determining the creativeness of the "I want to tell you" short video, the Court considers the following factors: First, the length of the video is not necessarily related to the determination of creativeness. Objectively speaking, if the video time is too short, it may be difficult to form original expressions. However, although some videos are not long, they can more completely express the thoughts and feelings of the producer, and then they have the possibility of becoming works. In this case, the shorter the video, the more difficult it is to create and the more likely it is to be creative. Second, the "I want to tell you" short video shows creativity. The producer of this video responds to the initiative of the party media platform. Given the theme and material, its creative space was limited to a certain extent, reflecting the higher creative difficulty. This short video shows a man in a masked black-faced hoodie standing in the post-disaster ruins and praying for blessing with gesture dance. Near the end of the gesture dance, it presents a vibrant scene. The light changed from gloomy to sunny, the ground from jagged to flat, the telephone poles from tilted to upright, the sleeves of the man in the black-faced hoodie turned red, and he finally made a gesture of love. The short video constitutes an organic and unified audio-visual whole, which contains the multi-faceted intellectual work of the producer, and is creative. Although the short video is created on the basis of existing materials, its arrangement, selection, and presentation to the audience are completely different from other short videos, reflecting the producer's personalized expression. Third, the "I want to tell you" short video evokes resonance from the audience. Constant self-improvement and the courage to face major disasters have always been the outstanding spiritual connotations of the Chinese nation. On the tenth anniversary of the Wenchuan earthquake, the "I want to tell you" short video delivered a rebirth comfort, a warm blessing and a forward force in a form that the public was willing to accept and responded to the public's nostalgia for the Wenchuan earthquake, the salute to the people in the disaster area, and the yearning for a better life. The spiritual enjoyment brought to the audience by the short video is also a concrete manifestation of the creativity of the short video. The sharing behavior of other users on the Douyin platform of the "I want to tell you" short video can also be used as proof that the video is creative. Therefore, this court determined that the "I want to tell you" short video meets the requirements of creativity.

In summary, "I want to tell you" short videos meet the originality requirements of the copyright law and constitute the work created in a way similar to cinematography.

3. Whether the two defendants constitute an infringement of the "I want to tell you" short video, and whether they are liable.

In this case, the evidence submitted by the plaintiff can show that the alleged infringing short video can be played on the Huopai video mobile phone software. The plaintiff claimed that the two defendants provided the accused infringing short video, and the defendant claimed that it only provided information storage space service. The dispute between the two parties lies in whether the two defendants provided the alleged infringing short video or only provided information storage space service; if the two defendants are only network service providers, whether their actions constitute infringement and whether they should be liable.

1) The two defendants provided the accused infringing short video or only provided information storage space services

In a case of infringing on the right of information network dissemination, the defendant shall bear the burden of proof if he maintains that only information storage space service is provided. The evidence submitted by the defendant is generally determined based on the following factors: the evidence provided by the defendant can prove that its website has the function of providing information storage space services for service objects; the relevant content on the defendant website clearly indicates the provision of information storage space services for service objects; The defendant was able to provide evidence such as the uploader's username, registered IP address, registration time, upload IP address, upload time, and contact information.

In this case, the plaintiff claimed that the two defendants deleted the watermark on the "I want to tell you" short video, which undermined the technical measures taken by the company. The Court believes that, in accordance with the industry practices and technical presentations recognized by both parties, "I want to tell you that" short videos downloaded from Douyin platform should be loaded with a watermark of Douyin platform and user ID. However, the alleged infringing short video disseminated on the Huopai mobile phone software does not show the above watermark, it can be presumed that the above watermark has been eliminated.

First of all, the nature of the above watermark is not a technical measure claimed by the plaintiff. According to the Article 26 of Regulation on the Protection of the Right to Communicate Works to the Public over Information Networks, "Technical measures" refers to the effective technologies, devices, or components used to prevent or limit others from browsing or enjoying works, performances, or audio-visual recordings without permission from the owner, or in providing the works, performances, or audio-visual recordings to the public through the network without the owner's permission. There are two main differences between the "technical measures" in the sense of copyright law and the "technical measures" in the sense of pure technology. First, the "technical measures" in the sense of copyright law are applied to specific objects in the copyright law, such as works, performances and sound recordings. The second is that the "technical measures" in the sense of copyright law have the function of preventing the specific actions against the above-mentioned specific objects. Only the technical means to prevent others from carrying out specific actions can realize the legislative purpose of copyright law. The watermark in this case obviously cannot achieve the above functions. From the public's perspective, watermarks are more capable of showing certain identity. The watermark in this case contains the user ID of the producer of the "I want to tell you" short video, which indicates the producer's information, and it is more appropriate to be regarded as rights management information. In addition, the words "Tik Tok" marked in the watermark indicate the communicator's information. The alleged infringing short video was uploaded by someone outside the case and the person who removed the watermark was not the two defendants.

Since the watermark is not a technical measure in the sense of copyright law and the person who eliminated the watermark is not the defendant, the plaintiff's claim that the two defendants infringed upon the right of information network dissemination by destroying the technical measure cannot be established. The Court does not support it.

2) If the two defendants are only a network service providers, whether their behavior constitutes infringement and whether they should bear legal responsibility

According to The second and third paragraphs of Article 36 of Tort Law of the People's Republic of China, Where a network user commits a tort through the network services, the victim of the tort shall be entitled to notify the network service provider to take such necessary measures as deletion, block or disconnection. If, after being notified, the network service provider fails to take necessary measures in a timely manner, it shall be jointly and severally liable for any additional harm with the network user. Where a network service provider knows that a network user is infringing upon a civil right or interest of another person through its network services, and fails to take necessary measures, it shall be jointly and severally liable for any additional harm with the network user. Therefore, there are two prerequisites for network service providers to assume responsibility: one is that network users commit tort by using Internet services, and the other is that network service providers are subjectively faulty in their implementation of the above infringements. According to Article 2 of Regulation on the Protection of the Right to Communicate Works to the Public over Information Networks, Under the following circumstances, a network service provider that provides information storage space to a service object or provides works, performances, or audio-visual recordings to the public through the information network, shall not be liable for compensation:

1. Having clearly mentioned that the information storage space is provided to the service object, and also having publicized the name, contact information, and web address of the network service provider;
2. Having not altered the work, performance, or audio-visual recording provided to the service object;
3. Having not known and having no justified reason to know that the works, performances, or audio-visual recordings provided by the service object have infringed upon an other's right;

4. Having not directly obtained economic benefits from the service object's provision of the work, performance, or audio-visual recording;
5. After receiving the notification from the owner, having deleted the work, performance, or audio-visual regarded as infringing on the right of the owner according to the provisions of this Regulation.

The second and third paragraphs of Article 36 of the Tort Law are constitutive elements of the tort liability of network service providers. If it does not comply with the safe haven principle, it should also be determined in accordance with Article 36 of the Tort Law whether the network service provider should bear the corresponding tort liability.

In this case, the two defendants made it clear that the Huopai mobile phone software was provided for the service target and disclosed the name, contact person and network address of Baidu Netcom company; the plaintiff did not submit evidence to prove that the defendant did not comply with the above-mentioned Article 22(2) to (4). Therefore, the key to whether the two defendants assumes responsibility lies in whether the two defendants fulfilled the obligation of "notification-delete".

The plaintiff presented evidence in the form of two emails, claiming that it had already notified the two defendants to delete the alleged infringing short video on August 24, 2018. The two defendants had not deleted the short video until September 10, which failed to perform its notification-deletion obligation within a reasonable time, so the two defendants should not apply the safe harbor principle and should bear corresponding legal liabilities. However, in the case that the two defendants claimed that they did not receive the above-mentioned email, the plaintiff could not prove that the above-mentioned email reached their email system. Therefore, the Court does not approve the above claims of the plaintiff.

Although the plaintiff did not recognize that the two defendants deleted the alleged infringing short video on September 10 after receiving the plaintiff's paper complaint letter on September 7, 2018, However, the plaintiff was unable to submit contrary evidence to overturn the background records of the deletion operation submitted by the two defendants. So the Court accepted all the above time nodes. Considering that although the two time nodes are four days apart, they include two weekends. Therefore, the Court believes that after receiving a valid complaint, the two defendants deleted the alleged infringing short video within a reasonable time limit. Therefore, the existing evidence cannot prove whether the two defendants knew or should have known subjective fault for the infringement of the alleged infringing short video, and after receiving the notice from the plaintiff, the two defendants promptly deleted the alleged infringing short video. The defendants' behavior met the requirements for entering a "safe haven." Under this circumstance, regardless of whether the user involved in the case of cooperating with the small video mobile phone software constituted an infringement, the two defendants, as network service providers, did not constitute an infringement and should not be liable.

It needs to be emphasized that the purpose of the "notification-delete" rule is to balance the interests of copyright owners and network service providers in the network environment, which is conducive to the healthy development of network platforms and the protection of copyright owners' rights., For the application of the "notice-delete" rule, the goodwill of the rule should be maximized based on the principle of good faith. In this case, the plaintiff should protect his rights in the most economical and direct way provided that he has access to public complaint channels. As a provider of platform services, it is not enough to rely solely on the safe haven principle. The two defendants are responsible for fulfilling platform obligations through more active and effective management.

In summary, this court holds that:

First of all, Xie is the producer of the "I want to tell you" short video. Based on Xie's permission, Weibo Vision Company has obtained the exclusive right of information network dissemination within a certain period of time. The company owes the right to file a lawsuit in this case;

Secondly, Baidu Online is the operator of the mobile phone software (Android system) that cooperates with Huopai video, and should bear the legal responsibility for the application platform of the software. Baidu Online Company is the eligible defendant in this case;

Thirdly, the "I want to tell you" short video is a selection and arrangement based on the existing material, which reflects the producer's personalized expression and brings positive spiritual enjoyment to the audience. It is original and constitutes the work created in a way similar to cinematography.

Fourth, the alleged infringing short video was provided by a mobile phone software user (ID 451670) who made a small video;

Fifth, Baidu Online Company and Baidu Netxun Company, as network service providers that provide information storage space, did not have subjective fault for providing alleged infringing short videos by mobile phone software users of Huopai video. After fulfilling the obligation of "notify-delete", they do not constitute an infringement and should not bear related responsibilities.

The court's decision is as follows:

Dismissed all claims of the plaintiff, Beijing Weibo Vision Technology Co., Ltd.

The case acceptance fee of 14,250 yuan shall be borne by the plaintiff Beijing Weibo Vision Technology Co., Ltd. (paid).

If you disagree with this judgment, you can submit an appeal petition to the court within 15 days from the date of service of the judgment, and submit a copy according to the number of the opposing parties, and appeal to the Beijing Intellectual Property Court.

1.2 Analysis of the Case

1. Facts

Beijing Weibo Vision Technology Co., Ltd. (hereinafter referred to as Weibo Vision Company) is the operator of the Douyin platform. Baidu Online Network Technology (Beijing) Co., Ltd. and Baidu Netcom Technology Co., Ltd. (collectively known as Baidu Company) are the operators of the partnership platform. On the tenth anniversary of the Wenchuan earthquake, on May 12, 2018, the V user "Black Face V" of the Douyin platform responded to the initiative of the national party media information platform (referred to as the party media platform) and the People's Daily Online to use given materials to produced and published the "5.12, I want to say to you" short video (short for "I want to say to you" short video) on the Douyin platform. Authorized by "Black Face V", Weibo Vision has the exclusive right of information network dissemination and exclusive rights for the "I want to say to you" short video on a global scale. A short video of "I want to say to you" was circulated on the mobile phone software of Huopai. The short video playback page did not display Douyin and the user ID watermark. Weibo Vision Company uses "I want to say to you" short videos to constitute works created in a similar way to filming movies (referred to as similar works). The aforementioned dissemination and removal of watermarks by Baidu Company violated the right of information network communication of Weibo Vision Company. The Beijing Internet Court held that the "I want to say to you" short video constitutes a similar electronic work, and Baidu, as a network service provider that provides information storage space, provided accused infringing short videos for cooperating with users of small video mobile phone software. There is no subjective fault. After fulfilling the obligation of "notice-delete", it does not constitute an infringement, and should not bear related responsibilities. The judgment rejected all the claims of Weibo Vision.

2. The focus of dispute

The focus of the dispute in this case is: 1. Is the short video creative? 2. Does Baidu Technology constitute an infringement and is it liable?

3. Legal regulations

Article 11 of the "Copyright Law of the People's Republic of China": copyright belongs to the author. If there is no proof to the contrary, the citizen, legal person or other organization that signed the work shall be the author.

Article 15 of the "Copyright Law of the People's Republic of China": the copyright of film works and works created in a method similar to film production shall be enjoyed by the producer.

Article 2 of the "Implementation Regulations of the Copyright Law of the People's Republic of China": the term "work" in the Copyright Law refers to the intellectual ability that is original in the fields of literature, art, and science and can be copied in a tangible form. Results.

Article 4 of the "Copyright Law of the People's Republic of China": film works and works created in a method similar to film production refer to a series of pictures with or without accompanying sound filmed on a certain medium, and they are projected with the help of appropriate devices. Or works disseminated in other ways.

According to Article 36, Paragraphs 2 and 3 of the Tort Liability Law of the People's Republic of China: if a network user uses a network service to commit infringement, the infringed person has the right to notify the network service provider. The person shall take necessary measures such as deleting, blocking, and disconnecting the link. If the network service provider fails to take necessary measures in time after receiving the notice, it shall be jointly and severally liable with the network user for the enlarged part of the damage. If a network service provider knows that a network user uses its network service to infringe the civil rights and interests of others, and fails to take necessary measures, it shall bear joint and several liability with the network user.

4. Application of the law

(1) Are short videos creative?

Short videos integrate text, pictures, voice, and video content to meet the diverse expression and communication needs of users intuitively and three-dimensionally. In this context, defining the creative standards of short video works has important practical significance to ensure the normal and orderly dissemination of short videos, promote cultural prosperity and development, and create social wealth. Judicial trials should adopt a cautious and positive attitude and properly use creativeness. Discretionary standards to facilitate the development and growth of emerging industries. Short video has the characteristics of low creation threshold, short recording time, clear theme, strong sociality and interaction, and easy dissemination. It is a new type of video format. The above characteristics generally simplify the short video production process, and the producers are mostly individuals or small teams. The creation and dissemination of short videos contributes to the diversified expression of the public and the prosperity of culture. Therefore, when judging whether the short video meets the creative requirements, the creation height should not be exacting, as long as it can reflect the producer's personalized expression, It can be considered creative.

(2) What are the conditions that the network service provider claims only providing information storage space?

In a case of infringing on the right to spread information on the Internet, if the defendant claims to only provide information storage space services, he shall bear the burden of proof. The evidence submitted by the defendant is generally determined based on the following factors: the evidence provided by the defendant can prove that its website has the function of providing information storage space services for service objects; the relevant content on the defendant's website clearly indicates the provision of information storage space services for service objects; The defendant was able to provide evidence such as the uploader's username, registered IP address, registration time, upload IP address, upload time, and contact information.

5. Conclusion and significance

The court determined that short videos belonged to works created with the similar way as film work, and Baidu only provided information storage space services for network service providers, and did not infringe upon the fulfillment of the "notice-delete" obligation. This case is one of the "Top Ten Media Law Cases in China" in 2018 and has attracted widespread attention from all walks of life. This case involves the resolution of a series of new types of legal issues such as whether short video programs can be protected by the copyright law and the degree of protection granted, and how the people's courts balance the creation and dissemination, right holders and network service providers in the judicial practice of copyright. The interest relationship between the public and the society presents new challenges. Compared with traditional film works, short videos are shorter in duration, and whether they have the "originality" requirements of the copyright law for the protection of the object is the focus of the dispute between the parties in this case. In this case, the People's Court fully implemented the judicial policy of reasonably determining the scope and intensity of protection of intellectual property rights in different fields, and in accordance with the characteristics of copyright in literary and artistic works, the characteristics of works, creative space, etc., and full consideration of innovation in the context of "Internet+". The needs and characteristics of this case reasonably determined the scale of the originality of the short video program in this case, correctly divided the boundaries between the scope of copyright and the public domain, and fully realized the protection of intellectual property rights, the promotion of innovation, and the promotion of industrial development.

(2) **The connotation of joint work and its liability of infringement—Hebei Shanren Sculpture Co., Ltd. v. People's Government of Sanhe Town etc.**

2.1 Case Judgement Guizhou Provincial High People's Court
Case No.: (2019) No. 449 of Qianmin Final
29-07-2019
The cause of the action: copyright infringment

The parties:
Appellant (plaintiff in the first instance): Hebei Shanren Sculpture Co., Ltd.
Appellant (defendant in the first instance): Hebei Zhongding Garden Sculpture Co., Ltd.
Appellee (defendant in the first instance): People's Government of Sanhe Town, Bozhou District, Zunyi City.
Appellee (defendant in the first instance): Zunyi Zhonghecheng Agricultural Development Co., Ltd.
Appellee (defendant in the first instance): Guizhou Huilong Construction Engineering Co., Ltd.
Appellee (defendant in the first instance): Guizhou Huilong Construction Engineering Co., Ltd. Zunyi Branch.

Shanren Sculpture Company appeal and request:
the determination of the facts of original judgment was unclear and the application of the law was wrong, which led to the wrong judgment. It requested to revoke the original judgment and revise to support all the claims of Shanren Sculpture Company. The litigation costs of the first and second instance shall be borne by Zhongding Sculpture Company, Sanhe Town Government, Zhonghe Chengnong Development Company, Huilong Construction Engineering Company, and Huilong Construction Engineering Zunyi Branch. The specific reasons are as follows: 1. The infringed works determined by the court of first instance are used for social welfare undertakings. If they are removed, it will inevitably cause a large waste of social resources. Therefore, the liability for stopping the infringement and removing the sculpture is changed to payment for fair use, the facts ascertained and the applicable laws are all wrong, although the alleged infringing sculptures were placed in the Martyrs Cemetery in Sanhe Town, ×××× District, Guizhou Province (hereinafter referred to as

the Sanhe Town Martyrs Cemetery) for social welfare undertakings. But this cannot be a legitimate reason for infringing on the copyright of others. 2. The court of first instance ruled that the Sanhe Town Government and Zhongding Sculpture Company jointly paid 100,000 yuan for the use of the works were unjustified.

Zhongding Sculpture Company appeal and request:
The facts found in the original judgment were unclear and the application of law was wrong, which led to the wrong judgment. It requested to revoke the original judgment. Zhongding Sculpture Company was not liable for infringement in accordance with the law. The first and second instance litigation costs shall be borne by Shanren Sculpture Company. The specific reasons are as follows: 1. The copyright of the works involved in the case created by Shanren Sculpture Co., Ltd. cannot be exclusively enjoyed by it. The Sanhe Town Government and Huilong Construction Engineering Zunyi Branch are co-authors; 2. Zhongding Sculpture Co., Ltd. just presses Sanhe Town Government and Huilong Construction Engineering Zunyi Branch to provide the plan drawings for the construction, subjectively without intentional infringement; 3. The alleged infringing sculpture was not actually completed and has not been evaluated and appraised. The court of first instance ruled that the Sanhe Town Government and Zhongding Sculpture Company jointly paid 100,000 yuan for the use of the works, which lacked basis.

Shanren Sculpture Company sued the court of first instance:
1. According to law, the Sanhe Town Government, Zhonghe Chengnong Development Company, Huilong Construction Company, Huilong Construction Zunyi Branch and Zhongding Sculpture Company shall Immediately dismantle the infringing relief "Daoba Dajie" located in the Martyrs Cemetery in Sanhe Town;; 2. According to law, the above five defendants were ordered to publish an apology letter in the "Zunyi Daily", and Zhonghe Chengnong Development Company shall publish an apology letter in a prominent position on its company website (duration not less than 30 days) to publicly apologize and eliminate the impact; 3. Litigation fees and related costs of 70,000 yuan shall be borne by the above five defendants.

The court of first instance found out after the trial:
In December 2017, under the introduction of Yang Yun, an outsider, Shanren Sculpture Company negotiated with Zunyi Zhonghecheng Agricultural Development Company about the relief. On December 29, 2017, Mr. Yang1, Manager of the Gardening Department of Zhonghe Chengnong Kai Company, sent an email to Yang Yun, informing him about the design of the sculpture theme for the victory of the battle of the sword and target, and attached the title "Sanhe·Drawing of the sword and target" Attached, Yang Yun forwarded the email to Fan Xiaoyu, an employee of Shanren Sculpture Company on the same day. At the beginning of January 2018, after Fan Xiaoyu completed the design drawings, he discussed the design and quotation of the relief project with Yang and the Sanhe Town Government. On February 6, 7, and 8, 2018, Shanren Sculpture Company informed Yang 1 of the parameters, materials and quotation information of the sculpture via WeChat. On February 10, 2018, Shanren Sculpture Company sent a notification letter to Yang 1 via WeChat,

stating that "the project originally planned to be completed by the end of March, due to contract and payment issues, needs to apply for a 15-day extension."

On March 5, 2018, Huilong Construction Engineering Zunyi Branch (Party A) and Zhongding Sculpture Company (Party B) signed the sculpture design and installation contract. Article 7.2.1 of the contract stipulates that "Party B shall complete all the work from the design, production, installation and transportation to the completion and acceptance of all sculptures according to the contract." Article 7.2.2 stipulates that "Party B shall be liable for any dispute with a third party arising from patent, copyright, intellectual property and other related matters designed in this contract".

In May 2018, Shanren Sculpture Company found that the relief sculpture located in the Daoba martyrs cemetery in Sanhe town infringed its copyright, so it sued to the court. In the trial of the first instance, Zhongding Sculpture Company recognized that the relief sculpture involved was designed, produced and installed by him.

It was also found out that: Sanhe Town Government (the developer) and Huilong Construction Engineering Zunyi Branch (contractor) signed the construction contract and the two parties reached an agreement on the construction of the Martyrs Cemetery in Sanhe Town (Phase I) and related matters, The project site is in Sanhe Town, the planned start date is May 28, 2017 and the planned completion date is June 28, 2017. The court of first instance held that the dispute point in this case is:

1. Whether Shanren Sculpture Company own the copyright to his work of "Daoba Dajie"; 2. Whether the "Daoba Dajie" sculpture located in the Dajie Martyrs Cemetery of Sanhe Town infringed the copyright of Shanren Sculpture Company; 3. If the fact of infringement exists, how should the Sanhe Town Government, Zhonghe Chengnong Development Company, Huilong Construction Company, Huilong Construction Zunyi Branch and Zhongding Sculpture Company bear corresponding civil liabilities.

1. Regarding the first dispute point, the court of first instance held that the "Daoba Dajie" was an art work created by Shanren Sculpture Company according to the content of the negotiation with the Sanhe Town Government and Zhonghe Chengnong Development Company. In accordance with the copyright law and the regulation of implementation, the relief sculpture of "Daoba Dajie" created by Shanren Sculpture Company is a work protected by the Copyright Law and Shanren Sculpture Company shall enjoy the corresponding copyright rights.

2. Regarding the second dispute point, the court of first instance compared the "Daoba Dajie" work created by Shanren Sculpture Company (hereinafter referred to as the work involved in the case) with "Daoba Dajie" sculpture accused of infringement made by Zhongding Sculpture Company (hereinafter referred to as the alleged infringing work) and determined that two are substantially similar. The specific comparison is as follows: the work involved in the case and the alleged infringing work are both composed of three parts. ① Comparison in the first part. The first part of the works involved in the case is a brief introduction to "Daoba Dajie" and consists of relief images of three red army shaking hands with two local people; the first part of the alleged infringing work also has a text introduction of "Daoba Dajie" and relief of three red army and three local people. From the perspective of the design of the characters, one of the three red army of the work involved in the case is kneeling

on one knee, one shaking hands with the aunt of the masses and one standing with a gun; the three red army of the alleged infringing work are all standing without a gun. The crowd had a child and a man and the child carried a basket contained something. ② Comparison in the second part. The second part of the two works is composed of the relief sculpture of the battle of "Blade Target Victory" in the middle and the red curtain walls on both sides. The works involved in the case have the design of "Chinese Workers and Peasants Red Army" and the emblem of the Communist Party of China on the red curtain walls. The works are accused of infringement. The red curtain wall has no words or patterns; in the main relief part in the middle, whether it is the posture, demeanor, overlapping of the characters falling to the ground, or the prominent prominent figure in the relief XX holding the telescope in the right hand, pointing the left finger forward, and XX holding the telescope in the left hand As well as the postures of XX, Deng Ping, and XX, the alleged infringing works are basically the same as the copyrighted works involved. ③ The third part of the comparison. The third part of the two works is a relief of the staff, both of which are selected from the Long March group songs. The court of first instance held that although the first part of the two works is different in terms of expression, the relief of "Blade Target Victory" is a whole composed of three parts, and the second part of the "Blade Target Victory" battle relief is the main part of the whole work., The second part of the alleged infringing work (that is, the main part of the entire relief) is basically the same as the right work involved, but Zhongding Sculpture Company did not submit evidence that the alleged infringing work was created by him, and Zhongding Sculpture Company's statement It also recognized exposure to works created by Shanren Sculpture Company. The court of first instance found that this part of the alleged infringing work had plagiarized the right work involved in the case, that is, the alleged infringing work was Zhongding Sculpture Company without the permission of Shanren Sculpture Company. It is made on the basis of modifying and copying works created by Shanren Sculpture Company, which is substantially similar to the rights involved in the case, and infringes Shanren Sculpture Company's right to modify and copy the art works of the "Band Target". right.

3. Regarding the third dispute point, how to identify the infringers and how to bear the liability for infringement.

First, with regards to the identification of infringers, The alleged infringing work was designed and constructed by Zhongding Sculpture Company so it should be the infringer. According to the relevant provisions of the Tort Law, Zhongding Sculpture Company shall bear the corresponding tort liability. The Sanhe Town government is the contracting party of the project and has not undertaken the design of the alleged infringing sculptures and shall not be liable for the infringement. Zhonghe Chengnong Development Co., Ltd., Huilong Construction Company, and Huilong Construction Company Zunyi Branch are not the designers and construction units of the alleged infringing works, and they should not be liable for infringement.

Secondly, with regards to how Zhongding Sculpture Company should bear the liability for tort. Shanren Sculpture Company requested that the alleged infringing works be removed. According to Article 47 of the Copyright Law of the People's Republic of China, its claim complies with the law. However, the court of first instance held that the alleged infringing work was placed in the Daoba Martyrs Cemetery in Sanhe Town, forming an integral part of the entire cemetery. The alleged infringing work is used for public welfare undertakings. If they are removed, it will inevitably cause a greater waste of social resources. Therefore, the court of first instance changed responsibility which should be born by Zhongding Sculpture Company's form removing the sculpture to pay a reasonable fee for use. Regarding the amount of the fee, considering the nature of the work involved, the way of use and the time of use, the court of first instance determined that Zhongding Sculpture Company should pay 100,000 yuan for the use of the work. At the same time, the Sanhe Town government clearly stated that it would not dismantle the alleged infringing sculpture and would continue to use the sculpture for exhibition visits and education on the red revolution. That is, the Sanhe Town government and Zhongding Sculpture Company should jointly bear the use fees. Regarding Shanren Sculpture Company's claim for an apology, Zhongding Sculpture Company modified the work involved in the case without the permission of Shanren Sculpture Company, infringing on the right of modification of Shanren Sculpture Company. The above right belongs to the personal rights in the copyright. Therefore, Zhongding Sculpture Company shall bear the civil liability of eliminating the influence and apologizing. Because the alleged infringing work was located in Sanhe Town, Banzhou District, Shanren Sculpture Company's request to eliminate the impact and make an apology in the local newspaper "Zunyi Daily" should be supported. Regarding Shanren Sculpture Company's claim for compensation of 70,000 yuan for other expenses, because Shanren Sculpture Company did not provide evidence to prove its actual losses, the court of first instance considered the nature, circumstances, subjective fault and the aforementioned confirmed use fees and the reasonable expenses paid by Shanren Sculpture Company to stop the infringement, it was determined that the Sanhe Town Government and Zhongding Sculpture Company should pay 20,000 yuan to Shanren Sculpture Company as reasonable expenses.

In summary, in accordance with the provisions of Articles 3, 10, 47, 48, and 49 of the Copyright Law of the People's Republic of China, the court of first instance decided: 1. Sanhe Town Government and Hebei Zhongding Garden Sculpture Co., Ltd. shall jointly pay Hebei Shanren Sculpture Co., Ltd. use fees of 100,000 yuan and reasonable expenses of 20,000 yuan within 10 days after this judgment becomes effective; 2. Hebei Zhongding Garden Sculpture Co., Ltd. Shall apologize to Hebei Shanren Sculpture Co., Ltd. in the Zunyi Daily within 10 days after this judgment becomes effective. The content must be reviewed by the court. If Hebei Zhongding Garden Sculpture Co., Ltd. refuses to perform, the court will publish the main content of this judgment in the Zunyi Daily and the expenses shall be borne by Hebei Zhongding Garden Sculpture Co., Ltd.; 3. The remaining claims of Hebei Shanren Sculpture Co., Ltd. shall be rejected. The acceptance fee of first instance is 500 yuan, which shall be borne by Hebei Zhongding Garden Sculpture Co., Ltd.

The court of second instance:
The court of second instance believes that this case is a copyright infringement dispute case caused by sculpture design and construction. Shanren Sculpture Company

believes that the sculpture involved in the case is a work of art and Zhongding Sculpture Company, Zunyi Zhonghecheng Agricultural Development Company, Sanhe Town Government, Huilong Construction Company, and Huilong Construction Zunyi Branch jointly infringed its copyright. So Shanren Sculpture Company request them to stop the infringement, dismantle the infringing sculpture and compensate Shanren Sculpture Company for losses; Zhongding Sculpture Company, Zhonghe Chengnong Development Company, Sanhe Town Government, Huilong Construction Engineering Company and Huilong Construction Engineering Zunyi Branch separately or jointly proposed the sculpture design of Shanren Sculpture Company does not constitute a work. Even though it is a work, Shanren Sculpture Company is not the copyright owner or the sole copyright owner; The use of the sculpture involved has a legal source; there is no contact with the creative design drawings of Shanren Sculpture Company; the amount of compensation claimed by Shanren Sculpture Company has no factual and legal basis and many other defense opinions.

According to the appeal request and reasons of the parties, the dispute points in the second instance are: 1. Whether the design of sculpture involved in the case is a work of art within the meaning of the Copyright Law; 2. If the sculpture design involved is protected by copyright law, to whom does the copyright belong? 3. Whether Zhonghe Hecheng Agricultural Development Company, Sanhe Town Government, Huilong Construction Company, Huilong Construction Zunyi Branch and Zhongding Sculpture Company constitute copyright infringement and whether they should bear corresponding civil liabilities.

Regarding the first dispute point, whether the design of sculpture involved in the case is a work of art within the meaning of the Copyright Law.

Copyright is a right created in accordance with the law based on literary, artistic, and scientific works. Authors and other copyright owners enjoy copyright of their creations. According to the Article 2 of the Regulation for the Implementation of the Copyright Law of the People's Republic of China, the term "works" as referred to in the Copyright Law means intellectual creations with originality in the literary, artistic or scientific domain, insofar as they can be reproduced in a tangible form. In this case, the disputed work is computer rendering created by Shanren Sculpture Company through computer graphics software. the relief "Daoba Dajie" created by it shows the structural layout of points, lines, surfaces and various geometric figures, and is based on the history of the red revolution. The unique facial features, body proportions, colors and lines of the characters give each image a vivid form and rich expression, which reflects the originality of the author and a certain artistic beauty. It has artistic value and reproducibility and shall be the work of art protected by copyright law.

Regarding the second dispute point, the copyright ownership of the design of sculpture involved in the case.

According to the provisions of the Copyright Law and the implementation regulation, unless otherwise stipulated by the Copyright Law, the copyright shall belong to the author; Where a work is created according to the intention and under the supervision and responsibility of a legal entity or another organization, such legal entity or organization shall be the author of the work. The citizen, legal entity or organization whose name is affixed to a work shall, without the contrary proof, be the author of the work. The term "creation" as referred to in the Copyright Law means intellectual activities in which literary, artistic or scientific works are directly created. Any organizational activity, consultation, material support or other auxiliary services conducted or offered for another person's creation shall not be deemed as creation.

This court believes that the art work involved in the case was specially created by Shanren Sculpture Company for the construction of the sculpture project of the Martyrs Cemetery in Sanhe Town, a staff member of Shanren Sculpture Company, had changed the draft several times. According to Article 7 of the Interpretation of the Supreme People's Court Concerning the Application of Laws in the Trial of Civil Disputes over Copyright, the manuscripts, original scripts, lawful publications, copyright registration certificates, attestations issued by authentication institutions, contracts for acquiring rights, etc. as submitted by the parties concerned may be adopted as evidences. According to the provision, in this case, design drawing of the relief submitted by Shanren Sculpture Company can be used as preliminary evidence to prove its copyright to the design of the sculpture. In the case that Zhongding Sculpture Company did not submit the opposite evidence, it can be determined that the copyright owner of the design of the sculpture involved in the case is Shanren Sculpture Company.

Zhongding Sculpture Company advocates that the Sanhe Town Government and Huilong Construction Engineering Zunyi Branch are also co-authors. However, co-authors should have the desire and consciousness to create together and should actually participate in creative activities and make original contributions. In this case, the Sanhe Town government mainly put forward requirements and amendments. This behavior belongs to the category of ideology, which cannot directly produce art works. The design department of Shanren Sculpture Company, through its own intellectual work, specifically expresses the design requirements of the Sanhe Town Government's ideological category through painting. This expression reflects Shanren Sculpture Company's design requirements for Sanhe Town Government. The individualized understanding and result are the original expressions carried out by Shanren Sculpture Company and its behavior belongs to independent creation. Moreover, Zhongding Sculpture Company did not provide evidence to prove that the Sanhe Town Government and Huilong Construction Zunyi Branch participated in the creation activities, so it is difficult to determine that the Sanhe Town Government and Huilong Construction Zunyi Branch are co-author.

Regarding the third dispute point, whether Zhonghe Chengnong Development Company, Sanhe Town Government, Huilong Construction Company, Huilong Construction Zunyi Branch and Zhongding Sculpture Company constitute copyright infringement, and whether they should bear corresponding civil liabilities.

First of all, the work created by Shanren Sculpture Company and the alleged infringing work made by Zhongding Sculpture Company have been compared and they are substantially similar. The reasons are as follows: One is the overall comparison: the sculptures of the two works are composed of three parts. From the overall visual observation, there is no obvious difference. The second is a sub-item comparison: Although the first part of the two works is slightly different in expression techniques, they also constitute similarities; the second part is the main part of the relief of the "Daoba Dajie", which is basically the same; the third part is the relief of the staff, because the expression of the music score is unique, and the works in this case are not musical works, but works of art, so the third part does not constitute infringement. After comparison, the corresponding parts (parts 1 and 2) of the alleged infringing work and the involved right work, as well as the whole, are basically indistinguishable visually, and they are of the same height and substantially similar in composition.

Second, the identification of the infringer. According to Article 6 of Tort Law of the People's Republic of China, One who is at fault for infringement upon a civil right or interest of another person shall be subject to the tort liability. The first is for Zhongding Sculpture Company. The alleged infringing work was designed and constructed by Zhongding Sculpture Company and the composition of the alleged infringing work was substantially similar to the copyrighted work involved. Since Zhongding Sculpture Company did not submit evidence to prove that the alleged infringing work was created by him and admitted that it comes into contact with the works created by Shanren Sculpture Company, so it can be determined that the alleged infringing work has plagiarized the work of Shanren Sculpture Company. Although Zhongding Sculpture Company argued that it had no intention of subjective infringement, Zhongding Sculpture Company, as a professional sculpture producer, did not perform reasonable duty of care, knowing that Huilong Construction's Zunyi Branch did not have copyright in the works involved in the case. Without the permission of the copyright owner, Shanren Sculpture Company, the Gongzunyi branch implemented minor modifications to the works of Shanren Sculpture Company, and implemented the act of copying the works involved in the case from flat to three-dimensional, and produced and installed infringing sculptures. In the cemetery of the martyrs in Sanhe Town. The actions of Zhongding Sculpture Company violated Shanren Sculpture Company's right to modify, copy, and exhibit the fine art works of "Daoba Dajie". The second is for Zhonghe Chengnong Development Company, Sanhe Town Government, Huilong Construction Company, and Huilong Construction Zunyi Branch. Since Zhonghe Chengnong Development Company, Sanhe Town Government, Huilong Construction Company, and Huilong Construction Company Zunyi Branch have all contacted the design drawings of Shanren Sculpture Company, they are related to Zhongding Sculpture Company's infringement., In line with the constituent elements of joint infringement. According to Article 130 of the "General Principles of Civil Law": "If two or more persons jointly infringe and cause damage to others, they shall bear joint liability." According to the provisions of Zhonghe Chengnong Development Company, Sanhe Town Government, Huilong Construction Company, Huilong Construction Engineering Zunyi Branch shall bear joint and several liability for compensation.

Thirdly, whether Shanren Sculpture Company's request for the destruction of the alleged infringing work should be supported. The original intention of Shanren Sculpture Compan is to obtain reputation and economic benefits through the dissemination of the work. In this case, The loss of Shanren Sculpture Company was mainly manifested in that the infringement activities of Zhongding Sculpture Company squeezed its market share and lost the benefits obtained from the sculpture involved, but it could be compensated by paying compensation. The alleged infringing sculpture was used for public welfare undertakings and was placed in the Martyrs Cemetery in Sanhe Town, forming an integral part of the entire cemetery. If it is removed, it will inevitably cause a great waste of social resources. As a large-scale modern sculpture work, its carrier itself has high value. From the perspective of following the principle of balance of interests and the benefit of effective use of public resources, the alleged infringing sculpture should not be judged to be removed. Moreover, the Martyrs Cemetery is an important place for revolutionary traditional education and patriotism education. In order to promote core values of socialism and establish a correct view of history, nation and culture, the local government should be encouraged and supported to take advantage of the red resources to carry out the creation, production and promotion of works based on the deeds of heroes and martyrs. In this case, the owner, Sanhe Town government, made it clear that it was unwilling to remove the sculpture and would continue to use the sculpture for exhibition visit and education on the red revolution. Adhering to the principle of respecting history, protecting rights and favoring inheritance, Shanren Sculpture Company's litigation request to destroy the alleged infringing sculpture is not supported in accordance with the law.

Fourth, how to determine the amount of compensation. Article 49 of the Copyright Law stipulates: "The infringer shall, when having infringed upon the copyright or the rights related to copyright, make a compensation on the basis of the obligee's actual losses; where the actual losses are difficult to be calculated, the compensation may be made on the basis of the infringer's illegal gains. The amount of compensation shall also include the reasonable expenses paid by the obligee for stopping the act of tort." Interpretation of the Supreme People's Court Concerning the Application of Laws in the Trial of Civil Disputes over Copyright stipulates in Article 25, paragraph 2: "When determining the amount of compensation, the people's court shall take into comprehensive consideration of the type of the work, reasonable royalties, nature and consequences of the infringing act, etc." As far as this case is concerned, Shanren Sculpture Company has no evidence to prove the specific amount of economic losses it suffered due to infringement, and there is no evidence. Prove the specific amount of economic benefits obtained by Zhongding Sculpture Company due to infringement, so the determination of the amount of compensation shall apply the principle of statutory compensation according to law. The academy's comprehensive considerations: First, the work of Shanren Sculpture Company is a graphic art work. Although the shape of the sculpture has a certain originality, its artistic beauty has not yet reached a high level, the originality is low, and the number of pictures is small, and the creation time is relatively long. Short, the economic cost of creation is not high; second, the infringer obtains the Shanren Sculpture Company's work through cooperation and uses it without authorization, subjectively infringing maliciously, and is at a greater fault; third, based on the Sanhe Town Government (issuer) and Hui Hui "Construction Contract for Construction Projects" signed by Long Jiangong Zunyi Branch (contractor), "Sculpture Design, Production and Installation Contract" signed by Huilong Construction Zunyi Branch (orderer) and Zhongding Sculpture Company (contractor), The amount and payment consideration agreed in the two contracts; fourth, referring to the general profit of the sculpture industry, necessary economic compensation and other factors, determine as appropriate Zhongding Sculpture Company, Zhonghe Chengnong Development Company, Sanhe Town Government, and Huilong Construction Engineering Company, Huilong Construction Engineering Zunyi Branch shall bear the amount of compensation for infringement and reasonable expenses for safeguarding rights of 200,000 yuan.

In summary, the first-instance judgment which determined that Zhonghe Chengnong Development Company, Sanhe Town Government, Huilong Construction Company and Huilong Construction Zunyi Branch did not constitute infringement and should not bear corresponding responsibilities was incorrect. The court shall correct it according to law. The grounds for appeal of Shanren Sculpture Company were partially established and part of its appeal was supported in accordance with the law. The grounds for appeal of Zhongding Sculpture Company lacks factual and legal basis and its appeal request should be rejected.

The judgment is as follows:

1. Uphold the second and third items of the civil judgment of the Intermediate People's Court of Zunyi City, Guizhou Province (2018) Qian 03 Min Chu No. 328;
2. Change the first item of civil judgment of the Intermediate People's Court of Zunyi City, Guizhou Province (2018) Qian03 Minchu No. 328 to: Hebei Zhongding Garden Sculpture Co., Ltd., Sanhe Town Government, Zunyi Zhonghecheng Agricultural Development Co., Ltd., Guizhou Huilong Construction Engineering Co., Ltd. and Zunyi Branch of Guizhou Huilong Construction Engineering Co., Ltd. shall jointly compensate Hebei Shanren Sculpture Co., Ltd. for economic losses and reasonable expenses of RMB 200,000 within ten days from the effective date of this judgment.

If the obligation to pay money is not fulfilled within the period specified in the judgment, the interest on the debt during the delayed performance period shall be doubled in accordance with Article 253 of the Civil Procedure Law of the People's Republic of China.

This decision is final.

2.2 Analysis of the Case

1. Facts

Hebei Shanren Sculpture Co., Ltd. (hereinafter referred to as Shanren Sculpture Company) and Hebei Zhongding Garden Sculpture Co., Ltd. (hereinafter referred to as Zhongding Sculpture Company) are professional institutions engaged in sculpture design, production and installation. In December 2017, Shanren Sculpture Company and the People's Government of Sanhe Town, Bozhou District, Zunyi City, Guizhou Province (referred to as Sanhe Town Government) negotiated a cooperation in the sculpture project of the Martyrs Cemetery in Sanhe Town. Shanren Sculpture Company will complete the creation of the case. The design drawings and display panels of the work "Blade Target Great Victory" were submitted to the Sanhe Town Government for review, and were revised several times according to the request of the Sanhe Town Government, but the two parties did not finally reach an agreement. Houshanren Sculpture Company filed a lawsuit with the Intermediate People's Court of Zunyi City, Guizhou Province, claiming that the alleged infringing sculpture designed and installed by the Zhongding Sculpture Company entrusted by the Sanhe Township Government in the Mausoleum of Martyrs of the Dao Target infringed its copyright. The Intermediate People's Court of Zunyi City, Guizhou Province in the first instance decided that the Sanhe Town Government and Zhongding Sculpture Company jointly paid Shanren Sculpture Company 100,000 yuan for the use of the works and 20,000 yuan for reasonable expenditures, and Zhongding Sculpture Company apologized. Both Shanren Sculpture Company and Zhongding Sculpture Company refused to accept the decision of the first instance and filed an appeal. The Guizhou High People's Court found that the infringement was established in the second instance, but at the same time it held that the cemetery for the martyrs of the sword target is an important place for revolutionary traditional education and patriotism education. From the perspective of following the principle of balance of interests and the effectiveness of use of resources, the alleged infringement sculpture is not advisable to dismantle. Therefore, under the condition that the rights of Shanren Sculpture Company can be adequately remedied by appropriately raising the infringement compensation standard, Shanren Sculpture Company's claim to stop the infringement and dismantle the infringing sculptures is not supported. According to this, the judgment was changed to Zhongding Sculpture Company, Sanhe Town Government and others to jointly compensate Shanren Sculpture Company for infringement compensation and reasonable expenses totaling 200,000 yuan.

2. The focus of dispute

(1) Whether the sculpture design involved is a work of art within the meaning of copyright law?
(2) If the sculpture design involved is protected by copyright law, who is the copyright holder?
(3) Whether Zhonghe Chengnong Development Company, Sanhe Town Government, Huilong Construction Company, Huilong Construction Zunyi Branch, and Zhongding Sculpture Company constitute copyright infringement, and whether they should bear corresponding civil liabilities.

3. Legal rules
(1) About the definition and attribution of works
Copyright law (2010):
Article 10, paragraph 1, item (3), item (5), item (8),
Article 47, paragraph 1, item (5),
Article 48
Article 49;
"Regulations for the Implementation of the Copyright Law:
Articles 2, 3, and 4
(2) Liability for copyright infringement

Articles 7 and 25 of the "Interpretation on Several Issues Concerning the Application of Law in the Trial of Copyright Civil Dispute Cases": Manuscripts, originals, legal publications, copyright registration certificates, certificates issued by certification bodies, contracts for obtaining rights, etc. provided by the parties involved in copyright may be used as evidence."

Articles 118 and 130 of the "General Principles of the Civil Law of the People's Republic of China".

Article 130 of the "General Principles of Civil Law": "If two or more persons jointly infringe and cause damages to others, they shall bear joint liability."

4. Application of law

(1) Regarding the identification of collaborative works

The copyright belongs to the author; the work that is presided over by a legal person, represents the will of the legal person, and is responsible for the legal person, the legal person is regarded as the author; if there is no proof to the contrary, the legal person who signs the work is regarded as the author; The organization of the creation of others, the provision of advisory opinions, material conditions, or other auxiliary work are not considered creations; those who do not participate in the creation cannot become co-authors.

In this case, the Sanhe Town government mainly put forward requirements and amendments. This behavior belongs to the category of ideology and is an ideological requirement for sculpture design. It cannot directly produce art works. The design department of Shanren Sculpture Company, through its own intellectual work, specifically expresses the design requirements of the Sanhe Town Government's ideological category through painting. This expression reflects Shanren Sculpture Company's design requirements for the Sanhe Town Government. The individualized understanding and result are the original expressions carried out by Shanren Sculpture Company, and its behavior belongs to independent creation. Moreover, Zhongding Sculpture Company did not provide evidence to prove that Sanhe Town Government and Huilong Construction Zunyi Branch participated in the creation activities of the involved sculpture design, so it is difficult to determine that Sanhe Town Government and Huilong Construction Zunyi Branch are joint creations author.

(2) The issue of liability

In this case, the losses of Shanren Sculpture Company were mainly manifested in that Zhongding Sculpture Company's infringement activities squeezed its market share and lost the benefits obtained from the sculpture works involved, but it could be compensated by paying compensation. The alleged infringing sculpture was used for social welfare undertakings and was placed in the Dao Target Martyrs Cemetery in Sanhe Town, forming an integral part of the entire cemetery. If it is removed, it will inevitably result in a greater waste of social resources. As a large-scale modern sculpture work, its carrier itself has high value. From the perspective of following the principle of interest balance and the benefit of effective use of public resources, the accused of infringing sculpture should not be judged to be demolished. And the Sanhe Town Knife Target Martyrs Cemetery is an important place for revolutionary traditional education and patriotism education. In order to promote the core values of socialism and establish a correct view of history, nation, and culture, the local government should be encouraged and supported to take advantage of the red resources and to carry out the creation, production and promotion of works based on the deeds of heroes and martyrs.

5. Conclusion and significance

In recent years, the people's courts have actively incorporated the core socialist values into the entire judicial process of intellectual property rights, and have incorporated the core socialist values throughout the entire process of legal interpretation and law application. Among them, the proper trial of copyright cases involving classic revolutionary works is an important link in spreading the positive energy of judicial protection of intellectual property rights. This case is a copyright dispute involving classic revolutionary works. The second-instance judgment adheres to the principles of respecting the law, respecting rights, and respecting classics. While the judgment does not stop the infringement, it also provides relief to the right holder by increasing the infringement compensation and royalties. The effective protection of rights is fully considered, and the inheritance of classics is also vigorously taken into account, so that the results of the judgment conform to the law and the social conditions and public opinions, and the organic unity of legal, political, and social effects is achieved.

(3) **The copyrightability of interactive game and its specific play rules—Chengdu Tianxiang Interactive Technology Co., Ltd. v. Suzhou Snail Digital Technology Co., Ltd.**

3.1 Case Judgement Jiangsu High People's Court
Case number: (2018) Su Minzhong No. 1054
31-12-2019
The cause of action: Infringement Disputes

The parties:
Appellant (defendant in the first instance): Chengdu Tianxiang Interactive Technology Co., Ltd.
  Appellant (defendant in the first instance): Beijing Aiqiyi Technology Co., Ltd.
  Appellee (plaintiff in the first instance): Suzhou Snail Digital Technology Co., Ltd.

Tianxiang Company appeal and request: revoke the judgment of the first instance, send back for retrial or revise the judgment to dismiss all claims of Snail Company. The litigation costs of the first and second instance shall be borne by Snail Company.

Facts and reasons:
1. There were major flaws in the first-instance trial procedure, which violated the relevant provisions of the Civil Procedure Law. (1) Snail Company failed to clarify the litigation request in this case within the statutory time limit, which greatly damaged the litigation rights of Tianxiang Company. Until the end of the trial procedure of the first instance, Snail Company did not clarify its specific petition. The court of first

instance accepted the written materials submitted by Snail Company after the court but did not transmit it to Tianxiang Company and did not re-designate the time limit for proof. (2) The court of first instance broke the regulations on the submission of "new evidence" and allowed Snail Company to submit new evidence many times to delay the lawsuit maliciously without meeting the statutory conditions.

2. Part of the facts on which the judgment of the first instance was based is inconsistent with the actual situation. (1) There are major flaws in the authenticity of the evidence of rights submitted by Snail Company. The server of the "Tai Chi Panda 1.1.1" version involved was temporarily constructed by Snail Company and the data also came from Snail Company, which has sufficient motivation and ability to modify relevant content. (2) There are major flaws in the completeness of the evidence. The court of first instance did not include music, text, art design into the scope of comparison nor did it compare all running screens of the two games. It only compared part of the game's running dynamic screens, so its rights basis was incomplete.

3. The court of first instance holds that the gameplay rules constitute the subject matter protected by the copyright law, which is groundless and belongs to the wrong application of law. (1) Many previous judgments have confirmed that the game play rules belong to ideas and are not protected by copyright law, and the interface layout can be protected as works of art if it is original, and the infringement comparison will belong to the interface of ideas The layout is eliminated, and the pattern and color of the interface are compared. If the pattern and color are different, it cannot be regarded as a copy. (2) There was a contradiction when the court of first instance determined that it constituted an infringement of the right of adaptation. The court of first instance tried to protect the plot behind the Tai Chi Panda.

4. The amount of compensation determined by the court of first instance without ascertaining the facts of the infringement involved is extremely high. The capital exchanges and invoicing between Tianxiang Company and Iqiyi Company do not necessarily only involve the cooperation of "Hua Qiangu" and there may be other cooperation possibilities that are not suitable for disclosure. Moreover, even if the content of the work that Snail Company claims to protect exists, it only accounts for a very small proportion of the "Hua Qiangu" game, and the entire income of the "Hua Qiangu" game should not be regarded as illegal income.

During the trial of the second instance, Tianxiang Company added the following appeal opinions: 1. The inquest procedure of the court of first instance was illegal. The inspection in the first-instance procedure is that the snail company provides servers and other software and game data materials. No court experts or technical investigators participated in the inspection process, which is equivalent to entrusting the court's power to the snail company, which is not legal in terms of procedures. 2. The court of first instance found that the rules of the game belong to the basic expression of the game and there is a logical error.

Iqiyi Company appeal and request: Revoke the first-instance judgment, re-trial or revise the judgment to dismiss all claims of Snail Company, the litigation costs of the first and second instance shall be borne by Snail Company.

Facts and reasons:
1. The court of first instance violated the law and provided Snail Company with unlimited opportunities to change the lawsuit request, which deprived iqiyi Company of its right of proof and defense. 2. The court of first instance violated the law and did not specify a time limit for proof during the three-year trial period, and gave Snail Company an unlimited time limit for proof, which violated iqiyi's litigation rights. 3. In the case that Snail Company did not provide objective, true and complete evidence of the rights version and the infringement of the game version, the court of first instance determined that the game rules of the two games were substantially similar, which was an error in fact determination. 4. The game should be recognized as a computer software work. The court of first instance determined that the overall operating screen of the online game constitutes a work created in a way similar to cinematography protected by the copyright law, which is an error in fact determination and legal application. 5. The court of first instance mistakenly identified the overall running screen of the game as a work created in a way similar to cinematography and completely ignored the fact that the screens and accompanying sound of the two games were completely different. It only determined that the two games had the same rules of play and that there was an adaptation infringement. It is a one-sided determination of facts and extreme use of the law. The rules of gameplay belong to the ideological level and should not be protected by copyright law. 6. The fact determination in the court of first instance was wrong and in the absence of infringement facts, the judgment of the amount of compensation is unwarranted and all the claims of Snail Company should be rejected.

During the trial of the second instance, iQiyi Company added the following appeal opinions: 1. There was an error in the evidence of the whole case in the court of first instance. Both iQiyi Company and Tianxiang Company raised objections to the similarity comparison analysis submitted by Snail Company, but the court of first instance took it as the evidence basis for the verdict. 2. The descriptions of the game comparison rules on pages 21–61 of the first-instance judgment are all statements submitted unilaterally by Snail Company and there is no other evidence to support it and should not be used as the basis for the verdict.

Snail Company argued that:
1. The first instance of this case has made it clear that the law of the Intellectual Property Department shall be applied as the legal basis for the trial of this case. 2. The appeal grounds of Tianxiang Company and Iqiyi Company regarding the time limit for proof cannot be established. The evidence proof provided by the court of first instance to both parties is fair and just, and it can be said to be tolerant to Tianxiang Company and Iqiyi Company. 3. The Snail Company has completed the burden of proof, and Tianxiang Company prevaricates the court on the grounds that the company is limited, which is a negative hindrance to the court's collection of evidence. 4. The court of first instance found that there was an infringement after comparing the game rules of the two games, which was not inappropriate. 5. The operating income and profit amount of the game "Hua Qiangu" as determined by the court of first instance are all based on the agreement, documents and objective

documentary evidence of Tianxiang Company and iQiyi Company. The data is true and the analysis is detailed. The appeal claims of Tianxiang Company and Iqiyi Company on the amount of compensation cannot be established. 6. As a large-scale mobile game, the development cycle of "Hua Qiangu" is much lower than normal. The main reason is that it has analyzed and copied the rules of "Tai Chi Panda" of Snail Company.

In summary, Snail Company requested the rejection of the appeals of Tianxiang Company and iQiyi Company and upheld the original judgment.

The court of first instance found the facts:

1. The basic situation of the works involved

Snail Company is the copyright owner of the mobile game software of "Tai Chi Panda". According to the computer software copyright registration certificate, the development of version 1.0 of this software was completed on May 15, 2014. According to public information on the software download platform of Anzhi Market, the earliest version 1.0.9 of the Android mobile game "Tai Chi Panda" was launched on October 31, 2014, and version 1.1.1 was launched on March 19, 2015. Snail Company submitted notarization No. 1389 as evidence of the work of right.

Tianxiang Company and Iqiyi Company are the copyright holders of the mobile game software "Hua Qiangu". According to the computer software copyright registration certificate, the development of version 1.0 of this software was completed on March 6, 2015. According to public information on the software download platform of Anzhi Market, the earliest version 1.1.0 of the mobile game "Hua Qiangu" on the Android system was launched on June 19, 2015. Snail Company submitted notarization No. 2352 as evidence of the alleged infringing works. In the lawsuit, both parties confirmed that there is no difference in the running results of the two mobile games involved in the Android system version and the IOS system version. At the same time, in order to illustrate the facts that the game version of "Hua Qiangu" has changed, Snail Company submitted the game running screen video of version 1.1.1 of "Hua Qiangu" on Android system and version 1.1.1 of "Hua Qiangu" on IOS system, which are listed in notarization No. 1671 and notarizationNo. 1723 respectively.

2. The factual dispute about the objectivity of the evidence of the work of right.

1) Regarding the notarization No. 1389. Tianxiang Company and Iqiyi Company argued that the server-side corresponding to version 1.1.1 of "Tai Chi Panda" running in the Notary Certificate No. 1389 was temporarily set up for this litigation by Snail Company. The same client can change the display content by modifying the server-side data. It cannot be ruled out that the Snail Company will adjust and modify a large amount of graphic information that does not exist on the server in advance to form a running interface similar to "Hua Qiangu". The evidence is not objective.

Snail Company confirmed the fact of temporary server construction, but believed that: due to the need for proof of the historical version of the works, it could only be carried out through temporary server construction. The game client running in the notarization No. 1389 is the historical version downloaded from Anzhi Market, which is objective and has a matching degree between the client and the server. If the 1.1.1 version of the client is inconsistent with the server, the game cannot run. Therefore, its evidence accords with the requirement of objectivity.

2) No. 889 notarization provided by Snail Company. In order to indicate the source of the server-side data used to set up the server in the No. 1389 notarization, Snail Company submitted the No. 889 notarization to the court of first instance. This notarization is a video notarization of the Tai Chi Panda SVN development recording software client running content and the process of copying game server-side data files (compressed package named server96353) from it. The snail company refers to the "server96353" compressed package file as 1389. The server resource file used to build the server in the notary certificate. Snail Company claims that it is the server resource file used to build the server in the No. 1389 notarization.

Tianxiang Company and Iqiyi Company do not recognize the authenticity, legality and relevance of No. 889 notarization. It is believed that the evidence is a notarization completed at the place where the Snail Company operates and using its company computer, and the notarization does not record the cleanliness inspection of the computer used. This piece of evidence is not relevant. First of all, SVN is open source software and is under the control of Snail Company. Its data content can be modified or deleted. Therefore, the previous version of the game server data on the SVN server provided by it may be modified. Moreover, in the course of litigation, it has the possibility to modify or falsify the evidence in favor of it, so the evidence does not possess objectivity and authenticity. Secondly, all the content of notarization involves professional technical content, which requires the professional judgment of the judicial expertise agency, and cannot be directly determined by the court. Thirdly, even if the server file involved in the notarization is authentic, it cannot prove that the file in the server involved in the notarization No. 1389 is the file copied from the SVN in the notarization No. 889.

3) On-site inspection by the court of first instance. On May 2, 2017, under the supervision of the court of first instance, the staff of Snail Company used the external computer of the court of first instance to demonstrate in detail and restore the specific process of server setup and deployment through the Shanda G cloud platform. Snail Company believes that the aforementioned process of setting up a server on site restores the process of setting up a server when it runs the 1.1.1 version of Tai Chi Panda game in No. 1389 notarization.

Tianxiang Company and iQiyi Company believe that the aforementioned server construction process cannot guarantee the authenticity and objectivity. First of all, the data saved in SVN can be deleted and changed by itself as mentioned above. Second, the third-party software downloaded from the Internet by Snail Company cannot confirm whether the version is correct or whether the content has been inserted into other content. If the software itself has problems or has been tampered with, the authenticity of the restoration process cannot be guaranteed.

Third, during the construction process, Snail Company copied many configuration files and script files, which exactly contained the similarities of the two games advocated by Snail company. The content and actual role of these documents cannot be determined during the investigation. In the process of restoring the server, there are a lot of operations such as inputting, importing scripts and configuration files, installing third-party software, and every link may insert undetected or other intentional codes and values. Fourth, the technical issues involved in on-site inspections require people with professional knowledge to judge in a professional environment. Snail Company's conclusion on server recovery relies on a large number of technical opinions and must be made by a specialized agency or a person with expertise.

4) In order to prove that in the case of running on the same client, the display content of the client can be changed by changing the content of the server, Tianxiang Company submitted the No. 57 judicial appraisal opinion issued by the Shanghai Oriental Computer Judicial Appraisal Institute.

Regarding the aforementioned evidence and the objectivity dispute between the two parties regarding the evidence of No. 1389 notarization, the court of first instance judged as follows:

1. As for SVN evidence, according to notarization No. 889, the SVN system has preserved the development content of Tai Chi Panda since the establishment of the game, with as many as 150,000 records. It is true that information such as log content and log time in the SVN system server can be tampered with by specific technical means.

However, the court of first instance held that, as a professional game developer, Snail Company used the SVN system to strictly manage the software development data involved in a single game development project. If it tampered with evidence in this case, and modified the SVN time record and corresponding log content, it would face the whole The risk of dirty reading of data in the mobile game software development system of "Tai Chi Panda", that is, the problem of invalid data reading. In the absence of preliminary evidence or other facts showing that there is a modification, the court of first instance recognizes the SVN attached to the Notary Certificate No. 889 The objectivity of the server data resources extracted in the system.

3. Comparison of game works between "Tai Chi Panda" and "Hua Qiangu"

Snail Company asserted that the game "Hua Qiangu" is substantially similar to the game "Tai Chi Panda" in terms of game structure, gameplay rules, numerical content, release rhythm and software documentation, and submitted relevant comparison documents. The court of first instance organized the two parties conducted a comparison.

Part 1: Game Structure

Snail Company advocates that its game structure includes four parts: battle function, expansion function, growth function and launch function. The battle function can be divided into PVP (player vs. player) and PVE (player vs. environment). The expansion function is divided into interaction, activity and shopping mall. The growth function is divided into the protagonist, equipment system and the Valkyrie system. The launch function is divided into novice guidance, function opening, colorful gift packs and level restrictions. The game "Hua Qiangu" uses basically the same game structure. The Snail Company submitted a comparison chart of the overall game structure it produced and believed that all 39 specific gameplay systems of "Hua Qiangu" came from "Tai Chi Panda". Upon investigation by the court of first instance, the content required for comparison only contained 29 gameplay systems so it was deemed that it advocated 29 gameplay systems.

In this regard, Tianxiang and iQiyi believe that: First of all, the game structure is an ideology which cannot be protected; Secondly, Tianxiang Company submitted the game structure of a Three Kingdoms theme card game "Let go of the Three Kingdoms" released by an outsider (Beijing Babel Times Technology Co., Ltd.) in 2013, and believes that the game also adopts the same game structure and specific gameplay. The game structure advocated by Snail Company is the industry-wide content, not its original creation.

Part 2: Gameplay rules

The expressions of the gameplay rules that Snail Company advocates for protection include: 1. The layout of the screenshots of each gameplay system interface in the aforementioned game structure and the content of the gameplay information reflected; 2. The specific gameplay rules summarized by operating the game. Snail company submitted detailed comparison opinions of a total of 29 gameplay systems mentioned above as well as the three gameplay system entrances: the main interface of the game, the experience (practice) interface and the copy selection interface.

Part 3: Numerical content

In addition to the 47 pieces of equipment attribute values mentioned above, Snail Company advocated that the numerical design of the character attribute enhancement of the spirit pets in the game "Hua Qiangu" after evolving to a certain level copied the design of the Valkyrie in "Tai Chi Panda", and submitted No. 7897 notarization. The notarization is performed on the page of the mobile game home website. The page contains the value of Valkyrie (spirit pet) in the two games. Upon investigation, the court of first instance found that the content of the notarized webpage could not correspond to the notarized game video involved in the case, so this part of the facts was rejected.

Part 4: Delivery rhythm

Snail Company believes that there are two main aspects to the game release rhythm: one is the rhythm of the user's exposure to the game functions, which mainly includes the function opening rules, that is, the rules for different gameplay in the game to be opened to the players; the second is the rhythm of users' growth, which mainly includes restrictive delivery rules and so on. Upon investigation by the court of first instance, they were all statements made by Snail Company regarding its design principles and design process, and no further evidence was submitted for verification.

Part 5: Software documentation

4. Comparison between "Tai Chi Panda" and "Let go of the Three Kingdoms"

Tianxiang Company advocates that the game "Tai Chi Panda" has completely copied the structure, interface and rules of the game "Let go of the Three Kingdoms", so it is not original. It submitted No. 73629 notarization and No. 87000 notarization to prove the content of "Let go of the Three Kingdoms".

The court of first instance organized a comparison between the two parties and found that: 1. In the No. 73629 notarization, the game "Let go of the Three Kingdoms" was downloaded on July 6, 2016 as its commercial version at that time. In the court hearing, Tianxiang Company confirmed that the game version in the video was the latest version at the notarization time, so it cannot be used as evidence of a complete prior work; 2. Even though the relevant content of No. 73629 notarization can be confirmed in No. 87000 notarization, most of the content of the comparison does not constitute similarity: (1) From the perspective of the interface layout, the interface of brave store, arena, honor store, diamond store, skills, star refining, equipment refining, runes, guilds, chat and Valkyrie in "Tai Chi Panda" is significantly different from the interface of the corresponding gameplay in "Let go of the Three Kingdoms". (2) From the perspective of gameplay rules, there is no direct correspondence of the gameplay of black market and backpack between "Tai Chi Panda" and "Let go of the Three Kingdoms". (3)The equipment enhancement interface of "Tai Chi Panda" is similar to the Valkyrie enhancement interface of "Let go of the Three Kingdoms", but one is to strengthen the equipment used by the protagonist and the other is to strengthen the character who goes on the battle with the protagonist. They are not the same. 3. The first charge of "Tai Chi Panda" is basically similar to the corresponding gameplay interface in "Let go of the Three Kingdoms" and the gameplay is also similar. The investment plan of "Tai Chi Panda" is basically similar to the corresponding gameplay value in "Let go of the Three Kingdoms", and the interface has a certain degree of similarity.

5. The Claim of Tianxiang Company on the unique design of "Flower Thousand Bone"

Tianxiang Company advocates that the plot design, level design, character design, prop design, game scene design and art design in the game "Hua Qiangu" are different from those of "Tai Chi Panda" and its design content is mainly derived from the novel "Hua Qiangu". Tianxiang Company submitted the No. 81793 notarization and the introduction to the unique design of "Hua Qiangu". The notarization contains 10 recorded plot animations from the 1.1.0 version of "Hua Qiangu" launched on June 25, 2015.

Snail Company recognizes that the aforementioned IP elements (story background), music and art in the game "Hua Qiangu" are different from those of "Tai Chi Panda", but believes that these contents are not protected in this case and therefore have no relevance to this case.

6. Other facts related to the allegation of infringement in this case

(1) On August 24, 2015, searching on Sina Weibo with "Tai Chi Panda Huaqiangu" as a keyword, some netizens commented as follows: "It is indeed almost the same...the Kung Fu Panda played by my cousin is so similar to the Hua Qiangu I played", "The Hua Qiang mobile game is extremely similar to Tai Chi Panda..." etc.

(2) The current running situation of the game "Hua Qiangu".

In the lawsuit, Tianxiang Company submitted No. 12426, No. 12427, and No. 12428 notarization to prove that the fact that Snail Company accused of infringement of the game "Hua Qiangu" in this case no longer exists.

The holding of the court of first instance:

1. The overall composition of the dynamic picture of the game "Tai Chi Panda" is a work created in a way similar to cinematography

In this case, Snail Company advocated that the entire game involved should be protected as other works stipulated in Article 3 (9) of the Copyright Law of the People's Republic of China (hereinafter referred to as the Copyright Law). Tianxiang Company and Iqiyi Company believe that, The Copyright Law does not make special categorization provisions for game works. The essence of game work is computer software work. Even if there are elements that can be protected by copyright in its running screen, the game screen cannot be protected as a whole, and it does not belong to works created in a way similar to cinematography, let alone other works stipulated by the Copyright Law. The court of first instance held that:

1) The overall running screen of the online game is the expression form of overall work.

First of all, the essence of online games is a collection of computer software programs (including server-side programs and client-side programs) and game information data (pictures, music, text, etc.). This essence determines that online games as a composite work presents two forms of expression. One is a collection of static computer code and information data and the other is a dynamic audiovisual output presented by the game software program in the intelligent terminal controlled by the player, and both can be copied in a tangible form. It can be seen that the overall picture of the network game finally displayed on the screen is driven by its computer program and its text, music, pictures, audio, video and other copyrightable elements are used to reflect and serve the gameplay and game rules. The overall running picture is the complete presentation of online game works and it is also the overall work form that players recognize and perceive.

Secondly, the elements and contents of the work that Snail Company claimed to protect in this case are game structure and game rules. Most of the foregoing content comes from the part embodied by the game as a whole work, and both parties in the litigation also believe that only the comparison of the overall program code of the computer software cannot judge and solve the substantial similarity of the foregoing content and it was confirmed that the two games used different game development engines. Therefore, in this case, the court of first instance, in accordance with the claims and evidence of the snail company, used the continuous dynamic images formed after the game was run as the form of expression of the online game "Tai Chi Panda".

2) The running screen of "Tai Chi Panda" game as a whole constitutes a work created in a way similar to cinematography as prescribed in Article 3 (6) of the Copyright Law.

First of all, Article 2 of the Regulation for the Implementation of the Copyright Law of the People's Republic of China "(hereinafter referred to as the Regulation for the Implementation of the Copyright Law) stipulates: "The term "works" as referred to in the Copyright Law means intellectual creations with originality in the literary, artistic or scientific domain, insofar as they can be reproduced in a tangible form." The "Tai Chi Panda" is a large-scale ARPG (action role-playing game). From the perspective of its overall screen performance, the design is beautiful and the gameplay level is rich. It contains a lot of intellectual achievements of the game design team. From the evidence of SVN record submitted by Snail Company, it can be clearly seen that it took more than one year for the game from the end of 2013 to the development of the notarized and preserved rights version, and more than 90,000 development records were formed. The work formed through the aforementioned development process is the crystallization of the wisdom of the main creators' labor and teamwork, and belongs to the original work in the field of art and science stipulated by the Copyright Law. It took more than one year from the project approval at the end of 2013 to the completion of development, and more than 90,000 development records were formed. The work formed through the aforementioned development process is the crystallization of the wisdom of the main creators' labor and teamwork, which belongs to the original work in the field of art and science stipulated by the Copyright Law.

Secondly, Article 4(11) of the Regulation stipulates "cinematographic works and works created by a process analogous to cinematography" means works which are recorded on some material, consisting of a series of images, with or without accompanying sound, and which can be projected with the aid of suitable devices or communicated by other means. Compared with video products, cinematographic works have higher requirements on the originality of the contents presented in their continuous pictures, which requires a certain plot. As mentioned above, from the perspective of its performance, the overall picture of "Tai Chi Panda" is a "continuous dynamic image" presented on the screen with the continuous operation of the player, which conforms to the definition of works created by a process analogous to cinematography. Furthermore, the gameplay settings of ARPG games are storytelling, that is, they mainly construct a virtual world with rich connotation, in which players can experience a series of events and plots such as role selection, pet development, growth and battle, providing an immersive audio-visual experience which is similar to the appreciation experience of "cinematographic works. In addition, as a mobile game, "Tai Chi Panda" also sets up a novice guide part that compulsory player operation, automatic battle during battle, automatic path finding and other game mandatory settings or automatic settings. In these Settings, the player has a very low degree of operation for the game, which makes the nature of the picture presented by the game is more similar to cinematographic works. On the other hand, with regard to another element "are recorded on some material", according to Article 2 of Berne Convention for the Protection of Literary and Artistic Works, the expression "literary and artistic works" shall include every production in the literary, scientific and artistic domain, whatever may be the mode or form of its expression. The essence of the description of works created in a way similar to cinematography in Article 2(1) of the aforementioned convention lies in the form of work rather than the method of creation. Therefore, the court of first instance held that as long as the performance of the work meets the originality requirements of works created in a way similar to cinematography, its production method should not be an obstacle to the quality of the work.

In summary, the overall dynamic screen of the game "Tai Chi Panda" is original. The overall running screen of the game can be recognized as works created by a process analogous to cinematography and there is no need to recognize it as other works under the Copyright Law.

2. The specific presentation of the gameplay rules in the overall picture of the game "Tai Chi Panda" constitutes the subject matter of copyright protection.

1) The rules of gameplay

First of all, the copyright law does not protect abstract ideas and methods, only the concrete expression of ideas. The original expression of game rules in online games can be protected by copyright law to a certain extent. To distinguish between the corresponding gameplay rules in the game work is thought or expression, it should be seen whether these gameplay rules belong to a general description or whether they are specific enough to produce a unique enjoyment experience perceiving the source of a particular work. If it is specific to this level where it is enough to reach the critical point of thought and expression, which can be regarded as expression. Specifically, the gameplay system design of the "Tai Chi Panda" involved in the case includes four parts: battle, growth, expansion and delivery systems. When describing each system, you can use the method of what gameplay function the system mainly implements. At this point, the aforementioned content should belong to the ideological part of the rules of gameplay and should not be monopolized by the author of the work. However, when further specific to each specific gameplay setting in the aforementioned system and the game interface design on which it depends, a careful judgment must be made. In this case, Snail Company claimed that the scope of comparison was specific to the basic layout of the game interface, content and detailed description of the gameplay. The court of first instance held that through the game interface in the continuous dynamic image of the game, the game designer expressed the specific gameplay rules of a single game system either through straightforward text in the interface or through the continuous game operation interface so that the player can clearly perceive and carry out interactive operations during the operation of the game, which is expressive. As mentioned above, in ARPG video games, the role selection, growth, battle and other gameplay settings are inherently narrative, relying on the detailed gameplay rules presented on the game interface, similar to the detailed movie plot. In the process of game development, the expression of the rules of the game is implemented by drawing and designing the game interface, which has a certain similarity with the production and communication of the plot based on the script in the film creation process. It can be said that the detailed game rules embodied in the design of the game interface constitute a specific way of presenting the rules of the game play and it is a fully described structure that constitutes the expression of the work.

Secondly, most of the specific presentation of the gameplay rules of "Tai Chi Panda" are original. From the current situation of the industry, the design and development of online games, especially ARPG mobile games, has gradually shown a trend of modularization. That is, the development and design of the overall gameplay system of a new game often does not start from scratch but is based on the existing mature individual gameplay system Therefore, it is obvious that "Tai Chi Panda" does not have a monopoly on a certain gamerule system itself. However, in this case, through the evidence provided by Tianxiang Company and the investigation of the court of first instance, the vast majority of the specific presentation of the aforementioned gamerules that Snail Company claimed in the game "Tai Chi Panda" does not exist in the game "Let go of the Three Kingdoms" so the court of first instance believes that the rules of gameplay of "Tai Chi Panda" can be considered as original.

Thirdly, when determining the scope of copyright protection, non-original expression, limited expressions and public domain expressions should be filtered out of the scope of protection. In this case, after comparison by the court of first instance, the basic interface layout and corresponding gameplay of "First charge" and "investment plan" in The game of tai Chi Panda appeared in the game of "Let go of the Three Kingdoms", which is not original and should be excluded. As for Tianxiang Company advocates the layout design of "Tai Chi Panda" is the common interface layout and composite interface layout, including vertical list, horizontal square, nine square grid, TAB, pop-up box, and vertical list combination, horizontal square combination, horizontal TAB combination, which are functional interface layouts and should not be protected. The court of first instance held that the aforementioned layout design was indeed a common layout design for mobile games, especially horizontal screen mobile games. However, as analyzed by the court of first instance, what Snail Company claims to protect in this case was not the common layout design itself, but the specific expression that includes the basic layout, content, and detailed gameplay. Therefore, Tianxiang Company's defense on this point shall not be adopted by the court of first instance. Regarding the opinion of Tianxiang Company that the the main interface and battle interface of "Tai Chi Panda" are common interface for special scenes in mobile games, the court of first instance held that mobile games are limited by the screen space and operating habits of players. In the common design of the main interface, there will be a layout where the bottom row is mostly functional area buttons and the left and right sides are vertical buttons. In the common design of the battle interface, the left and right bottom will appear. They are the layout of joysticks and skill keys. So this part of the content belongs to limited expression and public domain expression, Snail Company does not enjoy the exclusive copyright of the aforementioned design itself. However, the specific gameplay and connotation corresponding to the gameplay buttons and icons in the functional area, whether there are other characters and arrangement in the battle interface, the number of skill keys and design space, are not limited expressions.

2) Game structure, numerical content, delivery rhythm and software documentation
First of all, the game structure belongs to the idea of abstracting the game, which is not the subject matter protected by the copyright law; secondly, the numerical content has been reflected in the specific presentation of the game rules and will

not be reviewed separately; thirdly, the content of the release rhythm is the statement of the Snail Company on its design principles and design process. Even if the relevant facts are established, it can be proved to a certain extent that the similarities between the two games are not coincidental and there is no need to separately protect them under copyright law.; finally, Regarding computer software documents, Snail Company claimed that the pictures of "Tai Chi Panda" were used in the "Hua Qian Gu" document, and the essence of its claim is to prove that before the "Hua Qian Gu" computer software copyright registration and actual release, " "Hua Qian Gu" has already contacted "Tai Chi Panda". And it is also a plagiarism based on the analysis of the structure and details of the gameplay of "Tai Chi Panda". The relevant infringement content will be specifically identified in the game rules part, so this part will no longer be a separate infringement determination.

3. The specific presentation of the gameplay rules and its selection, arrangement and combination of "Hua Qiangu" use the basic expression of "Tai Chi Panda" as a whole, and on this basis, certain art, music, animation, text, etc. The re-creation of the content violates the right of adaptation enjoyed by the copyright owner.

(1) The specific presentation of the gameplay rules and its selection, arrangement and combination of "Hua Qiangu" substantively utilize the basic expression of "Tai Chi Panda".

The development of version 1.0 of "Tai Chi Panda" was completed on May 15, 2014 and its earliest online release on the Anzhi market was October 31, 2014, which was much earlier than the registration time of the software copyright of "Hua Qiangu". It can also be known from the contents of the registration documents that Tianxiang Company and iQiyi Company were fully exposed to the content of the game works of "Tai Chi Panda" before creating the game "Hua Qiangu".

Regarding the question of whether they are substantially similar: the two ARPG mobile games involved in the case both have a huge and complex gameplay system. To determine whether the subsequent game actually uses the overall expression of the previous game's rules, the overall gameplay rule system should be compared. First, determine whether the specific presentation of a single gameplay system are identical or substantially similar, and then see whether the overall selection, arrangement, and combination of a single gameplay system in the overall game architecture are substantially similar. The overall judgment should not only consider the number of individual gameplay systems that are substantially similar, but also consider the degree of influence of different gameplay systems on the game experience, whether it is the focus of game design, game profitability and other factors, to make a comprehensive judgment.

In this case, among the 39 gameplay systems of the game structure of "Hua Qiangu", gameplay 1, the gold coin copies 1 and 2 of gameplay 3, the competition and exchange part of gameplay 8, gameplay 17, 24–25, 27, 29, 31–32, 34, 36, 38–39, 41–42, 44–45, 48–49, a total of 20 gameplay systems have the same or similar basic layouts of the primary and secondary interfaces. The detailed gameplay information transmitted by the interface and the gameplay rules obtained through the operation of the game are highly similar. The basic layout and gameplay information of gameplay

5 and 11 are similar. Among them, gameplay 1, 3, 8, 29, 31, 32, 34, 36, 38, 39, 41, 42, 44 are the core gameplays of ARPG game action and role-playing growth. The seven main gameplays in the core area of the two games on the main interface are all substantially similar and have a one-to-one correspondence. The pricing for purchasing virtual currency and other gift packages in the two game malls is also the same and the novice guidance part of the game opening part is highly similar. In addition, judging from the arrangement and combination of the aforementioned gameplay systems, the two games have made most similar integration arrangements for gameplay entrances in the main interface, campaign (experience) interface, and experience (practice) interface.

Tianxiang Company and Iqiyi Company believe that the evidence of Snail Company is incomplete. There are still many gameplay rules and interfaces, such as the switching method of the god of war and the interface of the remaining chapter copies, and the value of the characters and battles in the "Tai Chi Panda" game are not presented in the notarized video. The court of first instance held that: judging from the content of the video, most of the gameplay content in the main interface has been involved.

During the litigation process, Snail Company has also extracted the server-side program and data resources of the corresponding version from its company's SVN system and set up a server on the computer of the court to re-run the Android 1.1.1 version of Tai Chi Panda for comparison, that is, it has submitted a complete version for comparison. However, during the on-site inspection, Tianxiang Company and iQiyi Company strongly objected to the objectivity of the server construction method, which made the comparison impossible. And when the court of first instance asked whether there is a method different from the plaintiff to a mobile client platform, Tianxiang Company replied that it was unable to judge whether there were other methods. Therefore, the court of first instance rejected the claims of Tianxiang Company and iQiyi Company regarding incomplete evidence of rights on the basis of determining the objectivity of the on-site server establishment.

As far as infringement comparison is concerned, Snail Company has submitted No. 2352 notarized video as evidence of infringing works. In the litigation, the court of first instance required Tianxiang Company to provide the server-side resource data of the allegedly infringing version of the game "Hua Qiangu" and set up the server in the same way. Tianxiang Company replied that the company has not kept the server resource data of the corresponding version due to a long time. However, the court of first instance noted that the case was filed in August 2015. At this time, the alleged infringement version of the game "Hua Qiangu" in the case was its normal commercial version, which must save complete game server-side program code and data resources, that is, when the case entered the litigation, Tianxiang Company should still keep the relevant data intact. Now it claims that it cannot provide it and there is no reasonable reason. Under this circumstance, the court of first instance held that in the process of designing, developing and implementing the game rules of "Hua Qiangu", it was not just a reference to the related gameplay of "Tai Chi Panda" or to innovate and re-innovate on the basis of it but it is the unidentified copying and duplication of the overall game rules design of "Tai Chi Panda", which goes far beyond the scope of fair use and constitutes copyright infringement.

Combined with the fact that the elements and interfaces of the Tai Chi Panda game are used in the computer software copyright registration documents of the "Flower Thousand Bone" game, as well as the fact that there are many similarities in text details and design defects in the game interfaces of both parties, it is believed that based on the current situation Evidence is sufficient to judge that in the process of designing, developing and implementing the game rules of the game "Flower Thousand Bone", it is not just a reference or reference to the game-related gameplay of "Tai Chi Panda", or to innovate and redesign based on it., But the unidentified copying and duplication of the content of the overall game rule design of "Tai Chi Panda", which goes far beyond the scope of fair use and constitutes copyright infringement.

(2) The game "Hua Qiangu" has undergone a certain degree of re-creation in art, music, and animation.

In this case, Snail Company claimed that Tianxiang Company and Iqiyi Company had infringed on its reproduction right, adaptation right and information network dissemination right. In this regard, the court of first instance held that: Article 10 (1) of the Copyright Law stipulates that the right of reproduction, that is, the right to produce one or more copies of the work by means of printing, Xeroxing, rubbing, sound recording, video recording, duplicating, or re-shooting, etc.; Article 10 (1) (14) stipulates that the right of adaptation, that is, the right to modify a work for the purpose of creating a new work of original creation; The key to distinguishing the right of reproduction and the right of adaptation is whether the alleged infringing work created a new work based on the basic expression of the original work.

In this case, the IP of the game "Hua Qiangu" comes from the TV series of the same name. It can be seen from the dynamic screen of the overall operation of the game, its plot animation, the level name, art scene corresponding to the plot design, the role of the player, the name and art image of the spirit pet, the name of the NPC, the name and art image of various props, the main interface scene, the name of the plot scene, the name of the practice scene and the art screen, the character design, the skill art effect, animation special effects, UI button design, UI icon design, loading page and switching page design, sound effect design, AI design and other designs are different from "Tai Chi Panda". The content and elements of this part are created based on the TV series and novel work of the same name "Hua Qiangu", so the player can recognize the difference from the original work to a certain extent from the appearance. The aforementioned creative act was implemented on the basis of the basic expression of the original game play rules. From the current legal provisions, the act is more like an act within the control of the right of adaptation. Therefore, the court of first instance found that the actions of Tianxiang Company and Iqiyi Company infringed Snail Company's right to adapt the original work. Regarding the infringement of reproduction right and information network dissemination right claimed by Snail Company, within the scope of the same claim, the infringement of reproduction right and adaptation right cannot be established at the same time. The information network dissemination right controls the act of providing works to the public through the information network. In this case, Tianxiang Company and Iqiyi Company did not implement the act and their act of providing infringing adaptations to the public fell within the scope of the right of adaptation. Therefore, the court of first instance no longer supported the two claims of Snail Company.

4. The civil liability of Tianxiang Company and iQiyi Company

Article 47 (6) of the Copyright Law stipulates that, exploiting a work by means of exhibition, making cinematographic productions or a means similar to making cinematographic productions, or by means of adaptation, translation, annotation, etc. without the permission from the copyright owner, he shall bear the civil liability for such remedies as ceasing the infringing act, eliminating the effects of the act, making a public apology or paying compensation for damages, depending on the circumstances:

In this case, the Snail Company demanded that Tianxiang Company and iQiyi Company immediately stop the infringement, that is, stop adapting the game "Tai Chi Panda" and remove all the client versions of "Hua Qiangu" currently available for download in the software application store, but In the litigation, Snail Company confirmed that the game "Hua Qiangu" has been iteratively updated and the content of version 1.8.0 released online on January 19, 2016 basically does not contain the content that Snail Company alleged infringement in this case. It is within the acceptable range of Snail Company and Snail Company did not again prove that there are infringing content in the current commercial version of the game "Hua Qiangu". Therefore, the court of first instance required Tianxiang Company and Iqiyi Company to stop adapting its rights. The work and the appeal of disseminating the infringing adapted work to the public are supported, and the content has been fulfilled by Tianxiang Company and Iqiyi Company, and the other claims of Snail Company on stopping the infringement are not supported.

Therefore, the court of first instance required Tianxiang Company and iQiyi Company to stop adapting their copyrighted works and provide them to the public. The petition for disseminating the infringing adapted work is supported, and the content has been fulfilled by Tianxiang Company and iQiyi Company, and the other claims of Snail Company on stopping the infringement are not supported.

Regarding Snail's request for Tianxiang Company and iqiyi Company to eliminate the impact, Tianxiang Company and iqiyi Company used their overall gameplay rules expressions without their permission. The two games have also caused misunderstanding among many players. It has caused a certain degree of influence in the common competitive market of both parties. The court supports Snail Company's request to ask Tianxiang Company and iQiyi Company to eliminate the influence.

Regarding the losses that Tianxiang Company and iQiyi Company should compensate: Snail Company maintains that the infringing party's illegal gains shall be used as the basis for calculation and the infringed party's losses shall be used as a reference. Regarding the profit from infringement, in accordance with the agreement between the two parties, four times the sum of the special value-added tax invoices issued by them is the total infringement income of Tianxiang Company and Iqiyi

Company. On the other hand, the total recharge turnover of "Hua Qian Gu" from June 2015 to March 2016 presented by the "Transaction Plan (Revised Draft)" and the profit margin in 2015 and 2016 presented by the "Second Reply Announcement" can be used to calculate the infringement profit of the game.

In this regard, Tianxiang Company believes that it cannot be ruled out that Tianxiang Company and iQiyi Company have other business transactions other than the "Hua Qian Gu" mobile game. There is no factual basis for judging the infringement income of the "Hua Qian Gu" mobile game only from the transaction of funds. Secondly, even if the relevant amount is indeed due to the occurrence of the "Hua Qian Gu" mobile game, it is not infringement income. Even if the content of the work claimed by the Snail Company in this case exists, it only accounts for a small proportion of the "Hua Qian Gu" game. The overall revenue of the game "Hua Qian Bone" should not be regarded as infringement revenue. Iqiyi added that the number of value-added tax invoices should not be used as the requested amount. According to the relevant tax laws of my country, only the actual deduction of value-added tax invoices can reflect the actual transaction between the two parties. Part of the special value-added tax invoice issued by the Tianxiang Company to Iqiyi Company was not actually deducted. The profit shown in the "Transaction Plan (Revised Draft)" and "Second Reply Announcement" has nothing to do with this case.

The court of first instance held that: First of all, according to the "Transaction Plan (Revised Draft)", the game recharge flow data of "Hua Qian Gu" is not directly recorded as Tianxiang Company's main business income. It needs to be recognized as business income after deducting the corresponding channel costs or sharing proportionally with the operator under different operating modes. Therefore, Snail's claim that the profit is calculated directly based on the recharge flow value and the revenue profit rate is not accurate; secondly, the relevant recharge flow data shown in the "Transaction Plan (Revised Draft)" not only involves The operating data of the defendant Tianxiang Company in this case also involves the operating income of Chengdu Tianxiang Interactive Digital Entertainment Co., Ltd., an outsider. Therefore, based on the aforementioned claims and evidence of Snail Company, It is impossible to determine exactly that Tianxiang Company and Iqiyi Company constitute infringement and make profit by providing the game work of "Hua Qian Gu" in this case. Thirdly, the "Special Audit Report of Suzhou Jinding Certified Public Accountants Co., Ltd." shows the decrease in net income of the game "Tai Chi Panda" since July 2015, but considering that online games have their specific market life cycle after they are launched, it cannot be determined The decrease in revenue was due to the launch of the game "Hua Qian Bone". Therefore, in this case, there is no definitive evidence to determine the actual loss of the right holder or the illegal gains of the infringer. The court of first instance combined the evidence in the case and comprehensively considered the following factual factors to determine the amount of compensation in this case:

(1) Time point of calculation: According to the claims of Tianxiang Company, the 1.8.0 version of the game "Hua Qian Gu" released on January 19, 2016 has undergone multiple updates and a big difference from the game "Tai Chi Panda" involved. The snail company also recognizes this opinion. So the launch time of the game "Hua Qian Gu" is from June 2015 to January 2016 as the estimated time interval.

(2) The funds in the bank accounts of both parties and the transaction data shown in the issuance of value-added tax invoices. From July 2015 to January 2016, Tianxiang Company paid iQiyi Company in two instalments on November 5, 2015 totaling 715,413.68 yuan, and the purposes were all marked as settlement payments.

During the aforementioned period, Tianxiang Company issued a total of 26 special value-added invoices to Iqiyi Company, with a total value of 16,917,299.33 yuan. Tianxiang certified 47 special value-added invoices issued by iQiyi, with a total value of 40,871,859.22 yuan. From the "<Huaqiangu> Mobile Online Game Cooperation Agreement", it can be seen that the actual amount of share paid by Tianxiang Company to iQiyi Company multiplied by 4 is the total game revenue of the channel part of the game operated by Tianxiang Company. The total amount of special value-added tax invoices issued multiplied by 4 is the total revenue shared by both parties for game operations.

Multiply the amount of funds in the aforementioned bank account by 4 to get 28,616,454.72 yuan; multiply the total value-added tax invoice issued by Tianxiang to iqiyi company by 4 to get 67,669,197.32 yuan, During the aforementioned period, Tianxiang Company issued a total of 26 special value-added invoices to Iqiyi Company, with a total value of 16,917,299.33 yuan. Tianxiang certified 47 special value-added invoices issued by iQiyi, with a total value of 40,871,859.22 yuan. From the "<Huaqiangu> Mobile Online Game Cooperation Agreement", it can be seen that the actual amount of share paid by Tianxiang Company to iQiyi Company multiplied by 4 is the total game revenue of the channel part of the two parties' game operations by Tianxiang Company. The total amount of special value-added tax invoices issued multiplied by 4 is the total revenue shared by both parties for game operations.

Multiply the amount of funds in the aforementioned bank account by 4 to get 28,616,454.72 yuan; multiply the total value-added tax invoice issued by Tianxiang to iqiyi company by 4 to get 67,669,197.32 yuan, the total amount of special value-added tax invoices issued by Tianxiang and certified by iqiyi company multiplied by 4 is 163,487,436.88 yuan, and the two items total 23,115,6634.2 yuan.

The "'Huaqiangu' Mobile Online Game Cooperation Agreement" stipulates that after the two parties have checked the operating income, according to the actual monthly payment amount and the share ratio between the two parties, confirm the amount of money that the two parties need to pay each other and issue special invoices for equal value of 6% value-added tax within 7 working days. And within 45 working days after receiving the corresponding invoice, the payment will be paid to the special account designated by both parties. However, the evidence in the case shows that there is a big difference between the aforementioned bank account data and the data of the special value-added tax invoice. According to the situation of Tianxiang Company disclosed in the "Transaction Plan (Revised Draft)", Tianxiang Company and iQiyi Company did not have any other major business transactions except for the IP sharing of the game involved. At the same time, taking into account the situation of the recharge flow of the game "Hua Qiangu" involved, The court of first instance considered the aforementioned value-added tax invoice data of 231,156,634.22 yuan as the basic consideration of the total game share of both parties, that is, the total unshared game revenue of the operating channel part of the Tianxiang Company is calculated as 163,487,436.88 yuan, and iQiyi Company is responsible for the unshared amount of the operating channel part. The total revenue from the game is calculated at 67,669,197.32 yuan.

(3) The income profit rate and specific estimated profit indicated in the "Second Reply Announcement".

a. Revenue and profitability data. According to the "Second Reply Announcement", the profit margin of the target company of "Hua Qiangu" in 2015 was 13.9%, and that of the target company from January to March 2016 was 32.68%. Although the income margin is not only calculated for the financial statements of Tianxiang Company, it still has great reference significance for the calculation of Tianxiang Company's income and profit. This data calculates the cost of sharing costs, server costs, period expenses, and income tax amounts for the IP party and R&D party of "Hua Qiangu", and takes into account the forecasted revenue and profit rate during the performance commitment period of the target company disclosed in the "Second Reply Announcement" Considering the average revenue and profit of other similar games, the court of first instance held that a 13.9% revenue profit rate should be a fair figure.

b. Estimate profit. Based on the total game share amount shown in the aforementioned value-added tax invoices of the two parties and based on the 13.9% revenue profit rate, It is estimated that the profit of the total game revenue from the operating channel part of the Tianxiang company and the iqiyi company is 32,130,772 yuan. For reference, if calculated at 32.68%, the profit amount reached 7,554,1988 yuan, both of which have exceeded the 30 million yuan claimed by the snail company. It should be pointed out that because the 13.9% revenue profit rate takes into account the cost of sharing, the aforementioned game revenue and profit calculated using this data does not include the profit sharing between Tianxiang Company and iQiyi Company from each other, that is, if this part of the profit is added to constitute the total operating profit data of the two parties, it will be further greater than the aforementioned amount. In this case, there is no direct reference for calculating the profit margin of iQiyi's operating game revenue. The court of first instance used the aforementioned Tianxiang Company's data as appropriate.

c. Other considerations. It is mentioned in the "Transaction Plan (Revised Draft)" that the game "Hua Qian Gu" received a high turnover recharge within four months of its launch, which to a certain extent is closely related to the TV series of the same name that was broadcast during the same period. Tianxiang Company also proposed that the entire income of the game "Hua Qian Gu" cannot be regarded as infringement income. In this regard, the court of first instance held that it is undeniable in this case that the high recharge turnover of the game "Hua Qian Gu" during the alleged infringement period is not only due to the playability of the game itself but also should consider the. contribution of the IP of "Hua Qian Gu". However, it should be pointed out that if it weren't for the original work, Tianxiang and iQiyi could not form a new work of "Hua Qian Gu" or at least could not launch the game on the market in a relatively short period of time during the popular TV series of the same name. The prerequisite for the game to obtain high overall revenue is the implementation of the infringement and adaptation involved in the case, so even if the profit contribution of the "Hua Qiangu" IP is considered, it can be moderate. In terms of specific calculations, the 13.9% profit margin has been deducted from the cost of IP sharing, which can be considered to have considered the contribution of IP to a certain extent. Combined with the litigation claim of the snail company on the total amount of compensation, the court of first instance held that it is unnecessary to allocate and convert the aforementioned estimated profit.

In summary, according to the above estimates, the profits made by Tianxiang Company and iqiyi from developing and operating the game "Hua Qiangu" have significantly exceeded the amount of compensation claimed by Snail Company. In summary, according to the above estimation, the profits made by Tianxiang Company and iQiyi Company from developing and operating the game "Flower Thousand Bone" have significantly exceeded the amount of compensation claimed by Snail Company. On this basis, the court of first instance comprehensively considered the nature of the infringement, the circumstances of the infringement and other factors, and supported Snail's claim that Tianxiang Company and Iqiyi Company should jointly compensate 30 million yuan.

In accordance with Article 15 of the "Law of Tort Liability of the People's Republic of China", Article 3, Article 10 (14), Article 47 (6), 49 Article 2, Article 2 and Article 4 (11) of the "Regulations for the Implementation of the Copyright Law of the People's Republic of China", Article 25 of the "Interpretation of the Supreme People's Court on Several Issues Concerning the Application of Law in the Trial of Copyright Civil Disputes" stipulates that the first instance.

The court ruled:

1. Tianxiang Company and iQiyi Company immediately stopped adapting the "Tai Chi Panda" Android 1.1.1 version of the game and providing the adapted works to the public through the information network (performed);
2. Tianxiang Company and iqiyi Company Within 30 days from the effective date of the judgment, jointly publish a statement in national newspapers approved by Snail Company or designated by the court of first instance in order to eliminate the impact of its infringement on Snail Company (the content of the statement shall be reviewed by the court of first instance. The court will publish the content of this judgment within the same scope, and the related expenses shall be borne by Tianxiang Company and Iqiyi Company;
3. Tianxiang Company and Iqiyi Company shall jointly compensate Snail Company for economic losses of 30 million yuan within ten days from the effective date of the judgment.
4. Dismissed other claims of Snail Company.

If the obligation to pay money is not fulfilled within the period specified in this judgment, the interest on the debt during the delayed performance period shall be doubled in accordance with Article 253 of the Civil Procedure Law of the People's Republic of China. The first-instance case acceptance fee was 191,800 yuan, which was jointly borne by Tianxiang Company and Iqiyi Company.

The holding of the court of second instance:

The dispute point of the second instance of this case is: 1. Whether the game "Tai Chi Panda" involved is a work protected by the Copyright Law; 2. If it is a work protected by the Copyright Law, whether the game "Hua Qian Gu" infringes the copyright of the "Tai Chi Panda" game; 3 If it constitutes an infringement, whether the amount of compensation determined by the court of first instance is appropriate.

1. Whether there are defects in the trial procedures of the court of first instance

The appeals of Tianxiang Company and iQiyi Company held that the trial procedures of the first-instance court were flawed, mainly focusing on the issue of the time for Snail Company to clarify the litigation request and the time limit for proof. First of all, based on the facts found in the second instance, at the hearing of the court of first instance on January 19, 2016, the entrusted litigation agent of Snail Company stated that "in the case of conflicts between anti-law and intellectual property law, We agree to follow the intellectual property law as our request law." At the first hearing of the court of first instance on August 9, 2016, the entrusted litigation agent of Snail Company clarified that his litigation request was that "the defendant shall be ordered immediately to stop copyright infringement…". At the same time, in the five sessions of the first-instance court, all parties fully stated their opinions and conducted fierce debates on whether the game involved can be protected by the copyright law. Therefore, Tianxiang Company and Iqiyi Company believed that Snail Company had not made clear the claims of the litigation until the end of the first-instance trial, which was inconsistent with the facts. Secondly, the second paragraph of Article 65 of the Civil Procedure Law of the People's Republic of China stipulates that A people's court shall, according to the claims of a party and the circumstances of trial of a case, determine the evidence to be provided by a party and the time limit for provision of evidence. Therefore, in the first-instance procedure of this case, the specific time limit for the parties to submit evidence should be determined by the first-instance court. Under the premise that this case is a new type of case, the facts involved in the case are very complicated and the parties involved are more controversial, in order to ascertain the facts of the case and protect the litigation rights of the parties, the court of first instance allows the parties to submit relevant evidence multiple times, and there is nothing wrong.

Iqiyi Company also appealed that the court of first instance failed to affirm the two pieces of evidence submitted by Snail Company, that is, the comparison analysis of the similarity between "Hua Qian Gu" and "Tai Chi Panda" and the explanation of the comparison of game rules. The basis for this is improper. In this regard, this court believes that the comparison of the similarity between "Hua Qiangu" and "Tai Chi Panda" and the comparison of game rules are one of the core focuses of the dispute between the two parties in this case. The court of first instance listened to the opinions of all parties in detail on the specific comparison. At the same time, in the judgment of the first instance, the two comparison documents were specifically determined based on the comparison during the trial. Therefore, the court of first instance did not directly determine the two pieces of evidence but based on the comparison during the actual trial of the case. Based on the fact finding and determination, there is no circumstance of improper procedures as claimed by iQiyi company.

In summary, the grounds for appeal of Tianxiang Company and Iqiyi Company regarding the flaws in the first-instance trial procedure cannot be established.

2. Whether there are defects in the foundation of Snail Company's rights

Both Tianxiang Company and iQiyi Company appealed that because the server corresponding to version 1.1.1 of Snail Company's "Tai Chi Panda" was temporarily built, there was a possibility of modification. So Snail Company's right foundation was flawed. Tianxiang Company also argued that the court of first instance did not introduce expert witnesses or technical investigators and other personnel with professional knowledge during the investigation, which is improper. In this regard, the court believes that: first of all, the data in the SVN server used by Snail Company can be modified. Snail Company has approved this during the first instance. The fourth set of evidence from Tianxiang Company in the second instance also proved this point. However, the possibility of modification does not mean that there must be modified behavior. According to Article 108 of the Interpretation of the Supreme People's Court on the Application of the Civil Procedure Law of the People's Republic of China, for evidence provided by a party who bears the burden of proof, where a people's court finds out high possibility of existence of the facts to be investigated upon examination in combination with relevant facts, it shall be deemed that the facts exist. For evidence provided by a party for the purpose of refuting the facts claimed by the party who bears the burden of proof, where a people's court believes whether the facts to be investigated are true or false is not clear upon examination in combination with relevant facts, it shall be deemed that the facts do not exist. In this case, in order to fulfill its burden of proof, Snail Company adopted methods such as notarization and the establishment of the on-site restoration of the game server environment and the recovery server set up by it can be interconnected with the client downloaded by the notarization. Therefore, Snail company has exhausted all the means of proof. Tianxiang Company and iQiyi Company believe that Snail Company's evidence is flawed but the evidence cited only proves that the data in the SVN server can be modified, and does not clearly point out any post-modification actions that Snail Company may make. Under this circumstance, the court of first instance, in conjunction with other facts ascertained in the case, approved the snail company's proof according to the high probability standard, and there was nothing wrong with it. Secondly, the law does not require the court to bring in expert witnesses or technical investigators and other personnel with professional knowledge when organizing an inspection when hearing a case. When participating in the inspection, Tianxiang Company can apply for its own expert witnesses to appear in court or ask expert witnesses for verification on the screen and video recording of the court of first instance. It is not inappropriate for the court of first instance to judge whether it is necessary to introduce personnel with professional knowledge and makes corresponding decisions based on the situation of the case.

3. Whether the game "Tai Chi Panda" is a work protected by copyright law.

First of all, Article 2 of Regulation for the Implementation of the Copyright Law of the People's Republic of China stipulates that the term "works" as referred to in the Copyright Law means intellectual creations with originality in the literary, artistic or scientific domain, insofar as they can be reproduced in a tangible form. The design of an ARPG-type online game includes original elements and content in many aspects such as storyline, gameplay rules, equipment values, screen art, dubbing and interface layout, including a large number of intellectual achievements of the game design team, preset the expression of the constantly changing specific scene and the scope of expression when the game is running, including the gameplay rules and various other elements combined and the overall running environment of the game can be tangibly copied. Therefore, the game "Tai Chi Panda" is an original intellectual achievement in the fields of literature, art, and science stipulated by the Copyright Law and should be protected by the Copyright Law.

Secondly, an online game is a collection of multiple elements such as text, music, pictures, videos and specific gameplay rules. It supports the realization and execution of gameplay rules through computer software programs. The rules of gameplay are not static and independent. You can use the setting of many condition items to form a specific expression that can be continuously perceived through the complex and diverse combination of different rules and different elements. Relying on the player's operation to retrieve game pictures, music, Video and other materials form original, changing, and continuous game screens. The overall running screen of the game is an organic, continuous, and dynamic presentation of the work formed by the combination of gameplay rules and all game materials. It is true that the protection of the rights of online games can be carried out from the perspective of writing, art, music, or computer software works according to the different elements, However, the protection of such subdivided rights only protects a certain element category in online games, and is not sufficient to achieve full and substantial protection of online games with integrity characteristics. This also makes it easy for infringers to evade infringement liability by evading and replacing certain types of elements in the overall game. Under this circumstance, the first-instance court used the overall picture of the game operation including the game play rules and all game materials as the basis for comparison in order to realize the overall protection of online games. It is a reasonable judgment within the framework of the current legal system and has corresponding factual and legal basis.

Third, Article 4 (11) of the Regulation for the Implementation of the Copyright Law of the People's Republic of China stipulates that "cinematographic works and works created by a process analogous to cinematography" means works which are recorded on some material, consisting of a series of images, with or without accompanying sound, and which can be projected with the aid of suitable devices or communicated by other means; In this case, the content design of the different characters of the game "Tai Chi Panda", the interaction between the characters and the storyline of the entire game are similar to the script creation in the film creation process; The overall running screen formed by the player's operation is similar to the process of filming and imaging under the framework of the script, and the expression presented by the player after the operation is also within the boundaries of the range set by the game developer. At the same time, the overall picture of the game includes a series of game pictures with or without sound, which can be spread through digital playback devices such as computers. Therefore, under the current situation that the copyright law adopts the enumeration method for the form of works, it is not obviously inappropriate to regard the overall running screen of the game "Tai Chi Panda" as a work created in a way similar to cinematography.

In summary, the overall operating screen of the game "Tai Chi Panda" can be regarded asa work created in a way similar to cinematography and the copyright protection shall be granted.

4. Whether the game "Hua Qian Gu" infringes the copyright of the game "Tai Chi Panda"

(1) The specific presentation method of the gameplay rules in the game "Tai Chi Panda" can be recognized as an subject matter protected by copyright law.

The copyright law only protects expression but not ideas. This is the basic principle of copyright law. The "expression" here does not only refer to the "form of expression" but also includes the original content. For example, the method of "synonym substitution" is used to rewrite the novels created by others, which makes the specific forms of expression (specific words and sentences) completely different, but because the two "content", that is, the storyline, characters, the sequence of events and the relationship between the characters are exactly the same, so the latter still constitutes copyright infringement against the former.

Regarding the boundary between "idea" and "expression", taking a novel as an example, it is not only the theme or central idea of the novel that can be classified as "idea", from every detail of the work to the coexistence and continuity of countless details, and then to the central theme conveyed to the reader by the final work, there is a step-by-step interpretation, from obscurity to clarity, from abstract to concrete, from complex to simple. The process is similar to a triangular structure from the bottom to the top. From the expression of each word, sentence and paragraph at the bottom of the triangle to the theme idea at the top of the triangle, there is a process of continuous abstraction and generalization. This process is equivalent to the gradually narrowing state of the triangle that is constantly approaching the top. The changes in this state are not distinct. Obviously, from the most basic expression at the bottom to the clearest thought at the top, there is a gradual process, which also incorporates expressions of different schedules, levels and methods. As far as works are concerned, although ideas can be expressed directly or indirectly, there are often intertwined parts of thought and expression in works, and it is not possible to simply define a clear dividing line. Generally speaking, for the comparison between the prior work and the subsequent work, the higher the convergent part below the top of the triangle, the closer the infringement in the sense of "expression". Obviously, the demarcation line for judging whether infringement or not cannot be drawn at the bottom, otherwise it means that only verbatim plagiarism is an act of infringement of "expression", which greatly reduces the scope of "expression"; similarly, this line cannot be drawn at the top, otherwise any abstract plot that is more specific than the main idea will be regarded as "expression", greatly expanding the scope of "expression". How to determine the dividing line between "idea" and "expression" still requires specific judgments based on the specific circumstances of the work.

In this case, first of all, the battle, growth, expansion and placement systems in the "Tai Chi Panda", as well as the PVE (player and computer), PVP (player and player) battle system, the protagonist system, equipment system, Valkyrie system, interaction, operation activities, mall system under the expansion system, novice guidance, function opening, colorful gift packs, level restriction system and other game play rules under the expansion system are specific and explicit The "idea" part of transformation should not be protected by copyright law. Secondly, the basic interface layout of the "first charge" gameplay and the "investment plan" gameplay in the "Tai Chi Panda" game, as well as the layout of the bottom row that appears in the main interface design are mostly function area buttons, and the left and right sides are vertical buttons, etc., These are non-innovative or limited expression and public domain expression content, and should also be excluded from the "expression" advocated by Snail Company.

After excluding the above related content, the remaining basic layout of the interface and specific content of the interface in the "Tai Chi Panda" game are independently designed by the snail company. And through the straightforward text in the interface or the continuous display of the game operation interface, the external narrative expression of some specific game rules is realized. Through these original interface layouts, interface texts and interface interactions, online game players can understand the specific gameplay rules and operating experience designed by the Snail Company in the "Tai Chi Panda" game. Therefore, the interface layout and interface content of this part can be regarded as a specific way of presenting the specific rules of the game, constituting the "expression" in the copyright law.

In addition, the court needs to further explain that in addition to considering the original interface layout, text and interaction design of snail company, the new interface layout or specific presentation of specific gameplay rules constituted by the selection, arrangement and combination of other elements such as public domain and limited expression, if it can already achieve the creative characteristics that distinguish it from other games, it will also be regarded as an original "expression".

In summary, the court believes that the specific presentation of the game rules in the game "Tai Chi Panda" can be regarded as the subject matter of copyright protection.

(2) Based on the existing evidence, it can be determined that the game "Hua Qian Gu" has implemented "skin-changing" plagiarism from the game "Tai Chi Panda" "Skin-changing" plagiarism generally refers to the use of IP image, music and other elements that are different from the previous game, and it is completely the same or substantially similar to the previous game in terms of gameplay rules, numerical planning, skill system and operation interface. Since gameplay rules, numerical

planning, skill system and operation interface are the core content of a game, it can be consistent with previous games in terms of operation habits and user experience. At the same time, by plagiarizing previous games, the development cost of the game can be greatly reduced and the development cycle can be shortened. In this case, the large amount of evidence submitted by the Snail Company can prove that the game "Hua Qian Gu" has implemented a "skin-changing" of the game "Tai Chi Panda".

First of all, according to the facts ascertained by the court of first instance, in the computer software copyright registration archives of the "Hua Qian Gu" game software V1.0, 26 UI interfaces use the elements and interfaces of the game "Tai Chi Panda". Tianxiang Company and Iqiyi Company argued that it was a third-party registration company entrusted by them to use the pictures freely, and this claim was obviously unreasonable. At the same time, this behavior confirms Snail Company's claim from another aspect that Tianxiang Company and iQiyi Company used "skin-changing" to plagiarize in order to launch the game as soon as possible during the hit period of "Hua Qian Gu" TV series.

Secondly, there are many substantial similarities between the game "Hua Qian Gu" and "Tai Chi Panda" in the core gameplay of ARPG games such as the battle copy, character skills, equipment and the Valkyrie (spiritual pet) system and their corresponding expression content. And the 24 attribute values of 47 equipment all show the same proportion of fine-tuning corresponding relationships. The court of first instance has conducted a very detailed investigation of the relevant content and the court will not repeat it here. At the same time, in some design flaws, the "Hua Qian Gu" game is completely consistent with the "Tai Chi Panda" game, which further proves that it has implemented "skin-changing" plagiarism, such as: on the "Tai Chi Panda" "Star Refining" interface In the eight circles in the main part of the gossip picture, only the bottom two circles are actually used. Only the bottom one can be clicked. Most of the overall screen is wasted. This is the failure of Snail's interface design. This design was also copied in the game "Hua Qian Gu".

Third, the perception of the similarity and operating experience of the two games of the end users of online games are also important considerations for judging whether the two games are similar. In this case, Snail Company listed some user comments in Sina Weibo and user reviews of the IOS system "Hua Qian Gu" game. These content proves that for players participating in online games, they can already clearly perceive the similarities between the two games in terms of gameplay rules, numerical planning, skill systems and operation interfaces.

(3) The game "Hua Qian Gu" essentially uses the specific expression content of the game rules in the game "Tai Chi Panda", which constitutes copyright infringement. Regarding the "Hua Qian Gu" game implemented the "skin-changing" plagiarism of the "Tai Chi Panda" game, the above content has been discussed in detail and will not be repeated here. What needs to be further elaborated is whether the act of "skin-changing" can be regarded as copyright infringement.

First of all, both Tianxiang Company and Iqiyi Company appealed that the game play rules advocated by Snail Company belonged to the category of "idea" and were not the subject matter of copyright protection. In this regard, the court believes that, as mentioned above, the original interface text, layout and interaction in "Tai Chi Panda" that show the specific game rules constitute a specific presentation method of the game rules and can be regarded as subject matter protected by copyright law. Specific interface graphics and interface texts can be regarded as specific "forms of expression", and a layer of abstraction and generalization on top of them can be deduced to the specific setting of a specific specific gameplay rule. This level The content of can be identified as "expressive content", and can also be identified as an object protected by copyright law. Of course, the gameplay and rules that are further abstracted and generalized to the next higher level should be regarded as belonging to the category of "idea". In this case, the court of first instance determined that the specific presentation mode of the game rules in the "Tai Chi Panda" game that needs to be protected still belongs to the level of "expression", so it does not belong to the category of "idea" and can be protected by copyright law.

Secondly, in the second instance, Tianxiang Company submitted new evidence containing a number of comparative analysis of different types of online games, intending to prove that games of the same category are not only very similar in game interface layout design but also very similar in game rules design. Games have a high degree of similarity in the design of gameplay rules, which has become an industry practice. In this regard, the court believes that the rules and interface comparisons of different games in the evidence cited by Tianxiang Company are still at a high level of abstraction, and have not been subdivided into the detailed presentation of certain specific game rules. The comparison interface content is also less.

Third, Tianxiang Company submitted a second set of new evidence in the second instance, which intends to prove that the three essential elements of a game are story, artistry and interactivity. The rules of the game are only a small part of the game's interactivity and cannot be equated to the entire game. If the rules of the game are equal to the game works and then the game rules are the same, the two game works are the same and constitute copyright infringement, which violates the general principles of game design and the general principles of the game industry. In this regard, the court believes that the basis for the court of first instance to determine the infringement of the game "Hua Qian Gu" is that it violated the specific presentation of the game rules of "Tai Chi Panda", not just the same rules of the two games. As mentioned earlier, the expression of the rules of gameplay in the game involves many aspects such as the overall structure of the game, the layout of the game interface, content, interaction, equipment values and the planning of the skill system. It does not only involve the interactivity of the game., It will also be involved in story and artistry. Therefore, Tianxiang Company's defense for this point cannot be established and the court will not accept it.

Finally, Tianxiang Company and iQiyi Company also appealed that the "Hua Qian Gu" game and the "Tai Chi Panda" game are completely different in story background, art design and dubbing. Therefore, even if there are some similarities in the game play rules, nor should it be deemed that the two components are similar as a whole. In this regard, the court believes that the game structure, gameplay rules, numerical planning, skill system, interface layout and interaction design belong to the core content of the entire game design, which is equivalent to the skeleton of the game, and the game character image, dubbing and soundtrack, etc. belong to the image design, which is equivalent to the skin or clothing of the game. Therefore, the behavior that only replaces the IP image, music and other elements but is substantially similar in game rules, numerical planning, skill system, operation interface, etc. is called "skin changing". "Plagiarism. The game involved in this case has many substantial similarities with the game "Tai Chi Panda" in the core gameplay of ARPG games such as battle copy, character skills, equipment a nd the Valkyrie (spiritual pet) system, and there are some details in some details. The similarity goes far beyond the possibility of creative coincidence. Therefore, it can be determined that the game "Flower Thousand Bone" has copied and copied the specific expression designed by the specific rules of the game "Tai Chi Panda" as a whole, which constitutes copyright infringement.

According to Article 4 (14) of the Copyright Law, the right of adaptation, that is, the right to modify a work for the purpose of creating a new work of original creation; and according to Article 12, Where a work is created by adaptation, translation, annotation or arrangement of a pre-existing work, the copyright in the work thus created shall be enjoyed by the adapter, translator, annotator or arranger, provided that the copyright in the original work is not infringed upon. In this case, although the "Hua Qian Gu" is different from the "Tai Chi Panda" in terms of IP image, music, storyline, etc., this does not change its plagiarism of the "Tai Chi Panda" game in some specific core gameplay. In the determination of infringement, the court of first instance determined that its behavior of changing the game's IP image, music and storyline was an infringement of the adaptation right of the "Tai Chi Panda" game, which has corresponding factual and legal basis.

In summary, the game "Hua Qiangu" has carried out "skin-changing" plagiarism against the "Tai Chi Panda" game, which constitutes copyright infringement. The relevant determination of the court of first instance was correct.

5. Whether the amount of compensation determined by the court of first instance is appropriate

First of all, Tianxiang Company and iQiyi Company both appealed and held that all the capital exchanges between the two parties could not be regarded as the income of the game "Hua Qiangu", because there may be other transactions between the two parties that should not be disclosed. In this regard, the court believes that in the process of civil litigation, the parties are obliged to provide evidence for their claims. Even if there are other transactions between Tianxiang and iQiyi that are not suitable for the general public, they can be submitted to the court as evidence and require the court to keep the relevant evidence confidential. However, from the first instance to the second instance of this case, Tianxiang Yuiqiyi did not submit any evidence to the court to prove its claim, so the reason for its appeal cannot be established without factual basis, and this is not supported.

Secondly, both Tianxiang and iQiyi appealed that a large part of the revenue from the game "Hua Qiangu" was derived from the popular TV series "Hua Qiangu". Even though some of the game rules are substantially similar to those of "Tai Chi Panda", the contribution of this part of the content is also very low, far less than the 30 million yuan of the first instance judgment. In this regard, the court believes that, on the one hand, the total game share revenue calculated by the court of first instance based on the value-added tax invoices of both parties is 23,115,6634.2 yuan, which is far lower than the amount of income is much lower than the amount of each party's share calculated based on the evidence submitted by the snail company in the second instance. Moreover, the profit margin of 13.9% considered by the court of first instance has also been deducted from the sharing cost of the IP party and the cost of the sharing cost of the R&D party, server costs, period expenses and income tax amount. The profit calculated on this basis is still more than 30 million yuan; on the other hand, On the other hand, it is precisely because of the aforementioned adaptation infringement by Tianxiang Company and iQiyi Company that they can shorten the development cycle and simultaneously launch the mobile game "Hua Qiangu" during the popular TV series of the same name. Under this circumstance, the court of first instance determined the amount of compensation of 30 million yuan based on the total revenue share between the two parties and other factors such as other ascertained facts, the nature and circumstances of the infringement, which was not obviously too high.

Third, iQiyi Company also appealed that the time point of compensation calculation should not be calculated until the time when "Hua Qiangu" version 1.8.0 is online, but should be calculated until the time when "Hua Qiangu" version 1.1.1 is offline. In this regard, the court believes that when online games are undergoing version changes, they generally do not suddenly change a large number of game interfaces, operations and rules of gameplay. Therefore, the Snail Company has proved that version 1.1.1 of the game "Hua Qiangu" is better than the game "Tai Chi Panda". Therefore, under the premise that the Snail Company has proved that version 1.1.1 of the game "Flower Thousand Bone" constitutes an infringement on the game "Tai Chi Panda", it is up to Tianxiang Company or iQiyi Company to further prove which version of the game "Hua Qiangu" no longer has substantially similar content to the game "Tai Chi Panda". In the process of the first instance, Tianxiang Company and iQiyi Company only proved that "Hua Qiangu" 1.8.0 version no longer contained infringing content and was approved by Snail Company. Therefore, the court of first instance determined that the listing date of version 1.8.0 of "Hua Qiangu" was the date on which the infringement ceased, which it was not inappropriate. IQiyi Company's claim that it should only count until the time when the 1.1.1 version of "Hua Qiangu" is offline has no factual and legal basis and the court will not accept it.

In summary, the appeals of Tianxiang Company and Iqiyi Company cannot be established and should be rejected; The first-instance judgment has clear facts and correct application of law, which should be maintained. In accordance with the provisions of the first paragraph (1) of Article 170 of the Civil Procedure Law of the People's Republic of China, the judgment is as follows:

The appeal was rejected and the original judgment was upheld.

The case acceptance fee of the second instance was 191,800 yuan, which was jointly borne by Chengdu Tianxiang Interactive Technology Co., Ltd. And Beijing Aiqiyi Technology Co., Ltd.

The decision is final.

3.2 Analysis of the Case

1. Facts

Suzhou Snail Digital Technology Co., Ltd. sued Chengdu Tianxiang Interactive Technology Co., Ltd. and Beijing Aiqiyi Technology Co., Ltd. for copyright infringement. The Suzhou Intermediate Court's judgment of 30 million yuan in compensation in the first instance caused even more waves. The Suzhou Intermediate People's Court recognized that "The specific presentation method and selection, arrangement, and combination of the game "HUA QIAN GU" game used the basic expression of "Tai Chi Panda" as a whole, and performed art, music, animation, and animation on this basis. The re-creation of certain content such as text violates the right of adaptation enjoyed by the copyright owner." The second-instance judgment determined that the presentation of the game rules in "Tai Chi Panda" can be regarded as the object protected by the copyright law. The game "Hua Qian GU" essentially uses the specific expression content of the game rules in the game "Tai Chi Panda", which constitutes copyright infringement. Affirmed that the specific presentation of game rules can be regarded as works in the sense of copyright law are protected.

2. The focus of dispute

(1) Is the game "Tai Chi Panda" involved in the case belonged to a work created in a similar way to filming a movie protected by the Copyright Law? (2) Is it possible that specific game play rules constitute the subject matter of copyright protection?

3. Legal regulations

"The Tort Liability Law of the People's Republic of China"

Article 6: The perpetrator shall bear the tort liability for infringement of the civil rights and interests of others due to his fault.

Article 15: Ways to bear tort liability.

"The Copyright Law of the People's Republic of China"

Article 3: The works mentioned in this law include works of literature, art, natural science, social science, engineering and technology created in the following forms:

Article 10 (14): The right of adaptation, that is, the right to change the work and create a new work with originality;

Article 47 (6): Where the work is used in exhibitions, filming, or similar to film-making methods, or using works by adaptation, translation, annotation, etc., without the permission of the copyright owner, this law provides otherwise Except.

Article 49: In case of infringement of copyright or copyright-related rights, the infringer shall pay compensation based on the actual loss of the right holder; if the actual loss is difficult to calculate, compensation may be based on the infringer's illegal income. The amount of compensation should also include the reasonable expenses paid by the right holder to stop the infringement.

"Regulations for the Implementation of the Copyright Law of the People's Republic of China"

Article 2: The term "work" as mentioned in the Copyright Law refers to the intellectual achievements in the fields of literature, art and science that are original and can be reproduced in some tangible form.

Article 4 (11): Film works and works created in a method similar to film production refer to a series of pictures with or without accompanying sound filmed on a certain medium, and are shown with the help of appropriate devices or Works disseminated by other means;

"Interpretation of the Supreme People's Court on Several Issues Concerning the Application of Law in the Trial of Copyright Civil Dispute Cases"

Article 25 stipulates that if the actual loss of the right holder or the illegal income of the infringer cannot be determined, the people's court shall determine the amount of compensation based on the request of the party or by applying the provisions of the second paragraph of Article 48 of the Copyright Law.

4. Application of law

(1) The overall operating picture of an online game is the expression form of its overall work, which is a work created with the similar way to a movie.

The essence of online games is a collection of computer software programs (including server-side programs and client-side programs) and game information data (pictures, music, text, etc.). This essence determines that a composite work of online games presents two forms of expression, one is a collection of static computer codes and information data forms, the other is the dynamic audiovisual output presented by the game software program controlled and run by the player in the intelligent terminal, and can be copied in a tangible form. The overall picture of the network game finally displayed on the screen is driven by its computer program, and its text, music, pictures, audio, video and other copyrightable elements are formed for the purpose of reflecting and serving game play and game rules. The organic, continuous, and dynamic combination of presentation, and its overall running picture is the complete presentation of online game works, and it is also the overall work form that players recognize and perceive. From the perspective of its performance effect, the overall picture of "Tai Chi Panda" is a "continuous dynamic image" presented on the screen with the continuous operation of the player, which conforms to the definition of film work. Furthermore, the gameplay settings of ARPG games are story-telling, that is, they mainly construct a virtual world with rich connotation, in which players can experience a series of games such as role selection, pet development, growth, and battle. Events and plots provide an immersive audio-visual experience, similar to the appreciation experience of movie works. Article 2 of the Berne Convention for the Protection of Literary and Artistic Works stipulates that the term "literary and artistic works" includes all works in the fields of science and literature and art, regardless of their manner of expression or form. The essence of the description of cinema-like works in Article 2(1) of the aforementioned convention lies in the form of expression of the work rather than the method of creation. Therefore, the court of first instance held that as long as the performance of the work meets the originality requirements of the film-like work, its production method should not be an obstacle to the characterization of the work.

(2) The specific presentation of game play rules constitutes the subject matter of copyright protection.

To distinguish between the corresponding gameplay rules in the game works as thoughts or expressions, it should be seen whether these gameplay rules belong to general descriptions, or whether they are specific enough to generate a unique enjoyment experience perceiving the source of a particular work. If this is specific to this, the degree is enough to reach below the critical point of thought and expression, and it can be used as expression. Through the game interface in the continuous dynamic image of the game, the game designer expresses the specific gameplay rules of a single game system either through straightforward text in the interface or through the continuous game operation interface to make the player clearly perceive and express based on this, interactive operations are expressive. In video games, the role selection, growth, battle and other gameplay settings are inherently narrative. Relying on the detailed gameplay rules presented in the game interface, similar to the detailed plot of the movie, the game development process is implemented through drawing and designing the game interface. The expression of game rules has a certain similarity with the production of sub-scene scripts based on text scripts and the transmission of the plot in the film creation process. It can be said that the detailed game rules embodied in the game interface design constitute a specific way of presenting the game rules. A fully described structure constitutes the expression of the work.

5. Conclusion and significance

The game "Tai Chi Panda" involved in the case is a work created in a similar way to filming movies protected by the Copyright Law; 2. The specific game play rules may constitute the subject matter protected by the Copyright Law. The "HUA QIAN GU" case was the first high-stakes case that clearly determined that the specific expressions of game rules could be protected. It embodies the court's attitude and philosophy on the protection of game intellectual property rights. It has greater impact on game industries and has strong research value as well.

3.3 Civil Cases on Trademark Infringement

3.3.1 Trademark Cases from United States

(1) **The source of "spectrum of distinctiveness" of trademark—Abercrombie Fitch Co. v. Hunting World, Inc.**

1.1 No. 21, Docket 74-2540

United States Court of Appeals, Second Circuit. 537 F.2d 4 (2d Cir. 1976) Decided Jan 16, 1976

No. 21, Docket 74-2540.

Argued September 18, 1975.

Decided January 16, 1976. Opinion on Limited Rehearing February 26, 1976.

Richard H. Wels, New York City (Moss, Wels Marcus, New York City, of counsel), for defendant-appellee.

Roy C. Hopgood, New York City (Paul H. Blaustein, and Hopgood, Calimafde, Kalil, Blaustein Lieberman, New York City, of counsel), for plaintiff-appellant.

Appeal from the United States District Court for the Southern District of New York.

Before FRIENDLY, TIMBERS and GURFEIN, Circuit Judges.

FRIENDLY, Circuit Judge:

This action in the District Court for the Southern District of New York by Abercrombie Fitch Company (AF), owner of well-known stores at Madison Avenue and 45th Street in New York City and seven places in other states,[56] against Hunting World, Incorporated (HW), operator of a competing store on East 53rd Street, is for infringement of some of AF's registered trademarks using the word 'Safari'. It has had a long and, for AF, an unhappy history. On this appeal from a judgment which not only dismissed the complaint but canceled all of AF's 'Safari' registrations, including several that were not in suit, we relieve AF of some of its unhappiness but not of all. AF also conducts a substantial mail order business.

I

The complaint, filed in January 1970, after describing the general nature of AF's business, reflecting its motto "The Greatest Sporting Goods Store in the World," alleged as follows: For many years AF has used the mark 'Safari' on articles "exclusively offered and sold by it." Since 1936 it has used the mark on a variety of men's and women's outer garments. Its United States trademark registrations include: *Trademark Number Issued Goods.*[57]

The mark 'Safari Mills' was acquired by assignment from original registrant, Robert Suffern.

Safari 358,781 7/26/38 Men's and Women's outer garments, including hats. Safari Mills 125,531 5/20/19 Cotton Piece goods. Safari 652,098 9/24/57 Men's and Women's outer garments, including shoes. Safari 703,279 8/23/60 Women cloth, sporting goods, apparel, etc. [3] AF has spent large sums of money in advertising and promoting products identified with its mark 'Safari' and in policing its right in the mark, including the successful conduct of trademark infringement suits. HW, the complaint continued, has engaged in the retail marketing of sporting apparel including hats and shoes, some identified by use of 'Safari' alone or by expressions such as 'Minisafari' and 'Safariland'. Continuation of HW's acts would confuse and

---

[56] https://casetext.com/_print/doc/abercrombie-fitch-co-v-hunting-world-inc?_printIncludeHighlights=false&_printIncludeKeyPassages=false&_printIsTwoColumn=undefined#25e88fcb-5034-4320-b8f8-484b36985de8-fn1.

[57] https://casetext.com/_print/doc/abercrombie-fitch-co-v-hunting-world-inc?_printIncludeHighlights=false&_printIncludeKeyPassages=false&_printIsTwoColumn=undefined#f476fd8a-2ebc-4edf-8371-03fa16dd99b5-fn2.

deceive the public and impair "the distinct and unique quality of the plaintiff's trademark." AF sought an injunction against infringement and an accounting for damages and profits.

HW filed an answer and counterclaim. This alleged, *inter alia*, that "the word 'safari' is an ordinary, common, descriptive, geographic, and generic word" which "is commonly used and understood by the public to mean and refer to a journey or expedition, especially for hunting or exploring in East Africa, and to the hunters, guides, men, animals, and equipment forming such an expedition" and is not subject to exclusive appropriation as a trademark. HW sought cancellation of all of AF's registrations using the word 'Safari' on the ground that AF had fraudulently failed to disclose the true nature of the term to the Patent Office.

HW having moved for summary judgment, Judge Lasker granted this only in part, 327 F.Supp. 657 (S.D.N.Y. 1971). He held, 327 F.Supp. at 662, that: Although "safari" is a generic word, a genuine issue of fact exists as to whether the plaintiff has created a secondary meaning in its use of the word "identifying the source" and showing that "purchasers are moved to buy it because of its source."

On the other hand, he concluded that AF had no right to prevent HW from using the word 'Safari' to describe its business as distinguished from use in the sale of a particular product[58]—a conclusion we do not understand to be disputed; that HW had not infringed AF's registered mark using the word 'Safari' under its brand name on a "classical safari hat" or in advertising this as "The Hat for Safari" since such use was purely descriptive, 327 F.Supp. at 664; that HW had also not infringed by using the term 'Minisafari' as a name for its narrower brimmed safari hats, and that HW was entitled to use the word 'afariland' as the description of an area within its shop and as the name of a corporation engaged in the wholesale distribution of products imported from East Africa by an affiliate, Lee Expeditions, Ltd., and in the "Safariland News," a newsletter issued by HW and Lee.

Expeditions, 327 F.Supp. at 664–65. With respect to shoes he concluded that both parties had used the word 'Safari' in a fanciful rather than a descriptive sense and hence that plaintiff might have a valid infringement claim it could establish a secondary meaning invalid. 327 F.Supp. at 665.

---

[58] He noted that HW had grown "from the operation of a company which actually organizes safaris and has common officers with that company," 327 F.Supp. at 663.

On AF's appeal this court reversed and remanded for trial, 461 F.2d 1040 (2 Cir. 1972). Most of Judge Thomsen's opinion for the court concerned the issue of appealability, as did most of Judge Timbers' concurring opinion and all of Judge Feinberg's dissent. Intimating no opinion on the ultimate merits, this court concluded "that genuine issues of fact exist which made it improper to enter a summary judgment finally denying even in part the injunctive relief sought by plaintiff." *Id.* at 1042.

Judge Ryan, before whom the action was tried on remand, ruled broadly in HW's favor. He found there was frequent use of the word 'Safari' in connection with wearing apparel, that AF's policing efforts thus had evidently been unsuccessful, and that AF had itself used the term in a descriptive sense not covered by its registration, e.g., in urging customers to make a "Christmas Gift Safari" to the AF store. After referring to statements by Judge Lasker that 'Safari' was a "weak" mark, 327 F.Supp. at 663, the judge found the mark to be.

'Safari,' the court held, "is merely descriptive and does not serve to distinguish plaintiff's goods as listed on the registration from anybody else's"; while such terms are afforded protection by the Lanham Act if they come to identify the company merchandising the product, rather than the product itself, AF had failed to establish that this had become the situation with respect to 'Safari'.[59] The opinion did not discuss AF's assertion that some of its marks had become incontestable under § 15 of the Lanham Act, 15 U.S.C. § 1065. The court entered a judgment which dismissed the complaint and canceled not only the four registered trademarks in suit but all AF's other registered 'Safari' trademarks.[60] AF has appealed.

This finding—that AF did not establish "secondary meaning" for its marks—is not here disputed.

There were, in addition to Nos. 358,781, 125,531, 652,098, and 703,279, *supra,* also plaintiff's New York Registration No. R-8008 (for 'Safari' applied to sporting goods apparel) and the following United States Registrations for 'Safari' not relied on by AF in its complaint: 768,332 (luggage); 770,336 (portable grills); 777,180 (insulated ice chests); 779,394 (camping tents); 803,036 (axes); 856,889 (smoking tobacco).

The judgment also enjoined HW from using the letters 'T.M.' and 'R.' after the terms 'Minisafari Hat' and 'Safariland'—a ruling from which HW has not appealed.

II

It will be useful at the outset to restate some basic principles of trademark law, which, although they should be familiar, tend to become lost in a welter of adjectives.

The cases, and in some instances the Lanham Act, identify four different categories of terms with respect to trademark protection. Arrayed in an ascending order which roughly reflects their eligibility to trademark status and the degree of protection accorded, these classes are (1) generic, (2) descriptive, (3) suggestive, and (4) arbitrary or fanciful. The lines of demarcation, however, are not always bright. Moreover, the difficulties are compounded because a term that is in one category for a particular product may be in quite a different one for another, because a term may shift from one category to another in light of differences in usage through time,[61] because a term may have one meaning to one group of users and a different one to others,[62] and because the same term may be put to different uses with respect to a single product.[63] In various ways, all of these complications are involved in the instant case.

---

[59] https://casetext.com/_print/doc/abercrombie-fitch-co-v-hunting-world-inc?_printIncludeHighlights=false&_printIncludeKeyPassages=false&_printIsTwoColumn=undefined#6e5dbb9b-a220-41f1-88f9-77512a7cc188-fn4.

[60] https://casetext.com/_print/doc/abercrombie-fitch-co-v-hunting-world-inc?_printIncludeHighlights=false&_printIncludeKeyPassages=false&_printIsTwoColumn=undefined#94cc08fc-cff6-4906-9c99-d26a304eb05e-fn5.

[61] See, e.g., *Haughton Elevator Co. v. Seeberger,* 85 U.S.P.Q. 80 (1950), in which the coined word 'Escalator', originally fanciful, or at the very least suggestive, was held to have become generic.

[62] See, e.g., *Bayer Co. v. United Drug Co.,* 272 F. 505 (S.D.N.Y. 1921).

[63] See 15 U.S.C. § 1115(b)(4).

To take a familiar example "Ivory" would be generic when used to describe a product made from the tusks of elephants but arbitrary as applied to soap.

It imakes an important exception with respect to those merely descriptive terms which have acquired secondary meaning, see § 2(f), 15 U.S.C. § 1052(f), it offers no such exception for generic marks. The Act provides for the cancellation of a registered mark if at any time it "becomes the common descriptive name of an article or substance," § 14(c). This means that even proof of secondary meaning, by virtue of which some "merely descriptive" marks may be registered, cannot transform a generic term into a subject for trademark. As explained in *J. Kohnstam, Ltd. v. Louis Marx and Company,* 280 F.2d 437, 440, 47 CCPA 1080 (1960), no matter how much money and effort the user of a generic term has poured into promoting the sale of its merchandise and what success it has achieved in securing public identification, it cannot deprive competing manufacturers of the product of the right to call an article by its name. See, accord, *Application of Preformed Line Products Co.,* 323 F.2d 1007, 51 CCPA 775 (1963); *Weiss Noodle Co. v. Golden Cracknel and Specialty Co.,* 290 F.2d 845, 48 CCPA 1004 (1961); *Application of Searle Co.,* 360 F.2d 650, 53 CCPA 1192 (1966). We have recently had occasion to apply this doctrine of the impossibility of achieving trademark protection for a generic term, *CES Publishing Corp. v. St. Regis *10 Publications, Inc.,* 531 F.2d 11 (1975). The pervasiveness of the principle is illustrated by a series of well-known cases holding that when a suggestive or fanciful term has become generic as a result of a manufacturer's own advertising efforts, trademark protection will be denied save for those markets where the term still has not become generic and a secondary meaning has been shown to continue. *Bayer Co. v. United Drug Co.,* 272 F. 505 (2 Cir. 1921) (L. Hand, D.J.); *DuPont Cellophane Co. v. Waxed Products Co.,* 85 F.2d 75 (2 Cir.) (A.N. Hand, C.J.), cert. denied, 299 U.S. 601, 57 S.Ct. 194, 81 L.Ed. 443 (1936); *King-Seeley Thermos Co. v. Aladdin Industries, Inc.,* 321 F.2d 577 (2 Cir. 1963). A term may thus be generic in one market and descriptive or suggestive or fanciful in another.

Some protection to descriptive marks which had acquired a secondary meaning was given by the law of unfair competition. The Trademark Act of 1920 permitted registration of certain descriptive marks which had acquired secondary meaning, see *Armstrong Paint Varnish Works v. Nu-Enamel Corp.,* 305 U.S. 315, 59 S.Ct. 191, 83 L.Ed. 195 (1938).

A generic term is one that refers, or has come to be understood as referring, to the genus of which the particular product is a species. At common law neither those terms which were generic nor those which were merely descriptive could become valid trademarks, see *Delaware Hudson Canal Co. v. Clark,* 80 U.S. (13 Wall.) 311, 323, 20 L.Ed. 581 (1872) ("Nor can a generic name, or a name merely descriptive of an article or its qualities, ingredients, or characteristics, be employed as a trademark and the exclusive use of it be entitled to legal protection"). The same was true under the Trademark Act of 1905,*Standard Paint Co. v. Trinidad Asphalt Mfg. Co.,* 220 U.S. 446, 31 S.Ct. 456, 55 L.Ed. 536 (1911), except for marks which had been the subject of exclusive use for ten years prior to its enactment. 33 Stat. 726 (https://casetext.com/_print/doc/abercrombie-fitch-co-v-hunting-world-inc?_printIncludeHighlights=false&_printIncludeKeyPassages=false&_printIsTwoColumn=undefined#034c0d22-6d97-4d66-a4f3-3f567b74b4a7-fn10). While, as we shall see, p. 10 infra, the Lanham Act.

The term which is descriptive but not generic[64] stands on a better basis. Although § 2(e) of the Lanham Act, 15 U.S.C. § 1052, forbids the registration of a mark which, when applied to the goods of the applicant, is "merely descriptive," § 2(f) removes a considerable part of the sting by providing that "except as expressly excluded in paragraphs (a)–(d) of this section, nothing in this chapter shall prevent the registration of a mark used by the applicant which has become distinctive of the applicant's goods in commerce" and that the Commissioner may accept, as prima facie evidence that the mark has become distinctive, proof of substantially exclusive and continuous use of the mark applied to the applicant's goods for five years preceding the application. As indicated in the cases cited in the discussion of the registrability of generic terms, "common descriptive name," as used in §§ 14(c) and 15(4), refers to generic terms applied to products and not to terms that are "merely descriptive." In the former case any claim to an exclusive right must be denied since this in effect would confer a monopoly not only of the mark but of the product by rendering a competitor unable effectively to name what it was endeavoring to sell. In the latter case the law strikes the balance, with respect to registration, between the hardships to a competitor in hampering the use of an appropriate word and those to the owner who, having invested money and energy to endow a word with the good will adhering to his enterprise, would be deprived of the fruits of his efforts.

See, e.g., *W. E. Bassett Co. v. Revlon, Inc.*, 435 F.2d 656 (2 Cir. 1970). A commentator has illuminated the distinction with an example of the "Deep Bowl Spoon":

"Deep Bowl" identifies a significant characteristic of the article. It is "merely descriptive" of the goods, because it informs one that they are deep in the bowl portion.... It is not, however, "the common descriptive name" of the article [since] the implement is not a deep bowl, it is a spoon.... "Spoon" is not merely descriptive of the article—it identifies the article—[and therefore] the term is generic.

Fletcher, Actual Confusion as to Incontestability of Descriptive Marks, 64 Trademark Rep. 252, 260 (1974). On the other hand, "Deep Bowl" would be generic as to a deep bowl.

The category of "suggestive" marks was spawned by the felt need to accord protection to marks that were neither exactly descriptive on the one hand nor truly fanciful on the other—a need that was particularly acute because of the bar in the Trademark Act of 1905, 33 Stat. 724, 726, (with an exceedingly limited exception noted above) on the registration of merely descriptive marks regardless of proof of secondary meaning. See *Orange Crush Co. v. California Crushed Fruit Co.*, 54 U.S.App. D.C. 313, 297 F. 892 (1924). Having created the category, the courts have had great difficulty in defining it. Judge Learned Hand made the not very helpful statement:

It is quite impossible to get any rule out of the cases beyond this: That the validity of the mark ends where suggestion ends and description begins. *Franklin Knitting*

---

[64] https://casetext.com/statute/united-states-code/title-15-commerce-and-trade/chapter-22-tradem arks/subchapter-i-the-principal-register/section-1052-trademarks-registrable-on-principal-reg ister-concurrent-registration.

Mills, Inc. v. Fashionit Sweater Mills, Inc., 297 F. 247, 248 (2 Cir. 1923), aff'd *per curiam,* 4 F.2d 1018 (2 Cir. 1925)—a statement amply confirmed by comparing the list of terms held suggestive with those held merely descriptive in 3 Callmann, Unfair Competition, Trademarks and Monopolies § 71.2 (3d ed.). Another court has observed, somewhat more usefully, that:

A term is suggestive if it requires imagination, thought and perception to reach a conclusion as to the nature of goods. A term is descriptive if it forthwith conveys an immediate idea of the ingredients, qualities or characteristics of the goods.

Stix Products, Inc. v. United Merchants Manufacturers Inc., 295 F.Supp. 479, 488 (S.D.N.Y. 1968)—a formulation deriving from *General Shoe Corp. v. Rosen,* 111 F.2d 95, 98 (4 Cir. 1940). Also useful is the approach taken by this court in *Aluminum Fabricating Co. of Pittsburgh v. Season-All Window Corp.,* 259 F.2d 314 (2 Cir. 1958), that the reason for restricting the protection accorded descriptive terms, namely the undesirability of preventing an entrant from using a descriptive term for his product, is much less forceful when the trademark is a suggestive word since, as Judge Lumbard wrote, 259 F.2d at 317.

The English language has a wealth of synonyms and related words with which to describe the qualities which manufacturers may wish to claim for their products and the ingenuity of the public relations profession supplies new words and slogans as they are needed.

If a term is suggestive, it is entitled to registration without proof of secondary meaning. Moreover, as held in the *Season-All* case, the decision of the Patent Office to register a mark without requiring proof of secondary meaning affords a rebuttable presumption that the mark is suggestive or arbitrary or fanciful rather than merely descriptive.

It need hardly be added that fanciful or arbitrary terms[65] enjoy all the rights accorded to suggestive terms as marks—without the need of debating whether the term is "merely descriptive" and with ease of establishing infringement.

As terms of art, the distinctions between suggestive terms and fanciful or arbitrary terms may seem needlessly artificial. Of course, a common word may be used in a fanciful sense; indeed, one might say that only a common word can be so used, since a coined word cannot first be put to a bizarre use. Nevertheless, the term "fanciful", as a classifying concept, is usually applied to words invented solely for their use as trademarks. When the same legal consequences attach to a common word, i. e., when it is applied in an unfamiliar way, the use is called "arbitrary." In the light of these principles, we must proceed to a decision of this case.

III

We turn first to an analysis of AF's trademarks to determine the scope of protection to which they are entitled. We have reached the following conclusions: (1) applied to specific types of clothing 'safari' has become a generic term and 'minisafari' may be used for a smaller brim hat; (2) 'safari' has not, however, become a generic term

---

[65] https://casetext.com/_print/doc/abercrombie-fitch-co-v-hunting-world-inc?_printIncludeHighlights=false&_printIncludeKeyPassages=false&_printIsTwoColumn=undefined#e2fa9096-2d9a-4304-8cc3-c6a73a0387d1-fn12.

for boots or shoes; it is either "suggestive" or "merely descriptive" and is a valid trademark even if "merely descriptive" since it has become incontestable under the Lanham Act; but (3) in light of the justified finding below that 'Camel Safari,' 'Hippo Safari' and 'Safari Chukka' were devoted by HW to a purely descriptive use on its boots, HW has a defense against a charge of infringement with respect to these on the basis of "fair use." We now discuss how we have reached these conclusions.

It is common ground that AF could not apply 'Safari' as a trademark for an expedition into the African wilderness. This would be a clear example of the use of 'Safari' as a generic term. What is perhaps less obvious is that a word may have more than one generic use. The word 'Safari' has become part of a family of generic terms which, although deriving no doubt from the original use of the word and reminiscent of its milieu, have come to be understood not as having to do with hunting in Africa, but as terms within the language referring to contemporary American fashion apparel. These terms name the components of the safari outfit well-known to the clothing industry and its customers: the 'Safari hat', a broad flat-brimmed hat with a single, large band; the 'Safari jacket', a belted bush jacket with patch pockets and a buttoned shoulder loop; when the jacket is accompanied by pants, the combination is called the 'Safari suit'. Typically, these items are khaki-colored.

This outfit, and its components, were doubtless what Judge Ryan had in mind when he found that "the word 'safari' in connection with wearing apparel is widely used by the general public and people in the trade." The record abundantly supports the conclusion that many stores have advertised these items despite AF's attempts to police its mark. In contrast, a search of the voluminous exhibits fails to disclose a single example of the use of 'Safari', by anyone other than AF and HW, on merchandise for which AF has registered 'Safari' except for the safari outfit and its components as described above.

What has been thus far established suffices to support the dismissal of the complaint with respect to many of the uses of 'Safari' by HW. Describing a publication as a "Safariland Newsletter", containing bulletins as to safari activity in Africa, was clearly a generic use which is nonenjoinable, see *CES Publishing Co. v. St. Regis Publications, Inc., supra.* AF also was not entitled to an injunction against HW's use of the word in advertising goods of the kind included in the safari outfit as described above. And if HW may advertise a hat of the kind worn on safaris as a safari hat, it may also advertise a similar hat with a smaller brim as a minisafari. Although the issue may be somewhat closer, the principle against giving trademark protection to a generic term also sustains the denial of an injunction against HW's use of 'Safariland' as a name of a portion of its store devoted at least in part to the sale of clothing as to which the term 'Safari' has become generic.

AF stands on stronger ground with respect to HW's use of 'Camel Safari', 'Hippo Safari' and Chukka 'Safari' as names for boots imported from Africa. As already indicated, there is no evidence that 'Safari' has become a generic term for boots. Since, as will appear, AF's registration of 'Safari' for use on its shoes has become incontestable, it is immaterial (save for HW's contention of fraud which is later rejected) whether AF's use of 'Safari' for boots was suggestive or "merely descriptive."

HW contends, however, that even if 'Safari' is a valid trademark for boots, it is entitled to the defense of "fair use" within § 33(b)(4) of the Lanham Act, 15 U.S.C. § 1115(b)(4). That section offers such a defense even as against marks that have become incontestable when the term charged to be an infringement is not used as a trademark "and is used fairly and in good faith only to describe to users the goods and services of such party, or their geographic origin."

Here, Lee Expeditions, Ltd., the parent company of HW, has been primarily engaged in arranging safaris to Africa since 1959; Robert Lee, the president of both companies, is the author of a book published in 1959 entitled "Safari Today—The Modern Safari Handbook" and has, since 1961, booked persons on safaris as well as purchased safari clothing in Africa for resale in America. These facts suffice to establish, absent a contrary showing, that defendant's use of 'Safari' with respect to boots was made in the context of hunting and traveling expeditions and not as an attempt to garner AF's good will. The district court here found the HW's use of 'Camel Safari', 'Hippo Safari', and 'Safari Chukka' as names for various boots imported from Africa constituted "a purely descriptive use to apprise the public of the type of product by referring to its origin and use." The court properly followed the course sanctioned by this court in *Venetianaire Corp. of America v. AP Import Co.*, 429 F.2d 1079, 1081-82 (1970), by focusing on the "*use* of words, not on their nature or meaning in the abstract" (emphasis in original). When a plaintiff has chosen a mark with some descriptive qualities, he cannot altogether exclude some kinds of competing uses even when the mark is properly on the register, *13 see 3 Callmann, *supra*, § 85.1; *Kiki Undies Corp. v. Alexander's Dep't Stores, Inc.*, 390 F.2d 604 (2 Cir. 1968); contrast *Kiki Undies Corp. v. Promenade Hosiery Mills, Inc.*, 411 F.2d 1097 (2 Cir. 1969), *cert. dismissed*, 396 U.S. 1054, 90 S.Ct. 707, 24 L.Ed.2d 698 (1970). We do not have here a situation similar to those in *Venetianaire, supra,* and *Feathercombs, Inc. v. Solo Products Corp.*, 306 F.2d 251 (2 Cir. 1962), in both of which we rejected "fair use" defenses, wherein an assertedly descriptive use was found to have been in a trademark sense. It is significant that HW did not use 'Safari' alone on its shoes, as it would doubtless have done if confusion had been intended.

We thus hold that the district court was correct in dismissing the complaint.

IV

We find much greater difficulty in the court's broad invalidation of AF's trademark registrations. Section 37 of the Lanham Act, 15 U.S.C. § 1119, provides authority for the court to cancel those registrations of any party to an action involving a registered mark.[66] The cases cited above, p. 13, establish that when a term becomes the generic name of the product to which it is applied, grounds for cancellation exist. The relevant registrations of that sort are Nos. 358,781 and 703,279. Although No. 358,751 dates back to July 20, 1938, and No. 703,279 was registered on August 23, 1960, and an affidavit under § 15(3), 15 U.S.C. § 1065(3), was filed on October 13, 1965, cancellation may be decreed at any time if the registered mark has become "the

---

[66] In contrast to the rule under the Trademark Act of 1905, see *Drittel v. Friedman*, 154 F.2d 653, 654 (2 Cir. 1946), § 37 of the Lanham Act permits cancellation on a counterclaim by a defendant who does not own a registered mark. See *Best Co. v. Miller*, 167 F.2d 374, 376-77 (2 Cir. 1948).

common descriptive name of an article or substance," § 14(c), see also § 15(4), 15 U.S.C. §§ 1064(c) and 1065(4). The whole of Registration No. 358,781 thus was properly canceled. With respect to Registration No. 703,279 only a part has become generic[67] and cancellation on that ground should be correspondingly limited.[68] Such partial cancellation, specifically recognized by § 37, accords with the rationale by which a court is authorized to cancel a registration, viz, to "rectify" the register by conforming it to court judgments which often must be framed in something less than an all-or-nothing way.

There remain eight other registrations and those terms not pared from No. 703,279. Three of these registrations, Nos. 652,098, 768,332 and 770,336, and the nongeneric portions of No. 703,279 appear to have become incontestable by virtue of the filing of affidavits under § 15(3), of five years continuous use.[69] There is nothing to suggest that the uses included in these registrations, except the uses described above with respect to 703,279 are the common descriptive names of either current fashion styles or African expeditions. The generic term for AF's 'safari cloth Bermuda shorts', for example, is 'Bermuda shorts', not 'safari'; indeed, one would suppose this garment to be almost ideally unsuited for the forest or the jungle and there is no evidence that it has entered into the family for which 'Safari' has become a generic adjective. The same analysis holds for luggage, portable grills, and the rest of the suburban paraphernalia, from swimtrunks and raincoats to belts and scarves, included in these registrations. HW alleged that these registrations were procured by fraud, *14 a claim which, if successful, would deny incontestability to AF's marks, see § 14(c), 15 U.S.C. § 1064(c). But these allegations seem to have meant no more than that HW believed the terms to be merely descriptive and hence unregistrable, and that the Patent Office must have been duped into registering them in the first place without proof of secondary meaning. However, we regard these terms as suggestive rather than "merely descriptive." Moreover, even if they were the latter, assuming that the person filing the applications made the required allegation that "no other person, firm, corporation, or association, to the best of his knowledge and belief, has the right to use such mark in commerce either in the identical form thereof or in such near resemblance thereto as might be calculated to deceive," see § 1(a)(1), 15 U.S.C. § 1051(a)(1), there is nothing to show that such statements were knowingly false when made. Cf. *Bart Schwartz Int'l Textiles, Ltd. v. F.T.C.*, 289 F.2d 665, 48 CCPA 933 (1961); *National Trailways Bus System v. Trailway Van Lines, Inc.*, 269 F.Supp. 352 (E.D.N.Y. 1965). The scheme of the Lanham Act forbids a denial of incontestability to a "merely descriptive" mark which would otherwise have become incontestable under § 14 on the basis of a mere allegation of fraud in obtaining registration, without supporting proof.

---

[67] To wit, pants, shirts, jackets, coats and hats.

[68] Similar partial cancellation is the proper remedy with respect to the New York registration.

[69] https://casetext.com/_print/doc/abercrombie-fitch-co-v-hunting-world-inc?_printIncludeHighlights=false&_printIncludeKeyPassages=false&_printIsTwoColumn=undefined#153d1bcd-152a-4a3a-b01b-b64c2f5dc381-fn16

In limiting ourselves to these four registrations we are proceeding solely on the basis of the certified copies of trademark registrations filed as exhibits. Since HW's answer challenged incontestability only on the ground of fraud, AF may not have been alerted to the desirability of informing the court of the filing of § 15(3) affidavits. In view of our holding that the other five registrations should not have been canceled, this is immaterial.

PER CURIAM:
We hold also that the registrations which have not become incontestable should not have been canceled. 'Safari' as applied to ice chests, axes, tents and smoking tobacco does not describe such items. Rather it is a way of conveying to affluent patrons of AF a romantic notion of high style, coupled with an attractive foreign allusion. As such, these uses fit what was said many years ago in upholding 'Ideal' as a mark for hair brushes:

The word "Ideal" has no application to hair brushes, except as we arbitrarily apply it, and the word is in no sense indicative or descriptive of the qualities or characteristics or merits of the brush except that it meets the very highest ideal, mental conception, of what a hair brush should be:

Hughes v. Alfred H. Smith Co., 205 F. 302, 309 (S.D.N.Y.), aff'd. *per curiam,* 209 F. 37 (2 Cir. 1913). It is even wider of the mark to say that 'Safari Mills' "describes" cotton piece goods. Such uses fit into the category of suggestive marks. We need not now decide how valuable they may prove to be; it suffices here that they should not have been canceled.

In sum, we conclude that cancellation should have been directed only with respect to No. 358,781 and portions of No. 703,279 and the New York registration. With respect to the remaining registration AF will have the benefits accorded by § 7(b) that registration shall be "prima facie evidence of the validity of the registration… and of [the] registrant's exclusive right to use the mark in commerce," 15 U.S.C. § 1057(b). This means "not only that the burden of going forward is upon the contestant of the registration but that there is a strong presumption of validity so that the party claiming invalidity has the burden of proof [and] must put something more into the scales than the registrant." *Aluminum Fabricating Co. of Pittsburgh v. Season-All Window Corp.,* 259 F.2d 314, 316 (2 Cir. 1958). In the case of registrations that have become incontestable AF will have the further benefit accorded by § 33(a), 15 U.S.C. § 1115(a), subject to the limitations contained therein and in § 33(b), 15 U.S.C. § 1115(b). Whether all this will suffice for a victory will depend on the facts in each case.

So much of the judgment as dismissed the complaint is affirmed; so much of the judgment as directed cancellation of the registrations is affirmed in part and reversed in part, and the cause is remanded for the entry of a new judgment consistent with this opinion. No costs.

On Petition of Appellant for Rehearing

By petition for rehearing plaintiff-appellant, Abercrombie Fitch Company (AF), *15 requested us to alter our opinion filed January 16, 1976, in two respects: one was that footnote 14, p. 13, describing the scope of cancellation of Trademark Registration No. 703,279, be modified by omitting the word "shirts". The other was that we should not uphold the "fair use" defense, pp. 13–14, as to Hippo Safari and Camel Safari shoes. We called upon defendant-appellee Hunting World, Inc. (HW) to answer.

We agree with AF that footnote 14 was in error in indicating that Safari had become generic with respect to shirts. Since the mark has become incontestable, it is of no moment, on the issue of cancellation, that, as HW urges, the mark may now be "merely descriptive," pp. 12–13. HW's answer adduces nothing to show that Safari has become the "common descriptive name" for this type of shirt; indeed, HW admits never having advertised its own shirts as such. While HW asserts that "the record is clear that the upper garment of the safari suit is referred to interchangeably as a safari bush jacket and as a safari shirt," the cited pages do not bear this out. On the other hand we see no force in AF's criticisms of the portion of our opinion relating to the fair use defense with respect to Hippo Safari and Camel Safari shoes sufficient to lead us to change the views previously expressed or, indeed, to require further discussion.

The petition for rehearing is granted to the extent of striking the word "shirts" from fn. 14 on p. 13 and is otherwise denied.

1.2 Analysis of the Case

Abercrombie & Fitch Co. v. Hunting World, Inc., 537 F.2d 4 (2d Cir. 1976).
The text of Abercrombie & Fitch Co. v. Hunting World, Inc. is available here:
https://casetext.com/case/abercrombie-fitch-co-v-hunting-world-inc

This is an opinion from Second Circuit U.S. Court of Appeals. This case is unusual because even though it was not decided by the U.S. Supreme Court, it is nonetheless very important and influential. This is because the opinion was written to establish a framework with which to analyze trademarks and articulate the appropriate levels of Lanham Act protection that particular trademarks should receive. It established a taxonomy of trademark distinctiveness in the US, breaking trademarks into classes which are accorded differing degrees of protection. Courts often speak of marks falling along the following "spectrum of distinctiveness," also known within the US as the "Abercrombie classifications" or "Abercrombie factors." Such a large number of courts have adopted its reasoning that it is a critical component of trademark law jurisprudence.

The underlying dispute was between Abercrombie & Fitch Company (A&F) and Hunting World, Incorporated (HW). A&F asserted that for many years it had used the mark 'Safari' on a variety of men's and women's outer garments. A&F claimed it had spent large sums of money in advertising and promoting products identified with its mark 'Safari' and in policing its rights in the mark, including via the successful conduct of trademark infringement suits. HW was a competitor of A&F and had engaged in the retail marketing of sporting apparel including hats and shoes, some identified by use of 'Safari' alone or within expressions such as 'Minisafari' and 'Safariland.'

A&F accused HW of infringing its trademarks. In response, HW argued that: "The word 'safari' is an ordinary, common, descriptive, geographic, and generic word" which "is commonly used and understood by the public to mean and refer to a journey or expedition, especially for hunting or exploring in East Africa, and to the hunters, guides, men, animals, and equipment forming such an expedition" and was therefore not subject to exclusive appropriation as a trademark. HW sought cancellation of all of A&F's trademark registrations that used the word 'Safari.'

To lay out the basic governing principles of relevant trademark law, the author of the opinion, Judge Friendly, explained:

It will be useful at the outset to restate some basic principles of trademark law, which, although they should be familiar, tend to become lost in a welter of adjectives.

The cases, and in some instances the Lanham Act, identify four different categories of terms with respect to trademark protection. Arrayed in an ascending order which roughly reflects their eligibility to trademark status and the degree of protection accorded, these classes are (1) generic, (2) descriptive, (3) suggestive, and (4) arbitrary or fanciful. The lines of demarcation, however, are not always bright. Moreover, the difficulties are compounded because a term that is in one category for a particular product may be in quite a different one for another, because a term may shift from one category to another in light of differences in usage through time, because a term may have one meaning to one group of users and a different one to others, and because the same term may be put to different uses with respect to a single product. In various ways, all of these complications are involved in the instant case.

A generic term is one that refers, or has come to be understood as referring, to the genus of which the particular product is a species. At common law neither those terms which were generic nor those which were merely descriptive could become valid trademarks, see Delaware & Hudson Canal Co. v. Clark, 80 U.S. (13 Wall.) 311, 323, 20 L.Ed. 581 (1872) ("Nor can a generic name, or a name merely descriptive of an article or its qualities, ingredients, or characteristics, be employed as a trademark and the exclusive use of it be entitled to legal protection"). The same was true under the Trademark Act of 1905, Standard Paint Co. v. Trinidad Asphalt Mfg. Co., 220 U.S. 446, 31 S.Ct. 456, 55 L.Ed. 536 (1911), except for marks which had been the subject of exclusive use for ten years prior to its enactment, 33 Stat. 726.10 While, as we shall see, p.—infra, the Lanham Act makes an important exception with respect to those merely descriptive terms which have acquired secondary meaning, see § 2(f), 15 U.S.C. § 1052(f), it offers no such exception for generic marks. The Act provides for the cancellation of a registered mark if at any time it "becomes the common descriptive name of an article or substance," § 14(c). This means that even proof of secondary meaning, by virtue of which some "merely descriptive" marks may be registered, cannot transform a generic term into a subject for trademark. As explained in J. Kohnstam, Ltd. v. Louis Marx and Company, 280 F.2d 437, 440, 47 CCPA 1080 (1960), no matter how much money and effort the user of a generic term has poured into promoting the sale of its merchandise and what success it has achieved in securing public identification, it cannot deprive competing manufacturers of the product of the right to call an article by its name. .... The pervasiveness of the principle is illustrated by a series of well-known cases holding that when a suggestive or fanciful term has become generic as a result of a manufacturer's own advertising efforts, trademark protection will be denied save for those markets where the term still has not become generic and a secondary meaning has been shown to continue. ... A term may thus be generic in one market and descriptive or suggestive or fanciful in another.

The term which is descriptive but not generic stands on a better basis. Although § 2(e) of the Lanham Act, 15 U.S.C. § 1052, forbids the registration of a mark which, when applied to the goods of the applicant, is "merely descriptive," § 2(f) removes a considerable part of the sting by providing that "except as expressly excluded in paragraphs (a)–(d) of this section, nothing in this chapter shall prevent the registration of a mark used by the applicant which has become distinctive of the applicant's goods in commerce" and that the Commissioner may accept, as prima facie evidence that the mark has become distinctive, proof of substantially exclusive and continuous use of the mark applied to the applicant's goods for five years preceding the application. As indicated in the cases cited in the discussion of the unregistrability of generic terms, "common descriptive name," as used in §§ 14(c) and 15(4), refers to generic terms applied to products and not to terms that are "merely descriptive." In the former case any claim to an exclusive right must be denied since this in effect would confer a monopoly not only of the mark but of the product by rendering a competitor unable effectively to name what it was endeavoring to sell. In the latter case the law strikes the balance, with respect to registration, between the hardships to a competitor in hampering the use of an appropriate word and those to the owner who, having invested money and energy to endow a word with the good will adhering to his enterprise, would be deprived of the fruits of his efforts.

The category of "suggestive" marks was spawned by the felt need to accord protection to marks that were neither exactly descriptive on the one hand nor truly fanciful on the other a need that was particularly acute because of the bar in the Trademark Act of 1905, 33 Stat. 724, 726, (with an exceedingly limited exception noted above) on the registration of merely descriptive marks regardless of proof of secondary meaning. See Orange Crush Co. v. California Crushed Fruit Co., 54 U.S. App. D.C. 313, 297 F. 892 (1924). Having created the category, the courts have had great difficulty in defining it. Judge Learned Hand made the not very helpful statement: "It is quite impossible to get any rule out of the cases beyond this: That the validity of the mark ends where suggestion ends and description begins." ....

A term is suggestive if it requires imagination, thought and perception to reach a conclusion as to the nature of goods. A term is descriptive if it forthwith conveys an immediate idea of the ingredients, qualities, or characteristics of the goods. Stix Products, Inc. v. United Merchants & Manufacturers Inc., 295 F. Supp. 479, 488 (S.D.N.Y.1968) a formulation deriving from General Shoe Corp. v. Rosen, 111 F.2d 95, 98 (4 Cir. 1940). Also useful is the approach taken by this court in Aluminum Fabricating Co. of Pittsburgh v. Season-All Window Corp., 259 F.2d 314 (2 Cir. 1958), that the reason for restricting the protection accorded descriptive terms, namely the undesirability of preventing an entrant from using a descriptive term for his product, is much less forceful when the trademark is a suggestive word since, as Judge Lumbard wrote, 259 F.2d at 317: "The English language has a wealth of synonyms and related words with which to describe the qualities which manufacturers may wish to claim for their products and the ingenuity of the public relations profession supplies new words and slogans as they are needed."

If a term is suggestive, it is entitled to registration without proof of secondary meaning. Moreover, as held in the Season-All case, the decision of the Patent [& Trademark] Office to register a mark without requiring proof of secondary meaning affords a rebuttable presumption that the mark is suggestive or arbitrary or fanciful rather than merely descriptive. It need hardly be added that fanciful or arbitrary terms12 enjoy all the rights accorded to suggestive terms as marks without the need of debating whether the term is "merely descriptive" and with ease of establishing infringement.

The court than applied these principles to the facts of the case and concluded: "(1) applied to specific types of clothing 'safari' has become a generic term and 'minisafari' may be used for a smaller brim hat; (2) 'safari' has not, however, become a generic term for boots or shoes; it is either "suggestive" or "merely descriptive" and is a valid trademark even if "merely descriptive" since it has become incontestable under the Lanham Act; but (3) in light of the justified finding below that 'Camel Safari,' 'Hippo Safari' and 'Safari Chukka' were devoted by HW to a purely descriptive use on its boots, HW has a defense against a charge of infringement with respect to these on the basis of "fair use.""

The court thus held that the trial court had been correct when it dismissed the complaint. The main takeaway concept from this case is that word (textual) trademarks should initially be sorted into one of the following categories:

Fanciful marks:
A fanciful textual trademark is one that is inherently distinctive and prima facie registrable because it comprises an entirely invented or "fanciful" word. For example, "Adidas" had no meaning before it was adopted and used as a trademark in relation to athletic shoes. Similarly "Xerox" is an invented word used as a trademark for photocopiers. Fanciful textual marks are sometimes referred to as "coined" marks. Fanciful marks enrich the global lexicon by adding new words to the universal discourse. This entitles them to expansive protections.

Arbitrary marks:
An arbitrary trademark is usually a common word which is used in a meaningless context (e.g. "Apple" for cell phones or "Thundercloud" for chewing gum). These marks consist of words that already have a dictionary meaning before being adopted as trademarks, but which are used in connection with products or services that are completely unrelated to that dictionary meaning. The pairing is therefore completely arbitrary. Arbitrary marks are also considered inherently distinctive, so they can be registered and defended as valid without a showing of secondary meaning.

Suggestive marks:
A suggestive trademark indicates or evokes the nature, quality, or a characteristic of the products or services in relation to which it is used, but does not specifically describe this characteristic, and requires imagination on the part of the consumer to

link the trademark with the good or service it represents. Suggestive trademarks are the most commonly used kind of word mark. The reason for this is that there is a clear differentiating advantage in branding; the suggestive trademark stands out and when done well, tends to be "sticky" in the minds of consumers. Since suggestive trademarks encourage imagination and perception, they can be strong marketing tools. They are also deemed inherently distinctive, like fanciful and arbitrary marks. Examples of suggestive trademarks include "Blu-ray," for a technology for high-capacity data storage, "Microsoft" for a well-known software and electronics company, and "Airbus" for a large passenger plane.

Descriptive marks:
A descriptive mark is a word with a dictionary meaning which is used as a mark in connection with products or services directly related to the word's meaning. Descriptive marks are not registrable without a showing that distinctive character has been established in the term through extensive use in the marketplace. This distinctive character is called secondary meaning or acquired distinctiveness. Secondary meaning is the connection consumers make between a mark and the pertinent goods and services, usually as a function of advertising and exposure. If secondary meaning has not been established, the mark is "merely descriptive" and cannot be registered. Merely descriptive marks cannot be registered because they do not identify and distinguish the source of products or services. Marks that are misdescriptive are also ineligible for registration. "American Airlines" was registrable as a servicemark for commercial air travel services in America because the company could show that people associated the mark with the airline, and it therefore had secondary meaning. "Lektronic" for electronic goods was refused registration by the US Patent & Trademark Office because it was deemed merely descriptive.

Generic terms:
A generic term is the common name for a product or service. It cannot be monopolized and protected as a mark for the product or service. In other words, "Ice" cannot be registered or protected as a mark for ice (frozen water), and "Salt" cannot be registered or protected as a mark for salt (sodium chloride). Ice could be registered as a trademark for dining room furniture, because in that context it is an arbitrary trademark. Generic terms cannot be valid trademarks because competitors would be disadvantaged if they could not use the appropriate word or words to describe their goods or services. For example, if one farmer could obtain an enforceable trademark on the word "Rice" for rice, what would all the other farmers call it? There are no tenable substitutes in English.

Some marks start out as fanciful or arbitrary, inherently distinctive and entitled to strong protection. However, if the consuming public starts using the mark as a generic term for the good or service itself, rather than as a trademark, it can lose its registration and protectability altogether. Marks which become generic after losing their distinctive character in this way are known as genericized trademarks. The process by which strong marks become generic terms is sometimes called genericide. Any strong mark is vulnerable if the consuming public begins using the mark generically. The mark holder can try to prevent this with advertising campaigns but is not always successful. Marks that went from fanciful to generic due to the genericizing manner of public usage include: Trampoline, Aspirin, Thermos and Cellophane tape.

(2) **Which should be considered: actual dilution or likelihood of dilution— Moseley et al., DBA Victor's Little Secret v.V Secret Catalogue, INC., et al.**

OCTOBER TERM, 2002

CERTIORARI TO THE UNITED STATES COURT OF APPEALS FOR THE SIXTH CIRCUIT

No. 01-1015. Argued November 12, 2002-Decided March 4, 2003

2.1 Syllabus

An army colonel sent a copy of an advertisement for petitioners' retail store, "Victor's Secret," to respondents, affiliated corporations that own the VICTORIA'S SECRET trademarks, because he saw it as an attempt to use a reputable trademark to promote unwholesome, tawdry merchandise. Respondents asked petitioners to discontinue using the name, but petitioners responded by changing the store's name to "Victor's Little Secret." Respondents then filed suit, alleging, *inter alia,* "the dilution of famous marks" under the Federal Trademark Dilution Act (FTDA). This 1995 amendment to the Trademark Act of 1946 describes the factors that determine whether a mark is "distinctive and famous," 15 U. S. C. § 1125(c)(1), and defines "dilution" as "the lessening of the capacity of a famous mark to identify and distinguish goods or services," § 1127. To support their claims that petitioners' conduct was likely to "blur and erode" their trademark's distinctiveness and "tarnish" its reputation, respondents presented an affidavit from a marketing expert who explained the value of respondents' mark but expressed no opinion concerning the impact of petitioners' use of "Victor's Little Secret" on that value. The District Court granted respondents summary judgment on the FTDA claim, and the Sixth Circuit affirmed, finding that respondents' mark was "distinctive" and that the evidence established "dilution" even though no actual harm had been proved. It also rejected the Fourth Circuit's conclusion that the FTDA "requires proof that (1) a defendant has [used] a junior mark sufficiently similar to the famous mark to evoke in ... consumers a mental association of the two that (2) has caused (3) actual economic harm to the famous mark's economic value by lessening its former selling power as an advertising agent for its goods or services," *Ringling Bros.-Barnum & Bailey Combined Shows, Inc.* v. *Utah Div. of Travel Dev.,* 170 F.3d 449, 461.

2.2 Reasoning:
(a) Unlike traditional infringement law, the prohibitions against trademark dilution are not the product of common-law development, and are not motivated by an interest in protecting consumers. The approximately 25 state trademark dilution laws predating the FTDA refer both to injury to business reputation (tarnishment) and to dilution of the distinctive quality of a trademark or trade name (blurring). The FTDA's legislative history mentions that the statute's purpose is to protect famous trademarks from subsequent uses that blur the mark's distinctiveness or tarnish or disparage it, even absent a likelihood of confusion. pp. 428–431.

(b) Respondents' mark is unquestionably valuable, and petitioners have not challenged the conclusion that it is "famous." Nor do they contend that protection is confined to identical uses of famous marks or that the statute should be construed more narrowly in a case such as this. They do contend, however, that the statute requires proof of actual harm, rather than mere "likelihood" of harm. The contrast between the state statutes and the federal statute sheds light on this precise question. The former repeatedly refer to a "likelihood" of harm, rather than a completed harm, but the FTDA provides relief if another's commercial use of a mark or trade name "*causes dilution* of the [mark's] distinctive quality," § 1125(c)(1) (emphasis added). Thus, it unambiguously requires an actual dilution showing. This conclusion is confirmed by the FTDA's "dilution" definition itself, § 1127. That does not mean that the consequences of dilution, such as an actual loss of sales or profits, must also be proved. This Court disagrees with the Fourth Circuit's *Ringling Bros.* decision to the extent it suggests otherwise, but agrees with that court's conclusion that, at least where the marks at issue are not identical, the mere fact that consumers mentally associate the junior user's mark with a famous mark is not sufficient to establish actionable dilution. Such association will not necessarily reduce the famous mark's capacity to identify its owner's goods, the FTDA's dilution requirement. pp. 432–434.

The evidence in this case is insufficient to support summary judgment on the dilution count. There is a complete absence of evidence of any lessening of the VICTORIA'S SECRET mark's capacity to identify and distinguish goods or services sold in Victoria's Secret stores or advertised in its catalogs. The officer who saw the ad directed his offense entirely at petitioners, not respondents. And respondents' expert said nothing about the impact of petitioners' name on the strength of respondents' mark. Any difficulties of proof that may be entailed in demonstrating actual dilution are not an acceptable reason for dispensing with proof of an essential element of a statutory violation. P.434.

259 F.3d 464, reversed and remanded.

STEVENS, J., delivered the opinion for a unanimous Court with respect to Parts I, II, and IV, and the opinion of the Court with respect to Part III, in which REHNQUIST, C. J., and O'CONNOR, KENNEDY, SOUTER, THOMAS, GINSBURG, and BREYER, JJ., joined. KENNEDY, J., filed a concurring opinion, *post*, p. 435.

James R. Higgins, Jr., argued the cause for petitioners.
With him on the briefs was *Scot A. Duvall.*
Walter Dellinger argued the cause for respondents. With him on the brief was *Jonathan D. Hacker.*

Deputy Solicitor General Wallace argued the cause for the United States as amicus curiae. With him on the brief were Solicitor General Olson, Assistant Attorney General McCallum, Irving L. Gornstein, Anthony J. Steinmeyer, Mark S. Davies, John M. Whealan, Nancy C. Slutter, Cynthia C. Lynch, and James R. Hughes.*

JUSTICE STEVENS delivered the opinion of the Court.

In 1995 Congress amended § 43 of the Trademark Act of 1946, 15 U. S. C. § 1125, to provide a remedy for the "dilution of famous marks." 109 Stat. 985–986. That amendment, known as the Federal Trademark Dilution Act (FTDA), describes the factors that determine whether a mark is "distinctive".

Briefs of *amici curiae* urging affirmance were filed for the American Bar Association by *Robert E. Hirshon, Robert W Sacoff,* and *Uli Widmaier;* for the American Intellectual Property Law Association by *Jonathan Hudis, Amy C. Sullivan,* and *Roger W Parkhurst;* for Best Western International, Inc., et al. by *Avraham Azrieli, Joel W Nomkin, Charles A. Blanchard,* and *Suzanne R. Scheiner;* for Intel Corp. by *Jerrold J. Ganzfried, Mark I. Levy,* and *Thomas L. Casagrande;* for Andrew Beckerman-Rodau et al. by *Mark A. Lemley, pro se;* for the Intellectual Property Owners Association by *Laurence R. Hefter, Elizabeth McGoogan,* and *Ronald E. Myrick;* for the International Trademark Association by *Theodore H. Davis, Jr.,* and *Marie V. Driscoll;* and for Ringling Bros. Barnum & Bailey Combined Shows, Inc., et al. by *Robert A. Long, Jr.*

Malla Pollack, pro se, filed a brief as *amicus curiae.* JUSTICE SCALIA joins all but Part III of this opinion and defines the term "dilution" as "the lessening of the capacity of a famous mark to identify and distinguish goods or services." The question we granted.

The FTDA provides: "SEC. 3. REMEDIES FOR DILUTION OF FAMOUS MARKS.
(a) REMEDIEs.—Section 43 of the Trademark Act of 1946 (15 U. S. C. 1125) is amended by adding at the end the following new subsection:
(c)
(1) The owner of a famous mark shall be entitled, subject to the principles of equity and upon such terms as the court deems reasonable, to an injunction against another person's commercial use in commerce of a mark or trade name, if such use begins after the mark has become famous and causes dilution of the distinctive quality of the mark, and to obtain such other relief as is provided in this subsection. In determining whether a mark is distinctive and famous, a court may consider factors such as, but not limited to:
(A) the degree of inherent or acquired distinctiveness of the mark;
(B) the duration and extent of use of the mark in connection with the goods or services with which the mark is used;
(C) the duration and extent of advertising and publicity of the mark;
(D) the geographical extent of the trading area in which the mark is used;
(E) the channels of trade for the goods or services with which the mark is used;
(F) the degree of recognition of the mark in the trading areas and channels of trade used by the marks' owner and the person against whom the injunction is sought;
(G) the nature and extent of use of the same or similar marks by third parties; and

(H) whether the mark was registered under the Act of March 3, 1881, or the Act of February 20, 1905, or on the principal register.

(2) In an action brought under this subsection, the owner of the famous mark shall be entitled only to injunctive relief unless the person against whom the injunction is sought willfully intended to trade on the owner's reputation or to cause dilution of the famous mark. If such willful intent is proven, the owner of the famous mark shall also be entitled to the remedies set forth in Secs. 35(a) and 36, subject to the discretion of the court and the principles of equity.

(3) The ownership by a person of a valid registration under the Act of March 3, 1881, or the Act of February 20, 1905, or on the principal register shall be a complete bar to an action against that person, with respect to that mark, that is brought by another person under the common certiorari to decide is whether objective proof of actual injury to the economic value of a famous mark (as opposed to a presumption of harm arising from a subjective "likelihood of dilution" standard) is a requisite for relief under the FTDA.

(4) The following shall not be actionable under this section:

(A) Fair use of a famous mark by another person in comparative commercial advertising or promotion to identify the competing goods or services of the owner of the famous mark.

(B) Noncommercial use of a mark.

(C) All forms of news reporting and news commentary.'

(b) CONFORMING AMENDMENT.—The heading for title VIII of the Trademark Act of 1946 is amended by striking 'AND FALSE DESCRIPTIONS' and inserting "FALSE DESCRIPTIONS, AND DILUTION." SEC. 4. DEFINITION.

Section 45 of the Trademark Act of 1946 (15 U. S. C. 1127) is amended by inserting after the paragraph defining when a mark shall be deemed to be 'abandoned' the following:

The term "dilution" means the lessening of the capacity of a famous mark to identify and distinguish goods or services, regardless of the presence or absence of:

(1) competition between the owner of the famous mark and other parties, or

(2) likelihood of confusion, mistake, or deception.109 Stat. 985–986.

I

Petitioners, Victor and Cathy Moseley, own and operate a retail store named "Victor's Little Secret" in a strip mall in Elizabethtown, Kentucky. They have no employees.

Respondents are affiliated corporations that own the VICTORIA'S SECRET trademark and operate over 750 Victoria's Secret stores, two of which are in Louisville, Kentucky, a short drive from Elizabethtown. In 1998 they spent over $55 million advertising "the VICTORIA'S SECRET brand, one of moderately priced, high quality, attractively designed lingerie sold in a store setting designed to look like a woman's bedroom." App. 167, 170. They distribute 400 million copies of the Victori's Secret catalog each year, including 39,000 in Elizabethtown. In 1998 their sales exceeded $1.5 billion.

In the February 12, 1998, edition of a weekly publication distributed to residents of the military installation at Fort Knox, Kentucky, petitioners advertised the

"GRAND OPENING Just in time for Valentine's Day!" of their store "VICTOR'S SECRET" in nearby Elizabethtown. The ad featured "Intimate Lingerie *for every woman*"; "Romantic Lighting"; "Lycra Dresses"; "Pagers"; and "Adult Novelties/ Gifts." *Id.,* at 209. An army colonel, who saw the ad and was offended by what he perceived to be an attempt to use a reputable company's trademark to promote the sale of "unwholesome, tawdry merchandise," sent a copy to respondents. *Id.,* at 210. Their counsel then wrote to petitioners stating that their choice of the name "Victor's Secret" for a store selling lingerie was likely to cause confusion with the well-known VICTORIA'S SECRET mark and, in addition, was likely to "dilute the distinctiveness" of the mark. *Id.,* at 190–191. They requested the immediate discontinuance of the use of the name "and any variations thereof." *Ibid.* In response, petitioners changed the name of their store to "Victor's Little Secret." Because that change did not satisfy respondents, they promptly filed this action in Federal District Court. After being advised of a proposal to change the store name to "VICTOR'S LITTLE SECRETS," respondents' counsel requested detailed information about the store in order to consider whether that change "would be acceptable." App. 13–14. Respondents filed suit two months after this request.

The complaint contained four separate claims: (1) for trademark infringement alleging that petitioners' use of their trade name was "likely to cause confusion and/ or mistake in violation of 15 U. S. C. § 1114(1)"; (2) for unfair competition alleging misrepresentation in violation of § 1125(a); (3) for "federal dilution" in violation of the FTDA; and (4) for trademark infringement and unfair competition in violation of the common law of Kentucky. *Id.,* at 15, 20–23. In the dilution count, the complaint alleged that petitioners' conduct was "likely to blur and erode the distinctiveness" and "tarnish the reputation" of the VICTORIA'S SECRET trademark. *Ibid.*

After discovery the parties filed cross-motions for summary judgment. The record contained uncontradicted affidavits and deposition testimony describing the vast size of respondents' business, the value of the VICTORIA'S SECRET name, and descriptions of the items sold in the respective parties' stores. Respondents sell a "complete line of lingerie" and related items, each of which bears a VICTORIA'S SECRET label or tag. Petitioners sell a wide variety of items, including adult videos, "adult novelties," and lingerie. Victor Moseley stated in an affidavit that women's lingerie represented only about five percent of their sales. *Id.,* at 131. In support of their motion for summary judgment, respondents submitted an affidavit by an expert in marketing who explained "the enormous value" of respondents' mark. *Id.,* at 195–205. Neither he, nor any other witness, expressed any opinion concerning the impact, if any.

Respondents described their business as follows: "Victoria's Secret stores sell a complete line of lingerie, women's undergarments and nightwear, robes, caftans and kimonos, slippers, sachets, lingerie bags, hanging bags, candles, soaps, cosmetic brushes, atomizers, bath products and fragrances." *Id.,* at 168.

In answer to an interrogatory, petitioners stated that they "sell novelty action clocks, patches, temporary tattoos, stuffed animals, coffee mugs, leather biker wallets, zippo lighters, diet formula, diet supplements, jigsaw puzzles, whyss, handcufs [sic], hosiery bubble machines, greeting cards, calendars, incense burners, car air fresheners, sunglasses, ball caps, jewelry, candles, lava lamps, blacklights, fiber optic lights, rock and roll prints, lingerie, pagers, candy, adult video tapes, adult novelties, t-shirts, etc." *Id.,* at 87. of petitioners' use of the name "Victor's Little Secret" on that value.

Finding that the record contained no evidence of actual confusion between the parties' marks, the District Court concluded that "no likelihood of confusion exists as a matter of law" and entered summary judgment for petitioners on the infringement and unfair competition claims. Civ. Action No. 3:98CV-395-S (WD Ky., Feb. 9, 2000), App. to Pet. for Cert. 28a, 37a. With respect to the FTDA claim, however, the court ruled for respondents.

Noting that petitioners did not challenge Victoria's Secret's claim that its mark is "famous," the only question it had to decide was whether petitioners' use of their mark diluted the quality of respondents' mark. Reasoning from the premise that dilution "corrodes" a trademark either by "'blurring its product identification or by damaging positive associations that have attached to it,'" the court first found the two marks to be sufficiently similar to cause dilution, and then found "that Defendants' mark dilutes Plaintiffs' mark because of its tarnishing effect upon the Victoria's Secret mark" *Id.,* at 38a-39a (quoting *Ameritech, Inc.* v. *American Info. Technologies Corp.,* 811 F.2d 960, 965 *(CA6 1987)).* It therefore enjoined petitioners "from using the mark 'Victor's Little Secret' on the basis that it causes dilution of the distinctive quality of the Victoria's Secret mark" App. to Pet. for Cert. 38a-39a. The court did not, however, find that any "blurring" had occurred. *Ibid.*

The Court of Appeals for the Sixth Circuit affirmed. 259 F.3d 464 (2001). In a case decided shortly after the entry of the District Court's judgment in this case, the Sixth Circuit had adopted the standards for determining dilution under the FTDA that were enunciated by the Second Circuit in *Nabisco, Inc.* v. *PF Brands, Inc.,* 191 F.3d 208 (1999). See *Kellogg Co.* v. *Exxon Corp.,* 209 F.3d 562 *(CA6 2000).* In order to apply those standards, it was necessary to discuss two issues that the District Court had not specifically addressed-whether respondents' mark is "distinctive," and whether relief could be granted before dilution has actually occurred. With respect to the first issue, the court rejected the argument that Victoria's Secret could not be distinctive because "secret" is an ordinary word used by hundreds of lingerie concerns. The court concluded that the entire mark was "arbitrary and fanciful" and therefore deserving of a high level of trademark protection. 259 F. 3d, at 470.

It is quite clear that the statute intends distinctiveness, in addition to fame, as an essential element. The operative language defining the tort requires that 'the [junior] person's ... use ... caus[e] dilution of the distinctive quality of the [senior] mark.' 15 U. S. C. § 1125(c)(I). There can be no dilution of a mark's distinctive quality unless the mark is distinctive." *Nabisco, Inc.* v. *PF Brands, Inc.,* 191 F.3d 208, 216 *(CA2 1999).*

The Second Circuit explained why it did not believe "actual dilution" need be proved:

"Relying on a recent decision by the Fourth Circuit, Nabisco also asserts that proof of dilution under the FTDA requires proof of an 'actual, consummated harm.' *Ringling Bros.-Barnum & Bailey Combined Shows, Inc.* v. *Utah Division of Travel*

Dev., 170 F.3d 449, 464 (4th Cir. 1999). We reject the argument because we disagree with the Fourth Circuit's interpretation of the statute.

"It is not clear which of two positions the Fourth Circuit adopted by its requirement of proof of 'actual dilution.' *Id.* The narrower position would be that courts may not infer dilution from 'contextual factors (degree of mark and product similarity, etc.),' but must instead rely on evidence of 'actual loss of revenues' or the 'skillfully constructed consumer survey.' *Id.* at 457, 464–65. This strikes us as an arbitrary and unwarranted limitation on the methods of proof." *Id.,* at 223.

"In this case, for example, although the word 'secret' may provoke some intrinsic association with prurient interests, it is not automatically linked in the ordinary human experience with lingerie. 'Secret' is not particularly descriptive of bras and hosiery. Nor is there anything about the combination of the possessive 'Victoria's' and 'secret' that automatically conjures thought of women's underwear-except, of course, in the context of plaintiff's line of products. Hence, we conclude that the 'Victoria's Secret' mark ranks with those that are 'arbitrary and fanciful' and is therefore deserving of a high level of trademark protection. Although the district court applied a slightly different test from the one now established the second issue, the court relied on a distinction suggested by this sentence in the House Report: "Confusion leads to immediate injury, while dilution is an infection, which if allowed to spread, will inevitably destroy the advertising value of the mark." H. R. Rep. No. 104–374, p. 3 (1995). This statement, coupled with the difficulty of proving actual harm, lent support to the court's ultimate conclusion that the evidence in this case sufficiently established "dilution." 259 F. 3d, at 475–477. In sum, the Court of Appeals held:

"While no consumer is likely to go to the Moseleys' store expecting to find Victoria's Secret's famed Miracle Bra, consumers who hear the name 'Victor's Little Secret' are likely automatically to think of the more famous store and link it to the Moseleys' adult-toy, gag gift, and lingerie shop. This, then, is a classic instance of dilution by tarnishing (associating the Victoria's Secret name with sex toys and lewd coffee mugs) and by blurring (linking the chain with a single, unauthorized establishment). Given this conclusion, it follows that Victoria's Secret would prevail in a dilution analysis, even without an exhaustive consideration of all ten of the *Nabisco* factors." *Id.,* at 477.8.

In this circuit, the court would undoubtedly have reached the same result under the *Nabisco* test. Certainly, we cannot say that the court erred in finding that the preliminary factors of a dilution claim had been met by Victoria's Secret." 259 F. 3d, at 470–471.

The court had previously noted that the "Second Circuit has developed a list of ten factors used to determine if dilution has, in fact, occurred, while describing them as a 'nonexclusive list' to 'develop gradually over time' and with the particular facts of each case. Those factors are: distinctiveness; similarity of the marks; 'proximity of the products and the likelihood of bridging the gap;' 'interrelationship among the distinctiveness of the senior mark, the similarity of the junior mark, and the proximity of the products;' 'shared consumers and geographic limitations;' 'sophistication of consumers;' actual confusion; 'adjectival or referential quality of the junior use;' 'harm to the junior user and delay by the senior user;' and the 'effect of [the] senior's prior laxity in protecting the mark.'" *Id.*, at 476 (quoting *Nabisco,* 191 F. 3d, at 217–222).

In reaching that conclusion the Court of Appeals expressly rejected the holding of the Fourth Circuit in *Ringling Bros. Barnum & Bailey Combined Shows, Inc.* v. *Utah Div. of Travel Development,* 170 F.3d 449 (1999). In that case, which involved a claim that Utah's use on its license plates of the phrase "greatest *snow* on earth" was causing dilution of the "greatest *show* on earth," the court had concluded "that to establish dilution of a famous mark under the federal Act requires proof that (1) a defendant has made use of a junior mark sufficiently similar to the famous mark to evoke in a relevant universe of consumers a mental association of the two that (2) has caused (3) actual economic harm to the famous mark's economic value by lessening its former selling power as an advertising agent for its goods or services." *Id.,* at 461 (emphasis added). Because other Circuits have also expressed differing views about the "actual harm" issue, we granted certiorari to resolve the conflict. 535 U. S. 985 (2002).

II

Traditional trademark infringement law is a part of the broader law of unfair competition, see *Hanover Star Milling Co.* v. *Metcalf,* 240 U. S. 403, 413 (1916), that has its sources in English common law, and was largely codified in the Trademark Act of 1946 (Lanham Act). See B. Pattishall, D. Hilliard, & J. Welch, Trademarks and Unfair Competition 2 (4th ed. 2000) ("The United States took the [trademark and unfair competition] law of England as its own"). That law broadly prohibits uses of trademarks, trade names, and trade dress that are likely to cause confusion about the source of a product or service. See 15 U. S. C. §§ 1114, 1125(a)(1)(A). Infringement law protects consumers from being misled by the use of infringing marks and also protects producers from unfair practices by an "imitating competitor." *Qualitex Co.*

Because respondents did not appeal the District Court's adverse judgment on counts 1, 2, and 4 of their complaint, we decide the case on the assumption that the Moseleys' use of the name "Victor's Little Secret" neither confused any consumers or potential consumers, nor was likely to do so. Moreover, the disposition of those counts also makes it appropriate to decide the case on the assumption that there was no significant competition between the adversaries in this case. Neither the absence of any likelihood of confusion nor the absence of competition, however, provides a defense to the statutory dilution claim alleged in count 3 of the complaint.

Unlike traditional infringement law, the prohibitions against trademark dilution are not the product of common law development and are not motivated by an interest in protecting consumers. The seminal discussion of dilution is found in Frank Schechter's 1927 law review article concluding "that the preservation of the uniqueness of a trademark should constitute the only rational basis for its protection." Rational Basis of Trademark Protection, 40 Harv. L. Rev. 813, 831. Schechter supported his conclusion by referring to a German case protecting the owner of the well-known trademark "Odol" for mouthwash from use on various noncompeting steel products. That case, and indeed the principal focus of the Schechter article, involved an established arbitrary mark that had been "added to rather than withdrawn from the human vocabulary" and an infringement that made use of the identical mark. *Id.,* at 829.10.

The German court "held that the use of the mark, 'ado!' even on noncompeting goods was '*gegen die guten Sitten*,' pointing out that, when the public hears or reads the word 'Odol,' it thinks of the complainant's mouth wash, and that an article designated with the name 'ado!' leads the public to assume that it is of good quality. Consequently, concludes the court, complainant has 'the utmost interest in seeing that its mark is not diluted *[verwassert]*: it would lose in selling power if everyone used it as the designation of his goods.'" 40 Harv. L. Rev., at 831–832.

Schecter discussed this distinction at length: "The rule that arbitrary, coined or fanciful marks or names should be given a much broader degree of protection than symbols, words or phrases in common use would appear to be entirely sound. Such trademarks or tradenames as 'Blue Ribbon,' used, with or without registration, for all kinds of commodities or services, more than sixty times; 'Simplex' more than sixty times; 'Star,' as far back as 1898, nearly four hundred times; 'Anchor,' already registered over one hundred fifty times in 1898; 'Bull Dog,' over one hundred times by 1923; 'Gold Medal,' sixty-five times; '3-in-1' and '2-in-1,' seventy-nine times; 'Nox-all,' fifty times; 'Universal,' over thirty times; 'Lily White' over twenty times;- all these marks and names have, at this late date, very little distinctiveness in the public mind, and in most cases suggest merit, prominence or other qualities of goods or services in general, rather than the fact that the product or service, in connection with which the mark or name is used, emanates from a particular source. On the other hand, 'Rolls-Royce,' 'Aunt Jemima's,' 'Kodak,' 'Mazda,' 'Corona,' 'Nujol,' and 'Blue Goose,' are coined, arbitrary or fanciful words or phrases that have been added to rather than withdrawn from the human vocabulary by their owners, and have, from the very beginning, been associated in the public mind with a particular product, not with a variety of products, and have created in the public consciousness an impression or symbol of the excellence of the particular product in question." Id., at 828–829.

Some 20 years later Massachusetts enacted the first state statute protecting trademarks from dilution. It provided:

"Likelihood of injury to business reputation or of dilution of the distinctive quality of a trade name or trademark shall be a ground for injunctive relief in cases of trademark infringement or unfair competition notwithstanding the absence of competition between the parties or of confusion as to the source of goods or services." 1947 Mass. Acts p. 300, ch. 307.

Notably, that statute, unlike the "Odol" case, prohibited both the likelihood of "injury to business reputation" and "dilution." It thus expressly applied to both "tarnishment" and "blurring." At least 25 States passed similar laws in the decades before the FTDA was enacted in 1995. See Restatement (Third) of Unfair Competition § 25, Statutory Note (1995).

III

In 1988, when Congress adopted amendments to the Lanham Act, it gave consideration to an antidilution provision.

During the hearings on the 1988 amendments, objections to that provision based on a concern that it might have applied to expression protected by the First Amendment were voiced and the provision was deleted from the amendments. H. R. Rep. No. 100–1028 (1988). The bill, H. R. 1295, 104th Cong., 1st Sess., that was introduced in the House in 1995, and ultimately enacted as the FTDA, included two exceptions designed to avoid those concerns: a provision allowing "fair use" of a registered mark in comparative advertising or promotion, and the provision that noncommercial use of a mark shall not constitute dilution. See 15 U. S. C. § 1125(c)(4).

On July 19, 1995, the Subcommittee on Courts and Intellectual Property of the House Judiciary Committee held a i-day hearing on H. R. 1295. No opposition to the bill was voiced at the hearing and, with one minor amendment that extended protection to unregistered as well as registered marks, the subcommittee endorsed the bill and it passed the House unanimously. The committee's report stated that the "purpose of H. R. 1295 is to protect famous trademarks from subsequent uses that blur the distinctiveness of the mark or tarnish or disparage it, even in the absence of a likelihood of confusion." H. R. Rep. No. 104–374, p. 2 (1995). As examples of dilution, it stated that "the use of DUPONT shoes, BUICK aspirin, and KODAK pianos would be actionable under this legislation." *Id.,* at 3. In the Senate an identical bill, S. 1513, 104th Cong., 1st Sess., was introduced on December 29, 1995, and passed on the same day by voice vote without any hearings. In his explanation of the bill, Senator Hatch also stated that it was intended "to protect famous trademarks from subsequent uses that blur the distinctiveness of the mark or tarnish or disparage it," and referred to the Dupont Shoes, Buick aspirin, and Kodak piano examples, as well as to the Schechter law review article. 141 Congo Rec. 38559–38561 (1995).

IV

The VICTORIA'S SECRET mark is unquestionably valuable and petitioners have not challenged the conclusion that it qualifies as a "famous mark" within the meaning of the statute. Moreover, as we understand their submission, petitioners do not contend that the statutory protection is confined to identical uses of famous marks, or that the statute should be construed more narrowly in a case such as this. Even if the legislative history might lend some support to such a contention, it surely is not compelled by the statutory text.

The District Court's decision in this case rested on the conclusion that the name of petitioners' store "tarnished" the reputation of respondents' mark, and the Court of Appeals relied on both "tarnishment" and "blurring" to support its affirmance. Petitioners have not disputed the relevance of tarnishment, Tr. of Oral Arg. 5–7, presumably because that concept was prominent in litigation brought under state antidilution statutes and because it was mentioned in the legislative history. Whether it is actually embraced by the statutory text, however, is another matter. Indeed, the contrast between the state statutes, which expressly refer to both "injury to business reputation" and to "dilution of the distinctive quality of a trade name or trademark," and the federal statute which refers only to the latter, arguably supports a narrower reading of the FTDA. See Klieger, Trademark Dilution: The Whittling Away of the Rational Basis for Trademark Protection, 58 U. Pitt. L. Rev. 789, 812–813.

The contrast between the state statutes and the federal statute, however, sheds light on the precise question that we must decide. For those state statutes, like several provisions in the federal Lanham Act, repeatedly refer to a "likelihood" of harm, rather than to a completed harm. The relevant text of the FTDA, quoted in full in n. 1, *supra,* provides that "the owner of a famous mark" is entitled to injunctive relief against another person's commercial use of a mark or trade name if that use "*causes dilution* of the distinctive quality" of the famous mark. 15 U. S. C. § 1125(c)(1) (emphasis added). This text unambiguously requires a showing of actual dilution, rather than a likelihood of dilution.

This conclusion is fortified by the definition of the term "dilution" itself. That definition provides:

"The term 'dilution' means the lessening of the capacity of a famous mark to identify and distinguish goods or services, regardless of the presence or absence of"

"(1) competition between the owner of the famous mark and other parties," or

"(2) likelihood of confusion, mistake, or deception." § 1127.

The contrast between the initial reference to an actual "lessening of the capacity" of the mark, and the later reference to a "likelihood of confusion, mistake, or deception" in the second caveat confirms the conclusion that actual dilution must be established.

Of course, that does not mean that the consequences of dilution, such as an actual loss of sales or profits, must also be proved. To the extent that language in the Fourth Circuit's opinion in the *Ringling Bros.* case suggests otherwise, see 170 F. 3d, at 460–465, we disagree. We do agree, however, with that court's conclusion that, at least where the marks at issue are not identical, the mere fact that consumers mentally associate the junior user's mark with a famous mark is not sufficient to establish actionable dilution. As the facts of that case demonstrate, such mental association will not necessarily reduce the capacity of the famous mark to identify the goods of its owner, the statutory requirement for dilution under the FTDA. For even though Utah drivers may be reminded of the circus when they see a license plate referring to the "greatest *snow* on earth," it by no means follows that they will associate "the greatest show on earth" with skiing or snow sports, or associate it less strongly or exclusively with the circus. "Blurring" is not a necessary consequence of mental association. (Nor, for that matter, is "tarnishing.").

The record in this case establishes that an army officer who saw the advertisement of the opening of a store named "Victor's Secret" did make the mental association with "Victoria's Secret," but it also shows that he did not therefore form any different impression of the store that his wife and daughter had patronized. There is a complete absence of evidence of any lessening of the capacity of the VICTORIA'S SECRET mark to identify and distinguish goods or services sold in Victoria's Secret stores or advertised in its catalogs. The officer was offended by the ad, but it did not change his conception of Victoria's Secret. His offense was directed entirely at petitioners, not at respondents. Moreover, the expert retained by respondents had nothing to say about the impact of petitioners' name on the strength of respondents' mark.

Noting that consumer surveys and other means of demonstrating actual dilution are expensive and often unreliable, respondents and their *amici* argue that evidence of an actual "lessening of the capacity of a famous mark to identify and distinguish goods or services," § 1127, may be difficult to obtain. It may well be, however, that direct evidence of dilution such as consumer surveys will not be necessary if actual dilution can reliably be proved through circumstantial evidence-the obvious case is one where the junior and senior marks are identical. Whatever difficulties of proof may be entailed, they are not an acceptable reason for dispensing with proof of an essential element of a statutory violation. The evidence in the present record is not sufficient to support the summary judgment on the dilution count. The judgment is therefore reversed, and the case is remanded for further proceedings consistent with this opinion.

It is so ordered

As of this date, few courts have reviewed the statute we are considering, the Federal Trademark Dilution Act, 15 U. S. C. § 1125(c), and I agree with the Court that the evidentiary showing required by the statute can be clarified on remand. The conclusion that the VICTORIA'S SECRET mark is a famous mark has not been challenged throughout the litigation, *ante,* at 425, 432, and seems not to be in question. The remaining issue is what factors are to be considered to establish dilution.

For this inquiry, considerable attention should be given, in my view, to the word "capacity" in the statutory phrase that defines dilution as "the lessening of the capacity of a famous mark to identify and distinguish goods or services." 15 U. S. C. § 1127. When a competing mark is first adopted, there will be circumstances when the case can turn on the probable consequences its commercial use will have for the famous mark. In this respect, the word "capacity" imports into the dilution inquiry both the present and the potential power of the famous mark to identify and distinguish goods, and in some cases the fact that this power will be diminished could suffice to show dilution. Capacity is defined as "the power or ability to hold, receive, or accommodate." Webster's Third New International Dictionary 330 (1961); see also Webster's New International Dictionary 396 (2d ed. 1949) ("Power of receiving, containing, or absorbing"); 2 Oxford English Dictionary 857 (2d ed. 1989) ("Ability to receive or contain; holding power"); American Heritage Dictionary 275 (4th ed. 2000) ("The ability to receive, hold, or absorb"). If a mark will erode or lessen the power of the famous mark to give customers the assurance of quality and the full satisfaction they have in knowing they have purchased goods bearing the famous mark, the elements of dilution may be established.

Diminishment of the famous mark's capacity can be shown by the probable consequences flowing from use or adoption of the competing mark. This analysis is confirmed by the statutory authorization to obtain injunctive relief. 15 U. S. C. § 1125(c)(2). The essential role of injunctive relief is to "prevent future wrong, although no right has yet been violated." *Swift & Co.* v. *United States,* 276 U. S. 311, 326 (1928). Equity principles encourage those who are injured to assert their rights promptly. A holder of a famous mark threatened with diminishment of the mark's capacity to serve its purpose should not be forced to wait until the damage is done and the distinctiveness of the mark has been eroded.

In this case, the District Court found that petitioners' trademark had tarnished the VICTORIA'S SECRET mark. App. to Pet. for Cert. 38a-39a. The Court of Appeals affirmed this conclusion and also found dilution by blurring. 259 F.3d 464, 477 (CA6 2001). The Court's opinion does not foreclose injunctive relief if respondents on remand present sufficient evidence of either blurring or tarnishment.

With these observations, I join the opinion of the Court.

2.3 Analysis of the Case

Moseley v. V Secret Catalogue, Inc., 537 U.S. 418 (2003).

The text of Mosely v. Victoria's Secret Catalogue is available here:

https://supreme.justia.com/cases/federal/us/537/418/

Moseley v. V Secret Catalogue, Inc., is a decision by the Supreme Court of the United States holding that, under the Lanham Act, a claim of trademark dilution requires proof of actual dilution. This decision was later superseded by the Trademark Dilution Revision Act of 2006 (TDRA), in which the U.S. Congress attempted to clarify what trademark dilution is, and to fix some mistakes in the previous dilution statute that the Supreme Court had made evident in its opinion.

Victoria's Secret is a registered trademark held by V Secret Catalogue, Inc., which was founded in 1988. Its stores sell moderately priced high-quality lingerie. By 1998 the company was spending $55 million in advertising its brand, operating 750 Victoria's Secret stores, including two in Louisville, Kentucky, and distributing 400 million copies of its catalogues. Also in 1998, a weekly publication distributed to residents of Fort Knox, Kentucky contained an ad for the grand opening of a store called Victor's Secret that was owned by Victor and Cathy Moseley which sold lingerie and adult novelties and gifts. An army colonel who saw the ad was offended by what he perceived to be an attempt to use a reputable company's trademark to sell "unwholesome, tawdry merchandise" and contacted Victoria's Secret, which then requested that the Moseleys immediately discontinue the use of the name Victor's Secret and "any variations thereof." In response the Moseleys changed the name of the store to Victor's Little Secret. Unsatisfied with this name change, V Secret Catalogue, Inc. filed suit alleging, among other claims, a violation of the Federal Trademark Dilution Act of 1996, then in effect.

The trial court held that the two names were sufficiently similar to cause dilution, and that the Victor's Little Secret mark diluted the Victoria's Secret mark through its tarnishing effect. The Sixth Circuit Court of Appeals affirmed, but noted that after the trial court's decision, the Court of Appeals had adopted standards for determining dilution under the FTDA of 1996 based on a test articulated in a Second Circuit case. Under this test, it was not necessary for the mark holder to establish that any economic harm had occurred because of the dilution. This analysis was in direct conflict with a Fourth Circuit case which held that proof of actual economic damages was necessary to prevail on a trademark dilution claim. The Supreme Court granted certiorari to resolve the legal conflict caused by this circuit split and addressed the question of whether the Federal Trademark Dilution Act of 1996 required objective proof of actual injury to the economic value of a famous mark for relief.

Justice John Paul Stevens wrote the opinion for an almost unanimous Court, which held that the Federal Trademark Dilution Act of 1996 required proof of actual dilution. The Court reasoned this standard (as opposed to a presumption of harm arising from a subjective "likelihood of dilution" standard) controlled. Many famous mark holders were upset with this holding and lobbied the U.S. Congress to amend the dilution statute. Congress was responsive and in 2006 the Trademark Dilution Revision Act of 2006 (TDRA) took effect. In the Trademark Dilution Revision Act of 2006, Congress adopted the "likelihood of dilution" approach rejected by the Supreme Court in its Moseley v. V Secret Catalogue opinion. The "likelihood of dilution" standard requires only that the famous mark holder demonstrate a likelihood of dilution, and not a showing of actual dilution. The TDRA has therefore made it easier for mark holders to obtain dilution protection, in contravention of the reasoning of the Supreme Court in this case.

(3) **The protection of trade dress under Lanham Act—Wal-Mart Stores, INC. v. Samara Brothers, INC.**

OCTOBER TERM, 1999
CERTIORARI TO THE UNITED STATES COURT OF APPEALS FOR THE SECOND CIRCUIT
No. 99–150. Argued January 19, 2000-Decided March 22, 2000.

3.1 Syllabus
Respondent Samara Brothers, Inc., designs and manufactures a line of children's clothing. Petitioner Wal-Mart Stores, Inc., contracted with a supplier to manufacture outfits based on photographs of Samara garments. After discovering that Wal-Mart and other retailers were selling the so-called knockoffs, Samara brought this action for, *inter alia,* infringement of unregistered trade dress under §43(a) of the Trademark Act of 1946 (Lanham Act). The jury found for Samara. Wal-Mart then renewed a motion for judgment as a matter of law, claiming that there was insufficient evidence to support a conclusion that Samara's clothing designs could be legally protected as distinctive trade dress for purposes of § 43(a). The District Court denied the motion and awarded Samara relief. The Second Circuit affirmed the denial of the motion.

3.2 Reasoning:
In a § 43(a) action for infringement of unregistered trade dress, a product's design is distinctive, and therefore protectible, only upon a showing of secondary meaning. Pp.209–216.
(a) In addition to protecting registered trademarks, the Lanham Act, in § 43(a), gives a producer a cause of action for the use by any person of "any ... symbo[l] or device ... likely to cause confusion ... as to the origin ... of his or her goods." The breadth of the confusion-producing elements actionable under § 43(a) has been held to embrace not just word marks and symbol marks, but also "trade dress"—a category that originally included only the packaging, or "dressing," of a product, but in recent years has been expanded by many Courts of Appeals to encompass the product's design. These courts have correctly assumed that trade dress constitutes a "symbol" or "device" for Lanham Act purposes. Although § 43(a) does not explicitly require a producer to show that its trade dress is distinctive, courts have universally imposed that requirement, since without distinctiveness the trade dress would not "cause confusion ... as to ... origin," as § 43(a) requires. In evaluating distinctiveness,

courts have differentiated between marks that are inherently distinctive—i.e., marks whose intrinsic nature serves to identify their particular source-and marks that have acquired distinctiveness through secondary meaning—i.e., marks whose primary significance, in the minds of the public, is to identify the product's source rather than the product itself. This Court has held, however, that applications of at least one category of mark-color-can *never* be inherently distinctive, although they can be protected upon a showing of secondary meaning. *Qualitex Co.* v. *Jacobson Products Co.,* 514 U. S. 159, 162–163. Pp. 209–212.

(b) Design, like color, is not inherently distinctive. The attribution of inherent distinctiveness to certain categories of word marks and product packaging derives from the fact that the very purpose of attaching a particular word to a product, or encasing it in a distinctive package, is most often to identify the product's source. Where it is not reasonable to assume consumer predisposition to take an affixed word or packaging as indication of source, inherent distinctiveness will not be found. With product design, as with color, consumers are aware of the reality that, almost invariably, that feature is intended not to identify the source, but to render the product itself more useful or more appealing. Pp.212–214.

(c) *Two Pesos, Inc.* v. *Taco Cabana, Inc.,* 505 U. S. 763, does not foreclose the Court's conclusion, since the trade dress there at issue was restaurant decor, which does not constitute product *design,* but rather product packaging or else some *tertium quid* that is akin to product packaging and has no bearing on the present case. While distinguishing *Two Pesos* might force courts to draw difficult lines between product-design and product-packaging trade dress, the frequency and difficulty of having to distinguish between the two will be much less than the frequency and difficulty of having to decide when a product design is inherently distinctive. To the extent there are close cases, courts should err on the side of caution and classify ambiguous trade dress as product design, thereby requiring secondary meaning. Pp. 214–215.

165 F.3d 120, reversed and remanded.

WAL-MART STORES, INC. *v.* SAMARA BROTHERS, INC.

SCALIA, J., delivered the opinion for a unanimous Court.

William D. Coston argued the cause for petitioner. With him on the briefs were *Kenneth C. Bass* III and *Martin L. Saad.*

Deputy Solicitor General Wallace argued the cause for the United States as amicus curiae urging reversal. With him on the brief were Solicitor General Waxman, Acting Assistant Attorney General Ogden, Edward C. DuMont, Barbara C. Biddle, Alfred Mollin, Albin F. Drost, and Nancy C. Slutter. *Stuart M. Riback* argued the cause for respondent. With him on the brief was *Mark 1. Levy.* *

*Briefs of *amici curiae* urging reversal were filed for the International Mass Retail Association by *Jeffrey* S. *Sutton* and *Robert J. Verdisco;* for the Private Label Manufacturers Association by *Arthur M. Handler;* and for Scott P. Zimmerman by *Charles W Calkins.*

H. Bartow Farr III, Richard G. Taranto, and *Stephen M. Trattner* filed a brief for Ashley Furniture Industries, Inc., et al. as *amici curiae* urging affirmance.

Briefs of *amici curiae* were filed for the American Intellectual Property Law Association by *Sheldon H. Klein, Michael A. Grow,* and *Louis T. Pirkey;* for the

International Trademark Association by *Theodore H. Davis, Jr., Morton D. Goldberg*, and *Marie V. Driscoll;* and for Payless Shoesource, Inc., by *William A. Rudy* and *Robert Kent Sellers.*

JUSTICE SCALIA delivered the opinion of the Court.

In this case, we decide under what circumstances a product's design is distinctive, and therefore protectible, in an action for infringement of unregistered trade dress under § 43(a) of the Trademark Act of 1946 (Lanham Act), 60 Stat. 441, as amended, 15 U. S. C. § 1125(a).

I

Respondent Samara Brothers, Inc., designs and manufactures children's clothing. Its primary product is a line of spring/summer one-piece seersucker outfits decorated with appliques of hearts, flowers, fruits, and the like. A number of chain stores, including JCPenney, sell this line of clothing under contract with Samara.

Petitioner Wal-Mart Stores, Inc., is one of the Nation's best known retailers, selling among other things children's clothing. In 1995, Wal-Mart contracted with one of its suppliers, Judy-Philippine, Inc., to manufacture a line of children's outfits for sale in the 1996 spring/summer season. Wal-Mart sent Judy-Philippine photographs of a number of garments from Samara's line, on which Judy-Philippine's garments were to be based; Judy-Philippine duly copied, with only minor modifications, 16 of Samara's garments, many of which contained copyrighted elements. In 1996, Wal-Mart briskly sold the so-called knockoffs, generating more than $1.15 million in gross profits.

In June 1996, a buyer for JCPenney called a representative at Samara to complain that she had seen Samara garments on sale at Wal-Mart for a lower price than JCPenney was allowed to charge under its contract with Samara. The Samara representative told the buyer that Samara did not supply its clothing to Wal-Mart. Their suspicions aroused, however, Samara officials launched an investigation, which disclosed that Wal-Mart and several other major retailers Kmart, Caldor, Hills, and Goody's-were selling the knockoffs of Samara's outfits produced by Judy-Philippine.

After sending cease-and-desist letters, Samara brought this action in the United States District Court for the Southern District of New York against Wal-Mart, Judy-Philippine, Kmart, Caldor, Hills, and Goody's for copyright infringement under federal law, consumer fraud and unfair competition under New York law, and most relevant for our purposes infringement of unregistered trade dress under § 43(a) of the Lanham Act, 15 U. S. C. § 1125(a). All of the defendants except Wal-Mart settled before trial.

After a weeklong trial, the jury found in favor of Samara on all of its claims. Wal-Mart then renewed a motion for judgment as a matter of law, claiming, *inter alia,* that there was insufficient evidence to support a conclusion that Samara's clothing designs could be legally protected as distinctive trade dress for purposes of § 43(a). The District Court denied the motion, 969 F. Supp. 895 (SDNY 1997), and awarded Samara damages, interest, costs, and fees totaling almost $1.6 million, together with injunctive relief, see App. to Pet. for Cert. 56–58. The Second Circuit affirmed the denial of the motion for judgment as a matter of law, 165 F.3d 120 (1998), and we granted certiorari, 528 U. S. 808 (1999).

II

The Lanham Act provides for the registration of trademarks, which it defines in § 45 to include "any word, name, symbol, or device, or any combination thereof [used or intended to be used] to identify and distinguish [a producer's] goods ... from those manufactured or sold by others and to indicate the source of the goods ...." 15 U. S. C. § 1127. Registration of a mark under § 2 of the Lanham Act, 15 U. S. C. § 1052, enables the owner to sue an infringer under § 32, 15 U. S. C. § 1114; it also entitles the owner to a presumption that its mark is valid, see § 7(b), 15 U. S. C. § 1057(b), and ordinarily renders the registered mark incontestable after five years of continuous use, see § 15, 15 U. S. C. § 1065. In addition to protecting registered marks, the Lanham Act, in § 43(a), gives a producer a cause of action for the use by any person of "any word, term, name, symbol, or device, or any combination thereof ... which ... is likely to cause confusion ... as to the origin, sponsorship, or approval of his or her goods ...." 15 U. S. C. § 1125(a). It is the latter provision that is at issue in this case.

The breadth of the definition of marks registrable under § 2, and of the confusion-producing elements recited as actionable by § 43(a), has been held to embrace not just word marks, such as "Nike," and symbol marks, such as Nike's "swoosh" symbol, but also "trade dress"—a category that originally included only the packaging, or "dressing," of a product, but in recent years has been expanded by many Courts of Appeals to encompass the design of a product. See, e.g., *Ashley Furniture Industries, Inc.* v. *Sangiacomo* N. A., *Ltd.,* 187 F.3d 363 *(CA4* 1999) (bedroom furniture); *Knit-waves, Inc.* v. *Lolly togs, Ltd.,* 71 F.3d 996 *(CA2 1995)* (sweaters); *Stuart Hall Co., Inc.* v. *Ampad Corp.,* 51 F.3d 780 *(CA8* 1995) (notebooks). These courts have assumed, often without discussion, that trade dress constitutes a "symbol" or "device" for purposes of the relevant sections, and we conclude likewise. "Since human beings might use as a 'symbol' or 'device' almost anything at all that is capable of carrying meaning, this language, read literally, is not restrictive." *Qualitex Co.* v. *Jacobson Products Co.,* 514 U. S. 159, 162 (1995). This reading of § 2 and § 43(a) is buttressed by a recently added subsection of § 43(a), § 43(a)(3), which refers specifically to "civil action[s] for trade dress infringement under this chapter for trade dress not registered on the principal register." 15 U. S. C. § 1125(a)(3) (1994 ed., Supp. V).

The text of § 43(a) provides little guidance as to the circumstances under which unregistered trade dress may be protected. It does require that a producer show that the allegedly infringing feature is not "functional," see § 43(a)(3), and is likely to cause confusion with the product for which protection is sought, see § 43(a)(1)(A), 15 U. S. C. § 1125(a)(1)(A). Nothing in § 43(a) explicitly requires a producer to show that its trade dress is distinctive, but courts have universally imposed that requirement, since without distinctiveness the trade dress would not "cause confusion ... as to the origin, sponsorship, or approval of [the] goods," as the section requires. Distinctiveness is, moreover, an explicit prerequisite for registration of trade dress under § 2, and "the general principles qualifying a mark for registration under § 2 of the Lanham Act are for the most part applicable in determining whether an unregistered mark is entitled to protection under § 43(a)." *Two Pesos, Inc. v. Taco Cabana, Inc.,* 505 U. S. 763, 768 (1992) (citations omitted).

In evaluating the distinctiveness of a mark under § 2 (and therefore, by analogy, under § 43(a)), courts have held that a mark can be distinctive in one of two ways. First, a mark is inherently distinctive if "[its] intrinsic nature serves to identify a particular source." *Ibid.* In the context of word marks, courts have applied the now-classic test originally formulated by Judge Friendly, in which word marks that are "arbitrary" ("Camel" cigarettes), "fanciful" ("Kodak" film), or "suggestive" ("Tide" laundry detergent) are held to be inherently distinctive. See *Abercrombie & Fitch Co. v. Hunting World, Inc.,* 537 F.2d 4, 10–11 *(CA2* 1976). Second, a mark has acquired distinctiveness, even if it is not inherently distinctive, if it has developed secondary meaning, which occurs when, "in the minds of the public, the primary significance of a [mark] is to identify the source of the product rather than the product itself." *Inwood Laboratories, Inc. v. Ives Laboratories, Inc.,* 456 U. S. 844, 851, n. 11 (1982).[70]

The judicial differentiation between marks that are inherently distinctive and those that have developed secondary meaning has solid foundation in the statute itself. Section 2 requires that registration be granted to any trademark "by which the goods of the applicant may be distinguished from the goods of others"—subject to various limited exceptions. 15 U. S. C. § 1052. It also provides, again with limited exceptions, that "nothing in this chapter shall prevent the registration of a mark used by the applicant which has become distinctive of the applicant's goods in commerce"— that is, which is not inherently distinctive but has become so only through secondary meaning. § 2(f), 15 U. S. C. § 1052(f). Nothing in § 2, however, demands the conclusion that *every* category of mark necessarily includes some marks "by which the goods of the applicant may be distinguished from the goods of others" *without* secondary meaning-that in every category some marks are inherently distinctive.

Indeed, with respect to at least one category of mark colors—we have held that no mark can ever be inherently distinctive. See *Qualitex, supra,* at 162–163. In *Qualitex,* petitioner manufactured and sold green-gold dry-cleaning press pads. After respondent began selling pads of a similar color, petitioner brought suit under § 43(a), then added a claim under § 32 after obtaining registration for the color of its pads. We held that a color could be protected as a trademark, but only upon a showing of secondary meaning. Reasoning by analogy to the *Abercrombie & Fitch* test developed for word marks, we noted that a product's color is unlike a "fanciful," "arbitrary," or "suggestive" mark, since it does not "almost *automatically* tell a customer that [it] refer[s] to a brand," 514 U. S., at 162–163, and does not "immediately ... signal a brand

---

[70] The phrase "secondary meaning" originally arose in the context of word marks, where it served to distinguish the source-identifying meaning from the ordinary, or "primary," meaning of the word. "Secondary meaning" has since come to refer to the acquired, source-identifying meaning of a nonword mark as well. It is often a misnomer in that context, since nonword marks ordinarily have no "primary" meaning. Clarity might well be served by using the term "acquired meaning" in both the wordmark and the nonword-mark contexts-but in this opinion we follow what has become the conventional terminology.

or a product 'source,'" *id.,* at 163. However, we noted that, "over time, customers may come to treat a particular color on a product or its packaging ... as signifying a brand." *Ibid.* Because a color, like a "descriptive" word mark, could eventually "come to indicate a product's origin," we concluded that it could be protected *upon a showing of secondary meaning. Ibid.*

It seems to us that design, like color, is not inherently distinctive. The attribution of inherent distinctiveness to certain categories of word marks and product packaging derives from the fact that the very purpose of attaching a particular word to a product, or encasing it in a distinctive packaging, is most often to identify the source of the product. Although the words and packaging can serve subsidiary functions—a suggestive word mark (such as "Tide" for laundry detergent), for instance, may invoke positive connotations in the consumer' mind, and a garish form of packaging (such as Tide's squat, brightly decorated plastic bottles for its liquid laundry detergent) may attract an otherwise indifferent consumer's attention on a crowded store shelf—their predominant function remains source identification. Consumers are therefore predisposed to regard those symbols as indication of the producer, which is why such symbols "almost *automatically* tell a customer that they refer to a brand," *id.,* at 162–163, and "immediately ... signal a brand or a product 'source,'" *id.,* at 163. And where it is not reasonable to assume consumer predisposition to take an affixed word or packaging as indication of source-where, for example, the affixed word is descriptive of the product ("Tasty" bread) or of a geographic origin ("Georgia" peaches)—inherent distinctiveness will not be found. That is why the statute generally excludes, from those word marks that can be registered as inherently distinctive, words that are "merely descriptive" of the goods, § 2(e)(1), 15 U. S. C. § 1052(e)(1), or "primarily geographically descriptive of them," see § 2(e)(2), 15 U. S. C. § 1052(e)(2). In the case of product design, as in the case of color, we think consumer predisposition to equate the feature with the source does not exist. Consumers are aware of the reality that, almost invariably, even the most unusual of product designs-such as a cocktail shaker shaped like a penguin—is intended not to identify the source, but to render the product itself more useful or more appealing.

The fact that product design almost invariably serves purposes other than source identification not only renders inherent distinctiveness problematic; it also renders application of an inherent-distinctiveness principle more harmful to other consumer interests. Consumers should not be deprived of the benefits of competition with regard to the utilitarian and esthetic purposes that product design ordinarily serves by a rule of law that facilitates plausible threats of suit against new entrants based upon alleged inherent distinctiveness. How easy it is to mount a plausible suit depends, of course, upon the clarity of the test for inherent distinctiveness, and where product design is concerned we have little confidence that a reasonably clear test can be devised. Respondent and the United States as *amicus curiae* urge us to adopt for product design relevant portions of the test formulated by the Court of Customs and Patent Appeals for product packaging in *Seabrook Foods, Inc. v. Bar-Well Foods, Ltd.,* 568 F. 2d 1342 (1977). That opinion, in determining the inherent distinctiveness of a product's packaging, considered, among other things, "whether it was a 'common'. basic shape or design, whether it was unique or unusual in a particular field, [and] whether it was a mere refinement of a commonly adopted and well-known form of ornamentation for a particular class of goods viewed by the public as a dress or ornamentation for the goods." *Id.,* at 1344 (footnotes omitted). Such a test would rarely provide the basis for summary disposition of an anticompetitive strike suit. Indeed, at oral argument, counsel for the United States quite understandably would not give a definitive answer as to whether the test was met in this very case, saying only that "[t]his is a very difficult case for that purpose." Tr. of Oral Arg. 19.

It is true, of course, that the person seeking to exclude new entrants would have to establish the nonfunctionality of the design feature, see § 43(a)(3), 15 U. S. C. § 1125(a)(3) (1994 ed., Supp. V)—a showing that may involve consideration of its esthetic appeal, see *Qualitex, supra,* at 170. Competition is deterred, however, not merely by successful suit but by the plausible threat of successful suit, and given the unlikelihood of inherently source-identifying design, the game of allowing suit based upon alleged inherent distinctiveness seems to us not worth the candle. That is especially so since the producer can ordinarily obtain protection for a design that *is* inherently source identifying (if any such exists), but that does not yet have secondary meaning, by securing a design patent or a copyright for the design—as, indeed, respondent did for certain elements of the designs in this case. The availability of these other protections greatly reduces any harm to the producer that might ensue from our conclusion that a product design cannot be protected under § 43(a) without a showing of secondary meaning.

Respondent contends that our decision in *Two Pesos* forecloses a conclusion that product-design trade dress can never be inherently distinctive. In that case, we held that the trade dress of a chain of Mexican restaurants, which the plaintiff described as "a festive eating atmosphere having interior dining and patio areas decorated with artifacts, bright colors, paintings and murals," 505 U. S., at 765 (internal quotation marks and citation omitted), could be protected under § 43(a) without a showing of secondary meaning, see *id.,* at 776. *Two Pesos* unquestionably establishes the legal principle that trade dress can be inherently distinctive, see, e.g., *id.,* at 773, but it does not establish that *product-design* trade dress can be. *Two Pesos* is inapposite to our holding here because the trade dress at issue, the decor of a restaurant, seems to us not to constitute product *design.* It was either product packaging—which, as we have discussed, normally *is* taken by the consumer to indicate origin—or else some *tertium quid* that is akin to product packaging and has no bearing on the present case.

Respondent replies that this manner of distinguishing *Two Pesos* will force courts to draw difficult lines between product-design and product-packaging trade dress. There will indeed be some hard cases at the margin: a classic glass Coca-Cola bottle, for instance, may constitute packaging for those consumers who drink the Coke and then discard the bottle, but may constitute the product itself for those consumers who are bottle collectors, or part of the product itself for those consumers who buy Coke in the classic glass bottle, rather than a can, because they think it more stylish to drink from the former. We believe, however, that the frequency and the difficulty of having to distinguish between product design and product packaging will be much less than the frequency and the difficulty of having to decide when a product design is inherently distinctive. To the extent there are close cases, we believe that courts should err on the side of caution and classify ambiguous trade dress as product design, thereby requiring secondary meaning. The very closeness will suggest the existence of relatively small utility in adopting an inherent-distinctiveness principle, and relatively great consumer benefit in requiring a demonstration of secondary meaning.

We hold that, in an action for infringement of unregistered trade dress under § 43(a) of the Lanham Act, a product's design is distinctive, and therefore protectible, only upon a showing of secondary meaning. The judgment of the Second Circuit is reversed, and the case is remanded for further proceedings consistent with this opinion.

It is so ordered.

3.3 Analysis of the Case

Wal-Mart Stores, Inc. v. Samara Brothers, Inc., 529 U.S. 205 (2000).
The text of Walmart v. Samara Brothers is available here:
https://supreme.justia.com/cases/federal/us/529/205/
Related case: Two Pesos, Inc. v. Taco Cabana, Inc., 505 U.S. 763 (1992).
The text of Two Pesos v. Taco Cabana is available here: https://www.law.cornell.edu/supct/html/91-971.ZO.html).

Wal-Mart Stores, Inc. v. Samara Brothers is a case in which the U.S. Supreme Court partially undid its unfortunate and ill-advised previous holding in Two Pesos v. Taco Cabana. Taco Cabana, a fast food Mexican restaurant chain in San Antonio, Texas, had developed a style of decorating its restaurants that it asserted was protectable "trade dress" under the Lanham Act. Two Pesos, another similar restaurant chain based in Houston, Texas, opened a few years later with restaurants that had an arguably similar look.

In 1992, Taco Cabana sued Two Pesos under the Lanham Act, alleging that Two Pesos copied Taco Cabana's distinctive trade dress. At trial, the judge instructed the jury that trade dress must be inherently distinctive or have acquired a secondary meaning to be protectable. The jury found that Taco Cabana's trade dress was inherently distinctive but had not acquired a secondary meaning. The trade dress was therefore protectable in the Fifth Circuit, because it was inherently distinctive. However, it would not have been protectable in the Second Circuit, which required a showing of secondary meaning before it would protect unregistered trade dress under the Lanham Act. In consequence, the U.S. Supreme Court granted certiorari so that it could resolve this circuit split. It had to decide whether trade dress could be inherently distinctive, or whether proof of a secondary meaning was required before trade dress received protection under the Lanham Act.

The U.S. Supreme Court decided to follow the jurisprudence of the Fifth Circuit and held that trade dress can be protected under the Lanham Act without a showing of secondary meaning if it is inherently distinctive. The Court held that there was no persuasive reason to treat unregistered trade dress differently from registered trademarks and asserted that requiring a showing of secondary meaning for protection would go against the purposes of the Lanham Act.

The U.S. Supreme Court's holding in Two Pesos v. Taco Cabana was not well received by several lower courts, because it did not provide a test or analytical framework with which to determine when trade dress was inherently distinctive. The opinion was also widely criticized for being anticompetitive because the unregistered nature of trade dress in something like restaurant décor meant that competitors did not have any notice about which elements of the decor the mark holder was asserting rights over. If Taco Cabana had festive Mexican sombreros hanging on the walls, did this mean that no other restaurant could do that? There was not any registration paperwork to refer to. Competitors might only find out definitively whether festive Mexican sombreros were "protected trade dress" after a long and expensive infringement trial. Taco Cabana had every incentive to claim Lanham Act protections over very simple design elements such as wall color. So did every other business owner that wanted a legal mechanism with which to needle its competitors.

Eight years later in 2000, the U.S. Supreme Court decided to revisit the issue in Wal-Mart v. Samara Brothers. Samara Brothers designed and manufactured a popular line of appliqued seersucker children's clothing. Wal-Mart Stores, Inc. contracted with a supplier to manufacture outfits based on photographs of Samara garments, which were sold under Wal-Mart's house label, "Small Steps." When the supplier manufactured the clothes, it copied sixteen of Samara's garments with some small modifications to produce the line of clothes required under its contract with Wal-Mart.

After discovering that Wal-Mart was selling the "Small Steps" knockoffs, Samara Brothers brought an action for infringement of unregistered trade dress under Sec. 43(a) of the Lanham Act. The jury found for Samara and awarded the company more than $1 million in damages. Wal-Mart unsuccessfully appealed the conclusion that Samara's clothing designs could be legally protected as trade dress in both the trial court and the Second Circuit Court of Appeals. Ultimately, however, Wal-Mart prevailed at the Supreme Court.

The Supreme Court had to decide whether unregistered trade dress comprised of product design features was protectable under the Lanham Act if it was inherently distinctive but lacked secondary meaning. In a unanimous opinion written by Justice Antonin Scalia, the Court held that: "[In a Sec. 43(a) action for infringement of unregistered trade dress, a product's design is distinctive, and therefore protectible, only upon a showing of secondary meaning. The fact that product design almost invariably serves purposes other than source identification not only renders inherent distinctiveness problematic; it also renders application of an inherent-distinctiveness principle more harmful to other consumer interests. Consumers should not be deprived of the benefits of competition with regard to the utilitarian and esthetic purposes that product design ordinarily serves by a rule of law that facilitates plausible threats of suit against new entrants based upon alleged inherent distinctiveness]."

The Court explained that the judicial differentiation between marks that are inherently distinctive and those that have developed secondary meaning (set out in cases like Abercrombie & Fitch v. Hunters World discussed above) also has a solid foundation in the Lanham Act itself. In addition, the Court had recently held in another case, Qualitex Co. v. Jacobson Products Co., Inc., 514 U.S. 159 (1995), that color marks could never be inherently distinctive and were only protectable as trademarks with a showing of secondary meaning. The Court concluded that this was also the best approach to take with respect to design as unregistered trade dress. Justice Scalia wrote: "The fact that product design almost invariably serves purposes other than source identification not only renders inherent distinctiveness problematic; it also renders application of an inherent-distinctiveness principle more harmful to other consumer interests. Consumers should not be deprived of the benefits of competition with regard to the utilitarian and esthetic purposes that product design ordinarily serves by a rule of law that facilitates plausible threats of suit against new entrants based upon alleged inherent distinctiveness. How easy it is to mount a plausible suit depends, of course, upon the clarity of the test for inherent distinctiveness, and where product design is concerned, we have little confidence that a reasonably clear test can be devised."

Although the Supreme Court did not use its opinion in Wal-Mart v. Samara Brother to fully overrule its holding in Two Pesos v. Taco Cabana, it suggested that this opinion only applied to some particular forms of trade dress, such as restaurant décor. Many observers were relieved that product features could no longer receive Lanham Act protection without a showing of secondary meaning (and no protection at all if the trade dress was functional), because that made the scope of trade dress more predictable to competitors.

3.3.2 Trademark Cases from China

(1) **The recognition of inherent and acquired distingctiveness of 3D trademark—Christian Dior Perfumes Llc v. Trademark Appeal Board of SAIC**

1.1 Case Judgement   Supreme People's Court of China
Administrative judgment
(2018) Zuigaofaxingzai No.26
Retrial applicant (Plaintiff in the first instance, appellant in the second instance): Christian Dior Perfumes Llc.
Authorized representative: Ludovic BAYLE, director.
Agents ad litem: Li Fengxian, lawyer of Beijing Yongxinzhicai Law Firm.
Agents ad litem: Pang Tao, lawyer of Beijing NTD Law Office.
Retrial respondent: Trademark Appeal Board of SAIC.
Legal representative: Zhao Gang, committee director.
Agents ad litem: Sun Mingjuan, examiner.
Agents ad litem: Zhuo Hui, examiner.

In the case of administrative dispute reviewing rejection of a trademark application between retrial applicant, Christian Dior Perfumes Llc. (hereafter "Dior") and retrial respondent, Trademark Review And Adjudication Board of SAIC (hereafter "Trademark Review And Adjudication Board"), Dior did not accept the judgment delivered by Beijing High People's Court (hereafter 'second-instance court') and applied to this court for retrial. This court made an administrative order on December 29, 2017, and referred the case for review. After the review, this court formed a collegial panel in accordance with the law and heard the case in open court sessions on April 26, 2018. Li Fengxian and Pang Tao, the agents ad litem of Dior as well as Sun Mingjuan and Zhuo Hui, the agents ad litem of Trademark Appeal Board, attended the court. This case is decided now.

On August 30, 2015, Dior filed a review application with the Trademark Appeal Board. It requested the Trademark Appeal Board to approve the application for territorial extension of the International Registration No. 1221382 (hereinafter "applied trademark") on all goods in Class 3. The main reasons for Dior's application for review are as follow: (a) The applied trademark is an artistic work specially for J'adore perfume, with strong originality and distinctiveness, and its use on designated goods has a significant role in identifying. (b) After a large amount of publicity and use, the applied trademark can completely distinguish the source of goods and services. The application for territorial extension protection in China should be approved. (c) The applied trademark has been approved for registration in New Zealand and other countries and regions, and this situation can serve as a reference for the approval of registration in China.

On February 22, 2016, the Trademark Appeal Board issued Decision No. 13584 of refusal to review (hereinafter "Decision No. 13584") and decided to reject the application for the territorial extension protection of the applied trademark in China.

Dior did not accept Decision No. 13584 and filed an administrative lawsuit with the Beijing Intellectual Property Court (hereinafter "first-instance court"), requesting the court to revoke the Decision No. 13584 and order the Trademark Appeal Board to make a new decision. The main reasons are: (a) The applied trademark is a three-dimensional trademark with a specified color, and Dior has submitted a three-sided view of the trademark to the Trademark Appeal Board during the review but it has not been commented. Therefore, there was a omission in review. (b) The applied trademark has a unique design and strong distinctiveness, and is not a general or common packaging for designated goods. In particular, the applied trademark contains the prominent text "j'adore", which can be used on designated goods to distinguish the origin of the goods without causing confusion and misunderstanding by the relevant public. (c) Through the long-term and extensive promotion and use of Dior, the applied trademark has gained stronger distinctiveness.

The findings of the first-instance court:

The applied trademark is the International Registration No. 1221382 Graphical Trademark (see the picture below); the applicant is Dior, and the filing date is April 16, 2014; the designated commodity (Class 3, similar group 0301; 0305–0306): Spice, aromatic shower gel, soap, perfume, strong perfume, toilet water, perfume essence, body lotion, oil, etc.

Appication No. 1221382号.

On July 13, 2015, the Trademark Office issued a notice of rejection. In accordance with Article 11 of the *Trademark Law of the People's Republic of China* (hereinafter "*the Trademark Law*"), the application for territorial extension protection of all the designated goods of the applied trademark in China was rejected.

Within the legal duration, Dior Company filed an application for review with the Trademark Appeal Board.

On February 22, 2016, the Trademark Appeal Board made Decision No. 13584, which determined that the applied trademark is a graphic composed of bottles which can be easily identified as a common container for designated goods. It is not easy for consumers to recognize it as a trademark, and it is difficult for consumers to distinguish the source of goods. Therefore, it lacks the distinctiveness. The trademark review adopts the principle of case-by-case review, and the reason that the similar trademarks mentioned by Dior have been approved for registration cannot be the natural reason for the application for applied trademark in this case. The evidence in the case is insufficient to prove that the applied trademark has formed a unique corresponding relationship with Dior through publicity and use, and has the distinctive features of the trademark. In accordance with the provisions of Item(3), Paragraph 1, Article 11, Article 30, and Article 34 of *the Trademark Law,* the Trademark Appeal Board has decided to reject the application of extended territorial protection on goods in Class 3 of applied trademark in China.

Dior did not accept Decision No. 13584 and filed an administrative lawsuit in the first-instance court.

In the first-instance trial, Dior claimed that the applied trademark was a three-dimensional and designated color trademark. The Trademark Office and the Trademark Appeal Board erroneously recorded the applied trademark as a common trademark with no designated color in the trademark document, which was a significant fact omission. In addition, Dior argued that Decision No. 13584 failed to comment on the evidence submitted by it during the review, which was a procedural error and omission.

The first-instance court also found that, in the application for review, Dior did not explicitly use the important fact that the Trademark Office ignored that the applied trademark is a three-dimensional and designated color trademark as the reason for the application.

The first-instance court held that, in this case, the applied trademark is generally a conical perfume bottle with golden thread wrapped around the neck. Although the combination of the shape of the bottle body and the appearance decoration of the applied trademark had certain characteristics, the relevant public generally regarded the applied trademark as the container of the commodity and will not recognize the bottle as a trademark. Therefore, the applied trademark lacked the inherent distinctiveness that a trademark should have. The evidence submitted by Dior cannot prove that the applied trademark had distinctiveness to distinguish the origin of the goods.

According to Article 13 and 43 of the Regulation on the Implementation of the Trademark Law of the People's Republic of China (hereinafter "Regulations on the Implementation of the Trademark Law"), Dior Company is obliged to voluntarily explain to the Trademark Office whether to apply for trademark registration with a three-dimensional mark. But Dior did not explain this fact in the application submitted to the Trademark Office. Secondly, whether there were errors in the trademark application information entered by the Trademark Office and the Trademark Appeal Board in the trademark file is not within the scope of the trial of this case. Dior can seek relief through other channels. Thirdly, Dior did not explicitly use the fact that the information on the trademark file was entered incorrectly as one of the reasons for the review. Finally, even considering the fact that the applied trademark is a three-dimensional mark and a designated color trademark, based on the aforementioned analysis, the applied trademark did not distinctiveness. In addition, Dior argued that Decision No. 13584 failed to comment on the evidence of trademark use submitted by it during the review stage, which was a procedural error and omission. However, the Trademark Appeal Board made a comprehensive review of the evidence submitted by Dior and did not omit the examination. The claim of Dior has no factual and legal basis.

To sum up, in accordance with Article 69 of *the Administrative Litigation Law of the People's Republic of China*, the first-instance court decided to dismiss Dior's clams.

Dior did not accept the judgment of the first instance and filed an appeal to the second-instance court, requesting to revoke the judgment of first instance and Decision No. 13584 as well as order the Trademark Appeal Board to make a new decision. The main reasons are: (a) The applied trademark is a three-dimensional trademark with a specified color, and Dior has submitted a three-sided view of the trademark to the Trademark Appeal Board during the review but it has not been commented. Therefore, there was a omission in review. (b) The applied trademark with the prominent text "J'adore" has a unique design and strong distinctiveness, and is not the usual packaging of designated goods. The applied trademark can distinguish the source of the goods and will not cause confusion and misunderstanding by consumers. (c) Through the long-term and extensive promotion of Dior Company, the applied trademark has gained stronger distinctiveness.

The Trademark Appeal Board obeyed the judgment of first instance.

The second-instance court affirmed that the findings of the first-instance court are true. And there were the trademark files, notice of rejection, Decision No. 13584, the evidence materials submitted by the parties in the trademark review and the original trial, the statements of the parties as well as other supporting evidence.

During the second instance of this case, Dior additionally submitted the following evidence:

(a) Sales agreements, invoices and delivery lists of J'adore perfumes in major cities such as Beijing, Shanghai, Guangzhou and Shenzhen (2012–2017);
(b) Customs declaration form and tax payment form for J'adore perfume;
(c) Advertising of J'adore perfume in more than 20 well-known magazines/pics (2012–2016);
(d) J'adore perfume's list of advertising expenditures and examples of advertising placement (2011–2016, television, paper media, digital and other advertising forms), advertising orders and invoices (2012–2016);
(e) The search report issued by the National Library of China with the "Special Seal for the National Library Science and Technology Novelty Search Center", a list of printed documents, relevant documents and relevant news media reports (No.: 2017-NLC-JSZM-0109);
(f) The sales ranking of J'adore perfume (the first in total value of all channels for women's perfume), certification documents (2011–2016 mid-term);
(g) J'adore perfume sales ranking table (2013–2016 third quarter);
(h) Honor of J'adore perfume (2012–2016).

The Trademark Appeal Board recognized the authenticity of the above-mentioned evidence, but did not recognize the relevance and the proof purpose.

The second-instance court also found that Dior stated on page 13 of the *Review Application* that "The applicant pointed out that the applied trademark is a three-dimensional trademark designed by the applicant and used exclusively on its J'adore perfume."

In the first supplementary statement of reasons submitted by Dior to the Trademark Appeal Board on November 30, 2015, the first reason was "The applied trademark is a three-dimensional trademark with a specified color, and the applicant shall submit the three-dimensional trademark to the board according to law" with a three-sided view of the applied trademark.

The second-instance court held that:

Paragraph 1, Article 5 of Interpretation of the Supreme People's Court on Issues concerning the Jurisdiction over Trademark Cases and Application of Law after the Entry into Force of the Decision on Amending the Trademark Law provides that: "Where an application for trademark registration or renewal is filed by a party before the Decision on Amending the Trademark Law comes into force, if the Trademark Office makes a decision not to accept the trademark application or not to renew the trademark after the Decision comes into force, and the party therefore files an administrative lawsuit, the people's court shall apply the Trademark Law as amended in its review." The application date for the applied trademark in this case was April 16, 2014, and the Trademark Office issued the trademark rejection notice on July 13, 2015. Therefore, this case shall apply to the Trademark Law amended on August 30, 2013 and the Regulations on the Implementation of the Trademark Law 2014.

Paragraph 3, Article 13 of *Regulation on the Implementation of the Trademark Law of the People's Republic of China* provides that: "Where an application is filed for registering a three-dimensional symbol as a trademark, it shall be stated in the application, the instructions for use of the trademark shall be provided, and a design including, at a minimum, the three-view drawing shall be submitted based on which the three-dimensional shape could be determined". Article 43 provides that: "Where an applicant for territorial extension to China requests protection of a three-dimensional symbol, a combination of colors, or a sound mark as a trademark or protection of a collective or certification mark, the applicant shall, within three months from the date when the trademark is entered into the International Register of the International Bureau, submit the relevant materials as listed in Article 13 of this Regulation to the Trademark Office through a legally formed trademark agency. If the required materials are not submitted within the prescribed time limit, the Trademark Office shall refuse the application for territorial extension."

In this case, Dior did not declare to the Trademark Office within three months from the date when the trademark is entered into the International Register of the International Bureau that the applied trademark is a three-dimensional mark and submit a trademark drawing containing at least three-sided views. It was only in the supplementary statement that it was clearly proposed to apply for the trademark as a three-dimensional mark and submit a three-sided view. In the case that Dior did not declare that the applied trademark was a three-dimensional mark and submitted relevant documents, it is not inappropriate that the Trademark Office examined the applied trademark as a common graphic trademark. Whether there was any error in the registration of the designated color and trademark form in the trademark file by the Trademark Office is not within the scope of the trial of this case. Dior may seek relief through other channels.

Paragraph 1, Article 52 provides that: "For a review case against a decision of the Trademark Office to refuse a trademark registration application, the Trademark Appeal Board shall try it based on the decision of refusal of the Trademark Office, the facts, grounds, and claims submitted by the applicant for review, and the factual status at the time of review." In this case, Dior did not clearly claim that the applied trademark is a three-dimensional mark when it filed an application for review with the Trademark Appeal Board, and the Trademark Office did not review the applied trademark as a three-dimensional mark. Therefore, it is not inappropriate for the Trademark Appeal Board to review the applied trademark as a common graphic trademark based on the trademark files registered by the Trademark Office. The reasons for the omission of the trademark review committee stated by Dior Company cannot be established and are not supported.

Article 11 of Trademark Law provides that: "The following signs may not be registered as trademarks: (1) A sign only bearing the generic name, design, or model of the goods. (2) A sign only directly indicating the quality, main raw materials, functions, uses, weight, quantity, or other features of goods. (3) Other signs lacking distinctiveness. If a sign listed in the preceding paragraph has obtained distinctiveness through use and can be easily identified, it may be registered as a trademark." To determine whether an applied trademark has distinctive features, it is necessary to comprehensively consider factors such as the trademark itself, the goods designated for the use of the trademark, the cognitive habits of the relevant public, and the actual use of the industry which the goods designated for the trademark belong to. In this case, the applied trademark is a graphic trademark composed of a conical perfume bottle pattern, and the pattern has certain characteristics in the shape and decoration of the bottle body. However, when it is used as a graphic trademark on commodities such as perfume and fragrance products, it is easy to be recognized as a packaging or decorative pattern according to the recognition ability of general consumers, and it is difficult to distinguish the source of the commodity. The applied trademark lacks inherent distinctive features and falls under the circumstance that it cannot be registered as a trademark stipulated in the paragraph 3, Article 11 of the Trademark Law. Dior's appeal reasons about the unique design and strong distinctiveness of the applied trademark cannot be established and is not supported.

In the case where the applied trademark itself lacks distinctive features, it should be combined with relevant evidence to determine whether the trademark has acquired distinctive features through actual use and whether it is easy to be identified. In this case, the evidence submitted by Dior can prove that the J'adore perfume series have been widely sold in the Chinese market.

However, it is not enough to prove that when the applied trademark was used as a common graphic trademark, the relevant public can identify the perfume and fragrance products by the applied trademark as a sign indicating the source of the goods to obtain distinctive features. Therefore, Dior's appeal grounds for the trademark application that has gained distinctiveness after long-term and extensive use cannot be established and is not supported.

To sum up, in accordance with item(1), paragraph 1, Article 89 of the Administrative Litigation Law of the People's Republic of China, the second-instance court decided to dismiss the appeal and affirm the original judgment.

Dior did not to accept the second-instance judgment and applied to this court for a retrial. The reasons are as follows: (a) The Trademark Appeal Board violated legal procedures and omitted to review important facts in this case. Dior has repeatedly emphasized that the applied trademark is a three-dimensional trademark with a specified color in administrative procedures, and has submitted a three-sided view of this three-dimensional trademark to the Trademark Appeal Board. However, the Trademark Office's file which the Trademark Appeal Board relied on in this case identified the applied trademark as a common trademark. Therefore, the basic facts of Decision 13584 are clearly wrong. At the same time, the decision did not comment on the Trademark Office's misidentification of the applied trademark, and violated legal procedures as well as omitted important facts. Specifically, the applied trademark is an international registered trademark. In accordance with the review process for international registered trademark applications for the protection of China's territorial extension, the International Bureau of the World Intellectual Property Organization (hereinafter "International Bureau"), instead of the trademark applicant, directly transfers the relevant materials to the Trademark Office for review. The international trademark registration file in this case has clearly stated that the applied trademark is a three-dimensional trademark with a designated color of gold. It is difficult for applicants of internationally registered trademarks to know the special provisions of the Trademark Office for three-dimensional trademark applications, and they have never received a supplementary notice asking them to supplement the three-sided view from the Trademark Office. Dior did not have the opportunity and channel to submit the application and drawings to the Trademark Office for explanation. After learning that the trademark application was rejected by the Trademark Office, Dior Company has submitted a three-sided view of the applied trademark in time during the review and has repeatedly emphasized that the applied trademark is a three-dimensional trademark. Therefore, the Trademark Appeal Board did not correctly determine that the applied trademark is a three-dimensional trademark, and its Decision No.13584 on the basis of common trademarks violated legal procedures. (b) The applied trademark has unique design and inherent distinctiveness. The applied trademark is the three-dimensional trademark of the famous J'adore perfume, which was tailored for J'adore perfume by French artist Jean-Michel Othoniel. The bottle body has exquisite details, and the perfect combination of glass and metal wire drawing, showing the image of a noble, capable and confident woman. It is neither a common product packaging nor a general perfume bottle design. It has become a personalized symbol and can be used as a three-dimensional trademark to identify the source of goods. In addition, the graphic trademark No. 7505828 (designated color) owned by Dior, which is exactly the same as the applied trademark, has been approved for registration. It can be seen that the applied trademark has inherent distinctiveness and should be approved for registration. (c) Through extensive use and promotion of the applied trademark, it has gained high popularity and distinctiveness. Since the J'adore perfume entered the Chinese market in 1999, it has consistently used the design of the applied trademark in this case. Dior has invested more than 100 million yuan in various advertising expenses for the J'adore perfume series. Since 2001, J'adore Perfume has been widely reported by Chinese media, and is known and recognized by the relevant public. To sum up, Dior requested this court to revoke the first and second instance judgments as well as Decision No. 13584, and order the Trademark Appeal Board to make a new review decision.

The opinions submitted by the Trademark Appeal Board are as follows: (a) The applied trademark is an international registered trademark that designated China for territorial extension protection. The International Bureau transferred the application materials to the Trademark Office on November 6, 2014, and entered the application information. Dior shall submit the materials stipulated in Article 13 of the Implementation Regulations of the Trademark Law to the Trademark Office within 3 months thereafter. Since Dior did not provide the Trademark Office with supplementary materials within the time limit, it was not inappropriate for the Trademark Office to examine the applied trademark as a common trademark. (b) The Trademark Office has conducted a comprehensive review of whether the applied trademark is a three-dimensional trademark and whether it lacks distinctiveness. (c) Dior did not use the fact that the information in the trademark application was entered incorrectly as one of the reasons for the review, and the Trademark Appeal Board did not violate the legal procedures. To sum up, the Trademark Appeal Board requested this court to reject Dior's application for retrial.

During this court's retrial, Dior submitted two exhibits to this court to support its claims. Based on the cross-examination opinions of the Trademark Appeal Board, this court held that:

Exhibit 1 is the international registration information of the applied trademark and its Chinese translation. The source of exhibit is the official website of the World Intellectual Property Organization. The main content is: The original country of the international registration trademark No. G1221382 (namely the applied trademark) is France, the basic registration date is April 16, 2014, and the international registration date is August 8, 2014. The name of the owner is Dior. The designated trademark type is three-dimensional trademark. The description of trademark is: The trademark is like the exquisite and elongated number "8", with a small ball on the upper part and an oval shape at the bottom. The bottle body is decorated in gold. A side view of the applied trademark is attached to the registration information. Exhibit 2 is the trademark status information page, and the source of evidence is the Trademark Appeal Board. The type of trademark is recorded as "common". The Trademark Appeal Board recognized the authenticity and legality of the above-mentioned exhibits, but considered that it was not sufficient to prove that the applied trademark has acquired distinctiveness through use.

Regarding the above-mentioned exhibits submitted by Dior, this court reviewed and determined as follows: Exhibit 1 and 2 are printed copies of trademark registration information, which may be obtained and verified through public channels, or come from the Trademark Appeal Board, and their authenticity and legitimacy have been recognized by the Trademark Appeal Board. So this court affirms their authenticity and legality. At the same time, the trademark application information reflected in the above evidence is relevant to this case, so it is affirmed by this court.

Combined with the existing evidence, this court has additionally found the following facts:

The original country of the trademark application is France, the registration date is April 16, 2014, and the international registration date is August 8, 2014. The owner of applied trademark is Dior. The trademark type designated by the international registration is "three-dimensional trademark". The specific shape of the trademark is described as: like the exquisitely elongated number "8", the upper part is a small sphere and the bottom part is an oval shape. The bottle body is decorated in gold. The applied trademark was designated to be used on perfumes, strong perfumes and other commodities in Class 3. After the applied trademark has been internationally registered, in accordance with the relevant provisions of the *Madrid Agreement Concerning the International Registration of Marks* (hereinafter "Madrid Agreement") and *Protocol Relating to the Madrid Agreement Concerning the International Registration of Marks* (hereinafter referred to as the "Protocol"), Dior Company, through the International Bureau, filed applications for territorial extension protection with Australia and Denmark, Finland, the United Kingdom, China and other countries. On July 13, 2015, the Trademark Office issued a notice of rejection of the trademark application to the International Bureau, rejecting all applications for territorial extension protection in China on the grounds of lack of distinctiveness.

On August 30, 2015, Dior did not accept the above-mentioned notice of rejection from the Trademark Office and filed an application for review with the Trademark Appeal Board. In the supplementary reason submitted by Dior on November 30, 2015, there was the following written record: The applied trademark is a three-dimensional trademark with a specified color, and the applicant (Dior) shall submit a three-sided view of the three-dimensional trademark in accordance with the law. As stated in the reasons for the review by Dior, the applied trademark is a three-dimensional trademark created and designed by Dior and it was used in its famous J'adore perfume. According the Trademark Law, applicants for three-dimensional trademarks must submit at least three views to explain how to use them. Since the applied trademark is an international registered trademark, Dior failed to explain to the Trademark Office of China in the application, and subsequently did not receive any official notice for making correction. Therefore, Dior has not been given the opportunity to make supplement. Dior also attached a three-sided view of the applied trademark in the statement of reasons.

It was also found that the applicant for the graphic trademark No. 7505828 was Dior, which was designated to be used on soaps, shampoos, essential oils, fragrances, cosmetics and other goods in the Class 3 of the International Classification. The trademark was approved for registration by the Trademark Office on August 7, 2011.

Registered Trademark No. 7505828

This court's retrial held that, based on Dior's grounds for retrial application and the Trademark Appeal Board's defense opinions, combing relevant evidence and facts, the key issues at the retrial stage of this case were: A. Whether Decision No. 13584 violated legal procedures; B. Whether the applied trademark has distinctiveness. In this regard, this court's analysis is as follows:

A. Whether Decision No. 13584 violated legal procedures

(a) Factual basis of Decision 13584

Dior claimed that, according to the international registration information of the applied trademark, the applied trademark is a "three-dimensional trademark" instead of the "common trademark" recorded in the file of the Trademark Office. Therefore, the factual basis of Decision No. 13584 is clearly wrong. The Court believes that, first of all, based on the trademark status information, the written record of "International Registered Graphic Trademark No. 1221382" in Decision No. 13584, and the

Trademark Appeal Board's defense opinions, the Trademark Office's rejection notice and Decision No. 13584 both review the applied trademark as a graphic trademark. Secondly, based on the fact that both parties have no dispute, the information on the international registration of the applied trademark clearly recorded that the type of applied trademark is "three-dimensional trademark", and its three-dimensional form was specifically described as: The trademark is like the exquisite and elongated number "8", with a small ball on the upper part and an oval shape at the bottom. The bottle body is decorated in gold. The Trademark Appeal Board recognized the above facts. In the absence of evidence to the contrary, the record of the specific type of the trademark in the international registration information of the applied trademark shall be regarded as the form of declaration by Dior that the applied trademark is a three-dimensional trademark. It can also be reasonably presumed that in the process of applying for territorial extension protection in China, the application information transmitted by the International Bureau to the Trademark Office is consistent with it, and the Trademark Office should be aware of the above information. Since applicant of international registered trademarks do not need to apply for registration again in designated countries, the trademark application information transmitted by the International Bureau to the Trademark Office should be the factual basis on which the Trademark Office can review and determine whether the application for territorial extension protection in China can be supported. According to the available evidence, the type of applied trademark is "three-dimensional trademark", not "common trademark" recorded in the file of the Trademark Office which was used as the basis for review by the Trademark Office and Trademark Appeal Board. The determination of the first-instance court that the application submitted by Dior to the Trademark Office failed to explain the fact that the applied trademark was a three-dimensional mark, was inconsistent with the trademark international registration procedure and lacked factual basis. This court shall correct it.

(b) Whether Decision No. 13584 violated legal procedures

Paragraph 1, Article 52 provides that: "For a review case against a decision of the Trademark Office to refuse a trademark registration application, the Trademark Appeal Board shall try it based on the decision of refusal of the Trademark Office, the facts, grounds, and claims submitted by the applicant for review, and the factual status at the time of review." Dior believed that it has applied for a three-dimensional trademark with a specified color in the review process and added a three-dimensional view. The Trademark Appeal Board's omission of the claim by Dior and its decision on the basis of the "common mark" violated due process. This court believes that, based on the facts supplemented by this court, the statement of reasons for review submitted by Dior clearly stated: The applied trademark is a three-dimensional trademark with a specified color. Because the it is an international registered trademark, Dior was unable to explain to the Trademark Office, nor to obtain an opportunity for making correction. Dior also submitted a three-sided view of the applied trademark to the Trademark Appeal Board during the review process. Based on the above facts, Dior has clarified in the review process that the specific type of the applied trademark is a three-dimensional trademark, and has required to supplement by submitting the three-sided view. In this regard, the Trademark Appeal Board did not truthfully record this in Decision 13584, nor did it verify whether the relevant facts of trademark Office's rejection were incorrect in view of the above-mentioned claims made by Dior. However, the Trademark Appeal Board still examined the applied trademark as a "graphic trademark" and rejected Dior's review application, which violated legal procedures and may harm the legitimate interests of administrative counterparts. It was corrected by this court. As the review department of the Trademark Office, in the case that Dior has clearly put forward the reasons for the review and provided relevant evidence to support its claims, the Trademark Appeal Board shall correct the errors made by the Trademark Office regarding the types of applied trademarks based on the true status of the applied trademarks. On this basis, the Trademark Office as well as the Trademark Appeal Board shall review the issues such as whether the applied trademark has distinctive features and based on the three-dimensional trademark in accordance with the provisions of the review procedure. The specific type of applied trademark is the factual basis of Decision No. 13584. The conclusion of the court of first instance and second instance regarding whether the related information is wrongly recorded is not within the scope of the trial of this case and Dior did not object in the review procedure, lacks factual and legal basis. This court shall correct it. In its defense, the Trademark Appeal Board also pointed out that since Dior did not follow the requirements of Article 43 of the Implementing Regulations of the Trademark Law to supplement materials to the Trademark Office within the legal duration, it is not inappropriate for the Trademark Office to examine the applied trademark as a graphic trademark.

According to the relevant provisions of the Implementing Regulations of the Trademark Law, combining with the defense reasons of the Trademark Appeal Board, this court believes that the main purpose of the Madrid Agreement and its Protocol is to establish and improve the procedures for international trademark registration through the establishment of an international cooperation mechanism, and to reduce and simplify registration procedures in order to to facilitate applicants to obtain trademark protection at the lowest cost. Combining the facts of the case, the application of applied trademark is a Madrid international registration of marks, and the relevant application materials shall be subject to the content transmitted by the International Bureau to the Trademark Office. Based on the existing evidence, it can be reasonably presumed that Dior has already declared the fact that the applied trademark is a three-dimensional trademark in the process of international trademark registration, explaining the specific use of the applied trademark and providing a side view of the applied trademark.

Based on the above facts, Dior has completed the international registration procedures, as well as the declaration and explanation obligations stipulated in Article 13 of the Implementation Regulations of the Trademark Law in accordance with the provisions of the Madrid Agreement and its Protocol. This should be a situation where the application procedures are basically complete. Where the application documents lack only formalities, within the meaning of the Implementing Regulations of the Trademark Law, the competent trademark authority should adhere to the principle of performing its obligations under international agreements, while giving the applicant a reasonable chance to submit supplements and make corrections to the documents. Specifically, first of all, the Trademark Office should truthfully record the type of applied trademark as a "three-dimensional mark" according to the content of the declaration and explanation made by Dior in the international registration. Secondly, Dior has clarified the type of applied trademark, and the application only lacked some of the formal requirements such as the trademark view. The Trademark Office shall give full consideration to the particularity of the international trademark registration, and give Dior the opportunity to supplement the application materials in accordance with paragraph 2, Article 40 of the Implementing Regulations of the Trademark Law in order to fully protect the legitimate interests of applicants of international registration including Dior. In this case, the Trademark Office did not truthfully record the declaration made by Dior on the trademark type in the international registration procedure, and did not give Dior a reasonable opportunity to make corrections. At the same time, in the absence of the party's request and factual basis, it changed the type of the applied trademark to common trademark and made an conclusion that was not conducive to Dior. The above situation and the practice of the Trademark Appeal Board that it did not any corrections lacked factual and legal basis and may harm the reasonable expected interests of the administrative counterpart. This court shall correct it.

B. Whether the applied trademark has distinctiveness

As mentioned above, since Dior has clearly defined the type of trademark applied for as a three-dimensional trademark in the international registration, the Trademark Office's practice of treating the applied trademark as a graphic trademark and judging that it does not have lacks distinctiveness lacked factual basis. Therefore, the Trademark Appeal Board should correct the improper determination of the Trademark Office based on the reasons for review related to the type of trademark proposed by Dior. And according to the judging criteria of whether the three-dimensional mark has distinctive features, the issue of whether the application for the territorial extension protection in China should be approved shall be re-examined. This court believes that the Trademark Office and the Trademark Appeal Board should focus on the following factors in review: (a) The distinctiveness of the applied trademark and the distinctiveness obtained through use; the time when the applied trademark entered the Chinese market; the actual use and promotion that can be proved by the evidence in the case; and the possibility of the function of identifying the source of the goods arising from the applied trademark; (b) The principle of consistency of review standards. Although trademark review and judicial review need to consider individual cases, the review is based on the trademark law and related administrative regulations, and the uniformity of law enforcement standards cannot be ignored on the grounds of individual review.

To sum up, this court believes that Decision No. 13584, the first-instance and second-instance judgments have errors in the facts and the applicable law and should be revoked.

In accordance with Article 70 and 89 of The Administrative Litigation Law of the People's Republic of China, and Article 119 and 122 of Interpretation of the

Supreme People's Court on Application of the Administrative Litigation Law of the People's Republic of China, it ordered as follows:

(a) Revoke the Administrative Judgment (2017) J.X.Z. No.744 of Beijing Higher People's Court;
(b) Revoke the Administrative Judgment (2016) J.73X.C No.3047 of Beijing Intellectual Property Court.
(c) Revoke Decision No. 13584 the Trademark Appeal Board.
(d) Order the Trademark Appeal Board to review the international registered trademark No. 1221382.

1.2 Analysis of the case

1. Facts:

The retrial applicant Christian Dior Fragrance Company (hereinafter referred to as Dior Company) was dissatisfied with the Beijing high people's court 's (2017) Jing Xing Zhong No. 744 Administrative Judgment in a case of administrative dispute over trademark application refusal reviewing by the Trademark Review and Adjudication Board of the State Administration for Industry and Commerce (hereinafter referred to as the Trademark Review and Adjudication Board), applied to this court for a retrial.

On August 30, 2015, Dior Company filed an application for reexamination with the Trademark Review and Adjudication Board, requesting to approve the application for territorial extension of the International Registration of trademark No. 1221382 on all designated goods in Category. The Trademark Review and Adjudication Board believes that the applied trademark is a graphic of a bottle, which can be easily identified as a common container for designated goods. It is designated as a trademark for use on Class 3 perfumes and other goods. It is difficult for consumers to recognize it as a trademark and play a role in distinguishing the source of goods, and so lack the distinctiveness that a trademark should have. They rejected the application. Dior refused to accept Decision No. 13584 and filed an administrative lawsuit with the Beijing Intellectual Property Court (hereinafter referred to as the court of first instance). The court of first instance held that the applied trademark was generally a perfume bottle with golden silk thread wrapped around the neck of the bottle. Although the combination of the shape of the bottle body and the appearance decoration of the trademark application has certain characteristics, the relevant public generally regard the trademark application as the container of the commodity, and will not recognize the bottle body as a trademark. Therefore, the applied trademark does not have the distinctive features that a trademark sign should have, and lacks the inherent distinctiveness that should be possessed by registration as a trademark. The evidence submitted by Dior cannot prove that the applied trademark has been used to distinguish the origin of the goods.

Dior refused to accept the judgment of the first instance and filed an appeal to the court of second instance (Beijing High People's Court), requesting to revoke the judgment of the first instance and Decision No. 13584 and order the Trademark Review and Adjudication Board to make a new decision. The court rejected the application for similar reason. Dior refused to accept the judgment of the second instance and applied to the Supreme People's Court for a retrial.

2. Focus of dispute

How to judge the distinctiveness of the trademark applied?

3. Rules

Article 11 of the Trademark Law:

"The following signs shall not be registered as trademarks: (1) Only the general name, graphics, and model of the product; (2) Only directly indicate the quality, main materials, functions, uses, and weight of the product, Quantity and other characteristics; (3) Other lack of distinctive characteristics."

Articles 13 and 43 of the "Regulations for the Implementation of the Trademark Law of the People's Republic of China":

(1) Article 13: Where an application is filed for registering a three-dimensional symbol as a trademark, it shall be stated in the application, the instructions for use of the trademark shall be provided, and a design including, at a minimum, the three-view drawing shall be submitted based on which the three-dimensional shape could be determined.
(2) Article 43: Where an applicant for territorial extension to China requests protection of a three-dimensional symbol, a combination of colors, or a sound mark as a trademark or protection of a collective or certification mark, the applicant shall, within three months from the date when the trademark is entered into the International Register of the International Bureau, submit the relevant materials as listed in Article 13 of this Regulation to the Trademark Office through a legally formed trademark agency. If the required materials are not submitted within the prescribed time limit, the Trademark Office shall refuse the application for territorial extension.

Article 89 Paragraph 1 of the Administrative Procedure Law of the People's Republic of China:

The civil court hears appeal cases and handles them separately according to the following circumstances:

(1) If the facts found in the original judgment or ruling are clear and the applicable laws and regulations are correct, the judgment or ruling shall reject the appeal and maintain the original judgment or ruling;

4. Reasoning

The supreme people's court thought that the Trademark Office and the Trademark Review and Adjudication Board should focus on the following factors in the re-examination and determination: First, the distinctiveness of the applied trademark and the distinctiveness obtained through use, especially the time when the applied trademark entered the Chinese market, and the actual use that can be proved by the evidence in the case; The situation with publicity and promotion, as well as the possibility of the function of identifying the source of the goods arising from the application for trademark; the second is the principle of consistency of examination standards. Although trademark review and judicial review procedures must consider individual cases, the basis for review is the trademark law and related administrative regulations, and the uniformity of law enforcement standards cannot be ignored on the grounds of individual review. Therefore, the TRAB was rejected, and the judgments of the first and second instance were sent back to the TRB for reconsideration.

5. Conclusion and enlightenment

In this case, the Trademark Review and Adjudication Board, the court of first instance and the court of second instance all adopted the same model of "description plus confirmation" in determining the distinctiveness of trademarks, that is, first describing some three-dimensional trademark features and then judging that they are not distinctive. It also caused continuous appeals by the plaintiffs dissatisfied with the results. The distinctiveness judgment of a trademark, especially for the judgment of distinctiveness obtained through use, cannot be subjectively judged whether there is distinctiveness or not. If some objective tests and experiments can be introduced as that in foreign countries, the results will be more convincing. Of course, this kind of work will also can be done by the plaintiff.

(2) Honda Motor Co., Ltd. v. Chongqing Hensim Taixin Trading Co., Ltd.

2.1 Case Judgement   Supreme People's Court of P.R.C.

Case No.: (2019) zuigaofaminzai No.138

Date of hearing: Sep 23, 2019.

Cause of action: tardemark infringement.

Retrial applicant (plaintiff in the first instance, appellee in the second instance): Honda Motor Co., Ltd.

Legal representative: Kuraishi Seiji, executive director.

Agents ad litem: Yu Zegang, lawyer of Zhejiang Harnest & Garner Law Firm.

Agents ad litem: Shang Shuangling, lawyer of Zhejiang Harnest & Garner Law Firm.

Retrial respondent (defendant in the first instance, appellant in the second instance): Chongqing Hensim Xintai Trading Co., Ltd.

Legal representative: Wang Xun, chairman.

Agents ad litem: Cao Bo, Chongqing Exceedon&Partners Law Firm.

Retrial respondent (defendant in the first instance, appellant in the second instance): Chongqing Hensim Group Co., Ltd.

Legal representative: Wang Xun, chairman.

Agents ad litem: Cao Bo, Chongqing Exceedon&Partners Law Firm.

In the case of trademark infringement dispute between Retrial applicant, Honda Motor Co., Ltd. (hereafter "Honda") and Retrial respondent Chongqing Hensim Xintai Trading Co., Ltd. (hereafter "Hensim Xintai"), Chongqing Hensim Group Co., Ltd. (hereafter "Hensim Group"), Honda did not accept the judgment delivered by Yunnan High people's Court and applied for retrial to this court. This court made a civil order on September 14, 2018, and referred the case for review. This court formed a collegial panel in accordance with the law and heard the case in open court sessions. The agents ad litem Yu Zegang and Shang Shuangling of Honda, and Cao

Bo, the agents ad litem of Hensim Xintai and Hensim Group, attended the court. This case is decided now.

Honda applied for retrial and stated that:

(a) The alleged infringement is a typical trademark infringement. 1. The trademark of the 220 sets of motorcycle parts involved (hereinafter "alleged infringing products") clearly highlighted the "HONDA" trademark of Honda, with the intention of attaching to the reputation of the trademark, which could easily cause confusion and misunderstanding by the relevant public. 2. The registered trademarks No. 314940, No. 1198975, and No. 503699 (hereinafter "the three involved trademarks") enjoyed a high reputation. 3. The previous case determined that the unregulated use of authorized trademarks constituted trademark infringement. 4. Article 10 of *the Provisions the Management of Trade Marks in Foreign Trade* and Article 8 of *the Administration of Trademarks for Export Commodities* all have provisions on the use of "trademarks designated or provided for use by others" in foreign trade operations.

(b) 1. The alleged infringement shall not be regarded as foreign-related OEM processing. 1. The trademark used by the alleged infringing products is not consistent with the overseas authorized trademark. To determine whether the use of foreign-related trademarks constitutes "foreign-related OEM processing", overseas authorized trademarks should be used as the object of comparison. The trademark used by the alleged infringing products should be exactly the same as the overseas authorized trademark, and should belong to the approved product category of the overseas authorized trademark (within the scope of self-use rights), that is, "double identical", otherwise it would not be "foreign-related OEM processing". The trademarks on the alleged infringing products were not consistent with the overseas authorized trademarks, and they were not legally authorized and there was no reasonable explanation. 2. Hensim Xintai and Hensim Group cannot prove that they have obtained the legal authorization of the foreign trademark holder in advance, nor have they used the foreign authorized trademark in a true and reasonable way. Therefore, it does not belong to foreign-related processing.

(c) The second-instance judgment determined that Hensim Xinta and Hensim Group's act of attaching trademark to the alleged infringing products did not belong to the use in the meaning of the *Trademark Law of the People's Republic of China* (2013 revision, hereinafter "Trademark Law"). The application of law is wrong. 1. The alleged infringement belongs to the use of trademarks on goods and product packaging to identify the origin of the goods. 2. The use of deformed Myanmar trademark on the alleged infringing products is no longer to attach an icon designated by an overseas customer, but to mislead consumers. 3. The relevant public may be exposed to the alleged infringing products. In the context of international trade, the relevant public includes workers on the production line, packaging and printing workers of the alleged infringing product labels, transportation workers, workers unpacking goods at the docks, and customs inspectors. Domestic consumers can access products and labels that have been exported overseas through the Internet. A large number of Chinese companies and individuals traveling abroad and doing business are also the relevant public. The three involved trademarks are well-known, and the public at home or abroad may confuse or misidentify the origin of the alleged infringing products. When the social and economic foundation changes, the legal provisions should be interpreted in line with the current economic characteristics. 4. If the act of attaching a trademark on exported goods is deemed to be not a use in the sense of trademark law, the customs' intellectual property border protection system will fail. 5. There have been previous judgments that clearly stated that the export is a use of trademark 0.6. The use of trademarks is an objective behavior, and it is not evaluated differently due to different users or different links of production and circulation.

(d) Hensim Xintai Company and Hensim Group Company failed to perform their duty of reasonable care and had the purpose of attaching the reputation of Honda, which violated the "principle of good faith." 1. Hensim Xintai and Hensim Group maliciously changed the overseas registered trademarks. 2. Hensim Xintai, Hensim Group are operators in the same industry as Honda. Knowing that the trademark of Honda is extremely well-known, they have not fulfilled the necessary duty of care and avoidance. 3. Hensim Xintai and Hensim Group failed to perform their duty of reasonable care. 4. Hensim Group tried to apply for the "HONDAKIT" trademark.

To sum up, Honda requested this court to revoke the second-instance judgment and maintain the first-instance judgment; the case acceptance fee shall be borne by Hensim Xintai and Hensim Group.

Hensim Xintai and Hensim Group submit opinions that:

(a) The evidence submitted by the two companies has formed a complete chain of evidence, proving that the actions of the two companies belonged to the OEM processing. 1. Hensim Group accepted the entrustment of Myanmar Meihua Co., Ltd. (hereinafter "Meihua Company") for contract processing. Hensim Xintai was responsible for handling export matters and all related products were exported to Myanmar. Therefore, the behavior of the two companies was contract processing. 2. The 220 sets of motorcycle parts involved are products rather than commodities. They are owned by Meihua Company and will not enter the Chinese market. 3. Myanmar citizen ThetMonAung enjoys the trademark rights of HONDAKIT in Myanmar and serves as the managing director of Meihua Company. Meihua Company commissioned Hensim Group to process and produce motorcycle parts. ThetMonAung authorized Hensim Group to attach the HONDAKIT trademark to the corresponding products. Hensim Xintai handled relevant customs declaration and export matters.

(b) Two companies did not infringe Honda's three involved trademarks in the case. 1. Use that does not play an identifying role is not a "use" as stipulated in paragraph 2, Article 57of the Trademark Law. 2. The 220 sets of motorcycle parts involved in the case are unlikely to enter the Chinese market. There is no use of trademark in the sense of trademark law and they did not destroy the identification function of the trademark involved. 3. The alleged infringement will not cause confusion and misunderstanding by the relevant public in China. The alleged infringing products were motorcycles, and the export destination was Myanmar, where cross-border e-commerce is very lagging behind. The possibility of returning to the domestic market is very low, and there is no possibility of causing confusion among the relevant domestic public.

(c) Response to the reasons for the retrial application. 1. The relevant judgments cited by the retrial applicant have no reference value for this case. The quantity of the alleged infringing products and the drawings attached to the trademark were all based on the requirements of the overseas entrusting party. Meihua Company has corresponding trademark rights in Myanmar. In this case, there is no domestic trademark registrant registered in a foreign market, nor is there the fact that the goods of both parties in the litigation are sold to the same overseas market. 2. Article 14 of *the Provisions the Management of Trade Marks in Foreign Trade* stipulates administrative penalties for operators who violate the regulations. Therefore, if it violates the provisions of Article 10, it shall bear administrative responsibility, which has nothing to do with whether it constitutes trademark infringement. 3. The definition of the relevant public and the possibility of contact. The workers and transportation workers on the production line mentioned by the applicant are not consumers and operators. If it is believed that a large number of Chinese companies and individuals traveling abroad and doing business may come into contact with the involved products in Myanmar, it is equivalent to denying the territoriality of trademark.

(d) The particularity and impact of the involved OEM processing. 1. Foreign-related OEM processing trade occupies a large proportion of my country's economy, especially foreign trade. In the current global economic downturn, business operations are difficult, and the advantage of cheap labor for Chinese companies is losing. If foreign-related OEM processing is defined as infringement of trademark rights, it will increase the burden of business operations. 2. Foreign trademark ownership and infringement disputes have nothing to do with foreign-related OEM processing. 3. In the case of a poor legal environment in the country where the ordering party is located, it is unrealistic to demand the domestic processing party to fulfill the high review obligation. To sum up, Hensim Taixin and Hensim Group requested this court to reject the retrial application.

Honda filed a lawsuit and request the first-instance court shall: (a) Order Hensim Xintai and Hensim Group Company to immediately stop infringing on the exclusive right of registered trademark of Honda; (b) Order Hensim Xintai and Hensim Group to compensate Honda for economic losses of RMB 3 million (including reasonable expenses paid by Honda to stop the infringement). Hensim Xintai and Hensim Group Company shall bear the joint liability for the compensation; (c) Order Hensim Xintai and Hensim Group to bear all litigation costs in this case.

The first-instance court affirmed that Honda is a large-scale multinational enterprise specializing in the production of motorcycles and other products. It was approved for registration by the Trademark Office of the State Administration for

Industry and Commerce (hereinafter "Trademark Office") on May 30, 1988, and obtained the registered trademark No. 314940. The trademark is approved for use on Class 12 goods, including airplanes, ships, vehicles and other means of transportation. The validity period of the trademark is until May 29, 2018. Honda was approved for registration by the Trademark Office on August 14, 1998, and obtained the registered trademark No. 1198975. The trademark is approved for use on Class 12 goods, including airplanes, ships, vehicles and other means of transportation. The validity period of the trademark is until August 13, 2018. Honda was approved for registration by the Trademark Office on December 17, 1998, and obtained the registered trademark No. 503699. The trademark is approved for use on Class 12 goods, including airplanes, ships, vehicles and other means of transportation. The validity period of the trademark is until November 9, 2019. Hensim Group is a limited liability company registered on September 29, 1998, Hensim Xintai is a limited liability company registered on June 19, 2001. Hensim Group is the parent company of Hensim Taixin, and the legal representative of this two companies is Wan Xun. On June 30, 2016, Kunming Customs issued the *Notice of the Kunming Customs of the People's Republic of China on Confirming the Intellectual Property Status of Imported and Exported Goods* to Honda, informing Honda that on June 28, 2016, Ruili Customs, a subsidiary of Kunming Customs, seized 220 motorcycles declared for export with the trademark "HONDAKIT". Kunming Customs believed that the goods may be suspected of infringing the intellectual property rights of Honda filed with the General Administration of Customs, and required Honda to submit a written application for custom protection measures for intellectual property rights before July 3, 2016, and submit a guarantee one hundred thousand yuan in accordance with Article 14 of *Regulation of the People's Republic of China on the Customs Protection of Intellectual Property Rights*. On August 22, 2016, Ruili Customs issued the *Notice of Ruili Customs Investigation Results of Suspected Infringement Goods* to Honda, informing Honda that Hensim Xintai entrusted Ruili Lingyun Freight Co., Ltd. to declare to Ruili Customs to export 220 motorcycles which bear the "HONDAKIT" logo, with a total declared price of 118,360 US dollars to Myanmar. Honda requested Ruili Customs to detain the above-mentioned goods on July 12, 2016 and it was found that the goods were processed and produced by Hensim Group under the authorization of Meihua Company. It is difficult for the customs to determine whether the exported motorcycles constitute infringement. According to Article 23 of the *Regulations of the People's Republic of China on the Customs Protection of Intellectual Property Rights*, Honda can apply to the People's Court for an order to stop the relevant infringement and for property preservation measures. If the customs does not receive the notice of the people's court on assisting execution within 50 working days as of the detainment, the customs shall release the detained suspected infringing goods. On September 13, 2016, Honda filed a lawsuit to the first-instance court.

The above facts are supported by evidence including the photos of the Ruili Customs seizure warehouse submitted by Honda, the sales contract of Meihua Company submitted by Hensim Xintai and Hensim Group, and the statements of the parties.

The first-instance court held that the key issues in this case were: (a) Whether the acts of Hensim Xintai and Hensim Group constituted an infringement of the exclusive right of registered trademark of Honda, and if so, whether their infringement should be stopped immediately; (b) Whether Hensim Xintai and Hensim Group should jointly compensate Honda Co., Ltd. for economic losses of 3 million yuan.

The first-instance court held that the case was a dispute over trademark infringement. Honda's domicile is in Japan, so this case is a foreign-related intellectual property dispute. According to Article 50 of *Law of the People's Republic of China on Choice of Law for Foreign-related Civil Relationships*, "The laws at the locality where protection is claimed shall apply to the liabilities for tort for intellectual property, the parties concerned may also choose the applicable laws at the locality of the court by agreement after the tort takes place." In this case, the locality where protection is claimed and the place of these court are both in China, so the law of the People's Republic of China shall be applied to this case.

Firstly, whether the acts of Hensim Xintai and Hensim Group constituted an infringement of the exclusive right of registered trademark of Honda, and if so, whether their infringement should be stopped immediately. The first-instance court held that Honda separately obtained the three involved trademarks in 1998, and their rights should be protected in accordance with the law. Hensim Xintai and Hensim Group used "HONDAKIT" text and graphics on the motorcycle hoods, engine covers, left and right windshields, and nameplates they produced and sold, and highlighted the text part of "HONDA" and reduced "KIT" text part. Hensim Xintai and Hensim Group argued that their behavior was OEM processing authorized by Meihua Company. However, the certified evidence submitted by them could not form a complete chain of evidence, and could not confirm that their behavior was OEM processing authorized by Meihua Company. And judging from the certified evidence they submitted, Meihua's authorized trademark "HONDAKIT" did not highlight the text of "HONDA" and reduce the text of "KIT". These two are text and graphics in the same font size. The drawings attached by Hensim Xintai and Hensim Group are also inconsistent with the authorization of Meihua Company. According to Article 57 of the Trademark Law, "Any of the following conduct shall be an infringement upon the right to exclusively use a registered trademark: …; (2) Using a trademark similar to a registered trademark on identical goods or using a trademark identical with or similar to a registered trademark on similar goods, without being licensed by the trademark registrant, which may easily cause confusion. (3) Selling goods which infringe upon the right to exclusively use a registered trademark".

Hensim Xintai and Hensim Group used "HONDAKIT" text and graphic trademarks and highlighted the text part of "HONDA" on motorcycles with the same and similar product categories as the Class 12 for which Honda obtained serial registered trademark trademark rights. At the same time, they reduced the text of "KIT", obviously highlighting and emphasizing the use and visual effects of "HONDA" text and graphics in the goods involved, which constituted the use of the same or similar trademarks as the registered trademarks on the same or similar goods. This act has infringed the exclusive right of registered trademark of Honda, and this infringement should be stopped immediately according to law.

Secondly, whether Hensim Xintai and Hensim Group should jointly compensate Honda Co., Ltd. for economic losses of 3 million yuan. The acts of Hensim Xintai and Hensim Group constitute trademark infringement, and shall bear civil liability for stopping the infringement and compensating for losses in accordance with the law. In this case, both parties failed to submit evidence to prove the loss of Honda, the benefits obtained by Hensim Xintai and Hensim Group, and the license fee for the registered trademark of Honda. Therefore, considering the reputation of the registered trademark of Honda, the subjective fault of Hensim Xintai and Hensim Group, the circumstances of the infringement, the possibility of profit, and the reasonable expenses of Honda to stop the infringement, the first-instance court held that Hensim Xintai and Hensim Group should jointly compensated Honda for economic losses of RMB 300,000.

To sum up, the first-instance court held that the acts of Hensim Xintai and Hensim Group constituted an infringement of the exclusive right of registered trademark of Honda, and their infringement should be stopped immediately, and partially supported the claim that Hensim Xintai and Hensim Group should compensate Honda for economic losses of RMB 3 million. It ordered as follows: (a) Hensim Xintai and Hensim Group immediately stop the infringement of the exclusive right of the three involved trademark of Honda; (b) Hensim Xintai and Hensim Group jointly compensated Honda for economic losses of RMB 300,000; (c) Dismiss Honda's other claims.

Hensim Xintai and Hensim Group refused to accept the judgment the first instance and appealed to the second-instance court, requesting it to: (a) Revoke the first and second items of the first-instance judgment, and dismiss all claims of Honda; (b) Order Honda to bear the litigation costs of the first instance and the second instance of this case.

The second instance found that the facts determined by the first instance court were true, and the second instance confirmed it. In the second instance, the two parties did not submit any new evidence, but there was a dispute over whether the act performed by Hensim Xintai and Hensim Group was an act of foreign-related OEM processing or commodity sales.

The second instance court held that, summarizing the views of both parties, the key issues in this case are: (a) whether the act performed by Hensim Xintai and Hensim Group was an act of foreign-related OEM processing or commodity sales. (b) Whether Hensim Xintai and Hensim Group's use of the involved sign is use of trademark in the sense of Trademark Law; (c) Whether the alleged acts of Hensim Xintai and Hensim Group constitute trademark infringement, and which trademark right has been infringed; (d) If the infringement is established, how should the compensation amount of Hensim Xintai and Hensim Group be determined.

Regarding the first key issue in the dispute, Hensim Xintai and Hensim Group's act was not commodities sales but foreign-related OEM processing. First of all, according to the evidence submitted by Hensim Xintai and Hensim Group in the first instance, the contract signed by Hensim Xintai and Meihua Company on April 3, 2016, called the "Sales Contract", is actually a foreign-related OEM processing contract. After reviewing the terms of the contract, it can be seen that the contract clearly stipulates the following main contents: The products ordered by the buyer are: 125CCMO-TORCYCLEINSKDFORM, BRAND: HONDAKIT (the second-instance judgment is mistakenly written as HONDKIT), and 125CCHONDAKIT motorcycle parts. The quantity is 220 sets, The unit price is US$538, The total price is US$118,360, The destination is Myanmar; The quality objection period after the buyer receives the goods is 30 days. These contract terms were in line with the conditions for OEM processing. Secondly, the relationship between Hensim Group and Hensim Xintai was not a sales relationship on the involved products. Hensim Xintai, a subsidiary of Hensim Group Company, was responsible for handling export matters for this batch of products. The company that actually produced the products is the Hensim Group. Such an arrangement belongs to the business arrangement within the Hensim Group, because they are related companies with the same legal representative and the same domicile. Meihua Company was clearly aware of this situation, which can be known from its trademark authorization letter. Third, all the products involved in the contracted processing were delivered to the ordering party. Without entering the Chinese market, it is impossible for the relevant public in China to have access to the batch of products. Fourth, Myanmar citizen ThetMonAung enjoys the right to the registered trademark "HONDAKIT" in Myanmar. In the first instance, Hensim Xintai and Hensim Group submitted the trademark registration-related ownership certificate obtained by ThetMonAung in Myanmar, namely the *Trademark Registration Declaration Contract* to the court. Hensim Xintai and Hensim Group hired the Yunnan Provincial Translators Association for translation and learned that Myanmar citizen ThetMonAung had registered the trademark "HONDAKIT" with the Contract and Document Registry of Mandalay on Myanmar on June 23, 2014. The category of goods for which the trademark was approved is vehicles and other goods. It can be seen that the registrant of the "HONDAKIT" trademark ThetMonAung has fulfilled the relevant procedural requirements of Myanmar's trademark registration system. Fifth, Hensim Group has obtained the trademark authorization from Myanmar citizen ThetMonAung. In the *Authorization* issued by Meihua Company and the company's executive director ThetMonAung, it was stated that Meihua Company entrusted Hensim Group to process and produce the motorcycle parts involved in the case, and attach "HONDAKIT" trademark. The trademark should be affixed to the engine cover, left and right windshield, and hood. ThetMonAung is the managing director of Meihua Company, and he is also the signatory of the Myanmar side on the *Sales Contract* dated April 3, 2016. These facts are sufficient to confirm that as the trademark holder ThetMonAung involved in the case, the registered trademark of "HONDAKIT" should be attached to the products under the contract, and it is also sufficient to confirm that Hensim Group's production of foreign-related OEM products was legally authorized by the Myanmar trademark owner. The first-instance judgment has examined the four documents including the *Sales Contract*, *Trademark Registration Declaration Contract*, and *Authorization*, and concluded that the evidence submitted by Hensim Xintai and Hensim Group cannot form a complete chain of evidence and cannot confirm that the behavior of Hensim Xintai and Hensim Group was authorized by Meihua Company. And on this basis, the first-instance judgment determined that the behavior of Hensim Xintai and Hensim Group was not an act of foreign-related OEM processing, but an act of selling goods, which constituted a trademark infringement. This is an error in the analysis and certification of the evidence, and it is an unclear fact and an error in the application of the law. The second-instance court corrected it.

Regarding the second key issue in this dispute, the use of the sign involved in the case by Hensim Xintai and Hensim Group is not a use of trademark in the sense of Trademark Law. Article 48 of the Trademark Law provides: "For the purposes of this Law, "use of a trademark" means using a trademark on goods, on the packages or containers of goods, in the trade documents of goods, or for advertisements, exhibitions, and other commercial activities for the purpose of identifying the origin of goods." According to this definition, the original intention of the trademark law in protecting the use of trademarks is to protect the distinctiveness of trademarks in commercial activities. It can be inferred from this meaning that if the use of a certain mark is not used to identify the origin of goods in commercial activities, it will naturally not meet the prerequisite requirements for "use" in paragraph 2, Article 57 of the Trademark Law. According to the circumstances of this case, the 220 sets of motorcycle parts handled by Hensim Xintai and Hensim Group were all exported to Myanmar. Without entering the Chinese market and participating in commercial activities, the relevant public in China would not have access to the products. Therefore, this act of Hensim Xintai and Hensim Group cannot play a role in identifying the origin of goods in China. So, this is not a use of trademark in the sense of Trademark Law.

Regarding the third key issue in this dispute, foreign-related OEM processing usually refers to domestic manufacturers that are legally authorized by foreign legal trademark owners to produce and export all the products they produce to countries and regions where the trademark owner has trademark rights. Whether the production under this model infringes the trademark rights of the relevant trademark owners in China should be analyzed in detail based on the specific circumstances of the case. In this case, the actions of Hensim Xintai Company and Hensim Group Company did not constitute an infringement of the three involved trademarks of Honda in the case.

First of all, from the analysis of the relevant provisions of the Trademark Law, Article 57 of the Trademark Law has revised the content of Article 52 of the former Trademark Law, from five acts to seven acts, and the content of the former paragraph 1 was split into two parts. That is, the first paragraph is "Using a trademark identical with a registered trademark on identical goods without being licensed by the trademark registrant". The paragraph 2 is "Using a trademark similar to a registered trademark on identical goods or using a trademark identical with or similar to a registered trademark on similar goods, without being licensed by the trademark registrant, which may easily cause confusion". It can be seen that "easily cause confusion" is new content. According to the provisions of this article, trademark indicate the origin of goods or services, enabling the relevant public to distinguish goods or services provided by different operators, So that it is not "easy to cause confusion". This is the core function of a trademark and the most basic value of a trademark. The fundamental purpose of trademark protection in trademark law is to ensure the trademark identification. The key to judging whether a trademark is infringing or not is to examine whether the use of a trademark is likely to cause confusion among the relevant public about the origin of goods or services. Only the acts that easily cause the relevant public to confuse the origin of goods or services can trigger the use of similar trademarks that infringe the trademark rights of others. There is no basis for talking about trademark infringement without these conditions and circumstances. Secondly, in this case, all 220 sets of motorcycle parts were exported to Myanmar. Without entering the Chinese market for sale, it is impossible for the relevant public in China to have access to the product. Therefore, there is no problem of causing confusion to the relevant public in China, and it has not harmed the actual interests of Honda. That is, it does not have the essential elements for trademark infringement. Thirdly, trademark right has territoriality. In this context, our country's trademark law can only protect trademark rights registered in our country, and the scope of protection cannot extend beyond our country's territory. The 220 sets of OEM products involved in this case are not in China but in Myanmar. Therefore, when Hensim Xintai Company and Hensim Group Company highlighted the HONDA part of in HONDAKIT, whether it is easy to cause the relevant public in Myanmar to confuse the origin of the goods is beyond the judging scope of our country's Trademark Law.

Regarding the fourth key issue in this dispute, since the acts of Hensim Xintai Company and Hensim Group Company did not constitute infringement, there is no issue of compensation for losses.

To sum up, the appeal grounds of Hensim Xintai Company and Hensim Group Company are established. The facts found in the judgment of first instance were unclear and the application of law was wrong, and should be corrected in accordance with law. It ordered as follows: (a) Revoke the first-instance judgment. (b) Dismiss the claims of Honda.

In retrial, this court also found that Hensim Xintai Company and Meihua Company signed a "Sales Contract" on April 3, 2016 to sell the alleged infringing goods. Ruili Customs seized the alleged infringing goods on June 28, 2016. The first and second instance courts applied the *Trademark Law of the People's Republic of China* (2013 revision, hereinafter "Trademark Law"), and the parties had no objections.

This court believed that the key issue in this dispute is the determination of the nature of the alleged infringement of Hensim Xintai Company and Hensim Group Company: (a) Whether it belongs to foreign-related OEM processing. (b). Whether it constituted the use of trademark. (c) Whether it constituted a trademark infringement. (a) Whether the alleged infringement of Hensim Xintai Company and Hensim Group Company belongs to foreign-related OEM processing. Based on the facts found in the first and the second instance, the second-instance court found that the alleged infringement of Hensim Xintai Company and Hensim Group Company is foreign-related OEM processing. The second-instance court conducted an in-depth analysis and found the facts clear. This court affirmed it.

(b) Whether the alleged infringement of Hensim Xintai Company and Hensim Group Company constituted the use of trademark. Article 48 of the Trademark Law provides: "For the purposes of this Law, "use of a trademark" means using a trademark on goods, on the packages or containers of goods, in the trade documents of goods, or for advertisements, exhibitions, and other commercial activities for the purpose of identifying the origin of goods". The term "identifying the origin of goods" mentioned in this article refers to the purpose of the user of the trademark to identify the origin of the goods, including the possible role of identifying the origin of goods and the actual role of identifying the origin of goods.

Use of Trademark is an objective behavior, which usually includes many links, such as physical attachment, market circulation, etc. Whether it constitutes the "use of a trademark" in the sense of the Trademark Law should be interpreted in a consistent manner in accordance with the Trademark Law, and should not separate an act to consider a only certain link. It is necessary to prevent a single link from concealing the behavior process, and at the same time to overcome the replacement of a single aspect of the behavior as a whole. Use of trademark means that a certain trademark is used for a certain commodity, which may conform to the common will of the commodity provider and the trademark owner, or may not conform to the common will of the commodity provider and the trademark owner. A certain trademark is used for a certain product so that the two are integrated into the observation object for consumers to identify the product and its origin, which may allow consumers to correctly identify the origin of the product, or may cause consumers to misidentify the origin of the product. There may even be complicated situations where some consumers correctly identify the origin of the products, while others misidentify the origin of the products. These phenomena are complicated and are all dominated by the use of trademark. These interests are repeatedly gamed and are all dominated by Trademark Law. Therefore, if a trademark is used in labeling or other ways on products, as long as it has the possibility of distinguishing the origin of the goods, the state of use should be deemed to be a "use of trademark" in the sense of Trademark Law.

Article 8 of Interpretation of the Supreme People's Court Concerning the Application of Laws in the Trial of Cases of Civil Disputes Arising from Trademarks provides: "The "relevant general public" as mentioned in the Trademark Law refers to the consumers relating to a certain type of commodities or services to which the trademark represents and other business operators that are closely connected with the marketing of the aforesaid commodities or services". In addition to the consumers of the alleged infringing goods, the relevant public in this case should also include operators who are closely related to the marketing of the alleged infringing goods. In this case, the operators in the transportation of the alleged infringing goods may had access to the goods. Moreover, with the development of e-commerce and the Internet, even if the alleged infringing goods are exported abroad, there is still the possibility of returning to the domestic market. At the same time, with the continuous development of China's economy, there are a large number of Chinese consumers who travel and consume abroad, and there is also the possibility of contact and confusion about "OEM products". The court of second instance found that the 220 sets of motorcycle parts handled by Hensim Xintai Company and Hensim Group Company were all exported to Myanmar. Without entering the Chinese market and participating in commercial activities, the relevant public in China could not have access to the products. Therefore, this act of Hensim Xintai Company and Hensim

Group Company cannot play a role in identifying the origin of goods in China. This is not use of trademark in the sense of Trademark Law. There were errors in the facts found in the second instance and the applicable laws, and this court corrected them. (c) Whether the alleged infringing act of Hensim Xintai Company and Hensim Group Company constituted trademark infringement. The paragraph 2, Article 57 of Trademark Law provides: "Any of the following conduct shall be an infringement upon the right to exclusively use a registered trademark:... Using a trademark similar to a registered trademark on identical goods or using a trademark identical with or similar to a registered trademark on similar goods, without being licensed by the trademark registrant, which may easily cause confusion". The basic function of a trademark is to distinguish the origin of goods or services. Infringement of trademark rights is essentially the destruction of the trademark identification function, causing general consumers to confuse and misidentify the origin of goods. From the perspective of legal provisions, the principle of liability for trademark infringements should belong to the principle of no-fault liability, and the actual damage should not be the constitutive requirement of infringement. The term "easily cause confusion" in the aforementioned trademark law refers to the possibility of confusion if the relevant public comes into contact with the alleged infringing goods. It does not require the relevant public to have actual access to the alleged infringing goods, nor does it require that the fact of confusion has occurred.

In this case, Hensim Xintai and Hensim Group used "HONDAKIT" text and graphics on the alleged infringing motorcycle they produced and sold, with highlighting the text part of "HONDA" and reducing "KIT" part. At the same time, they marked the H letter and parts with similar wing shapes in red, which constituted similar trademarks on the same or similar products with the three involved trademarks of Honda. As mentioned above, the alleged infringing act constituted the use of trademark, and it also had the possibility of causing confusion and misunderstanding by the relevant public.

Our country's economy has shifted from a stage of rapid growth to a stage of high-quality development. Faced with the ever-increasing degree of globalization of economic development, the increasingly complex division of international trade and economic and trade cooperation, and the ever-changing trade policy conflicts of various countries, the people's courts hearing trademark infringement disputes involving foreign-related OEMs should fully consider the domestic and international economies. At the same time, the people's court shall conduct specific analysis of trademark infringement disputes in specific periods, specific markets and specific forms of transactions, and accurately apply the law, reflecting the judicial policy orientation of intellectual property rights of "judicial leadership, strict protection, classified policies, and proportional coordination". It is also necessary to strengthen the creation, protection and use of intellectual property rights, and actively create a good legal environment, market environment, and cultural environment for intellectual property. Since the reform and opening up, foreign-related OEM processing trade has been an important method of our country's foreign trade. With the transformation of our country's economic development mode, people's awareness and dispute resolution of trademark infringement issues arising from foreign-related licensing processing are constantly changing and deepening. In the final analysis, to resolve disputes through justice, in the application of law, the unity of the legal system must be maintained, and certain trade methods (such as the foreign-related OEM processing method in this case) cannot be simply solidified as an exception that does not infringe on trademark rights. Otherwise, it will violate the basic rules of trademark infringement judgment in the Trademark Law. This is an issue that must be clarified and emphasized.

Hensim Xintai Company and Hensim Group Company held that Hensim Group Company has obtained the Myanmar Company's trademark authorization, and therefore did not constitute infringement. In this regard, as an intellectual property right, trademark rights have a territoriality. For trademarks that are not registered in China, even if they are registered in foreign countries, they do not enjoy the exclusive right to register trademarks in China. Correspondingly, the so-called "trademark authorization" obtained by civil entities in China does not belong to the legal rights of trademark protected by our country's trademark law, and cannot be used as a defense against infringement of trademark right. Therefore, it was an error in the applicable law that the second-instance court held that "the products involved in the case produced by the Hensim Group Company were legally authorized by the Myanmar trademark owner". This court shall correct it.

To sum up, the alleged infringing act of Hensim Xintai Company and Hensim Group Company constituted an infringement of the registered trademark rights of the three involved trademarks of Honda. Hensim Xintai Company and Hensim Group Company shall bear civil liability for stopping the infringement and compensating for losses in accordance with law. Considering the reputation of the registered trademark of Honda, the subjective fault of Hensim Xintai and Hensim Group, the circumstances of the infringement, the possibility of profit, and the reasonable expenses of Honda to stop the infringement, the first-instance court order that Hensim Xintai and Hensim Group should jointly compensated Honda for economic losses of RMB 300,000. Honda did not file an appeal or raise an objection in the application for retrial. This court maintained it.

To sum up, the judgment of the second instance that the act of Hensim Xintai Company and Hensim Group Company did not constitute infringement is wrong. The reasons for Honda's retrial application are partially established and supported.

In accordance with Article 48, paragraph 2 of Article 57 of the *Trademark Law of the People's Republic of China*, paragraph 1, Article 207 and item (2), paragraph 1, Article 170 of the *Civil Procedure Law of the People's Republic of China*, it ordered as follows:

(a) Revoke the civil judgment (2017) Y.M.Z No.800 of Yunnan Provincial Higher People's Court.
(b) Maintain the civil judgment (2016) Y.31 M.C. No.52 of Intermediate People's Court of Dehong Dai and Jingpo Autonomous Prefecture, Yunnan Province.

2.2 Analysis of the Case

1. Facts

Honda Co., Ltd. filed a lawsuit with the court of first instance: (1) Order Hengsheng Xintai Company and Hengsheng Group to immediately stop infringing on the exclusive right to use the registered trademark of Honda Co., Ltd.; (2) Order Hengsheng Xintai Company and Hengsheng group company compensates Honda Co., Ltd. for economic losses of RMB 3 million; (3) Order Hengsheng Shengxintai Company and Hengsheng Group Company shall bear all litigation costs in this case.

The alleged infringement is a typical trademark infringement. (2) The alleged infringement shall not be regarded as foreign-related licensing processing. (3) It is err for the second-instance court to not define the act of attaching trademark logos to the alleged infringing goods as "use" within the meaning of the "2013 Trademark Law." (4) Hengsheng Xintai Company and Hengsheng Group Company failed to perform their duty of reasonable care and had the purpose of attaching to the reputation of Honda Co., Ltd., which violated the "principle of good faith." In summary, this court is requested to revoke the second-instance judgment and maintain the first-instance judgment; the case acceptance fee shall be borne by Hengsheng Xintai Company and Hengsheng Group Company. The decision of the first and second instance:

The court of first instance held that (1) Hengsheng Xintai Company and Hengsheng Group Co., Ltd. immediately stopped infringing the exclusive right to use the three trademarks; (2) Hengsheng Xintai Company and Hengsheng Group Co., Ltd. Jointly compensate Honda Co., Ltd. for economic losses of RMB 300,000; (3) Dismiss other claims of Honda Co., Ltd. Hengsheng Xintai Company and Hengsheng Group Company refused to accept the judgment of the first instance and filed an appeal to the court of second instance. The appeal court held: (1) Revocation of the first-instance judgment; (2) Dismissed Honda's litigation request.

2. Focus of dispute

The Honda compamy applied the retrail to the supreme people's court. The court believes that the focus of the dispute in this case is the determination of the nature of the alleged infringement of Hengsheng Xintai Company and Hengsheng Group Company, namely: 1. Whether it is a foreign-related licensing process activities; 2. Whether it constitutes a trademark use behavior; 3. Whether it constitutes a trademark infringement.

3. Rules

"Trademark law (2013)".

Article 48: For the purposes of this Law, "use of a trademark" means using a trademark on goods, on the packages or containers of goods, in the trade documents of goods, or for advertisements, exhibitions, and other commercial activities for the purpose of identifying the origin of goods.

Article 57: Any of the following conduct shall be an infringement upon the right to exclusively use a registered trademark: Using a trademark similar to a registered trademark on identical goods or using a trademark identical with or similar to a registered trademark on similar goods, without being licensed by the trademark registrant, which may easily cause confusion.

"Regulation of the People's Republic of China on the Customs Protection of Intellectual Property Rights (2018 Revision)"

Article 32: An intellectual property right holder may, after filing an application with the customs for taking protection measures, apply in accordance with the Trademark Law of the People's Republic of China, the Copyright Law of the People's Republic of China, the Patent Law of the People's Republic of China or other relevant laws to the people's court for taking the measures of ordering to stop the acts of infringement or taking property preservation with regard to the suspected infringing goods detained.

Interpretation of the Supreme People's Court Concerning the Application of Laws in the Trial of Cases of Civil Disputes Arising from Trademarks.

The "relevant general public" as mentioned in the Trademark Law refers to the consumers relating to a certain type of commodities or services to which the trademark represents and other business operators that are closely connected with the marketing of the aforesaid commodities or services.

4. Reasoning

1) Belonging to foreign-related licensing processing activities.

The behaviors carried out by Hengsheng Xintai Company and Hengsheng Group Company are not commodity sales behaviors but foreign-related licensing processing behaviors. First of all, according to the evidence submitted in the first instance of Hengsheng Xintai Company and Hengsheng Group Company, the contract signed between Hengsheng Xintai Company and Meihua Company on April 3, 2016 is called the "Sales Contract", which is actually a foreign-related brand processing contract. After reviewing the terms of the contract, the contract clearly stipulated the following main content: The products ordered by the buyer were: 125CCMOTORCY-CLEINSKDFORM, BRAND: HONDAKIT, 125CCHONDAKIT motorcycle parts; 220 sets in quantity; unit price: US$538; total the price is 118,360 US dollars; the destination is Myanmar. These contract terms are in line with the custom-made conditions for OEM processing. Second, all the products involved in the contracted processing are delivered to the ordering party. Without entering the Chinese market, it is impossible for the relevant public in China to have access to the batch of products. Fourth, Myanmar citizen Wu De Meng Ang enjoys the registered trademark right of "HONDAKIT" in Myanmar. Fifth, Hengsheng Group has obtained the trademark use authorization from Myanmar citizen Wu De Meng Ang. All these indicate that this behavior belongs to the processing behavior of a designated brand.

2) Constitutes trademark use

Trademark use behavior is an objective behavior, which usually includes many links, such as physical attachment, market circulation, etc. Whether it constitutes a "trademark use" in the sense of trademark law should be interpreted consistently in accordance with the trademark law. The use of a trademark means that a certain trademark is used for a certain commodity, which may conform to the common will of the commodity provider and the trademark owner, or may not conform to the common will of the commodity provider and the trademark owner; Therefore, As long as the product has the possibility of distinguishing the source of the product, in manufacturing or processing, it should be determined that the state of use is a "trademark use" in the sense of trademark law if the trademark is used in labeling or other ways.

3) Constitutes trademark infringement

Hengsheng Xintai Company and Hengsheng Group Company used "HONDAKIT" text and graphics on the alleged infringing motorcycles produced and sold by them, and emphasized the part of "HONDA" and the reduction of the part of "KIT". At the same time, the letter H and similar wing shapes are marked in red, which constitutes similar trademarks on the same or similar products with the three trademarks requested by Honda Co., Ltd. for protection. As mentioned earlier, the alleged infringement constitutes the use of a trademark, and it also has the possibility of causing confusion and misunderstanding by the relevant public, which is easy to confuse the relevant public.

5. Enlinghtenment

How to define whether or not an activity is foreign-related licensing processing activity?

To define the designated-brand processing, we should examine the clauses of contract rather than the title of the contract. But to define the trademark infringement, we should examine the possibility of confusion. We can not infer that no infringement is found as long as it is a foreign-related licensing processing activity, and it depends on how to use the authorized trademark correctly.

How to define the "use" in trademark law?

If a trademark is used in a labeling or other manner on a product manufactured or processed, as long as it has the possibility of distinguishing the source of the goods, it should be determined that the state of use belongs to the "use of a trademark" in the sense of trademark law.

How to define "relevant public"?

In this case, in addition to the consumers of the alleged infringing goods, the relevant public should also include operators who are closely related to the marketing of the alleged infringing goods. In this case, the operators in the transportation of the alleged infringing goods may be contacted. Moreover, with the development of e-commerce and the Internet, even if the alleged infringing goods are exported abroad, there is still the possibility of returning to the domestic market. At the same time, with the continuous development of China's economy, there are a large number of Chinese consumers who travel and consume abroad, and there is also the possibility of contact and confusion for "branded products".

How to define "easy to cause confusion"?

The term "easy to cause confusion" under the Trademark Law refers to the possibility of confusion. If the relevant public comes into contact with the alleged infringing goods, it does not require the relevant public to actually be in contact with the alleged infringing goods. The fact of confusion is not required to be certain. The alleged infringement in this case constitutes the use of a trademark, and it also has the possibility of causing confusion and misunderstanding by the relevant public, which is easy to confuse the relevant public.

(3) **How to identify the "other adverse effects" stipulated in Trademark Law?—Shanghai Junke Commerce Co., Ltd. v.Trademark Appeal Board of SAIC**

3.1 Case Judgement: Beijing High People's Court
Case No.: (2018)jingxingzhong No.137
Date of judgment: Feb 03, 2019
Cause of action: tardemark administrative management
Appellant (plaintiff in the original trail): Shanghai Junke Commerce Co., Ltd.
Legal representative: Li Suping, Executive Director.
Attorney: Wang Ying, lawyer of Beijing Daoning Law Firm.
Attorney: Xian Yi, lawyer of Beijing Daoning Law Firm.
Appellee (defendant in the original trail): Trademark Review and Adjudication Board of SAIC.
Legal representative: Zhao Gang, Director.
Authorized proxy: Ke Peipei, examiner of Trademark Appeal Board of SAIC.
Third party in the original trail: Yao Hongjun
Authorized proxy: Meng Yujie, lawyer of Shanghai Capitallaw Law Firm

The appellant, Shanghai Junke Commerce Co., Ltd. (hereinafter referred to as Shanghai Junke Company), refused to accept the Administrative Judgment (2016) Jing 73 Xingchu No. 6871 of the Beijing Intellectual Property Court and appealed to this court in the case of an administrative dispute over a request for invalidation of trademark rights. After this court accepted the case on January 10, 2018, a collegial panel was formed in accordance with the law to conduct the trial. On March 7, 2018, Wang Ying and Xian Yi, the attorneys of the appellant, Shanghai Junke Company, and Ke Peipei, the authorized proxy of theTrademark Appeal Board of SAIC (hereinafter referred to as theTrademark Appeal Board), and Meng Yujie, the third party's authorized proxyin the original trial, came to this court for questioning. This case is decided now.

The Beijing Intellectual Property Court affirmed that the No. 8954893 trademark "MLGB" (hereinafter referred to as the disputed trademark) was applied for registration by Shanghai Junke Company on December 15, 2010 and was approved for registration on December 28, 2011. This trademark has been approved for use on the 25th category of clothing, wedding dresses, shoes, hats, socks, ties, scarves, belts (for clothing), sweatshirts, and baby outfits. The disputed trademark is valid until December 27, 2021.

On October 9, 2015, Yao Hongjun filed an application for invalidation of disputed trademark to theTrademark Appeal Board. The main reasons are: disputed trademark tend to make people think of uncivilized terms; the use of disputed trademark which has undesirable effects on clothing, hats and other commodities is harmful to socialist morals and customs. Yao Hongjun requested that the disputed trademark should be declared invalid in accordance with item (8), paragraph 1, Article 10 and paragraph 1, Article 44 of *Trademark Law of the People's Republic of China* (hereinafter referred to as the *Trademark Law 2013*).

To prove his claim, Yao Hongjun submitted the following evidence to theTrademark Appeal Board:

(a) Related web page documents, including "an inventory and essays triggered by the Internet", are used to prove that "MLGB" has been used as an abbreviation for uncivilized terms long before the disputed trademark application date. Until now, according to the understanding of the public, "MLGB" is still an abbreviation for uncivilized terms.
(b) Relevant web page documents, including "I didn't expect MLGB to be a brand", "What brand is MLGB?", "MLGB, it turned out to be a brand", etc., are used to prove that "MLGB" printed as a trademark on the clothes and hats caused adverse effects and cannot accepted by the public.

To prove its claim, Shanghai Junke Company submitted the following evidence to the Trademark Appeal Board:

(a) A screenshot of the discussion about whether the disputed trademark has adverse effects.
(b) The performance of Shanghai Junke Company.
(c) The publicity and use of the disputed trademark.

On November 9, 2016, the Trademark Appeal Board issued the Shangpingzi (2016) No. 93833 *Decision on No. 8954893 Trademark "MLGB" Dispute* (hereinafter referred to as the accused decision), which determined that the letter combination of the disputed trademark is widely used on social platforms such as the Internet, with negative meaning and low style. Its use as a trademark is harmful to socialist ethics and tends to produce adverse effects. Shanghai Junke Company argued that the disputed trademark refers to "My Life's Getting Better". However, the evidence submitted by Shanghai Junke Company is still difficult to prove that the meaning has been widely recognized by the public. On the contrary, the public is more likely to recognize "MLGB" as an uncivilized term. In accordance with item (8), paragraph 1, Article 10 of the *Trademark Law of the People's Republic of China* (hereinafter referred to as the *Trademark Law 2001*), the Trademark Appeal Board decided that the disputed trademark shall be declared invalid.

Shanghai Junke Company refused to accept the accused decision and filed an administrative lawsuit with the Beijing Intellectual Property Court within the legal duration.

In the original trial, Shanghai Junke Company additionally submitted the following evidence:

(a) The registration records of the "MLGB" trademark on different goods and services show that the "MLGB" trademark has been registered in 45 categories of goods and services, Which are used to prove that the Trademark Appeal Board has made the invalidation of registration in 25 categories based on the same examination standard, which violates the principle of administrative certainty.
(b) *Information Statement* and *Electronic Tax Payment Voucher* issued by Shanghai Enbixi Trading Co., Ltd, which are used to prove that the production and sale of "MLGB" brand clothing is one of the businesses of Shanghai Junke Company. Through years of hard work, the company has formed a consumer group of fashion brand clothing, with good sales and tax records.

(c) Screenshot of infringement websites on Taobao and protected records in Taobao's intellectual property complaint platform, which are used to prove that the "MLGB" brand is well-known, and Shanghai Junke Company actively protected its trademark rights and goodwill.
(d) BYD, SB, NND, NMD, CD, CNM, MLB, NMB, NB, TMD, TNND, MD, MB, NMD application and registration information, which are used to prove that a large number of registered trademarks including well-known trademarks similar to the disputed trademarks in this case are in use at home and abroad and in related industries.
(e) Evidence of brand promotion, which is used to prove that Shanghai Junke Company has invested a lot of manpower and material resources in the promotion of the disputed trademark and has formed a good reputation. When using and publicizing the disputed trademark, Shanghai Junke Company highlighted the publicity of the trademark meaning "My Life is Getting Better" in a prominent way, which is sufficient to enable relevant consumer to form an understanding of the correct meaning of the trademark.

In the original trial, Yao Hongjun additionally submitted the following evidence:

(a) Shanghai Junke Company has successfully registered the trademarks "caonima" and "草泥马" while applying for the registration of "MLGB" trademark. It is used to prove that the registration of disputed trademark of Shanghai Junke Company is malicious.
(b) Articles written by relevant professional staffs after the Trademark Appeal Board made the accused decision to prove that the public knows the meaning of "MLGB" in Chinese is not high in style.

The Beijing Intellectual Property Court held that when a trademark with a relatively fixed meaning is applied for registration as a trademark, whether it violates ethical customs does not always cause differences in judgment, because the code of conduct and values are relatively stable for a certain period of time. For example, words such as "underworld" will be forbidden to be approved for registration because they are harmful to socialist morals. However, with the development of the Internet, changes in information carriers have led to changes in the way of people's expression. Word combinations with new meanings, including the use of pinyin letters instead of Chinese vocabulary expressions, continue to appear. The habits, styles, and methods of language use in the network environment have formed their own distinctive characteristics, and even formed "network language" with relatively fixed meanings in certain groups. And they gradually merge into people's daily language environment, producing new words or new meanings that are widely accepted by society. There were disagreements when determining whether such terms belonged to "harmful to socialist morals or have other adverse effects" as stipulated in item (8), paragraph 1, Article 10 of the *Trademark Law 2001*. The collegial panel has different opinions on whether the registration of disputed trademark is harmful to socialist morality or has other adverse effects.

A minority of opinions held that the registration of the disputed trademark did not violate the provisions of item (8), paragraph 1, Article 10 of the *Trademark Law*

2001, and the accused decision should be revoked. These opinions are mainly based on the following reasons: (a) As an Internet buzzword, the letter combination of the disputed trademark has not been formed for a long time and is limited to the Internet environment, mainly among young people, which is not common in daily life. Social morality depends on the cognition of most people. We cannot think that the two have established a fixed connection just because some people understand the uncivilized meaning of Internet buzzwords. In Chinese, there is no habit of understanding the meaning of English combinations with the initials of Pinyin. It should not be considered that the mark of the disputed trademark itself has the meaning of endangering the morals and customs because the improper association has produced the meaning of endangering social morals and customs. Otherwise, the use of language characters or Pinyin letters will be improperly restricted. (b) In the trademark invalidation procedure, after the disputed trademark was registered, the trademark owner had invested a lot of resources in the promotion and publicity of the trademark based on the trust in the administrative authorization. The disputed trademark has actually been continuously used and had a certain scale. With regard to the development and evolution of the meaning of the disputed trademark after the date of registration, which is "harmful to socialist morality" or has "other adverse effects", the admissibility and determination of evidence should be particularly cautious. Relatively stricter standards in the authorization procedure should be adopted to protect the right holder's trust in trademark registration. (c) Item (8), paragraph 1, Article 10 of the *Trademark Law 2001* is used to evaluate whether the mark itself and the use of the mark in the approved goods will harm the socialist morals and customs. As for whether the disputed trademark registered by Shanghai Junke Company intends to cater to some of the vulgar tastes on the Internet, it does not fall within the scope of the regulation of item (8), paragraph 1, Article 10 of the *Trademark Law 2001*.

The majority opinion believes that the disputed trademark registration on Category 25 commodities is a situation harmful to socialist morals as stipulated in item (8), paragraph 1, Article 10 of the Trademark Law 2001, and should be declared invalid. So the accused is deemed correct. These opinions are mainly based on the following reasons: (a) The legislative purpose of item (8), paragraph 1, Article 10 of the Trademark Law of 2001 is to maintain the ethics in social life, which is an absolute clause for trademark prohibition. From the legislative purpose, when applying this article, attention should be paid to the maintenance of social public interests and moral order when the judgment is made. When reviewing whether a registered trademark needs to be invalidated under this article, full consideration should be given to the meaning of the trademark in dispute when the judgment is made to ensure that the continuous existence of the trademark does not violate social ethics, not only the meaning of the trademark on the date of application or registration. Therefore, the evidence generated after the registration date and used to prove the current meaning of the trademark in question can be used as the basis for the determination. Existing evidence shows that the uncivilized meaning of the disputed trademark already existed before the date of approval for use of the disputed trademark. And the uncivilized meaning was used by a certain group of people, especially some young Internet users, and had a certain influence. After the disputed trademark was approved for registration, the scope of such referential use and cognition gradually expanded with the development of the Internet, and even expanded to appear in daily life. Although Shanghai Junke Company claimed that the "MLGB" is the abbreviation of "My life is getting better", and there was no evidence to show that this abbreviation is a common expression in English. There was also no evidence that this usage was known to the public or can eliminate the disgust that the disputed trademark had uncivilized meaning. (b) The commodities approved to use the disputed trademark are the 25th category of clothing, shoes, hats and other commodities. It can be seen from the advertising and other evidence provided by Shanghai Junke that the disputed trademarks stand out as novel, avant-garde and distinctive in brand positioning. The main consumer groups are youth groups with strong curious minds and pursuit of individuality. It is precisely that almost 100% of these groups are Internet users and almost all know the uncivilized meaning of the disputed trademark. Although the intention at the time of is not a necessary element that constitutes a violation of item (8), paragraph 1, Article 10 of the *Trademark Law 2001*. However, this determination further confirms the possibility that the registration of the disputed trademark would cause consequences that would endanger socialist morals and customs. (c) Like the minority opinions, the majority opinions also believe that the current evidence shows that the recognition of the uncivilized meaning of the disputed trademark is mainly limited to young people who often socialize online. However, the recognition scope of the meaning of a mark is not equivalent to the scope of the possible impact of the meaning, and the impact of a specific meaning of the a mark is not limited to the scope of the recognized meaning. A mark that only has a negative meaning for a specific group can also affect the morality of the entire society. Social networking has increasingly become an indispensable part of teenagers' lives. Teenagers have a strong sense of curiosity and rebellion, and the three views are still in the forming stage. The disputed trademark was registered and used on clothing, shoes and hats and other commodities. Evidence such as advertisements showed that the main marketing selling points were "fashion", "individuality" and "trend", and the target group was teenagers. The disputed trademark has a vulgar meaning to the youth group, and the maintenance of registration is more likely to produce bad guidance to regard vulgarity as the pursuit of fashion. This kind of bad guidance directly affects the youth group, and the harmful consequences will inevitably affect the morality of the entire society. The Internet is not a place outside the law, and the network environment is also based on real social relationships. When applying item (8), paragraph 1, Article 10 of the *Trademark Law 2001* to evaluate trademark based on internet language, it is still the basic values to follow to resist vulgar and evil customs, promote the true, the good and the beautiful, spread positive energy, and maintain socialist spiritual civilization and moral trend. Therefore, the disputed trademark which is harmful to socialist morality and other adverse effects is under the regulation of item (8), paragraph 1, Article 10 of the *Trademark Law 2001* and theTrademark Appeal Board's decision should be maintained.

The deliberations of the collegiate panel follow the principle of minority submission. In accordance with Article 69 and Article 101 of *The Administrative Litigation Law of the People's Republic of China*, and Article 42 of *The Civil Procedure Law of the People's Republic of China*, the Beijing Intellectual Property Court delivered a judgement and dismissed the claims of Shanghai Junke Company.

Not accepting the judgement, Shanghai Junke Company filed an appeal and requested to revoke the judgment of original trail and the accused decision. The main points that it contended were as follows: (a) The judgment of the original trial that the disputed trademark has formed a relatively fixed and uncivilized meaning lacks basis. When Shanghai Junke Company promoted the brand, the meaning of the disputed trademark was clearly defined as "My life's getting better" (b) The judiciary should understand the cognition of the parties and the public from a kind perspective, and believe that people are noble. This is in line with the spirit of the legal system and existing precedents, and the law can play a positive role in guiding noble and kind customs. (c) Under the background that there is no actual one-to-one correspondence between the disputed trademark and the uncivilized meaning, the conclusion of the original trail has an adverse impact and is contrary to the original intention of the public to apply for trademark registration.

The Trademark Appeal Board and Yao Hongjun obeyed the judgment of original trail.

The finding: The facts found in the original trail are clear, and the evidence are admissible. In addition, the accused decision, the disputed trademark file, the evidences submitted by Shanghai Junke Company and Yao Hongjun in the administrative and litigation procedures, and the statements of the parties are supporting the case. This court confirms them.

During the trial by this court, Shanghai Junke Company supplemented printed copies of the results of the Internet search, *Electronic Tax Payment Voucher*, judgment documents for other cases, and *Prohibited Words in Xinhua News Reports* published by Xinhua News Agency to prove that there was no relevant meaning when the disputed trademark was applied for registration. At the same time, Shanghai Junke Company invested a lot of material resources in the use and promotion of the disputed trademark, and "MLGB" was not included in the prohibited words on the Internet. The Trademark Appeal Board and Yao Hongjun recognized the authenticity of the above evidence but did not recognize its relevance.

During the trial by this court, Yao Hongjun supplemented the review articles that the "MLGB" trademark was rejected by the court, the 40th "Statistical Report on China's Internet Development Status" issued by the China Internet Center, and related news reports to prove that the disputed trademark had adverse effects. Shanghai Junke Company recognized the authenticity of the above evidence but did not recognize the relevance; theTrademark Appeal Board recognized the above evidence.

The above facts are supported by evidence submitted by Shanghai Junke Company and Yao Hongjun in the second-instance as well as the statements of the parties.

This court affirmed that the disputed trademark was approved for registration before the implementation of *the Trademark Law 2013*. According to the principle of non-retroactivity, the relevant substantive issues in this case apply to *the Trademark Law 2001*, and the procedural issues apply to *the Trademark Law 2013*.

According to item (8), paragraph 1, Article 10 of *the Trademark Law of 2001*, signs that are harmful to socialist morals or have other adverse effects shall not be used as trademarks. According to Article 5 of *Provisions of the Supreme People's Court on Several Issues concerning the Trial of Administrative Cases involving Trademark Authorization and Confirmation,* "Where a trademark sign or its constituent elements may cause passive and negative effect on the social and public interests and public order of China, the people's court may determine that it falls under the circumstance of 'having other adverse effect' as prescribed in item (8), paragraph 1, Article 10 of the Trademark Law"; According to Article 31, "These Provisions shall come into force on March 1, 2017. These Provisions may apply, mutatis mutandis, to the administrative cases involving trademark authorization and confirmation tried by the people's courts according to the Trademark Law amended in 2001". Since the "other adverse effects" in item (8), paragraph 1, Article 10 of *the Trademark Law 2001* is the definition of the absolute circumstances in which the use of relevant marks is prohibited as trademarks, it is necessary to avoid unduly expanding the scope of identification and limiting the space for free expression and creation of business operators in commercial activities. It should also avoid improperly narrowing the scope of identification, which may cause signs that may have a negative and negative impact on my country's public interests and public order to be approved for registration. Therefore, whether a trademark or its constituent elements belong to the "other adverse effects" stipulated in item (8), paragraph 1, Article 10 of *the Trademark Law 2001* should be comprehensively judged from the following four aspects:

(a) Subject of judging "other adverse effects". The subject of determining whether the trademark or its constituent elements are under "other adverse effects" should be the "public". Because the above clauses are for the prohibition of related signs as trademarks. It is based on the premise that relevant signs may harm the public interest and public order, and from the perspective of protecting "public order and good customs". Therefore, the subject of judgment on this issue should be the entire public, not the "relevant public" of the goods or services pointed by the disputed trademark. Otherwise, the conclusion are likely to be "partially generalized", which is not conducive to social public interest and protection of public order.

(b) Time of judging "other adverse effects". When examining whether a trademark or its constituent elements have "other adverse effects", generally the factual status at the time of application shall prevail. If the application does not fall under the above circumstance, but the disputed trademark already has "other adverse effects" when the registration is approved, considering that to avoid negative effects on the public interest and public order of our country, the disputed trademark can also be determined to constitute circumstances stipulated in item (8), paragraph 1, Article 10 of *the Trademark Law 2001*.

In addition, a distinction should be made between the system of trademark authorization and confirmation procedures. Especially in trademark confirmation cases, even if the public's habits and ways of using words have changed, the registered trademark are given other meanings. However, from the perspective of protecting the trust interests of trademark owners, the relationship between private rights and public interests should be balanced reasonably. Unless there is a situation where maintaining the registration of a disputed trademark would obviously violate public order and good customs, it is generally inappropriate to use the factual status after the registration date as a basis for evaluating whether the disputed trademark has "other adverse effects".

(c) Standard of judging the meaning of "other adverse effects". When determining whether a disputed trademark or its constituent elements have "other adverse effects", the judgment should generally be based on its "inherent meaning". In particular, for trademark composed of individual letters or combinations of letters, the understanding of the meaning of the disputed trademark or its constituent elements should be based on the common perception of the Chinese public, which are official publications such as dictionaries and reference books or the content determined by the information carrier with credibility. However, if the public in our country has formed a general understanding of the relevant content based on common sense of life, it can also be determined by full explanation.

It should be avoided that the unusual meaning formed in special contexts, occasions is placed on the disputed trademark or its constituent elements as the criterion for determining that it has "other adverse effects." Otherwise, it will inevitably result in an improper restriction of the space for free expression and creation of business operators in business activities, and it will also be detrimental to the positive guidance of our country's socialist moral culture. If there are differences in the understanding of the meaning of the disputed trademark, in order to reach a conclusion that is more in line with the general public perception, one can refer to factors such as the applicant, the method of use, and the designated goods or services to formed a "highly probable" confirmation on whether the use of the disputed trademark is likely to have a negative impact on the public interest and order of our country. For example, when applying for the registration of the names of public figures in a particular economic field as trademarks, differences in the subject of registration may result in different conclusions on whether there are "other adverse effects".

(d) Burden of proof for "other adverse effects". When examining whether a trademark or its constituent elements have "other adverse effects", the party claiming the disputed trademark has "other adverse effects" should generally bear the burden of proof. If the parties claim the inherent meaning of the trademark, they shall submit a dictionary, reference book, etc. for proof. However, if the meaning of the disputed trademark has been established based on common sense of life, it can be accepted after full explanation. However, it should be avoided to give a specific meaning to the disputed trademark based on the psychological presupposition of a specific group when the meaning of the disputed trademark is uncertain or has not formed a general recognition.

Based on the above analysis, the disputed trademark in this case consists of the letters "MLGB". The number of Internet users in our country is large and the Internet is closely related to the public life. Although these letters are not fixed foreign vocabulary, combined with the screenshots of relevant web pages submitted by Yao Hongjun during the administrative review stage that were formed before the application of the disputed trademark, there are already specific groups that believe "MLGB" has an adverse effect in the network environment. In order to actively purify the network environment, guide the young generation to establish a positive mainstream culture and values, stop the "three vulgar" behaviors and give full play to the role of justice in the mainstream cultural awareness inheritance and value guidance, the disputed trademark itself should be recognized as having negative meaning. At the same time, considering that although Shanghai Junke Company used the disputed trademark together with the English expression, it also applied for trademarks such as "caonima" while applying for the disputed trademark. Therefore, its intention to cater to adverse cultural tendencies in a vulgar way is relatively obvious, and there are vulgar commercial publicity of the disputed trademark in the actual use.

Therefore, based on the circumstances of the case, the judgment original trail and the accused decision which determined that the registration of the disputed trademark violated the item (8), was proper, and this court affirmed it. The reasons for the appeal of Shanghai Junke Company lacked facts and legal basis, and this court did not support it.

To sum up, the appeal of Shanghai Junke Company lacked facts and legal basis, and its appeal was not supported by this court. The facts of the first-instance judgement are clear and its applicable law is correct, and it should be affirmed in accordance with the law. In accordance with the item(1), paragraph 1, Article 89 of *The Administrative Litigation Law of the People's Republic of China*, the judgment is as follows:

Dismiss the appeal and affirm the original judgment.

3.2 Analysis of the case

1. Facts

The trademark "MLGB" No. 8954893 (referred to as the disputed trademark) was applied for registration by Shanghai Junke Company on December 15, 2010, and was approved for registration on December 28, 2011. It was approved for use on 25th category: clothing.

On October 9, 2015, Yao Hongjun filed an application for invalidation of a registered trademark with the Trademark Review and Adjudication Board. The main reason is: disputed trademarks are easy to think of indelicate terms. The use of trademarks on clothing, hats and other commodities is harmful to socialist morals and customs and has adverse effects. Request that the disputed trademark be declared invalid in accordance with the provisions of Article 10, Paragraph 1, Item 8, and Article 44, Paragraph 1 of the "Trademark Law of the People's Republic of China" (referred to as the 2013 Trademark Law) revised in 2013. The Trademark Review and Adjudication Board declared the trademark invalid. The Beijing Intellectual Property Court rejected Shanghai Junke's litigation request.

Shanghai Junke Company refused to accept the original judgment and filed an appeal to the Beijing High People's Court, requesting to revoke the original judgment and the adjudication. The main reasons are: 1. There is no evidence to show that the disputed trademark has formed a relatively fixed and indelicate meaning in first instance. When Shanghai Junke Company promotes the brand, the meaning of the disputed trademark is clearly defined as "My life's getting better"; 2. The judiciary should understand the cognition of the parties and the public from the perspective of kindness, and believe that people are noble. This is in line with the spirit of the legal system and existing precedents, and the law can play a positive role in guiding noble and kind customs; 3. Under the background that the disputed trademark and the uncivilized meaning did not actually form a one-to-one correspondence, the conclusion of the original judgment has an adverse effect, which is contrary to the original intention of the public to apply for trademark registration.

2. The focus of dispute

How to identify the "other adverse effects" stipulated in Article 10, Paragraph 1, Item 8 of the 2001 Trademark Law?

3. Rules

"Trademark Law" (2001) Article 10, Paragraph 1, Item 8: Signs that are harmful to socialist morals or have other adverse effects shall not be used as trademarks.

The Provisions of the Supreme People's Court on Several Issues Concerning the Trial of Administrative Cases for the Authorization and Confirmation of Trademarks, Paragraph 1 of Article 5: "Where a trademark sign or its constituent elements may have a negative or negative impact on my country's social public interests and public order, the people's court may It is determined that it belongs to the 'other adverse effects' stipulated in Article 10, Paragraph 1, Item 8 of the Trademark Law";

4. Reasoning

The Beijing Higher People's Court held that the facts ascertained in the original judgment were clear, the application of the law was correct, and it should be upheld in accordance with the law. The court clarified that the determination of whether a trademark sign or its constituent elements belong to the "other adverse effects" should be comprehensively judged from the following four aspects:

1). Who is entitled to decide "other adverse effects"?

The public should be entitled to decide whether the trademark sign or its constituent elements belong to the "other adverse effects" situation. Since the prohibited clauses are based on the absolute circumstances in which the relevant signs are prohibited from being used as trademarks, and on the premise that the relevant signs may harm the public interest and public order, from the perspective of protecting "public order and good customs", so the subject of judgment on this issue should be all The public, not the "relevant public" of the goods or services designated by the disputed trademark, otherwise the conclusions drawn are likely to be "partially generalized", which is not conducive to the protection of social public interests and public order.

2) When to recognized?

When examining whether a trademark sign or its constituent elements have "other adverse effects", the factual status at the time of the disputed trademark registration shall generally prevail. Generally, it is not appropriate to use the factual status after the registration date as the basis for evaluating whether the disputed trademark has "other adverse effects".

3) How to recognized?

Generally, judgments should be made on the basis of its "intrinsic meaning", especially for signs composed of individual letters or combinations of letters, the understanding of the meaning of the trademark sign in dispute or its constituent elements should be based on the common cognition of the Chinese public, that is, the dictionary, the content determined by official publications such as, reference books, or information carriers with "credibility" that can be widely contacted by the public shall prevail. However, if the public in our country has formed a general understanding of the relevant content based on common sense of life, it may also can be determined by full explanation.

4) How to allocate the burden of proof?

When examining whether a trademark sign or its constituent elements have "other adverse effects", the party claiming that the trademark in question has "other adverse effects" should generally bear the burden of proof. If the parties claim the inherent meaning of the mark, they should submit dictionaries, reference books, etc. to prove it. However, if the meaning of the disputed trademark is based on common sense of life, it can be accepted after sufficient explanation at this time. However, it should be avoided to give a specific meaning to the disputed trademark based on the psychological presupposition of a specific group when the meaning of the disputed trademark is uncertain or has not formed a general recognition.

3.4 Civil Cases on Unfair Competition

3.4.1 Cases from China

(1) **Guangdong Jiaduobao Beverage and Food Co., Ltd. v. Guangzhou Wanglaoji Health Industry Co., Ltd.**

1.1 Case Judgement : Supreme People's Court of P.R.C.
Case No.: (2015) Min San Zhong Zi No. 2
Date of judgment: Jul 27, 2017
Cause of action: Dispute over the use of unique packaging and decoration of well-known commodities
Appellant (plaintiff in the first instance): Guangdong Jiaduobao Beverage and Food Co., Ltd.
Legal representative: Zhang Shurong, general manager of the company.
Litigation representative: Yang Xiaoyan, lawyer of Beijing Xinrui Law Firm.
Litigation representative: Yao Huanqing, associate professor of Law School of Renmin University of China.
Appellee (defendant in the first instance): Guangzhou Wanglaoji Health Industry Co., Ltd.
Legal representative: Xu Wenliu, chairman of the company.
Litigation representative: Ni Yidong, male, executive vice chairman of the company.
Litigation representative: Hu Fuchuan, lawyer of Guangdong Mingjing Law Firm (appointed litigation agent before January 16, 2017).

Litigation representative: Zhao Xiaobo, male, deputy manager of the company's compliance and legal affairs department (appointed litigation agent since January 16, 2017).

The appellant Guangdong Jiaduobao Beverage and Food Co., Ltd. (hereinafter referred to as Jiaduobao Company) was dissatisfied with the case of a dispute over the use of unique packaging and decoration of well-known commodities without authorization with the appellee, Guangzhou Wanglaoji Health Industry Co., Ltd. (hereinafter referred to as the Wanglaoji Company), which is decided by (2013) YueGaoFaMinSanChuZi No. 1 Civil Judgment made by Guangdong Higher People's Court, therefore appealed to the court. After the court received the case on March 23, 2015, a collegial panel was formed in accordance with the law, and the trial was held in public. Yang Xiaoyan and Yao Huanqing, appointed litigation representatives of the appellant JDB and Ni Yidong and Hu Fuchuan, appointed litigation representative s of the appellee Wanglaoji, appeared in court to participate in the litigation. The case has now been concluded.

Jiaduobao Company's appeal requested:

The first-instance judgment should be revoked and the judgment should be changed to support all Jiaduobao Company's claims. The specific facts and reasons are as follows:

(1) There was a serious error in the definition of the "well-known commodity" involved in the case by the court of first instance.

First, the well-known product involved in the case is the red canned herbal tea operated by Jiaduobao Company for many years using the secret recipe of Wang Zebang's descendants, namely, the red canned herbal tea operated by Jiaduobao Company that used to bear the Wanglaoji trademark and now bears the Jiaduobao trademark. To define a well-known commodity, it is necessary to examine the use value of the commodity when it is "well-known" that has been generally recognized by consumers. According to the large amount of evidence submitted by Jiaduobao during the first instance, it can be proved that the involved red canned herbal tea products were launched on the market by Dongguan Hongdao Food Co., Ltd. (hereinafter referred to as Dongguan Hongdao Company) in 1996, and after the cancellation of Dongguan Hongdao Company in 1998, Jiaduobao Company has inherited the production and operation till now. Through Jiaduobao Company's large-scale production, continuous market promotion, and extensive media promotion, the involved red canned herbal tea has become a veritable "famous commodity" with its excellent quality and unique taste derived from the secret recipe of Wang Zebang's descendants.

Second, even if the red canned herbal tea produced by Guangzhou Pharmaceutical Group Co., Ltd. (hereinafter referred to as GPHL) and Wanglaoji Health Company bears the "Wanglaoji" trademark, it is not the same product as the aforementioned "well-known product". The court of first instance directly equated the unique name "Wanglaoji Herbal Tea" with a well-known product without identifying what is the "well-known commodity" in the case, which was an error in fact determination.

First of all, Wang Zebang's descendants have made it clear that they have never granted the ancestral secret recipe to GPHL for use. This is enough to show that the secret recipes of red canned herbal tea produced by Da Health Company and Jiaduobao Company are different. Herbal teas with different recipes and production processes are of course different commodities.

Secondly, both the GPHL and the Wanglaoji Company clearly stated in the first instance that the red canned herbal teas produced by the GPHL, the Jiaduobao Health Company and the Jiaduobao Company are not the same product. On this basis, they certainly have no right to become the right holders of the packaging and decoration rights of the well-known goods involved in the case and claim any rights in this case.

Finally, because the red canned herbal tea produced by both parties in this case is completely different in terms of production standards, craftsmanship, quality, formula, taste and source of goods, even during the period of undisputed trademark license use by both parties, "Wanglaoji Herbal Tea" is still cannot uniquely refer to any of the products of both parties, nor can it be used as the unique name of a well-known commodity to refer to a "well-known commodity". The court of first instance, on the basis of confusing the related products of Jiaduobao Company and GPHL, on the evidence 1, evidence 7, evidence 12, evidence 32, evidence 38, evidence 45, evidence 48 provided by Jiaduobao Company, and Evidence 1, Evidence 5, Evidence 6, Evidence 8, Evidence 10, Evidence 12–13, Evidence 21–25, and Evidence 27–34 provided by the Wanglaoji Health Company made a wrong determination, thereby transferring all the rights and interests of the well-known goods involved in the case to on the basis of completely different products produced by GPHL, the product name "Wanglaoji Herbal Tea", which cannot be the only corresponding to the well-known product involved, was identified as a "famous product" in the case. This conclusion is wrong.

(2) The special packaging and decoration rights of the well-known commodities involved belonged to Jiaduobao Company, and the conclusion made by the first-instance court that should be enjoyed by GPHL was a factual error and harmed the interests of consumers.

First, the unique packaging and decoration of the well-known goods involved in the case, from creativity and design to actual use in product production and promotion, until the unique packaging and decoration of well-known goods, are all derived from the actions of Jiaduobao and its affiliates, and the specific information marked "produced by Jiaduobao on the goods themselves" has established a stable and unique relationship with Jiaduobao. Jiaduobao should be the right holder of the special packaging and decoration of the well-known goods involved. The above facts have been previously effective, which is confirmed by the previous judgment.

Second, the packaging and decoration of the well-known commodities involved in the case already has the function of distinguishing the source of the commodities, and is not inseparable from the three characters "Wanglaoji". The first-instance court's determination that the packaging and decoration rights must be dependent on the exercise of trademark rights and that "Wanglaoji" was the most attractive feature of the packaging and decoration in the case was wrong. Trademark rights and well-known commodity packaging and decoration rights are two equal and independent rights protected by different laws, and there is no subordination or inclusion relationship between the two. The packaging and decoration involved in the case has the visual effect of red background color with yellow logo text and black auxiliary text, which is significantly different from other similar product packaging patterns, color matching, logo background color, etc., even if the "Wanglaoji" text is removed, it still constitutes unique packaging and decoration. The court of first instance declared that the trademark of "Wanglaoji" and packaging and decoration are integrated and inseparable, and the relevant public will not deliberately distinguish the trademark right from the special packaging and decoration right is wrong.

Third, the conclusion made by the court of first instance that Hongdao (Group) Co., Ltd. (hereinafter referred to as Hongdao Group) and Jiaduobao Company signed a trademark license agreement based on the popularity and market value of the "Wanglaoji" brand, and the Wanglaoji red canned herbal tea launched after authorization by GPHL, therefore, GPHL can simultaneously withdraw the trademark rights and the special packaging and decoration rights of well-known products with affiliated relationships, and believes that the conclusion that Jiaduobao should expect the results lacks factual and legal basis. Before the signing of the trademark license agreement, Hongdao Group had obtained the herbal tea secret recipe authorized by Wang Zebang's descendants in Hong Kong and produced and operated herbal tea products. At that time, the "Wanglaoji" trademark had been registered by others in the mainland, in order to cooperate with the product use by Wang Zebang's descendants. Because of the characteristics of the secret recipe, Hongdao Group used the "Wanglaoji" trademark by signing a trademark licensing agreement. In addition, when the earliest trademark licensing contract was signed, the packaging and decoration involved in the case did not yet exist. Of course, GPHL could not license others to use the rights that did not exist.

(3) The court of first instance did not support the claim that Wanglaoji Company's infringement of the special packaging and decoration rights of the well-known commodities involved constituted unfair competition, which was an error in determining facts.

First, the source of the goods identified in the unique packaging and decoration of the well-known goods involved and the packaging and decoration of the alleged infringing goods all point to Jiaduobao, which will not confuse the relevant public.

Second, the packaging and decoration of the alleged infringing product produced by Wanglaoji Company is similar to the packaging and decoration of well-known products produced by Jiaduobao Company. Wanglaoji Company has also recognized the fact that the two packaging decorations are similar.

Third, the packaging and decoration of the alleged infringing product produced by the Wanglaoji Company is similar to that of the well-known product produced by Jiaduobao Company, which will make consumers mistakenly believe that the alleged infringing product has the same source as the well-known goods involved in the case, which will damage Jiaduobao Company and the legitimate rights and interests of consumers. It constitutes unfair competition.

(4) The court of first instance violated legal procedures.

Specifically, the court of first instance adopted 13 pieces of evidence submitted by Wanglaoji on the day of the trial and after the expiration of the proof period, violating legal provisions and the principle of fairness, depriving and restricting Jiaduobao's legal litigation rights.

In summary, the facts found in the first-instance judgment are unclear, the law is improperly applied, and the legal procedure is violated, which has serious social adverse effects. Based on this, Jiaduobao Company requested the court to revoke the judgment of the first instance on the basis of ascertaining the facts, and amend the judgment in accordance with the law to support all the claims of Jiaduobao Company.

Wanglaoji Company argued that the facts in the first-instance judgment were clear, the procedures were legal, the application of the law was correct, and the judgment results were fair and just, and requested to dismiss the appeal and maintain the first-instance judgment. The main reasons are:

(1) The first-instance judgment determined that the well-known commodity involved in this case was "Wanglaoji Herbal Tea", which had legal and factual basis.

Jiaduobao's claim that the well-known product involved in the case is "red canned herbal tea produced by Jiaduobao using the authentic and exclusive formula of Wang Zebang's descendants" cannot be established. Before the "Wanglaoji" trademark license agreement was signed, "Wanglaoji Herbal Tea" was already a very well-known product in the whole country, especially in Guangdong, and the transformation of "Wanglaoji Herbal Tea" from medicine to food was a huge achievement of GPHL (and its predecessor), contribute. In addition, "well-known products" should be called by "name" instead of the content of the product, and the relevant claims of Jiaduobao are obviously inconsistent with consumers' identification habits, addressing habits, and memory habits.

(2) The packaging and decoration involved is an inseparable whole composed of the red can body, the "Wang Lao Ji" written in yellow in the middle of the can body, and related auxiliary text and drawings. The decision of this issue made by first instance determined is correct.

(3) The judgment of the first instance was correct to determine that the special packaging and decoration rights of the well-known "Wanglaoji Herbal Tea" were enjoyed by GPHL and not by Jiaduobao Company.

The unique packaging and decoration of well-known commodities are closely related to well-known commodities. As the trademark owner and trademark licensor of "Wanglaoji" and the owner of the famous commodity "Wang Lao Ji Herbal tea", GPHL shall also enjoy the rights and interests of the packaging and decoration involved in the famous commodity "Wang Lao Ji Herbal tea". Jiaduobao Company claims that its design, use, promotion and promotion of the special packaging and decoration of the well-known commodities involved are based on the implementation of the trademark license contract and cannot generate independent rights or rights attributable to Jiaduobao Company. In addition, the time point for judging the ownership and infringement of the rights in this case should be the fact that GPHL filed another lawsuit (July 6, 2012). The continued infringement of Jiaduobao Company cannot become the reasons having its right to use for the packaging and decoration involved in the case.

(4) The packaging and decoration used by the Wanglaoji Company on its herbal tea products has obtained the permission of GPHL, and has not infringed any rights of Jiaduobao Company.

Jiaduobao sued the court of first instance:

(1) On February 13, 1997, Hongdao Group signed the agreement with the original owner of the Wanglaoji trademark, Guangzhou Yangcheng Pharmaceutical Co., Ltd. Wanglaoji Food and Beverage Branch (hereinafter referred to as Yangcheng Pharmaceutical) the "Trademark Licensing Contract", which stipulates that Yangcheng Pharmaceuticals permits Hongdao Group and its investment enterprises to exclusively use the Wanglaoji trademark to produce red canned herbal tea. On May 2, 2000, Hongdao Group and GPHL signed the "Trademark License Agreement", and the license conditions were basically the same as the above agreement. Jiaduobao Company is a wholly-owned subsidiary established by Hongdao Group in Dongguan, Guangdong Province, responsible for the production and sales of red canned Wanglaoji herbal tea. On June 14, 1997, Chen Hongdao obtained the patent for the appearance design of the red canned Wanglaoji herbal tea, and licensed it to be implemented by Jiaduobao Company for the production of Wanglaoji herbal tea. The product formula of red canned Wanglaoji herbal tea also belongs to Jiaduobao Company.

(2) At the beginning when Jiaduobao Company started to produce red can Wanglaoji herbal tea, there were no other red can Wanglaoji herbal tea products on the market. The market awareness and market share of red can Wanglaoji herbal tea was very low. The total sales of red can Wanglaoji herbal tea in 2000 are only 8.66 million yuan. Moreover, as a regional product, Wanglaoji herbal tea has very uncertain market prospects. From 2002 to 2010, the market sales of red canned Wanglaoji herbal tea have been greatly increased, and this increase is due to the large-scale investment in the construction of factories by Jiaduobao Company and other Jiaduobao Group Companies and the large-scale expansion of red canned Wanglaoji herbal tea products. Formed by advertising and market promotion, the sales volume of red canned Wanglaoji herbal tea has ranked first in the country for many years in canned beverages, and has won various honors, thus becoming a well-known brand in the country. In the long-term business activities of Jiaduobao, the "red cans", "red cans of herbal tea" and "red cans of Wanglaoji" have obtained specific directivity and precise identification functions.

(3) On June 3, 2012, Wanglaoji Company held a public celebration of red canned Wanglaoji herbal tea at the Great Wall at Badaling Shuiguan Great Wall in Beijing, and publicly sold the red cans of "Wanglaoji" herbal tea produced by it. The packaging of its products was similar with which made by Jiaduobao Company. The red canned Wanglaoji herbal tea products produced are very similar. At the same time, the Wanglaoji Company also distributed a press release "Newly designed red cans

Wanglaoji shocked the Great Wall to achieve sales of 30 billion in five years", which particularly emphasized the "new design" of the "red cans". Numerous media have carried out extensive reports on the aforementioned matters. The above actions of Wanglaoji Company constitute a counterfeit of the unique packaging and decoration of the famous Jiaduobao Company red canned Wanglaoji t herbal tea, which infringes on the unique packaging and decoration rights of Jiaduobao Company famous products and the unique name rights of Jiaduobao Company red canned, red canned herbal tea and red canned Wanglaoji. It is sufficient to cause buyers to confuse the quality and source of the red cans of Wanglaoji herbal tea produced by Wanglaoji Company, which constitutes an act of unfair competition and should be prohibited according to law.

Therefore, the court is requested to order the Wanglaoji Company to:

1. Immediately stop using the unique packaging and decoration of Wanglaoji herbal tea, a well-known product of Jiaduobao Company;
2. Immediately stop using the unique names of well-known commodities such as "Red Can", "Red Can of Herbal Tea" and "Red Can Wang Lao Ji" of Jiaduobao Company;
3. Immediately stop the production of Wanglaoji herbal tea in red canned;
4. Compensation for the economic loss of Jiaduobao Company caused by its unfair competition behavior is 500,000 yuan;
5. Bear all litigation costs in this case.

On March 6, 2013, Jiaduobao changed its litigation request into a request to order the Wanglaoji Company:

1. Immediately stop using packaging decorations that are the same as or similar to the unique packaging decorations of Jiaduobao's well-known herbal tea products; stop producing and selling products with the same or similar products as the unique packaging and decoration of Jiaduobao's well-known products, and destroy all inventory of infringing packaging and decoration;
2. Publicly publish a statement in the relevant newspaper to eliminate the use of the same or similar products as Jiaduobao's well-known herbal tea products or similar packaging and decoration caused adverse effects on Jiaduobao Company;
3. Compensation for economic losses caused to Jiaduobao Company due to the above-mentioned unfair competition behaviors (the final specific compensation amount is based on the results of court investigations or actual audits);
4. Bear all litigation costs in this case.

On May 15, 2013, Jiaduobao changed its litigation request into a request to order the Wanglaoji Company:
1. Immediately stop using packaging decorations that are the same as or similar to the unique packaging decorations of Jiaduobao's well-known herbal tea products; stop producing and selling products with the same or similar packaging and decorations as those of Jiaduobao's well-known products, and destroy all inventory of infringing packaging and decorations;

2. In relevant media including but not limited to CCTV, various provincial-level television stations, and various provincial-level and above newspapers, the large portal website and its official website publicly issued a statement to eliminate the adverse effects on the Jiaduobao company due to its use of the same or similar packaging as the well-known herbal tea products of the Jiaduobao company; 3. Compensation for the economic loss caused by the above-mentioned unfair competition behavior to Jiaduobao Company temporarily amounts to 30.96 million yuan (the final specific compensation amount is subject to the audit result and the larger profit in the annual report); Jiaduobao Company reserves the right to claim for continued infringements by Wanglaoji Company after February 2013.

4. Bear all litigation costs in this case.

Wanglaoji Company replied:

(1) The well-known product in this case refers to the Wanglaoji herbal tea with the trademark "Wanglaoji". It is precisely because "Wanglaoji" herbal tea is a product that has a certain reputation in the market and is known to the relevant public, it is recognized as a well-known product. "Wanglaoji" herbal tea has a long history of becoming a well-known commodity. It is not because of the red canned of Wanglaoji herbal tea that it became a well-known commodity after 1996. It is not that Hongdao Group bred the well-known product Wanglaoji herbal tea after operating the red canned Wanglaoji herbal tea, but the well-known product Wanglaoji herbal tea made the red canned Wanglaoji herbal tea. Hongdao Group uses the registered trademark "Wanglaoji" and actually enjoys the goodwill of the well-known product Wanglaoji.

(2) Chen Hongdao is not the owner of the name, packaging and decoration of the well-known red canned Wanglaoji herbal tea. Jiaduobao provided evidence to prove that the existing red can Wanglaoji decoration was designed by Chen Hongdao and obtained a design patent. Although the design patent is genuine and legal, the patent should not be exclusive to Chen Hongdao because the patent has many other design factors. After analysis and comparison, it can be seen that the three characters "Wanglaoji" in the decoration are the unique name of the product, and the other notable one is the registered trademark of Wanglaoji, which belongs to the trademark registrant GPHL. The time Chen Hongdao entrusted others to design is after Hongdao Group signed the "Trademark Licensing Contract" with Yangcheng Pharmaceutical, based on the agreement of the "Trademark Licensing Contract", the background color was limited to red, the name of Wanglaoji was used as a distinctive sign, and Wanglaoji's registration was added, with the trademark formed by the inner elements. Therefore, under the premise that the "Wanglaoji" trademark already exists, its design must be used with the permission of the exclusive right holder of the "Wanglaoji" registered trademark. The decoration dedicated to the red canned Wanglaoji herbal tea must belong to the GPHL.

(3) The particularity of the formation of the subject matter of this case determines that the special decoration of the red canned Wanglaoji herbal tea is inseparable from the "Wanglaoji" trademark. The decoration of Wanglaoji herbal tea in red canned occurred during the trademark licensing period of Wanglaoji. After more than ten years of development, it has become one of the well-known products "Wanglaoji" herbal tea series and has huge impact in the market. The reason why Jiaduobao

Company was able to win in the twenty-four-flavor case was that the legal basis for the decoration rights enjoyed by Jiaduobao Company was the "Trademark Licensing Agreement" between GPHL and Hongdao Group. It was GPHL that granted the right to use the "Wanglaoji" trademark of Hongdao Group. Based on the right to use the Wanglaoji trademark, its decoration right would receive the court's support during its legal operation.

(4) The legal relationship between the owner of the well-known commodity and the operator determines that the packaging and decoration of the red canned Wanglaoji herbal tea ultimately belongs to the owner of the Wanglaoji trademark and the owner of Wanglaoji herbal tea, and the operator loses its using right without legal authorization. Jiaduobao Company is a newly established enterprise producing and selling Wanglaoji herbal tea by Hongdao Group after the cancellation of Dongguan Hongdao Company. It is still within the term of the "Trademark License Agreement" with GPHL to produce red canned Wanglaoji herbal tea. It inherited this right. Hongdao Group used to be the operator of red canned Wanglaoji herbal tea, but after the expiration of the license contract, it will no longer be an operator and no longer enjoy any rights to the well-known product Wanglaoji. All rights are borne by the new operator, Wanglaoji Company and are exclusive rights. Jiaduobao, as the original operator, cannot take away the product brand nor goodwill. Jiaduobao's publicity and use of the "Wanglaoji" trademark and decoration are only acts of fulfilling the "Trademark License Agreement" between GPHL and Hongdao Group.

(5) GPHL is the owner of the packaging and decoration rights of Wanglaoji herbal tea, a well-known commodity red can. It can license the trademark to Wanglaoji Company, and at the same time grant the legal operator Wanglaoji Company the right to use the unique decoration on the well-known commodity. It was determined by arbitration that Hongdao Group ceased to use the Wanglaoji trademark since May 2, 2010, which means that while GPHL took back the "Wanglaoji" trademark, it would also take back the decorations unique to the "Wanglaoji" well-known goods. Now it is authorized to produce red cans of Wanglaoji herbal tea to Wanglaoji Company, then the Wanglaoji Company is the legal operator of red canned Wanglaoji herbal tea, and it enjoys the unique decoration rights of well-known products, so the decoration rights for the well-known products of "Wanglaoji" should be protected by law. Jiaduobao Company is not qualified to claim the special name, packaging and decoration rights of the famous Wanglaoji herbal tea from the legal operators of the well-known Wanglaoji herbal tea. As the plaintiff in this case, the claim that the red can decoration right is not qualified, and the court shall dismiss the lawsuit in accordance with the law. The actions of Jiaduobao have constituted infringement and shall bear the legal responsibility for infringement. As mentioned above, Jiaduobao does not enjoy the packaging and decoration of the well-known product Wanglaoji herbal tea. It is no longer a legal operator to reproduce products with similar packaging and decoration to the Wanglaoji Company, which constitutes unfair competition.

In summary, Jiaduobao Company's litigation request lacks a legal basis and should not be supported by the court.

The court of first instance found the facts:

(1) The situation of the relevant company involved in this case

1. The situation of GPHL and its related companies
Wanglaoji brand herbal tea was founded in 1828 AD (the eighth year of Daoguang in the Qing Dynasty) by Wang Zebang. In 1956, with a public–private joint venture, Wanglaoji and Jiabaozhan and other eight companies formed the "Wanglaoji Joint Pharmaceutical Factory". In 1965, it was renamed as Guangzhou Chinese Medicine No. 9 Factory, and in 1982, it was renamed Guangzhou Yangcheng Pharmaceutical Factory. In 1992, Yangcheng Pharmaceutical Factory was transformed into a joint-stock enterprise. Guangzhou Yangcheng Pharmaceutical Co., Ltd. was established. On August 7, 1996, GPHL was formally established. Intangible assets such as the Wanglaoji trademark were placed in the possession of GPHL. On February 28, 2012, GPHL established a wholly-owned subsidiary, Wanglaoji Company.

2. The situation of Jiaduobao and its related companies
Dongguan Hongdao Company was established on September 19, 1995 and cancelled on August 31, 1998; Hongdao Group invested and established Dongguan Jiaduobao Food and Beverage Co., Ltd. (hereinafter referred to as Dongguan Jiaduobao) on September 17, 1998. On May 21, 2000, the corporate name of Dongguan Jiaduobao Company was changed to Guangdong Jiaduobao Beverage and Food Co., Ltd. JDB Group has 6 domestic companies. In addition to the establishment of Jiaduobao Company in this case in 1998, the other five JDB companies were established as follows: on March 3, 2004, JDB (China) Beverage Co., Ltd. was established as a wholly foreign legal person; on August 31, 2004, Zhejiang Jiaduobao Beverage Co., Ltd. was established as a wholly foreign legal person; on October 14, 2005, Fujian Jiaduobao Beverage Co., Ltd. was established as a wholly foreign legal person; On December 27, 2006, Hangzhou Jiaduobao Beverage Co., Ltd. was established as a sole proprietorship by Taiwan, Hong Kong and Macao legal persons; on March 28, 2007, Wuhan Jiaduobao Beverage Co., Ltd. was established as a sole proprietorship by Taiwan, Hong Kong and Macao legal persons.

(2) Regarding the registration of the "Wanglaoji" trademark
The registered trademark No. 328241 approved the use of herbal teas as category 37. The registered person is Guangzhou Yangcheng Nourishing Products Factory. The registration period is from October 30, 1988 to October 29, 1998. On October 30, 1998, it was approved to renew the registration on the 30th category of the International Classification of Commodities. In September 1998, with the approval of the Trademark Office of the State Administration for Industry and Commerce (hereinafter referred to as the Trademark Office), the registrant of the trademark was changed to Yangcheng Pharmaceutical. After being approved by the Trademark Office, the trademark was transferred to GPHL. The trademark has been renewed until October 29, 2018.

The registered trademark No. 626155 approved the use of non-alcoholic beverages and solid beverages in the 32nd category. The registered person is Guangzhou Yangcheng Tonics Factory. The registration is valid from January 20, 1993 to January

19, 2003. On September 1, 1993, with the approval of the Trademark Office, the registrant of the trademark was changed to Yangcheng Pharmaceutical. On August 28, 1997, with the approval of the Trademark Office, the trademark was transferred to GPHL. The trademark has been renewed until January 19, 2023.

The registered trademark No. 3980709 approved the use of goods as the 32nd category of beer; fruit juice; water (drinks); cola; non-alcoholic beverages; syrups for making beverages; beverage preparations; milk tea (non-dairy-based); soy milk; vegetable beverages. The registrant is GPHL, and the registration is valid from March 7, 2006 to March 6, 2016.

The registered trademark No. 9095940 approved the use of goods as the 32nd category of beer; fruit beverages (non-alcoholic); whey beverages; water (beverages); sodas; non-alcoholic beverages; soft drinks; plant beverages; fruit powder; beverage preparations. The registrant is GPHL, and the registration is valid from February 7, 2012 to February 6, 2022.

(3) Honors Brand Wanglaoji Obtained

On May 9, 1991, Guangzhou Yangcheng Pharmaceutical Factory and Guangzhou Light Industry Research Institute signed the "Guangzhou Technology Development Contract" for the "Wanglaoji Brand Herbal Tea Beverage" project, and agreed that Guangzhou Light Industry Research Institute would use Wanglaoji brand Guangdong herbal tea extract provided by Guangzhou Yangcheng Pharmaceutical Factory, research and determine the Wanglaoji brand herbal tea beverage formula, technological conditions and equipment requirements for industrial production.

On October 8, 1991, the record number QB/440100X751-91 "Guangzhou Enterprise Standard Record Receipt" of the Standards Management Office of the Guangzhou Municipal Administration of Standards and Metrology showed that: It has received one product standard from Guangzhou Yangcheng Pharmaceutical Factory and Guangzhou Yangcheng Tonic Factory., The standard name is ""Wanglaoji" Brand Herbal Tea Beverage", standard number is Q/(WS)YS1-91.

On October 15, 1991, Guangzhou Yangcheng Pharmaceutical Factory and Guangzhou Yangcheng Tonic Factory submitted the "Guangdong Province Food New Product Application Approval Form" to the Guangdong Provincial Food Hygiene Supervision and Inspection Institute, and declared the product name as "Wanglaoji" brand herbal tea. On January 18, 1992, Guangzhou Food Hygiene Inspection Institute agreed the report, and on March 24 of the same year, Guangdong Food Hygiene Inspection Institute approved the production and sale of "Wanglaoji" brand herbal tea products.

Guangzhou Yangcheng Nourishing Products Factory applied to the Guangzhou Municipal Bureau of Standards and Metrology for approval of the food label used for "Wanglaoji" brand herbal tea, which approved the use after examination on October 23, 1991.

On December 2, 1991, Guangzhou Food Hygiene Supervision and Inspection Institute issued Food Supervision and Inspection No. 893932 "Inspection Certificate", stating that the 250 ml/box Wanglaoji Herbal Tea submitted by Guangzhou Yangcheng Tonics Factory for inspection meets food hygiene requirements. On

March 19, 1992, the Guangdong Provincial Food Sanitation Inspection and Inspection Institute issued the Yueshi Sanitation Inspection Zi (1992) No. 27 "Inspection Report", stating that the composite paper packaging Wanglaoji Herbal Tea produced by Guangzhou Yangcheng Tonics Factory complies with the national GB2759-81 hygiene standards.

On January 11, 1992, the third edition of the "Guangdong-Hong Kong Information Daily" published the "Solemn Statement" of Guangzhou Yangcheng Pharmaceutical Factory and Guangzhou Yangcheng Tonic Factory. The content was: Guangzhou Yangcheng Pharmaceutical Factory and Guangzhou Yangcheng Tonic Factory's "Wanglaoji" trademarks have been registered by the State Administration for Industry and Commerce, and packaging and decoration designs have been accepted and filed by the State Patent Office. However, in recent years, incidents of infringement of our trademarks and patent rights have continued to occur in the market. ... For this reason, our factory solemnly declares: The relevant manufacturers should immediately stop the infringement of ours, and must not print, produce, or sell products and packaging products that counterfeit our logo and packaging design. Otherwise, we will sue and the printers, manufacturers and sellers should be subject to legal liabilities.

In November 1992, the famous trademark selection committee of Guangdong Province recognized the "Wanglaoji" trademark of Guangzhou Yangcheng Pharmaceutical Factory as a famous trademark of Guangdong Province in 1992. On March 1, 1993, Guangzhou Municipal People's Government awarded Yangcheng Pharmaceutical the "Wanglaoji Brand" trademark as "Guangzhou Famous Brand". In September 1995, the organizing committee of the 95 China (Guangdong) Top Ten Beverage Selection Campaign recognized that the Wanglaoji brand herbal tea (Tetra Pak) produced and distributed by Yangcheng Pharmaceutical won the "95 China (Guangdong) First Top Ten Most Popular Beverage Award" "In February 1998, the Guangdong Provincial Administration for Industry and Commerce recognized the "Wanglaoji" trademark of Yangcheng Pharmaceutical as a famous trademark in Guangdong Province. On August 24, 2005, February 18, 2006, and July 30, 2007, the Guangdong Provincial Food Cultural Heritage Recognition Committee recognized the herbal tea of Guangzhou Wanglaoji Pharmaceutical Co., Ltd. (hereinafter referred to as Wanglaoji Pharmaceutical) as the food cultural heritage of Guangdong Province-one of "the formula and specific terms of herbal tea". In April 2008, the "Wanglaoji" brand of Wanglaoji Pharmaceuticals was awarded the 2007 Guangdong Provincial Excellent Independent Brand by the Guangdong Provincial Excellent Independent Brand Evaluation Committee. In October 2008, the Guangdong Provincial Food Industry Association recognized Wanglaoji Pharmaceutical "Wanglaoji" as "the most influential brand in the herbal tea industry in the past 30 years of reform and opening up". On April 24, 2009, the Trademark Office recognized the registered trademark "Wanglaoji" used by GPHL on the 32nd category of non-alcoholic beverages as a well-known trademark. On November 10, 2010, Beijing Famous Brand Assets Appraisal Co., Ltd. assessed the value of the "Wanglaoji" brand of GPHL as RMB 108.015 billion. In December 2011, the "Wanglaoji (boxed)" brand of Wanglaoji Pharmaceuticals was recognized by the Guangdong Food Industry

Association as having a very high reputation in the industry, and was rated as the "leading brand in the herbal tea industry in Guangdong". In December 2011, the sales of Wanglaoji Herbal Tea from Wanglaoji Pharmaceuticals exceeded 5 billion boxes. On July 15, 2012, Wanglaoji Pharmaceutical's "Wanglaoji" herbal tea won the Most Consumer Favorite Product Award at the 2012 China International Light Industry Consumer Goods Exhibition. In July 2012, the China Market Research Center and the China Social and Economic Decision-making Consultation Center issued Wanglaoji Pharmaceutical's "Certificate of Honor", stating that "Wanglaoji, a national brand that was founded in the Daoguang period of the Qing Dynasty for a century, was recognized as the ancestor of herbal tea."

(4) Circumstances concerning the licensing of Wanglaoji trademark

On March 28, 1995, Yangcheng Pharmaceutical and Hongdao Group signed the "Trademark Licensing Contract", stipulating that Yangcheng Pharmaceuticals allowed Hongdao Group to exclusively use the registered trademark No. 626155, limited to red paper packaging herbal tea beverages. Hongdao Group could entrust other factories to process and manufacture the above products and send them to Yangcheng Pharmaceutical for the record; all the packaging patterns and colors on the herbal tea products produced by both parties shall not be the same as those of the other party; the herbal tea products produced by Hongdao Group with the three words "Wang Lao Ji" products must meet relevant Chinese food hygiene standards, and the name and address of the manufacturer must be indicated on the packaging. The product packaging and trademark use templates can only be produced after the approval of Yangcheng Pharmaceutical. The use of the above trademark by Hongdao Group is valid from March 28, 1995 to January 2003; Regarding the trademark license fee, the first year is 600,000 yuan, which will increase by 20% annually from the second year onwards.

On September 14, 1995, Yangcheng Pharmaceutical and Hongdao Group signed the "Supplementary Agreement on Trademark Licensing Contract (1)" and "Supplementary Agreement on Trademark Licensing Contract (2)". The license period and trademark license fee in the "Trademark License Contract" have been supplemented. Among them, the license period is from September 14, 1995 to January 2003. Regarding trademark licensing fees, RMB 100,000 is paid annually for the first three years, and 300,000 yuan for the fourth year, with an increase of 23% annually thereafter.

On February 13, 1997, Yangcheng Pharmaceutical and Hongdao Group signed the "Trademark Licensing Contract", which stipulated that Hongdao Group had obtained the exclusive rights to use the "Wanglaoji" trademark from Yangcheng Pharmaceutical in 1995 and to produce and sell red paper packaging and red tin cans of herbal tea beverages. During the term of this agreement, Hongdao Group has the right to use the Wanglaoji trademark (trademark category: Class 32, No. 626155, Class 30), this right is exclusive and exclusive, and "licensed goods" can be taken in iron cans (or aluminum cans). The two parties also agreed that after this contract takes effect, Yangcheng Pharmaceutical can retain the production and sale of the original Wanglaoji herbal tea packaged in paper, but the packaging color cannot be red, and the packaging design pattern shall not be the same as the "licensed commodities" produced by Hongdao Group. "The license period is from February 13, 1997 to December 31, 2011. Regarding the trademark license fee, the two parties agreed to pay RMB 2 million in 1997 and RMB 2.5 million annually starting in 1998.

On May 2, 2000, GPHL and Hongdao Group signed the "Trademark Licensing Agreement" (hereinafter referred to as the "2000 License Agreement"), which stipulated that GPHL granted Hongdao Group the exclusive use of No. 626155 "Wanglaoji" Trademark, the scope of products used is the production and sale of red canned and red bottled Wanglaoji herbal tea. The geographical scope is within China, excluding Hong Kong, Macau and Taiwan. The period of use is from May 2, 2000 to May 2, 2010. Regarding trademark licensing fees, the two parties agreed as follows: RMB 4.5 million per year for the first and second years, RMB 4.725 million per year for the third to sixth years, and RMB 4.914 million per year for the seventh to tenth years. The two parties also agreed that if Hongdao Group knows that any third party has committed any infringement, it can notify GPHL of the details in writing. When GPHL decides to take legal measures to stop the infringement, Hongdao Group must report and provide relevant information and assistance to GPHL. All expenses (including litigation costs, attorney fees and other costs) and risk responsibilities incurred shall be borne by the Hongdao Group, and the benefits obtained from this shall belong to the Hongdao Group; the Hongdao Group knows when any third party commits any infringement, it can directly take any legal measures in the name of Hongdao Group to stop any infringement. The expenses arising therefrom shall be borne by Hongdao Group, and Hongdao Group shall enjoy the relevant compensation benefits.

On November 27, 2002, GPHL and Hongdao Group signed the "Supplementary Agreement for "Wanglaoji" Trademark License" (hereinafter referred to as "Supplementary Agreement for 2002"), which changed the license period of the "2000 license agreement" from 10 to 20 years. The period is from May 2, 2000 to May 1, 2020; and the license period is divided into 6 time periods, and the license fee increases from 4.5 million yuan to 5.37 million yuan per year according to the time period.

On March 3, 2003, GPHL issued the "Power of Attorney", authorizing Hongdao Group to take legal measures to stop all infringements of the registered trademark "Wanglaoji" (Registration No. 626155) in Zhejiang and Guangdong provinces. It can also conduct litigation activities in the name of Hongdao Group, and the authorization period is from March 3, 2003 to December 31, 2003.

On June 10, 2003, GPHL and Hongdao Group signed the "Supplementary Agreement Regarding the "Wanglaoji" Trademark License Contract" (hereinafter referred to as the "2003 Supplementary Agreement", the "2003 Supplementary Agreement" and the "2002 Supplementary Agreement" collectively referred to as the "Two Supplementary Agreements"), stipulating that Hongdao Group shall go through the registration renewal procedures before the expiry date of the validity period of the trademark No. 626155 "Wanglaoji" (January 19, 2013), and handle the registration procedures of "Wanglaoji" thereafter, which would enable Hongdao Group to use the "Wanglaoji" trademark in accordance with the 2000 license agreement and two supplementary agreements within the license period.

(5) The packaging and decoration involved in this case

On December 18, 1995, Chen Hongdao applied to the State Intellectual Property Office for a design patent named "Beverage Box Label", which was published on February 12, 1997. The publication number was CN3054638, and the application number was 95318534.6, requesting color protection. The design patent is shown in attached Fig. 1.

On June 5, 1996, Chen Hongdao applied to the State Intellectual Property Office for a design patent named "Can Paste", which was published on July 2, 1997. The publication number was CN3059953, and the application number was 963055194. He requested color protection. The design patent is shown in attached Fig. 2.

On August 15, 2012, Pan Liangsheng made a "Declaration (Declaration of Decision of the Sole Proprietor)" in front of the appointed notary public in China and Hong Kong lawyer Zhang Demin at Zhang Yongxian·Li Huanglin Law Firm, Des Voeux Road, Hong Kong, stating that he is the sole proprietor of SUNNING-PRINTING&DESIGNCO. He has designed many canned, cartoned, and bottled projects for Chen Hongdao. Red Can Wanglaoji packaging was designed since 1995, the first design phase was in 1995, the second design phase was in February 1996, and the third design phase was in July 1998.

On September 19, 2012, Liang Shihe issued a personal statement stating: I, Liang Shihe, from July 1, 1990 to October 15, 1999, served as chairman of the board of Guangdong Nanfang Beverage Factory. During my tenure, our factory was commissioned by Dongguan Hongdao Company to process and produce herbal tea. The attached red herbal tea Tetra Pak paper packaging box [produced by (Hong Kong) Wanglaoji (Enterprise) Co., Ltd., 250 ml, standard code Q/GDNF101-89, label approval number 441900–207] is an herbal tea commissioned by our factory product packaging box. The packaging box is marked that June 26, 1993, to drink before this date. According to the product quality requirements of the year, the shelf life of the product is one year, so the production date of the product should be June 26, 1992. The statement is accompanied by a photo of the herbal tea packaging box produced by (Hong Kong) Wanglaoji (Enterprise) Co., Ltd. Beijing Chang'an Notary Office issued (2012) Beijing Chang'an NeiMinZhengZi No. 9906 "Notarization" on September 21, 2012, proving that Liang Shihe came to the notary office on September 19, 2012 and signed the previous "Personal Statement" in front of the notary.

On May 1, 1996, Dongguan Hongdao Company and Guangdong International Container Co., Ltd. signed the "Entrusted Processing Contract", stipulating that the former would entrust the latter to process and produce 240,000 sets of "Wanglaoji" 300 ml easy-open lid three-necked three-piece cans. On May 15, 2003, Guangdong International Container Co., Ltd. issued a "Certificate", certifying that Dongguan Hongdao Company, a subsidiary of Hongdao Group, has been entrusting it to manufacture empty cans of "Wanglaoji" since May 1, 1996. Now the certificate provided the design color picture of "Wanglaoji" herbal tea (canned) is consistent with the jars made by our company. On January 28, 1997, Hongdao Group and Guangdong International Containers Co., Ltd. signed the "Agreement on Clearing Out and Processing Empty Cans", in which it was agreed that the latter would process and produce the iron samples of the new version of Wanglaoji empty cans confirmed by the former in 1997 during the Spring Festival.

The court of first instance held that the focus of the dispute in this case is:

1. What is the content of the well-known goods involved and their unique packaging and decoration;
2. How to determine the ownership of the unique packaging and decoration rights of the well-known goods involved;
3. Whether Wanglaoji Company produce and sell "Wanglaoji", the packaging and decoration of the red canned herbal tea, constitutes unfair competition.

(1) Questions about the contents of the well-known goods involved and their unique packaging and decoration

1. Regarding the objects of the well-known commodities in this case

Article 5, Item 2 of the Anti-Unfair Competition Law stipulates: Unauthorized use of the unique name, packaging, or decoration of a well-known commodity, or use of a name, packaging, or decoration similar to that of a well-known commodity, causing confusion with other people's well-known commodities and causing buyers misunderstanding that it is the well-known commodity constitutes unfair competition. "The Supreme People's Court's Interpretation on Several Issues Concerning the Application of Law in the Trial of Unfair Competition Civil Cases" (hereinafter referred to as the "Judicial Interpretation of the Anti-Unfair Competition Law") Article 1, paragraph 1, stipulates: The goods that are known by relevant consumers shall be deemed to be "well-known goods" as stipulated in Article 5, Paragraph 2 of the Anti-Unfair Competition Law. Therefore, a well-known commodity refers to a commodity name that is not commonly used by related commodities and has significant distinguishing characteristics, and through its use on the commodity, enables consumers to distinguish the commodity from similar commodities of other operators. In this case, Jiaduobao Company sued and claimed that the well-known product in this case refers to the red canned herbal tea produced by Jiaduobao Company and "using the authentic and exclusive formula of Wang Zebang's descendants", while the Wanglaoji Company called the well-known product in this case as "Wanglaoji Herbal Tea".

Starting from the knowledge and cognitive ability of general consumers, defining the well-known product in this case as "Wanglaoji herbal tea" is sufficient to enable consumers to distinguish this product from similar products of other operators. Jiaduobao Company believes that the well-known product in this case refers to "red canned herbal tea produced by Jiaduobao Company and using the authentic and exclusive formula of Wang Zebang's descendants". It cannot be established, and the court of first instance would not support it.

2. Question about whether "Wanglaoji Herbal Tea" is a well-known product
According to the provisions of Article 1 Paragraph 1 of the Judicial Interpretation of the Anti-Unfair Competition Law, the people's court shall, when affirming well-known commodities, take into consideration the time, region, volume and targets for selling such commodities, the duration, degree and scope for any publicity of such commodities, as well as the protection situation as well-known commodities, and make comprehensive judgments.

Considering the sales time, sales area, sales and sales targets of the "Wanglaoji Herbal Tea" product involved, the duration, degree and geographic scope of the promotion, and the protection status of a well-known product, the "Wanglaoji Herbal Tea" should be identified as a well-known commodity.

3. Objects pointed to by the unique packaging and decoration of well-known commodities in this case
The packaging and decoration of Wanglaoji herbal tea, a well-known product involved in the case, uses red as the background color. In the center of the main view, there are three prominent and eye-catching regular script characters "Wang Lao Ji" decorated in yellow, with the sentence "The ancestor of herbal tea, Wanglaoji, was founded in Daoguangnian of the Qing Dynasty for more than a hundred years" on the right. The lower left part of "Wanglaoji" has a brown background and the white text "Herbal tea" in Song typeface. The upper part of the tank has a dark brown decorative line with yellow English "herbal tea" and "Wang Lao Ji" in small letters in regular script. The lower part of the tank has a thick decorative line and a thin decorative line; the rear view is basically the same as the front view; the left view is the ingredient list and anti-counterfeiting barcode in Chinese and English; the upper part of the right view is the "Wanglaoji" trademark and the words "Wanglaoji Herbal Tea", and the lower part is "Dongguan Hongdao Food Co., Ltd. Company" and its address, telephone number, fax number, shelf life and other information about the producer of the product. Since then, Wanglaoji canned herbal tea has been used in the packaging and decoration. Although there were some changes during the period, only a few changes were made in the text of the can. The Judgment No. 212 made by the court of first instance has determined: "The decoration on the 'Wanglaoji' canned herbal tea beverage in this case is unique in terms of text, color, pattern and arrangement and combination. The background color, pattern and name of the decoration are integrated in one body, with significant distinguishing characteristics, is not common to related products, but unique to that product, and should be a unique decoration for well-known products."

The content of the unique packaging and decoration of the well-known commodities involved in this case is the indicator that the body of the Wanglaoji red canned herbal tea product includes the yellow font "Wanglaoji" and other texts, the red background color and other colors, patterns and their permutations and combinations. The overall content within are the objects.

(2) How to determine the ownership of the rights and interests of the special packaging and decoration of the well-known commodities involved in the case

The unique packaging and decoration of well-known commodities are protected by the Anti-Unfair Competition Law, because they have the function of identifying the source of the commodities through use. The identification function of the source of a commodity is produced by its popularity. Therefore, it is the statutory requirement that the commodity has the popularity and the actual use of its packaging and decoration, forming uniqueness and distinctiveness, which is a legal requirement for the packaging and decoration to be protected by the Anti-Unfair Competition Law. Therefore, in order to determine whether the Wanglaoji Company infringed the rights of Jiaduobao Company in this case, the first thing to determine is the ownership of the special packaging and decoration rights and interests of the Wanglaoji red canned herbal tea involved. In this case, in the Wanglaoji trademark licensing contract between GPHL and Jiaduobao Company, there was no clear agreement on the ownership of the packaging and decoration rights of the Wanglaoji red canned herbal tea involved. Both parties claimed the right that they had the special packaging decoration of the Wanglaoji red canned herbal tea involved.

The court of first instance held that, the special packaging and decoration rights of the well-known commodities involved in this case should be enjoyed by GPHL, and Jiaduobao Company is not entitled to this right.

(3) Regarding whether the packaging and decoration used in the production and sale of "Wanglaoji" herbal tea in red cans by the Wanglaoji Company constitutes unfair competition

The second provision of Article 5 of the Anti-Unfair Competition Law stipulates that "causing confusion with other people's well-known goods and making buyers mistakenly believe that it is the well-known goods" is one of the constituent elements of this type of unfair competition. Article 4 of the Judicial Interpretation of the Anti-Unfair Competition Law stipulates that: if it is sufficient to cause the relevant public to misunderstand the source of the goods, including the misconception that it has a specific connection with the operator of a well-known commodity, such as a license to use, an affiliate relationship, etc., it shall be deemed as an anti-unfair competition according to the second paragraph of Article 5 of the Anti-Unfair Competition Law, "causes confusion with other people's well-known goods and makes buyers mistakenly believe that it is the well-known goods".

In this case, Jiaduobao Company believes that the production and sale of red canned herbal tea marked with the words "Wang Lao Ji" in yellow font by Wanglaoji Company since June 2012 infringed on its unique packaging and decoration rights for the well-known goods involved in the case. The court of first instance held that, as mentioned above, the exclusive packaging and decoration rights of the well-known commodities involved belonged to GPHL, not Hongdao Group or Jiaduobao Company. After the China International Economic and Trade Arbitration Commission's arbitration ruling on May 9, 2012, GPHL withdrew the license to Hongdao Group to use the "Wanglaoji" trademark, the GPHL licensed the "Wanglaoji" trademark and the corresponding packaging and decoration to Wanglaoji Company for use. Wanglaoji Company produces and sells Wanglaoji red cans of herbal tea. Therefore, the production and sale of Wanglaoji red canned herbal tea is legally authorized and legitimate. Jiaduobao Company does not have rights to the special packaging and decoration of the well-known commodities involved. Therefore, Jiaduobao Company accuses the Wanglaoji Company of producing and selling Wanglaoji red cans of herbal tea infringing on the special packaging and decoration rights of the well-known commodities involved and constitutes unfair competition. The claim lacked sufficient facts and legal basis, and the court of first instance would not support it.

To sum up, Jiaduobao Company believes that the Wanglaoji red canned herbal tea produced and sold by Wanglaoji Company infringes the special packaging and decoration rights of Jiaduobao's well-known products, and requested that Wanglaoji Company be ordered to stop immediately. After discussion by the trial committee of the court of first instance, the claims for terminating infringement, elimination of adverse effects, compensation for economic losses, and payment of litigation costs all lack factual and legal basis, and cannot be established, and should be rejected in accordance with the law. In accordance with Articles 1 and 2 of the Anti-Unfair Competition Law, and Article 142 of the Civil Procedure Law of the People's Republic of China, all claims of Jiaduobao Company were rejected. The first-instance case acceptance fee was 196,600 yuan, the evidence preservation fee was 30 yuan, and the audit fee was 400,000 yuan, all of which should be borne by Jiaduobao.

The court of second instance found that the facts ascertained by the court of first instance were basically true, and the court confirmed it.

According to opinion of the court of second instance, based on the appeal request of Jiaduobao Company and the defense opinion of Wanglaoji Company, as well as the relevant evidence and facts, there are four main issues in dispute in this case. The comments from the court are as follows:

1. The content and orientation of the unique packaging and decoration of the well-known goods involved in the case

According to Article 5, Item 2 of the Anti-Unfair Competition Law, unauthorized use of the unique name, packaging, or decoration of a well-known commodity, or use of a name, packaging, or decoration similar to that of a well-known commodity, may cause confusion with others' well-known commodities and cause the buyer mistakenly believes that it is the well-known commodity, which constitutes unfair competition. The unique packaging and decoration of well-known commodities are, in essence, the protection of commercial identification rights. Therefore, to determine whether there are legitimate rights and interests related to packaging and decoration that should be protected by law in this case is the first issue that needs to be commented.

(1) Questions about the content of the packaging and decoration involved and whether it is unique

1. Regarding the content of the packaging and decoration involved in the case

The court of first instance held that the content of the unique packaging and decoration of the well-known commodities involved in this case refers to the composition of the yellow font "Wang Lao Ji" and other characters on the body of the Wanglaoji red canned herbal tea product, the red background color and other colors, patterns and their permutations and combinations including parts. Jiaduobao believes that the visual effect of the red background color with yellow logo text and black auxiliary text of the packaging and decoration involved is significantly different from other similar product packaging in the pattern layout, logo background color, text color, text arrangement position, the color matching and so on, instead of the content of the text.

In this regard, the court believes that, first of all, based on the facts ascertained by the court of first instance, the products provided by Jiaduobao Company and Wanglaoji Company during the trial of the court of first instance to prove the specific form of packaging and decoration involved in the case are all marked on both sides. The packaging and decoration of the red cans with the words "Wanglaoji" is in accordance with the judgment of the court of first instance. In the production and sales of the red canned Wanglaoji herbal tea, except for some changes to the text content on the can body, the packaging and decoration form has been used, and it always contains the words "Wanglaoji" in yellow font.

Secondly, in the course of the lawsuit of this case, Jiaduobao Company has repeatedly used "Red Can Wanglaoji" to refer to the well-known goods that it requested protection in this case, and cited the content of judgment No. 212 as the basis for its claims. The judgment also found that "Wanglaoji" the decoration on the canned herbal tea beverage is unique in terms of text, color, pattern and their permutation and combination. It is not common to related products, but unique to that product, and should be unique to well-known products. This shows that Jiaduobao's claim that the meaning of the text should be ignored when determining the content of the packaging and decoration involved is inconsistent with the facts on which the rights are based.

Finally, the packaging and decoration of commodities is usually an overall image composed of text, patterns, colors and other components. The text part generally points to the name or trademark of the commodity that uses the packaging and decoration. In the actual use of packaging and decoration, trademarks can be used as one of the components of packaging and decoration, or they can be explicitly excluded. This depends entirely on the packaging and decoration design or the user's own wishes. In the actual use of the packaging and decoration involved, in addition to the use of the No. 626155 "Wanglaoji" registered trademark pattern on the packaging and decoration as stipulated in the trademark license agreement, the three characters "Wang Lao Ji" written in yellow font were also placed on the prominent position on the packaging. Jiaduobao Company has never made any substantial changes to the above-mentioned way of packaging and decoration in the process of producing and selling the red canned Wanglaoji herbal tea.

Therefore, Jiaduobao Company not only has the subjective willingness to use "Wanglaoji" as a component of packaging and decoration in the actual use process, but also through long-term and stable use behavior and use methods, the "Wanglaoji" text has become a reality. It is a component of the packaging and decoration involved and is closely integrated with other contents in the packaging and decoration. In the packaging and decoration, the words "Wanglaoji" and the registered trademark of Wanglaoji are the content used by Jiaduobao Company with the permission of GPHL. Other parts including red background, patterns and permutations and combinations are for Jiaduobao Company's own creation. According to this, the conclusion made by the court of first instance that "the overall content of the Wanglaoji red canned herbal tea product including the yellow Wanglaoji text, red background and other colors, patterns, and their permutations and combinations on the can body" is the unique packaging and decoration content involved in the case is nothing wrong.

2. Regarding whether the packaging and decoration involved in the case are unique
Article 2 of the Judicial Interpretation of the Anti-Unfair Competition Law stipulates that the name, packaging, and decoration of commodities with distinctive features that distinguish the source of goods shall be recognized as the "special name, packaging, decorate".

The packaging and decoration involved in the case was mainly red, and the three characters "Wang Lao Ji" in the center of the packaging and decoration were written in yellow fonts with bright colors and strong contrast with the main color, and the three characters "Wang Lao Ji" included in the decoration were allowed to be used. "Wanglaoji" Trademark logos, brown or black text, patterns, line combinations, etc., are organically combined with other constituent elements. Therefore, although the main color of red is not uncommon in the packaging and decoration design of canned beverage products, considering that the packaging and decoration forms of beverage products have a large design space, the packaging and decoration involved in the case adopted the color, and made the selection and combination of design elements such as text, patterns, etc., which presents a certain unique visual effect and distinctive features that have nothing to do with the functional effects of the product. Through long-term and large-scale publicity and actual use behavior, the packaging and decoration involved in the case played a role in indicating the source of goods which has been continuously strengthened. In fact, both parties did not question whether the packaging and decoration involved in the case were unique. Therefore, the packaging and decoration involved in the case meets the protection conditions of "unique packaging and decoration" in the Anti-Unfair Competition Law, and the court supports the relevant determination of the court of first instance.

(2) About the commodities involved in the packaging and decoration and their popularity

Packaging and decoration have distinctive identifying characteristics and are used on commodities with a certain degree of popularity, which is a condition for commercial identification rights related to packaging and decoration to be protected by the Anti-Unfair Competition Law. When applying the provisions of Article 5, Item 2 of the Anti-Unfair Competition Law, the relationship between "special packaging and decoration" and "well-known commodities" should be correctly understood, that is, the two have an inseparable relationship. Only commodities with unique packaging and decoration can become the object of review of the Anti-Unfair Competition Law. On the contrary, abstract product names, or product concepts with no definite connotations, are separated from the specific products on which the packaging and decoration are attached, lack actual use behaviors for evaluation, and do not comply with the meaning of evaluation in the provisions of Article 5, Paragraph 2 of the Anti-Unfair Competition Law.

1. Regarding the goods involved in the packaging and decoration of the case

Article 1 of the Judicial Interpretation of the Anti-Unfair Competition Law stipulates that commodities that have a certain market reputation in China and are known to the relevant public should be recognized as "well-known commodities" as stipulated in Article 5, Item 2 of the Anti-Unfair Competition Law. When it comes to the definition of well-known products in this case, Wanglaoji Company believes that "Wanglaoji Herbal Tea" is a well-known product in this case. Jiaduobao Company believes that "the red canned herbal tea produced by Jiaduobao Company and using the authentic and exclusive formula of Wang Zebang's descendants" is a well-known commodity in this case. The court of first instance held that a well-known commodity refers to a commodity name that is not commonly used by related commodities and has significant distinguishing characteristics, and through its use on the commodity, enables consumers to distinguish the commodity from similar commodities of other operators. The well-known product in this case refers to "Wanglaoji herbal tea", of which "herbal tea" belongs to the generic name of this type of product, and "Wanglaoji" belongs to the unique name. In this regard, the court believes that:

First of all, based on the orientation and attachment relationship between the unique packaging and decoration and well-known commodities, combined with the content of the unique packaging and decoration that the court has identified as the case, that is, it is used on the body of the red canned Wanglaoji herbal tea product, including yellow "Wanglaoji" text, red background and other colors, patterns and their permutations and combinations, etc. Based on the facts ascertained by the court of first instance, combined with the basis of the parties' claims, the aforementioned packaging and decoration forms are used by Jiaduobao Company. Therefore, the red canned Wanglaoji herbal tea produced and operated by Jiaduobao Company should be the commodity attached to the unique packaging and decoration of this case. In addition, for whether Jiaduobao's herbal tea in red cans with "Wanglaoji" on one side, "Jiaduobao" on the other side, and "Jiaduobao" on both sides used by Jiaduobao since December 2011, as well as the red canned Wanglaoji herbal tea authorized by GPHL since June 2012 are well-known products, the court believes that neither of the products are the factual basis for determining the specific content of packaging and decoration during the first instance. Therefore, the court will not comment on the above claims of GPHL and Jiaduobao Company.

Secondly, on whether "Wanglaoji herbal tea" is a "well-known commodity" in the case. According to the facts ascertained by the court of first instance, "Wanglaoji Herbal Tea" as a commodity name can at least refer to the green carton tea produced by GPHL and the red can tea produced by Jiaduobao when the dispute occurs between the two parties, with independent packaging and decoration. The purpose of defining "well-known commodities" in this case is to determine whether the specific packaging and decoration form attached to it meets the requirements of the Anti-Unfair Competition Law to provide protection for commercial marking rights. Therefore, the "well-known commodity" should have a clear directional relationship with the packaging and decoration involved in the case. The court of first instance broke away from the dependent relationship between the goods and the packaging and decoration, and identified the non-unique commodity name "Wanglaoji Herbal Tea" as the "famous commodity" in this case, which lacked factual and legal basis. The court corrected this. In addition, since the case involved a dispute over the special packaging and decoration of well-known commodities, the court of first instance's determination of whether "Wang Lao Ji" belongs to a special name has nothing to do with the case, and the court shall also correct it.

Finally, whether the formula or taste has an impact on the identification of well-known commodities. Jiaduobao believes that the well-known commodities in this case should also include the content of "using the authentic and exclusive secret recipe of Wang Zebang's descendants". The court believes that since the establishment of a trademark licensing relationship in 1995, the two parties have separately carried out the production and operation activities of Wanglaoji herbal tea. However, there is no evidence to show that in the process of producing and selling red canned Wanglaoji herbal tea, Jiaduobao has emphasized the differences in formula and taste so that consumers can distinguish between the Wanglaoji herbal teas produced by both parties. Based on this, Jiaduobao Company's claim that the content or source of the formula should be used to further limit the connotation of the "well-known commodity" in this case is not supported by the court.

2. Regarding whether the red canned Wanglaoji herbal tea produced and operated by Jiaduobao Company is well-known

Article 1 of the Judicial Interpretation of the Anti-Unfair Competition Law stipulates that the people's court shall consider the sales time, sales area, sales and sales target of a well-known commodity, as well as the duration, degree and geographical scope of any publicity, as a well-known commodity to make comprehensive judgments based on factors such as the protected situation. Accordingly, the following factors should be comprehensively considered for the question of whether the red canned Wanglaoji herbal tea is a well-known product in the case:

(1) The historical origin of the "Wanglaoji" brand. The "Wanglaoji" brand was founded by Wang Zebang in the Daoguang period of the Qing Dynasty and is known as the ancestor of herbal tea. After a public–private partnership in 1956, it has been operated by Guangzhou Yangcheng Pharmaceutical Factory and Yangcheng Pharmaceutical, and has been recognized as a famous trademark in Guangdong Province and Guangzhou City since 1992. Therefore, before the court of first instance established the trademark licensing relationship between the two parties, the "Wanglaoji" brand has been known to the relevant public in Guangdong and has a certain degree of market awareness. It is related to evidences provided by Wanglaoji Company. As for Jiaduobao's objection to the above evidence, the court will not support.

(2) The market sales and advertising of red canned Wanglaoji herbal tea. After Yangcheng Pharmaceutical and Hongdao Group signed the "Trademark Licensing Contract", Jiaduobao Company and its affiliates carried out large-scale production and sales of red canned Wanglaoji herbal tea, and carried out continuous marketing and promotion activities. The production and sales of red canned Wanglaoji herbal tea have been rising year after year, and have been among the best-selling products of canned beverage products in China for many years. It has also won many honorary titles including "the first brand in the Chinese herbal tea industry". The

above-mentioned production and operation activities of Jiaduobao Company have greatly enhanced the popularity of the red canned Wanglaoji herbal tea during this period. On the basis of lack of relevance or uncertainty of authenticity, the evidence 12, 32, 38, 45, 48 provided by Jiaduobao Company has not been accepted. The court would not support the objection raised by Jiaduobao.

(3) The record that the red canned Wanglaoji herbal tea is a well-known commodity protected by the effective judgment of the people's court. Judgment No. 212 has determined that the Wanglaoji canned herbal tea beverages involved in the case are known to consumers in Guangdong, occupy a large share in the herbal tea beverage market, enjoy a relatively high reputation, and should be well-known commodities in Guangdong. The above facts prove that the red canned Wanglaoji herbal tea meets the qualification requirements for well-known commodities. Based on this, comprehensively considering the historical origins of the "Wanglaoji" brand, the sales, promotion, and protection records of the red canned Wanglaoji herbal tea products produced and operated by Jiaduobao, as well as the relevant public's awareness of the formation of the products on this basis, it should be determined that it was a well-known commodity in the case.

2. Determination of the ownership of the unique packaging and decoration rights and interests of the well-known commodities involved in the case

In this case, Jiaduobao Company believes that it is the main body of rights and interests in the packaging and decoration involved in the case. Wanglaoji Company believes that GPHL is the right holder of the packaging and decoration involved, and Wanglaoji Company is based on the legal authorization of GPHL to produce and sell red cans of herbal tea marked with the words "Wanglaoji" in yellow font. Therefore, determining the ownership of the packaging and decoration rights involved in the case is a prerequisite for judging whether the actions of the Wanglaoji Company constitute infringement. The court of first instance held that the special packaging and decoration rights of the well-known commodities involved should be enjoyed by GPHL, and Jiaduobao clearly objected to this during the appeal process. Based on the facts of the case, combined with the claims made by both parties on the ownership of rights, the court commented on the ownership of the packaging and decoration rights of the red canned Wanglaoji herbal tea as follows:

(1) Whether the trademark licensing contract has stipulated the ownership of the rights and interests of the packaging and decoration involved in the case. Wanglaoji Company believes that according to the agreement of the trademark licensing contract, the red decoration was first proposed by GPHL and licensed to Hongdao Group. Therefore, the packaging and decoration design of "Wanglaoji" products is based on the authorization of the trademark owner. The court believes that the unique packaging and decoration of the well-known commodities involved is a comprehensive form of expression that contains multiple elements such as text, patterns, and color matching. In the "Wanglaoji" series of trademark licensing contracts, although Hong Dao Group has the right to exclusively use the "Wanglaoji" trademark on red canned herbal tea beverages, as well as the production and sale of red canned

Wanglaoji herbal tea, the contract did not clarify the specific manifestation of packaging and decoration. The expression of "red canned" used in the license contract is not sufficient to indicate that the packaging and decoration involved in a combination of multiple elements already exists, and there is no evidence to show that although there is no clear agreement in the license contract, GPHL has completed the design or actually used the packaging and decoration involved in the case, and has the factual basis for authorizing Hongdao Group to use it. Accordingly, the court of first instance determined that GPHL and Jiaduobao Company did not clearly agree on the ownership of the packaging and decoration rights of the Wanglaoji herbal tea in the Wanglaoji trademark in the Wanglaoji trademark licensing. The court maintained the determination made by the court of first instance.

(2) Whether the manufacturer's information can be a direct basis for determining the ownership of rights and interests. Jiaduobao believes that the manufacturer's name and other information marked on the packaging and decoration involved in the case are sufficient to determine the ownership of the packaging and decoration rights and interests. Jiaduobao Company further believes that the information about the producer and manufacturer marked on the packaging and decoration involved is directly related to Jiaduobao Company, and there is no information indicating that GPHL is the source of the goods. It has been able to enable consumers to establish a solid and unique connection between the packaging and decoration and Jiaduobao, and the related rights and interests of packaging and decoration should be enjoyed by Jiaduobao.

The court believes that, first of all, the manufacturer's labeling of information such as the manufacturer's name on the packaging and decoration is an act of fulfilling its product quality responsibilities and obligations as a manufacturer in accordance with the "Product Quality Law of the People's Republic of China" and other legal provisions. The information such as the name of the manufacturer is certainly indicative of the source of the product, but whether the name of the manufacturer can be used as a direct basis for obtaining intellectual property rights related to the product still needs a specific analysis.

Secondly, as far as this case is concerned, the packaging and decoration involved in the case as an overall image that contains multiple components, including the "Wanglaoji" text and trademark logo, as well as the matching and selection of lines and colors, and the name of the manufacturer, etc. Other text content. The above-mentioned constituent elements are combined with each other, so that the packaging and decoration involved in the case play a role of indicating the source of the goods as a whole. Therefore, although the Jiaduobao Company marked the manufacturer's information on the red can of Wanglaoji herbal tea and indicated to consumers that it was the actual operator of the red can of Wanglaoji herbal tea, the relevant public had been involved in the packaging and decoration of the case and Jiaduobao. The company has established a certain connection, but it is undeniable that the "Wanglaoji" brand has already gained a certain degree of market awareness, and the separation of brand controllers and actual operators brought about by the licensing system has become more and more common. It is difficult for consumers to ignore the word "Wanglaoji" and the trademark used in the packaging and decoration involved in the case, as well as the connection between the word and the trademark owner. Therefore, Jiaduobao's claim that the ownership of the packaging and decoration rights in this case can be determined directly based on the manufacturer's name and other information, lacking sufficient facts and legal basis, the court does not support it.

(3) The influence of the content of the existing judgment on the determination of the ownership of rights and interests. Jiaduobao Company believes that Judgment No. 212 has clearly determined that Jiaduobao Company is the legal operator of "Wanglaoji" canned herbal tea beverages and has inherited the rights and interests of Dongguan Hongdao Company's unique packaging and decoration of well-known products. It is a well-known product in this case, with the main body of unique packaging and decoration rights and interests. The court believes that the disputes involved in the foregoing judgment occurred during the duration of the series of trademark licensing contracts signed by both parties. In this case, Jiaduobao was able to file a lawsuit in its own name on the intellectual property disputes related to the red canned Wanglaoji herbal tea, based on the clear authorization given to Hongdao Group by GPHL. Based on the previous agreement between the two parties on the disposition of litigation rights, the fact that GPHL did not participate in the above-mentioned litigation and jointly asserted rights with Jiaduobao does not necessarily mean that it has given up its intellectual property rights related to the red canned Wanglaoji herbal tea. In addition, as far as the foregoing judgment itself is concerned, there is no determination of the relationship between GPHL and Jiaduobao regarding the rights and interests of packaging and decoration involved in the case, and it is not sufficient to directly conclude that Jiaduobao is the sole right holder of packaging and decoration involved in the case. Therefore, in the case that GPHL also claims rights to the packaging and decoration rights in the case, the court does not support Jiaduobao's claim that the ownership of the packaging and decoration rights in the case can be directly determined based on the foregoing judgment.

(4) Determining the ownership of the unique packaging and decoration rights and interests of the well-known commodities involved in the case. The dispute over the special packaging and decoration of the well-known commodities involved in this case arises from the fact that the two parties did not make a clear agreement on how to divide the derivative benefits that may arise during the licensing period in the process of signing and performing the trademark licensing contract. Under normal circumstances, after the termination of the trademark licensing relationship, the licensee should stop the use, and the goodwill accumulated on the licensed use of the trademark should be returned to the licensor at the same time. However, the particularity of the dispute in this case is that the unique packaging and decoration formed during the period of license use is not only closely related to the use of the licensed trademark, but also because of its independent rights and interests under the Anti-Unfair Competition Law, which has caused spillovers which are goodwill features other than trademark rights. Both GPHL and Jiaduobao Company claim to have rights in the special packaging and decoration of red canned Wanglaoji herbal tea. Specifically, as the right holder of the registered trademark of part of the division,

and played a significant role in identifying the source of the goods. Consumers will of course think that the red canned Wanglaoji herbal tea comes from the owner of the trademark "Wanglaoji", and the formula and taste will not affect consumers' recognition and identification of the product. As the former actual operator of red canned Wanglaoji herbal tea, Jiaduobao believes that the ownership of the packaging and decoration rights and the trademark rights of "Wanglaoji" is independent and does not affect each other. Consumers love the red canned Wanglaoji herbal tea produced by Jiaduobao and selected specific formulas. The packaging and decoration of this case is used by Jiaduobao and closely integrated with the aforementioned products. The related rights and interests of packaging and decoration should belong to Jiaduobao. The court believes that the claims made by both parties not only involve general legal application issues related to the protection of commercial identity rights and interests, but also reflect the complex historical and practical factors involved in the formation of the unique packaging and decoration rights and interests in this case. Therefore, when determining the ownership of its rights, the following factors need to be comprehensively considered:

1. The role of the "Wanglaoji" brand in the formation of the packaging and decoration rights involved in the case

From the perspective of the inheritance and development of the "Wanglaoji" brand, before the two parties signed the first licensing contract in 1995, the "Wanglaoji" brand was already a century-old "Chinese time-honored brand". The rights holders of GPHL and its affiliates have maintained the historical heritage and market value of the "Wanglaoji" brand through the development of "Wanglaoji Brand Herbal Tea" beverages and other production and operation activities. It is also based on the historical origin and brand effect of the "Wanglaoji" brand in mainland China that after obtaining the right to use the "Wanglaoji" trademark, Jiaduobao Company chose to use eye-catching and prominent fonts in the packaging and decoration of the case. It has been used in China, and once the red canned Wanglaoji herbal tea is launched on the market, it has a better consumer perception foundation and market prospects. Therefore, as the owner of the trademark of "Wanglaoji", GPHL maintains its brand awareness and reputation, which is an important foundation for the creation, continuation and development of the popularity of red canned Wanglaoji herbal tea.

From the perspective of the role played by the "Wanglaoji" brand in the packaging and decoration involved, the packaging and decoration involved in the case includes text, patterns, colors and their permutations and combinations, and they belong to the decoration form of text and patterns. Among them, the main red color used in packaging and decoration, and the three characters "Wang Lao Ji", which are located in the center of the tank and form a strong visual contrast with the background color, should be the most eye-catching design elements in packaging and decoration. Regarding the packaging and decoration of the Wanglaoji herbal tea in the red can involved, from the initial market circulation to the time when the dispute occurred in this case, the yellow font of "Wanglaoji" was used in the packaging and decoration in a consistent, stable and continuous manner. Consumers have continuously strengthened the recognition that the word "Wanglaoji" has been integrated with packaging and decoration, and in fact played a role in revealing the source of goods to consumers, that is, when the relevant public purchases red cans of Wanglaoji herbal tea, they would both think of Jiaduobao as the actual operator, and GPHL, the owner of the trademark "Wanglaoji". Therefore, through the actual use of Jiaduobao Company, the word "Wanglaoji" has in fact become an important part of the packaging and decoration of Wanglaoji herbal tea in red cans. It lacks factual and legal basis to deny that it has also played the function of source identification for the packaging and decoration involved in the case.

2. The role played by Jiaduobao's operation of red canned Wanglaoji herbal tea in in the formation of the packaging and decoration rights involved in the case

As the actual business entity of red canned Wanglaoji herbal tea, Jiaduobao has not only clearly conveyed to consumers that red canned Wanglaoji herbal tea is actually operated by Jiaduobao through years of continuous and large-scale publicity and use behaviors, but also has significantly increased the market visibility of Jiaduobao Company and red canned Wanglaoji herbal tea. Jiaduobao Company has made important contributions to the formation of the packaging and decoration rights involved in the case.

Judging from the role of Jiaduobao Company's business activities in the formation of the packaging and decoration rights and interests involved, the second provision of Article 5 of the Anti-Unfair Competition Law is to provide legal protection for the unique packaging and decoration of well-known commodities. Packaging and decoration have the ability to identify products. The salient characteristics of the source and the packaging and decoration attached to a certain well-known commodity are the statutory requirements for the packaging and decoration involved in the case to be protected by the Anti-Unfair Competition Law. Obviously, the emergence of unique packaging and decoration rights is inseparable from the actual use of relevant market operators. In this case, from the launch of the red canned Wanglaoji herbal tea on the market to the occurrence of the dispute in this case, Jiaduobao Company was the actual business entity of the red canned Wanglaoji herbal tea. Its continuous and stable use behavior significantly increased the popularity of the red canned Wanglaoji herbal tea. It also makes the packaging and decoration that contain the red background color and yellow "Wanglaoji" characters and other distinguishable parts have the conditions to be protected by the Anti-Unfair Competition Law. At the same time, during this process, consumers have gradually developed a clear understanding of the fact that Jiaduobao Company was the actual operator of red canned Wanglaoji herbal tea during this period. Therefore, denying the important role of Jiaduobao's operating behavior in the formation of the packaging and decoration rights involved in the case is also contrary to the facts and the law.

3. Consumer perception and the measurement of fairness principles

This case is a dispute over the unauthorized use of special packaging and decoration of well-known goods under the framework of the Anti-Unfair Competition Law. Although the dispute itself originated from the trademark licensing relationship that existed between the two parties, it is the core law in this case to resolve the ownership of packaging and decoration rights. It is still necessary to return to the legal provisions of the Anti-Unfair Competition Law on the unique packaging and decoration protection system. The so-called unique packaging and decoration of well-known commodities refers to the packaging and decoration forms of well-known commodities that have distinctive features that distinguish the source of the commodity. When determining the rights and interests of unique packaging and decoration, it is necessary to encourage honest labor on the premise of following the principle of honesty and credibility, but also to respect consumers' cognition of the source of the commodity based on the distinctive characteristics of the packaging and decoration itself.

Considering the above factors comprehensively, combined with the historical development process of red canned Wanglaoji herbal tea, the background of cooperation between the two parties, the perception of consumers and the consideration of the principle of fairness, GPHL and its predecessor, Jiaduobao Company and its affiliates, both parties made great contribution to the formation and development of the packaging and decoration rights involved in the case.

The judgment of the packaging and decoration rights involved in the case to one party would lead to an apparently unfair result and may harm the public interest. Therefore, the special packaging and decoration rights and interests of the well-known commodities involved in the case can be shared by GPHL and Jiaduobao jointly under the principle of good faith and respecting consumer cognition and not harming the legitimate rights and interests of others. The court of first instance determined that the special packaging and decoration of the well-known commodities involved should be enjoyed by GPHL and not by Jiaduobao Company, lacking factual and legal basis, and contrary to social effects, and the court shall correct it.

3. Whether the alleged infringement of the Wanglaoji company constitutes unfair competition

Article 5, Paragraph 2 of the Anti-Unfair Competition Law stipulates that unauthorized use of the unique name, packaging, or decoration of a well-known commodity without permission, or using any name, packaging, or decoration similar to that of a well-known commodity, causing confusion with another's commodity so that purchasers would mistake its commodity for the well-known commodity, constitutes an act of unfair competition.

Jiaduobao believes that the Wanglaoji Company began to produce and sell red canned herbal tea marked with the words "Wanglaoji" in yellow fonts in June 2012, infringing on its unique packaging and decoration rights for the well-known goods involved in the case. The court believes that, first of all, the foregoing has confirmed that the reputation and popularity of GPHL and its "Wanglaoji" brand is an important foundation for the creation, continuation and development of the popularity of the red canned Wanglaoji herbal tea. More importantly, since the red canned Wanglaoji herbal tea actually operated by Jiaduobao has been put on the market, the word "Wanglaoji" has always been an important part of the packaging and decoration. Consumers will naturally consider the packaging and decoration involved in the case with Jiaduobao and GPHL at the same time. Therefore, without prejudice to the legitimate interests of others, Jiaduobao Company and GPHL can jointly enjoy the packaging and decoration rights involved in the case.

Secondly, after the China International Economic and Trade Arbitration Commission ruled that GPHL took back the right to use the "Wanglaoji" trademark, Jiaduobao has no right to continue to use the "Wanglaoji" trademark, that is, the red canned Wanglaoji herbal tea produced by Jiaduobao was actually withdrawn from the market. Sharing the rights and interests of packaging and decoration involved in the case, GPHL has the right to authorize Wanglaoji company to use the trademark "Wanglaoji" to produce and sell red cans of herbal tea, which does not constitute unauthorized use of the special packaging and decoration of other people's well-known commodities. After the termination of the trademark licensing relationship, Wanglaoji Company is authorized to produce and sell red canned herbal tea using the "Wanglaoji" trademark, and the red canned Wanglaoji herbal tea produced and sold by Jiaduobao Company may appear to a certain extent. Confusion of sources is a market phenomenon that appears under a specific historical background, and will gradually fade as the two parties strengthen their respective brands and update their products in their business activities. To sum up, Jiaduobao Company's claim that the Wanglaoji Company infringes on the rights and interests of its well-known products' unique packaging and decoration lacks sufficient facts and legal basis, and the court would not support it.

4. Whether the court of first instance violated legal procedures

Jiaduobao Company believes that the court of first instance allowing Wanglaoji Company to submit additional evidence during the trial violated legal procedures. After investigation, the Wanglaoji Company supplemented and submitted part of the evidence on the day of the trial of the court of first instance. In this regard, the court believes that during the trial of the court of first instance, both parties have submitted additional evidence. The court of first instance comprehensively considered the complexity of the case and the difficulty of the parties to collect and submit evidence. While supplementing the evidence submitted on the same day, the court of first instance also gave Jiaduobao Company the opportunity and time to issue cross-examination opinions, which equally protected the litigation rights of both parties. There was nothing improper in its related practices, nor did it violate the law. The objection raised cannot be established, and the court would not support it.

Throughout this case, the court believes that the intellectual property system is to ensure and encourage innovation. The behavior of workers to create and accumulate social wealth in the manner of honest work and honest management shall be protected by law. Judicial protection of intellectual property rights should take the maintenance of an orderly and standardized, fair competition, and vibrant market environment as its own responsibility, and provide the public with clear legal expectations. Intellectual property disputes often arise from complex historical and realistic backgrounds, and the division of rights and the balance of interests are often intertwined. The handling of such disputes requires us to fully consider and respect various factors such as the historical causes of the disputes, the current status of use, and consumer perceptions. The basic principles of maintaining honesty and credibility and respect for objective reality are required to strictly follow the guidelines of the law, to resolve disputes fairly and reasonably. Based on the above-mentioned position and basic principles, the court confirms that both parties can jointly enjoy the unique packaging and decoration rights of the well-known commodities involved without harming the legitimate interests of others. Both GPHL and Jiaduobao Company have made positive contributions to the accumulation of the goodwill of the "Wanglaoji" brand. While effectively enhancing the company's reputation, it has also obtained huge market benefits. However, after the termination of the "Wanglaoji" trademark licensing relationship, the two parties involved in continuous intellectual property disputes and the amount of money involved in the lawsuit was huge, which aroused some concerns and worries of the public, and may damage the social evaluation of the company. In this regard, the two parties should implement the judgment in good faith in the spirit of mutual understanding and reasonable avoidance, uphold the corporate social responsibility, cherish the business results, respect the trust of consumers, and act for the national brand with honest, trustworthy and standardized market behaviors. Be bigger and stronger, and work hard to provide consumers with better products.

In summary, although the law applicable to the first-instance judgment is improper, the result of the judgment is correct, so Jiaduobao Company's appeal request is not supported. After discussion and decision by the Judicial Committee of the court, in accordance with Article 1, Article 2, Paragraph 1, Article 5, Item 2 of the Anti-Unfair Competition Law of the People's Republic of China, Articles 1 and 2 of the Interpretation of Certain Issues, Article 170, Paragraph 1, Item 1 of the Civil Procedure Law of the People's Republic of China, and Article 334 of the Interpretation of the Supreme People's Court on the Application of the Civil Procedure Law of the People's Republic of China, the judgment is as follows:

The appeal is rejected and the original verdict is upheld.

The first-instance case acceptance fee is RMB 19,600,000, the evidence preservation fee is RMB 30, the audit fee is RMB 400,000, and the second-instance case acceptance fee is RMB 19,600, all of which should be borne by Guangdong Jiaduobao Beverage and Food Co., Ltd.

This judgment is final.
Presiding Judge: Song Xiaoming
Judge: Xia Junli
Judge: Zhou Xiang
Judge: Qian Xiaohong
Acting judge: Tong Shu
July 27, 2017
Clerk: Zhang Bo
Clerk: Cao Jiayin

1.2 Analysis of the case

1. Basic facts:
On July 6, 2012, Guangzhou Pharmaceutical Holdings Limited (hereinafter referred to as "GPHL") and Guangdong Jiaduobao Beverage and Food Co., Ltd. (hereinafter

referred to as "JDB Company") respectively instituted legal proceedings in a court on the same day, each asserting its rights and interests of the packaging and decoration specific to a famous commodity, "Red-Canned Wanglaoji Herbal Tea", and alleging on this basis that the packaging and decoration of the red-canned herbal tea produced and sold by the other party constituted infringement. Specifically speaking, GPHL, as the holder of registered trademark "Wanglaoji" believes that since "Wanglaoji" is an inseparable part of the packaging and decoration and distinctively indicates the source of commodity, consumers would take it for granted that the Red-Canned Wanglaoji Herbal Tea originates from the holder of trademark "Wanglaqji", and the recipe and taste would not affect the consumers identification and judgment of the commodity. JDB Company, as the former actual operator of Red-Canned Wanglaoji Herbal Tea, believes that the rights and interests of the packaging and decoration and the ownership of trademark right of "Wanglaqji" are independent from, and do not affect, each other. What consumers love is the Red-Canned Wanglaoji Herbal Tea produced by JDB Company with specifically selected recipe, and the packaging and decoration in this Case is used by JDB Company and closely integrated with the said commodity; thus the rights and interests relating to the packaging and decoration shall belong to JDB Company.

2. The focus of dispute

(1) What are the contents of the well-known goods involved and their unique packaging and decoration; (2) How to determine the ownership of the unique packaging and decoration rights of the well-known goods involved; (3)Whether the packaging and decoration used by the big health company for the production and sale of "Wanglaoji" red cans of herbal tea constitutes unfair competition.

3. Rules

"Anti-unfair Competition Law of the People's Republic of China 1993"

Article 5: A business shall not conduct market transactions by the following unfair means to damage competitors: (2) Using the unique name, packaging, or decoration of a well-known commodity without permission, or using any name, packaging, or decoration similar to that of a well-known commodity, causing confusion with another's commodity so that purchasers would mistake its commodity for the well-known commodity.

"Interpretation of Anti-unfair Competition"

Article 1: Commodities that have a certain degree of market awareness in China and are known to the relevant public should be recognized as "well-known commodities" as stipulated in Article 5, Paragraph 2 of the Anti-Unfair Competition Law.

Article 2: The name, packaging, and decoration of commodities with distinctive features that distinguish the source of the commodity shall be recognized as the "special name, packaging, and decoration" stipulated in Article 5, Paragraph 2 of the Anti-Unfair Competition Law.

Article 4: If it is sufficient to cause the relevant public to misunderstand the source of the goods, including the misconception that it has a specific connection with the operator of a well-known commodity, such as a license to use, an affiliated company relationship, etc., it shall be deemed as the "Article 5 Paragraph 2 of the Anti-Unfair

4. Reasoning

In the first instance, Guangdong High People's Court held that the rights and interests of the packaging and decoration of "Red-Canned Wanglaoji Herbal Tea" shall belong to GPHL and that the production and sale of red-canned herbal tea by Guangzhou Wanglaoji Health Industry Co., Ltd. (hereinafter referred to as "Health Company") with the authorization by GPHL did not constitute infringement. Since JDB Company did not own the rights and interests of the packaging and decoration concerned, its production and sale of both red-canned herbal tea with "王老吉(Wanglaoji)" and "加多宝(JDB)" on either side and that with "加多宝(JDB)" on both sides constituted infringement. Hence, the Court in the first instance ordered JDB Company to cease the infringement, publish a statement to eliminate the effect, and compensate GPHL 150 million yuan for economic losses and more than 260,000 yuan for reasonable enforcement costs. JDB Company appealed both judgments of the first instance to the Supreme People's Court. The Supreme People's Court made the second-instance judgment on July 7, 2017, dismissing all the claims of both GPHL and JDB Company.

5. Reasoning

The Court held in the effective judgment that distinctive features of packaging and decoration for recognition and their application to fairly famous commodities are the conditions for the rights and interests of the commercial indications connected with packaging and decoration to be protected by the Anti-unfair Competition Law. The application of Item 2, Article 5 of the Anti-unfair Competition Law shall correctly understand the relationship between "specific packaging and decoration^, and "famous commodity", as being mutually interdependent and inseparable. Only the commodity that uses the specific packaging and decoration is evaluable by the Anti-unfair Competition Law. On the contrary, abstract commodity names or commodity concepts without definitive connotations are detached from the concrete commodities on which packaging and decoration depend, short of evaluable conducts of actual usage, and thus unevaluable under Item 2, Article 5 of the Anti-unfair Competition Law. When dispute occurred between the two parties, t4Wanglaoji Herbal Tea", as a kind of commodity name, could at least refer to variously packaged and decorated herbal tea products such as the green-boxed one produced by GPHL and red-canned one produced by JDB Company. The purpose of defining "famous commodity" is to judge whether the specific packaging and decoration attached thereto meet the conditions for the rights and interests of commercial indications to be protectable by the Anti-unfair Competition Law. Hence, such "famous commodity", shall be clearly directed to the packaging and decoration concerned. The court of first instance disregarded the dependence of the packaging and decoration on the commodity, and found the commodity name "Wanglaqji Herbal Tea", which has non-specific references, as the "famous commodity" in this case. This decision lacks factual and legal basis and is hereby corrected.

This dispute over the packaging and decoration specific to the famous commodity arose from the failure of both parties to clearly contract, while entering into and performing the trademark license contract, how to allocate the derivative benefits accruable during the term of license. Usually, once the trademark license terminates, the licensee shall immediately stop its use, and the goodwill accumulated on the licensed trademark shall be simultaneously returned to the licensor. The dispute in this Case occurred in an unusual way in the sense that the specific packaging and decoration introduced during the licensed use not only closely related to the licensed trademark, but also created features of goodwill beyond trademark rights due to their attribute as independent rights and interests under the Anti-unfair Competition Law. The claims proposed by the parties both entail the general application of law on the protection of rights and interests of commercial indications, and reflect the complex historical and realistic factors involved in the formation process of the rights and interests of the specific packaging and decoration in this Case. The registered trademark system and the protection system of the rights and interests of the packaging and decoration specific to famous commodities have different sources of rights and conditions fbr protection though they both belong to the legal system to protect the rights and interests of commercial indications. Registered trademarks and packaging and decoration can each play an independent role of recognition, and respectively belong to different rightholders. After the Red-canned Wanlaoji Herbal Tea was launched to the market and effectively marketed by JDB Company and its affiliates, the packaging and decoration used on the Red-canned Wanlaoji Herbal Tea has generated independent rights and interests of commercial indications due to its popularity and specificity. This Case is exceptional because in the course of design, use and promotion, JDB Company, as the actual operator of the packaging and decoration concerned, always highlighted the word 66Wanglaoji? A registered trademark of GPHL, on its packaging and decoration, and never intended to break and clearly distinguish the relation between the packaging and decoration and the registered trademark contained therein, which objectively caused the packaging and decoration to simultaneously refer to JDB Company and GPHL. Consumers would not deliberately differentiate, in the legal sense, the trademark rights and the rights and interests of the packaging and decoration specific to famous commodities, but would naturally relate the Red-canned Wanglaoji Herbal Tea to GPHL and JDB Company at the same time. Actually, the packaging and decoration concerned did contain the influence of GPHUs brand "Wanglaoji" and the commodity populanty formed and developed by JDB Company through production, operation and promotion for more than ten years as well as the remarkable recognitive effects of the packaging and decoration.

In an overall consideration of the abovementioned factors, as well as the development history of Red-canned Wanglaoji Herbal Tea, cooperation background between the parties, consumers cognition and the principle of equity, on account of the positive role of GPHL and its predecessor and that of JDB Company and its affiliates in the forming and developing the rights and interests of the packaging and decoration concerned and establishing the goodwill, it would result in obvious unfairness and might harm public interests if the rights and interests of the packaging and decoration are all awarded to either party. Therefore, on the premise of compliance with the principle of good faith and respect for consumers cognition, without prejudicing the lawful rights and interests of others, the rights and interests of the packaging and decoration specific to the famous commodity concerned may be jointly owned by GPHL and JDB Company.

6. Conclusion and significance

"The People's Republic of China Anti-Unfair Competition Law" Article 5 (2) stipulates that "well-known goods" and "special packaging and decoration" have a mutually exclusive and inseparable relationship, and only those using special packaging and decoration Commodities can become the object of adjustment of the Anti-Unfair Competition Law. Abstract product names or product concepts with no definite connotations, separated from the specific products to which the packaging and decoration are attached, lack of actual use behavior for evaluation, and do not comply with Article 5 (2) of the "People's Republic of China Anti-Unfair Competition Law" Stipulates the meaning of evaluation.

When determining the ownership of the rights and interests of unique packaging and decoration, it is necessary to encourage honest labor under the premise of the principle of honesty and credibility, but also to respect consumers' cognition of the source of the commodity based on the distinctive characteristics of the packaging and decoration itself.

(2) **Review and Application of Act Preservation Measures in Trade Secret Infringement Litigation—Eli Lilly and Company, Eli Lilly (China) R & D Company v. Huang Meng Wei**

2.1 Case Judgement:: Shanghai First Intermediate People's Court
Case By: infringement dispute know-how (technology secret)
Case No.: (2013) Huyi Zhongmin Five (Zhi) Chuzi No. 119
Date of judgment: Dec 25, 2013
Cause of action: infingement of trade secret
The plaintiff: Eli Lilly and Company (Eli Lilly and Company).
The legal representative: Michael J. Harrington.
The plaintiff: Eli Lilly (China) R&D Co., Ltd.
The legal representative: BeiBettyZhang, the chairman of the company.
Attorney: Wang Xuan, lawyer of Shanghai Guotai Law Firm.
The defendant: Huang Mengwei.
Attorney: Hou Jie, lawyer of Shanghai Xinwenhui Law Firm.

The plaintiff, Eli Lilly and Company (hereinafter referred to as Eli Lilly and Company) and Eli Lilly (China) R&D Co., Ltd. (hereinafter referred to as Eli Lilly and Company) sue Huang Mengwei, the defendant in the case of a dispute over infringement of trade secret, was accepted by this court on July 2, 2013 Later, a collegial panel was formed in accordance with the law to hear the case. The case has now been concluded.

The two plaintiffs claimed that: Eli Lilly is a world-renowned American pharmaceutical company, and Eli Lilly China is a wholly-owned subsidiary of the Eli Lilly Group. In May 2012, Eli Lilly China signed a "Labor Contract" with the defendant and hired the defendant to work as a chemistry chief researcher. According to the supplementary clauses of the "Labor Contract", the defendant must abide by the "Employee Handbook", "Confidentiality Agreement", "Company Policy Guidelines", "Red Book", "Protection of Eli Lilly" and other company rules and regulations. In January 2013, the defendant violated the above-mentioned company rules and regulations and the provisions of the "Non-disclosure Agreement" by downloading 21 plaintiff's core confidential business documents from Eli Lilly China's servers and storing the above-mentioned documents privately in a storage owned by the defendant In the device. After negotiations, the defendant admitted to the plaintiff that it had downloaded the above-mentioned confidential files from the company's server, and allowed the company to check its personal devices to ensure that the information in the confidential files was not leaked or used, and also authorized the company to delete the information. However, since then, the defendant ignored the plaintiff's negotiations and efforts and refused to fulfill the promise. The plaintiff believes that the 21 core confidential business documents involved in the GPR receptor (G-Proteincoupledreceptor), MetAP2 (methionineaminopeptidase-2) and DPP4 (dipeptidylpeptidase-4) are the know-how (technology secret) of the plaintiff. They have never been disclosed to the public in any form. They are of great commercial value and constitute the "Anti-Unfair Competition Law". Protected know-how (technology secret). The defendant has the right to log in to the company's server from the Internet with a work password and download the above-mentioned confidential business documents. However, transferring the above-mentioned confidential business documents to his personal mobile hard drives and laptops is an act of theft and violation of the company's rules and regulations. It constitutes a trade secret infringement. Due to the defendant's failure to fulfill the promise, the semi-finished products and finished product development results that the plaintiff invested in a large amount of resources were exposed to the risk of being disclosed, leaked and used, and caused the plaintiff to adjust the protection strategy and file patent applications in advance, causing serious losses to the plaintiff. The 21 confidential business documents involved GPR142 and many other projects, of which only the actual total cost of the GPR142AgonistG protein-coupled receptor 142 agonist project was USD 3,131,458.61; the reasonable cost of this case was RMB 173,006.88 (the same currencies below), which were notarized. The fee is 13,500 yuan, the translation fee is 5,683 yuan, and the lawyer's fee is 153,823 yuan.

Now the lawsuit is filed in the court, requesting an order: 1. The defendant immediately ceases the infringement of the plaintiff's trade secrets, that is, immediately and permanently deletes the 21 confidential business documents of the plaintiff illegally stolen and possessed, and shall not disclose, use or allow others to use the 21 secrets. Commercial documents; 2. The defendant compensated the plaintiff for the economic losses and the plaintiff's reasonable expenses to stop the defendant's infringements totaling 20 million yuan, of which the reasonable expenses were 173,006.88 yuan.

The defendant argued:

1. The defendant is an individual worker, not a market operator, and has no competitive relationship with the two plaintiffs. This case is an internal labor dispute within the company, not an unfair competition dispute.

2. The technical information claimed by the plaintiff for protection does not constitute a trade secret. The reasons are: ① The content of the technical information involved was not invented by the plaintiff, and all the compounds are public and known, and are easily obtained by technicians in the same industry, so it is not confidential (do not process secrecy); ② Part of the information is discussion and meeting records, R&D, forecasting, etc., and the information involved in the case only involves the first stage in the 11 stages of drug R&D, so it is not practical; ③ The defendant is a senior researcher and has the authority to download and copy the files involved in the case according to company regulations. As far as the defendant's behavior is concerned, the plaintiff has no targeted confidentiality measures and confidentiality regulations, so it is not confidential. 3. The defendant had no infringement. The defendant had no intention of infringement, and the plaintiff had no restrictions on the transfer of the information involved before or during the incident. The defendant cooperated with the company's investigation and proactively informed the company about the transfer situation, and also promised to cooperate with the company's inspection and deletion, but the company refused to accept it and made a decision to dismiss. Therefore, the state of the dispute in this case was deliberately caused by the plaintiff. 4. The plaintiff had no substantial damages and no actual losses. The related expenses were caused by the plaintiff's malicious litigation, and the attorney's fees, notary fees, translation fees, etc. incurred during the labor arbitration of both parties have nothing to do with this case. Request the court to dismiss the original complaint.

The investigation found that:

Eli Lilly was established in Indiana, USA in 1901 and is a world-renowned pharmaceutical company. Eli Lilly China was founded on March 4, 2011 by the foreign legal person Eli Lilly Finance S.A., and its business scope covers the research and development of medical, pharmaceutical, biotechnology products and related technologies, the transfer of its own technological achievements, and the provision of related technical consultation and technology service. Eli Lilly China is a wholly-owned subsidiary of the Eli Lilly Group of Companies.

On May 3, 2012, Eli Lilly China signed the "Labor Contract" as Party A and Huang Mengwei as Party B. Party A hires Party B as the chief researcher of the chemical research and development group (level I). Article 8 of the "Labor Contract" stipulates that the "Consultation Clause" stipulates: "1. If Party B's work involves Party A's business secrets and intellectual property-related confidential matters, Party A may negotiate with Party B in advance and agree to protect business secrets or restrict competition. And sign a trade secret protection agreement or a non-competition agreement. 2. If Party A contributes to Party B's professional technical training and requires Party B to perform the service period, it shall obtain Party B's prior consent and sign an agreement to clarify both parties Rights and obligations. 3. Other matters that need to be agreed by both parties: see the supplementary clauses." The fourth "discipline and internal rules" of the supplementary clause stipulates: "1. Party B must abide by the "Employee Handbook", "Confidentiality Agreement" and "Company Policy" "Guide", "Red Book" and "Protection of Eli Lilly" and all applicable rules and systems in the training contract and job description." Article 5 stipulates: "Party B must abide by the "Confidentiality Agreement" reached by the two parties. (1) For Those confidential and proprietary information that Party B may disclose to Party B before or during the employment period, and the confidential and proprietary information related to Party A's production may be obtained during Party B's employment with Party A. Party B Should: (A) keep these secrets; (B) not to disclose to any other individual or organization, unless it is to other employees of Party A who need to know the above-mentioned information due to work reasons and need to know the above information for work reasons; (C) The above-mentioned information shall not be used for any other purpose, except for the implementation of the obligations and responsibilities stipulated in this contract."

The "Confidentiality Agreement" stipulates: "2. The employee further agrees and guarantees that the" Return all documents involving confidential company information to the company within [2] days after the notice of termination of the "Labor Contract". Employees whose employment relationship is terminated without 30 days' notice should return the above documents to the company immediately upon receiving the notice of termination of the contract. "Documents involving company confidential information" include documents involving the following matters: (1) product process flow, raw material specifications, manufacturing data or procedures; (2) product quality standards; (3) engineering and technical information; (4) Marketing information, sales data, sales revenue and customer information, etc.; (5) Future planning of the factory; (6) know-how (technology secret), sales strategies, methods and plans; (7) All other confidential or company-specific information.

The "Confidentiality Regulations" section of the "Employee Handbook" states: "Since an employee is employed by the company, the employee has continued to have the following legal obligations: not to disclose the company's confidential information, not to use the company's confidential information for private purposes or without Purposes permitted by the company.... Employees should only use confidential information for the purpose of performing the duties arranged by the company, and shall not copy, reproduce, copy, distribute or otherwise use or allow any third party to use confidential information in any way for any other purpose ...Employees are obliged to read and understand the "Professional Conduct", "Antitrust and Competition Law", "Trade Secrets", "Securities Transaction/Substantial Information" and other contents related to confidential information in the Code of Business Conduct (Red Book). "The code of Business conduct" Red Book "," electronic resources "section states:" the safe use of electronic resources (for example: not to disclose your password to others; do not open suspicious e-mail attachments; at the same time is not personal devices or media storage company information). Do not make changes to electronic resources (for example: disable anti-virus software; install disabled software; or install hardware that is not provided by the company). The "Employee Handbook Responsibility Statement" stated: "I have read Eli Lilly China 2011 in detail. Version of the "Employee Handbook", on the basis of fully understanding the contents of the "Employee Handbook", to ensure compliance with the "Employee Handbook" rules and regulations. At the same time, I understand that the company will from time to time in accordance with the requirements of laws and regulations and the company's management needs Revise and update this manual. If the company updates the content of the "Employee Handbook", all employees will be notified in writing. I am willing to check the company intranet frequently or through other companies to learn about the content of the changes and updates, and I am willing to comply The revised and updated "Employee Handbook" and various rules and regulations." The defendant signed and confirmed on May 3, 2012.

The "Training Confirmation Statement" states: "I have received training, and read and understood the topics covered in this training course. To the extent permitted by local laws, I will comply with the training introduced during the contract period of service to Eli Lilly. All Eli Lilly's policies and legal requirements." The training content includes the 2011 Red Book and the 2011 Ethics White Paper.

On May 9 and November 5, 2012, the plaintiff organized employees to conduct intellectual property training. The content mainly involved Eli Lilly's intellectual property policies and trade secret protection requirements. Among them, "employees' obligations" clearly prohibited work outside of Eli Lilly's work. Purpose to use the company's confidential information; "Key Principles" refer to the "Red Book" and "Global Policy on the Information Assets of the Company and Other Parties". The defendant signed on the signature page to confirm his participation in the training.

Eli Lilly's "Global Policy on the Information Assets of the Company and Other Parties" that took effect on October 1, 2009 stated: "This policy applies to all company employees worldwide.": According to the value and sensitivity of the information to the company, use appropriate and safe methods and suitable media to prepare, process, store and dispose of this confidential information. The company's information assets are used only for the company's business purposes. The reference materials for the formulation of this policy include: The global policy on the use of electronic resources protects LillyNet's website." The "Inventor Remuneration Company System for Inventions Completed by Lilly in China" stipulates: "All employees of Lilly China agree to: 1. Information about products, processes, services, research and development, and other business information that can obtain economic value from outside Lilly generally not known to have ownership. 2. Unless written authorization from Lilly, employees of Lilly will not The above information is disclosed to anyone outside of Eli Lilly and will not be used in any occasions outside of Eli Lilly's work.... 3. Eli Lilly employees acknowledge all these ideas, inventions, discoveries, and improvements to inventions and discoveries All are the assets of Eli Lilly." The "Employee Confidentiality Agreement and Invention and Creation Agreement" stipulates: "Lilly treats all information about products, processes, services, and R&D that are generally not known to outside Eli Lilly that can obtain economic value from it. And other business information have ownership rights. Unless I have written authorization from Eli Lilly, I will not disclose the above information to anyone other than Eli Lilly, and I will not use this information on any occasion outside of Eli Lilly's work." The defendant signed the above-mentioned documents for confirmation on May 3, 2012.

On February 1, 2013, the defendant signed a power of attorney with the following content: "I have been employed by Eli Lilly (China) R&D Co., Ltd. since May 3, 2012, which is a subsidiary of the Eli Lilly Group of Companies. 2013 On January 19, I downloaded 33 confidential documents (company documents) belonging to the company from the company's server to my work computer (company computer) assigned by the company, and then transferred the company documents to my private ownership or private Used a non-company device or storage device (first-hand non-company device), and then transferred company documents to a second non-company device or storage device that I owned or used privately through the first-hand non-company device (Second-hand non-corporate devices). I hereby allow the company or company-designated personnel to inspect non-corporate devices in my presence to evaluate my use, forwarding (if any) and/or deleting (if any) company files Specifically, I allow the company or its designated personnel to inspect first-hand non-company devices and second-hand non-company devices to make sure that I have not further forwarded, modified, used or printed any company documents. If the company or its designated personnel If any company files or content are found on non-company devices, I authorize the company or its designated personnel to delete these company files and related content. As a consideration for this authorization, the company agrees not to take legal actions against my downloading of these company files, but only if I have never disclosed, distributed, disseminated or released documents or any other confidential business information of the company to anyone without the authorization of the company, nor have I performed any actions that are too relevant to harm the interests of the company."

February 1, 2013, Eli Lilly The Chinese company issued a notice of suspension to the defendant, notifying the defendant to suspend the relevant functions of Chief Researcher I on January 28, 2013. On the same day, the defendant submitted a letter of resignation to Eli Lilly China, stating that due to personal career development, he hoped to quit his job at Eli Lilly China immediately. The last working day was February 28, 2013.

On February 26, 2013, Eli Lilly China issued a notification letter to the defendant through Shanghai Xiangxiang Express Co., Ltd., informing the defendant: "1) Bring non-company equipment to the office of Eli Lilly China at 9 am on February 27, 2013 Cooperate with the company in the inspection; 2) If you still refuse to cooperate, the company will have to terminate the labor relationship with you immediately; 3) The company will take all feasible legal measures to protect the legitimate interests of the company to resolve the dispute without notice." But the defendant did not sign for it.

On February 27, 2013, Eli Lilly China issued a notice of termination of labor relations to the defendant, notifying the defendant that the Labor Contract entered into force on May 3, 2012 was signed with Eli Lilly China, on the date of this letter. Immediately terminate; and require the defendant to immediately return all property belonging to the company, including but not limited to company computers, all work-related documents and electronic data, other work equipment, and any company information you copied from the company.

On June 3, 2013, Eli Lilly China applied for notarization of preservation evidence to Shanghai Luwan Notary Public Office. The content was that a user named C160732 connected to the server of Eli Lilly China from the Internet and downloaded 48 files, including 21 files that the plaintiff claimed to be protected as trade secrets. The download time is 0:58–1:01, January 19, 2013, the download device number is

GH3XPCNU2091DLN, and the file storage address is SEAGATE mobile hard disk. For this purpose, Shanghai Luwan Notary Office issued the (2013) Hulu Zhengjing Zi No. 1705 notarization. According to the records in the information technology equipment equipment form for employees of Eli Lilly China, the user name and download equipment were all equipped for the defendant's use.

On August 28, 2013, Eli Lilly China applied for notarization of preservation evidence to Shanghai Luwan Notary Public Office. It mainly involved the sending of emails between the defendant and Eli Lilly China over the Internet. Among them, the defendant sent a letter to Eli Lilly China on February 26, 2013: "I am using Internet cafes to send letters to everyone. Before the matter was resolved, I do not sign for any documents from the Eli Lilly R&D Center.... If no dismissal decision is made, I will go through the formalities with the equipment on No. 2.28 and Eli Lilly China will send the defendant a "Letter of Termination of Labor Relations" and "Cooperate with the investigation" "Notification letter" and the content of the related emails" The company sent the attached investigation notice letter to your home but it was rejected by you. Now we will send this letter to your private mailbox by email. Please check it. I hope you will be nine tomorrow morning. Click to cooperate with the investigation as required by the notification letter." Shanghai Luwan Notary Public Office issued a (2013) Hulu Zhengjing Zi No. 2717 for this purpose.

On July 19, 2013, the defendant applied to the Shanghai Jing'an District Notary Office for notarization of evidence preservation. The defendant entered the Internet through the computer of the notary office, accessed the www.mitbbs.org website, entered the pharmaceutical discussion area, and took screenshots of some pages and pasted them into the file. The following content is involved: "Sender: bouy (BB) Pharmeceutical Title: Lilly China R&D Center has only been opened for one year, and there have been reports of theft of data by researchers. Sending station: BBS Unnamed Space Station (July 2013, Eastern Time) on the 3rd Wednesday 09:45:53) Abstract Lilly company and by the actions of former employees to court, Lilly an employee of China R & D company to a non-storage facility to download confidential business, in violation of Lilly's policy. This An employee who later left the company refused to return the confidential information. His actions prompted Lilly to file a lawsuit in a Chinese court to protect the information... These stolen information and data are very important—including intellectual property rights and industry secrets As well as other confidential information. However, although the situation is serious, this accident has not caused major concerns at present." The Shanghai Jing'an Notary Office issued a (2013) Shanghai Jing Zhengzi No. 1917 notarization for this.

In the litigation, the plaintiff submitted to this court the names and background descriptions of 21 information documents claiming to be protected as know-how (technology secret), and proposed that the above information involved the plaintiff's work on GPR receptors for the development of drugs for the treatment of diabetes, cancer and other diseases., MetAP2 and DPP4 antagonist research, including the chemical structure of a number of compounds, data, valuable biological targets, activity information, proposals for future research, etc. The defendant confirmed the name and content of the above-mentioned information file.

The above facts submitted by the plaintiff of the disputed name of the directory 21 business documents, background, labor contract, confidentiality agreement, offer letter, employee handbook (excerpt), Employee Handbook responsibility statement acknowledgment of training courses completed table grid, Letter of Commitment, Notarization, Form of Staff Information Equipment Provision, Business Code of Conduct "Red Book" (excerpt), Notice of Suspension, Letter of Resignation, Notice of Termination of Labor Relations, Notice of Request for the Defendant to Cooperate in Investigation, Xiangxiang Express Delivery Receipt, Shanghai Statement of situation issued by Xiangxiang Express Co., Ltd., (2013) Hulu Zhengjingzi No. 2717, monthly statistics of direct and indirect costs, employee working hours statistics, order statistics, notarization fee invoices, translation fee invoices, lawyers Payment certificate, legal fee tax invoice, certificate issued by Shanghai Wanya Information Consulting Co., Ltd.; email submitted by the defendant to the plaintiff (January 28, 2013, February 26, 2013), damage to the defendant's electronic equipment The photographs, (2013) Hujing Zhengzi No. 1917 notarization and the court hearing statements of both parties are confirmed. The (2013) Huluzhengjingzi No. 1706 notarial certificate submitted by the plaintiff only reflects the fact that the plaintiff has sealed the defendant's work laptop and has no proving effect on the plaintiff's accusation of the defendant's infringement of trade secrets. This court will not accept it. The definition of material in the 21st Century English-Chinese Dictionary submitted by the defendant cannot be confirmed because of its authenticity. The media submitted reports on commercial bribery by Eli Lilly and Lilly China, the defendant's medical invoices and prescription notes, Shanghai Labor and Personnel Dispute Arbitration Commission's arbitration acceptance notice, notice of hearing, and the cover of arbitration evidence bound book are not relevant to this case, so this court will not accept it.

Based on the opinions of both parties, this court believes that the main disputes in this case are as follows: 1. Whether the defendant is an "operator (business)" regulated by the Anti-Unfair Competition Law; 2. Whether the content of the 21 information documents claimed by the plaintiff It is a technical secret; 3. Whether the defendant has committed any trade secret infringement; 4. Whether the plaintiff's claim for compensation for losses and reasonable expenses has a factual and legal basis. Based on relevant laws and regulations, this court has now issued the following comments and opinions based on the facts ascertained:

1. Regarding whether the defendant is a "operator" regulated by the Anti-Unfair Competition Law, the plaintiff believes that although the defendant has not directly engaged in business activities, But it improperly obtained the plaintiff's trade secrets, which undermined the plaintiff's competitive advantage and was subject to the adjustment of the Anti-Unfair Competition Law. The defendant believed that he was an ordinary worker, did not operate himself or participated in the business of others, had no competitive relationship with the two plaintiffs, and did not belong to the business operators stipulated in the Anti-Unfair Competition Law. This case should be a labor dispute rather than an unfair competition dispute.

The Court finds that, "Anti-Unfair Competition Law," Article 2 paragraph 3: "'business' means legal persons, other economic organizations, and individuals that trade in commodities or provide for-profit services (commodities and services are hereinafter collectively referred to as "commodities")." According to its literal meaning, operators refer to economic entities engaged in commodity operations or paid services. According to the "Anti-Unfair Competition Law of" article 10 paragraph 1 (3) provisions, Disclosing, using, or allowing another person to use a trade secret under its control in violation of an agreement or the requirements of the right holder for confidentiality of trade secrets, which is the act of infringing on trade secrets. The objects regulated by this article are generally the trading partners or employees of the trade secret right holder. It can be seen that the employees of the trade secret right holder are also the objects regulated by the Anti-Unfair Competition Law. The Court finds that, according to the Anti-Unfair Competition Law article 1, "This Law is enacted for the purposes of maintaining the sound development of the socialist market economy, encouraging and protecting fair competition, preventing acts of unfair competition, and safeguarding the lawful rights and interests of businesses and consumers." This law is enacted according to the regulations, the legislative purpose of the Anti-Unfair Competition Law is to regulate the order of market competition and promote the healthy development of the market economy. Therefore, based on the legislative purpose of the law and the standpoint of system interpretation, the operators referred to in the Anti-Unfair Competition Law essentially refer to the entities that participate in or influence market competition activities. As an employee of the plaintiff, the defendant obtained the plaintiff's know-how (technology secret), which could affect the plaintiff's market competition strategy, and was the subject of adjustment by the Anti-Unfair Competition Law. The plaintiff has the right to bring a lawsuit against the defendant on the grounds of unfair competition.

2. Regarding the issue of whether the contents of the 21 documents claimed by the plaintiff are know-how (technology secret)

The plaintiff believes that the contents of the 21 documents in dispute mainly involve the pathological principles and treatment pathways of diabetes treatment, and related drug candidates developed for certain pathologies The compounds, the drug action of the compounds, the roadmap of clinical research and development, and the internal compound database of Eli Lilly are the most confidential content of pharmaceutical companies. They have never been disclosed to the public in any form and cannot be easily obtained by those skilled in the art. The plaintiff spent a lot of manpower, material and financial resources and obtained the above-mentioned information content through countless experiments. As a staged research result of new drug research and development, it has extremely high, potential and predictable value. To this end, the plaintiff took a variety of confidentiality measures for the above-mentioned information, limiting the scope of the personnel who knew it, adopting encryption measures on the files, marking confidentiality signs, monitoring the reading and downloading of the files, signing confidentiality agreements with employees, and conducting confidentiality training. Therefore, the above information should be protected as trade secrets. The defendant believes that the contents of the above-mentioned documents are not confidential, practical and confidential, and are not commercial secrets. The reasons are: 1. The above documents are meeting, summary and confirmatory experiment records, the basic compounds involved are publicly known information, and the experimental data involved are simple arrangements and attempts made on the basis of publicly known information, which can be easily obtained by those skilled in the art; 2. The content of the above documents only relates to the first stage of the 11 stages of drug research and development, which is a conceptual and abstract idea. There are no formed data or formulas, and no practical value; 3. The defendant is the head researcher and has the right to After copying and consulting the above-mentioned documents, the plaintiff did not have any contract or rules to prohibit the defendant from transferring company information files to personal mobile hard drives and laptop computers. The confidentiality measures were not targeted.

The Court finds that, Anti-Unfair Competition Law, article10 states: "For the purpose of this Law, "trade secret" means the applied technology or business information unknown to the public and capable of bringing economic benefits to the right holder, for which the right holder has taken confidentiality measures." In this case, the defendant did not deny the content of the information file, but argued that the basic compound involved was publicly known information, and the experimental data was a simple combination. Those skilled in the art Easy to get. However, the defendant failed to provide rebuttal evidence to confirm the argument. The various effective secrecy measures adopted by the plaintiff can precisely reflect that the content of the information file is not easy to obtain. At the same time, this court believes that the public knowledge of basic compounds does not mean that the method of combining the use of known compounds is also publicly known. This way of using the wisdom of the right holder can completely become the right holder's trade secret. Regarding the issue of the practical value of the disputed information, our hospital believes that the long-term research and development cycle of new drugs and the large investment. In the initial stage of new drug research and development, the requirement that its technical information can bring economic benefits does not conform to the characteristics and laws of new drug research and development. This initial stage of research and discussion of research and development data such as compound selection, biological targets, activity information, etc. is an indispensable stage in the new drug development process, which helps to choose the correct research and development route, thereby speeding up the process of experimentation and productization, and establishing the competitive advantage of pharmaceutical R&D companies has potential commercial value. Regarding the issue of confidentiality measures, the plaintiff, as a professional drug research and development company, has restricted the scope of personnel who are aware of the disputed information files, adopted encryption measures for the files, marked confidentiality marks, monitored the viewing and downloading of the files, signed confidentiality agreements with employees, Carrying out a variety of multi-effect security methods such as confidential training, which meets the requirements of confidentiality. The defendant argued that his actions were not specific to the facts ascertained by this court and were not accepted. In summary, this court confirmed that the contents of the 21 information files in this case in dispute constitute know-how (technology secret) protected by the Anti-Unfair Competition Law.

3. Regarding whether the defendant has committed trade secret infringements, the plaintiff believes that the defendant's transfer of trade secret documents to his personal mobile hard drives and laptops is an act of theft and violation of the company's rules and regulations, and constitutes a trade secret infringement. Behavior; the defendant believes that the subjective purpose of transferring business documents is to learn business and better research and develop company projects. The transfer behavior is not prohibited in the company's rules and regulations known to him, and it has not been disclosed to the outside world, and all information has been deleted in time, and the storage equipment has been damaged. It does not constitute a trade secret infringement.

The Court finds that, according to Anti-Unfair Competition Law, A business shall not acquire a trade secret from the right holder by theft, inducement, coercion, or any other illicit means. In this case, the plaintiff accused the defendant of transferring trade secret documents to his personal mobile hard drives and laptops as a form of theft and violation of company rules and regulations, which constituted a trade secret infringement. This court believes that theft refers to the act of secretly stealing a large amount of public and private property or multiple thefts for the purpose of illegal possession. The so-called secret theft means that the perpetrator takes a method that he believes is not for the victim to take away the property secretly. The facts of this case show that, in accordance with the rules and regulations of the plaintiff's company, the defendant has the right to obtain the disputed information documents. In other words, the defendant did not need to resort to secret means to obtain the disputed information file, and therefore, his behavior did not meet the characteristics of theft. However, the defendant transferred the disputed information file to personal electronic equipment without authorization, which violated the company's rules and regulations and was improper. It was classified as "or any other illicit means." stipulated in the Anti-Unfair Competition Law constitutes a trade secret infringement. The defendant argued that the transfer was not prohibited in the company's rules and regulations known to him. This court believes that the Plaintiff's "Global Policy on the Information Assets of the Company and Other Parties" stipulates in principle the handling of information, that is, "appropriate and safe methods are adopted based on the value and sensitivity of the information to the company. And appropriate media to prepare, process, store and dispose of this confidential information". The reference materials for the formulation of this policy include the "Global Policy on the Use of Electronic Resources", "Protecting the LillyNet Website of Eli Lilly and Company" and so on. In the "Global Policy on the Use of Electronic Resources" and the "Code of Business Conduct" (Red Book), further provisions have been made for information processing, that is, no company information can be downloaded or stored in electronic devices or media that are not Eli Lilly. The defendant also confirmed that he had participated in the training of regulations such as "Global Policy on the Information Assets of the Company and Other Parties", "Protection of Eli Lilly", "Code of Business Conduct" (Red Book), etc. The defendant argued that the company's Red Book exists in multiple versions, But did not provide evidence of rebuttal, this court rejected it; the defendant also argued that Eli Lilly's rules and regulations do not apply to employees of Eli Lilly China. The company's policy does not comply with the legal requirements, so it is not accepted. As for whether the defendant deleted the trade secret documents or damaged the relevant electronic equipment, it was a subsequent act after the defendant obtained the trade secret by improper means, and did not affect the establishment of the trade secret infringement.

4. Regarding the Plaintiff's request for compensation for losses and reasonable expenses, the plaintiff believes that the defendant illegally obtained the plaintiff's trade secrets and continued to possess them, putting the plaintiff's trade secrets at risk of being disclosed at any time, causing some important items of the plaintiff to be shelved at any time Risks, and adjust trade secret protection strategies for this, and apply for patents in advance. The dispute \dispute information file involves multiple projects such as GPR142, of which only GPR142 project investment cost has exceeded 20 million yuan. The damage caused by the defendant's tort to the plaintiff is in fact inevitable. In order to stop the defendant's infringement, the plaintiff paid attorney fees, notarization fees, translation fees and other related expenses. The above-mentioned expenses were directly related to the defendant's infringement. Therefore, the defendant should compensate the plaintiff for losses and reasonable expenses of 20 million yuan. The defendant believed that the plaintiff had no actual losses, the plaintiff's claim was subjectively guessed, and the continuing state of the dispute was triggered by the plaintiff's actions. The plaintiff was responsible for the consequences of the dispute and did not agree to compensation; and the attorney's fee and notary fee overlapped with the corresponding costs of labor arbitration cases. It should not be supported.

The Court finds that, according to the " Anti-Unfair Competition Law of" Article twenty provisions, "Where a business violates this Law, causing damage to another business, the victim, it shall assume compensatory liability for the damage. The amount of the compensation shall be equal to the profits earned by the tortfeasor from the infringement during the period of infringement if it is difficult to measure the amount of loss incurred by the victim, and the tortfeasor shall also assume the reasonable expenses paid by the victim in investigating the acts of unfair competition that infringe upon the lawful rights and interests of the victim." In this case, the plaintiff claimed that due to the defendant's infringement, the plaintiff adjusted its trade secret protection strategy and filed a patent application in advance, which caused serious losses. However, the plaintiff did not provide evidence to confirm this claim. Therefore, the plaintiff claimed that the defendant should compensate for the economic losses. The evidence is insufficient and this court does not support it. Attorney fees, notarization fees, translation fees, etc., are necessary expenses paid by the plaintiff for investigating trade secret infringements, directly related to the defendant's trade secret infringements, and should be supported in accordance with the law. Based on the complexity of the legal relationship in the case, the difficulty of investigating and obtaining evidence, the fact that the lawyers participated in the litigation and labor arbitration cases at the same time, the use of relevant notarizations, and translated texts, the court determined a reasonable fee of 120,000 yuan.

To sum up, this court believes that the defendant violated the company's rules and regulations by downloading and transferring the plaintiff's technical secret files to personal electronic equipment without fulfilling his promise, and cooperated with the plaintiff to delete the above technical secret files, so that the plaintiff There is a risk of losing control of the know-how (technology secret) of the company, which constitutes a trade secret infringement, and shall bear corresponding civil liabilities in accordance with the law. Accordingly, in accordance with the "People's Republic of China Against Unfair Competition Law of" two paragraph 3, the first ten of the first paragraph (a), the first article twenty provisions, ruling as follows:

First, the defendant Huang Meng Wei entry into force of this decision Stop infringing on the know-how (technology secret) of the plaintiffs Eli Lilly and Company and Eli Lilly (China) R&D Co., Ltd., that is, delete 21 information files obtained by them, and shall not disclose, use or allow others to use them until the know-how (technology secret) are known to the public only;

Second, the day the defendant Huang Meng Wei entry into force of this decision within fifteen days to pay the plaintiff Eli Lilly and company, Eli Lilly (China) R & D Co., Ltd. reasonable expenses of RMB 120,000 yuan;

Third, dismissed the plaintiff Eli Lilly and company, Eli Lilly (China) The remaining litigation claims of R&D Co., Ltd.

During the obligations of paying money if the defendant fails to Huang Meng Wei specified in this decision shall be in accordance with the "Civil Procedure Law of People's Republic of China first" two hundred fifty-three stipulated, [pay double interest on the debt during the delay in performance. Thecase acceptance fee was RMB 141,800, the property preservation fee was RMB 5,000, and the total litigation cost was RMB 146,800. The plaintiff, Eli Lilly and Eli Lilly (China) Research and Development Co., Ltd., paid RMB 72,960, and the defendant, Huang Mengwei, paid RMB 73,840.

If you disagree with this judgment, the plaintiff, Eli Lilly and Company of the United States, may submit an appeal to this court within 30 days from the date of service of the judgment. Appeal to the Shanghai Higher People's Court of the People's Republic of China.

Presiding Judge Tang Zhen Acting Judge Chen Yaoyao People's Juror Chen Rongxiang December 25, 2013 Clerk Shi Weili UPI Beijing-Shanghai Branch.

2.2 Analysis of the Case

1. Basic Facts:
Claimant (Plaintiff): Eli Lilly and Company
Claimant (Plaintiff): Lilly (China) Research and Development Co., Ltd. (hereinafter referred to as "Lilly China").
Respondent (Defendant): Huang Mengwei

On July 2, 2013, Eli Lilly and Company and Lilly China filed a lawsuit with Shanghai No. 1 Intermediate People's Court (hereinafter referred to as "Shanghai No. 1 Intermediate Court") against Huang Mengwei fbr infringing technological secret and applied to the court for behavioral preservation, requesting the court to order the Defendant not to disclose, use or allow others to use the 21 confidential documents stolen from the Claimants.

The Claimants alleged that the Respondent joined Lilly China in May 2012 as a chief chemistry researcher. Lilly China signed a Confidentiality Agreement with the Respondent and provided corresponding trainings. In January 2013, the Respondent downloaded 48 documents owned by the Claimants from the server of Lilly China (including 21 core confidential documents of the Plaintiffs) and stored such documents in the device owned by the Respondent without authorization. Upon negotiation, the Respondent signed a letter of consent in February 2013, admitting to the Claimants, "I downloaded thirty-three (33) confidential documents belonging to the company from the company's server..., 9, and undertaking, T allow the company or persons designated by the company to check the first-hand device not belonging to the company and the second-hand device not belonging to the company to determine that I did not forward, modify, use or print any company document. If the company or persons designated by the company find any document or information of the company in device not belonging to the company, 1 authorize the company or persons designated by the company to delete such document or information. ..." After that, the Claimants repeatedly designated persons to contact the Respondent and required him to delete confidential commercial documents. The Claimants also designated persons to check and confirm whether the confidential commercial documents were deleted. However, the Respondent ignored the negotiations and efforts of the Claimants and refused to perform the obligations agreed in the letter of consent. As the Respondent seriously violated the rules and regulations of the company, the Claimants sent a letter to the Respondent on February 27, 2013, announcing the termination of their labor relation.

The Claimants believed that the 21 core confidential commercial documents downloaded by the Respondent without authorization were trade secrets of the Claimants and the Respondent knew and admitted it in the letter of undertaking. The Respondent's failure to fulfill his undertaking had exposed the Claimants9 trade secrets to the danger of leakage due to disclosure or use by the Respondent or use by others permitted by him, which would cause irreparable harm to the Claimants. Therefore, in accordance with law, the Claimants requested the court to order the Respondent not to disclose, use or allow others to use the 21 trade secret documents stolen from the Claimants. To support their application, the Claimants also provided the court with the names and content of the 21 trade secret documents involved, the Respondenfs letter of undertaking, the certificate of notarization, table of information devices allocated to employees, the termination notice of labor relation, the statistical statement of direct and indirect costs and other evidentiary materials. The Claimants also deposited RMB 100,000 with the court as security bond for the above application.

2. Focus of dispute

1. Whether the defendant is a "operator" regulated by the Anti-Unfair Competition Law; 2. Whether the contents of the 21 information files claimed by the plaintiff are technical secrets; 3. Whether the defendant has committed trade secret infringements; 4. whether there is a factual and legal basis for the plaintiff's compensate for the loss and reasonable expenses.

3. Rules

"Anti-unfair Competition Law of the People's Republic of China 1993"

Article 2, Para 3: For the purposes of this Law, "business" means legal persons, other economic organizations, and individuals that trade in commodities or provide for-profit services (commodities and services are hereinafter collectively referred to as "commodities").

Article 10: Businesses shall not infringe upon trade secrets by the following means: (3) Disclosing, using, or allowing another person to use a trade secret under its control in violation of an agreement or the requirements of the right holder for confidentiality of trade secrets.

Article 20: Where a business violates this Law, causing damage to another business, the victim, it shall assume compensatory liability for the damage. The amount of the compensation shall be equal to the profits earned by the tortfeasor from the infringement during the period of infringement if it is difficult to measure the amount of loss incurred by the victim, and the tortfeasor shall also assume the reasonable expenses paid by the victim in investigating the acts of unfair competition that infringe upon the lawful rights and interests of the victim.

4. Reasoning

As the first case where behavioral preservation was applied to a trade secret dispute under the new Civil Procedure Law (effective as of January 1, 2013), this case highlighted the practical efforts made by the people9 court in the new era to comply with societal needs, and strengthen the judicial protection of intellectual property according to law. During the trial, the court mainly considered the following factors:

I. Factors to be considered for behavioral preservation in trade secret infringement litigations.

In trade secret infringement litigations, a preliminary injunction plays an important role in protecting the interests of the obligee in a timely and effective manner. However, as a special relief, preliminary injunctions can not only ensure the smooth enforcement of the upcoming effective judgment, but also enable its claimant to obtain, in advance, all or part of the interests of the final relief Therefore, in judicial practice, the court shall not enter an injunction simply when there exist general possibilities of unauthorized disclosure or use. Before entering an injunction, the court shall usually consider such factors as the substantial possibility of the plaintiff wining the case, the substantial danger of irreparable harm caused by denial of injunction, the possible harm to the plaintiff outweighing any potential harm to the defendant, and injunction's non-infringement on public interests. What makes this case special is that: 1) the Respondent Huang Mengwei had confirmed that he downloaded 33 confidential documents belonging to the company (including 21 documents claimed by the obligees fbr trade secret protection) in violation of rules and regulations of the company, and undertaken to authorize persons designated by the company to delete such documents. Therefore, it is obvious that the Respondent obtained by illegal means the confidential documents claimed by the obligees for trade secret protection. 2) A trade secret, once lost, is lost forever. The commercial documents involved were already under the control of the Respondent. Once disclosed by the Respondent, the content of such electronic documents may be known to competitors or enter the public domain and then lose its confidentiality, leaving the interest of the obligees irreparably harmed. 3) Based on the facts of this case, the Respondent, as a natural person in contrast with the obligees, would not be harmed if he was prohibited from disclosing, using or allowing others to use the commercial documents. In addition, the obligees deposited security bond to the court fbr any damage that might occur. Based on the above facts, the collegial panel granted a behavioral injunction against the Respondent and informed him of the time limit for applying for reconsideration to facilitate the exercise of his right of defense.

IL Key points to be considered for behavioral preservation in trade secret infringement litigations.

As the first case fbr the application of behavioral preservation to trade secrete infringement litigation, this case had no precedent to follow with respect to the application of law. During the trial, the collegial panel mainly considered the following key points: 1) the consistency between the claims of the Plaintiffs and the application for injunction. When filing the lawsuit, the obligees requested the court to order the Respondent to stop infringing the trade secrets of the Plaintiffs, and specifically, to order the Respondent to delete and not disclose, use or allow others to use the 21 commercial documents involved. The collegial panel held that its review of the obligees9 injunction application shall be limited to their litigious claims without allowing additions, and shall conform to the means of trade secret infringement as set forth in Article 10 of the Anti-unfair Competition Law (Article 9 in the law as amended at the 30th Session of the Standing Committee of the 12th National People's Congress held on November 4, 2017). Therefore, the Respondent was ordered "not to disclose, use or allow others to use the 21 documents involved^^. 2) The relation between the preliminary injunction and the final judgment. When the trial was underway, it was pending whether the documents involved constituted trade secrets and belonged to the legal interests protected by the Anti-unfair Competition Law. As a temporary litigious measure, the injunction order shall be free from the danger of conflicting with the final judgment. Therefore, the order was worded as "the Respondent Huang Mengwei be prohibited from disclosing, using or allowing others to use the 21 documents claimed by Eli Lilly and Company and Lilly China Research and Development Co., Ltd. as protected trade secrets", which means that the 21 documents involved were just documents claimed by the applicant to be protected as trade secrets, instead of information finally confirmed by the court to be protected is trade secrets upon review under law. 3) Balance between trial and mfbrcement. As the content of the 21 documents involved was not Hear in the text of the order, the enforcement departments would ack specificity and feasibility during enforcement. Therefore, we ppendixed a list of the names of the 21 documents involved to the text of the order. This suggested that although the Respondent downloaded 33 documents in violation of the rules and regulations of the company, he shall only be legally liable for disclosing, using or allowing others to use the 21 appendixed documents in violation of the order.

III. Enforcement models of behavioral preservation in trade secret infringement litigations A behavioral injunction is about the court ordering a party to do or not to do a certain activity. Different from property preservation, a behavioral injunction is enforced against a person's behavior, instead of a property per se. Due to a behavioral injunction's special characteristics, its enforcement requires the party9s cooperation. Moreover, enforcement is more difficult when the injunction orders the party not to do something than doing something because a positive action by a party is perceivable from outside, and sometimes completable instantaneously while the prohibition of a party 9 s behavior depends on his conscientiousness, which is not objectively perceivable by the enforcement staff of the court, and makes the enforcement of court orders less certain. The collegial panel held that such negative injunctions mainly depend on deterrent force of effective legal instruments. Only by strengthening the deterrent force of effective legal instruments can the parties 9 conscientious compliance with court orders be ensured. Therefore, after entering the judgment, the court not only serviced the legal instrument, but also summoned the Respondent to the court and informed him of the content of the order and the consequence of violating it. In fact, in case a party refuses to comply with effective court judgments or orders, the court may. in accordance with Article 111 of the Civil Procedure Law, fine or detain the party based on the severity of circumstances, and hold him criminally liable if crime is committed. It is fair to say that such warning has generated good legal effect. In the court, the Respondent undertook in writing that it was willing to comply with the court order and then represented in later submission to the court that it had destroyed the hard disks that stored the downloaded documents, and attached photos to corroborate such representations.

5. Conclusion and significance

The "Civil Procedure Law of the People's Republic of China" that came into effect on January 1, 2013 provides for behavior preservation measures, which is conducive to the timely and effective seeking of remedies for trade secret rights holders. The court must comprehensively consider: the substantial possibility of the plaintiff winning the case, the substantial threat of irreparable loss if the injunction is not issued, the possible damage to the plaintiff is greater than any potential damage to the defendant, and the issuance of the injunction does not violate the public interest and other factors. In actual judgments, attention should also be paid to issues such as the unification of the original complaint and the application for the injunction, the relationship between the temporary injunction and the final judgment, and the consideration of the trial and execution. The enforcement of the injunction of omission requires the cooperation of the respondent, and the court shall notify the respondent to appear in court, serve the ruling and inform the legal obligation, so as to enhance the respondent's consciousness of fulfilling the effective legal documents.

Open Access This chapter is licensed under the terms of the Creative Commons Attribution 4.0 International License (http://creativecommons.org/licenses/by/4.0/), which permits use, sharing, adaptation, distribution and reproduction in any medium or format, as long as you give appropriate credit to the original author(s) and the source, provide a link to the Creative Commons license and indicate if changes were made.

The images or other third party material in this chapter are included in the chapter's Creative Commons license, unless indicated otherwise in a credit line to the material. If material is not included in the chapter's Creative Commons license and your intended use is not permitted by statutory regulation or exceeds the permitted use, you will need to obtain permission directly from the copyright holder.

MIX
Papier aus verantwortungsvollen Quellen
Paper from responsible sources
FSC® C105338

If you have any concerns about our products,
you can contact us on
ProductSafety@springernature.com

In case Publisher is established outside the EU,
the EU authorized representative is:
**Springer Nature Customer Service Center GmbH
Europaplatz 3, 69115 Heidelberg, Germany**

Printed by Libri Plureos GmbH
in Hamburg, Germany